A Commentary on
the Jewish Roots of

ROMANS

A Commentary on the Jewish Roots of ROMANS

Joseph Shulam
with Hilary Le Cornu

LEDERER

Messianic Jewish Publishers
a division of
The Lederer Foundation
Baltimore, Maryland

Printed in the United States of America
Cover design by Elhanan Ben-Avraham

04 03 02 01 00 99 98 7 6 5 4 3 2 1

Library of Congress Cataloging-in-Publication Data

Shulam, Joseph, 1946–
A commentary on the Jewish roots of Romans/by Joseph Shulam, Hilary Le Cornu.
p. cm.
Includes bibliographical references.
ISBN: 1-880226-69-3
1. Bible. N.T. Romans—Commentaries. 2. Bible. N.T. Romans—Theology.
3. Christianity and other religions—Judaism. 4. Judaism—Relations—Christianity.
I. Le Cornu, Hilary, 1959–. II. Title.
BS2665.3.S57
227'.107—dc21 98-12000
CIP

Messianic Jewish Publishers
a division of
The Lederer Foundation
6204 Park Heights Avenue
Baltimore, Maryland 21215-3600

(410) 358-6471
order line 1-800-410-7367
Email ledmessmin@aol.com

What the scholars are saying . . .

"An interesting approach to Paul's Letter to the Romans. Although abreast with modem scholarship, the comments reflect the yeshiva rather than the seminary, the first century rather than the twentieth. The numerous references to the Hebrew Bible, Qumran, and rabbinic literature make this book a must for all who wish to inquire into the meaning of the most important document in Paul's writings. Shulam and Le Cornu have done a masterful job."

George Howard
Author of *Hebrew Gospel of Matthew*
Professor of Religion, University of Georgia

"I know of no one with greater ability than Joe Shulam in showing the Pharisaic and Jewish background for understanding Paul. Standing in the tradition of W. D. Davies, David Daube, Peter Tomson and C. G. Montefiore, Shulam takes our position that Paul was a Pharisee who put forth a theology fully within a Jewish Biblical world view while correcting wrong viewpoints. Contrary to E. P. Sanders, Shulam sees Paul as loyal to Torah rightly applied. This book is a treasure chest."

Daniel C. Juster
Author of *Jewish Roots*
Director, Tikkun Ministries Inc.

"This work will prove an indispensable resource for all scholars interested in the early Jewish context of Romans and the Jewishness of the faith of first-century believers in Jesus. Although the work makes more of later rabbinic sources than some American scholars will feel comfortable with, extra sources are always better than not enough, and the authors draw from an impressive and commendably wide range of early Jewish sources."

Craig S. Keener
Author of *The IVP Bible Background Commentary: New Testament*
Visiting Professor of Biblical Studies, Eastern Seminary

"Joe Shulam's commentary on the Book of Romans comes as a refreshing addition to the growing body of Pauline scholarship which places the epistle in its proper Jewish context. The chief values of this thoroughly-researched volume are two: First, the rabbinic and other early Jewish materials cited add genuine insight as we seek to understand what the epistle does and does not teach. Second, the myriad of quotes from these sources help the Western-oriented student of Scripture enter into the feeling/thought world of our ancient Jewish people who produced the New Testament. Serious students of Scripture will use *A Commentary on the Jewish Roots of Romans* with profit."

Richard C. Nichol
Messianic Rabbi, Congregation Ruach Israel

"This commentary by Joseph Shulam is unique in both its methodology and quality. It is written from the perspective of a Jewish believer in Jesus, who wishes to approach the content of Paul's letter to the Romans from the same perspective as the Jewish believer who wrote it, the Apostle Paul. . . . The volume contains a treasure of references and lengthy citations of passages from the Talmud, Apocrypha, Pseudepigrapha, Dead Sea Scrolls, and Tanach that bear directly on the understanding of the text. Extensive cross references to New Testament passages abound, providing a rich source for comparative analysis of Pauline expressions. . . . For every scholar who is truly interested in putting the book of Romans in its first century context, this book will demonstrate that Paul was not a 16th century Protestant Reformer but a first century Jewish Rabbi who accepted Jesus as his savior. I strongly recommend it for those who have more than a cursory interest in the Jewish backgrounds of the New Testament."

John McRay
Professor of New Testament and Archaeology
Wheaton College Graduate School

"A Commentary on the Jewish Roots of Romans offers many interesting possible parallels with Second Temple and rabbinic literature."

Mark D. Nanos
Author of *The Mystery of Romans*

"Joseph has done a superb job excavating and presenting the vast Jewish milieu from which Paul derived much of his theological orientation as presented in the letter to the Romans. The commentary is a virtual encyclopedia of cross references from Paul's letter to the Romans to the Jewish world-especially as interpreted through the rabbinical tradition. The commentary provides an alternative to the hundreds of Protestant readings of Romans published since Luther."

David M. Young
Ph.D., New Testament, Vanderbilt University
Minister, North Boulevard Church of Christ

Table of Contents

GLOSSARY AND ABBREVIATIONS

'Aggadah

The term denotes all scriptural interpretation which is non-*halakhic* in character and came to refer mainly to homiletic material and stories.

Halakhah

The term comes from the Hebrew root "to walk" and refers generally to the body of legal rulings derived by various forms of exegesis from Scripture and specifically to a particular ruling.

Intertestamental Literature

The body of literature ascribed to the post-Biblical period until the New Testament writings. It traditionally includes the *apocryphal literature*, documents preserved in the Greek Old Testament (the Septuagint) but not in the Hebrew Tanakh; and the *pseudepigrapha*, extra- and post-canonical Jewish and Christian texts whose authorship is ascribed to Biblical characters (cf. "with false superscription").

The *apocrypha* includes the books of 1 Esdras (= 2 Ezra) and 2 Esdras (= 4 Ezra), Tobit, Judith, Additions to Esther, Wisdom of Solomon, Sirach (Ecclesiasticus), 1 Baruch, Letter of Jeremiah, Prayer of Azariah with the Song of the Three Men, Susanna, Bel and the Dragon, 1 and 2 Maccabees, and the Prayer of Manasseh.

The *pseudepigrapha* (under which the apocrypha is sometimes subsumed) includes nine collections: the works of Philo (c. 20 B.C.E. - 50 C.E.); the writings of Josephus Flavius (c. 37 C.E. - c. 100 C.E.); the Qumran texts; the *targums* or Aramaic translations of the Tanakh; Jewish magical papyri; the *Hermetica*, texts of the first few centuries C.E. attributed to Hermes and describe the means to personal salvation; the Coptic codices from Nag Hammadi (C1-4 C.E.), which are mostly gnostic writings; and the New Testament apocrypha and pseudepigrapha, usually legendary expansions of the New Testament texts.

LXX (Septuagint)
The "official" Greek translation of the Tanakh, dating from the third century B.C.E. through the fourth century C.E. The original translation was of the *Torah* (Pentateuch, the first five books), which the Letter of Aristeas records was made by seventy(-two) Jewish scholars in Alexandria (Egypt) from which it gained its name (*Septuaginta*). It is commonly referred to by the abbreviation, *LXX* (70).

Masoretic Text
The "official" text of the Hebrew Bible (*Tanakh*) edited by the "Masoretes" or Jewish grammarians during the sixth to tenth centuries C.E. This text is "pointed" with vowel signs (and accents) which were lacking in the previous texts.

Midrash
Midrash is a comprehensive term for the Jewish exegesis of Scripture and individually collected works of Scriptural interpretation (cf. "Genesis Rabbah" or "Midrash Psalms"). It also refers to a specific mode of interpretation, based primarily on "verbal analogy" in which one Scriptural text is interpreted through a second text (cf. Paul's use of Ps.32.1-2 in order to interpret Gen.15.6 in chapter 4). It can then refer to a specific midrash on a specific Scriptural verse or theme (cf. the midrash on Job 3.19, whose theme is the impossibility of serving two masters [chapter 6]). It may thus refer to both a text and a mode of interpretation (the term comes from the post-Biblical root "to search out" or "expound"), according to the context.

Mishnah
The first body of the "oral Torah" which comprises the *Talmud*. It is composed of midrashic texts or exposition of Scripture; *halakhah* (*halakhot*) or traditional and categorical statements of law; and *'aggadah* (*'aggadot*), Scriptural expositions in the form of narrative, parables and proverbs. The Mishnah is attributed to the *Tannaim* or early Sages (Rabbis) and its editing is usually ascribed to Judah haNasi around 200 C.E. It is divided into six *Orders* which contain a number of *tractates*. The Tannaitic material is complemented by two further sources: the *Tosefta*, "addition" or "supplement," which is a collection of Tannaitic statements and traditions which were not included in the Mishnah and follows the divisional order of the Mishnah; and *braitot* (*baraita*), Tannaitic statements "extraneous" to R. Judah's Mishnah.

Qumran
The documents which were discovered at Khirbet Qumran on the Dead Sea and sometimes known as the *Dead Sea Scrolls*. These texts include

copies of most of the biblical books, apocryphal writings (such as Enoch) and texts produced by the community itself (cf. the manual of Discipline and the Thanksgiving Hymns). These texts are referred to according to the number of the cave in which they were discovered at Qumran (e.g., 1QS [Community Rule], 1QH [Thanksgiving Hymns]). The biblical commentaries are especially good examples of the genre of *pesher* characteristic of these texts, a technical means whereby biblical passages are interpreted by application to contemporary events ("the explanation of this is . . .").

Talmud
The major body of Rabbinic literature which embodies the "oral law" of Jewish tradition. The name is given both to the whole corpus of the "oral Torah" (*Mishnah* and *Gemara*) and to the *Gemara* alone. The *Mishnah* was written in Hebrew by the Tannaim and is generally held to have been edited around 200 C.E.. It consists of legal rulings based on the Tanakh; the *Gemara* is a later commentary upon the *Mishnah*, written in Aramaic by several generations of *Amoraim* (as well as some Savoraim [C6] and Geonim). The Talmud exists in two recensions, the earlier Jerusalem (Palestinian) Talmud and the later Babylonian Talmud (c. 500 C.E.). The Babylonian Talmud is often considered more authoritative in the Western Jewish intellectual tradition, which is reflected in the fact that only the Palestinian Talmud is noted as such in the present volume (e.g., PPeah, PSotah). The Talmud is divided into six *Orders* (e.g., Mo'ed, Nashim) which contain a number of *tractates* (e.g., Shabbat, Ketubot). Some tractates contain only *Mishnah* with no *Gemara* (e.g., Peah, Shekalim). Each Talmud page is divided into a folio page and numbered "a" and "b," although the Palestinian Talmud is referred to according first to the chapter, then to the *halakhah* and finally to the folio page (e.g., PNed.9.1, 41b). Each page contains, in addition to the *Mishnah* and *Gemara*, Rashi's commentary on the text, written in "Rashi script" and found on the inner side of the page, the commentary of the *Tosafot* (medieval commentators), printed on the outer column of the page, and several other commentaries. In the Soncino English translation used here, the *Mishnah* is printed in capital letters and appears in capitals wherever it is cited in the *Gemara* as a *piska* (the verse or phrase which is being commented upon).

Tanakh
The Hebrew acronym denoting the three sections of the Hebrew Bible: the Torah, the Prophets (*Nevi'im*), and the Writings (*Ketuvim*).

Targumim
The Aramaic translations of the *Tanakh*, which were read aloud in the synagogue as a vernacular aid to understanding the biblical text.

Torah
The term refers comprehensively to the Hebrew Bible in its entirety; more strictly speaking, it is restricted to the first five books of Moses (the Pentateuch or *Chumash*). In Jewish thought, the *Torah* is primarily used in the latter sense, and is also divided into the "Written Torah" and the "Oral Torah." The latter is embodied in the *Talmud* (*Mishnah* and *Gemara*) and its *halakhah* and constitutes the "tradition" or commentary of later generations on the original Biblical text. In Jewish thought, both the Written and the Oral Torah are "inspired" and authoritative texts, since the Oral Torah is held to be have been given to Moses on Mount Sinai simultaneously with the Written Torah.

Abbreviations

Talmud
The Talmud (20 volumes), Soncino Press (London: 1952).

Name	Tractate	Order
Arak.	‘Arakin	Kodashim (Holy Things)
AZ	‘Abodah Zarah	Nezikin (Damages)
BB	Baba Bathra	Nezikin (Damages)
Bek.	Bekorot	Kodashim
Ber.	Berakot	Zera‘im (Seeds)
Betza	Bezah	Mo‘ed (Festivals)
Bik.	Bikkurim	Zera‘im
BK	Baba Kamma	Nezikin
BM	Baba Mezi’a	Nezikin
Chul.	Hullin	Kodashim
Demai	Demai	Zera‘im
Eduy.	‘Eduyyot	Nezikin
Eruv.	‘Erubin	Mo‘ed
Git.	Gittin	Nashim (Women)
Hag.	Hagigah	Mo‘ed
Hor.	Horayot	Nezikin

Kel.	Kelim	Toharot (Purity)
Ker.	Kerithot	Kodashim
Ket.	Ketubot	Nashim
Kid.	Kiddushin	Nashim
Kil.	Kil'ayim	Zera'im
Mak.	Makkot	Nezikin
Maksh.	Makshirin	Toharot
Meg.	Megillah	Mo'ed
Men.	Menahot	Kodashim
Mid.	Middot	Kodashim
MK	Mo'ed Katan	Mo'ed
Nazir	Nazir	Nashim
Ned.	Nedarim	Nashim
Nid.	Niddah	Nashim
Oh.	Ohalot	Toharot
Orla	Orla	Zera'im
PA	(Pirkei) Avot	Nezikin
Par.	Parah	Toharot
Pe'ah	Peah	Zera'im
Pes.	Pesachim	Mo'ed
RH	Rosh Hashanah	Mo'ed
San.	Sanhedrin	Nezikin
Sem.	Semahot	Minor Tractates
Shab.	Shabbat	Mo'ed
Shek.	Shekalim	Mo'ed
Shevu.	Shebuot	Nezikin
Shev.	Shebi'it	Zera'im
Sot.	Sotah	Nashim
Suk.	Sukkah	Mo'ed
Ta'anit	Ta'anit	Mo'ed
Tam.	Tamid	Kodashim
Ter.	Terumot	Zera'im
Yad.	Yadayim	Toharot
Yev.	Yebamot	Nashim
Yoma	Yoma	Mo'ed
Zev.	Zebachim	Kodashim
Tos.	Tosefta (Zuckermandel)	

Midrashim

Ag.Ber.	*Aggadat Bereshit*
ARN	*Aboth D'Rabbi Nathan*, version A (ARN[a]) (*Minor Tractates of the Talmud*, Soncino; version B (ARN[b]), *The Fathers According to Rabbi Nathan*, ed. A. Saldarini (Leiden: Brill, 1975)
Ber.Rab.	*Bereshit Rabbati*
Cant.R.	*Canticles* (Song of Solomon) *Rabbah* (*Shir Hashirim Rabbah*)
DER	*Derek 'Erez Rabbah* (*Minor Tractates of the Talmud*, Soncino)
DEZ	*Derek 'Erez Zuta* (*Minor Tractates of the Talmud*, Soncino)
Dt.R.	*Deuteronomy Rabbah* (*Midrash Rabbah*, Soncino) (*Devarim Rabbah*)
Eccl.Rabbah	*Ecclesiastes Rabbah* (Op. cit.) (*Kohelet Rabbah*)
Esth.R.	*Esther Rabbah* (Op. cit.)
Ex.R.	*Exodus Rabbah* (Op. cit.) (*Shemot Rabbah*)
Gen.R.	*Genesis Rabbah* (Op. cit.) (*Bereshit Rabbah*)
Kall.Rab.	*Kallah Rabbati* (*Minor Tractates of the Talmud*, Soncino)
Lam.R.	*Lamentations Rabbah* (*Midrash Rabbah*, Soncino) (*Eikha Rabbah*)
Lev.R.	*Leviticus Rabbah* (Op. cit.) (*Vayikra Rabbah*)
Mekh.	*Mekilta de-Rabbi Ishmael* (Lauterbach; JPS: 1961)
Mekh.de Rashbi	*Mekilta de Rabbi Ishmael*
MHG	*Midrash Ha-Gadol*
Mid.Tannaim	*Midrash Tannaim*
Mid.Ps.	*Midrash Psalms* (Braude; Yale University Press: 1959)
Num.R.	*Numbers Rabbah* (*Midrash Rabbah*, Soncino) (*Bamidbar Rabbah*)
PB	*Prayer Book* (Hertz; Bloch: 1982)
Pes.Zut.	*Pesikta Zutra*
Pes.Rab.	*Pesikta Rabbati* (Braude; Yale University Press: 1968)
PRE	*Pirkei de Rabbi Eliezer* (Friedlander; Sepher-Hermon Press: 1981)
PRK	*Pesikta de-Rab Kahana* (Braude and Kapstein; JPS: 1975)
Ruth.R.	*Ruth Rabbah* (*Midrash Rabbah*, Soncino)
SER	*Seder Eliyyahu Rabbah*
SEZ	*Seder Eliyyahu Zuta*
Sifra	*Sifra on Leviticus* (*Torat Cohanim*)
Sifre Num	*Sifre Numbers*
Sifre Dt.	*Sifre Deuteronomy*
SOR	*Seder Olam Rabbah*
Tanh.	*Tanhuma*

Tanh.B.	*Tanhuma*, ed. S. Buber
TBE	*Tanna debe Eliyyahu* (Braude and Kapstein; JPS: 1981)
Yalkut	*Yalkut Shimoni*

Qumran

A. Dupont-Sommer, *The Essene Writings from Qumran* (Mass.: Peter Smith, 1973).

CDC	Damascus Document
CDC[b]	Damascus Document, manuscript B
1QH	(Thanksgiving) Hymns
1QpH	Commentary on Habakkuk
1QM	War Rule
1QMyst	Book of Mysteries (= 1Q 27)
1QS	(Community) Rule
1QS[a]	Rule Annexe (= 1Q 28[a])
1QS[b]	Book of Blessings (= 1Q 28[b])
4QFlor.	Florilegium
4QpHos	Commentary on Hosea
4QpIsa	Commentary on Isaiah
4QpMic	Commentary on Micah
4QpNah	Commentary on Nahum
4QpPs37	Commentary on Psalm 37
4QPat.Bless.	Patriarchal Blessings
4QTest	Testimonia
11QMelch	Melchizedek text

Pseudepigrapha

The Old Testament Pseudepigrapha, ed. J. Charlesworth, 2 vols. (NY: Doubleday, 1985)

Ap.Bar.	Apocalypse of Baruch (KJV)
Apoc.Abr.	Apocalypse of Abraham
Apoc.Mos.	Apocalypse of Moses
Bar.	Baruch (2, 3, and 4)
Corp.Herm.	Corpus Hermeticum
En.	Enoch (1, 2, and 3)
4 Ez.	4 Ezra
Hell.Syn.Pray.	Hellenistic Synagogal Prayers
Jos.and As.	Joseph and Aseneth
Jub.	Jubilees
Let.Arist.	Letter of Aristeas
Macc.	Maccabees (1 and 2, KJV; 3 and 4, Charlesworth)

Odes Sol.	Odes of Solomon
Poim.	Poimandres
Ps.-Philo	Pseudo-Philo
Ps.-Phoc.	Pseudo-Phocylides
Ps.Sol.	Psalms of Solomon
Sir.	Ben Sirach (Ecclesiasticus) (KJV)
Sib.Or.	Sibylline Oracles
Test.Abr.	Testament of Abraham
Test.Adam	Testament of Adam
Test.Asher	Testament of Asher (Testament of the Twelve Patriarchs)
Test.Ben.	Testament of Benjamin (Testament of the Twelve Patriarchs)
Test.Dan	Testament of Dan (Testament of the Twelve Patriarchs)
Test.Gad	Testament of Gad (Testament of the Twelve Patriarchs)
Test.Isaac	Testament of Isaac
Test.Iss.	Testament of Issachar (Testament of the Twelve Patriarchs)
Test.Jac.	Testament of Jacob
Test.Job	Testament of Job
Test.Jud.	Testament of Judah (Testament of the Twelve Patriarchs)
Test.Levi	Testament of Levi (Testament of the Twelve Patriarchs)
Test.Mos.	Testament of Moses
Test.Naph.	Testament of Naphtali (Testament of the Twelve Patriarchs)
Test.Reub.	Testament of Reuben (Testament of the Twelve Patriarchs)
Test.Sim.	Testament of Simeon (Testament of the Twelve Patriarchs)
Test.Zev.	Testament of Zebulun (Testament of the Twelve Patriarchs)
Vis.Ezra	Vision of Ezra
Wis.Sol.	Wisdom of Solomon (KJV)

Philo

Loeb Classical Library

Conf.Ling.	De Confusione Linguarum (On the Confusion of Tongues)
De Abr.	De Abrahamo (On Abraham)
De Aeter.	De Aeternitate Mundi (On the Eternity of the World)
De Cher.	De Cherubim (On the Cherubim)
De Fuga	De Fuga et Inventione (On Flight and Finding)
De Mig.Abr.	De Migrationes Abrahami (On the Migration of Abraham)
De Opif.	De Opificio Mundi (On the Creation)
De Praem.	De Praemiis et Poenis (On Rewards and Punishments)
De Prov.	De Providentia (On Providence)
De Spec.Leg.	De Specialibus Legibus (On the Special Laws)

De Virt.	De Virtutibus (On the Virtues)
De Vit.Cont.	De Vita Contemplativa (On the Contemplative Life)
Leg.All.	Legum Allegoriae (Allegorical Interpretation)
Rer.Div.Her.	Quis Rerum Divinarum Heres (Who is the Heir of Divine Things)
Vit.Mos.	De Vita Mosis (On the Life of Moses)
Quod Omnis	Quod Omnis Probus Liber sit (Every Good Man is Free)

Josephus

Loeb Classical Library

Ant.	(Jewish) Antiquities
Bell.	Bellum (The Jewish War)
Contra Ap.	Contra Apion (Against Apion)

New Testament Apocrypha

Act.Paul	*Acts of Paul*
Act.Philip	*Acts of Philip*
Did.	*Didache* (Loeb Classical Library)
Ep.Barn.	*Epistle of Barnabas* (Loeb Classical Library)
Ep.Jacob	*Epistle of Jacob*
Shep.Hermas	*Shepherd of Hermas* (Loeb Classical Library)

Patristic Writings:

Clem.Hom.	Clement of Alexandria, *Homilies*
1 Clem.	*First Letter of Clement* (Loeb Classical Library)
Const.Ap.	*Apostolic Constitutions*
Orig.Con.Cel.	Origen, *Contra Celsum* (*Against Celsus*)
Just.Apol.	Justin Martyr, *Apologetics*
Just.Dial.	Justin Martyr, *Dialogues*

Maimonides (Rambam):

Guide	*Guide of the Perplexed*
MT/Yad	*Mishneh Torah*

Technical Notes

Since we have quoted from a multiplicity of texts, from all the above sources, there inevitably exists a plethora of diverse styles regarding content, form, and mode of citation. This will at times lead to confusion for the reader not yet readily acquainted with the various texts. Several notes are therefore given as aids to identification.

1. **Cross-references**

The cross-references are given at the top of the each "piska" (the verse or phrase which is being commented upon). The various sources follow a consistent order, are separated by a semi-colon: the references are first from the Tanakh, then from the New Testament (not separated); then from the Qumran scrolls; the apocryphal and pseudepigraphal writings (not separated); Josephus; the rabbinic texts, first the Mishnah, Tosefta, and midrashim, followed by the talmudic (Gemara) references; Philo; the New Testament apocrypha and patristic writings (not divided). This order is followed throughout the Commentary wherever lists of verses are cited.

2. **Modes of citation**

Wherever they exist, we have used the standard English translations of the original texts. Since these follow different rules, no standard mode of citation is available. Thus certain forms will be used in different ways by various texts. (Both English and American spellings are therefore also used, although the Commentary follows normal American usage in most areas.) A brief review of the major usages will perhaps help to clarify the resultant situation, however:

A. Capital letters
   i. These are used in the Soncino edition of the Talmud to mark the Mishnah; i.e., the Mishnah is capitalized, whereas the Gemara is printed in ordinary letters.
   ii. The Soncino edition of Midrash Rabba; however, sometimes uses capitals to mark the biblical text, although at other times it uses italics.

B. Italics: nearly all of the sources, normally excluding the intertestamental literature, use italics to mark the citation of a biblical text.

C. References within a quoted text:
   i. Following the Soncino Midrash Rabbah edition, we have standardized the use of bracketed references following the citation of a biblical text; e.g. (Ps.14.1), even where these are only noted in the footnote in the original English edition.

ii. The regular exceptions to this rule are the Qumran texts, where, since round brackets are used for missing but understood words (in contrast to lacunae which are marked by square brackets), we have marked any additional references by inverted brackets; e.g., {Zech.1.4}.

D. Inverted commas or quotation marks: these are used by different sources to mark biblical citations. Some sources use quotation marks (either double or single) in conjunction with italics, others, particularly the intertestamental literature, use only (usually double) quotation marks without italics. A notable exception is Aboth, which, because it is a Mishnah, has no notation marks at all since we have also chosen not to capitalize it.

E. Brackets

i. Round ( ): used for biblical references within quoted texts and to indicate the source cited after its end.

ii. Square [ ]: in the Qumran texts, these indicate a gap in the original text, which the translator at times speculatively fills in and at other times leaves blank due to the illegibility of the text. In rabbinic texts, they usually mark an interpolation or explanation of the text, at times taken from a footnote in the original English edition.

iii. Inverted { }: used mainly in the Qumran texts, to mark either a biblical citation or an explanatory note.

Introduction

The Book of Romans as a Jewish Text

Since there already numerous commentaries on all the different books of the New Testament, our first obligation to the reader is to justify the addition of yet another volume. Our basic premise is a very simple one. Simply put, it rests on the conviction that the book of Romans is a Jewish text. In this introduction we shall elaborate the meaning of this phrase and review the fundamental ramifications which it holds for understanding the New Testament in general and the book of Romans in particular.

The first element of our thesis lies in the fact that we are confronted with a piece of literature—a letter—which possesses the characteristics of all written material. These include the fact that it was written (not spoken)—and thus preserved in a set form. In conjunction with the issue of the canon, which we will address below, written material lays itself before the reader as a definitive and determined text. In contrast to oral material, which is flexible and can be retold in innumerable styles, the written text is black on white, and the order, layout, and content are a given. A text is an artifact, or a "piece of work." Texts are also written by specific people, with specific personal histories, in a specific historical time period, to a specific addressee, with a specific agenda. They further possess certain linguistic constraints: Paul's letters were written in Greek, but by a person trained in a rabbinic tradition which thought and wrote in Hebrew. These linguistic constraints include grammatical and syntactical rules, again both Greek and Hebrew in this case.

In the course of the commentary, it will become evident, both through the content and the particular structure, that in a very fundamental and profound sense, "textual" and "Jewish" can in fact be used as interchangeable adjectives. In addition to the peculiarities of the written text noted above, the notion of a text goes hand in hand with that of the "canon" or what constitutes "sacred writ." Because the text is fixed (written), it possesses an innate authority, especially over those readers who accept its claim to be inspired by God. In order to change it, the reader must grant himself a modicum of authority over what he has himself received. To the extent that a community recognizes a text as "Scripture" and therefore imbued with a sacred quality it also becomes what is frequently called a "textual community" or a community whose sense of identity derives from a specific written text to which the community attributes authority. It is no accident, for example, that Jews (and Christians) are frequently known as "the people of the Book."

The association between "textual" and "Jewish" is also true in regard to the other attributes of what is identified as "written." Our basic premise that the book of Romans (as part of the New Testament as a whole) is a Jewish text is conveyed in two further significant areas which derive one from another. The first of these is that the New Testament is indissolubly bound to what Christianity has traditionally erred in calling the "Old Testament." *The New Testament as a written text is both a continuation of and a commentary on or explication of the Tanakh, the Hebrew Bible.* It cannot be understood without reference to the Tanakh, which provides it with its primary interpretive context. This is one of the primary justifications for our premise that the New Testament is a Jewish text. Because of this fact, the issue of exegesis or interpretation is also bound to the content and context of the Tanakh. In addition, however, our claim of a Jewish text and Jewish mode of interpretation for the New Testament is tied to the specific historical period in which its books were written and the thought of the people who wrote them, who may be accepted as authentic examples of the Jewish world of the first centuries.

During this period, known generally as the Second Temple and Mishnaic period, the various strands within the Jewish community were producing variant interpretations and applications of the Tanakh to contemporary Jewish life. The earliest body of these is the "intertestamental literature," so named because it relates to the period between the two testaments (see the glossary). The earliest rabbinic document is the Mishnah, commonly identified with the legal rulings, known as halakhot, derived by the pharisaic rabbis from the biblical text. The Mishnah then becomes the subject of a further commentary in the form of the Gemara (literally, completion, in the sense of further study). These two texts compose the Talmud. (Although the Talmud was edited around 500 C.E., it contains material of a much earlier period, prior to and contemporaneous with the New Testament writings; see below.) Moreover, during this general period, specific exegetical (hermeneutical) principles for the proper interpretation of Scripture were evolved within Jewish thought.

Since the New Testament numbers within the body of Jewish interpretation, our premise that the book of Romans is a Jewish text means that it also shares the same interpretive principles as those developed in other strands of Second Temple and Mishnaic Jewish thought, particularly those of rabbinic literature. If we apply the four basic rules governing the relationship between the Gemara and the Mishnah to those between later Jewish texts and the Tanakh, we see that the Tanakh is incontrovertibly accepted and regarded as the source material for the search for truth; that these sources are precise and accurate in every detail; that a common, shared basis underlies all the biblical writings; and that all statements in Scripture have independent and significant meaning. These general principles are then broken down into more specific exegetical rules, which we shall elaborate separately.

Jewish Background

Paul himself, of course, was Jewish, and his language, terminology, methodology, and style all reflect the Jewish education which he received and the Jewish traditions in which he was brought up. An additional reason for looking at Romans (as representative of the New Testament as a whole) as a Jewish text is the fact that it reflects, mediates, passes on, and builds on interpretations of biblical passages already current in Second Temple Judaism. The Targumim, for example—the early Aramaic translations of the Tanakh—make explicit references to the Messiah in verses which make no outright mention of him. Much of Paul's understanding of the Tanakh and therefore of the arguments which he puts forward is filtered through these contemporary interpretations. These are themselves diverse in character, representing the various streams and tendencies within Second Temple Jewish thought. Moreover, his arguments and goals are those which emanate from the vision of Israel's prophets. Paul's pathos is therefore that of Israel and his eschatology, including his "messiology" (doctrine of the Messiah), is part of that of Second Temple Judaism. Finally, most of Paul's writings are dedicated to working out the participation of Gentile believers within the early community—how God's plans, announced through His prophets, were to elect a chosen people, Israel, through whom He could bless all the nations of the earth.

Without knowledge of these contemporary interpretations and the methods which they used to exegete the biblical text, the most logical assumption, drawn almost by default by most Christian commentators trained in the anti-Judaic atmosphere of institutional scholarship, is that Paul's conclusions were completely new. This attitude is largely the consequence of scholarly emphasis on the Hellenistic background of the New Testament and a corresponding neglect, at times even rejection, of the Jewish and rabbinic character of its writings. We do not intend to ignore either the Hellenistic elements within Second Temple Judaism or in the book of Romans. However, the reader who is aware of the claim that Second Temple Judaism was to a large degree already hellenized will also recognize that although this may well be true, Paul was still writing within a Jewish and rabbinic context. Our claim is simply that the Jewish character of the New Testament writings is far more important for their correct understanding than is an emphasis on their difference from the Jewish thought of the time.

Exegetical Background

Of all the New Testament epistles attributed to Paul, no other letter has played a more significant role in the formation of modern "evangelical" Christianity than the book of Romans. Because of the great influence that this letter has exerted on Christianity and because many of the passages in this letter have become standard clichés, it is difficult to examine the book of Romans with historical and linguistic, not to speak of theological, objectivity. For over two thousand years of history, both Jews and Christians have referred to Romans to reinforce their biases. This makes the understanding of Romans difficult for both the scholar and the layman. Much of the Reformation interpretation of Romans, for example, has formed the basis for the Protestant doctrine of "grace *versus* Law." Paul has been frequently portrayed as the champion of the "theology of grace" as it was articulated in Reformation thought and thus also regarded as the main exponent of the "gentilization" of Jewish Scripture which gave rise to the new Christian faith. This view, which has also been adopted by many Jewish thinkers, formed an integral element in the historical and theological trends which reinforced the schism between the two "religions," forcing them to develop independently and antagonistically, and inculcated the Jewish view that the New Testament is the book of the Christians and that Jews who believe in Yeshua (Jesus) become Christians and are no longer Jewish. It has become obvious through time that this neglect or contempt of the Jewish character of the New Testament has played a large part in the formation of the claim that Paul was in fact the author of a new religion (Christianity). We are endeavoring as far as possible to redress this "historical aberration" and to demonstrate that the New Testament is a Jewish book and that Jews who believe in Yeshua remain Jews. Our primary concern is to remain faithful to the text, and our conviction is strong that to do so means examining the New Testament writings in their original Jewish context and milieu—historical, cultural, social, political, literary, and theological.

Style and Methodology

We have somewhat simplified things in a historical context by saying that "Jewish" and "textual" are interchangeable adjectives. We have identified Romans as a Jewish text, but it is also a Jewish text from the Second Temple and Mishnaic period. Scholars, particularly following Neusner's work and the influence of other disciplines, have determined that what was once regarded as "normative" or mainstream Judaism at that time was in fact far more diversified than previously assumed.[1] When we start talking in terms of textual sources, we can number a half dozen or so various Jewish groupings within the contemporary literature and thought. These include the intertestamental writings, comprised of the apocryphal and pseudepigraphal texts; historical documents such as the books of Josephus; the Dead Sea Scrolls (Qumran) and circles close to their theology; the various forms of rabbinic Jewish thought, including the Mishnah, Talmud, and midrash; and philosophical works like those of Philo. Each of these bodies of literature represents a particular literary genre with its own style and methodology. Since they all form the general textual and theological background of Romans they are all relevant to a differing number of Paul's points and the way in which he makes them. In general, they not only provide us with examples of the Jewish thought of the period but they also demonstrate that the New Testament documents were written in a specific setting and can be helpfully interpreted through an understanding of their contemporary conceptual framework.

Our primary marker in distinguishing their influence on Romans as a Jewish text is that Paul was a diaspora Jew (born in Tarsus), who spoke Greek and wrote his letter in Greek to a community in Rome whose own language was largely Greek. Despite this fact, however, Paul chose to be educated in Jerusalem under one of the leading rabbinic scholars of the day, Rabban Gamaliel the Elder. This means that his main identity lay with rabbinic Judaism, since Gamaliel was one of the leading Rabbis in the pharisaic stream of rabbinic Judaism (who took as his students only those pupils who showed promise for a career in the "rabbinate"). Paul explicitly identifies himself as a Pharisee (cf. Phil.3.5), and his training under Gamaliel made him a master in rabbinic thought and forms.

The Talmud

Although Paul is writing a letter, the book of Romans does not fall into the category of private correspondence since it is addressed to the whole community at Rome. Instead it acts as a forum for the presentation of Paul's views regarding certain issues of public concern. Consequently, when we come to read the letter the genre or style of rabbinic thought takes precedence over that of private communication. If we can easily read a letter, however, we cannot read the Talmud (Mishnah and Gemara) in any similar sense of the word "reading." Just as one of the extended meanings of the word "Gemara" is "to study," the Talmud as a whole must be studied in order to be understood. It follows a tightly-knit argument structure which is based on a peculiar dialectic or reasoning.[2] This dialectic is unique in that it takes nothing for granted. It is only satisfied with proofs that approach absolute certainty. It constantly tries to sharpen these proofs, cull the evidence, and reach the very essence of the problems (the truth), with the greatest possible precision. Since Paul is not engaged in talmudic debate with other Rabbis, his letter is not as tightly bound by the constraints of dialectic argument as is the Talmud itself. This makes it much easier to study at the same time as this study is also made easier by knowing that Paul employs many of the same linguistic usages and structural elements of the Talmud.

In order to study the Talmud it is necessary to know and recognize the meaning of its peculiar language. For instance, the Rabbis use a number of key phrases indicating agreement and disagreement with a particular legal ruling (*halakhic* decision); justification for such agreement or disagreement; the rebuttal of a certain argument or decision; its modification; the reasons how and why it differs from another ruling which otherwise appears to be identical; and so forth. Paul utilizes these phrases at the pertinent points in his argument. One of his most characteristic questions, "what shall we then say?," is an example of the talmudic terminology used to introduce an erroneous conclusion. What follows the question is a proposed solution to the particular problem which, sooner or later, will be refuted. The refutation is marked by the rejoinder, "may it never be!" or "God forbid!" One of the most significant exegetical findings based on reading these markers demonstrates, contrary to most understandings, that in Romans 9.30-11.10 Paul is in fact presenting what he views as a mistaken idea (namely, that the Gentiles attained righteousness although not pursuing it while Israel did not attain it although they pursued it). He refutes this view in Romans 11.11. The consequences of reading this passage as an answer to a limited question rather than as part of the mistaken conclusion affect our whole understanding of what part the behavior of the people of Israel plays in the maintenance of their own election and in the inclusion of the Gentiles in the kingdom of God.

Midrash

The second form of rabbinic literature which plays an even greater role in Paul's writings is that of midrash. The Mishnah and Gemara (the Talmud) are predominantly concerned with arriving at the precise meaning of the biblical ordinances. (The process, as understood by the talmudic Rabbis, was that those injunctions needed to be spelled out where they were vague and general, and made relevant to the present generations. The Mishnah was the first stage of this interpretive endeavor, the Gemara the second, taking the Mishnah as its basic source.) Wider than but still part of the talmudic dialectic were the general rules of biblical interpretation (exegesis or hermeneutics). These are more apparent in midrash, because the fundamental nature of midrash is the exposition of the biblical text. In many ways, Romans could be added to the list of contemporary midrashic compilations of the period. Although it is modified because it is addressed to an actual community, with specific historical, social, cultural, and theological circumstances, as a piece of written text it demonstrates a large number of the characteristics of midrash.

First of all, the Epistle is an exposition of Scripture. Paul bases his entire argument on the Tanakh, and frequently cites scriptural prooftexts in similar fashion to midrash as an interpretive genre, although in contrast to other midrashim he does not follow the strict order of any particular biblical text. He thus uses the same fixed principles of interpretation known as "the principles through which the Torah is expounded" which all midrashic literature, whether part of the talmudic corpus or independent works, followed. Rabbinic literature provides us with different lists of such principles: the seven hermeneutic rules of Hillel; the thirteen of Rabbi Ishmael; the thirty-two principles of Rabbi Eliezer the son of Rabbi Jose Ha-Gelili, but none of the lists give a complete description of all the interpretive rules found in all the forms of midrash.

Paul mainly employs those principles which directly pertain to scriptural exegesis, in contrast to those which are more intimately connected to the precise delineation of halakhot (legal rulings). Many of these principles rest on common sense and logic. Paul demonstrates a predilection for the forms related to inference and analogy: verbal analogy (*gezerah shavah*), analogy (*binyan av*), and *a fortiori* inference (*kal ve-chomer*); for example, since these help structure an argument based on scriptural verses. Romans 5 is a masterful illustration of an analogy built upon a string of variations of *a fortiori* inferences: "if while we were enemies, we were reconciled to God . . . how much more . . . we shall be saved by his life;" "if by the transgression of the one, death reigned through the one, how much more those who receive the abundance of grace . . . will reign in life through the one, Yeshua the

Messiah." The passage in Romans 12.9ff is based on two principles, one transmitted through the pharisaic Rabbi, Hillel, the other known from the Qumran documents. Hillel taught that in order to "win converts," a person should weep when he weeps and rejoice when he rejoices, based on the verses in Ecclesiastes 3.1-8. The community at Qumran adopted the notion that they should submit to the evil authorities while they are in power so that God could wreak His final vengeance on them in the Day of Judgment. In chapter 14, Paul appeals to a string of contemporary *halakhic* rulings governing family and social relations under the rubric of "peace": for example, the principles of "shelom beit" or "peace in the house" and of human dignity, which demands respect for one's brothers. We have argued, on the other hand, that the section in 8.26-28 and following is best understood through an already existent interpretation of Proverbs 20.27, and this, too, changes the whole idea of "groaning" of the Spirit to that of man's own spirit.

Rabbinic Sources

If Paul's style and methodology are primarily based on talmudic hermeneutics, his thought is also largely influenced by rabbinic literature. Here again we enter the area of source-criticism. Attempts to interpret the New Testament writings in the light of rabbinic literature are often the butt of the objection that most of this material is much later than the time period of the New Testament texts and therefore an invalid source. It is a truism to say that all the extant literature has been edited. The Mishnah and Talmud, for example, are texts collected and preserved by the pharisaic school and not the Sadducean; they also demonstrate the fact that the *halakhah* was determined (in the majority of cases) according to the House of Hillel rather than the rival House of Shammai. Since the Talmud, and the midrashim, are compilations which range over an enormous time-span—from the first and second centuries B.C.E. to the fifth century C.E. (and much later for some of the midrashim)—the matter of dating particular sections and attributing ideas to specific periods is a matter of much controversy. Here, however, we would emphasize once again that we are largely treating the text as it stands before us as a coherent and independent textual unit (i.e., not endeavoring to trace its "original" sources). Our general attitude towards the use of rabbinic (talmudic and midrashic) material to compare and clarify New Testament texts conforms to the view expressed by Professor David Flusser in this regard:

> I do not deny the possibility that post-Christian Judaism could have created parallel motifs similar to those that appear in early Christian writings from mutual resources. Moreover I cannot completely exclude the possibility that in some case later rabbinic sayings may have been influenced by primitive Christian material. Nevertheless for the most part, it can be easily shown that on the one hand, later rabbinic parallels to New Testament passages provide great help for the elucidation of the New Testament. But on the other hand, these Christian texts shed little light on the interpretation of the later rabbinic parallels. In my opinion this fact demonstrates that even if the rabbinic sources are later, they still preserve evidence of an earlier stage which gave birth to the New Testament concepts and motifs. . . . The entire corpus of rabbinic literature is an expression of a constant stream of oral transmission. . . . Thus the specific character of rabbinic literature not only permits us, but even obligates us to include post-Christian rabbinic sources as an inseparable part of the investigation of the Jewish roots of Christianity.[3]

The textual approach which we have adopted here primarily deals with the letter as a whole text and not with source or historical-traditional criticism. (Those readers familiar with contemporary literary theory will recognize that our approach exhibits strong affinities with the concept of "intertextuality," according to which any written text is composed of a mosaic of other texts and the key to its understanding lies in the reader's hands rather than that of the original author.) Since, however, part of the way to demonstrate that Romans (and the New Testament writings as a whole) is a Jewish text, we are also engaged in demonstrating the direct sources of certain passages from contemporaneous Jewish thought. Where we (fairly rarely) feel justified in claiming direct influence, we have indicated this fact. In the majority of all the other places, no such claim is intended, and the quoted source is brought as a parallel to Paul's text or as a clarificatory or explanatory text.

Qumran

This situation differs more substantially when we consider the Qumran texts. As is known, the discovery of these texts has given rise to a wide range of speculations. Although some of these, such as that the "Teacher of Righteousness" was John the Baptist and the "Wicked Priest" and the "Liar" were two different code names for Yeshua (cf. Thiering) are insupportable, there is no doubt that the milieu from which the texts sprung had a formative influence on early Christian history.[4] In both the commentaries written by the Qumran community (e.g., the commentary on Habakkuk) and in Paul's letters, there are similar methods used in interpreting the text of the *Tanach* (Old Testament). The Qumran community and the early Messianic community drew from the same sources to express their ideas. These were the sources that all of the Jewish people considered inspired and divine. As with all the other contemporary texts of the general period, we have treated the Qumran documents more textually (and theologically) than historically. Where source criticism is concerned, however, they do seem to occupy a special place in the source of Paul's thought (though less in his style. Thus, for example, the exegetical formula called *pesher* which is characteristic of the Dead Sea Scrolls is not part of Paul's stock methodology). On the other hand, Paul's theological outlook is very close to that of the Qumran authors. In the majority of cases where we have suggested a direct influence on Paul's thought the source comes from Qumran or its related circle. A large part of the reason for this both draws from and supports Flusser's contention that a pre-Pauline stratum of textual material emanating from "Essene theology" existed, which has been visibly retained in most of the New Testament epistles, the Gospel and letters of John, and the author of the Book of Hebrews. Flusser comments that:

> Our last observation—namely, that no doctrine of central importance resembling Qumran theology (such as election or dualism) is restricted to any single NT book—seems to indicate that no single NT author (e.g. Paul) introduced such doctrines into Christian thought. Therefore a common source of influence is to be postulated. It is highly improbable that each of the New Testament authors under consideration was directly and independently influenced by the Qumran sectarians (or by Jewish circles close to them). If this had been the case, we should expect marked differences in the manner in which these ideas were worked into Christianity by the different authors. But no such differences exist. Therefore we must suppose that there existed a stratum of Christian thought which was especially influenced by Sectarian ideas, and that John the Evangelist, Paul and the authors of most other NT Epistles based themselves on the theological achievements of this stratum. . . . All this means practically that the whole body of ideas described above could have come into Christianity only from the Qumran Sect: it is not sufficient to presume that we are dealing with ideas that were generally diffused among Jews. Of course, it is not our contention to argue that the body of ideas passed into Christianity directly from the Sect; it is quite probable that it passed through several groups

> and movements (which were more or less influenced by Sectarian thought) before arriving at the points where it can be observed through some writings of the New Testament.[5]

This quote, in combination with the large number of parallels brought from the Qumran texts, may create in the reader the impression that Paul adhered to much of the theology of its authors. We therefore want to emphasize yet again that our use of contemporary Jewish literature, which includes the Dead Sea Scrolls, is primarily to demonstrate the ways in which the book of Romans is the product of its time and context; i.e., that it is a Jewish text whose comparison with and clarification through other contemporary Jewish texts form the most authentic means for its proper interpretation. (Or in the terminology of "intertextuality," these other documents are the uncited texts out of which the book of Romans is composed.)

Many of the terms and principles used in the commentary will probably be unfamiliar to our readers. We have tried to give brief explanatory remarks wherever terms and sources are referred to the first time, but we have also provided a glossary for quick reference for the main sources. It is our hope that the reader will not be put off by the quotes and feel that they intrude into the commentary. They should in fact be regarded as the main body of the commentary itself, allowing Paul's text to be interpreted through contemporary texts of the period which reflect ideas close to those which Paul presents; our own commentary is more of an attempt to let Paul's text speak for itself through bringing other clarifying texts. Where these texts require explanation we have generally put the material in the footnotes. When the ideas, both Paul's and those of other sources cited, are unfamiliar, unclear, unusual, or can be traced through a known textual path, we have given our interpretations as our contribution to the exegesis of Paul's thought.

Authorship and Place

There is little or no scholarly debate concerning Paul's authorship of Romans, although several theories claim that chapter 16 is not original. Our own research points out the textual affinities of chapter 16 with the rest of the letter and thus confirms Paul's authorship. Paul himself states in Romans 16.22-23 that he is writing from Gaius' house, where the community also meets. Paul speaks of baptizing a believer named Gaius at Corinth (1 Cor. 1.14), and Cenchrea, where Phoebe, the bearer of the letter to Rome, is a part of the fellowship, was the harbor of Corinth. Further external evidence from the field of archaeology corroborates the claim that Romans was written from Corinth. What is now known as the "Erastus inscription," an inscription discovered at Corinth, identifies its donator as the *aedile* or city treasurer who paved the pavement adjoining the theater in Corinth at his own expense in return for receiving the position. This matches Paul's mention of "Erastus, the city treasurer" in Romans 16.23 (cf. Acts 19.22, 2 Tim.4.20).

Paul—the Person

The New Testament provides us with more autobiographical details about Paul's life than about any of the other apostles: he was born in Tarsus, a city in Cilicia, which possessed the status of a Roman city (cf. Acts 9.11, 21.39); the citizens of Tarsus were given Roman citizenship. Thus, Paul states that he was born a Roman citizen. This could have been because his parents were already Roman citizens or because he was born in a Roman city; he was educated in Jerusalem (cf. Acts 22.3), probably under Rabban Gamaliel the Elder (cf. Acts 5.34) who was a Pharisee of the School of Shammai. Paul calls himself a Pharisee (cf. Acts 23.6, 26.5, Phil.3.5) and suggests that his parents were also Pharisees (cf. Acts 23.6), and encouraged him to seek a good rabbinic education in Jerusalem. It is possible that Paul's family remained in Tarsus, since he is often mentioned as being in the city (cf. Acts 9.30, 11.25); he lived his life in the manner of a Pharisee, Torah-observant, obedient to rabbinic regulations, and proud of his Jewish heritage (cf. Acts 22.3, 23.6, 26.4-7, 28.17, Rom.9.3, 2 Cor.11.22, Phil.3.5-6); he had a close relationship and was in good standing with the Sanhedrin since he was given letters of recommendation by the High Priest to the community in Damascus to bring the followers of Yeshua to trial in Jerusalem (cf. Acts 9.2, 22.); this relationship may be reflected in his role at Stephen's execution. Paul is said to have guarded the cloaks of those who stoned Stephen. Luke, in ignorance of the *halakhic* significance of his action may have missed the point that during the stoning of a condemned man, an official was appointed to stand at the door of the court with a cloak. If further witnesses appeared, or the accused man himself wished to plead another item in his favor, the cloak acted as a signal to a horseman in sight of the condemned man, who was brought back even four or five times (cf. San.42b).

Date

The dating of the letter can be determined according to Paul's stated itinerary. Although he planned to visit the community in Rome on his way to Spain, this wish is subject to his even more immediate need to reach Jerusalem for the feast of *Shavuot* because he has just completed his collection for the "saints in Jerusalem" (cf. 1.11-13, 15.23-29). He has gathered these contributions through Greece almost to Illyricum, and Luke says of Paul in Acts 19.21 that at the end of his stay in Ephesus Paul had "purposed in the spirit" to go to Rome after he had made the offering in Jerusalem. Paul speaks retrospectively of this trip in Acts 24.17, where he tells the governor Felix that after several (or many) years he came to Jerusalem to bring alms and present offerings to his nation. The contribution of the Gentile believers in Macedonia and Achaia are the fruit which he intends giving to the Temple as his priestly-prophetic offering as apostle to the Gentiles. Since both Timothy and Sopater (Sosipater), who send greetings (16.21) were Paul's travelling companions on his last journey from Greece to Jerusalem (cf. Acts 20.1ff), Romans can therefore fairly confidently be dated to his departure from Corinth on his third missionary journey *en route* for Jerusalem around the early part of 58 C.E. This is further confirmed by fact that Gallio's appointment to the proconsular office at Corinth, before whom Paul was brought by the Jewish population of the city, is known to have taken place around 57-58 C.E. (cf. Acts 18.12-18). Although scholars debate whether Paul was imprisoned more than once in Rome, he never reached Spain and according to tradition was martyred in Rome around 66-67 C.E.

Purpose of the Letter

It is traditional to evaluate the specific purpose for which the New Testament books were written in the light of the particular author's intention and/or the circumstances of the audience to whom he was writing. Although there is no doubt that both these elements are legitimate historical concerns, we would once more here again stress the predominance of our textual concerns. Our first intent is to demonstrate the way in which the book of Romans both reflects and represents the varied body of Jewish thought of the Second Temple period. Historical and other considerations are rarely mentioned, while the body of the commentary is taken up with textual illustrations of Paul's thought from similar passages in contemporary Jewish literature. Therefore, if we do not attribute certain themes of the letter to Paul's personal psychology, for example, or claim that he is obviously responding to the specific social and historical situation of the Roman community, we do intend to demonstrate that the book of Romans presents us with a textual picture of certain prevalent and controversial theological debates within Second Temple Jewish thought.

The Congregation at Rome

It is also certain, of course, that locating Romans within this historical period not only confirms its Jewish nature but also reflects the historical circumstances of the early community. Not only do these two positions not necessarily conflict with one another but they also necessarily overlap. Several factors indicate the origin and nature of the congregation in Rome. Paul explicitly dismisses the idea that he founded the community (cf. Rom.15.20), but his statement of not wishing to "build upon another man's foundation" does not necessarily indicate that the congregation in Rome was established by any one person, or even by St. Peter, to whose credit the early Christian tradition attributes its establishment (cf. 1 Pet.5.13). In fact, the various references to different people in chapter 16 suggest that the believers met in small groups within the city, who presumably distributed Paul's letter among themselves (cf. 16.5, 14, 15). Acts 2.10 notes "sojourning Romans" among those who heard Peter's speech at *Shavuot*, and many of these, together with the regular Jewish pilgrims to Jerusalem, probably returned to Rome permanently. Since it was the center of the Empire the city attracted a great number of people for varying purposes, and the Jewish community of Rome dated from the Babylonian exile. It seems most likely, therefore, that the community was composed of a mixture of Jewish and Gentile believers (see the greetings in chapter 16) whom Paul might have wished to visit specifically because they had formed themselves without any apostolic presence. The mixed nature of the congregation may also have been a source of friction in consequence of the fact that Christianity had not yet been recognized as a separate "religion" by Roman rule during the period. Claudius' banishment of the Jewish community from the city in 52 C.E. may therefore have left a vacuum in the early community which the Gentile believers came to fill. This might have created rivalry over leadership when the Jewish believers began returning, as Priscilla and Aquila are known to have (cf. Acts 18.2, Rom.16.3). Such social tensions frequently touched off and were the focus of the theological debates concerning the relationship between Jews and Gentiles especially within the early communities.

Theological Issues

The theological discussions common to the period included the relationship of the people of Israel to the Gentile nations, and since the early community was composed of both Jewish and Gentile believers the "ins and outs" of the debate over the Jewish-Gentile relationship was a central focus. What did the inclusion of the Gentiles into God's kingdom mean for Israel's election?

Since the Jewish people's election was sealed in their covenant with God, would they retain their position if the Gentiles were admitted without being circumcised and without observing the Torah as the seal of the covenant and election? If the Gentiles were admitted to God's kingdom without being required to convert to Judaism, what meaning would Israel's election retain? If the Gentiles received God's righteousness through faithfulness to God in Yeshua, what purpose would the Torah serve for them (would they need to observe it in order to be righteous?) and for Israel (does not faithfulness make the Torah superfluous?).

The Argument in Romans

It is clear that the practical issue of presenting the offering at *Shavuot* defined Paul's chronological timetable. At the same time, however, it also indicated his theological priorities. The issue directly relates to Paul's apostleship to the Gentiles, a fact which underlies the major textual themes of the letter. Paul's belief that God has indeed made room for the Gentiles in His kingdom, and appointed him as their apostle, generates a sustained and argued thesis to support his position. This is grounded, first of all, in Paul's conviction that God has permanently elected the people of Israel, demonstrated through His covenant of the Torah given on Mount Sinai. This claim commonly drew in its wake two possibilities regarding the Gentiles: either they would convert and become full members of the Jewish faith at the end of times; or they would remain Gentiles with lesser rights and rewards than those received by the people of Israel since they were not commanded to observe the Torah. The Torah and its commandments therefore became the focal point for Jewish identity. Not only did Torah-observance serve to mark Israel off from all the other nations but it also generated an internal Jewish debate, stemming from the prophetic literature, concerning the proper grounds of its observance. Second Temple Jewish thought contained a range of ideas, from the view that the commandments should be observed simply because they were commanded to the opinion that the "real" "sons of Abraham" were only those who were motivated by a love of God. Paul was not only convinced that ritual observance alone was not pleasing to God but also that anyone could be motivated by love and faithfulness—including the Gentiles who did not convert. He was therefore also convinced that the Torah did not cover all evils, as it were, nor did it automatically guarantee God's acceptance (cf. chapter 2). This idea went hand in hand with the belief that all mankind is equal before God: first in their sinfulness (cf. chapters 2 and 3) and consequently in their eligibility to receive God's righteousness "apart from the Torah" (cf. chapters 3 and 5). At this point (chapter 3) his argument takes on the form of a sustained dialectic between the various objections implied by various aspects of his thesis. First of all, the idea that all mankind are equal before God raises the possibility that Israel's election can in fact be called into question and nullified (cf. 3.1f). Paul digresses from his immediate defense of Israel's election to show that the people's unfaithfulness can never annul God's election (3.3f). This subsequently raises the theme of libertinism against which Paul fights throughout the length of the letter. Although man's sinfulness enables him to receive God's righteousness, this can never be made into a principle for sinning so that God's grace may increase or for presuming on God's goodness (cf. 3.5, 8, 6.1, 15, 7.13, 11.18f, 12.3, 14.1ff). He confronts the possibility of moral license by interpreting baptism in the light of the motif of serving two masters (chapters 6 and 8), and the view that Jewish believers are neither any longer responsible to the Torah nor able to overcome their evil inclination through Torah-observance alone (chapters 7-8).

Simultaneously, however, Paul insists that it was the Torah itself which witnessed to God's righteousness which is available to all mankind (cf. 3.21). The true goal or *telos* of the Torah is found in Yeshua's faithfulness (cf.1.1-2, 16-7, 3.22f, 10.4). This brings him back full circle to his conviction, based on God's promise to Abraham and repeated by the biblical prophets who foretold of God's plan, that the Gentiles would be included in God's kingdom (chapters 4, 9-11, 15.8-16). Israel may be redeemed from their sins because God's grace overcomes transgressions against the Torah; and therefore the Gentiles can also be redeemed from their sins, even though sin is determined through the Torah (chapter 5). Paul resumes his defense of Israel's election in 8.26, where he is led back to the idea that God judges the secrets of men's hearts (cf. 2.16), and develops the central point of his whole proposition, that God's promise to Israel was based on his promise to Abraham that through his descendants all the nations of the world would be blessed. Israel and the Torah were the means to bring the Messiah to the world (chapter 11). In chapters 12-13 he deals with the separate issue of "serving the time," according to which he establishes the principles of love, respect, and non-retaliation in the face of the wicked, and in chapters 14-15 he lays out a beautifully sustained argument for mutual love and respect based on the principles of peace and human dignity and the belief that God does not need man to keep His commandments in order to defend God's own honor.

This principle of equality between all believers leads him finally to demonstrate how Israel's Messiah, who is the example of pleasing one's neighbor, extended God's grace also to the Gentiles (15.7-13) and how he is fulfilling God's prophetic plan by bringing the contribution of the Gentiles to the Temple in Jerusalem at Shavuot (15.14ff). He ends the letter by sending personal greetings to those whom he knows in the community in Rome, and reiterating two main themes: peace between the brethren and the final great mystery of how all mankind is saved through righteousness and faithfulness.

We offer this commentary on the book of Romans as a Jewish text in the hope that it will bring to the reader a broader and deeper appreciation of the Jewish nature of the New Testament writings as a whole. In addition to new light which we trust has consequently been thrown on the interpretation of the letter in general and of specific passages in particular by situating it in its Jewish setting, elaborating the exegetical rules and terminology prevalent in the period, and bringing comparative sources from contemporary Jewish literature, we also hope that this volume will go some way in redressing the historical mistake committed by the Church of cutting itself off from its own roots. Our most fervent desire is perhaps that this commentary will also serve to return Yeshua himself to his own people, in demonstrating that the New Testament is not a Christian book representing a different faith but a Jewish text embodying an authentic Jewish interpretation of the Tanakh.

The Outline of Romans

- I. Introduction (1:1–15)
  - A. Address and greeting (1:1–6)
  - B. Paul's purpose in writing the letter (1:7–15)
- II. The Kerygma of the letter (1:16–17)
- III. The world's need for God's Messiah (1:18–32)
  - A. Introduction to the problem of God's wrath on the world (1:18)
  - B. The fall of mankind; i.e., the Gentiles (1:19–32)
    1. Mankind's ability to perceive God through nature (1:19–20)
    2. Mankind's fall into idolatry (1:21–25)
    3. Mankind delivered into gross immorality and perversion of nature (1:26–32)
- IV. No justification for mankind's sinful state—for Jew or a non-Jew (2:1–13)
  - A. "When you condemn others you will condemn yourselves"

[Paul employs a method like Nathan the prophet in the case of David and *Bath-Sheva*. He makes a general statement with which all would agree and then turns it around to include the Jews.] (2:1–4)

B. God's judgment requires repentance of both Gentiles and Jews (2:5–12)
 1. God's wrath: Every deed justly rewarded or punished (2:5–6)
 2. God's judgment: Mankind judged by their deeds (2:7–10)
 3. God's judgment: Equivalent for Jews and Gentiles (2:11–13)

V. Gentiles judged by same standard as Jews (2:14–16)

VI. Jews ought to have known better because they had the Torah (2:17–29)
 A. Over-confidence of the Jew (2:17–20)
 B. Hypocrisy of those who claim to have the Torah (2:21–24)
 C. Value of the Torah and living according to Torah (2:25)
 D. Being Jewish requires circumcision of the heart (2:26–29)

VII. Answer to the question, "What advantage has the Jew?" (3:1–2)

VIII. Disobedience of Jews affect God's character and plan? (3:3–7)

IX. Accusation against Paul, Why should we not do evil so that good might come out of it? (3:8)

X. Jews are no better than the Gentiles: All have sinned and fallen away from God's will (3:9–20)
 A. All mankind is sinful (3:10–18)
 B. Torah alone is ineffective to justify mankind before God [It is a tool that reflects mankind's sinfulness] (3:19–20)

XI. God's righteousness being revealed now in Yeshua the Messiah (3:21–26)

XII. All mankind are justified by their faith (3:27–28)

XIII. There's only one God for Jew and Gentile: Justification by faith does not contradict the Torah, but upholds it (3:29–31)

XIV. Abraham as a case study for the way God deals with mankind (4:1–25)
 A. Abraham is justified by faith (4:1–3)
 B. Faith's reward is righteousness; Work's reward is the earnings (4:4–5)
 C. King David is a witness to God's grace (4:6–8)
 D. Is God's grace only for the Jews? (4:9–11b)
 E. Abraham is father of all who believe—Jews and Gentiles (4:11b–12)
 F. Abraham's faithfulness benefits all mankind (4:13–22)
 G. Lessons learned from Abraham: Proof that faith's principle still works through Yeshua the Messiah (4:23–25)

XV. Introduction to Yeshua's role in justification of the believer (5:1–11)
   A. Direct benefits of one's faith in Yeshua (5:1–5)
   B. God's salvation through Yeshua is an act of His love (5:6–11)

XVI. Effects of justification by faith: Everlasting life of righteousness (5:12–21)
   A. First Adam analogy (5:12–18)
   B. Messiah's analogy (5:19–21)

XVII. How does release from sin work out practically? (6:1–7:6)
   A. Antinomian question that follows the teaching of salvation by grace (6:1–2)
   B. Dying with Messiah in order to live for God (6:3–14)
   C. Analogy of changing masters that changes our ability to do acts of righteousness (6:15–23)
   D. Analogy of marriage (7:1–3)
   E. Dying with Messiah and serving God in newness of spirit (7:4–6)

XVIII. Mankind and Torah in relationship to a system of faith (7:7–25)
   A. Purpose of the Torah (7:7–13)
   B. Mankind's final despair and the divine release (7:14–25)

XIX. Results of the Messiah's work: Life in the Spirit of God (8:1–17)

XX. Advantage of life in the Spirit in a world full of suffering; i.e., having hope in the Messiah (8:18–30)

XXI. Introduction to Israel's situation in relationship to the Gospel (God's love is irrevocable and stands even under conditions of extreme suffering) (8:31–39)

XXII. Israel and the Gentiles in God's purpose (9:1–11:36)
   A. Paul's desire for Israel (9:1–3)
   B. Israel's status in God's election (9:4–5)
   C. God has not failed when He chose Israel's seed for His election (9:6–13)
   D. Is God's election just? (9:14–18)
   E. If God has sovereignly elected Israel, why is He condemning them? (9:19–29)
   F. God's choice of Israel was not arbitrary, nor unjust (9:30–10:21)
      1. Israel's unfaithfulness was built into the system (9:30-33, 10:18-21)
      2. Israel did not understand the purpose of the Torah (10:1-4)
      3. Moses knew that faith is the essence of the Torah (10:5-13)
   G. Has God rejected His people? (11:1–32)
      1. God has not rejected His people Israel (11:1-2a)
      2. God is not left without a witness in Israel (The Elijah Syndrome

and the Church's attitude toward Israel) (11:2b-12)
3. What should the Church learn from the way God dealt with Israel? (11:13-24)
4. God will vindicate His choice of Israel: He will save all Israel (11:25-32)
5. Paul enters spiritual ecstasy (11:33-36)

XXIII. The *Halakhik* outworking of the Gospel in the lives of individuals and the Church (12:1–15:13)
- A. A fair trade-off: God gave mankind His mercy; mankind, through its conduct, ought to offer its body as a living sacrifice to God (12:1–2)
- B. General principles (*kelalim*) that regulate the life of individuals in the community (12:3–8)
- C. Rules and morals that shape the character of God's people (12:9–21)
- D. Attitude toward the state (13:1–7)
- E. Principle of love and keeping of the Torah (13:8–14)
    1. Practical implication of love in the Torah (13:8-10)
    2. Time demands a special attention to moral conduct (13:11-14)
- F. Special relationship of the Church to differences of culture and tradition (14:1–23)
- G. Conclusion of the *Halakhik* section (15:1–13)
    1. Encouragement to stand firm through hard times (15:1-6)
    2. Admonition to the Jews to understand the place of the Gentiles in the Church (15:7-13)

XXIV. Closing remarks and edification (15:14–30)
- A. Reason for writing this letter (15:14–22)
- B. Plans to visit Rome on the way to Spain (15:23–24)
- C. The collection for Jerusalem (15:25–33)

XXV. Greetings, introductions, and warnings against heretics (16:1–23)
- A. Introducing Phoebe (16:1–2)
- B. Greetings to Paul's acquaintances in Rome (16:3–16)
- C. Warning against heretics and problem makers (16:17–20)
- D. Greetings from Paul's companions (16:21)
- E. The signature of the Amanuenses, Tertius (16:22–23)

XXVI. Final doxology (16:25–27)

Selected Bibliography

Davies, W.D. *Paul and Rabbinic Judaism*, 4th ed. Philadelphia, PA, 1980.

Jervell, Jacob. *The Unknown Paul.* Minneapolis: Augsburg Publishing House, 1984.

Koester, Helmut. *Ancient Christian Gospels: Their History and Development.* London: SCM Press Ltd., 1990.

Maccoby, A. *The Myth Maker: Paul the Inventor of Christianity.* NY: Harper and Row, 1986.

Meeks, Wayne A. *The First Urban Christians.* New Haven, CT, 1983.

Räisänen, Heikki. *Paul and the Law*, 2nd ed. Tübingen, 1987.

Sanders. E.P. *Paul.* Oxford: Oxford University Press, 1991.

______.*Paul and Palestinian Judaism.* Philadelphia, 1977.

______.*Paul, the Law, and the Jewish People.* Philadelphia, 1983.

Schoeps, H.J. *Paul.* Philadelphia: Westminster Press, 1959.

Schweitzer, Albert. *Paul and His Interpreters.* London, 1912.

______.*The Mysticism of Paul the Apostle.* London, 1931.

Endnotes

1 See, for example, J. Neusner, *Judaism in the Beginning of Christianity* (Philadelphia: Fortress Press, 1984), 28f et al; M. Stone, "Judaism at the Time of Christ," *Scientific American* (January 1973), 80-87.

2 For the following discussion, see A. Steinsaltz, *The Talmud: A Reference Guide* (NY: Random House, 1989), 3f, 97, 147-48.

3 D. Flusser, *Judaism and the Origins of Christianity* (Jerusalem: Magnes Press, 1988), xiii-xv.

4 B. Thiering, *Jesus and the Riddle of the Dead Sea Scrolls: Unlocking the Secrets of His Life Story* (SF: 1992).

5 D. Flusser, *Judaism*, 24, 73.

ROMANS

1

Introduction

Paul introduces the main themes of his letter to the Roman community. He identifies his readers in verses 6-15, and presents his credentials as the apostle to the Gentiles (verses 1-5 and 11-17), a motif which he picks up again in chapter 15. He defines his first main theme: the gospel which he is preaching, which concerns the resurrection of Yeshua (verses 1-4), and which is the "power of salvation to all who believe" (verses 16-17). He then begins to describe the unrighteousness of the Gentile nations, whom God justifies, together with Israel, through his gift of righteousness in Yeshua, and which man receives through his faithfulness to God (verses 18-32).

Verse 1:
"Paul": cf. 1 Cor.1.1, 2 Cor.1.1, Gal.1.1, Eph.1.1, Phil.1.1, Col.1.1, 1 Tim.1.1, 2 Tim.1.1, Titus 1.1, Philem.1.

Paul was born in the Jewish community of Tarsus in Asia Minor (Cilicia; cf. Acts 9.11, 21.39, 22.3), of the tribe of Benjamin (cf. Phil.3.5). He inherited dual Tarsan (cf. Acts 21.39) and Roman citizenship from birth (Acts 22.28; cf. Acts 16.37, 22.25), but grew up in Jerusalem (cf. Acts 22.3).[1] He studied in Jerusalem under Rabban Gamaliel, one of the leading pharisaic authorities of his day (Acts 22.3; cf. 5.34), and identified himself as a Pharisee (cf. Acts 23.6, Phil.3.5) acting in accordance with pharisaic principles (cf. Acts 18.18, 20.16, 21.23-26, 22.3, 23.1, 6, 24.17, 26.5, 1 Cor.16.8, Phil.3.5).[2] He was known by his Hebrew name of Sha'ul (cf. Acts 7.58, 8.1, 9.1, 11, 17 etc.) and by his Roman name of Paul (cf. Acts 13.9).[3] He spoke Hebrew (cf. Acts 21.40) and Greek (cf. Acts 21.37), the *lingua franca* of the period, and signed his letters "Paul" in keeping with the fact that he wrote in Greek.

Paul's authorship of Romans is generally recognized.[4] The various designations with which Paul introduces himself to his readers ("bond servant," "apostle," "set apart . . . ") initially function as his "credentials," since he is writing to communities (cf. 16.5, 14-15) which he had not founded (cf. 15.20-22). Such introductory salutations were common in Jewish literature of the period.[5] Paul's writings also establish the (apostolic) authority for his teaching, which is grounded in his commission to preach the gospel to the Gentiles.[6] Verses 1-7 therefore introduce Paul to his readers in the communities in Rome, in which he presents the main theme of his letter. Since the communities in Rome are of mixed Jewish and Gentile believers (cf. 1.5-6, 13, 7.1, 16.5), Paul addresses the central issue of God's "creation" of the Gentiles (cf. 4.17) as a nation like Israel, who will provoke Israel back to the God of Abraham, Isaac, and Jacob after their temporary rejection of His Messiah, Yeshua.

"Bond-servant": cf. Mt.20.25-28, 23.11, Mk.9.35, 10.43, Rom.6.12-23, 1 Cor.7.22-23, Phil.1.1, 2.7, Tit.1.1, Jas.1.1, 2 Pet.1.1, Jude 1.1.

The biblical leaders and prophets are often characterized as servants.[7] Paul describes himself as though "bought by Yeshua" (cf. 1 Cor.7.23), and thus introduces the theme of the "two masters," based on a midrash on Job 3.19, which runs throughout the letter:

> R. Simon said: . . . "*And the servant is free from his master,*" he who performs the will of his creator (*yotzer*) angers his evil inclination (*yetzer*), but once he is dead he emerges into freedom, as it is said, "*And the servant is free from his master.*" (Ruth R.3.1)[8]

"Called": cf. Ex.31.2, 35.30, Num.1.16, 16.2, 26.9, Ps.78.70, 105.26, Jer.1.1ff, Rom.1.7, 8.33, 1 Cor.1.1-2, 9.1, Eph.1.1, Col.1.1, 1 Thess.2.12, 5.24; 1QS 2.2, 9.14, 11.7-8, 1QM 2.7, 3.2, 7, 4.10-11, CDC 4.3-4, 1QpHab 8.9.

Paul's "service" (cf. "bond-servant") to God is his personal response to God's election of Israel, since God's "calling" is His "setting apart" or "sanctification" of a nation to be His people (cf. Ex.19.6, Dt.7.6, 14.2), as the Qumran community similarly understood (although for different reasons):

> For [the man of understanding that he may instruct the sai]nts to li[ve according to the ru]le of the Community; to seek God with [all their heart] and [all their soul] [and] do what is good and right before Him, as He commanded by the hand of Moses and all His servants the Prophets; and to love all that He has chosen and hate all that He has despised; and to depart from all evil and cling to all good works; and to practice truth and righteousness and justice on earth, and to walk no more in the stubbornness of a guilty heart, nor with lustful eyes committing every kind of evil; and to cause all the volunteers to

enter who wish to practise the precepts of God in the Covenant of Grace, that they may be united in the Council of God and behave perfectly before Him. . . . (1QS 1.1-8)[9]

Paul has similarly been "converted from all evil" to God's "Covenant of Grace" to "volunteer . . . for His truth and to walk in His will," "to be separated from all perverse men who walk in the way of wickedness" (1QS 5.1-11) because he has been "bought" by Yeshua, and has made his Creator his master instead of his own (evil) inclination.

"As an apostle": cf. Mt.10.2, Jn.13.16, Acts 1.25-26, 11.13, 1 Cor.9.1, 15.9, 2 Cor.12.11, Gal.1.19, 1 Tim.2.7, 2 Tim.1.11; Tanh.Vayishlach 3, Mid.Ps.78.5, Ex.R.5.14, Ber.5.5, Ta'anit 2a, San.113a, Kid.23b, Yoma 19a-b, Hag.10b.

The Greek noun ἀποστολος (*apostolos*) originally derived from seafaring terminology referring to the sending out of merchant and military expeditions; eventually, the term was applied to the people conducting the expeditions who were recognized as "representatives" of those who commissioned their services.[10] The title and the function of the apostle in the New Testament more directly reflects, however, the rabbinic development of biblical ideas of "agency."[11] The legal implications of being "sent" were set out in Jewish law (*halakhah*) as the principle of "agency": "The one sent by a man [שליח; *shaliach*] is as the man himself" (Ber.5.5).[12] The principle of agency applied to most areas covered by *halakhah* when a "third party" was empowered to perform business on behalf of the person who sent him. The agent was thus invested with the power and authority of his sender and was regarded as equal to him in the business with which he was entrusted. The New Testament שליח was commissioned by Yeshua in the same way and on the same model as Yeshua himself is God's supreme שליח (cf. Jn.3.31-35, 5.36-38, 8.18, 17.1-3). The apostle's "agency" is the service of the kingdom of God. He is commissioned to preach the gospel throughout the world, corresponding to several of the functions of the rabbinic שליחים, among whose tasks were those of regulating the calendar for the Diaspora (cf. Yev.16.7), teaching the Tanakh (Bible) and Mishnah to the Diaspora communities (cf. Tos.Meg.2.5), collecting money from them, and carrying letters of accreditation. The New Testament apostles were God's representatives, whose appointment God affirmed through the Body of the Messiah on its behalf.[13] Christian history has traditionally perceived the early community to have laid down qualifications for the title (function) of the "twelve apostles." They were to have "accompanied us all the time" during Yeshua's ministry, and thus be fit to "become a witness with us of his resurrection" (Acts 1.22).[14] Here Paul connects the principle of agency with "service" (cf. "bond-servant"), based on a midrash (interpretation of Scripture) on Genesis 32.26, apparently used also by Yeshua (cf. Jn.13.16):

> R. Meir, R. Judah, and R. Simeon each made an observation. R. Meir said: Who is greater: the guardian or the guarded? Since it is written, *For He will give His angels charge over thee, to guard thee in all thy ways* (Ps.91.11), it follows that the guarded is greater than the guardian. R. Judah said: Who is greater, the bearer or the borne? Since it says, *They shall bear thee upon their hands* (ibid. 12), it follows that the borne is greater than the bearer. R. Simeon said: Who is greater: the sender or the sent? From the verse, AND HE SAID: LET ME GO [lit. 'send me away'] (Gen.32.26), it follows that the sender is greater than the sent. (Gen.R.78.1)[15]

Paul acted as an "agent" on behalf of the rabbinic authorities in bearing a letter of authorization to seek out the earliest believers in the Diaspora (cf. Acts 9.1ff). After his conversion he was "sent out" by various communities to preach in other places (cf. Acts 12.25, 13.1-4). The early communities also exercised the Jewish custom of סמיכה (*semichah*), or ordination (cf. San.13b-14a). Paul understands his agency most importantly, to be to "bear" the name of the Lord (cf. Gen.R.78.2) "before the Gentiles and kings and the sons of Israel" (Acts 9.15). His at times vehement defense of his apostolic authority (cf. 1 Cor.15.7-10, 2 Cor.12.11-12, Gal.1.6-2.10) is based on a midrashic association (cf. Test.Abr.12.12-13, Mid.Ps.122) of the twelve apostles with the twelve tribes of Israel who would judge the world at the final Judgment (cf. Mt.19.28, Lk.22.30, Rev.21.12, 14). Paul thus regards himself as a "thirteenth" apostle to the nations which would come before Israel to be judged (but also to provoke them to jealousy), a theme on which he elaborates throughout the letter.

"Set apart": cf. Ex.28.38, 41, 29.1, Lev.11.44, 20.7, Dt.7.6, 14.2, 32.8-9, Acts 9.15, 13.2; 1QS 5.1-2, 10, 8.11-16, 9.5-11, 19-20, CDC 6.17-20, CDC[b] 2.22-24.

Paul uses a number of synonyms in his writings for the idea of election (cf. "bond-servant," "called," "set apart"). As an "Israelite, a descendant of Abraham, of the tribe of Benjamin" (Rom.11.2), he represents (is an "agent" of) God's chosen people. He also represents (is an agent of) Yeshua. Just as the people of Israel were chosen and set apart to be witnesses of God (cf. Isa.43.10, 12), the apostles in the New Testament (whose number corresponds to the twelve tribes of Israel) are chosen and set apart to be witnesses of God through Yeshua (cf. Acts 5.32). God's "calling" and "setting apart" (His election) of men is for holiness, just as the Qumran community volunteered to separate themselves in order to "depart from all evil and cling to all good works" (1QS 1.4-5):

> When they join the Community, let whoever comes to the Council of the Community enter into the Covenant of God in the presence of all the volunteers, and let him undertake by oath to be converted to the Law of Moses according to all His commands, with all his heart and all his soul, following all that is revealed of it to the sons of Zadok the priests who keep the Covenant and seek His will, and to the majority of the members of their Covenant, they who volunteer together for His truth and to walk in his will. And let him undertake by the Covenant to be separated from all perverse men who walk in the way of wickedness. . . . In those days, they shall separate the members of the Community (into) the House of holiness for Aaron that infinite holiness may be assembled together, and (into) the House of community for Israel for those that walk in perfection. (1QS 5.7-11, 9.5-6)

"For the gospel of God": cf. Isa.40.9, 52.7, 61.1, Nah.1.15, Mk.1.14, Rom.15.16, 2 Cor.2.12, 4.3-4, 8.18, 9.13, 10.14, 11.7, Gal.1.6-16, 2.2, 1 Thess.3.2; 1QH 18.14.

The "holiness" to which Paul is "called" and "set apart" is the (preaching of the) "gospel of God," which parallels the "Mysteries" which were "revealed" to the Teacher of Righteousness in the Qumran community. Paul's calling is to preach the "mystery of the Messiah" to the Gentiles (cf. Eph.3.3-7), in a manner similar to the way in which the Teacher of Righteousness also perceived his calling:

> And Thou hast opened [his] foun[tain] to reprove the deeds of the creature of clay and the transgressions of him that is born of woman, in conformity with his works; and to open Thy l[aws] of truth to the creature whom Thou hast upheld by Thy might, that according to Thy truth [he may be] the one who announces good tidings [in the ti]me of Thy goodness [מבשר טובכה], preaching the gospel [לבשר] to the humble according to the abundance of Thy mercy . . . And [Thou hast] created [me] for Thy sake to [ful]fil the Law, and [to te]a[ch by] my mouth the men of Thy council in the midst of the sons of men,

> that Thy marvels may be told to everlasting generations and Thy mighty deeds be [contemp]lated without end. And all the nations shall know Thy truth and all the peoples, Thy glory. (1QH 18.12-14, 6.10-12)

The term "gospel of God" (εὐαγγελιον; *euangelion*; good news) derives, among many other verses, from Isaiah 52.7, which associates the "good news" with "salvation," and Isaiah 61-62, which speak of the "favorable year of the Lord" (or "the year of good-will").[16] Paul (cf. also the Teacher of Righteousness) understands these passages as messianic texts, and describes the gospel as "concerning [God's] son" (verse 3).[17] The good news of Yeshua is the "power of God" (1 Cor.1.18) for redemption, wisdom, righteousness, and sanctification (1 Cor.1.30), first to Israel and then also to the Gentiles.

"Promised beforehand": cf. Job 38.4f, Ps.72.17, Isa.42.9, 44.7, 46.8ff, 48.3ff, 61.1, Lk.1.70, Jn.1.1, 2, 8.56, 58, 13.19, 14.29, 16.4, 17.5, Rom.3.21, 4.13ff, 8.29, 9.4, 11.2, Gal.3.6f Eph.3.4-5, 2 Tim.1.9, Tit.1.1-3, Heb.6.13-20, 1 Pet.1.10-12, 20, Rev.13.8; 1 En.48.3, 62.7f, Odes Sol.41.15; Gen.R.85.1.

God's "promise" of "good news" is given in order to be fulfilled at a later time. In Second Temple Jewish thought, God's promises were interpreted as having existed from the beginning of time, and the Rabbis associated "foreknowledge" and "promises" with "pre-existence," especially in regard to the "birth" of the Messiah:

> Seven things were created before the world was created, and these are they: The Torah, repentance, the Garden of Eden, Gehenna, the Throne of Glory, the Temple, and the name of the Messiah. (Pes.54a)[18]

Verse 2:

"Through His prophets": cf. Gen.20.7, Ex.7.1, Dt.13.1ff, 18.15, 1 Sam.9.9, Jer.23.18, Amos 3.7-8, Hab.2.2-3, Mt.13.17, Lk.1.70, 10.23-24, 24.25-27, 44-48, Acts 13.27, Rom.16.25, Eph.3.3-5, Heb.1.1, 1 Pet.1.10-12; 1QS 1.3, 8.16, 1QpHab 2.5-10, 7.1-8; San.99a, Ber.34b.

One of the major functions of the biblical prophets, who were privy to the council of God and were entrusted with His secrets, was to declare God's promises for the future generations. The Sages commonly pronounced that "all the prophets prophesied only for the days of the Messiah" (Ber.34b). The Teacher of Righteousness at Qumran also saw himself as the "prophet like me" (a new Moses), to whom all the people would listen:

> And God told Habakkuk to write down the things which will come to pass in the last generation, but the consummation of time He made not known to him. And as for that which He said, *That he might read it easily that reads it* {Hab.2.2}, the explanation of this concerns the Teacher of Righteousness to whom God made known all the Mysteries of the words of His servants the prophets. *For there is yet another vision relating to the appointed time; it speaks of the end and does not deceive.* (2.3a) The explanation of this is that the final time will last long and will exceed everything spoken of by the Prophets; for the Mysteries of God are marvelous. . . . [*But the righteous will live by his faith.*] (2.4b) The explanation of this concerns all those who observe the Law in the House of Judah. God will deliver them from the House of Judgment because of their affliction and their faith in the Teacher of Righteousness. (1QpHab 7.1-8, 8.1-3; cf. 1QH 2.6-19, 7.12)

"In the holy Scriptures": cf. Gen.18.19, Ex.20.1ff, 31.18, 32.15-16, 34.27-28, Ps.19.7-11, 119.1ff, Prov.3.ff, 8.22ff, 30.5-6, Isa.30.8, Jer.30.2, Hab.2.2, Mt.26.56, Lk.24.44, Jn.5.39-47, 20.9, Rom.15.4, Gal.3.8, 2 Tim.3.15-16, 1 Pet.1.10-12, 2 Pet.1.21, 2 Pet.3.15, Rev.1.11; 4QMiksei Ma'asei HaTorah[b] 2.9ff; Sir.Prologue, 1 En.103.2; Jos.*Contra Ap.*1.38-42; PA 3.7, 8, 5.21, Pes.Rab.5.1, Shab.16.1, Eruv.10.3, Meg.1.8, 3.1, Pes.77a, BB 1.6, Par.10.3, Yad.3.5, 4.6; Philo, *De Vita Cont.*1f, 25, 28f; 1 Clem.53.1.

The "holy Scriptures" to which Paul refers are the Tanakh, which contains the Torah (תורה; *Torah*), Prophets (נביאים; *Nevi'im*), and Writings (כתובים; *Ketuvim*).[19] In the various Jewish debates concerning the contents of the "canon" of Scripture—what books should be regarded as authoritative for the community—three major criteria are identified as sources of holiness: the inspiration of the Holy Spirit; ritual purity (whether a book made the hands "unclean" or not); and the authority of the Covenant made on Mount Sinai:

> It therefore naturally, or rather necessarily, follows (seeing that with us it is not open to everybody to write the records, and that there is no discrepancy in what is written; seeing that, on the contrary, the prophets alone had this privilege, obtaining their knowledge of the most remote and ancient history through the inspiration which they owed to God, and committing to writing a clear account of the events of their own time just as they occurred)—it follows, I say, that we do not possess myriads of inconsistent books, conflicting with each other. Our books, those which are justly accredited, are but two and

> twenty, and contain the record of all time. Of these, five are the books of Moses, comprising the laws and the traditional history from the birth of man down to the death of the lawgiver. . . . [T]he prophets subsequent to Moses wrote the history of the events of their own time in thirteen books. The remaining four books contain hymns to God and precepts for the conduct of human life. From Artaxerxes to our own time the complete history has been written, but has not been deemed worthy of equal credit with the earlier records, because of the failure of the exact succession of the prophets. (Jos.*Contra Ap.*1.37-41)[20]

All the Holy Scriptures render the hands unclean. The Song of Songs and Ecclesiastes render the hands unclean. . . . R. Simeon says: Ecclesiastes is one of the things about which the School of Shammai adopted the more lenient, and the School of Hillel the more stringent ruling. . . . The [Aramaic] version that is in Ezra and Daniel renders the hands unclean. If an [Aramaic] version [contained in the Scriptures] was written in Hebrew, or if [Scripture that is in] Hebrew was written in an [Aramaic] version, or in Hebrew script, it does not render the hands unclean. [The Holy Scriptures] render the hands unclean only if they are written in the Assyrian character, on leather, and in ink. (Yad.3.5, 4.5)[21]

Verse 3:

"Concerning His son": cf. Gen.6.2,4, 2 Sam.7.14, Job 1.6, 2.1, Ps.2.7-12, 80.17, 110.1f, Prov.30.4, Isa.7.14, 9.6-7, 11.1f, Dan.3.25, Mt.1.21-23, 2.5, 3.17, 16.16, 26.63f, Mk.1.1-4, 5.7, Lk.2.29f, 3.22, Jn.5.18f, 5.39f, Heb.1.1-2; 1QH 3.7ff; 4 Ez.2.46f, 7.28-29, 13.32f, 14.9, Odes Sol.36.3, 1 En.62.7f, 105.2; Mid.Ps.2.9, 21.1-5, 72.6, Ber.17a, San.97a-99a.

The appellation "son(s) of God" primarily refers to Israel (cf. Ex.4.22, Isa.63.16, Jer.31.9, Hos.11.1). It is given also to the angels (cf. Gen.6.2, 4, Job 1.6, 2.1, 38.7) and to the kings of Israel (cf. 2 Sam.7.14, Ps.2.6-7, 89.26-27). Since the kings of Israel were referred to as both God's "son" and "anointed," the royal Messiah was therefore also expected to be God's son:

> In the decree of the Writings it is written, *The Lord said unto my lord: Sit thou at My right hand, until I make thine enemies thy footstool* (Ps.110.1). . . . R. Berechiah said in the name of R. Samuel: One verse reads of the king Messiah that *One like the son of man . . . came to the Ancient of days, and they brought him near before Him* (Dan.7.13). (Mid.Ps.2.9, 21.5)

"Born of a descendant of David": cf. 2 Sam.7.12f, Ps.89.3-4, 132.11, Mt.1.1, 9.27, Lk.1.32, 69, Acts 13.22-23, Rev.22.16; Ps.Sol.17.21, Test.Levi 18.3, Test.Jud. 24.1-6; CDC 7.18-20, 4QFlor.1.10f, 4QPat.Bless.1f; Hell.Syn.Pray.6.2; Pes.Rab.36.2, Mid.Ps.21.1, Ruth R.8.1, Cant.R.5.2.2, 7.14.1, San.97a, 98a, Yoma 10a.

According to a concept widespread in Second Temple Jewish circles, based on various biblical passages, Davidic descent was one of the characteristics of the Messiah:

> *[And] Yahweh [de]clares to thee that He will build thee a house; and I will raise up thy seed after thee, and I will establish his royal throne [for ev]er. I wi[ll be] a father to him and he shall be my son.* (2 Sam.7.11c, 12b-c, 13, 14a) This is the Branch of David who will arise with the Seeker of the law and who will sit on the throne of Zion at the end of days; as it is written, *I will raise up the tabernacle of David which is fallen* [Amos 9.11]. This *tabernacle of David which is fallen* (is) he who will arise to save Israel. (4QFlor.1.10-13)[22]

"According to the flesh": cf. Mt.1.1, 13.55, Lk.3.23-38, 4.22, Jn.1.11, 14, Rom.9.3-5, 1 Tim.3.16, 1 Jn.3.5, 8.

Genealogical lines and lineage were considered important in Second Temple Judaism. A text in Genesis Rabbah 98.8, for example, relates the story of the discovery of a genealogical scroll in Jerusalem ascribing Davidic descent to Hillel, while the Qumran community also placed great emphasis on genealogy, although in the priestly framework of Zadok over the royal line of David, to support their claim to be the "true Israel."[23]

Verse 4:

"Declared the Son of God . . . from the dead": cf. Mt.3.17, 11.27, 16.21, 17.5, Mk.8.28-31, 10.34, Lk.9.22-27, 11.24-25, Acts 1.22, 2.31, 4.33, Rom.4.24-25, 6.5, 1 Cor.15.12ff, Phil.3.10, 1 Pet.3.21; CDC 6.10-11, 7.20; Test.Jud.25.1, 1 En.91.9-11, 2 Bar.30.1, 49.2, 51.5, Hell.Syn.Pray.5.6; Ex.R.44.2, San.10.1, 90b, 91b, Ket.111a-b.

Paul identifies Yeshua's "earthly" descent and then associates his divine sonship directly with his resurrection by the Spirit of God. The belief in resurrection was developed in the Second Temple period from clear biblical references; Josephus records that the doctrine of resurrection was contested between the Pharisees and Sadducees in the first century C.E.[24] The "pre-existence" of the Messiah was also a common subject in midrashic literature, whose "resurrection" or non-death of the messianic figure was pre-figured in such cases as Melchizedek, Enoch, and Elijah.[25] Paul's reference to the "declaration" (the Greek verb ὁρίζω [*horidzo*] means "to decree" or "to appoint") of Yeshua as the "son of God" reflects God's "decree" in Psalm 2.7: "I will surely tell of the decree of the Lord: He said to Me, 'Thou art My Son, today I have begotten Thee' ":

> In another comment, the verse is read *I will tell of the decree: The Lord said unto me: Thou art My son . . . Ask of Me, and I will give the nations for thine inheritance, and the ends of the earth for thy possession* (Ps.2.7-8). R. Yudan said: All these goodly promises are in the decree of the King, the King of kings, who will fulfil them for the Lord Messiah. (Mid.Ps.2.9)[26]

"According to the Spirit of holiness": cf. Ps.51.11, Isa.63.10-11, Mt.3.11, Mk.1.8, Jn.1.33, 14.26, Acts 1.8, 2.4, 33, Rom.9.1, 1 Cor.12.3; 1QS 4.18ff, CDC 5.11, 7.3-4, 1QH 7.6-7, 8.11-12, 9.32, 12.12, 14.11, 16.6, 12, 17.26; Tos.Sot.13.3, Tanh.Vayechi 14, Mekh.Beshall.7, SOR 6, Sot.9.15.

Resurrection is frequently identified with purification, and thus also with renewal and recreation, in Jewish texts of the period:

> Behold, I was brought forth in iniquity, and in sin my mother conceived me. . . . Purify me with hyssop, and I shall be clean; wash me, and I shall be whiter than snow. . . . Create in me a clean heart, O God, and renew a steadfast spirit within me. Do not cast me away from Thy presence, and do not take Thy Holy Spirit from me. Restore to me the joy of Thy salvation, and sustain me with a willing spirit. (Ps.51.5-12)

Other Jewish sources strengthen and confirm the association between holiness and resurrection:

> . . . R. Phineas b. Jair said: Study leads to precision, precision leads to zeal, zeal leads to cleanliness, cleanliness leads to restraint, restraint leads to meekness, meekness leads to saintliness, saintliness leads to [the possession of] the holy spirit, the holy spirit leads to life eternal [lit. resurrection of the dead]. . . . (AZ 20b)[27]

The Messiah himself was expected, in one tradition, to die, although this Messiah of Joseph, "the son of Ephraim," was a precursor of the Messiah son of David:

> Our Rabbis taught: The Holy One, blessed be He, will say to the Messiah, the son of David (May he reveal himself speedily in our days!), 'Ask of Me anything, and I will give it to thee', as it is said, *I will tell of the decree* etc. *this day have I begotten thee, ask of me and I will give the nations for thy inheritance* (Ps.2.7-8). But when he will see that Messiah the son of Joseph is slain, he will say to Him, 'Lord of the Universe, I ask of Thee only the gift of life'. 'As to life', He would answer him, 'Your father David has already prophesied this concerning you', as it is said, *He asked life of thee, thou gavest it him* [*even length of days for ever and ever*] (Ps.21.4). (Suk.52a)[28]

"Yeshua HaMashiach our Lord": cf. Jn.13.13, Rom.4.24, 8.9f, 10.9, 14.8-9, 1 Cor.4.5, 12.3, Phil.2.10-11, Col.2.6; Odes Sol.17.17, 24.1, 39.11, Ps.Sol.17.32, 18.7.

The title "Lord Messiah" (Χριστος Κυριος; *Christos Kurios*) is derived from the biblical phrase "Messiah of God (YHWH)" (cf. 1 Sam.2.10, 35, 24.6, 10, 2 Sam.1.14, 16). It first appears in post-biblical literature in the Psalms of Solomon, in a text based on Jeremiah 23.5-6: "There will be no unrighteousness among them in his days, for all shall be holy, and their king shall be the Lord Messiah" (cf. Ps.Sol.17.32). God promises that He will "raise up" for David a "righteous branch," and calls his name "the Lord our righteousness."[29] Romans 10.9 confirms Paul's view that Yeshua's lordship is based upon his resurrection, since "confession" of his lordship parallels faithfulness to his being raised from the dead: Yeshua's resurrection makes him Lord of both the dead and the living (cf. Rom.14.9).

Verse 5:

"Through whom . . . apostleship": cf. Rom.11.13, 12.3, 15.15, 1 Cor.3.10, 15.10, 2 Cor.1.1, Gal.1.6, 2.9, Eph.1.1, 3.7, Col.1.1, 1 Tim.1.1; 1QS 4.3-5, 1QH 4.36-37, 6.9, 7.35, 11.28-34, 12.14; Odes Sol.9.5, 34.6, Wis.Sol.3.9.

Paul employs "grace" as a technical term which grounds his apostolic authority.[30] It represents his "calling" by God to serve Him in holiness, and as God's gift it empowers him to act as God's שליח (*shaliach*). A similar view of the apostolic task is described in a document attributed to the Teacher of Righteousness in Qumran:

> And it is Thou who in Thy mercy and in the greatness of Thy favors hast strengthened the spirit of man in the face of blows, [and hast redeemed] and cleansed him from much iniquity that he might recount Thy marvels in the presence of all Thy works. [And I, I will

> rec]ount [unto men] the judgments which have smitten me and all Thy marvels unto the sons of men because Thou hast manifested Thy power [in me . . .] . . . [And Thou hast proclaimed] Thy marvelous [me]ssages [by his mouth] that they may shine before the eyes of all that hear them. [For Thou hast upheld Thy servant] with Thy strong Right Hand to guide the[m] by the strength of Thy might . . . [For] Thou hast opened a [fount]ain in the mouth of Thy servant and upon his tongue Thou hast graven [Thy precepts] on a measuring-cord, [that he] may proclaim them unto creatures because of his understanding and be an interpreter of these things unto that which is dust like myself. (1QH 1.31-34, 18.6-12)

"Obedience of faith": cf. Gen.49.10, Acts 6.7, Rom.5.19, 15.18, 16.26, 2 Cor.2.9, 10.5, Phil.2.8, Heb.5.8, 1 Pet.1.14; 1QH 2.8-15, 6.10-14, 7.12, 1QpHab 7.2-3.

The phrase "obedience of faith" probably derives from the expression "the obedience of the peoples" (יקהת עמים; *yikhat 'amim*) with which Jacob blesses Judah in Genesis 49.10. This blessing is associated in Jewish literature with the Messiah, who will draw the Gentiles to himself and bring salvation to the whole world, just as in Psalm 2.7-8, according to the decree by which God pronounces him to be His son, he will receive the nations for his inheritance.[31] At the beginning of his letter Paul thus identifies his שליחות (*shelichut*; commission) with God's plan to redeem the whole world. The gospel which he is preaching is the "power of God for salvation to everyone who believes, to the Jew first and also to the Greek" (verse 16). This gospel is Yeshua himself, God's power and righteousness (cf. 1 Cor.1.18, 24, 30). Yeshua "belongs" first of all to Israel, whose are the "adoption as sons, the glory, the covenants, the giving of the Law, the Temple service, the promises, whose are the fathers, and from whom is the Messiah" (Rom.9.4-5). God's "mystery," however, which is hidden and predetermined from the foundation of the world like the Messiah, is that by Israel's partial and temporary rejection of the Messiah the Gentiles will be grafted into the commonwealth of Israel and provoke the people to jealousy for their own God and His Messiah.[32]

"For His name's sake": cf. Ex.32.12, Num.14.13, 1 Sam.12.22, Ps.23.3, 44.22, Isa.42.21, Mt.16.25, Lk.6.22, 18.29, Rom.8.36, 14.8, 1 Cor.9.23, Phil.1.29, 2 Jn.2; Sifre Dt.Ekev 48, Mid.Ps.31.1, 94.5, Suk.49b, Ned.62a, Ber.17a.

Paul ascribes God's plan to bring the Gentiles to the "obedience of faithfulness" to His concern for His "name" or reputation. God is unable to let people be excluded from His grace without compromising His sovereign power and attributes. Paul knows that he has received his "authority" as the apostle to the Gentiles because God wants to keep His name and His character pure. Paul's authority comes from Yeshua, in whose name Paul is teaching and preaching as God's agent (שליח; *shaliach*). He is thus acknowledging and publicly transmitting (cf. 1 Cor.15.1ff) the "gospel concerning God's son" in the same way as the Sages also each taught in the name of (משום; *mishum*) the teacher from whom they learned the tradition which they then passed on to their students (cf. PA 3.8, 6.6, 8).[33]

Verse 6:

"Among whom you also": cf. 13, 15.15-32, 1 Thess.2.12, 5.24.

Paul identifies part of the Roman community as those Gentiles whom Yeshua has commissioned him to bring to obedience.[34] The reference to "I am speaking to those who know the law" in 7.1, as well as the list of greetings in chapter 16, indicates that the community in Rome was mixed, containing both Jewish and Gentile believers (cf. Rom.2.17, 18, 25, 27, 11.13). The preponderance of Jewish and slave names amongst those whom Paul greets in chapter 16 also reflects the nature of the mixed community.

Verse 7:

"To all . . . beloved of God": cf. Isa.63.9, Jer.31.3, Hos.3.1, 11.4, 14.4, Mt.3.17, 17.5, Jn.13.23, 21.7, 20, Rom.5.5-8, 8.35-39, Eph.1.6, 2.4, Col.1.13, 2 Tim.1.2, Phlm.16, Heb.6.9, 1 Jn.2.7, 3.1-2, 4.7, 16, 19, Jude 1, Rev.3.19.

The term "beloved" is synonymous with the terms "chosen," "called," and "saints," and includes both Jews and Gentiles:

> He [R. Akiva] [also] used to say: Beloved is man in that he was created in the image [of God]; [it is a mark of] superabundant love [that] it was made known to him that he had been created in the image [of God] . . . Beloved are Israel in that they were called children of the All-Present. [It was a mark of] superabundant love that it was made known to them that they were called children of the All-Present . . . Beloved are Israel, in that a desirable instrument was given to them. [It was a mark of] superabundant love [that] it was made known to them that the desirable instrument wherewith the universe had been created was given to them, as it is said, For I give you good doctrine forsake not My teaching (Prov.4.2). (PA 3.14)[35]

"Called as saints": cf. Dt.7.6, 1 Sam.2.9, Ps.97.10, 135.4, Isa.41.8-9, Dan.7.18-27, 8.24, Rom.8.27-30, 9.24, 1 Cor.1.2, 6.2-3, Eph.1.18, 2.19, 3.18-19,

4.12, Phil.1.1, Col.1.12, 26, 1 Thess.3.13, 2 Thess.1.10, Jude 1-3, Rev.14.12; 1QS 5.13, 18, 8.11, 17, 20, 9.8, 11.7-8, 1QM 10.10; Ps.Sol.17.26, 1 En.58.1ff, 103.1, Asc.Isa.1.5, Test.Jac.8.2, Wis.Sol.3.9, 5.5.

Paul concludes his introductory greetings by once again acknowledging the members of the community in Rome as brethren in the Lord.[36]

"Grace to you and peace": cf. Gen.18.2-5, Num.6.24-26, Ruth 2.4, 2 Sam.20.9-18, 2 Kings 4.26, 29, 1 Cor.1.3, 2 Cor.1.2, Gal.1.3, Eph.1.2, Phil.1.2, 1 Thess.1.1, 1 Tim.1.2, 2 Tim.1.2, Tit.1.4, Phlm.3; Wis.Sol.3.9; Tanh.B.Vayeshev 7, Tos.AZ 1.3, Num.R.21.1, Shab.89a, MK 15a, 29a.

Paul greets both the Jewish and Gentile believers, using a traditional Jewish form:

> R. Helbo further said in the name of R. Huna: If one knows that his friend is used to greet him, let him greet him first. For it is said: *Seek peace and pursue it* (Ps.34.14). (Ber.6b)[37]

"God . . . Yeshua": cf. Dt.32.6, Isa.63.16, 64.8, Jer.31.9, Mal.1.6, 2.10, Mt.6.9, 1 Cor.1.3, 2 Cor.1.2, Gal.1.3, Eph.1.2, 2.11ff, Phil.1.2, 1 Thess.1.1, Phlm.3; Ps.Sol.13.9, 17.32, 18.4, 7, Test.Job 33.3, Hell.Syn.Pray.4.41, 12.14, Sir.23.1, 4, 2 Bar.7.3; TBE p.65, Sifre Dt.He'azinu 309, Ex.R.34.1, 3, Cant.R.2.16.1, Ber.35b.

God is the author and source of all blessings (cf. 2 Cor.1.3, Eph.1.3, Jas.1.17). Because He is One (cf. Dt.6.4), He is the God and Father of both Jews and Gentiles (cf. 3.30). Yeshua, His Messiah and שליח (agent) has brought peace (reconciliation and grace; cf. 5.15-18) between man and God, as well as between Jews and Gentiles (cf. Eph.2.12ff).

Verse 8:

"First I thank my God": cf. Rom.7.25, 1 Cor.1.4-9, 15.57, Phil.1.3-11, Col.1.3-14, 1 Thess.1.2-10, 2 Thess.1.3-12, Phlm.4-7.

Following the presentation of his credentials (verses 1-5) and his salutation to the community in Rome (verses 6-7), Paul begins to elaborate the reasons for which he is writing the letter. He first of all wants to thank God for their faithfulness to Him, because, both as a brother in the Lord and as the apostle to the Gentiles, he is planning to visit them on his anticipated journey to Spain (cf. 15.22-32). The "blessing" or thanks comes directly through Yeshua, who has also made the Gentiles obedient to God, and thus broken down the "barrier of the dividing wall" between Israel and the nations (cf. Eph.2.15).

"Your faith is being proclaimed . . . ": cf. 16.19.

Reports of the "obedience" of the believers in Rome have spread throughout "the whole world" (i.e., the whole known world) within the believing communities, as well as the non-believing circles (Jewish and non-Jewish) who were antagonistic to "the Way" (cf. Acts 9.2, 19.9, 23, 22.4, 24.14, 22, 28.22).

Verse 9:

"For God . . . my witness": cf. Gen.31.50, Josh.22.27, Judg.11.10, 1 Sam.12.5, Job 16.19, Ps.89.37, Jer.29.23, 42.5, Jn.8.14, Rom.1.1, 8.13-14, 9.1f, 12.1, 2 Cor.1.23, Heb.10.15, Rev.1.5.

Paul describes his being "set apart" for the preaching of "the gospel concerning (God's) son" in terms of "serving in my spirit," anticipating the metaphor of the "living and holy sacrifice" which he develops in 12.1-2.[38] His prayers were on behalf of the community in Rome (and other places), but also for his own desire to visit them personally, in order to impart to them some spiritual gift and be mutually encouraged in faith (cf. verses 11-12), and in emphasizing in his "unceasing" prayers, in which he is "always" making mention of the Roman community, he demonstrates his longing to visit the congregations in the city. God will attest how frequently Paul prays for the believers in Rome. In this respect, his service can also be associated with the rabbinic concept of prayer as the "worship of the heart": "It has been taught: *Love the Lord thy God and to worship Him with all your hearts*—What is service of Heart? You must needs say, Prayer" (Ta'anit 2a). In Ephesians 6.19, Paul further asks the brethren to pray also on his behalf that "utterance may be given to me in the opening of my mouth, to make known with boldness the mystery of the gospel."[39]

Verse 10:

"By the will of God . . . to you": cf. Acts 18.21, Rom.15.32, 1 Cor.4.19, 16.7, Heb.6.3, Jas.4.15, 1 Pet.3.17; PA 2.4, ARN[b] 32, Mekh.Beshall.3.

Paul's own wish is to visit the community in Rome, on his way to Spain. He follows his teacher's advice, however, in seeking to act according to God's will:

> He [Rabban Gamaliel] used to say: Do His will as [thou wouldst do] thine own will, so that He may do thy will as [He does] His own will. (PA 2.4)[40]

Verses 11-13:

"That I may impart some spiritual gift to you . . . ": cf. 12.3 8, 15.14-16, 1 Cor.12.1, 4, 14.1, Eph.4.7f, Heb.2.4; 1QS 4.2ff, 1QH 1.35, 2.7, 9, 7.6, 8.13; 3 En.8.1f, 10.6; PA 6.1.

Paul specifies the reason for his desire to visit the congregation in Rome as mutual spiritual edification. As the apostle to the Gentiles he apparently feels some responsibility for a community which he himself did not found, at the same time as he does not want to encroach on another evangelist's territory (cf. 15.20-22).[41] He immediately modifies his apostolic authority by saying that his intention is to "establish" (build up, or edify) the congregation, and explains that intention by indicating that he is seeking *mutual* encouragement. As he makes clear in chapter 15, Paul sees his ministry as a priest of the gospel, and his offering of the Gentiles as the "fruit" of his service.[42] The fruit of his "service in the spirit" (verse 9), however, is unambivalently intended to "establish" the congregation in Rome by building up their faithfulness, through which he will also be edified. He wishes to impart a spiritual gift to the congregation in a similar way to the "spiritual gifts" which the Qumran community saw as given to them by God as an "everlasting possession to those whom He has chosen":

> And these are the ways of these (Spirits) in the world. It is < of the Spirit of truth > to enlighten the heart of man, and to level before him the ways of true righteousness, and to set fear in his heart of the judgment of God. And (to it belong) the spirit of humility and forbearance, of abundant mercy and eternal goodness, of understanding and intelligence, and almighty wisdom with faith in all the works of God and trust in His abundant grace, and the spirit of knowledge in every design and zeal for just ordinances, and holy resolution with firm inclination and abundant affection . . . and modesty with universal prudence, and discretion concerning the truth of the Mysteries of Knowledge. Such are the counsels of the Spirit to the sons of truth in the world. And as for the Visitation of all who walk in this (Spirit), it consists of healing and abundance of bliss, with length of days and fruitfulness, and all blessings without end, and eternal joy in perpetual life, and the glorious crown and garment of honour in everlasting light. . . . The fountain of righteousness, the reservoir of power, and the dwelling-place of glory but God has given them as an everlasting possession to those whom He has chosen. He has granted them a share in the lot of the Saints, and has united their assembly, the Council of the Community, with the Sons of Heaven. And the assembly of the holy Fabric shall belong to an eternal planting for all time to come. (1QS 4.2-8, 11.6-9)[43]

Verse 14:

"I am under obligation": cf. Acts 4.19-20, Rom.8.12, 13.7-8, 15.27.

Paul expresses his apostolic authority in terms of being "indebted" to preach the gospel to all men (in the same way as he is "under obligation" to live according to the Spirit), bringing forth fruit in them because he himself has received God's grace. He further understands his calling to the Gentiles on the basis of his sharing in Israel's election (cf. 11.12-15). Because he partakes in Israel's spiritual blessings (cf. 3.2, 9.4-5) he is under obligation to share them with the nations of the world—just as the Gentiles themselves are "indebted" to minister to Israel (cf. 15.27):

> Thou shalt not turn away the needy, but shalt share everything with thy brother, and shalt not say that it is thine own, for if you are sharers in the imperishable, how much more in the things which perish. [For the Lord's will is that we give to all from the gifts we have received.] (Did.4.8)[44]

"Both to Greeks and to barbarians": cf. Acts 28.2, 4, 1 Cor.14.11, Col.3.11; 3 Macc.3.24; Jos.*Bell*.1.264, 268, 4.239, 5.345, *Ant*.12.222, 15.130, 18.328; Philo, *Vit.Mos*.2.19f, *De Spec.Leg*.2.44.

"Greeks" and "barbarians" were both "pagans" in Jewish thought; the distinction (cf. "both") was a Greek one, which distinguished "civilized" from uncultured peoples.[45] Paul places "Greeks and barbarians" in parallel with "the wise and the foolish" (cf. verse 22), a phrase which in 1 Corinthians 1.18ff corresponds to "Jews and Gentiles." This reflects the traditional rabbinic distinction between "Israel" and the "nations of the world" (אומות העולם; *'umot ha-'olam*) or the "goyim" (גוים).[46]

Verse 15:

"So I am eager . . . ": cf. 15.22-32.

Paul very much wants to visit the believers in Rome, despite the fact that he has previously been unwilling (or hindered) because he had not founded it.[47] Since it is unlikely that he is referring here to opposition to his visit from the congregation in Rome, the rider "for my part," which is evidently supposed to give further explanation about Paul's motivation, in fact gives little extra information, and adds no more than an emphasis to Paul's personal wish to visit Rome. The fact that he does not hesitate to state clearly that his wish to visit the congregation is based on his desire to "preach the gospel" to them further reflects his ambivalence.

Verse 16:

"I am not ashamed . . .": cf. Ps.25.2, 3, 20, 31.1, 69.6, 119.6, 80, 116, Isa.28.16, 29.22, 49.23, 50.7, Mk.8.38, Lk.9.26, Rom.5.5, 6.21, 9.33, 10.11, Phil.1.20, 2 Tim.1.8, 12, Heb.2.11, 11.16.

Paul is convinced that his gospel has the power to effect its purpose (cf. Isa.55.11), and is thus also "eager" to preach it to all men, both Jews and Gentiles. He appeals to the biblical word associated with disappointment and lack of security (חוש; *chush*, "to hasten"), connected most closely with Isaiah 28.16, a verse which he repeatedly recalls throughout the letter.[48] He knows that the gospel possesses God's "power" for salvation, since it concerns His son, "the Lord our righteousness" (cf. Jer.23.6). Not only will it bring redemption to Israel, but it will also "create" the Gentiles, who were once "not-My-people" (cf. Hos.1.10, 2.23), without God and without "hope" in the world, into becoming part of the "commonwealth of Israel" (cf. Eph.2.12f).

"Gospel . . . power of God": cf. Ex.15.3, 6, 1 Chron.29.11, Job 12.13, Ps.24.8, 44.1-3, 110.2, Isa.9.6, 49.26, Mt.6.13, Mk.5.30, 9.1, 13.26, 14.62, Lk.1.35, 4.14, 22.69, Acts 1.8, 8.10, Rom.1.4, 1 Cor.1.18, 24, 2 Cor.12.9, Eph.1.19, 21, 3.16, 4.10, Phil.3.21, 1 Thess.1.5, 2 Tim.1.8, Heb.1.3, Rev.5.12; 1QM 10.5, 1QH 3.34, 7.17, 19, 11.29, 12.35, 14.23; 1 En.49.2, Wis.Sol.12.16; PA 2.8, 4.10, 6.1, PRK 12.25, Mekh.Shirata 7, Tanh.Shemot 25.

In the Second Temple period, a number of epithets were developed as circumlocutions, enabling God to be described without infringing on His sovereign dignity. Among the attributes adopted to designate His name, such as המקום (*ha-Makom*), "the Place," השמים (*ha-Shamayim*), "Heaven," was the epithet הגבורה (*ha-Gevurah*), "the Power." The Sages frequently used the epithet of "Power," particularly in the context of God's revelation of His Torah to all the nations of the world, since His word came forth מפי הגבורה (*mipi ha-Gevurah*):

> *And all the People Saw the Thunderings* (Ex.20.18). R. Akiva says: They saw and heard that which was visible. They saw the fiery word coming out from the mouth of the Almighty [מפי הגבורה] as it was struck upon the Tables. . . . R. Johanan said: what is meant by the verse, *The Lord giveth the word: They that publish the tidings are a great host?*—Every single word that went forth from the mouth of the Omnipresent [מפי הגבורה] was divided into seventy languages. (Shab.88b)[49]

In this way, God's attributes became personified as independent entities ("hypostases").[50] The titles of the Messiah in Isaiah 9.6 begin with the words "Wonderful Counselor, Mighty God" (cf. Isa.11.2 and 53.11).[51] "Wisdom" is subsequently personified in Job 28 and Proverbs 8, and these texts become the basis for the later identification between Wisdom and the Torah.[52] Wisdom then becomes linked with God's "power":

> Thy power is the beginning of righteousness . . . [wisdom] is the breath of the power of God, and a pure influence flowing from the glory of the Almighty. . . . For she is the brightness of the everlasting light, the unspotted mirror of the power of God, and the image of His goodness. (Wis.Sol.12.16, 7.25-26)

> For God's truth is the rock of my steps and His power [גבורה], the stay of my right hand, and from the fount of His Righteousness comes my justification. From His wondrous Mysteries is the light in my heart, in the everlasting Being has my eye beheld Wisdom: because Knowledge [תושיה] is hidden from men and the counsel of prudence from the sons of men. The fountain of righteousness, the reservoir of power [גבורה], and the dwelling place of glory [כבוד] are denied to the assembly of flesh; but God has given them as an eternal possession to those whom He has chosen. (1QS 11.4-8; cf. 10.11-12)

Paul thus perceives Yeshua as the expression (manifestation or "representation") of God's wisdom, His power, and His Torah (cf. 1 Cor.1.18, 24, [30]), attributes ascribed to the Messiah. Paul "personifies" Yeshua as God's "Power," and describes the gospel "concerning His son" as the "power of God for salvation to all who believe" (verse 16).

"To the Jew first . . . ": cf. Acts 3.26, Rom.2.9, 3.1-2, 9.23 29, 11.25-26, 28, Gal.3.8.

Paul states the main theme of his whole letter: God's "wisdom" is His purpose to redeem the whole world through His own people, Israel, "to whom belongs the adoption as sons and the glory and the covenants and the giving of the Law and the (Temple) service and the promises, whose are the fathers, and from whom is the Messiah" (9.4-5). The people of Israel are the bearers of God's promise to Abraham (cf. 4.13f) that in him "all the nations of the world would be blessed" (cf. Gen.12.2, 18.18, 22.18). Yeshua is the fulfilment of God's promise since he is "the righteousness of God" (Jer.23.5-6, Rom.3.21). He has broken down the wall of partition and hostility (cf. Eph.2.12f), and thus provided the way for God to make the Gentiles part of the commonwealth of Israel. The nations will then turn all of Israel back to the God of Abraham, Isaac, and Jacob by provoking them to jealousy through their service of Him, following Israel's temporary rejection of God's Messiah (cf. 11.11).

Verse 17:

"Righteousness of God": cf. Gen.15.6, Dt.32.4, Ps.7.9, 11.7, Isa.45.24, Jer.23.5-6, 33.15-16, Rom.3.5, 21-22, 4.3ff, 5.17-21, 6.13ff, 9.30-10.10; 1QS 10.25, 11.4-7, 15, 1QH 1.26, 30, 7.18-22, 11.7, 18, 12.31, 13.19, 16.9-18, 17.20; Ps.Sol.4.24, 9.2, 17.26, 32, 18.7-8; Ber.Rab.p.37, PRK S6.5, Pes.Rab.307, Mid.Ps.21.2, 72.2, Num.R.18.21, Lam.R.1.16.51, BB 75b, Kall.Rab.51b.

Paul explains the messianic allusions of the "power of God" in direct reference to Jeremiah 23.5-6, one of the central rabbinic messianic prooftexts associated with the "Branch of David" (cf. 2 Sam.7.14, Jer.33.15, Zech.3.8, 6.12):

> The letters menatzpak {מ.נ.צ.פ.כ.} have double {ordinary and final} forms, and were instituted by the prophets. . . . The double *tzade* {צ} is hinted at in the verse, *Behold, a man whose name is the shoot* (tzemach), *and who shall shoot up* (yitzmach), *etc.* (Zech.6.12). This refers to the Messiah, of whom it also says, *I will raise unto David a righteous shoot* (tzemach tzaddik), *and he shall reign as king and prosper, and he shall execute justice and righteousness in the land* (Jer.23.5). (Num.R.18.21; cf. ibid., 1.11)[53]

The Teacher of Righteousness, who founded and led the Qumran community, understood his function according to similar messianic interpretations, which linked Isaiah 9.6 with Zechariah 8.3 and thus to a series of other Davidic prooftexts:

> [And] I was confused like the Woman about to bring forth at the time of her first child-bearing. . . . For she shall give birth to a man child in the billows of Death, and in the bonds of Sheol there shall spring from the crucible of the [Pregnant one] a Marvelous Counselor with his might [גבורה]; and he shall deliver every man from the billows because of Her who is big with him. . . . And through me Thou hast illuminated the face of many and caused them to grow until they are numberless; for Thou hast given me to know Thy marvelous Mysteries and hast manifested Thy power unto me in Thy marvelous counsel and hast done wonders to many because of Thy glory and to

> make known Thy mighty works to all the living . . . And Thou hast made me a father to the sons of Grace and as a foster-father to the men of good omen. (1QH 3.7-10, 4.27-28, 7.20-21)[54]

"Revealed from faith to faith": cf. Hab.2.4, Rom.3.26-30, Gal.2.19-20, 3.8; 1QS 4.2-6, 1QH 5.11-12, 11.16-18, 14.16; Mekh.Beshall.7, Tanh.Beshall.10, Mid.Ps.27.1-3, Gen.R.1.11, Eccl.R.3.9.1, Ber.63a, Hag.12b.

Paul picks up the idea of being comforted by the faithfulness of the community in Rome (cf. verse 12), and begins to describe the manner in which God reveals His righteousness to mankind, from Faithful to faithful, from Righteous to righteous, from mouth to mouth, and from hand to hand:

> R. Simon said in the name of R. Joshua b. Levi: *Manzapak* {מ.נ.צ.פ.כ.} is a Mosaic *halachah* from Sinai. R. Jeremiah said in the name of R. Hiyya b. Abba: They are what the *tzofim* [i.e. Seers] instituted. It once happened on a stormy day that the Sages did not attend the House of Assembly [i.e. the Academy]. Some children were there and they said, "Come and let us study [the letters instituted by] the Seers. Why are there two forms for *mem, nun, tzade, peh, and kaf*? It teaches [that the Torah was transmitted] from utterance to utterance, from Faithful to faithful, from Righteous to righteous, from mouth to mouth, and from hand to hand. (From utterance to utterance—from the utterance of the Holy One, blessed be He, to the utterance of Moses. From Faithful to faithful—from the Almighty, who is designated, "God, faithful King," to Moses, who is designated faithful, as it is written, *He* [sc. Moses] *is faithful* (i.e., "*trusted*") *in all My house* (Num.12.7). From Righteous to righteous—from God, who is designated righteous, as it is written, *The Lord is righteous in all His ways* (Ps.145.17), to Moses who is designated righteous, as it is written, *He executed the righteousness of the Lord* (Dt.33.21). From mouth to mouth—from the mouth of the Holy One, blessed be He, to the mouth of Moses. From hand to hand:) from the hand of the Holy One, blessed be He, to the hand of Moses." (Gen.R.1.11)[55]

God has also given His faithfulness to all men, in fulfilment of His promise to Abraham's faithfulness. God reveals His righteousness in His Messiah, "the Lord our righteousness." He is the fulfilment of God's promise to Abraham to bless all the nations in his "seed" (cf. Gal.3.16). God's promise "reckons righteousness" to Abraham because of his "faithfulness" (Gen.15.6), and Abraham's "faithfulness" then becomes the model for God's righteousness in His Messiah, so that the original faithfulness (of Abraham) is fulfilled and embodied in the faithfulness of the Messiah (cf. 3.21, Gal.2.20).[56] Genesis 15.6 is thus interpreted by Habakkuk 2.4, which is also used as a rabbinic prooftext for the essence of the Torah:

> [THEREFORE GAVE HE THEM TORAH (TEACHINGS) AND MANY COMMANDMENTS . . .] R. Simlai when preaching said: Six hundred and Thirteen precepts were communicated to Moses . . . David came and reduced them to eleven [principles] . . . Isaiah came and reduced them to six [principles] . . . Micah came and reduced them to three [principles] . . . Again came Isaiah and reduced them to two [principles], as it is said, *Thus saith the Lord, [i] Keep ye justice and [ii] do righteousness* [etc] (Isa.56.1). Amos came and reduced them to one [principle], as it is said, *For thus saith the Lord unto the house of Israel, Seek you Me and live* (Amos 5.4). To this R. Isaac b. Nahman demurred, saying: [Might it not be taken as,] Seek me by observing the whole Torah and live?—But it is Habakkuk who came and based them all on one [principle], as it is said, *But the righteous shall live by his faith* (Hab.2.4). (Mak.24a)[57]

Verse 18:

"Wrath of God": cf. Dt.29.28, Ps.6.1, 89.38, Isa.30.27, 66.15, Jer.4.4, 6.11, 21.12, 30.23, Ezek.5.13, Nah.1.6, Mt.3.7, Jn.3.36, Rom.2.5, 3.5, Col.3.5-6, Heb.3.11, Rev.6.16; 1QS 4.12, 19-26, 5.12-13, 9.23, 10.19, 1QM 1.5ff, 1QH 3.16f, 27-28, 11.16-18, 15.17-25; Ap.Bar.1.13, 1 En.91.7, 94.1ff; RH 17a.

Paul begins to develop the implications of his claim that the gospel is the "power of God for salvation to everyone who believes." It is God's power for redemption not only for Israel, whom God has chosen to be His people (cf. Dt.7.6), but also for the Gentiles. In the following verses, Paul addresses the means whereby God has "revealed" His righteousness to the Gentiles.[58] Since the Gentiles were, in standard Jewish thought, "unrighteous" by nature, God's wrath was automatically called forth against them and against the forces of evil whom they served:

> In these (two Spirits) walk the generations of all the sons of men, and into their (two) divisions all their hosts are divided from age to age. . . . And as for the Visitation of all who walk in this (Spirit), it consists of an abundance of blows administered by all the Angels of destruction in the everlasting Pit by the furious wrath of God's vengeance, of unending dread and shame without end and of the

> disgrace of destruction by the fire of the regions of darkness. And all their times from age to age are in most sorrowful chagrin and bitterest misfortune, in calamities of darkness till they are destroyed with none of them reviving or escaping. . . . For God has allotted these (two Spirits) in equal parts until the final end, and has set between their divisions eternal hatred. An abomination to Truth are the deeds of Perversity, and an abomination to Perversity are all the ways of Truth. And a fighting ardour (sets one against the other) on the subject of all their ordinances, for they walk not together. (1QS 4.15, 12, 16-18)[59]

Rabbinic sources further associated God's wrath with Sheol or "eternal damnation":

> R. Oshaia said: He who is haughty falls into Gehenna, as it is said, *A proud and haughty man, scoffer is his name, worketh for arrogant wrath* (Prov.21.24). And by wrath nought but Gehenna is meant; as it is said, *That day is a day of wrath* (Zeph.1.15). (AZ 18b)

"Ungodliness and unrighteousness": cf. Dt.12.31, Prov.6.16f, 11.31, Isa.59.20, 61.8, Jer.44.4, Zech.8.17, Rom.4.5, 5.6, 1 Tim.1.9, 2 Tim.2.16, Tit.2.12, 2 Pet.2.6, 3.7, Jude 15; 1QS 4.9f, 11.9-10, 1QH 13.16, 14.9-12, 15.24; Wis.Sol.14.9.

The terms "ungodliness" and "unrighteousness" correspond to both the Hebrew and Greek concepts of "sinfulness" which God hates and therefore punishes. They are attributes which characterize those under the "dominion of Belial," ruled and defiled, in the terms used by the Qumran community, by the "spirit of flesh":

> [I give Thee thanks,] O Adonai, who hast put understanding into the heart of Thy servant [that he may do what is good and right before Thee . . .] and that he may show himself stout hearted against the cri[mes] of ungodliness and that he may bless [Thy Name . . .] [and choose all th]at Thou lovest and loathe all that [Thou hatest] [. . .] of man. For in accordance with the [ever]lasting Spirits [Thou hast cast a lot for all the sons of men] between goodness and ungodliness, [and hast sea]led their reward. . . . For none of them that approach Thee can rebel against the commands of Thy mouth, and none that know Thee can hate Thy words. For Thou art righteous and all Thine elect are truth, and all perversity [and ungod]liness Thou wilt destroy for ever

> and Thy righteousness shall be revealed to the eyes of all Thy works. (1QH 14.8-16; cf. 6.22, 7.7)

"Who suppress the truth": cf. 1QS 5.12, 1QH 4.10-20, 15.16 25; Wis.Sol.12.27, 2 Bar.54.17-19.

Paul assumes that God has clearly manifested Himself and His will to mankind.[60] Since God has revealed His righteousness to the whole world, man has deliberately rebelled against His will in refusing to acknowledge Him as the Creator and sustainer of the world:

> For Thou, O God, despisest every thought of Belial: it is Thy counsel that shall remain, and it is the thought of Thy heart that shall stand fast for ever. As for them, they are hypocrites; the schemes of Belial which they conceive and they seek Thee with a double heart and are not firm in Thy truth. A root is in their thoughts bearing fruits that are poisoned and bitter and it is with stubbornness of heart that they seek Thee. And they have sought Thee out among idols and have set that before their face which causes them to fall into sin, and they have gone in to seek Thee according to the preaching of the prophets of falsehood, they who are led astray by error. . . . For [they have] not [heeded] Thy [voice] nor lent their ear to Thy word; for they have said of the vision of knowledge, It is not true! and of the way of Thy heart, That is not it! (1QH 4.13-18)

Some of the Rabbis also acknowledged the existence of some innate sense (cf. the idea of "natural law") within man which recognizes a supreme Being. They speak of Abraham, Isaac, Jacob, Judah, Joseph, Job, Hezekiah—and the Messiah—as all recognizing the existence of God unaided or of their own accord, and distinguished between knowledge gained through the mediation of Torah and knowledge obtained independently of Torah:

> Our Rabbis taught: *Mine ordinances shall ye do,* i.e., such commandments which, if they were not written [in Scripture], they should by right have been written and these are they: [the laws concerning] idolatry, immorality and bloodshed, robbery and blasphemy. *And My statutes shall ye keep*, i.e., such commandments to which Satan objects, they are [those relating to] the putting on of *sha'atnez*, the *chalitzah* [performed] by a sister-in-law, the purification of the leper, and the he-goat-to be-sent-away. (Yoma 67b)[61]

Several extant versions of an early midrash exist which claim that Abraham discovered the "true faith" by meditating on nature:

> NOW THE LORD SAID TO ABRAM: GET THEE OUT OF THY COUNTRY, ETC. (Gen.12.1). R. Isaac commenced his discourse with, *Hearken, O daughter, and consider, and incline thine ear; forget thine own people, and thy father's house* (Ps.45.10). Said R. Isaac: This may be compared to a man who was travelling from place to place when he saw a building in flames. Is it possible that the building lacks a person to look after it? he wondered. The owner of the building looked out and said, "I am the owner of the building." Similarly, because Abraham our father said, "Is it conceivable that the world is without a guide?" the Holy One, blessed be He, looked out and said to him, "I am the Guide, the Sovereign of the Universe." (Gen.R.39.1)

Verse 19:
"That which is known about God . . . ": cf. Ps.19.1-6, Acts 14.17, 17.24-28, 31; Wis.Sol.13.1ff; Philo, *De Spec.Leg.* 1.46f

God "reveals" His nature and will in His "works" of creation:

> Wherefore, whereas men have lived dissolutely and unrighteously, thou hast tormented them with their own abominations. For they went astray very far in the ways of error, and held them for gods, which even among the beasts of their enemies were despised, being deceived, as children of no understanding. Therefore unto them, as to children without the use of reason, thou didst send a judgment to mock them. But they that would not be reformed by that correction, wherein he dallied with them, shall feel a judgment worthy of God. For, look, for what things they grudged, when they were punished, that is, for them whom they thought to be gods; [now] being punished in them, when they saw it, they acknowledged him to be the true God, whom before they had denied to know; and therefore came extreme damnation upon them. (Wis.Sol.12.23-27)

"Evident within them": cf. 2.12-14, 8.29, Col.3.10.

Paul's denunciation of the Gentile nations for perceiving, yet rejecting, "that which is known about God" is "evident within them" (φανερον ἐστιν ἐν αὐτοις; *phaneron estin en autois*) corresponds to his more positive statement that, not having been given the Torah they yet observe it "instinctively" (φυσει; *phusei*—"by nature;" cf. 2.12-14):

> R. Johanan observed: If the Torah had not been given we could have learnt modesty from the cat, honesty from the ant, chastity from the dove, and good manners from the cock who first coaxes and then mates. (Eruv.100b)[62]

He may also be referring to the fact that man is made in God's "image" (cf. verses 23f), so that he "embodies" God's nature in his own body:

> He [R. Akiva] [also] used to say, Beloved is man in that he was created in the image [of God]; [It is a mark of] superabundant love [that] it was made known to him that he had been created in the image [of God], as it is said: 'For in the image of God made He man' (Gen.9.6). (PA 3.14).

Paul describes idolatry (cf. 1.23) as the transference of God's image to man or to creatures ("images") made by human hands. This further reflects the motif of the Two Ways or Two Spirits (masters): if man does not serve His creator, he serves his evil inclination:

> R. Yannai said: He who harkens to his evil inclination is as if he practised idolatry; for it is said, *There shall be no strange God within thee: thou shalt not worship any foreign God* (Ps.81.9). (PNed.9.1, 25b)

Verse 20:

"For since . . . invisible attributes": cf. Ex.33.20, 34.5-7, 1 Chron.29.11, Job 38-40, Ps.8.3-8, 19.1-6, Mk.10.6, 13.19, Jn.1.1, Acts 17.23f, Rom.8.22, 1 Cor.2.10-11, Col.1.15-16, 1 Tim.1.17, 6.16, Heb.11.27, 2 Pet.3.4, 1 Jn.4.12, 20, 3 Jn.11; 1QS 5.10-13, 11.5-8, CDC 3.13-14; Wis.Sol. 13.1-9, 13.10-15.19, Ap.Bar.6.45-52; Pes.Rab.53.1-2, Gen.R.1.4, 10, PRE 3, Mid.Ps.93.3, Pes.54a, Ned.39b, San.98b, Zev.116a; Philo, *De Mig.Abr.*181.

Paul associates God's revelation with His creation, as well as with man who is created in his image, and adopts terminology also used by Greek philosophers to specify God's characteristics which have been known through nature and creation.[63] The Greek word ἀορατα (*aorata*) here refers to "the invisible (things)" of God which are not seen in or by the world, and therefore should probably not be identified with the concept of the נסתרות (*nistarot*), the "hidden things" (cf. Dt.29.29, Mt.13.11, CDC 3.13-14, Sir.3.21-22, Hag.13a). Even the נסתרות, however, might be matters concerning which, although not openly revealed, God still holds man accountable:

And let him undertake by the Covenant to be separated from all perverse men who walk in the way of wickedness. For they are not counted in His Covenant: for they have not inquired nor sought Him concerning His precepts in order to know the hidden matters in which they have guiltily strayed; and they have treated with insolence matters revealed that Wrath might rise unto Judgment . . . and solemn judgment be fulfilled against them unto eternal destruction. . . . (1QS 5.10-13)

"Eternal power": cf. Ex.15.6, 1 Chron.29.11-12, 2 Chron.20.6, Job 36.5, Ps.29.4, 66.7, 145.11, Isa.45.24, Mt.6.13, Rom.1.16, 2 Cor.12.9, Eph.1.21, Heb.1.3; 1QM 1.14, 3.5, 8, 4.12, 6.2, 6, 10.5, 11.9, 1QH 1.13, 34, 4.28-33, 5.15, 6.11-12, 9.17; Pes.Rab.307, Sifre Dt.319, Lam.R.1.6.33, San.98b; Philo, *De Opif.* 8, *De Fuga* 9-95, *De Spec.Leg.*1.45f, *De Mig.Abr.*182f.

God's power embodies His will and purpose for the whole world:

And in Thy wisdom [Thou hast established the world from] former times, and before ever creating them Thou knewest all the works which creatures would accomplish during all ages for ever; for [without Thee] nothing is made and nothing is known without Thy will. It is Thou who hast formed every spirit g[ood and] ba[d] [together with their ways] and the judgment of all their works. It is Thou who hast spread out the heavens for Thy glory [and] hast [created] all [their hosts] according to Thy will together with the mighty winds according to the laws which governed them before they became [Thine] angels of hol[iness]; and to the everlasting spirits in their dominions [hast Thou entrusted] the heavenly lights according to their mysterious (laws) . . . It is Thou who hast created the earth by Thy strength, the seas and the deeps [and the rivers]. And Thou hast established [all] their [inhabi]tants by Thy wisdom, and all that is in them hast Thou di[spo]sed according to Thy will. (1QH 1.7-15)[64]

"Divine nature": cf. Ex.15.11f, 33.17f, 34.6, Isa.40.18ff, 46.5ff, Jn.1.18, Acts 17.29, Col.2.9, 1 Tim.1.17, 2 Pet.1.4; PRK 12.25, Tanh.Shemot 20, Tanh.B.Vayera 5, Yitro 17, Gen.R.4.4, 68.9, Ex.R.3.6, 29.5, Lev.R.4.8, Num.R.12.3, Dt.R.2.37, Lam.R.1.6.33.

God's "eternal power" expresses His sovereignty and therefore His "divinity." Idolatry, or worshipping something which is not God, is sometimes referred to as "weakening God's power" or His "attributes" (מידות; *middot*) in rabbinic literature:

> . . . Moses said to the Holy One, blessed be he, *Show me now Thy ways* (Ex.33.13), He showed them to Moses, as is said *He made known His ways unto Moses* (Ps.103.7). But when Moses said: *Show me, I pray Thee, Thy glory* (Ex.33.18), that is to say, "Show me the rule whereby Thou guidest the world," God replied, "My rules thou canst not fathom." . . . *Of the Rock that begot thee thou wast unmindful* (Dt.32.18): Whenever I want to do good things for you, you weaken the power of heaven. You stood at the (Red) Sea and said, *This is my God, and I will glorify Him* (Ex.15.2) . . . you relapsed and said, *Let us make a captain, and let us return to Egypt* (Num.14.4). When you stood before Mount Sinai and said, *All that the Lord hath spoken we will do and obey* (Ex.24.7), I wanted to do good things for you, but you relapsed and said to the calf, *This is thy god, O Israel* (Ex.32.4). Thus whenever I want to do good things for you, you weaken the power [גבורה] of heaven. (Mid.Ps.25.6, Sifre Dt.He'azinu 319; cf. Lam.R.1.6.33)

"Clearly seen . . . made": cf. Job 12.7-9, Ps.8.1-9, 19.1-6, 50.6, 89.5, 97.6, 104, 136.5-9, Rom.2.14; Wis.Sol.13.1f, Hell.Syn.Pray.12.43, 69, 2 Bar.54.18-19.

Man has a responsibility to acknowledge and recognize God's nature and His attributes from what God has made known of them. Man is "accountable" to God because God has given him the means to know his Creator:

> Surely vain are all men by nature, who are ignorant of God, and could not out of the good things that are seen know him that is: neither by considering the works did they acknowledge the work-master . . . With those whose beauty if they being delighted took them to be gods; let them know how much better the Lord of them is: for the first author of beauty hath created them. But if they were astonished at their power and virtue, let them understand by them, how much mightier is he that made them. For by the greatness and beauty of the creatures proportionally the maker of them is seen. But yet for this they are the less to be blamed: for they peradventure err, seeking God, and desirous to find him. For being conversant in his works they search (him) diligently, and believe their sight: because the things are beautiful that are

> seen. Howbeit neither are they to be pardoned. For if they were able to know so much, that they could aim at the world; how did they not sooner find out the Lord thereof? (Wis.Sol.13.1-9)

Paul describes man's corruption and error in verses 28ff as the "darkening of the minds," so that they no longer "see clearly" what God has made (cf. 1 Cor.13.12).[65]

Verse 21:

". . . they did not honor Him as God": cf. Ex.20.12, 1 Sam.2.30, 1 Chron.29.12, Ps.50.23, Isa.29.13, Mt.15.8-9, Jn.5.23, 1 Tim.6.16, Rev.5.13; Ps.Sol.1.4-8, Hell.Syn.Pray.12.68, Wis.Sol.14.27-30; PA 4.1, Sifre Num.Behealot.99, Gen.R.1.3, Hag.2.1; Philo, *De Virt.*179f.

Paul presumes that the Gentiles in fact knew God and rejected Him as the Creator, a common view in contemporary Jewish literature (see the cross-references). To "honor" God is to acknowledge His sovereignty by obeying and serving the Creator rather than one's own inclination, to recognize and imitate His attributes (מידות; *middot*):

> Forthwith the Holy One, blessed be He, took counsel with the Torah whose name is Tushijah (Stability or Wisdom) with reference to the creation of the world. (The Torah) replied and said to Him: Sovereign of the worlds! if there be no host for the king and if there be no camp for the king, over whom does he rule? If there be no people to praise the king, where is the honour of the King? (PRE 3)

> *And I will glorify Him* (Ex.15.2). R. Ishmael says: And is it possible for a man of flesh and blood to add glory to his Creator? It simply means: I shall be beautiful before Him in observing the commandments. . . . Abba Saul says: O be like Him! Just as He is gracious and merciful, so be thou also gracious and merciful. R. Jose says: I shall proclaim the glories and the praise of Him by whose word the world came into being, before all the nations of the world . . . [T]he Israelites say to the nations of the world: "Do you know Him? Let us but tell you some of His praise: 'My beloved is white and ruddy' (Cant.5.10)." As soon as the nations of the world hear some of His praise, they say to the Israelites: "We will join you," as it is said: "Whither is thy beloved gone, O thou fairest among women? Whither hath thy beloved turned him, that we may seek him with thee?" (ibid., 6.1). (Mekh.Shirata 3)

"Or give thanks": cf. 1 Chron.16.28ff, Ps.29.1, 96.7f, 103.21, 104.1, 105.1, 106.1, 118.1, 136.1, Isa.12.1, 4, Rom.7.25, 9.5, 11.33-36, 14.6, 1 Cor.15.57; 4 Ez.8.60; Ber.9.1-3, Mid.Ps.19.1, 101.1, 145.1, Sot.10b.

"Thanksgiving" and "blessing" are the ways in which man acknowledges God's works and His sovereign righteousness for the goodness of His creation, for His mercy upon them, and for His grace and gift of righteousness:

> Their wealth was extended to the whole earth, and their glory to the end of the earth. They exalted themselves to the stars, they said they would never fall. They were arrogant in their possessions, and they did not acknowledge (God). Their sins were in secret, and even I did not know. Their lawless actions surpassed the gentiles before them; they completely profaned the sanctuary of the Lord. (Ps.Sol.1.4-8)[66]

The proper affirmation of God's nature acknowledges man's helplessness, in place of his arrogant self-dependence:

> Blessed be Thou, O my God, who hast opened unto Knowledge the heart of Thy servant! Establish all his works in righteousness . . . For without Thee no way is perfect, and without Thy will nothing is done. It is Thou who hast taught all Knowledge, and all that is brought into being exists by Thy will. And there is none other beside Thee to dispute Thy decision and to comprehend all Thy holy Thought and to contemplate the depth of Thy Mysteries and to understand all Thy marvels and the power of Thy might. Who then shall contain Thy Glory? And what is the son of man himself amidst all Thy marvelous works? And he that is born of woman, what is his worth before Thee? Truly this man was shaped from dust and his end is to become the prey of worms. Truly, this man is a mere frail image in potter's clay and inclines to the dust. What shall clay reply, the thing which the hand fashions? What thought can it comprehend? (1QS 11.15-22)[67]

"They became futile": cf. 2 Kings 17.15, Ps.94.11, Isa.6.10, Jer.5.21, Ezek.12.2, Rom.11.8, 10, Eph.2.1-3, 4.17-19; 1QS 3.2-4, 4.9-11, 21, 23, 5.18-19; Wis.Sol.13.1; Philo, *De Virt.* 179, 221 12.2.

The Greek verb ματαιοω (*mataioo*; together with its other forms) is used in the LXX to translate the various terms used for "idols," which, because they have no life of themselves and are merely man-made creations, are worthless and useless.[68] In serving his own inclination and worshipping his own "images," man "walks after vanity" (cf. 2 Kings 17.15) in accordance with the "Spirit of perversity":

> But whoever scorns to enter the ways of God in order to walk in the stubbornness of his heart, he shall not pass into the Community of truth. For his soul has loathed the teachings of Knowledge, he has not established (within him) the ordinances of righteousness by conversion of his life. Therefore he shall not be counted among upright men, and his understanding and powers and possession shall not be brought into the Council of the Community. For his silence (is invaded) by confusion of wickedness and defilements (are hidden) within his calm. When he dissembles the stubbornness of his heart he shall not be justified, nor when he beholds the ways of light (being himself) darkness. . . . For all who are not counted in His Covenant shall be set apart, together with all that is theirs; and the holy shall not rely on any work of vanity. For they are all vanity who know not His Covenant, and He will destroy from the world all them that despise His word. . . . (1QS 2.25-3.3, 5.18-19)

"Foolish heart": cf. Dt.29.18, 32.6, 28, Job 5.3, Ps.2.1, 14.1, Prov.1.7, 29-33, 24.7, Isa.44.9-20, Jer.2.5, 7.24, 11.8, 13.10, 16.12, Hos.11.7, Acts 4.25, 1 Cor.1.18ff, Gal.4.8-9, Eph.4.17-19, Col.2.18, 23; Wis.Sol.11.15.

All through this section (verses 21-32), Paul repeats the same thought in different expressions. Man's "foolish heart" is the source and outcome of becoming "futile in their speculations," and corresponds to the term "spirit of perversity" or "spirit of flesh" in the Qumran texts (cf. 1QS 3.18-19, 4.9, 20, 1QH 1.22, 11.12, 13.13, 17.25). The heart in this sense combines both mind and heart as the "seat" and the "reins" of man's evil inclination, which rebels against God's will.

"Was darkened": cf. 2 Sam.22.29, Ps.107.10, Eccl.2.14, Isa.9.2, Isa.45.7, Jn.1.5, Acts 26.18, Rom.2.19, 2 Cor.6.14, Eph.4.18, 5.11, 1 Pet.2.9; 1QS 3.21ff, 1QM 1.1ff, 1QH 9.27; Test.Reub.3.8, Jos.Asen.8.10, 1 En.103.7; Gen.R.1.6, 2.3, Ber.17a.

Paul continues the theme of darkness as representing ignorance and error. According to the doctrine of the "Two Spirits" or "Two Ways" (masters), man partakes either of the Spirit of Light or of the Spirit of Darkness. In one he walks in light according to Truth, in the other in darkness according to Perversity:

> And He allotted unto man two Spirits that he should walk in them until the time of His Visitation; they are the Spirits of truth and perversity. The origin of Truth is in a fountain of light, and the origin of Perversity is from a fountain of darkness. Dominion over all the sons of righteousness is in the hand of the Prince of light; they walk in the ways of light. All dominion over the sons of perversity is in the hand of the Angel of darkness; they walk in the ways of darkness. (1QS 3.18-21)[69]

Verse 22:

"Professing to be wise . . . ": cf. Ps.14.1, 53.1, Prov.1.7, 3.7, Jer.9.23-24, Rom.1.14, 12.16, I Cor.1.19, 25f, 3.18-20, 10.14-15, 2 Cor 1.12, Eph.5.15, 2 Tim.3.15, Jas.3.13; 1 En.99.8.

Since the fear of the Lord is "the beginning of wisdom" (Prov.1.7), being "wise in one's own eyes" corresponds to serving one's own inclination. This produces "futile speculations" because man has not allowed his heart to be "enlightened" by the Spirit of God's truth:

> For God's truth is the rock of my steps and His power [גבורה], the stay of my right hand, and from the fount of His Righteousness comes my justification. From His wondrous Mysteries is the light in my heart, in the everlasting Being has my eye beheld Wisdom: because Knowledge [תושיה] is hidden from men and the counsel of prudence from the sons of men. The fountain of righteousness, the reservoir of power [גבורה], and the dwelling place of glory [כבוד] are denied to the assembly of flesh; but God has given them as an eternal possession to those whom He has chosen. (1QS 11.4-8; cf. 10.11-12)[70]

Verse 23:

"And exchanged the glory of God . . . creatures": cf. Ex.16.7, Num.16.19, Dt.5.24, Ps.24.8ff, 62.7, 106.20, Jer.2.11, Hos.4.7, 9.11, 10.5, Hab.1.11, Zech.2.5, Rom.3.23, 2 Cor.4.4, Phil.3.21, Heb.2.7; 1QS 10.12, 11.20, CDC 3.20, 1QM 4.6, 8, 1QH 10.8-12, 11.8, 15.17, 17.15; Wis.Sol.12.24, 13.10-19, 14.21, 15.17-19, Hell.Syn.Pray.12.68, Test.Naph.3.1--5; Gen.R.1.5; Philo, *De Virt.* 179.

In the following sections (verses 23-25, 26-27, 28-32), Paul creates a midrash on the theme of idolatry based on Psalm 106.20 and Jeremiah 2.11, analogous to other Jewish interpretations of similar biblical texts:

> When Israel disregarded *Thou shalt have no other gods before Me* (Ex.20.3), He forgave them, for in idolatry there is only jealousy, as

it says, *They roused Him to jealousy with strange gods, with abominations did they provoke Him* (Dt.32.16), and it also says, *Thus they exchanged their glory for the likeness of an ox* (Ps.106.20). (Ex.R.30.21; cf. Mekh.Beshall.7)

In Psalm 106.20, the expression "their glory" refers to God, who has given His "glory" to Israel (cf. Isa.46.13). Biblical texts frequently associate God's glory with His signs, His deeds, His holiness, and with the "knowledge of the Lord" which will "fill the earth as the waters cover the seas" (cf. Num.14.21-22, Dt.10.21, Ps.72.19, Isa.6.3, 11.9-10, 66.18-19, Hab.2.14). God's "glory" is one of His central characteristics (cf. Ex.33.18f), being one of His attributes, such as Wisdom and Righteousness, which later became personified in Second Temple Jewish literature:

> From His wondrous Mysteries is the light in my heart, in the everlasting being has my eye beheld Wisdom: because Knowledge is hidden from men and the counsel of Prudence from the sons of men. The fountain of righteousness, the reservoir of power, and the dwelling-place of glory are denied to the assembly of flesh; but God has given them as an everlasting possession to those whom He has chosen. . . . But to God I will say, My righteousness! (and) to the Most High, Support of my goodness! Source of Knowledge! Fountain of Holiness! Infinite Glory and Might of Eternal Majesty! I will choose whatever He teaches me and will delight in His judgment of me. (1QS 11.5-7, 10.11-13)

Since God's glory is also associated with His שכינה (*Shekinah*; God's "Presence;" cf. Num.16.19, 42, 20.6), which is sometimes treated as an independent entity in targumic and rabbinic texts, it was also easy to associate it with His Messiah, who is His "image" and His "representation" (cf. Heb.1.3) or "representative" (שליח; *shaliach*).[71] Thus Paul says in 3.23 that man has (literally) "missed the mark" and thus "fallen short" of God's glory, and demonstrates how God bestows his righteousness on those who are faithful to Him in Yeshua, "the Lord our righteousness" (Jer.23.6).[72]

"An image": cf. Ex.20.4, Lev.26.1, Num.33.52, Dt.4.15-19, 5.8, 7.25, 29.17, 2 Chron.34.3-4, Ps.97.7, Isa.10.10-11, 41.29, 42.17, 115.4-8, Jer.8.19, 10.14-15, Ezek.7.20, 37.23, Hab.2.18-19, Acts 17.29; 1QpHab 12.10-14; Wis.Sol.12.23-15.19, Ap.Bar.6.4-73; Philo, *De Virt*.221.

The word "image" is one of the biblical terms for idols, objects of worship created by man out of lifeless natural materials in exchange for the Living God. An "image" or idol is a "making of destruction":

> . . . he provided for it that it might not fall, knowing that it was unable to help itself; for it is an image, and hath need of help: then maketh he prayer for his goods, for his wife and children, and is not ashamed to speak to that which hath no life. For health he calleth upon that which is weak: for life prayeth to that which is dead: for aid humbly beseecheth that which hath least means to help: and for a good journey he asketh of that which cannot set a foot forward: and for gaining and getting, and for good success of his hands, asketh ability to do of him, that is most unable to do any thing. (Wis.Sol.13.16b-19)

"In the form of corruptible man . . . ": cf. Ex.20.4, 23, 32.1-8, 31, Dt.4.16-18, 28, Judg.2.13, 10.6, 1 Sam. 7.3-4, Ps.115.4-8, 135.15-18, Isa.2.8, 20, 31.7, 40.18-19, 44.9-20, 45.20, 46.1-7, Ezek.14.3-4, 20.7-8, 23.37, Hos.13.2, Hab.1.11, 1 Cor.15.36ff, 47ff, Heb.12.27, Rev.9.20; CDC[b] 2.9, 1QpHab 6.1-5; Mekh.Bechodesh 6, Ex.R.43.7, San.102a.

Man has exchanged the image of God for images of his own creation. These are idols which, because they are either in man's image or in the image of other creatures, are perishable and "mortal" (cf. 1 Cor.15.46-54):

> But miserable are they, and in dead things is their hope, who called them gods, which are the works of men's hands, gold and silver, to show art in, and resemblances of beasts, or a stone good for nothing, the work of an ancient hand. Now a carpenter that felleth timber, after he hath sawn down a tree meet for the purpose, and taken off all the bark skilfully round about, and hath wrought it handsomely, and made a vessel thereof fit for the service of man's life; and after spending the refuse of his work to dress his meat, hath filled himself; and taking the very refuse among those which served to no use, being a crooked piece of wood, and full of knots, hath carved it diligently, when he had nothing else to do, and formed it by the skill of his understanding, and fashioned it to the image of a man or made it like some vile beast, laying it over with vermilion, and with paint colouring it red, and covering every spot therein. . . . For man made them, and he that borrowed his own spirit fashioned them: but no man can make a god like unto himself. For being mortal, he worketh a dead thing with wicked hands: for he himself is better than the

> things which he worshippeth: whereas he lived (once), but they never . . . [and] went without the praise of God and his blessing. (Wis.Sol.13.10-14, 15-19)

Verse 24:

"God gave them over": cf. Job 8.4, Ps.81.12, Isa.64.6 (7), Acts 7.42; Test.Jos.7.8, Test.Naph.3.3.

Paul seems to be influenced by two biblical traditions here. One derives from Psalm 81.12, which emphasizes God's active "sending" (ואשלחהו; *va-'ashallechehu*) of man's heart towards "stubbornness" (בשרירות; *bisherirut*) (cf. also Job 8.4). God's anger over man's rebellion leads Him to "hand [him] over" to his own evil inclination, so that he has brought destruction upon himself. God can be said however, to hold ultimate responsibility for man's destruction, since He created his will to do evil (יצר הרע; *yetzer ha-ra'*).[73] The second tradition (cf. Isa.64.6) associates God's "handing over" of man to his evil inclination with the hiding of His face (הסתר פנים; *hester panim*).[74] God's "turning away" in punishment and removing His presence and His favor "allows" man to follow his own ways.[75] Paul tends towards the second tradition in this passage, a view which is strengthened by the LXX reading of Isaiah 64.6 (7). The Greek translators apparently understood the Hebrew Masoretic text ותמוגנו (*vatmugenu*; "melted") as ותמגננו (*vatmagenenu*; "covered").[76] The root, גנן, to cover or defend, corresponds to the piel form of the root סגר (*sagar*; to shut or close). The LXX thus read Isaiah 64.6 to refer to "delivering up" in the sense of "shutting one up to" or "leaving no other opening."[77] Paul employs this phrase in Romans 11.32 and Galatians 3.22 (cf. also Rom.3.9), where he says that God (Scripture) has "shut up" all men in disobedience. He has left man ("given them over") to his own devices, to walk according to his own ways, by turning away His face from him.

"In the lusts of their hearts": cf. Gen.6.5, Eccl.8.11, 9.3, Jer.17.10; Philo, *De Spec.Leg.*2.50.

Man must serve either his Creator or his own inclination, since he may be "mastered" either by sin or by God's righteousness. Even "good" men must "master" their own hearts, giving them instructions rather than being led by their lusts:

> AND THE LORD SAID TO HIS HEART [Gen.8.21]. The wicked stand in subjection to their heart [i.e. passions]. [Thus it says] *The fool hath said* in *his heart* (Ps.14.1); *And Esau said* in *his heart* (Gen.27.41); *And Jeroboam said* in *his heart*' (1 Kings 12.26); '*Now Haman said* in *his heart*' (Est.6.6). But the righteous have their hearts under their

> control; hence it is written, *Now Hanna, she spoke* at *her heart*' (1 Sam.1.13); *And David said* to *his heart*' (1 Sam.27.1); *But Daniel purposed* to *his heart*' (Dan.1.8); *And the Lord said* to *His heart*. (Gen.R.34.10)[78]

"Impurity, that their bodies might be dishonored . . . ": cf. Rom.6.19, Gal.5.19, Eph.2.3, 4.19; 1QS 4.9-14, 1QH 11.12, 13.13, 17.25; Ps.Sol.8.9, Jub.16.5-6, 33.10ff, Vis.Ezra 1.22, Sib.Or.5.386-94, 7.43-45; Philo, *De Spec.Leg*.2.50.

Idolatry turns man who is made in God's image into an object of worship, and his body becomes defiled by the "spirit of flesh" and the "spirit of perversity," according to the description in the Qumran texts:

> And in all those years Belial shall be unleashed against Israel; as God said by the hand of the prophet Isaiah son of Amoz, *Terror and pit and snare are upon thee, O inhabitant of the land*' {Isa.24.17}. The explanation of this (is that) these are Belial's three nets, of which Levi son of Jacob spoke, by which he (Belial) ensnared Israel, and which he set [be]fore them as three sorts of righteousness: the first is lust, the second is riches, (and) the third is defilement of the Sanctuary. . . . The builders of the wall, they who walked after *zaw—zaw* is a preacher of whom He said, *They only preach*—{Mic.2.6} have been caught by lust in two things: by marrying two women in their lifetime, whereas nature's principle is *Male and female created He them* {Gen.1.27}. . . . And they marry every one the daughter of his brother or the daughter of his sister. Now Moses said, *Thou shalt not approach the sister of thy mother; it is the flesh of thy mother* {Lev.18.13}. The law of incest is written for men but also for women, and if a brother's daughter uncovers the nakedness of the brother of her father, whereas it is the flesh < . . . >. Moreover, they have defiled their Holy Spirit, and with a blaspheming tongue have opened their mouth against the precepts of the Covenant of God. . . . They are all kindlers of fire and lighters of brands {Isa.50.11}; their webs are spider webs and their eggs are adder eggs {cf. Isa.59.5}. (CDC 4.12-21, 5.7-14)[79]

Verse 25:

"For they exchanged the truth of God": cf. Ps.106.20, Jer.2.11.

Paul continues his midrash on the theme of "exchanging the glory" of God for idols. Here he interprets "the glory of the knowledge of the Lord" (cf. Hab.2.14; 2 Cor.4.4) as God's "truth," in a similar way to Thanksgiving Scroll:

> And they, they [have led] Thy people [astray]. [Prophets of falsehood] have flattered [them with their wor]ds and interpreters of deceit [have caused] them [to stray]; and they have fallen to their destruction for lack of understanding for all their works are in folly. . . . And they, interpreters of falsehood and seers of deceit, devised plans of Belial against me, bartering [להמיר] Thy law which Thou hast graven in my heart for the flattering words (which they speak) to Thy people. . . . [And] I will [not] barter [אמיר] Thy truth for riches and all Thy laws for a gift. . . . And I will not enter the assembly of the m[en of Belial], of them that have turned far [away from] Thy [Covenant]. (1QH 4.6-10, 14.20-22)[80]

"For a lie": cf. Ps.59.12, 116.11, Jer.10.14, Ezek.13.8, Jn.8.44, Rom.3.4, 7, Col.1.9, 1 Tim.2.4, Jas.3.14, 1 Pet.2.6-12; Gen.R.1.5.

The opposite of God's truth and sovereignty is man's idolatry and "futile speculation," the consequences of which Paul further describes in the following verses. God's "glory" and "knowledge" are a "stumbling stone" (Isa.28.16) which distinguishes between those who have "volunteered" to be "converted" to His Covenant from the "assembly of Belial" (cf. 1QS 1.1ff). Those who believe in this stumbling stone will not be "disappointed" (יחיש; *yachish*) or "ashamed" (καταισχυνθεσεται; *kataischunthesetai*; "dishonored"); those who do not, but rely on their own reasoning, serve the cause of the "Preacher of Lies":

> *Woe to him who builds a town on murder and founds a city on crime! Is it not from the Lord of Hosts? The people labour for fire and the nations exhaust themselves for nothingness* (Hab.2.12-13). The explanation of this word concerns the Preacher of Lies who led many astray to build his town of vanity on murder and to found a congregation on deceit for the sake of his glory, that many people might labour in his service of vanity and conceive in [wo]rks of deceit; that their labour might be for nothingness, that they might come to judgement of fire for having insulted and outraged the elect of God. *For the earth will be filled with the knowledge of the glory of Yahweh as waters cover the se[a]* (Hab.2.14). The explanation of this word [is that] when they are converted [. . .] the lie, and afterwards knowledge will be revealed to them *as the waters of the sea*, abundantly. (1QpHab 10.6-11.2)[81]

Verse 26:
"For this reason": Paul repeats the thought of verses 21-23 and 24-25 in verses 26-27. Because man did not "honor" God alone and professed to be wise in his own right, he became futile in his speculations, and became foolish. Paul sums this thought up in verse 23, saying that man exchanged God's image for his own; he repeats this series of acts and consequences in verses 24-25, playing between the idea of God "giving (men) over" to impurity (dishonor/lies) and man's "exchanging" God's glory and truth for his own creations.

"Degrading passions": cf. Lev.18.3, Dt.18.9f, Prov.14.30, Gal.5.19, Eph.2.3, 4.19, Col.3.5, 1 Thess.4.5; 1QS 4.9-11, CDC 2.16, 4.17, 1QH 11.12, 20, 17.25; Test.Dan 5.5, Jub.21.21-24, Wis.Sol.14.22f, 4 Macc.7.16f, Jub.15.31, Test.Jud.23.2, Test.Naph.3.3; BB 10b, Yev.61a, 103a-b; Philo, *De Spec.Leg.*2.50, 3.37-50, *De Abr.*134-35; Lev.R.23.7.

Paul describes the immoral practices of pagan nations, whose denigration was a common theme in contemporary Jewish literature:

> The land of the Sodomites, a part of the land of Canaan afterwards called Palestinian Syria, was brimful of innumerable iniquities, particularly such as a rise from gluttony and lewdness, and multiplied and enlarged every other possible pleasure with so formidable a menace that it had at last been condemned by the Judge of all. All the inhabitants owed this extreme license to the never-failing lavishness of their sources of wealth . . . and the chief beginning of evils, as one has aptly said, is goods in excess. Incapable of bearing such satiety, plunging like cattle, they threw off from their necks the law of nature and applied themselves to deep drinking of strong liquor and dainty feeding and forbidden forms of intercourse. Not only in their mad lust for women did they violate the marriages of their neighbors, but also men mounted males without respect for the sex nature which the active partner shares with the passive; and so when they tried to beget children they were discovered to be incapable of any but a sterile seed. Yet the discovery availed them not, so much stronger was the force of the lust which mastered them. Then, as little by little they accustomed those who were by nature men to submit to play the part of women, they saddled them with the formidable curse of a female disease. For not only did they emasculate their bodies by luxury and voluptuousness but they worked a further degeneration in their souls and, as far as in them lay, were corrupting the whole of mankind. (Philo, *De Abr.*133-36)

"Exchanged the natural function . . . ": cf. Ex.22.19, Lev.18.22-23, 20.13f, Dt.27.20-23, 1 Cor.6.9; CDC 3.19-511; Ps.-Phoc.3, 189, Let.Arist.152, Sib.Or.2.73, 3.185-86, 596, 764, 5.166, 387-93, 430, Test.Jac.7.20, Test.Levi 17.11, Ps.Sol.2.13, 8.9, Ps.-Phoc.1.1; Philo, *De Spec.Leg.* 2.50, 3.37-50, *De Abr.* 135-36, *De Vit.Cont.*59-62; Shab.65a, Yev.76a.

Both homosexuality and bestiality were considered to be "unnatural" sexual practices from the biblical period (cf. Ex.19.22, Lev.18.22ff, 20.13f).[82] The Greco-Roman world manifested similar sexual habits, which contemporary Jewish literature commonly attributed to idolatrous practices:

> For the devising of idols was the beginning of fornication, and the invention of them the corruption of life. (Wis.Sol.14.12)

Homosexuality was commonly practiced in Greek society, where friendship between men was considered to be the noblest form of love; it was engaged in regularly, particularly by young men in their teens and early twenties. Although the Emperor Augustus passed legislation in 18/19 B.C.E. under which a man could be charged for homosexual activities, some scholars suggest that his purpose was to bring family life under the laws of the state in order to increase the birth rate rather than for political or moral considerations.[83] Bestiality was also a recognized pagan practice:

> . . . Moses, recognizing the way in which this [hybrid] animal is produced contravenes nature, stringently forbade it under the wider order by which he refused permission for animals of either sex to breed with those of an unlike species. In making this provision he considered what was in accord with decency and conformity to nature, but beyond this he gave us as from some far-off commanding height a warning to men and women alike that they should learn from these examples to abstain from unlawful forms of intercourse. Whether then, it is the man who uses a quadruped for this purpose, or the woman who allows herself to be used, the human offenders must die and the beasts also; the first because they have passed beyond the limits of licentiousness itself by evolving abnormal lusts, and because they have invented strange pleasures than which nothing could be more unpleasing, shameful even to describe; the beasts because they have ministered to such infamies, and to ensure that they do not bear or beget any monstrosity of the kind that may be expected to spring from such abominations. (Philo, *De Spec.Leg.*3.47-49)

Verse 27:

"Receiving in their own persons": cf. 24; Test.Gad 5.10.

Man "defiles his spirit" and becomes "strange flesh" and "animals" (cf. 2 Pet.2.12-16, Jude 7-16) when he walks according to the Spirit of Perversity (cf. 1QS 3.2-6, 18ff, 4.9-21, CDC 5.11). Paul recalls the principle of מידה כנגד מידה (*middah keneged middah*), or "measure for measure," in suggesting that God punishes man's offences according to the manner in which they were committed:

> But for the foolish devices of their wickedness, wherewith being deceived they worshipped serpents void of reason, and vile beasts, thou didst send a multitude of unreasonable beasts upon them for vengeance; that they might know, that wherewithal a man sinneth, by the same also shall he be punished. . . . Wherefore, whereas men have lived dissolutely and unrighteously, thou hast tormented them with their own abominations. (Wis.Sol.11.15-16, 12.23)

> *That the Waters May Come Back upon the Egyptians, upon Their Chariots, and upon Their Horsemen* (Ex.14.26). Let the wheel {of fortune} turn against them and bring back upon them their own violence. For with the same device with which they planned to destroy Israel I am going to punish them. They planned to destroy My children by water, so I will likewise punish them only by water. For it is said: "He diggeth a pit, and hollowed it, and is fallen into the ditch which he made" (Ps.7.15). "He that diggeth a pit shall fall into it; and whoso breaketh through a fence, a serpent shall bite him. Whoso quarrieth stones shall be hurt therewith; and he that cleaveth wood is endangered thereby" (Eccl.10.8-9). And it also says: "His mischief shall return upon his own head" (Ps.7.16). And it says: "Whoso that diggeth a pit shall fall therein" (Prov.26.27). . . . (Mekh.Beshall.7)

"The due penalty for their error": cf. Mt.16.27, Rom.2.6, 1 Cor.3.12-15, 2 Cor.5.10, Col.3.25, Rev.2.23, 20.12, 22.12; 1QS 4.9ff, CDC 2.4-5, 1QH 4.16, 20; Wis.Sol.11.15-20, 12.23-24, 13.6, 14.22, 16.1f, Test.Sim.2.12, Test.Jud.13.8.

Paul demonstrates how in the same way as faith leads to faith (cf. 1.17), so unrighteousness leads to wrath. God renders to every man according to his deeds:

> And so did King Solomon, peace be upon him, say: "A man shall be satisfied with good by the fruit of his mouth, and the doings of a

man's hands shall be rendered unto him" (Prov.12.14). Likewise, the prophet Isaiah, peace be upon him, said: "According to their deeds, accordingly will He repay" (Isa.59.18). And he also says: "Therefore will I first measure their wage," etc. (ibid., 65.7). Likewise the prophet Jeremiah said: "Great in counsel, and mighty in work; whose eyes are open upon all the ways of the sons of men, to give every one according to his ways, and according to the fruit of his doing" (Jer.32.19). And he also says: "Recompense her according to her work, according to all that she hath done, do unto her" (ibid., 50.29). (Mekh.Beshall.7)

Verse 28:

"They did not see fit . . . "

Paul repeats the previous sections in verses 28-32, and elaborates on the specific improprieties which men committed. His thought also fits in very neatly to the motif of the "two masters," as it is expressed in a series of rabbinic midrashim based on Genesis 2.7. The *plene* (full) text is written וייצר (*va-yitzer*); i.e., and God created (man), out of which anomaly the Rabbis interpreted that man is subject to two masters:

> . . . *And He formed* [va-yitzer] was written in Scripture with two *yods* . . . [It may be explained] in agreement with R. Simeon b. Pazzi, for Simeon b. Pazzi said, "Woe to me on account of my evil inclination [יצרי]; woe to me on account of my creator [יוצרי]." (Eruv.18a)

In terms of this midrash, Paul is saying that man "exchanged" obedience to ("did not see fit to acknowledge") his Creator [יוצר; *yotzer*] for obedience to his own inclination [יצר; *yetzer*]—his "depraved mind."[84]

"Those things which are not proper": cf. 2 Macc.6.4f, 3 Macc.4.16.

The comprehensive Greek word καθηκοντα (*kathekonta*), "things which are proper," was used in Stoic thought to refer to "what is morally fitting." It corresponds in some sense to the Hebrew phrase שלא כהוגן (*she-lo' ke-hogen*) which is used frequently in the *Derekh Eretz* literature (ethical and moral teachings).[85] Paul is suggesting here predominantly sexual perversions, but those things which are not "proper" cover any and all transgression of the commandments, and fall under the classification of those "natural" laws which, "if they were not written [in Scripture], they should by right have been written and these are they: [the laws concerning] idolatry [star-worship], immorality and bloodshed, robbery and blasphemy" (Yoma 67b).

Verses 28-31:
"Being filled with . . . unmerciful": cf. Ps.5.5, Mt.15.19, 1 Cor.5.10f, 6.9f, 2 Cor.12.20-21, Gal.5.19-21, Eph.4.19, 31, 5.3-5, Col.3.5, 8, 1 Tim.1.9f, 6.4f, 2 Tim.3.2-4, Tit.3.3, 1 Pet.4.3, Rev.9.21, 21.8, 22.15; 1QS 4.9-11, CDC 3.10-12, 8.4-10, CDC^b 1.17-22, 1QH 4.13-19; 4 Macc.1.26, Jub.7.20f, Test.Reub.3.1-9, Test.Jud.14.8, Wis.Sol.5.6-14.

Verses 28-32 list the particular manifestations of "the lusts of (man's) heart" (verse 24), his "degrading passions" (verse 26), and "depraved mind" (verse 28)—all those things which are "not proper."[86] The actions correspond to all the sins of action, of thought, of intention, of omission, of speech, between man and his fellows, between man and God, physical, mental, moral, and spiritual:

> But to the Spirit of perversity belong cupidity, and slackness in the service of righteousness, impiety and falsehood, pride and haughtiness, falsity and deceit, cruelty and abundant wickedness, impatience and much folly, and burning insolence, (and) abominable deeds committed in the spirit of lust, and the ways of defilement in the service of impurity, and a blaspheming tongue, blindness of eye and hardness of ear, stiffness of neck and heaviness of heart causing a man to walk in all the ways of darkness, and malignant cunning. (1QS 4.9-11)

In addition to all is an eighth spirit: sleep, with which is created the ecstasy of nature and the image of death. With these are commingled the spirits of error. First, the spirit of promiscuity resides in the nature and the senses. A second spirit of insatiability, in the stomach; a third spirit of strife, in the liver and the gall; a fourth spirit of flattery and trickery, in order that through excessive effort one might appear to be at the height of his powers; a fifth spirit of arrogance, that one might be boastful and haughty; a sixth spirit of lying, which through destructiveness and rivalry, handles his affairs smoothly and secretively even with his relatives and his household. A seventh spirit of injustice, with which are thefts and crooked dealings, in order that one might gain his heart's desire. For injustice works together with the other spirits through acceptance of bribes. With all these the spirit of sleep forms an alliance, which results in error and fantasy. (Test.Reub.3.1-7)

> There is a city . . . in the land of Ur of the Chaldeans, whence comes a race of most righteous men. They are always concerned with good counsel and noble works for they do not worry about the cyclic course

> of the sun or the moon . . . Neither do they practice the astrological predictions of the Chaldeans nor astrology. For all these things are erroneous, such as foolish men inquire into day by day, exercising themselves at a profitless task. And indeed they have taught errors to shameful men from which many evils come upon mortals on earth so that they are misled as to good ways and righteous deeds. But they care for righteousness and virtue and not love of money, which begets innumerable evils for mortal men, war, and limitless famine. They have just measurements in fields and cities and they do not carry out robberies at night against each other . . . nor does neighbor move the boundaries of neighbor, nor does a very rich man grieve a lesser man nor oppress widows in any respect . . . fulfilling the word of the great God, hymn of the law, for the Heavenly One gave the earth in common to all. . . . [T]hey lift up holy arms towards heaven, from their beds, always sanctifying their flesh with water, and honor only the Immortal who always rules, and then their parents. Greatly surpassing all men, they are mindful of holy wedlock, and they do not engage in impious intercourse with male children, as do Phoenicians, Egyptians, and Romans . . . transgressing the holy law of immortal God, which they transgressed. (Sib.Or.3.218-47, 591-600)

Verse 32:

"Know the ordinance of God"

Paul follows contemporary Jewish thought in judging transgression against the standards and precepts of the Torah:

> They are those that have departed from the way . . . bringing low the everlasting heights and departing from the paths of righteousness and removing the bound which their forefathers had established in their inheritance . . . Because they sought pleasant things and chose illusion, and because they spied out breaches and chose the beauty of the neck, and because they declared the wicked righteous and the righteous wicked, and because they transgressed the Covenant and violated the Precept . . . and their works were as a defilement before Him. . . . For they shall be sick < without > any healing and all the < chastisings shall crush > them . . . because they defiled themselves in the ways of lust and in the riches of iniquity, and because they took revenge and bore malice, each towards each brother, and because each man hated his fellow, and because they refused their help . . .

> and because they had shameful commerce, and because they made themselves strong for the sake of riches and gain, and because each man did what was good in his eyes, and because each man chose the stubbornness of his heart and because they kept not themselves from the people but lived in license deliberately, walking in the way of the wicked, of whom God said, *Their wine is the poison of serpents and the head of asps is cruel* {Dt.32.33}. (CDC 1.13-2.1, 8.4-10)

"Worthy of death": cf. 1 Cor.6.9-10, Gal.5.21, Eph.5.5; 1QS 4.9-14; PA 1.13, 2.11, 3.4, 7, 8, 10; Mak.23b; Philo, *De Spec.Leg.*3.38.

The phrase ἀξιοι θανατου (*axioi thanatou*; "worthy of death") reflects the Jewish concept of extra-legal punishment, in contradistinction to the penalties prescribed by the Torah (cf. חייב/מתחייב בנפשו ; *chaiyav/mitchaiyav be-nafsho*). This expression is frequently used in rabbinic texts as a parallel to the phrase אשר מוציא אדם מהעולם (*'asher motzi' 'adam me-ha'olam*), "which removes a man from the world."[87] These are transgressions which are punishable only by the "heavenly court" (בית דין של מעלה; *beit din shel ma'alah*), or by God Himself, not by the rabbinic (human) court (בית הדין; *beit ha-din*) instituted by the Torah.[88] Paul thus indicates that punishment may be incurred for "those things which are not proper" in the world to come.

"Give hearty approval": cf. Ps.50.18, Ezek.13.22, Mt.5.19, Lk.11.48; Ps.Sol.14.6, Test.Jud.14.8; PA 5.18, RH 17a.

Man's "exchange" of God's glory and truth for his own futile speculations, lies, and degrading passions indicates his service of his own evil inclination rather than obedience to his Creator:

> But to the wicked God says, "What right have you to tell of My statutes, and to take My covenant in your mouth? For you hate discipline, and you cast My words behind you. When you see a thief, you are pleased [lit. run together] with him, and you associate with adulterers. . . . Now consider this, you who forget God, lest I tear (you) in pieces, and there be none to deliver. He who offers a sacrifice of thanksgiving honors Me; and to him who orders (his) way (aright) I shall show the salvation of God." (Ps.50.16-18, 22-23)

The wicked shun good rather than evil; they cleave to evil and run from good:

> For [the man of understanding that he may instruct the sai]nts to li[ve according to the ru]le of the Community; to seek God with [all their heart] and [all their soul] [and] do what is good and right before Him, as He commanded by the hand of Moses and all His servants the Prophets; and to love all that He has chosen and hate all that He has despised; and to depart from all evil and cling to all good works . . . that they may love all the sons of light, each according to his lot in the Council of God; and that they may hate all the sons of darkness, each according to his fault in the Vengeance of God. (1QS 1.1-11)[89]

"To those who practice them"

Men have "exchanged" the image of God for their own image yet must serve either the Creator or their own inclination. Therefore, they act hypocritically towards both God and man through being "two-faced":

> The soul, they say, may in words express good for the sake of evil, but the outcome of the action leads to evil. There is a man who has no mercy on the one who serves him in performing an evil deed; there are two aspects of this, but the whole is wicked. And there is a man who loves the one who does the evil, as he himself is involved in evil, so that he would choose to die in evil for the evildoer's sake. There are two aspects of this, but the whole situation is evil. . . . But you, my children, do not be two-faced like them . . . For those who are two-faced are not of God, but they are enslaved to their evil desires, so that they may be pleasing to Beliar and to persons like themselves. . . . One cannot say that truth is a lie, nor a righteous act is unjust, because all truth is subject ultimately to the light, just as all things are ultimately subject to God. . . . The two-faced are doubly punished because they both practice evil and approve of others who practice it; they imitate the spirits of error and join in the struggle against mankind. (Test.Asher 2.1-3, 3.1-2, 5.3, 6.2)

Paul adapts this principle of "double-mindedness" and "two-faced" hypocritical behavior in the following chapter, and there begins to warn Israel of the dangers of engaging in similarly hypocritical behavior.[90]

Endnotes on Chapter 1

1 Roman citizenship could be obtained from parents who were Roman citizens; through manumission of a slave in Rome; on discharge from service in the auxiliaries; on enlistment in the legions in cases of emergency recruitment; or as a favor for special services rendered to the Empire. Paul himself was born a Roman citizen, and his parents may have received citizenship for some such service. See E. Ferguson, *Backgrounds of Early Christianity* (Michigan: Eerdmans, 1987), 48-49.

2 Rabban Gamaliel I (c.10-80 C.E.) was the grandson of Hillel, but himself belonged to the rival pharisaic school of *Beit Shammai*; cf. Orla 2.12, Yev.16.7, Shab.15a.

3 People were frequently known by their Roman or Hebrew names, as well as by "nicknames." Peter, for example, was known as Simon Cepha (cf. Mt.4.18, Mk.3.16); James and John were given the nickname Boanerges, "the sons of thunder" (cf. Mk.3.17); Joseph was called Barsabbas in Aramaic and Justus in Greek (cf. Acts 1.23); Barnabas' Hebrew name was Joseph (cf. Acts 4.36); and Tabitha was known as Dorcas in Greek (cf. Acts 9.36).

4 Scholars have traditionally placed Romans, 1 and 2 Corinthians, Galatians, Philippians, 1 Thessalonians, and Philemon in the category of "authentic" Pauline letters; a considerable body of scholarly opinion also regards Colossians and 2 Thessalonians as authentic as well; seeG.W. Kümmel, *Introduction to the New Testament* (NY: 1975).

5 Cf. 1 Macc.11.30, 32, 12.6, 20, 2 Macc.1.1, Jos.*Ant.*16.166-171, 17.131-141, Tanh.Vayishlach 3, Gen.R.75.5, 2 Clem.6.1-6. Paul's writings are referred to within other New Testament letters. Peter refers to "all [Paul's] letters" in addition to what Paul had specifically written to Peter's readers (2 Pet.3.15-16).

6 Cf. Acts 9.15, 22.21, 26.17, Rom.1.5, 11.13, 15.15-16, Gal.1.16, 2.9, Eph.3.2, 8, 1 Tim.2.7, 2 Tim.4.17.

7 Cf. Gen.26.24, Num.12.7, 1 Kings 14.8, Isa.42.1-5, 49.5-6. Chapters 42-53 of Isaiah include those sections known as the "Servant Songs," which refer to the Messiah who brings redemption to Israel and light to the nations.

8 Paul elaborates the midrash and the theme of "slavery" or servanthood explicitly in chapter 6. The midrash reflects the doctrine of the Two Ways or the Two Spirits, according to which man must choose between serving either God or his own (evil) inclination.

9 The terms "elect," "chosen," and "called" are synonymous in Greek, linked by the common idea of being "called out" (ἐκκαλεω; *ekkaleo*). The same idea is reflected in Hebrew, where being "called by God's name" indicates being chosen by Him (קרואי אל, the "called of God;" see the references above.) This text is from the beginning of the Scroll of the Rule (1QS) found at Qumran, which is one of the documents ascribed to the (Essene) community who settled there and were probably responsible for writing the Dead Sea Scrolls. The "Teacher of Righteousness" was the founder and leader of the Qumran community. (The identity of the Essenes, and their residency at Qumran has long been the subject of scholarly debate; for a convenient review of the discussion, as well as the major texts, see A. Dupont-Sommer, *The Essene Writings from Qumran* [Massachusetts: Peter Smith, 1973]. This is the translation we have used in the present volume. The most recent claims that the "Qumran community" itself is a "myth" are unfounded, in our opinion. On the contrary, the evidence of the textual influence of the Qumran documents, particularly on Paul's writings, is one of the clearest facts to emerge from the Commentary. The best statement of the connection between Qumran and the New Testament texts in this respect, is D. Flusser, "The Dead Sea Sect and Pre-Pauline Christianity," in *Judaism and the Origins of Christianity* [Jerusalem: Magnes Press, 1988], 23-74. The square brackets [ ] mark a lacuna or gap in the text, which the translator at times speculatively fills in.)

10 See G. Kittel, *Theological Dictionary of the New Testament* (Michigan: Eerdmans, 1964), 1:407ff; (henceforth referred to as TDNT).

11 Abraham becomes God's שליח when he leaves Ur (cf. Gen.12.1ff); Eliezer is Abraham's "agent" in looking for a wife for Isaac (cf. Gen.24.1ff); Moses and the prophets are called "apostles" (cf. Ex.3.14-15, 4.1, 10-13, 1 Kings 14.6, Isa.6.8, 55.11, Ezek.3.5); and Jehoshaphat sends "emissaries" to teach in the cities of Judah (cf. 2 Chron.17.7-9, Jer.49.14, Ezek.23.40).

12 Cf. Hag.10b, BK 113b. The Rabbis themselves traced back the institution of the שליח (*shaliach*) to the Torah (cf. Ned.72b).

13 This process of affirmation reflects some of the functions of the שליח ציבור (*shaliach tzibor*) or the official responsible for leading prayers in the synagogue; cf. Ber.5.5, RH 4.9, 17b.

14 Paul regarded the office of "apostleship" as an "agency" as well as a title (cf. 1 Cor.12.29, 2 Cor.8.23, Eph.4.11), which might have included women as well as men (cf. Rom.16.7), even though *halakhah* did not usually recognize women as "agents" (cf. Kid.23b).

15 All these three Rabbis are attempting to prove that the righteous are in fact greater than angels. Yeshua adopts the same principle in Jn.13.16, in order to encourage humility and servitude amongst his disciples.

16 See also the comments on 8.28.

17 For contemporary (and later) Jewish messianic understandings of Isa.52.7 and 61.2, cf. Lk.4.16-22, 1QH 15.15, 18.14-15, PRK S5.4, Lev.R.9.9.

18 Cf. PRE 3, Mid.Ps.93.3, Gen.R.1.4, Ned.39b, San.98b.

19 The word "Tanakh" is the acronym—תנ"ך—for these three groups of text. The designations for Scripture in Hebrew include כתבי הקודש (*kitvei ha-kodesh*; "[the] holy writings"); המקרא (*ha-mikra'*; lit. "the read"); הכתוב(ים) (*ha-ketuv[im];* "[what is] written"); and הספרים (*ha-sefarim*; "the books"). In the New Testament the term "holy" or "sacred" Scripture is used in 2 Tim.3.15, but the normal usage is simply "Scripture." See M. Mulder, ed., *Mikra: Text, Translation, Reading and Interpretation of the Hebrew Bible in Ancient Judaism and Early Christianity* (Philadelphia: Fortress Press, 1990), 39-40, 45-55.

20 Despite the fact that Josephus emphasizes the historical truth of the biblical books, it is also clear that he regards them as authoritative equally because of their prophetic inspiration.

21 Holiness causes the hands to be "unclean" because it brings the sacred into contact with the profane. Any book, therefore, which did *not* make the hands unclean when they touched it did not possess a degree of sanctity. Some of the other considerations according to which the canon was determined included the fact that a book's content might appear to be "secular" (cf. Ecclesiastes), that it was "erotic" (cf. Canticles), or that it possessed contradictions to other biblical books (cf. Ezekiel). For the tripartite division of the Tanakh (Torah, Prophets, Writings) and its significance, see M. Mulder, *Mikra*, 39-86, 653-90.

22 Cf. Jer.23.5-6, 33.15-16, Zech.3.8, 6.12, Lk.1.68f, 2.25-32, 24.21, 4QpIsa.[d] 1, 4QPat.Bless.1f. This Qumran "pesher" (interpretation of Scripture) interprets 2 Sam.7.14 in the light of Amos 9.11, so that the "king" is associated with David and David is associated with the Messiah, who in Jer.23.6 is said to save Israel.

23 Cf. 1QS 5.7-11, 1QS[a] 1.1-3, 24, 1QS[b] 1.22-25, CDC 4.4f. The lacuna (gap) in the latter text probably continued with a list of the genealogy, dates, and titles of the members of the community. The phrase "flesh and blood" was also frequently used in rabbinic literature to distinguish human behavior from God's characteristics (cf. Ex.R.21.4, Dt.R.5.14, Lev.R.18.5).

24 Cf. Dt.32.20, Ps.56.13, Isa.26.19, Dan.12.2, Jos.*Bell.*2.162-166, *Ant.*18.11-17; see also Mt.22.23-33, Lk.20.27-40, Acts 23.8, San.91b.

25 Elijah was regarded as the precursor of the Messiah at least partially by virtue of his mysterious demise; cf. 2 Kings 2.11, Mt.11.14, 16.14, 17.10-13, Mk.6.15, 9.2-13, Lk.1.17, 9.8, Jn.1.21. See J. Tabor, "'Returning to the Divinity': Josephus's Portrayal of the Disappearances of Enoch, Elijah, and Moses," *Journal of Biblical Literature* 108.2 (1989), 225-38. For the Melchizedek tradition, cf. Gen.14.18, Ps.110.4, Heb.6.20-7.3, 11QMelch.2.7f, 2 En.71.12ff, Num.R.14.1 [MS.M], Suk.52b.

26 Cf. the messianic interpretations of Ps.72.17 and 93.2 in Mid.Ps.72.6, 93.3, San.98b, Pes.54a, Ned.39a. The "decree" may refer to "today," when God publicly proclaims him to be His "son" (cf. Mt.3.17); or to the day when God "begot" him—either revealed him or, possibly, resurrected him.

27 Cf. Sot.9.15, where the version slightly differs. This passage is sometimes called the "Saint's Progress." The phrase תחית המתים (*techiyat hametim*), "the resurrection of the dead," may also refer to the power of restoring life to the dead; see also the comments on verse 9.

28 Cf. 4 Ez.7.27-30, Num.R.14.1, PSuk.55b, Suk.52b. For the tradition of the Messiah son of Joseph, see J. Klausner, *The Messianic Idea in Israel* (NY: 1955), 483-501; see also the comments on 5.6.

29 For the series of messianic interpretations of Jer.23.5-6, cf. Targum Jonathan on Jer.23.5-6 and 33.15, Mid.Ps.21.2, Num.R.18.21, Lam.R.1.16.51, BB 75b.

30 See also the comments on 12.3 and 15.15.

31 Cf. Num.24.17-18, Ps.2.6-9, 60.7-8, 72.8-11, 108.7-9, Isa.42.6-13, 49.6-7, 51.4-5, Gen.R.97 (NV), 98.8, 99.8, Lam.R.1.16.51, 1QS^{b} 5.27-28, CDC 7.18-21, 4QPat.Bless.1-6.

32 Cf. Dt.32.17ff; see also the comments on 15.18.

33 "Agency" here becomes an expression of the rabbinic principle of לשמה (*lishmah*; intention [lit. "for the name of"]); cf. Suk.49b, Ned.62a, Ber.17a; see also the comments on chapter 14.

34 The Jewish community of Rome was large, dating from the fall of Jerusalem to Pompey in 63 B.C.E., and Paul's letter further reflects the banishment and dispersion of the Jewish community in Rome as a result of Claudius' decree in 52 C.E. (cf. Acts 18.2; Seutonius, *Claudius*, 25).

35 See also the comments on 8.28.

36 See the comments on verses 1 and 6.

37 Cf. MK 15a, 29a. For the use of God's name in greetings, cf. Ruth R.4.5, Ber.54a.

38 The motif is also based, however, on the theme (midrash) of the "two masters" which Paul introduces in chapter 6, the foundation for the subsequent chapters.

39 For Paul's role as an intercessor on behalf of his people, see 9.1-5 (where he appeals to the witness of the Holy Spirit to confirm his longing for the salvation of his people), and 11.1-6, as well as God's intercession through the Holy Spirit and Yeshua in 8.26-39.

40 For the details of Paul's itinerary, and the reasons and motives which guided him, see the comments on 15.22-32.

41 For the ambiguities of this situation, see the comments on 15.20-22. Paul seems to resolve the difficulty over impinging on someone else's ground ("wanting to obtain some fruit among you also" [verse 13]) by emphasizing his wish to receive as well as to give. This mitigates his appeal to his apostolic authority, and in some sense turns the visit into a more "personal" than "professional" trip.

42 Paul's desire to "impart a spiritual gift" possibly reflects his wish to prove his authority to the Roman congregation. In Acts 8, Peter and John are called to Samaria in order to lay hands on the Samaritan converts so that the latter might receive the Holy Spirit; Philip and the other evangelists apparently did not possess the authority to perform this function.

43 This list from Qumran corresponds to many of the "gifts" to which Paul refers: abundant mercy and abundant grace (cf. 1 Cor.1.4, Phil.1.7, Col.1.6); almighty wisdom with faith (cf. Phil.1.9, Col.1.4, 9, 1 Thess.1.3, 2 Thess.1.3); the spirit of knowledge and discretion concerning the truth of the Mysteries of Knowledge (cf. Rom.16.25, 1 Cor.1.5, Phil.1.9, Col.1.9, 26-27); abundant affection towards all the sons of truth (cf. Phil.1.9, Col.1.4, 1 Thess.1.3, 2 Thess.1.3, Phlm.5). Paul also wants to bring the Gentiles themselves (symbolized in their financial contribution) as an offering of "first fruits" to the "saints in Jerusalem;" see the comments on 15.16, 25ff.

44 See the comments on 15.27. Paul further appeals to the "proselytizing" aspect of "debt," in which putting oneself in another's place is a way of bringing him to faithfulness to God in Yeshua in 12.9ff and 13.7-8.

45 See TDNT 1:546f.

46 The term βαρβαροι (*barbaroi*; barbarians) corresponds to the Hebrew term לועז (*lo'az*), which denotes every nation and tongue not of Israelite offspring or extract (cf. Ps.114.1). In the Tanakh, the term "goyim" referred to all the nations, including Israel (cf. Gen.10.5, 12.2, 18.18, 25.23, 35.11, Ex.19.6, Dt.4.6, Ps.106.5, Isa.9.1, Jer.5.15, Ezek.4.13, 36.13-14, Mic.4.2, 3). In later usage, during the Second Temple period and onwards, it was referred exclusively to the Gentiles, who were idolaters and "sinners [by nature];" cf. Gal.2.15, Test.Dan.5.8, Test.Naph.3.3-5, Ps.Sol.2.1f, AZ 1.1, Tos.AZ 3.4.

47 See the comments on verse 11 and 15.20-22.

48 The LXX translates לא יחיש (*lo' yachish*; NASB, "will not be disturbed") by the verb καταισχυνω (*kataischuno*), "to be ashamed," which has influenced most of the other translators.

49 For the various usages of the epithet "Power," see E.E. Urbach, *The Sages* (Jerusalem: Magnes Press, 1979), 80-96.

50 See D. Flusser and S. Safrai, "The Essene Doctrine of Hypostasis and R. Meir," *Immanuel* 14 (1982), 46-57.

51 See also the comments on 8.34.

52 Cf. Dt.4.5-6, Prov.3.1-4, 13, 16, 4.2, 6.23-24, 7.4-5, Sir.1.4-5, 15.1ff, 21.11, 24.3-9, 23ff, Ap.Bar.4.1, Wis.Sol.7.25, Let.Arist.31, 313; Sifre Dt.48, Mekh.Shirata 3, PRE 3, Mid.Ps.21.2, Gen.R.1.1, 4, 43.6, 70.5, Ned.39b; Philo, *De Spec.Leg*.1.46-48, *De Mig.Abr*.179-83. See also Paul's midrash on Lev.18.5 in 10.5ff.

53 See also the comments on 3.21-23.

54 The psalmist (identified by many scholars with the Teacher of Righteousness) compares himself to the woman who is to give birth to the Messiah at the end of time; the "crucible" is the womb. His "power" is the ability to deliver from the waves of Sheol, Death, and perdition. The reference to the "men of good omen" derives from Zech.3.8, a messianic passage which speaks of the coming of the "Branch (of David)."

55 The midrash discusses the issue of whether the dual (ordinary and final) forms of these five letters were instituted at the giving of the Torah on Mt. Sinai or were instituted by the Seers (Sages). The bracketed passage ("From . . . hand:") is added from various manuscripts, but obviously comes to explain the same dictum.

56 Cf. the Qumran "pesher" or interpretation of Hab.2.4: "The explanation of this concerns all those who observe the Law in the house of Judah. God will deliver them from the house of Judgment because of their affliction and their faith in the Teacher of Righteousness" (1QpHab 7.1-3).

57 See also the comments on 10.9-10.

58 In 1.18-32, Paul refers to the deeds of the Gentiles. It is clear that Paul assumes that God has revealed Himself to Israel in the Torah (cf. 3.2, 9.4). He must now also explain how He has revealed His righteousness to the Gentiles.

59 Cf. 1QS 4.19-26, 5.12, 8.10, 9.23, 10.19, 1QM 1.5ff, 1QH 3.16ff, 15.17-25.

60 Cf. Gal.4.9, where Paul distinguishes between "having come to know God" and "being known by God," as well as 1 Cor.8.3 and 1 Jn.4.7-12.

61 Cf. Apoc.Abr.8.1-6, ARN[a] 4, Sifra Acharei Mot 44b, Gen.R.61.1, Lev.R.2.10, Num.R.14.2, Philo, *De Abr*.6.

62 Cf. Yoma 67b. "Honesty" is literally "(objection to) robbery," and "chastity" is literally "forbidden intercourse." The point of R. Johanan's saying is that moral etiquette could have been known to man without God's revelation in the Torah. According to Paul, the Gentiles could also have learnt the same lessons from what God had created, and therefore have "no excuse" for rejecting His sovereignty.

63 See J. Weiss, *The History of Primitive Christianity* (London: 1837), 1:240; C.H. Dodd, *The Bible and the Greeks* (London: 1935), 36.

64 See also the comments on 1.16-17.

65 The image of darkness for ignorance and error, and light as goodness and wisdom is widespread in contemporary Jewish texts; cf. the Qumran designations of the "sons of light" and the "sons of darkness": 1QS 3.13-4.26; see also Ps.119.130, Isa.9.2, 42.6, 49.6, Lk.2.32, Acts 13.47, 26.18, 23, 1 Pet.2.9, Test.Jos.19.3, Test.Abr.B 7, Jos.Asen.8.10, 12.2, 15.13, 2 En.30.15, 3 Bar.6.13, Wis.Sol.18.4, Philo, *De Virt.*179, 221, Did.1.1f, Ep.Barn.18.1-20.2; see also the comments on 2.19.

66 The subject of this section of the psalm is obviously the Gentiles, who did not "acknowledge" God by paying Him tribute (cf. Ps.29.1, 96.7f), or possibly, did not bring (offerings) (cf. Ps.68.29, 76.11). Although they were in possession of God's blessings, they were not properly thankful to Him.

67 Paul gives his own personal thanks for being released and delivered from "this body of death" in which he is enslaved to sin in 7.25; he picks up the image of the potter's clay in regard to God's election of the Gentiles in 9.19ff; and he uses the idea of "blessing" or giving thanks as a way of sanctifying "profane" or "secular" things in 14.6f.

68 Cf. ריק/הבל (*rek/hevel*; emptiness); שוא (*shav'*; vanity); שקר/כזב (*sheker/kazav*; lies).

69 See the comments on verse 20 and 2.19.

70 Paul picks up this theme again in the conclusion to the letter, where he inserts a strong warning against false teaching which causes strife (also based on motifs from Qumran); see the comments on 16.17-18.

71 Cf. E.E. Urbach, *Sages*, 37-65; see also the comments on 3.23.

72 See the comments on 3.21f.

73 Cf. 1 Sam.16.14, 1 Kings 22.22, Isa.45.7, Ezek. 20.25, 2 Thess. 2.10-12. See, for example, those midrashim which complain about God creating the יצר הרע (*yetzer ha-ra'*), the evil inclination; cf. TBE p.62, Gen.R.27.4, 34.10, Ex.R.43.7, 46.4, MHG Gen.4.9, PRK 4.2, Suk.52b, Kid.30b.

74 Cf. Deut. 31.17-18, 32.20f, Ps.27.9, 30.7, 44.23-4, 69.17, 88.14f, 102.2, 143.7, Isa. 8.17, 54.8, 64.7, Jer.33.5, Ezek.39.29, Mic.3.4. For the

midrashim which speak of man being "delivered into the hands of the evil inclination who lies at the door," cf. ARN[b] 16, 30, Pes.Rab.9.2, PRK S3.2, Kid.30b, Suk.52b, San.91b, Ber.61a.

75 On the other hand, God's "turning a blind eye," "winking at," or "overlooking" is a sign of His mercy; cf. Acts 14.16, 17.30.

76 The first verb derives from the root מוג (*mug*), "to melt," the second from the root גנן (*ganan*), "to cover or defend;" cf. Gen.14.20, Prov.4.9, Hos.11.8. The LXX therefore translates Isa.64.6 (7) with the normal Greek for "to hand over" (παραδωκας ὑμας; *paradokas humas*; "handed us over"), the same verb as Paul uses in this verse.

77 The piel verb form is also used with the phrase "into the hand of" (ביד; *be-yad*); cf. 1 Sam.17.46, 24.19 (18), 26.8; cf. 2 Sam. 18.28.

78 Cf. Gen.R.67.8. The midrash makes literal use of the different prepositions "in," "at," and "to," in these verses to imply that the wicked speak in (subjection to) their hearts, while the righteous speak to their hearts, giving orders, as it were, to their hearts.

79 The word *zaw* comes from Hos.5.11 but refers in Isa.28.10 to the "prating" of a prophet; "Levi son of Jacob" alludes to the Testament of Levi, although the passage does not appear in the extant text. The Torah forbids the marriage of a nephew to his aunt, but the Qumran community further prohibited the marriage between a niece and uncle, arguing that although the law may seem to involve men only because it is addressed to men, it really concerns women (nieces) as well; for the rabbinic discussion of the inclusion or exclusion of nieces, see Tos.Yev.1.10f.

80 Cf. 1QH 2.18-19, 36. The verb "to barter" comes from the root (מור; *mor*), "to change," which is used in Jer.2.11 and Ps.106.20.

81 The word "lie" is the last word of a phrase the remainder of which has disappeared in the lacuna (gap) at the bottom of column 10. According to the Qumran community, the "Preacher of Lies" (cf. also the "Man of Lies") refers to the "Wicked Priest" who was the "arch-enemy" of the Teacher of Righteousness, and whom various scholars identify with Hyrcanus II. Yeshua also describes Satan as the "father of lies" (cf. Jn.8.44).

82 Cf. also the reputation of Sodom, whose name was given to the practice of "sodomy;" cf. cf. 2 En.34.1, Test.Isaac 5.27, Test.Levi 14.6-8, Test.Naph.3.4, Test.Ben.9.1f, Jub.16.5-6, 20.5f, Pes.Rab.5.7, 40.2, ARN[a] 12, Mekh.Shirata 2, Num.R.13.2.

83 See E. Ferguson, *Backgrounds*, 52, 57.

84 This midrash, as developed by R. Simeon in connection with Job 3.19, is perhaps the most basic of Paul's themes throughout the letter, although he begins to develop it most thoroughly in chapter 6.

85 Cf. DEZ 6, Shab.88b, 114a, Ber.61b. The reference in 2 Maccabees, on the other hand, relates specifically to profanation of sacred objects and commandments.

86 Paul is convinced, on the other hand, that the members of the community in Rome are "full of goodness, filled with all knowledge, and able also to admonish one another" (15.14) to do what is "proper."

87 Cf. the "offences" listed in the mishnayot in PA above.

88 Cf. Num.R.18.4, Kid.43a, BK 55b, 56a, 91a, 98a, Git.53a, Mak.13b.

89 Cf. Rom.12.9, 1 Cor.10.20-21, 2 Cor.6.14-16, 1 Thess.5.22, Jas.4.4, 1QS 4.18, CDC 2.15, 1QH 14.10, 15.19, 17.24, PA 1.4, 7, 2.9. Paul addresses the issue of loving those who do evil in chapters 12-13; see the comments on 12.9ff.

90 The author of the Testament of Asher does not address the condition of the Gentiles and their denial of God and His commandments, but warns against allowing men to use evil (means) for good ends. Paul counters a similar attitude throughout his letter, especially where that attitude overlaps with the dangers of "libertinism," or thinking that God's mercy licenses immoral actions; cf. Rom.3.3f, 8, 31, 6.1ff, 7.7ff, (14.16). Cf. also Paul's comments in Gal.2.13-14, regarding Peter's hypocritical behavior.

ROMANS 2

Introduction

Paul begins to develop his main theme, stated in 1.16-17, of God's righteousness through faithfulness. He now turns to Israel's election, however, and rejects their "excuses" which parallel the excuses of the Gentiles in 1.20. He makes a series of points in order to establish two related principles, in two parallel sections of the chapter (verses 1-16 and 17-29). God renders to every man according to his deeds (verse 6), and since the people of Israel engage in the same improper things which the Gentiles practice, they will receive the same judgment as do the Gentiles (verses 1-3). This principle (cf. God's punishment of "measure for measure") means that Israel cannot presume upon their privileged status as God's people, since God's criteria are impartial (verse 11). Paul makes these two points in general in verses 1-16, and then breaks them down into particular examples in verses 17-29. This section subdivides in turn, where Paul first lists the particular elements of Israel's election (verses 17-20), and then describes how they are given to misuse (verses 21-29). Verse 16 establishes the grounds for both elements of his argument, since God judges every man according to the faithfulness of his deeds and not according to his possession of the Torah. The Gentiles who are faithful to the will of God can therefore become "sons of Abraham" together with those among Israel whose hearts are circumcised.

Verse 1:
"Therefore . . ."

Paul continues arguing that no man has an excuse before God for his behavior (cf. 1.20). In chapter 1 he describes how the Gentiles' refusal to acknowledge God's sovereignty over the world leads them to encourage one another to practice things which they know to be worthy of death. Just as the Gentiles' excuse that they were unable to see clearly God's attributes from His creation cannot justify them, so, too, Paul says, every Jew who points a finger at the ungodly behavior of the Gentiles is also without an excuse. Among the people who engage in and "give hearty approval" to such deeds are those within the nation of Israel who also practice the same improper things. He thus repeats his denunciation of "those things which are not proper," for the same reasons and on the same grounds, the only difference lying in the fact that here he identifies Israel as being those who practice such deeds. This switch in tactics, as it were, forms the basis for his argument in chapter 2, in which he warns Israel that their election is not an automatic guarantee of redemption. They must also obey God's commands in order to receive His rewards and avoid His punishments, just like the Gentile nations. Since God thus treats both Jews and Gentiles according to the same principle, Israel must recognize, and maybe reassess, the grounds of their election.

"Every man of you . . . ": cf. 2.3, 9.20, 10.10-11.

Paul immediately begins to remind Israel of their solidarity with the whole of mankind. He uses the inclusive phrase איש איש (*'ish 'ish*; each man [lit. "man man"]) to demonstrate that every person who denounces other people's behavior is usually included in their company.[1] He first generalizes concerning the guilt of all mankind (1.18-32) and then turns to Israel as the particular example of the guilty party.[2] Since no man has an excuse for excluding himself from God's judgment, and the people of Israel are not excluded from mankind in general, God will punish them for practicing the same things of which they accuse the Gentile nations.

"Who passes judgment . . . ": cf. Mt.7.1, Mk.4.24, Lk.6.37-38, Rom.12.3f, 14.1ff, 1 Cor.4.3-5, 5.12-13, 8.1f, Jas.4.11, 5.9; 1QS 5.25-6.1, 7.5-9, 10.18-11.2, CDC 7.2-3, 9.2-8; Test.Zev.8.1-6, Sir.17.20; PA 1.6, 2.4, 4.1, 3, ARN[a] 15.1, 16.4, ARN[b] 23, 26, DEZ 3.1, Lam.R.3.41.9, Shab.127a, Meg.28a, Yoma 23a, Arak.16b, BB 60b, Kid.70a-b, AZ 18b.

Paul now combines the two principles of (inclusive) repetition and the general and the particular with the principle of מידה כנגד מידה (*middah keneged middah*) or "measure for measure." Since at least a part of the people of Israel engage in the same things which are not proper amongst the Gentiles, as a nation (or as individuals) they are liable to the same judgment which God will mete out to the Gentiles. Because God's judgment of the Gentiles is based on their deeds, "whosoever" among the people of Israel who practices the same things will receive the same punishment. These two points are central to Paul's argument in this chapter: since God renders to every man according to the faithfulness of his deeds, the Gentiles can become "sons of Abraham" (cf. verses 25-29); and Israel may not claim privileged and exclusive spiritual rights because of their possession of God's will in the Torah. Here Paul applies the idea of a "double moral standard" to Israel's attitude towards the Gentile nations, and claims that Israel cannot presume superiority over the Gentiles, or even immunity from God's punishment, because of their election.[3] If God punishes according to a person's deeds (cf. 1.27), then Israel will receive the same judgment as the Gentiles when they practice the same deeds. In the same way, when they judge the Gentiles for wicked acts, they too will be judged for their own iniquities. Paul also applies the principle of "measure for measure" to God's judgment of men. He follows here a tradition based on a "new understanding" of Leviticus 19.18 and the command to "love thy neighbor as thyself."[4] The principle of a "measure for measure" is linked with altruistic love, and the "compensation" (that which you receive in return for your action) leads to the love of one's fellow-man. If you love your fellow-man, you may rely on divine reward; if you do not love him, you may be certain of punishment:

> Rabbi Hanina, the Prefect of the Priests, says: An oath from Mount Sinai has been sworn on (this) saying upon which the whole world depends: If (you) hate your fellowman whose deeds are evil like yours, I the Lord am judge to punish that same man and if you love your neighbor whose deeds are proper like your own, I the Lord am faithful and merciful toward you. (ARN[b] 26)[5]

Verses 2-3:
"And we know . . . judgment of God": cf. Dt.32.35, Ps.2.10f, 9.8, 96.13, 98.9, 110.6, Isa.63.1ff, Jer.31.30, Ezek.7.1ff, Dan.9.14, Joel 1.15, 2.1f, 11, 31, 3.14, Amos 5.18-20, Obad.1.15f, Zeph.1.14f, Mal.4.5, Mt.3.7-10, 6.19-20, 7.2, 23.33, Lk.12.33, Jn.3.18-19, 5.24, 27, 8.16, Acts 10.42, 17.30-31, Rom.1.18-32, 9.22, 1 Thess.1.10, 2 Thess.1.5, 1 Tim.6.19, Rev.6.16-17, 14.19, 15.1, 7, 16.1ff; 1QS 3.18ff, 4.11ff, CDC 7.9f, 1QM 1.1ff, 11.14, 13.10-16, 1QH 1.26, 4.20-26, 40, 6.29f, 5.4, 6.29-33, 7.12, 28-29, 9.9, 14-16, 10.34f, 11.8; 4 Ez.7.33f, [77]f, 8.36, Test.Jud.23.1-5, Ps.Sol.2.15, 32, 9.2-5, 15.8, Sib.Or.2.218f, 4.183, 1 En.91.7; PA 3.1, 4.2, 11, 20, 22, 5.19, 6.6, ARN[a] 16.4, ARN[b] 32, Mid.Ps.36.7, DER 2.1-4, 7, Lev.R.27.1, AZ 3b.

Paul accepts the biblical and Jewish doctrine that God rewards good deeds and judges evil deeds, a fact which he says that the Gentiles know (cf. 1.32). He repeats the statement here for the benefit of the people of Israel, who also know that God rewards good deeds and punishes iniquity. His warning is forceful because he has just warned Israel against judging the Gentiles for ungodly practices. Not only will Israel be punished for their transgressions, but they will also be judged for judging others for those same deeds (in measure for measure). He further repeats the warning in verse 5.

Verse 4:

"Do you think lightly": cf. Gen.27.12 (Hebrew), Dt.7.6-11, Ps.50.16-23, Hos.6.7 (Hebrew), Amos 3.2; PA 1.3, 2.12, 3.11, 15, 4.22, ARN[b] 32, Lev.R.27.1, BB 8a.

Paul returns to the theme of honoring God which he introduces in 1.21ff.[6] He now applies exactly the same warning against dishonoring God to Israel. Where in 1.21ff he refers to the Gentiles' disparagement of God, here he also accuses Israel of despising God, by seeing in His goodness a guarantee of their redemption. This verse is often understood to relate to God's attributes, since He is "compassionate and gracious, slow to anger and abounding in lovingkindness and truth; who keeps lovingkindness for thousands, who forgives iniquity, transgression and sin . . . " (Ex.34.6-7). The Greek verb καταφρονεω (*kataphroneo*), "to think lightly," is used in the LXX for several Hebrew terms.[7] Those who despise God's compassion denigrate God's character and His attributes in the same way as those who practice other forms of idolatry (cf. Hab.1.13), and while God seemingly allows the wicked to prosper, the righteous man must wait until the wicked receives his punishment instead of complaining against God's mercy (cf. Psalm 37). Paul is speaking here more specifically, however, of Israel's "presumption" of God's kindness in electing them as His people. The tendency to "despise" His kindness is not a sign of belittling God's kindness, but of presuming upon His intention to redeem those whom He has chosen. God's kindness in this regard does not make Israel's election a guarantee of salvation.[8] Here Paul combines the three elements of God's choice based upon faithfulness, His acceptance of the Gentiles who are "a law to themselves," and the "sons of Abraham." He expresses this thought in the most general terms in verses 1-6 (11), repeats it in the Jewish thought that it is not the hearers of the Torah who are just before God but the doers, thus expressly declaring to Israel that the Gentiles are acceptable in God's eyes, and finally spells it out to Israel in terms of the motif of the "sons of Abraham."[9]

"The riches of His kindness": cf. Ex.34.6-7, Ps.103.8, Acts 14.16-17, 17.30, Rom.3.25, 9.23, 11.22, 33, Eph.1.7, 2.7, 3.8, Phil.4.19, Col.1.27, 2.2, Tit.3.4, 1 Pet.2.3; 1QS 4.3-5, 1QH 1.32, 4.36-37, 6.9, 18, 7.27, 30, 35, 9.14, 10.14ff, 11.28f, 12.14, 13.17, 15.16, 16.12; Wis.Sol.11.23f, 12.13f, 1 En.50.3, Ps.Sol.9.7; Jos.*Ant.*11.144; Mekh.Shirata 9, Mid.Ps.51.2, 55.6, 71.2, 72.1, 89.2, 119.55, Sifre Num.Ma'asei 160, Gen.R.60.2, Dt.R.2.1.

Paul elaborates the attributes of God which He displays towards Israel (and to the whole world), but which His people must not take as a guarantee of redemption (verses 4-10), based on Exodus 34.6-7. God's kindness "overlooks," "winks at," or "passes over" men's transgressions when the time for their punishment has long passed:

> I answered and said, "I know, my lord, that the Most High is now called merciful because he has mercy on those who have not yet come into the world; and gracious, because he is gracious to those who turn in repentance to his law; and patient, because he shows patience toward those who have sinned, since they are his own works; and bountiful, because he would rather give than take away; and abundant in compassion, because he makes his compassion abound more and more to those now living and to those who are gone and to those yet to come, for if he did not make them abound, the world with those who inhabit it would not have life; and he is called giver because if he did not give out of his goodness so that those who have committed iniquities might be relieved of them, not one ten-thousandth of mankind could have life; and judge, because if he did not pardon those who were created by his word and blot out the multitude of their sins, there would probably be left only very few of the innumerable multitude." (4 Ez.7.62-70)[10]

"Forbearance": cf. Ex.34.6, Joel 2.13, Acts 14.16, 17.30, Rom.3.25, 9.22; 4 Ez.7.62f, Test.Gad 4.7, Sir.17.21; PA 5.2, Mid.Ps.77.1, PRK 24.11.

The Greek word ἀνοχη (*anoche*), "forbearance," can mean "acceptance" or "reconciliation" (cf. 2 Cor.11.1, 19). God's forbearance in the Tanakh lies in His "restraining" Himself from destroying man (cf. LXX Isa.64.12) out of the abundance of His mercy (cf. LXX Isa.42.14).[11] This idea also underlies the frequent rabbinic dicta in which God conquers His attribute of wrath with His attribute of mercy (so that He does not give "measure for measure"):

> R. Samuel bar Nahman, citing R. Johanan, said: The text, not saying "long in patience," but saying *long in acts of patience* (Joel 2.13), is intimating that God exercises patience before deciding to requite the wicked, and even when He decides to requite them, in patience he requites them [for only one wicked deed at a time]. . . . R. Issachar of Kefar Mindu interpreted the verse *For He knoweth false men; indeed he seeth iniquity, but considereth it not* (Job 11.11) as follows: It is man's way in the world to heap up iniquities, but once he vows repentance, then, though God seeth [his] iniquity, He considereth it not, if one dare say such a thing. (PRK 24.11, 13)

"Patience": cf. 3.25, 9.22; 4 Ezek. 3.8, 7.62f, 8.36, Sir.17.21, 18.11-12, Wis.Sol.11.23, 1 En.60.5, 25, Test.Gad 4.7, Test.Abr.10.14f; PA 5.2, Mid.Ps.77.1, Pes.Rab.11.2, PRK 24.11, 25.1, Tanh.Shemot 20, Eccl.R.8.11.1, Ber.7a; Philo, *Leg.All*.3.106.

God's kindness allows Him to "overlook" acts which are "worthy of death" (cf. Acts 17.30, Rom.1.32):

> Let it not be your will to destroy those who have had the ways of cattle; but regard those who have gloriously taught your Law. Be not angry with those who are deemed worse than beasts; but love those who have always put their trust in your glory. For we and our fathers have passed our lives in ways that bring death, but you, because of us sinners, are called merciful. For if you have desired to have pity on us, who have no works of righteousness, then you will be called merciful. . . . But what is man, that you are angry with him; or what is a mortal race, that you are so bitter against it? For in truth there is no one among those who have been born who has not acted wickedly, and among those who have existed there is no one who has not transgressed. For in this, O Lord, your righteousness and goodness will be declared, when you are merciful to those who have no store of good works. (4 Ez.8.29-36)[12]

"Not knowing . . . ": cf. 3.19-20, 10.2-3.

God's "kindness" is meant to provoke man to repentance, not to encourage him to feel contempt for what he perceives as God's "weakness":

> But to the wicked God says, "What right have you to tell of My statutes, and to take My covenant in your mouth? For you hate discipline, and you cast My words behind you. When you see a thief, you are pleased with him, and you associate with adulterers. You let your mouth loose in evil, and your tongue frames deceit. You sit and speak against your brother; you slander your own mother's son. These things you have done, and I have kept silence; you thought that I was just like you; I will reprove you, and state (the case) before your eyes. Now consider this, you who forget God, lest I tear (you) in pieces, and there be none to deliver. He who offers a sacrifice of thanksgiving honors Me; and to him who orders (his) way (aright) I shall show the salvation of God. (Ps.50.16-23)[13]

Man must therefore not make the mistake of presuming God's kindness to give him the license to transgress His will:

> BECAUSE SENTENCE AGAINST AN EVIL WORK IS NOT EXECUTED SPEEDILY (Eccl.8.11): because a man sins and the Attribute of Justice does not overtake him, THEREFORE THE HEART OF THE SONS OF MEN IS FULLY SET IN THEM TO DO EVIL. What do they say? 'Behold, the haughty go in and come out without stumbling.' [Because punishment does not befall them immediately after their sin, they think they will escape altogether.] BUT IT SHALL NOT BE WELL WITH THE WICKED (Eccl.8.13). (Eccl.R.8.11.1)

"Kindness . . . leads to repentance": cf. Ps.50.16-23, 73.11, Eccl.8.11, Isa.57.11, Tit.3.4, 2 Pet.3.9; Wis.Sol.11.23, Test.Abr.10.14f, Hell.Syn.Pray.11.4; Pes.Rab.44.7, 9, PRK 24.7, 11; Philo, *Leg.All.*3.106.

God's "overlooking" of man's transgressions should lead him to turn from his iniquity and repent:

> . . . thou hast ordered all things in measure and number and weight. For thou canst show thy great strength at all times when thou wilt; and who may withstand the power of thine arm? For the whole world before thee is as a little grain of the balance, yea, as a drop of the morning dew that falleth down upon the earth But thou hast mercy upon all; for thou canst do all things, and winkest at the sins of men, because they should amend. For thou lovest all the things that are, and abhorrest nothing which thou hast made; for never wouldest thou have made any thing, if thou hadst hated it. And how could any thing have endured, if it had not been thy will? or been preserved, if not called by thee? But thou sparest all: for they are thine, O Lord, thou lover of souls. (Wis.Sol.11.20-26)[14]

Verse 5:

"Stubbornness and unrepentant heart": cf. Ex.32.9, 33.3, 34.9, Dt.9.6, 13, 27 (LXX), 31.27, 2 Chron.30.8, Ps.75.5, (Hebrew) 95.8, Isa.48.4, Jer.5.3, 17.23, Ezek.2.4, 3.7, Acts 7.51, Rom.9.18-23, Eph.4.18; 1QS 1.6-7, 2.14, 3.3, 4.11, 5.4-5, CDC 2.17-18, 3.11-12; 1 En.50.4-5, Hell.Syn.Pray.11.4; PRK 17.5.

Because of Israel's rebelliousness towards God, the nation is characteristically described in the Tanakh as a "stiff-hearted" or "stiff-necked" (obstinate) people (קשי ערף וחזקי-לב; *keshei 'oref ve-chizkei lev*; cf. Ex.33.3, Ezek.2.4).

Stubbornness is a form of pride, and of refusing to submit to someone else's authority. The Qumran community adopted the reflexive form of the root for Jewish *halakhah* (הלך/התהלך; to walk) to describe the "sons of darkness" (and renegades from the community) who walked according to their own ways, and stubbornly refused to be "converted" (שוב; *shuv* [lit. "to turn" or "repent"]) from their evil ways:

> For [the man of understanding that he may instruct the sai]nts to li[ve according to the ru]le of the Community; to seek God with [all their heart] and [all their soul] [and] do what is good and right before Him, as He commanded by the hand of Moses and all His servants the Prophets; and to love all that He has chosen and hate all that He has despised; and to depart from all evil and cling to all good works; and to practice truth and righteousness and justice on earth, and to walk no more in the stubbornness of a guilty heart, nor with lustful eyes committing every kind of evil. . . . But whoever scorns to enter the ways of God in order to walk in the stubbornness of his heart, he shall not pass into His Community of truth. . . . Let no man walk in the stubbornness of his heart to stray by following his heart and eyes and the thoughts of his (evil) inclination. But in the Community they shall circumcise the foreskin of the (evil) inclination and disobedience in order to lay a foundation of truth for Israel. . . . (1QS 1.1-7, 2.25-26, 5.4-5)

"Storing up . . . judgment of God": cf. Dt.32.35, Ps.9.8, 96.13, 98.9, 110.5, Isa.63.1ff, Jer.31.28, Ezek.7.1ff, Dan.9.14, Hos.13.12, Joel 1.15, 2.1f, 11, 31, 3.14, Amos 5.18-20, Obad.15f, Zeph.1.14f, Mal.4.5, Mt.3.7, 7.2, 23.33, Jn.3.18-19, 5.24, 27, 8.16, Acts 10.42, 17.30-31, Rom.1.18-32, 9.22, 1 Thess.1.10, 2 Thess.1.5, 1 Tim.6.19, Rev.6.16-17, 14.19, 15.1, 7, 16.1ff; 1QS 3.18ff, 4.11ff, CDC 7.9f, 1QM 1.1ff, 11.14, 13.10-16, 1QH 1.26, 4.20-26, 40, 6.29f, 5.4, 6.29-33, 7.12, 28-29, 9.9, 14-16, 10.34f, 11.8; 4 Ez.7.[77]f, 8.36, Test.Jud.23.1-5, Ps.Sol.2.15, 32, 9.2-5, 15.8, Jub.24.30, 1 En.91.7; PA 3.1, 4.2, 11, 20, 22, 5.19, 6.6, ARN[a] 16.4, ARN[b] 32, Mid.Ps.36.7, Sifre Dt.307, DER 2.1-4, 7, Lev.R.27.1, AZ 3b, 18b, BB 10a.

Paul appeals to the rabbinic doctrine of reward and punishment (and measure for measure), and knows that man will be punished on the Day of Judgment in the world to come, even when in this world the wicked at times appear to escape punishment (cf. Psalms 37 and 73).[15] Several of the Rabbis perceived that, in the same way as "the reward of a mitzvah is a mitzvah," so a man is also punished for his transgression by committing yet another transgression:

> Ben Azzai said: Run to [perform] an easy precept, as [you would] in [the case of] a difficult one, and flee from transgression; for [one] precept draws [in its train another] precept, and [one] transgression draws [in its train another] transgression; for the recompense for [performing] a precept is a precept, and the recompense for [committing] a transgression is a transgression . . . He who violates a light command will ultimately violate a heavy one; he who violates, Love they neighbor as thyself will ultimately violate, Thou shalt not take vengeance nor bear any grudge. (PA 4.2, Sifre Dt.Shoftim 187)[16]

God will punish a man's transgressions even if He "overlooks" his disobedience for a period and gives him time in which to repent. He will prove Himself to be right and just in ultimately judging the practice of those things which are "not proper":

> He [R. Eleazar ha-Kappar] used to say: The born [are destined] to die, the dead to be brought to life, and the living to be judged; [it is, therefore, for them] to know and to make known, so that it become known, that He is God, He the Fashioner, He the Creator, He the Discerner, He the Judge, He the Witness, He the Complainant, and that He is of a certainty to judge, blessed be He, before whom there is no unrighteousness, nor forgetting, nor respect of persons, nor taking of bribes, for all is His. And know that all is according to the reckoning. And let not thy [evil] inclination assure thee that the grave is a place of refuge for thee; for without thy will wast thou fashioned, without thy will wast thou born, without thy will wilt thou die, and without thy will art thou of a certainty to give an account and reckoning before the King of the Kings of Kings, the Holy One, blessed be He. (PA 4.22)

Verse 6:
"Render . . . according to his deeds": cf. Job 34.11, Ps.62.12, Prov.24.12, Isa.59.18, 65.7, Jer.17.10, 32.19, Ezek.33.20, Mt.17.24-35, 1 Cor.3.13, 2 Cor.5.10, Eph.6.8, Col.3.25, Jas.1.22-25, Rev.2.23, 20.12, 22.12; 1QS 2.7-8, 3.14-15, 26, 4.2ff; Test.Naph.8.4-6, Test.Abr.12.18, 1 En.41.1, 2 En.52.15, Ps.Sol.17.8, 4 Ez.3.34; PA 2.1, 14, 15, 16, 3.16, 4.11, 16, 6.5, DER 2.12, Sifre Dt.307.

Paul firmly establishes the principle that Israel's election is still based upon obedience to God's will. God acts according to the principle of a "measure for measure" in judging those who judge their fellow-man:

> I shall prove you right, O God, in uprightness of heart; for your judgments are right, O God. For you have rewarded the sinners according to their actions, and according to their extremely wicked sins. . . . For none that do evil shall be hidden from your knowledge, and the righteousness of your devout is before you, Lord. Where, then, will a person hide himself from your knowledge, O God? Our works (are) in the choosing and power of our souls, to do right and wrong in the works of our hands, and in your righteousness you oversee human beings. The one who does right saves up life for himself with the Lord, and the one who does what is wrong causes his own life to be destroyed; for the Lord's righteous judgments are according to the individual and the household. . . . For God's mark is on the righteous for (their) salvation. Famine and sword and death shall be far from the righteous; for they will retreat from the devout like those pursued by famine. But they shall pursue sinners and overtake them, for those who act lawlessly shall not escape the Lord's judgment. They shall be overtaken as those experienced in war, for on their forehead (is) the mark of destruction. And the inheritance of sinners is destruction and darkness, and their lawless actions shall pursue them below into Hades. . . . And sinners shall perish forever in the day of the Lord's judgment, when God oversees the earth at his judgment. (Ps.Sol.2.15-16, 9.3-5, 15.6-12)[17]

Paul elaborates the elements of God's reward and punishment in the following verses, which illustrate the "doctrine" of the "Two Ways" of Two Spirits (masters).[18]

Verse 7:

"Perseverance in doing good . . . ": cf. Dan.12.2, Mt.25.46, Jn.3.15f, 36, 5.24, 29, 17.2f, Acts 13.46, Rom.6.23, 12.9-15, 21, 14.16, 15.2, Gal.6.8, 1 Tim.4.8, 2 Tim.1.10, 1 Pet.1.7, 1 Jn.5.11; 1QS 1.1-9, 16-17, 3.7, 12, 4.7-8, 5.1ff, 24, 8.1ff, 9.23-26, CDC 6.14, 7.6, 1QH 1.35-36, 6.23-27, 11.10-14, 13.16-18, 17.13-15, 18.28-30; Test.Reub.4.1, Test.Ben.10.8, Sib.Or.8.409f, 1 En.50.1, 58.11, Wis.Sol.1.15, 3.41, Ps.Sol.3.7, 12, 9.5, 14.1-3, 10, 4 Macc.16.13, 17.12; PA 1.3, 2.16, 20, 21, 5.2, 10, PRK 15.5, DER 2.23, DEZ 1.6, Tanh.Ber.1, PPeah 1.1, Sot.9.15, Ex.R.52.3, Cant.R.1.1.3, 5.2.2, AZ 3b, 19b, Ber.28b.

These are the qualities of the Spirit of Truth, and those who walk according to it will receive their reward both in this life and in the world to come:

> And these are the ways of these (Spirits) in the world. It is < of the Spirit of Truth > to enlighten the heart of man, and to level before him the ways of true righteousness, and to set fear in his heart of the judgment of God. And (to it belong) the spirit of humility and forbearance, of abundant mercy and eternal goodness, of understanding and intelligence, and almighty wisdom with faith in all the works of God and trust in His abundant grace, and the spirit of knowledge in every design and zeal for just ordinances, and holy resolution with firm inclination and abundant affection towards all the sons of truth. . . . And as for the Visitation of all who walk in this (Spirit), it consists of healing and abundance of bliss, with length of days and fruitfulness, and all blessings without end, and eternal joy in perpetual life, and the glorious crown and garment of honour in everlasting light. (1QS 4.2-8)

Verse 8:
"Selfishly ambitious . . . ": cf. Dt.9.7, 24, Judg.2.17, 19, Jn.8.44, Rom.5.21, 6.23, 2 Cor.12.20, Gal.5.20, Eph.2.2, Phil.2.3, Jas.3.14, 16; 1QS 1.6-7, 5.3f, 4.9-11, CDC 1.13-2.1, 2.5f, 3.4ff, 5.15ff, 7.9-10, 1QH 15.16-25; Ps.Sol.4.24, 15.10-12, Test.Jud.14.8, Test.Gad 2.3-4.7, 10.8; PA 1.13, 2.2, 12, 3.5, 10, 12, 4.3, 12, ARN[a] 2.2, 4, DEZ 1.9, 10, 2.5.

These are the qualities of the "Spirit of perversity," which the Book of Judges describes by saying that "the sons of Israel did evil in the sight of the Lord . . . every man did what was right in his own eyes" (cf. Judg.17.6, 21.25), and whose punishment, according to the Qumran texts, will be eternal:

> But to the Spirit of perversity belong cupidity, and slackness in the service of righteousness, impiety and falsehood, pride and haughtiness, falsity and deceit, cruelty and abundant wickedness, impatience and much folly, and burning insolence, (and) abominable deeds committed in the spirit of lust, and the ways of defilement in the service of impurity, and a blaspheming tongue, blindness of eye and hardness of ear, stiffness of neck and heaviness of heart causing a man to walk in all the ways of darkness, and malignant cunning. And as for the Visitation of all those who walk in this (Spirit), it consists of an abundance of blows administered by all the Angels of destruction in the everlasting Pit by the furious wrath of the God of vengeance, of unending dread and shame without end, and of the disgrace of destruction by the fire of the regions of darkness. And all their times from age to age are in the most sorrowful chagrin and

bitterest misfortune, in calamities of darkness till they are destroyed with none of them surviving or escaping. (1QS 4.9-14)

Verses 9-10:
"The Jew first . . . also to the Greek": cf. Amos 3.2, Acts 3.26, 13.46, Rom.1.16, 3.9, 29-30, 9.14f, 10.12f; Test.Ben.10.9; PRK 15.5, Sifre Dt.Re'eh 97, Sifra Shemini 57b, Emor 99d, Lev.R.27.1.

Paul recalls his key statement in 1.16, where he says that the gospel is the "power of God for salvation to all who believe, to the Jew first. . . . " In 1.18-32, he lays out the deeds deserving punishment committed by the Gentile nations. Now he particularizes the argument by including Israel among those who practice those things which are not proper, which are right in their own eyes but evil in God's sight. Both because they are part of mankind (cf. "every man of you" [2.1, 3]), and because God has chosen them to be a "holy nation," set apart as His lot, Israel shares the punishment of those (both Jews and Gentiles) who practice things which are not proper (2.1ff). They cannot therefore claim that their election by God exempts them from His judgment. In fact, they are the first to receive retribution as well as the first to receive salvation, because God has chosen them: "You only have I chosen among all the families of the earth; therefore, I will punish you for all your iniquities" (Amos 3.2).[19] Paul makes this very clear in the next verse, by emphasizing that God is impartial both in His reward and in His punishment.

Verse 11:
"For there is no partiality with God": cf. Lev.19.15f, Dt.10.17, 2 Chron.19.7, Job 34.19, Ps.36.6, 145.9, Isa.19.19-25, 26.2, Jon.4.10-11, Mal.2.9, Mt.5.45, Acts 10.34-35, Rom.3.29-30, 9.14f, Gal.2.6, Eph.6.9, Col.3.25, 1 Pet.1.17; Jub.5.12-16, Wis.Sol.6.7, 1 En.63.8, Ps.Sol.5.15; PA 4.22, TBE p.8, p.48, p.65, DER 3.1, Tanh.B.Vayetzei 10, Sifra Achare Mot 86b, Mekh.Bachodesh 1, Amalek 3, Pes.Rab.48.4, Yalkut 76, 429, AZ 2b, San.59a, BK 38a, 50b.

Paul clearly lays down the principle that God renders to "every man" (cf. verses 1 and 3) according to his deeds—to the Jew first (and also to the Greek). The people of Israel do not possess the right of special appeal to God simply because He has elected them, nor can they expect Him to exempt them from punishment for transgressions against His commandments: God is impartial not only concerning the rich and the poor, but also regarding Israel and the Gentile nations.[20] A sinner may therefore repent, and a righteous man may fall; a Gentile may do what is right in God's eyes, and a Jew may stumble and transgress the Torah:

> God said to Moses: 'Is there respect of persons with Me? Whether it be Israelite or Gentile, man or woman, slave or handmaid, whoso doeth a good deed shall find the reward at his side; as it says, *Thy righteousness is like the everlasting hills: man and beast alike Thou savest, O Lord* (Ps.36.6).' (Yalkut 76)

> . . . the Holy One turned to placate Moses, saying: Am I not He whose sons are you and the children of Israel, sons whose Father I am? You and they are My brothers and I am your Brother. You are My friends and I am your Friend. You are My beloved and I am your Beloved. Have I ever deprived you of anything? Since I examined My attributes of mercy and found eleven to be the number of such attributes, I ask of you only that your lives display these eleven attributes of mercy: Let each of you be one (1) *who lives without blame*, (2) *who does what is right*, (3) *and in his heart acknowledges the truth* that I am God; (4) *one whose tongue is not given to evil*, (5) *who has never done harm to his fellow*, (6) *or endured reproach for [mistreatment of] his neighbor*; (7) one to *whom a contemptible man is abhorrent*, (8) *but who honors those who fear the Lord*, (9) *who stands by his oath even to his own hurt*; (10) *who has never lent money at interest*, (11) *or accepted a bribe to the hurt of the innocent* (Ps.15.2-5). Then the Holy One continued to placate Moses, saying to him: Do I show any partiality as between a heathen and an Israelite, between a man and a woman, or a manservant and a maidservant? The fact is that when any sort of person obeys a Divine command, the reward therefore is immediate . . . Hence it is said, when a man thinks much of the glory of Heaven, the glory of Heaven is magnified and his own glory is likewise magnified. When a man thinks little of the glory of Heaven, however, and much of his own glory, the glory of Heaven remains undiminished, but his own glory is diminished. (TBE p.65)

Verse 12:

"Sinned without the Law . . . ": cf. Rom.1.18-32, 3.9f, 19-21, 4.15, 5.13-14, 7.1, 1 Cor.9.21, Gal.2.15, 3.19ff, 2 Thess.2.7, 1 Tim.1.8f; Pes.Rab.40.3/4, Mid.Ps.9.11, P RH 1.3, 57a.

Paul repeats the thought of 1.18-32 (cf. verses 1-5 and 6-10), although he deals with the relationship between sin and the giving of the Torah only in chapter 5.[21] The Gentiles "suppress" God's truth, what they know of Him from His works and His creation. This is sin, although Paul usually states that sin is determined according to the Torah.[22] Paul identifies the Jewish believers in the community at Rome as "those who know the Torah" (Rom.7.1), since the people of Israel were called בני ברית (*benei berit*), "sons of the Covenant," in order to distinguish them from the Gentiles who were "sinners" (by nature) (cf. Gal.2.15):

> THE VALUATION [IS MADE] IN MONEY [BUT MAY BE PAID] BY MONEY'S WORTH, IN THE PRESENCE OF THE COURT AND ON THE EVIDENCE OF WITNESSES WHO ARE FREE MEN AND PERSONS UNDER THE JURISDICTION OF THE LAW [בני ברית]. . . . 'FREE MAN' excludes slaves [from giving evidence]; 'PERSONS UNDER THE JURISDICTION OF THE LAW' excludes heathens. Moreover, it was essential to exclude each of them. . . . Had . . . the exemption been referred only to a heathen, we should have thought it was on account of his not being subject to the commandments [of the Law], whereas a slave who is subject to the commandments might have been thought not to have been excluded. (BK 14b-15a; the *Mishnah* is capitalized)[23]

Verse 13:

"Hearers . . . doers of the Law": cf. Ex.19.5, 24.3, 7, Dt.5.27-29, 6.1-3, Mt.7.17f, 24f, 21.28-32, Jn.13.17, Rom.2.28-29, 3.4, 4.2f, 5.1, Gal.3.8f, 24, 5.4, Jas.1.22f; 1QS 9.5, 11.2ff; PA 1.17, 2.4, 3.9, 17, 4.5, 6.5, ARN[a] 22.1, 24.1-4, PRK S1.2, Sifra Bechuk.110c, Num.R.14.10, Lev.R.25.1, 35.7, Dt.R.11.6, AZ 17b, Kid.40b; Philo, *De Praem.*79, 82.

Paul appeals to the traditional rabbinic debate over the respective merits of "wisdom" (Torah-study) over "deeds" (Torah-observance); "hearing" was one of a number of terms used to contrast "study" over "deeds," "Talmud-Torah" over "derekh eretz," "wisdom" over "practice":

> R. Eleazar said: When the Israelites gave precedence to '*we will do*' over '*we will hearken*', a Heavenly Voice went forth and exclaimed to them, Who revealed to My children this secret, which is employed by the Ministering Angels, as it is written, *Bless the Lord, ye angels of his: Ye mighty in strength, that fulfil his word, That hearken unto the voice of his word* (Ps.103.20): first they fulfil and then they hearken? R. Hama son of R. Hanina said: What is meant by, *As the apple tree among the trees of the wood, [So is my beloved among the sons]* (Cant.2.3): why were the Israelites compared to an apple tree? To teach you: just as the fruit of the apple tree precedes its leaves, so did the Israelites give precedence to '*we will do*' over '*we will hearken*'. (Shab.88a; cf. Cant.R.2.3.1)

Here Paul cites the difference between hearing and doing primarily as a sign of hypocrisy, and builds on the distinction between "hearing" and "doing" in order to establish that God regards both Israel and the Gentile nations as equal in so far as He renders to each man according to his deeds:

> When God was about to give the Torah, no other nation but Israel would accept it. It can be compared to a man who had a field which he wished to entrust to metayers [sharecroppers]. Calling the first of these, he inquired: 'Will you take over this field?' He replied: 'I have no strength; the work is too hard for me.' In the same way the second, third, and fourth declined to undertake the work. He called the fifth and asked him: 'Will you take over this field?' He replied 'Yes'. But as soon as he took possession of it, he let it lie fallow. With whom is the king angry? With those who declared: 'We cannot undertake it,' or with him who did undertake it, but no sooner undertook it than he left it lying fallow. Surely with him who undertook it. Similarly, when God revealed Himself on Sinai, there was not a nation at whose doors He did not knock, but they would not undertake to keep it; as soon as He came to Israel, they exclaimed: *All that the Lord hath spoken will we do, and obey* (Ex.24.7). Accordingly, it is only proper that you should hearken; hence, 'Hear ye the words of the Lord, O House of Jacob' (Jer.2.4). For if you do not, you will be punished on account of your pledge. . . . (Ex.R.27.9)[24]

Verse 14:

"Do instinctively . . . the Law": cf. Acts 10.35, Rom.2.15, 27, 11.21, 24, 1 Cor.11.14, Gal.2.15, 4.8, Eph.2.3; Hell.Syn.Pray.1.4, 2.9, 11.3, 12.43, 69, Sir.25.12; Tanh.Ekev 3.

The Gentiles, although not possessing the Torah, are free either to suppress the truth of God which is evident in the world (cf. 1.19-20), or to act according to His ways. Such practices which are pleasing to God are (part of) the things which, had they not been written in the Torah, are nevertheless still intelligible without God's revelation:

> Our Rabbis taught: *Mine ordinances shall ye do* (Lev.18.4), i.e., such commandments which, if they were not written [in Scripture], they should by right have been written and these are they: [the laws concerning] idolatry [star worship], immorality and bloodshed, robbery and blasphemy. *And My statutes shall ye keep* (ibid.), i.e., such commandments to which Satan objects, they are [those relating

> to] the putting on of *sha'atnez*, the *chalitzah* [performed] by a sister-in-law, the purification of the leper, and the he-goat-to-be-sent-away. And perhaps you might think these are vain things, therefore Scripture says: *I am the Lord* (ibid.), i.e., I, the Lord have made it a statute and you have no right to criticize it. (Yoma 67b; cf. Num.R.19.5)[25]

"Are a law unto themselves"
The Gentiles act in accordance with the existence of the "natural laws" of the universe (see above).[26] Because God judges them according to the deeds which they perform, rewarding those which conform to His will and punishing those which do not, they cannot be considered totally immoral or "lawless":

> R. Joseph said: '*He stood and measured the earth; he beheld*' etc. What did he behold? He beheld the seven commandments which had been accepted by all the descendants of Noah, and since [there were clans that] rejected them He rose up and granted them exemption. Does this mean that they benefited [by breaking the law]? And if so, will it not be the case of a sinner profiting [by the transgression he committed]?—Mar the son of Rabana thereupon said: 'It only means that even were they to keep the seven commandments [which had first been accepted but subsequently rejected by them]they would receive no reward.' Would they not? But it has been taught: 'R. Meir used to say, Whence can we learn that even where a gentile occupies himself with the study of the Torah he equals [in status] the High Priest? We find it stated: . . . *which if a man do he shall live in them* it does not say "priests, Levites and Israelites", but *"a man"*, which shows that even if a gentile occupies himself with the study of the Torah he equals [in status] the high Priest.'—I mean [in saying that they would receive no reward] that they will receive reward not like those who having been enjoined perform commandments, but like those who not having been enjoined perform good deeds: for R. Hanina has stated: Greater is the reward of those who having been enjoined do good deeds than of those who not having been enjoined [but merely out of free will] do good deeds. (BK 38a)[27]

Verse 15:
"In that they show . . . hearts": cf. Ps.119.11, Jer.31.33, Ezek.36.26f, Gal.2.16; 1QS 10.24; Sir.25.12, 2 Bar.48.39-40, 57.2; PA 3.17, 6.2, Mekh.Amalek 4, Vayassa 1, TBE p.31, Lam.R.2.10.13, Cant.R.1.2.3, BK 38a, BM 83a.

Paul boldly makes use of the messianic idea that God will write His covenant (Torah) on man's heart (cf. Jer.31.33f, Ezek.37.26f), to demonstrate how God truly judges man.[28] He looks at "the secrets of men" (verse 16), the intentions and motives of their hearts, in order to know whether they are serving Him or not:

> R. Eliezer asked R. Joshua, "What should a man do to escape the judgment of hell?" He replied, "Let him occupy himself with good deeds." R. Eliezer said, "If that be so, then the nations can do good and pious deeds, and so escape the judgment of hell." (Mid.Prov.17.1)[29]

> . . . God gave to the heathen only some odd commandments, but when Israel arose, He said to them, 'Behold the whole Torah is yours,' as it says, '*He hath not dealt so with any nation.*' R. Eliezer said: It can be compared to a king who went out to war with his legions. When he slaughtered an animal, he would distribute to each one a piece proportionately. His son, beholding this distribution, asked him, 'What wilt thou give me?'—He replied, 'Of that which I have prepared for myself.' So God gave to the heathen commandments as it were, in their raw state, for them to toil over, not making any distinction among them between uncleanness and purity; but as soon as Israel came, He explained each precept separately to them, both its punishment [for non-fulfilment] and reward, as it says, *Let him kiss me with the kisses of his mouth* (Cant.1.2). (Ex.R.30.9)[30]

"Their conscience . . . defending them": cf. Job 27.6, Prov.16.1, 9, 19.21, Jer.10.23, Acts 23.1, 24.16, Rom.9.1, 13.5, 1 Cor.8.7, 1 Tim.3.9, 4.2, Heb.9.14, 10.22, 1 Pet.3.16, 1 Jn.3.19-22; 2 Bar.48.39-40, Test.Reub.4.3, Test.Sim.4.5, Test.Jud.20.1-5, Wis.Sol.17.11f, Hell.Syn.Pray.1.4f, 2.11, Sir.25.12, 4 Ez.16.51-67; Hag.16a.

Paul understands the Greek term συνειδησις (*suneidesis*), "conscience" as "consciousness" or "awareness," in the biblical sense of that which God examines when He searches the "heart" or "thoughts" of man (cf. Ps.7.9, Jer.11.20, 17.10, 20.12). He expresses the "natural law" (the commandments in their "raw" state; see above) which the Gentiles observe in terms associated with the doctrine of the "Two Ways." According to this principle, a choice between good and evil is set before man, and each person will be recompensed according to the master whom he serves. His "conscious awareness" or his will must therefore either make his own evil inclination master over him, or make his Creator, God, his master:

> So understand, my children, that two spirits await an opportunity with humanity: the spirit of truth and the spirit of error. In between is the conscience of the mind which inclines as it will. The things of truth and things of error are written in the affections of man, each one of whom the Lord knows. There is no moment in which man's works can be concealed, because they are written on the heart in the Lord's sight. And the spirit of truth testifies to all things and brings all accusations. He who has sinned is consumed in his heart and cannot raise his head to face the judge. (Test.Jud.20.1-5)

Verse 16:

"According to . . . Yeshua haMashiach": cf. Ps.7.9, 9.8, 44.21, 94.9, 96.13, 98.9, Isa.8.14, 28.16, Jer.11.20, 17.10, 20.12, Mt.10.26, 12.41, Lk.2.34-35, 8.17, 11.29-32, Rom.8.27, 14.10, 1 Cor.4.5, Col.3.25; 1QS 2.8-9, 3.13-15, 4.26, 5.11, 7.12, 9.12-16, 17, 1QH 7.13, 1QpHab 7.2-3; Sir.17.19-23, 44.14-16, 1 En.49.3-4, 61.8-9, 2 En.36.3, Jub.4.23-24, 10.17, Test.Jud.20.3-5, Wis.Sol.1.6f, 4 Ez.16.57-67, Hell.Syn.Pray.2.4, 7, Ps.Sol.14.8, Sib.Or.8.369f; DER 2.12; 1 Clem.21.1-2, 9.

Paul's interjected reference to "my gospel" here seems to suggest that he feels the need either to defend an idea that was potentially controversial, or to emphasize that such an idea, which was known from other sources, was in fact to be regarded as authoritative.[31] He states in 1.1-6 that his "gospel" concerns (God's) Son, and one of the roles of the "Son of man," a title favored by Yeshua, was to "recompense every man according to his deeds" in "judging" both their deeds and their thoughts.[32] A tradition apparently then arose in which Enoch (associated also with Noah and Jonah) was related to the Son of man, since both figures are set as "signs" for the Day of Judgment:

> He (God) placed the Elect One on the throne of glory; and he shall judge all the works of the holy ones in heaven above, weighing in the balance their deeds. And when he shall lift up his countenance in order to judge the secret ways of theirs, by the word of the name of the Lord of the Spirits, and their conduct, by the method of the righteous judgment of the Lord of the Spirits, then they shall speak with one voice, blessing, glorifying, extolling, sanctifying the name of the Lord of the Spirits. For the Son of man was concealed from the beginning, and the Most High One preserved him in the presence

> of his power; then he revealed him to the holy and elect ones. . . . And they blessed, glorified, and extolled (the Lord) on account of the fact that the name of that (Son of) Man was revealed to them. . . . Thenceforth nothing that is corruptible shall be found; for that Son of Man has appeared and has seated himself upon the throne of his glory; and all evil shall disappear from before his face. . . . (1 En.61.8-9, 62.7, 69.27-29)[33]

Paul's statement here also recalls Luke's pronouncement that Yeshua is "appointed for the fall and rise of many in Israel, and for a sign to be opposed . . . to the end that thoughts from many hearts may be revealed" (Lk.2.34-35). Paul refers to the "day on which" the "secrets of men" will be judged in similar fashion to Enoch's testifying against generation unto generation on the day of judgment, and may thus want to legitimize an idea taken from the tradition concerning Enoch, which was not widely accepted in contemporary Jewish thought:

> And he [Enoch] was taken from among the children of men, and we led him to the garden of Eden for greatness and honor. And behold, he is there writing condemnation and judgment of the world, and of all the evils of the children of men . . . for the work of Enoch had been created as a witness to the generations of the world so that he might report every deed of each generation in the day of judgment. (Jub.4.23-24, 10.17)[34]

Verse 17:

"Bear the name 'Jew'": cf. cf. Ex.19.5, Est.8.17, Ps. 95.7, 100.3, Isa.43.10, 12, 44.5, Zech.8.23, Rom.9.4, 6, 24, 27, 31f, 10.21, 11.1, 2, 7, 1 Cor.10.18, 2 Cor.10.12, Gal.3.28, 6.16, Eph.2.12, Col.3.11, Rev.2.9, 3.9; CDC 4.3-6; Sib.Or.7.135, Wis.Sol.17.1, Ap.Bar.57.2; Jos.*Ant*.13.171f; PRK 1.3, Ex.R.42.9, Esth.R.6.2, Meg.12b, 13a; Philo, *De Virt*.108, 226, *De Spec.Leg*.2.163.

Paul begins to detail the particular elements which characterize Israel's election.[35] Israel are God's people and His possession, called by His name and witnesses to His Oneness (see the references above). The Greek verb ἐπονομαζω (*eponomadzo*), "to bear the name," means "to name after," "to give a nickname," or "to give a second name" to someone:

> *There was a certain Jew in Shushan the castle*, etc. *a Benjamite* (Esth.2.5). What is the point of this verse? If it is to give the pedigree of Mordechai, it should trace it right back to Benjamin! [Why then were (only these

> three names) specified?]—A Tanna taught: All of them are designations [of Mordechai]. 'The son of Yair' means, the son who enlightened [*heir*] the eyes of Israel by his prayer. 'The son of Shimei means, the son to whose prayer God hearkened [*shama*]. 'The son of Kish' indicates that he knocked [*hikkish*] at the gates of mercy and they were opened to him. He is called 'a Jew' [*yehudi*] which implies that he came from [the tribe of] Judah, and he is called 'a Benjamite', which implies that he came from Benjamin. [How is this]?—R. Nahman said: He was a man of distinguished character. . . . R. Johanan said: He did indeed come from Benjamin. Why then was he called 'a Jew'? Because he repudiated idolatry. For any one who repudiates idolatry is called 'a Jew', as it is written, *There are certain Jews* etc. (Dan.3.12). (Meg.12b-13a)[36]

"Rely upon the Law": cf. 2 Chron.16.7-8, Prov.3.5, Isa.10.20, 31.1, 50.10, Mic.3.11, Mt.23.2, 7; 2 Bar.48.22, Sir.33.3; Corp.Herm.9.10; PA 1.13, 2.8, 12, 4.7, 6.11, Sifre Dt.Ve'etchanan 32, Ekev 48, Eccl.R.4.1.1, Ta'anit 7a, Suk.49b, Ned.25a, 62a, Ber.17a, Sot.21b.

According to the majority of the Sages, acceptance of the Torah was tantamount to repudiating idolatry. Its observance is therefore one of the most basic definitions of being "a Jew." The Torah was given to be studied so that it would be practiced, and its practice was designed to create good character:

> . . . the Torah [is acquired] in [the form of] forty-eight things, and these they are in: [the form of] study, attentive listening, ordered presentation [of one's study-matter] with [one's] lips, reasoning of the heart, intelligence of the heart, awe, fear, humility, joyousness . . . [knowledge of] Scripture, [knowledge of] the oral learning, moderation in sleep, moderation in gossip, moderation in [worldly] pleasure, moderation in hilarity, moderation in worldly intercourse, long-suffering, a good heart, the conscientiousness of the Sages, [uncomplaining] acceptance of [divine] chastisements. . . . [The possessor of the Torah is one] who recognizes his place, who rejoices in his portion, who makes a fence to his words, who claims no credit for himself, is loved, loves the All-Present, loves [his fellow] creatures, loves righteous ways, welcomes reproofs [of himself], loves uprightness, keeps himself far from honour[s], lets not his heart become swelled on account of his learning, delights not in giving legal decision, shares in the bearing of a burden with his colleague, uses his weight with him on the scale of merit, places him upon [a

groundwork of] truth, places him upon [a groundwork of] peace, composes himself at his study, asks and answers, listens [to others], and [himself] adds [to his knowledge], learns in order to teach, learns in order to practice, makes his teacher wiser, notes with precision that which he has heard, and says a thing in the name of him who said it. (PA 6.5-6)[37]

Verses 17-18:

"Boast . . . out of the Law": cf. Ex.6.7, 7.16, 19.8, 24.3, Lev.26.12, Num.24.16, Dt.5.27, 7.6ff, 29.13, 1 Chron.15.22, 17.22, Neh.8.7-8, Ps.34.2, 40.8, 44.8, 119.15, 24, 30 66, 168, Prov.25.14, Isa.41.16, 43.3-4, Jer.7.23, 9.23-24, 24.7, 30.22, 32.38, Ezek.11.20, 36.28, Dan.12.3, Mt.6.10, 7.21, 21.31, 23.15, 27f, Mk.3.35, Jn.6.38-40, Rom.4.2, 12.2, 15.4, Gal.6.6, Eph.5.17, Phil.1.10, 2.13-14, 1 Thess.4.3, Heb.13.20; 1QS 1.1f, 3.13f, 5.9, 9.10-24, 1QS [a] 1.6-8, CDC 3.15, 4.8, 10.6, 13.2, 7ff, 14.8, 1QH 17.23; 2 Bar.48.22-24, Sir.9.16, 10.22, 39.1, Wis.Sol.2.13, 16, Odes Sol.4.3, 2 Bar.48.22, Ps.Sol.17.1; PA 2.4, 8, 12, 6.1, 5, Sifre Dt.Ekev 48, Num.R.14.10, 21.12, 27.9, BM 85b, Ket.66b, Ber.17a, 35b, Ned.62a.

God has chosen Israel to be His people, and promised that He will be their God (cf. Ex.6.7, Dt.7.6ff, Dt.29.13, Jer.7.23, 30.22, Ezek.36.28). They bear God's name (cf. Isa.43.1, 7, 56.5, 62.2, Dan.9.19), are witnesses to His name (cf. Isa.43.10), and have agreed "to do and to hear" all the words that God has spoken to them in His covenant (Torah):

> For the (ungodly) said, reasoning with themselves, but not aright . . . let us lie in wait for the righteous; because he is not for our turn, and he is clean contrary to our doings: he upbraideth us with our offending the law, and objecteth to our infamy the transgressings of our education. He professeth to have the knowledge of God: and he calleth himself the child of the Lord. He was made to reprove our thoughts. He is grievous unto us even to behold: for his life is not like other men's, his ways are of another fashion. We are esteemed by him as counterfeits: he abstaineth from our ways as from filthiness: he pronounceth the end of the just to be blessed, and maketh his boast that God is his father. Let us see if his words be true: and let us prove what shall happen in the end of him. For if the just man be the son of God, he will help him, and deliver him from the hand of his enemies. Let us examine him with despitefulness and torture, that we may know his meekness, and prove his patience. Let us condemn him with a shameful death: for by his own saying he shall be respected. (Wis.Sol.2.1, 12-20)

God's will in the Torah "instructs" (cf. 15.4) men in the "things which are essential." The Greek term διαφεροντα (*diapheronta*) can mean "those things which are different," "those things which are excellent," or "exceeding." It therefore corresponds linguistically to δοκιμαζω (*dokimadzo*), to distinguish.[38] In the LXX the verb διαφερω (*diaphero*) at times translates the Hebrew root שנה (*shanah*; to repeat), a root which later became a technical term in rabbinic literature for biblical exposition and interpretation:

> Finally, brethren, whatever is true, whatever is honorable, whatever is right, whatever is pure, whatever is lovely, whatever is of good repute, if there is any excellence, and if anything worthy of praise, let your mind dwell on these things. The things which you have learned and received and heard and seen in me, practice these things. . . . (Phil.4.8-9; cf. TBE p.37)[39]

Verse 19:

"Confident": cf. Prov.3.5, Isa.36.7, Ezek.33.13, Mt.23.1ff, Lk.18.9, Eph.3.12, Heb.3.6, 4.16, 10.19; PA 2.4, 8, 12, 6.6, DER 4.1, PRK 15.6, 24.2, Gen.R.76.2, Ta'anit 20b, Ned.62a.

Paul once again begins to introduce a note of warning into his defense of Israel's election, a warning which he develops and details in verses 21-29. "Confidence" comes from the knowledge that the people of Israel are indeed God's people, have been chosen by Him, are beloved by Him, and have been given the "desirable instrument" through which the world was created (cf. PA 3.14). This is designed to inculcate in them a sense of "shame" which leads to the fear of sin, since the only boast man may make is that he "understands and knows Me, that I am the Lord who exercises lovingkindness, justice, and righteousness on earth" (Jer.9.24):

> It was taught: [*And Moses said unto the people, fear not: for God is come to prove to you,*] *that his fear may be before your faces*: By this is meant shamefacedness; *that ye sin not*—this teaches that shamefacedness leads to fear of sin: hence it was said that it is a good sign if a man is shamefaced. Others say: No man who experiences shame will easily sin; and he who is not shamefaced—it is certain that his ancestors were not present at Mount Sinai. (Ned.20a; cf. PA 5.20, Yev.79a)

Paul cautions Israel, however, that it is humanly characteristic to distort God's gifts through self-"reliance" and "boasting" (cf. verses 17-18):

> R. Nehorai said: Go as a [voluntary] exile to a place of Torah—and say not that it will come after thee—for [it is] thy fellow[student]s who will make it permanent in thy keeping and lean not upon thine own understanding . . . Fit thyself to study Torah for it is not [a thing that comes] unto thee [as] an inheritance . . . If thou hast learnt much Torah, do not claim credit unto thyself, because for such [purpose] wast thou created. (PA 4.14, 2.12, 8)[40]

"A guide . . . in darkness": cf. Lev.19.14, Dt.16.19, 27.18, Job 29.15, Ps.19.7-11, 119.24, 105, 130, Prov.6.23, Isa.9.1-2, 29.18, 35.5, 42.6-7, 43.8, 49.6, Mt.15.14, 23.16ff, Lk.6.39f, Jn.1.4-5, 8.12, 9.5, 12.36, Acts 26.18, 2 Cor.4.4, Eph.5.8, Col.1.13, 1 Thess.5.5, 1 Pet.2.9, 2 Pet.1.9, 1 Jn.1.6-7, 2.9-11; 1QS 3.22f, 4.2f, 11.3-6, 19-216f; 2 Bar.59.2, 77.16, Sib.Or.3.195, 4 Ez.7.21, 14.20f, Test.Levi 14.4ff, 18.9, 19.1, Wis.Sol.2.1ff, 7.26, 18.4, Sir.24.27, 32; Corp.Herm.10.21, Poim.4ff; Gen.R.33.1, Dt.R.7.3, Sot.21b, BK 52a, Ber.28a; Philo, *De Virt.*7.

Paul appeals to the common motif of light as goodness and darkness as evil (which is a characteristic element of much dualistic thought, such as that reflected in the doctrine of the "Two Spirits"), and describes the task of the Torah as illuminating and enlightening man.[41] Those who "walk in the light," however, have no cause to "lord it over" those whom they regard to be less righteous or "enlightened":

> All the commandments which a man obeys in this world radiate no more light than the light of a single lamp, but the Torah gives light from one end of the world to the other. . . . As for him who knows how to provide guidance and does provide it for multitudes, such a man gives delight to Him at whose word the world came into being, for it says, *As for them who provide guidance, everyone of them gives delight, and so the blessing of the Good comes upon them* (Prov.24.25). The text does not say "blessing . . . upon him [who provides guidance]," but *blessing . . . upon them*, that is, upon him who provides guidance and also upon him who is willing to receive it. Then, too, he who acknowledges the justice of chastisements which he receives and indeed manages to rejoice in them, is given life without end both in this world and in the world-to-come, for it is said, *The commandment is, [to be sure], a lamp, and the Torah is light, but the way to life [eternal] is through heeding of chastisements* (Prov.6.23). (TBE pp.16-17)[42]

Verse 20:
"A corrector of the . . . immature": cf. Ps.10.1ff, 14.1f, 53.1f, 94.10, 12, 119.1ff, 130, Prov.9.7-12, Jer.2.19, 10.23-24, Hos.5.2, Mt.18.3, 20.25-26, 1 Cor.1.18f, 2.4f, 3.18f, 2 Cor.1.24, Eph.4.13, 1 Tim.2.7, 2 Tim.2.25, 3.16, Tit.2.12, Heb.12.5ff, Jas.3.13f; Wis.Sol.6.11, 25, 12.24f, Sir.6.32, 18.13, 4 Macc.5.34; PA 1.6, 10, 2.4, 5, 5.7, ARN[b] 26, RH 2.9, BK 8.6, Ber.47b, Sot.21b, Ta'anit 20a-b.

In the same way as other rabbinic dicta, Paul warns that in the same measure that a master is unwilling to learn from his disciple, so he himself will become ignorant—at the hands of God Himself. A man can only guide another man if he himself is willing to learn the way, and may only correct another man if he is willing to learn from him:

> It is said: "The poor man and the man of means meet together; the Lord giveth light to the eyes of both" (Prov.29.13). And it also says: "The rich and the poor meet together—the Lord is the maker of them all" (ibid. 22.2). If the disciple attends the master and the master is willing to let him learn, then "the Lord giveth light to the eyes of both"—the one acquires eternal life and so does the other. If the disciple attends the master and the master is unwilling to let him learn, then "the Lord is the maker of them all." He who had made the one wise will in the end make him ignorant, and He who had made the other ignorant will in the end make him wise. (Mekh.Amalek 4)

"Having in the Law . . . knowledge and truth": cf. Ps.19.7-9, 119.34, 43, 66, 73, 100, 104, 130, 142, 144, 151, 160, 172, 2 Tim.3.15; 1QS 1.12, 26, 3.1, 4.6, CDC[b] 2.30-31, 1QH 5.26, 11.9-10, 12.11-14; Sir.1.4-5, 26, 21.11, 24.3 9, 23f, Wis.Sol.2.13, 6.22, 9.9, Ap.Bar.4.1; PA 1.8, 2.7, 3.14, 3.23, 5.22, 6.1, 10, Mekh.Shirata 3, Sifre Dt.37, 48, PRE 3, DER p.37, Gen.R.1.1, 4, Dt.R.11.6, Ned.39b, Shab.88b-89a; Philo, *De Spec.Leg.*1.46-48, *De Mig.Abr.*179-83.

Although the Torah can be identified as the personification of Wisdom (cf. 1.16), and possess insight, understanding, counsel, knowledge, and truth, Paul again emphasizes that it must not only be "heard" but also be observed (cf. Ex.24.7):

> A favourite saying of Raba was: The goal of wisdom is repentance and good deeds, so that a man should not study Torah and Mishnah and then despise his father and mother and teacher and his superior in rank, as it says, *The fear of the Lord is the beginning of wisdom, a*

good understanding have all they that do thereafter (Ps.111.10). It does not say, 'that do', but '*that do thereafter*', which implies, that do them for their own sake and not for other motives. If one does them for other motives, it were better that he had not been created. (Ber.17a)

Verses 21-23:

"You, therefore": cf. 2.1.

Paul now starts making explicit his claim of hypocritical conduct on Israel's behalf. Although it is true that they possess all the "advantages" (cf. 3.1) of God's chosen people, since God renders to "every man" (cf. 2.1, 3) according to his deeds, the people of Israel must fulfil their promise "to do and to hear" (obey) all of God's words in His Torah:

AND KEEP MY COMMANDMENTS, AND DO [lit. MAKE] THEM (Lev.26.3). R. Hama son of R. Hanina expounded: 'If you keep the Torah.' [says God], 'I shall consider it as though you had made the commandments,' [for the text may be read]: AND *YE* MAKE THEM. R. Hanina b. Pappi expounded: He told them: If you keep the Torah I shall consider it as if you had made yourselves, [this being the implication of] AND YE MAKE THEM. R. Hiyya taught: This refers to one who learns with the intention of practising and not to one who learns with the intention of not practising. He who learns with no intention of practising had been better unborn. (Lev.R.35.7)

The people of Israel who do not intend to "do" the commandments of the Torah which God has given them (i.e., to practice what they preach) cannot claim to be any better than the Gentile nations who rejected God's offer of the Torah, openly acknowledging that its commandments were too hard for them to perform.[43] In the same measure which Israel judges the nations, both for not accepting the Torah, and for refusing to obey God's will, God will judge them for having accepted His Torah but not having performed its commandments:

Why are you sitting in the council of the devout, you profaner? And your heart is far from the Lord, provoking the God of Israel by lawbreaking; excessive in words, excessive in appearance above everyone, he who is harsh in words condemning sinners at judgment. And his hand is the first one against him as if in zeal, yet he himself is guilty of a variety of sins and intemperance. His eyes are on every

> woman indiscriminately, his tongue lies when swearing a contract. At night and in hiding he sins as if no one saw. With his eyes he speaks to every woman of illicit affairs; he is quick to enter graciously every house as though innocent. May God remove from the devout those who live in hypocrisy; may his flesh decay and his life be impoverished. May God expose the deeds of those who try to impress people; (and expose) their deeds with ridicule and contempt. And the devout will prove God's judgment to be right when sinners are driven out from the presence of the righteous, those who please men, who deceitfully quote the Law. (Ps.Sol.4.1-8)

Verse 21:

"Who teach another": cf. Ps.50.16-20, Mt.5.19f, 23.3f; Ps.Sol.3.4, 19, Test.Levi 14.6; PA 1.11, 17, 2.5, 3.9, 17, 5.14, 6.5, TBE pp.16-17, 167, 197, DEZ 3.10, ARN[b] 23, 32, PBer.1.2, Num.R.7.5, Eccl.R.4.1.1, San.99b, Betza 9a, Ber.17a, BM 49a.

The authority of the pharisaic teachers was widely discussed within Second Temple Jewish literature. They were reproved both by internal and external sources, among whom Yeshua was merely one. Paul therefore follows in a distinguished tradition:

> AND THE PLAGUE OF PHARISEES etc. Our Rabbis have taught: . . . There are seven types of Pharisees: the *shikmi* Pharisee—he is one who performs the actions of Shechem. The *nikpi* Pharisee—he is one who knocks his feet together. The *kizai* Pharisee—R. Nachman b. Isaac said: He is one who makes his blood to flow against walls. The 'pestle' Pharisee—Rabba b. Shila said: [His head] is bowed like [a pestle in] a mortar. The Pharisee [who constantly exclaims] 'What is my duty that I may perform it?—but that is a virtue! Nay, what he says is, 'What further duty is there for me that I may perform it?' The Pharisee from love and the Pharisee from fear—Abaye and Raba said to the tanna [who was reciting this passage] Do not mention 'the Pharisee from love and the Pharisee from fear'; for Rab Judah has said in the name of Rab: A man should always engage himself in Torah and the commandments even though it be not for their own sake, because from [engaging in them] not for their own sake, he will come [to engage in them] for their own sake. R. Nahman b. Isaac said: What is hidden is hidden, and what is revealed is revealed; the Great Tribunal will exact punishment from those who rub themselves against the walls. (Sot.22b)[44]

Just as Paul states that God's kindness leads to repentance (cf. verse 4), so the study of the Torah should lead to its performance, and he joins the Rabbis in censoring hypocritical behavior:

> *Within and without shalt thou overlay it.* (Ex.25.11). Raba said: Any scholar whose inside is not like his outside is no scholar. Abaye, or as some say, Rabba b. 'Ulla, said: He is called abominable, as it is said: *How much less one that is abominable and impure, man who drinketh iniquity like water. . . .* Once R. Judah after having had a seminal issue was walking along a river bank, and his disciples said to him, Master, repeat to us a section from the Laws of Derekh Eretz, and he went down and bathed and then repeated to them. They said to him, Have you not taught us, Master, 'He may repeat the laws of Derekh Eretz'? He replied, Although I make concessions to others, I am strict with myself. (Yoma 72b, Ber.22a)[45]

"Steal . . . commit adultery": cf. Ex.20.14, Lev.18.1-18, 20.10ff, Dt.5.18, Ps.50.16, Jer.7.8-11, Mal.3.8f, Mt.5.28, 15.3f, 19.9, Mk.7.7f, Jn.8.3-11, Rom.7.1-7, Jas.2.11, 4.4, 2 Pet.2.14; CDC 6.16; Ps.Sol.8.11, Test.Levi 14.5-8, Odes Sol.4.5, 8.10-11; Did.2.2, 3.3f; Pes.Rab.24.2-3, PRK 15.9, Gen.R.26.5, Lev.R.23.12, Num.R.8.5, 9.1, 17.6, Yoma 29a, 85b, San.74a, BK 38a; Philo, *Conf.Ling.*163, *Leg.All.*3.241.

Paul adduces further examples of hypocritical conduct within the nation, following the list of "improper" deeds (cf. 1.28) in Jeremiah 7.8-11.[46] Temple robbery was frequently associated with stealing, breaking-in, kidnapping, murder, and adultery:

> And now, my children, I know from the writings of Enoch that in the endtime you will act impiously against the Lord, setting your hands to every evil deed; because of you, your brothers will be humiliated and among all the nations you shall become the occasion for scorn. For your father, Israel, is pure with respect to the impieties of the chief priests . . . as heaven is pure above the earth; and you should be the lights of Israel as the sun and the moon. For what will the nations do if you become darkened with impiety? You will bring down a curse on our nation, because you want to destroy the light of the Law which was granted to you for the enlightenment of every man, teaching commandments which are opposed to God's just ordinances. You plunder the Lord's offerings; from his share you steal choice parts, contemptuously eating them with whores. You

> teach the Lord's commands out of greed for gain; married women you profane; you have intercourse with whores and adulteresses. You take gentile women for your wives and your sexual relations will become like Sodom and Gomorrah. You will be inflated with pride over your priesthood, exalting yourselves not merely by human standards but contrary to the commands of God. With contempt and laughter you will deride the sacred things. (Test.Levi 14.1-8)

Verse 22:

"Abhor idols . . . rob temples": cf. Dt.7.25-26, 32.16, Isa.2.8, 20, 17.7-8, 44.19, 66.3, Jer.4.1, 7.8-11, Mt.21.13, Mk.7.11-13, 11.17, Lk.19.46; CDC 6.16; Test.Levi 14.5; Jos.*Contra Ap.*1.249f, 310f; Sifre Num.Shelach 111, Meg.13a, Ned.25a.

The Greek text plays on the "abomination" of idols, since idols are things which are unclean and defiled (defiling).[47] Although the context requires a literal parallel between hatred of idolatry and yet benefiting in some way from pagan temples, Paul may be referring to robbing God of that which He is owed (cf. Mk.7.11-13) rather than to the known claims that Jews were accused of "breaking and entering" pagan temples in order to desecrate them.[48] People also stole from God or from His Temple when they kept something "consecrated" to God for a "common" (profane) purpose:

> If a man said to his fellow, *Konam* or *Konah* or *Konas*, these are substitutes for *Korban*, an Offering [a thing as forbidden to him for common use as a Temple offering]. . . . To vows not expressly defined the more stringent ruling applies, but to vows expressly defined the more lenient ruling applies. Thus [if a man said,] 'May it be to me as salted flesh!' [or] 'as wine of the Drink-offering!' and his vow was of the things offered to Heaven [i.e., offered in the Temple; cf. Lev.2.13, Num.15.6], it is binding; and if his vow was of the things offered to idols it is not binding; but if neither was expressly defined, it is binding. [If he said,] 'May it be to me as a devoted thing!' and meant 'as a thing devoted to heaven' [cf. Lev.27.28], it is binding; and if he meant 'as a thing devoted to the priests', it is not binding; but if neither was expressly defined, it is binding. (Ned.1.2, 4)[49]

Verse 23:

"Boast . . . dishonor God": cf. Num.15.31, 20.12, 27.14, 1 Sam.2.29-30, Isa.29.13, 43.23, 58.13-14, Dan.5.23, Mal.1.6f, 2.2, Jn.8.49, Rom.2.17; Test.Naph.8.6; Mid.Ps.52.1, Eccl.R.4.1.1.

Paul sums up all the actions which express "relying upon the Torah" and "boasting in God" (verse 17). For the people of Israel to "dishonor" God means breaking (transgressing or violating) His covenant (cf. Ezek.16.59, 17.15f) and "abusing" it for unlawful purposes, just as Paul accuses the Gentiles of doing, without the Torah, in chapter 1, when they "became futile in their speculations, and their foolish heart was darkened" (verse 21):

> In commenting on the passage, *Then shall ye return and discern between the righteous and the wicked, between him that serveth God and him that serveth Him not* (Mal.3.18), R. Aha bar Ada said that the words *between the righteous and the wicked* mean "between him who has faith and him who has not; that he *that serveth God* is he who is willing to serve God's need, and he *that serveth Him not* is he who is not willing to serve God's need. Thus a man should not make the words of the Torah an edged tool for his own use, nor make them a crown to crown himself. *The Lord repayeth the others who would act proudly* (Ps.31.23) refers to the disciples who study Torah not for the sake of heaven but for the sake of doing themselves proud in this world, and to such others who expect a reward in this world for their study of it. (Mid.Ps.31.9)

Verse 24:

"The name of God is blasphemed . . . ": cf. Ex.32.12, Num.14.13-16, Dt.9.28, Josh.7.9, Ps.42.3, 79.10, 115.2, Isa.52.5, 66.3-6, Ezek.36.20-21, 23, Joel 2.17, 2 Pet.2.2; Tos.BK 10.15, Mid.Ps.10.4, 52.3, BK 94a.

Paul understands, as do many other rabbinic dicta, that Israel's boasting dishonors God's name when it leads to חלול ה' (*chilul ha-Shem*; profanation of God's name), particularly amongst the Gentiles.[50] By transgressing God's commandments, Israel impeaches God's character in the eyes of the Gentiles, since such behavior does not honor His name, which they bear. Moreover, treating the Gentiles disparagingly also leads the people of Israel to violate the Torah:

> See that you art beloved by human beings, and keep thyself from sin and theft from Jew, Gentile or any man. He who begins by stealing from a Gentile ends by stealing from a Jew, and the same applies to robbery by violence, perjury, circumvention and murder. Now Torah was given only to sanctify God's great Name, as it says, 'And I will put a sign on them (Israel) . . . and they shall declare My glory among the Gentiles' (Isa.66.19). (Yalkut 837)

Verse 25:

"Circumcision is of value . . . ": cf. Gal.5.3; 1QS 5.5, CDC 16.4-6, 1QH 2.18; Test.Naph.8.4-6; BK 94a.

Paul repeats his argument of the preceding sections (cf. verses 1-10, 11-16, 17-20), this time appealing, according to Jewish tradition, to circumcision as the symbol of God's covenant, the Torah (cf. PA 3.11, Gen.R.48.2, Ned.32a). He reminds the people of Israel that to be circumcised as a sign or a "seal" of membership in God's covenant people means not only to study the Torah, but also to practice it.[51] Since God renders to "every man" (cf. verses 1 and 3) according to his deeds, the "value" of circumcision is the value of observing the Torah, a principle to which the Qumran community also strongly adhered:

> Let no man walk in the stubbornness of his heart to stray by following his heart and eyes and the thoughts of his (evil) inclination. But in the Community they shall circumcise the foreskin of the (evil) inclination and disobedience. . . . But to the uncir[cumcision] of my lips Thou hast given a reply of the tongue and hast upheld my soul with strength of loins and strong endurance; and Thou hast confirmed my steps in the realm of ungodliness. . . . [And all] the men of deceit roared against me like the clamour of the roaring of great waters, and ruses of Belial were [all] their [thou]ghts; and they cast down towards the Pit the life of the man by whose mouth Thou hast established the teaching and within whose heart Thou hast set understanding that he might open the fountain of Knowledge to all the understanding. But they bartered it for uncircumcision of the lips and for the foreign tongue of a people without understanding that they might be lost in their straying . . . And on the day on which a man undertakes to be converted to the Law of Moses, the Angel of Hostility will depart from him if he fulfils his promises. For this reason Abraham circumcised himself on the day on which he knew. (1QS 5.4-5, 1QH 2.7-8, CDC 16.4-6)[52]

The Sages similarly sometimes ascribed the "evil inclination," among other things, to a state of "uncircumcision":

> The Evil Inclination has seven names. The Holy One, blessed be He, called it *Evil*, as it is said, *For the imagination of man's heart is evil from his youth* (Gen.8.21). Moses called it *Uncircumcised*, as it is said, *Circumcise therefore the foreskin of your heart* (Dt.10.16). (Suk.52a)[53]

"Transgressor . . . uncircumcision": cf. Gen.17.9ff, 34.14, Ex.4.25, Lev.12.3, Dt.10.16, 30.6, Jer.4.4, 9.25-26, Acts 7.8, 11.3, Rom.3.30, 4.9, 10, 12, 1 Cor.7.18-19, Gal.2.7, 5.6, 6.15, Eph.2.11, Col.2.13, 3.11; 1QS 5.5, CDC 16.4-6, 1QH 2.7, 18-19, 6.20-21, 18.20, 1QpHab 11.13; Jos.*Ant*.12.5.1; PA 1.5, 13, 2.11, 3.3, 5, 11, 4.5, 5.19, San.11.1, 99a, Suk.52a, BK 94a; Ep.Barn.9.5, 13.7.

If a man does not practice the Torah he is considered an evil man (cf. PA 5.12, 14), but if a man also does not observe the Torah in order to honor God in the performance of His commandments, he is no better than the man who has made no commitment to honor Him:

> R. Eliezer b. Jacob says: If one misappropriated a *seah* of wheat and kneaded it and baked it and set aside a portion of it as *hallah*, how would he be able to pronounce the benediction? He would surely not be pronouncing a blessing but pronouncing a blasphemy, as to such a one could be applied the words: *The robber pronounceth a benediction* [*but in fact*] *contemneth the Lord* (Ps.10.3). (BK 94a)[54]

The Sages enumerated five kinds of uncircumcised things (עורלה; *'orlah*) in the world, one of which refers to trees (cf. Lev.19.23), and four to man. All the items referring to man relate to the moral attitude and behavior of the people, rather than to their physical circumcision, and the Rabbis were clearly aware that the uncircumcision of the people's heart made them equal with the Gentile nations who were not physically circumcised (and thus, in their eyes, not bound to observe the moral standards of the Torah):

> Rabbi Ze'era said: There are five kinds of 'Orlah (things uncircumcised) in the world: four with reference to man . . . Whence do we know this concerning the four (terms) applying to man? (Namely,) the uncircumcision of the ear, the uncircumcision of the lips, the uncircumcision of the heart, and the uncircumcision of the flesh. Whence do we know of the uncircumcision of the ear? Because it is said, "Behold, their ear is uncircumcised" (Jer.6.10). Whence do we know of the uncircumcision of the lips? Because it is said, "For I am of uncircumcised lips" (Ex.6.12). Whence do we know of the uncircumcision of the heart? Because it is said, "Circumcise the foreskin of your heart" (Dt.10.16); and (the text) says, "For all the nations are uncircumcised, and all the house of Israel are uncircumcised in heart" (Jer.9.26). Whence do we know of the uncircumcision of the flesh? Because it is said, "And the uncircumcised male who is not circumcised

> in the flesh of his foreskin" (Gen.17.14). And "all the nations are uncircumcised" in all the four cases, and "all the house of Israel are uncircumcised in heart." The uncircumcision of the heart does not suffer Israel to do the will of their Creator. And in the future the Holy One, blessed be He, will take away the uncircumcision of the heart, and they will not harden their stubborn (heart) any more before their Creator, as it is said, "And I will take away the stony heart out of your flesh, and I will give you an heart of flesh" (Ezek.36.26); and it is said, "And ye shall be circumcised in the flesh of your foreskin" (Gen.17.11). (PRE 29)

In a similar fashion to this midrash, Paul understands that the "circumcision of the heart" refers, as the biblical passages make clear, to a time when God will put His Spirit in man's heart in order to "suffer Israel to do the will of their Creator."[55]

Verse 26:

"Uncircumcised man . . . as circumcision": cf. Lev.18.5, Dt.30.16, Rom.2.13; San.59a.

Just as at the beginning of the chapter, Paul specifically charges Israel of the practice of "those things which are not proper," and "judges" them, in Jewish tradition, according to the judgments which they pass on others, so here he demonstrates that "circumcision" can become equal to "uncircumcision" (and vice versa). If transgression of the Torah means that a person does not keep the Torah, the person who practices the Torah "keeps" it—whether he is a Jew or a Gentile (cf. verses 12-14). If, therefore, a Gentile "practices" the Torah, he has "circumcised" his heart and has made the Creator his master (rather than serving his own evil inclination), just as Israel promised to "hear and do" when they accepted God's covenant in the Torah:

> R. Jeremiah said: Whence can you know that a Gentile who practices the Law is equal to the High Priest? Because it says, *Which if a man do, he shall live through them* (Lev.18.5). And it says, *This is the law [Torah] of man* (2 Sam.7.19). It does not say: 'The Law of Priests, Levites, Israelites,' but, This is the Law of *man*, O Lord God. . . . And it does not say, 'Rejoice ye, Priest and Levites and Israelites,' but it says, *Rejoice ye righteous* (Ps.33.1). And it does not say, 'Do good, O Lord, to the Priest and the Levites and the Israelites,' but it says, *Do good, O Lord, to the good* (Ps.125.4). So even a Gentile, if he practices the Law, is equal to the High Priest. (Sifra 86b)[56]

Verse 27:

"Judge you": cf. Mt.7.1-5, Rom.2.1-3, 12, Jas.4.11-12.

Once again Paul appeals to the principle of מידה כנגד מידה (*middah keneged middah*) in regard to judging other people. In the measure in which Israel judges (2.1f) the Gentile nations for their "improper practices" (cf. 1.18-32), the Gentiles also "judge" Israel when they (the Gentiles) perform the commands of the Torah which the people of Israel do not keep. While Paul accuses the Gentile nations of refusing to honor God by obeying Him in chapter 1, he then warns Israel against judging the Gentiles, since God will punish Israel for the practice of the same deeds (and in the same measure by which they judge others). He incriminates Israel not merely for their disobedience before God, but also for their boasting and reliance on being chosen by God to be His people, but throughout chapter 2 also argues that the righteous Gentiles have the equal right to "judge" the "unrighteous" amongst Israel; moreover, they may also accuse Israel of not practicing what they themselves do practice. Israel should therefore know that God can and will make "sons of Abraham" out of those who possess Abraham's qualities:

> Whoever possesses these three things, he is of the disciples of Abraham, our father; and [whoever possesses] three other things, he is of the disciples of Balaam, the wicked. The disciples of Abraham, our father, [possess] a good eye, a humble spirit and a lowly soul. The disciples of Balaam, the wicked, [possess] an evil eye, a haughty spirit and an over-ambitious soul. What is [the difference] between the disciples of Abraham, our father, and the disciples of Balaam, the wicked? The disciples of Abraham, our father, enjoy [their share] in this world, and inherit the world to come, as it is said: That I may cause those that love Me to inherit substance and that I may fill their treasuries, but the disciples of Balaam, the wicked, inherit Gehinnom, and descend into the nethermost pit, as it is said: But Thou, O God, wilt bring them down to the nethermost pit; men of blood and deceit shall not live out half their days; but as for Me, I will trust in Thee (Ps.55.23). (PA 5.19)[57]

"Letter (of the Law)": cf. Ex.32.16, Jer.31.31, Ezek.37.26f, Rom.14.5f, 2 Cor.3.2ff, Jas.1.25; 1QS 9.16-21, 10.8, 11, 11.1-2; PA 6.2, Mekh.Amalek 4, PGit.6.6, BM 30b, 83a, 108a, BK 99b.

The phrase "letter (of the Law)" (γραμματος; *grammatos*) literally refers to the written (and Oral) Torah (cf. verses 17-18), which God has given as His covenant to His people.[58] Although most Christian commentators understand Paul's dichotomy between "spirit" and letter" as a reference to the Holy Spirit which overcomes the "letter of the Law (Torah)," the Sages in fact debated the same issue as Paul raises here in terms of the rabbinic principle known as לפנים משורת הדין (*lifnim mi-shurat ha-din*), which literally means "within the line of the law" (cf. Ber.7a).[59] At times they described the principle as behavior which goes "beyond the strict measure ['letter'] of the law;" at other times they described by it actions performed which remain "within the strict letter of the Torah" when a man was in fact legally permitted to refrain from performing them.[60] The principle reflected a situation in which the Rabbis were undecided as to whether the codified Torah (the "letter" of the Law) represented the highest possible ethical standard, or whether it itself pointed to a morality above and beyond its written ordinances—the "spirit" of the law. Several talmudic stories of events in the lives of particular Rabbis reflect the way in which this principle was debated:

> There was a certain woman who showed a denar [coin] to R. Hiyya and he told her that it was good. Later she again came to him and said to him, 'I afterwards showed it [to others] and they said to me that it was bad, and in fact I could not pass it.' He therefore said to Rab: Go forth and change it for a good one and write down in my register that this was a bad business. But why [should he be different from] Danchko and Issur [two renowned money changers of the day] who would be exempt because they needed no instruction? Surely R. Hiyya also needed no instruction?—R. Hiyya acted within the 'margin of the judgment,' on the principle learnt by R. Joseph: *And thou shalt show them* (Ex.18.20) means the source of their livelihood; *the way* (ibid.) means deeds of lovingkindness; *they must walk* (ibid.) means the visitation of the sick; *wherein* (ibid.) means burial, *and the work* (ibid.) means the law; *which they must do* (ibid.) means within the 'margin of the judgment.' (BK 99b-100a)[61]

> Some porters [negligently] broke a barrel of wine belonging to Rabbah son of R. Huna. Thereupon he seized their garments; so they went and complained to Rab. 'Return them their garments,' he ordered. 'Is that the law?' he enquired. 'Even so,' he rejoined: *That thou mayest walk in the way of good men* (Prov.2.20). Their garments having been returned, they observed, 'We are poor men, have worked all day, and are in need: are we to get nothing?' 'Go and pay them,' he ordered. 'Is that the law?' he asked. 'Even so,' was his reply: *and keep the path of the righteous* (ibid.). (BM 83a)[62]

Verses 27-28:
"And circumcision . . . flesh": cf. Col.2.11f.

Paul once again refers to circumcision as a symbol of Torah-observance and the covenant (cf. verse 25). Obedience to God's commandments must be performed by "walking in the ways of good men" and "keeping the paths of the righteous," one of the prooftexts used by the Rabbis to indicate the highest possible form of moral behavior:

> R. Eleazar of Modin said: One who profanes things sacred, and one who slights the festivals, and one who causes his fellow-man's face to blanch in public, and one who nullifies the covenant of our father Abraham, peace be upon him, and he who exhibits impudence towards the Torah, even though he has to his credit [knowledge of the] Torah and good deeds, he has not a share in the life of the world to come. (PA 3.11)[63]

The term "outwardly" corresponds to the "physical" act of circumcision (cf. verse 27), and metaphorically to observance of the "letter" of the law without regard for its "goodness" or "righteousness" (cf. Prov.2.20).[64]

Verse 29:
"Jew . . . of the heart": cf. Dt.10.16, 30.6, Jer.4.4, Col.2.11f; 1QS 5.5, 1QH 2.7, 18-19, 6.20-21, 18.20, 1QpHab 11.13.

The expression "of the heart" parallels the phrase "by the Spirit," and stands in contrast to the "letter (of the law)" (verse 27).[65] The heart is also the seat of a person's "voluntary conversion" to keep the will of God, and to serve the Creator by "angering" his evil inclination.[66] According to the doctrine of the Two Ways or Spirits (masters), a person must choose in the "conscience of his mind" between the way of "God and good," and Belial (the Devil) and evil:

> And this is the rule for the members of the Community, for those who volunteer to be converted from all evil and to cling to all His commands according to His will; to separate themselves from the congregation of perverse men . . . They shall practice truth in common, and humility, and righteousness and justice and loving charity, and modesty in all their ways. Let no man walk in the stubbornness of his heart to stray by following his heart and eyes and the thoughts of his (evil) inclination. But in the Community they shall circumcise the foreskin of the (evil) inclination and

> disobedience in order to lay a foundation of truth for Israel, for the Community of the everlasting Covenant. . . . (1QS 5.1-5)

"By the Spirit": cf. Acts 7.51, Rom.7.6; AZ 20b.

Paul combines the principle of לפנים משורת הדין (*lifnim mi-shurat ha-din*) (see above) with a doctrine very similar to the "Two Spirits":

> And the Lord said to Moses, "I know their contrariness and their thoughts and their stubbornness. And they will not obey until they acknowledge their sin and the sins of their fathers. But after this they will return to me in all uprighteousness and with all of (their) heart and soul. And I shall cut off the foreskin of their heart and the foreskin of the heart of their descendants. And I shall create for them a holy spirit, and I shall purify them so that they will not turn away from following me from that day and forever." . . . My heart was pruned and its flower appeared, then grace sprung up in it, and it produced fruits for the Lord. For the Most High circumcised me by his Holy Spirit, then he uncovered my inward being toward him, and filled me with his love. And his circumcising became my salvation, and I ran in the Way in his peace, in the Way of truth. (Jub.1.22-23, Odes Sol.11.1-3)[67]

"Praise . . . from God": cf. 1 Sam.2.30, Ps.50.23, 51.17, 102.17, Prov.3.3-4, Jn.5.44, 12.43, 1 Cor.4.5, 2 Cor.10.18; Sir.15.10; PA 3.10, 4.1; Philo, *Rer.Div.Her.*90, 129, *Leg.All.*3.77, *De Abr.*262.

Paul sums up his warning to Israel against presuming upon their election and disregarding the fact that God renders to "every man" (cf. verses 1 and 3), perhaps playing here on the Hebrew root for "Jew" (יהודי; *Yehudi;* "the one who praises" [cf. Gen.29.35, 49.8]). One of the purposes of the principle of לפנים משורת הדין (*lifnim mi-shurat ha-din*) was to encourage love and respect for one's brethren, rather than maintaining one's own prestige.[68] Paul combines this idea with the "new interpretation" of Leviticus 19.18 in the Second Temple period, which understood love of God as love for one's fellow-man.[69] Thus to honor one's brethren is to honor God and to be honored by Him:

> Who is he that is honoured? He who honours his fellow-men, as it is said: For them that honour Me I will honour, and they that despise Me shall be lightly esteemed (1 Sam.2.30). (PA 4.1)

True honor comes from God, and the measure in which a man honors his fellow-man who is created in God's image, is the measure of honor which God receives.[70] Paul thus combines in this saying the motifs of "within the strict letter of the law," "measure for measure," loving man as an expression of love for God, service to the Creator rather than to one's evil inclination (the two Ways or Spirits), and the "sons of Abraham."

Endnotes on Chapter 2

1 Cf. Lev.17.10, 13, 18.6, 20.2, 24.15, BB 10b (interpreting Prov.14.34). These texts are all referred to in a discourse in San.57a concerning the laws pertaining to Benei Noah, the sons of Noah. In each case, the double repetition (*ish ish*) is understood to extend the prohibitions under discussion (adultery, bloodshed, and blasphemy) to the sons of Noah as well. Here, however, Paul turns the extension around to include Israel under the prohibitions of the Gentiles. For a review of some of the rabbinic anti-Gentile attitudes and *halakhot*, see Y. Cohen, "The Attitude to the Gentile in the *Halakhah* and in Reality in the Tannaitic Period," *Immanuel* 9 (1979), 32-41.

2 Paul repeats the same technique in verses 9-10, where he breaks down the generalization into the particular first of the Jew and then of the Gentile, and finally generalizes back to the whole of mankind in chapter 3.

3 Cf. Amos 3.2, Sifra 110b, BK 38a, San.56a-59b, Yad, *Hil.Gezela ve-Aveda*, concerning robbery; AZ 26b, Yad, *Hil.Avadim* 1.7, 9.1, concerning slaves.

4 See D. Flusser, "A New Sensitivity in Judaism and the Christian Message," in *Judaism*, 469-89, and the comments on 12.9ff.

5 The saying appears in PA 2.11 and in ARN[a] 26 under R. Joshua's statement that hating mankind puts one out of this world, which recalls 1.32 ("worthy of death"). For the development of the "new sensitivity" and Paul's further use of the same material, see also the comments on 12.9ff and 14.10ff.

6 Cf. especially Ps.50.17-23, where God originally addresses the people of Israel.

7 Cf. בוז/בזה (*buz/bazah*), "to despise;" בגד (*bagad*), "to betray;" חבל (*chaval*), "to writhe;" and תעה (*ta'ah*), "to err." Cf. the play on the same root (φρονεω; *phroneo*) in 12.3, where Paul encourages "sound judgment" amongst the members of the Body.

8 Paul returns to this theme again at the end of the chapter, where Israel's disparagement of God's goodness influences His reputation amongst the

Gentiles (verses 23f). Thus Israel's redemption is also for the sake of God's glory and reputation; cf. Mid.Ps.44.1.

9 See the example of John the Baptist, who plays on the Hebrew association between אבנים (*'avanim*; stones) and בנים (*banim*; sons) in order to demonstrate to the Pharisees and Sadducees the need to bear fruit in keeping with repentance (cf. Mt.3.7-9).

10 Paul picks up this theme (cf. verses 4-8) again in 9.18ff (cf. 11.22), in relation to the election of the Gentiles; see also the comments below on "patience."

11 Nachmanides (1194-1270 C.E.) notes in his commentary on Ex.20.5 ("I am a jealous God, visiting the iniquity of the fathers on the children ...") that the root פקד (*pakad*) should be understood both in Ex.20.5 and in Ex.34.7 as "storing up" rather than as "visiting," which is its most frequent meaning; see also verse 5.

12 God as it were "sanctifies" man's sins by His patience and longsuffering. In chapter 14 Paul applies this argument to the "profanation" of attitudes and practices which, if they did not offend a brother in the community, a person would otherwise hold sacred as divine commandments. Man, too, may "sanctify" or hold as "profane" God's commandments where their observance offends a brother, since Paul states that loving one's neighbor is the highest possible principle and takes precedence over any other commandments; see the comments on chapter 14; cf. also Tit.3.4-5.

13 See also the comments on 3.25.

14 See also the sequential list in 5.3-5, where tribulation "brings about" (leads to) perseverance, and perseverance, proven character, and proven character, hope. The verb "leads" carries the same connotations as "storing up," in that it anticipates consequences from present deeds in the future. Paul specifically associates God's "preservation" of the ungodly with His "creation" of the Gentiles in 4.17.

15 This is one of the classical issues of theodicy, knowing how to justify God's goodness in the face of the prosperity of the wicked. The Rabbis often resolved the question by suggesting that the righteous receive their punishment in this world so that they might be totally righteous in the world to come, while the punishment of the wicked is deferred to the world to come so that it might be even more weighty; cf. Hor.10b. Paul appeals to a similar concept in 12.19ff; see the comments there, and on chapter 13.

16 Cf. ARN[b] 33, 36, DEZ 3.3.

17 See the understanding of "forbearance" as derived from the root פקד (*pakad*)—"to visit" in the sense of "to store up"—in verse 4. The com-

munity at Qumran inherited this usage and, conjoined it with a policy of "non-retaliation" practiced by the members of the community during the "dominion of Belial." This commitment to loving their enemies and not repaying evil with evil enabled the wicked, so to speak, to "store up" their iniquity until God "visited" His final punishment upon them and utterly destroyed them. Paul reflects the same viewpoint in chapters 12 and 13; see the comments on 12.9ff.

18 See also the comments on verse 16.

19 Paul builds his whole argument in this chapter around the theme of "measure for measure." Israel practice the same evil deeds of which they accuse the Gentiles, and they will be judged as they judge the pagan nations; God will render to each man according to his deeds; Israel will be punished first because God chose them first; they will also be redeemed first because they were chosen first; cf. Yev.121b.

20 God's impartiality in returning judgment with judgment ("measure for measure") can be found in Leviticus 19. When the phrase "loving thy neighbor as thyself" in Lev.19.18 was later interpreted in Second Temple Jewish thought to mean that "your neighbor" has the same nature as your own, Paul was able to apply the principle to demonstrate that Jews and Gentiles are equal before God, who renders to each man according to his deeds.

21 Paul's difficulty lies in the fact that if "sin entered the world through one man" (Adam), then it cannot be determined according to the Torah, which was given only to Moses; if, on the other hand, sin is determined according to the Torah, Adam's sin can only be a direct transgression of a specific command, not of the Torah itself (cf. 5.12-14). It is important for Paul to associate sin with Adam, however, because Yeshua's salvation and atonement pertains to all men, not merely to Israel. Paul makes the same argument also here, combining it with the principle that God renders to every man according to his deeds, in order to show, on the other side of the coin, that a Gentile who does what pleases God is just as acceptable to God as a "son of the Covenant," and a Jew who transgresses is punished equally with the Gentile to whom God has not given His Torah. Paul goes on to develop both aspects of mankind's equality—in their sinfulness and their righteousness through Yeshua's faithfulness in chapter 3.

22 Although the noun ἄνομια (*anomia*) means "lawless" in the sense of "wicked" or "rebellious," the adverb ἄνομος (*anomos*) here refers to the Gentiles who are not part of God's covenant. The Torah and the

covenant were regarded as synonymous in Second Temple Judaism; cf. Dt.7.9f, 2 Kings 23.2, Ps.25.10, 103.18, 105.8, 45, Jer.31.31f, Rev.11.19, 1QS 1.7-8, 16-17, 2.18, 5.2-3, 7ff, CDC 3.12-16, 6.19, 7.5-6, Ber.16b.

23 Cf. BK 38a. Rabbinic tradition frequently states that the Gentile nations were offered the Torah but refused to accept it, for various, usually unworthy, reasons; cf. PRK 5.2, PRK S2.1, Pes.Rab.21.3, Mekh.Bachodesh 5, Sifre Dt.Berakah 343, Ex.R.27.9, AZ 2a and following.

24 The midrash exhibits close parallels to Mt.21.28-32 and 33-46, two parables given by Yeshua to illustrate his authority. The second parable (the "Parable of the Landowner") is often used to interpret God's replacement of Israel with the Church. In the light of the midrash, however, and of the "Parable of the Two Sons" which precedes the Parable of the Landowner, God both chose Israel because no other people would accept it, and, by the same token, also imposes greater duties and responsibilities on Israel as His people, punishing them for not obeying what they promised to do. This idea is probably based, like many other midrashim, on Ex.24.7: "All that the Lord has spoken we will do and hear," an illogical order, since hearing usually precedes doing. The Rabbis frequently cited the reversal of hearing and doing in order to emphasize Israel's complete acceptance of God's will, since they were prepared to obey whatever God might *subsequently* command them (i.e., before they heard what they were) (cf. Ex.R.1.36, Lev.R.1.1); see also the comments on 10.6f.

25 This text forms part of the rabbinic discussion over טעמי המצוות (*ta'amei ha-mitzvot*), or the "reasons" for the commandments), and concerns the "rational" and "irrational" aspects of certain of the commandments. For the form of the argument (i.e., that "natural" laws should have in fact been written in Scripture in order to be recognized as such), cf. the comparison of the Noachide covenant to the covenant on Sinai in San.58a and following.

26 Paul describes the rebelliousness of the pagan world in 1.18-32 and not the laws which govern it. These laws may be observed by those who are "groping" after God (cf. Acts 10.35, 17.27); see also 11.24.

27 Cf. BK 87a, San.59a, AZ 3a. This passage combines a series of different principles, not all of which relate to the present discussion but which are of general interest in demonstrating the various rabbinic attitudes towards the Gentiles. R. Hanina's statement (cf. Kid.31a), which is the most relevant of the themes, relates to the dilemma which Paul deals with in chapter 5: how does sin relate to the Gentiles when transgressions are regulated by the Torah? R. Hanina, whose ruling was apparently widely

accepted (cf. BK 87a), resolved the issue by awarding greater reward to those who have been commanded to observe God's commandments than to those who have not been commanded to perform them. The argument in this section of Baba Kamma questions R. Joseph's interpretation of Hab.3.2, that when God "beheld" the inability of the Gentiles to keep merely the seven Noachide laws He exempted them from these seven as well. (For the textual support for the argument, see AZ 2b-3a.) The Talmud asks Paul's question of 3.5 and 6.1: how can a person benefit by sinning? R. Hanina's ruling comes to answer this question, since the interim resolution (that the Gentiles receive no reward at all for good deeds) is disproved by R. Meir's dictum that a Gentile may possess the same status as a High Priest (cf. San.59a). R. Hanina's principle is founded upon the conviction that moral acts are only firmly based when they are prompted by God's command and not by man's free will; God's commands hold greater authority over man than his own autonomous will. Thus the Gentiles may in fact do the deeds of the Torah (just as non-Christians may do good deeds or be good people), but their reward will be less. This idea corresponds, at least partially, to Paul's dictum that the Gentiles are "a law unto themselves."

28 See also the comments on verses 25f.

29 I.e., the nations can "live" and thus escape hell by doing deeds of goodness and charity; cf. AZ 3a (R. Meir).

30 The midrash understands the verse in Cant.1.2 to mean that God lovingly taught His Torah to Israel, whereas the Gentiles were vouchsafed only the rudiments of law, as it were. The idea is reminiscent of another midrash in which Scripture is described as "wheat out of which the fine flour of Mishnah was to be produced and as flax out of which the fine linen cloth of Mishnah was to be produced" (TBE [EZ] p.172); or the concept, in other words, the interpretation and application of Scripture ("tradition") is a necessary part of the original giving of the Torah (מתן תורה; *mattan Torah*).

31 See Gal.1.6ff, where Paul describes God's revelation of Yeshua to him, which is the basis of his message. In Gal.1.6f, however, he appeals to this gospel (and its sources) as the authority for his apostolic commission, although the content of any other gospel (of which by definition there can in fact be none), carries no authority because it does not come from God.

32 Cf. Mt.13.41, 16.27, 19.28, 24.30, 39, 25.31. See D. Flusser, "Jesus and the Sign of the Son of Man," in *Judaism*, 526-34, and for this whole discussion.

33 Cf. 1 En.49.3-4, 4 Ez.16.62-63, Ps.Sol.17.21ff. For the tradition of the role of the Son of man as judge, see D. Flusser, "Melchizedek and the Son of Man," in *Judaism*, 186-92.

34 There are several linguistic parallels between Paul's thought and the Enochic tradition in this passage. Enoch is a "witness" who writes down the "condemnation" (accusation) of the generations. Flusser claims that Yeshua knew the Enoch tradition in the book of Jubilees, but did not mention him because he "did not intend to invite an unnecessary critique by his hearers. In addition, it is quite probable that Yeshua himself considered Enoch to be a problematic personality. Although Yeshua used a source which spoke favorably about Enoch, he transferred Enoch's eschatological task to the Son of Man." D. Flusser, *Son*, 533. Paul may have been aware both of the tradition and of its controversial nature; Yeshua himself never mentions Enoch in his extant sayings, and Enoch never appears in the entire Tannaitic and Talmudic traditions, according to Flusser, because of the exaggerated praise given to him in Jewish mystical and apocalyptic circles; ibid. If Paul is adapting the tradition, he transfers part of the role of judgment to the conscience of the Gentiles who are a "law to themselves." According to the sign of Jonah, God's judgment was intended to bring repentance—among the Gentiles. This fits Paul's warning here against Israel's boasting in their possession of the Torah without doing works in keeping with repentance. Paul picks up the same theme in 8.27f, on the basis of the same motif, this time taken from Prov.20.27, on which Lk.2.34-35 is also based. It is a central theme, since repentance and righteousness are obtained through faithfulness to Yeshua. The Teacher of Righteousness also adopted some of the same Messianic passages (cf. Isa.8.14, 28.16) in this respect; cf. 1QS 8-9, 7.12, 1QpHab 7.2-3.

35 For the general structure of the chapter, see the introduction, and the comments on verses 1-2. In the first section, Paul describes the general principles upon which God rewards and punishes. In verses 17-20, he lists the central tenets of Judaism, which constitute the grounds of Israel's election. In verses 21-29 he then cites the ways in which the people of Israel mistake the grounds of their election, and in fact engage in exactly the same sort of conduct for which God punishes the Gentiles (cf. 1.18-32).

36 The phrase, "He was a man of distinguished character" is rendered literally, "crowned with his *nimus*." *Nimus* means "manner" or "way" in the Talmud (cf. νομος; *nomos*, law), and thence "bearing" or "character." Rashi translates the term as "with his names," as if *nimus* corresponds to the Greek ὀναματι (*onamati*). Some variant readings add כעדי (*ke-'adi*),

"as an ornament," and the Ruch (*Chaim Vital*) explains in this connection that Mordechai was "adorned" with the precepts of the Torah as with an ornament. The term *Yehudi* as applied to Mordechai does not then denote a tribal name (cf. Judah or Benjamin) but is an epithet of distinction. See the notes in the Soncino Talmud there.

37 Cf. PA 6.1, ARN[a] 11.2, Sifre Dt.Ekev 48, Berakah 343, Cant.R.1.2.3.

38 Cf. LXX Dan.7.3, 2 Macc.15.13, 3 Macc.6.26. Delitzsch translates ותבין בין טוב לרע (*ve-tavin bein tov lera'*), "and know good and evil," presumably based on Gen.3.5, but this seems an arbitrary interpretation, although cf. TBE p.37.

39 Cf. משנה, the Mishnah, which "repeated" traditional law or legend derived from the Tanakh; see H. Strack, *Introduction to the Talmud and Midrash* (NY: Atheneum, 1983), 3. The verb κατηχεω (*katecheo*), "to teach by word of mouth" (cf. "catechism"), functions in the same way in the New Testament; cf. 1 Cor.12.28, Gal.6.6, Eph.4.11.

40 See especially Prov.3.5.

41 The "blind" are frequently associated with those who are "ignorant," whose eyes God has not "enlightened" with His Torah; cf. Ps.119.130, Isa.9.2, 42.6, 49.6, Lk.2.32, Acts 13.47, 26.18, 23, 1 Pet.2.10, Test.Jos.19.3, Test.Abr.B7, Jos.Asen.8.10, 12.2, 15.13, 2 En.30.15, 3 Bar.6.13, Wis.Sol.18.4, Philo, *De Virt.*179, 221, Did.1.1, Ep.Barn.18.1-20.2. The motif of causing someone to stumble is based on Lev.19.14. Paul picks up the theme of stumbling, which itself is a metaphor for falling into unrighteousness (cf. 1QH 6.21, 27, 7.6-7, Ps.Sol.3.5, 9), in chapters 9-11 and 14; see the comments on 9.30f and 14.13.

42 The midrash is based on the verse in Prov.6.23: "A commandment is but one lamp, but the Torah is light," and reads the term מוכיחים (*mokhichim*), "they who decide justly," as "they who provide guidance;" the term ינעם (*yina'am*), "shall be delight," as "gives delight;" and the phrase ברכת-טוב (*birkhat tov*), "a good blessing," as "the blessing of the Good." For the idea of humility, even before a heathen, cf. also TBE [EZ] p.167 and p.197.

43 Cf. Mekh.Bachodesh 5, Ex.R.27.9. The rabbinic dicta go further than Paul, in the sense that they contend that it was better for someone not to have been born than to live and not to obey God's will. Paul's point here, however, is not so much the internal Jewish debate which this reflects as the fact that Israel boast of superiority over the Gentiles because of their possession of the Torah and their election by God.

44 Cf. ARN[a] 37, PSot.5.5, 20c, PBer.9.5, 14b. The remarks relate to: a) the Pharisee who was either circumcised from an unworthy motive or who ostentatiously carried his religious duty on his shoulder (*shekem*); b) the

Pharisee who walked with exaggerated humility; c) either the Pharisee who, in his anxiety to avoid looking at a woman, beat his face against the wall, or the Pharisee who calculatedly performed a bad deed after a good deed in order to set one off against the other; d) the Pharisee whose head was bowed in mock humility. R. Nahman's remark is taken to refer to simulated humility, since hypocrisy does not avail against the Judge who reads the hearts; (the text is sometimes also rendered: those who wrap themselves in their cloaks).

45 The verse cited from Job 15.16 is understood to refer to the person who drinks the water of the Torah and yet still has iniquity in him and performs wrong deeds; cf. ARN[b] 23, 32, Mid.Ps.52.3, 101.3, Eccl.R.4.1.1, MK 15a, Sot.41b, Ber.28a.

46 The continuation of the passage in Jer.7.21f is part of the well-known prophetic critique of the sacrificial cultus. This critique of ritual performed without inner motivation underlies the rabbinic denunciation of hypocrisy, as well as the motif of the "sons of Abraham" to which Paul appeals at the end of the chapter.

47 The Greek verb βδελυσσω (*bdelusso*), "to abhor," means "to loathe" in the active voice and "to defile" in the middle/passive voice; idols are called βδελυγμα (*bdelugma*), things which are "abhorred" and "defiled;" see the references above.

48 Cf. especially Jer.7.8-11, which associates idolatry with robbery, and Mal.3.8-11. Josephus suggests that the name Jerusalem (Ἱεροσολυμα; *Hierosoluma*) itself derives from ἱεροσυλος (*hierosulos*, temple robber) as a result of the inhabitants' sacrilegious propensities (cf. *Contra Ap.*1.249f, 309f). According to Augustus' edict, anyone stealing sacred books or funds from the Jews is a temple robber (cf. *Ant.*16.164, 168). Paul also associates idolatry and adultery (cf. the previous clause) in 7.1-6; see the comments on 7.3, and the whole of Jeremiah 3, to which Paul alludes in chapter 7. The author of the Damascus Document (CDC) makes a similar accusation against the Temple Establishment of his day. He warns the members of the community who have insulated themselves at Qumran to "separate themselves from the unclean riches of iniquity (got) with a vow or anathema, or by robbing the goods of the Sanctuary, or by stealing from the poor of His people to make of widows their prey. . . . " The phrase "robbing the goods of the Sanctuary" seems to refer here to a perversion of the "exact tenor of the Law," i.e., a pollution of the Temple in Jerusalem. The lust after wealth was one of the Qumran community's most serious accusations against the Temple priesthood.

49 Cf. BK 9.10, Tos.Ned.1.1. The context in Nedarim is the validity of vows and their formulas. The concept of קורבן (*korban*) is linked to the making of vows, since dedicating things to God validates and makes the vow binding; cf. also the principle of הפקר (*hefker*), the exploitation of something which is "ownerless;" cf. BM 30b.

50 Cf. Test.Naph.8.4, 6, Hag.13b, Git.56a, San.104b.

51 Paul is therefore not proposing here the doctrine that "in order to fulfil the Law you must fulfil all of the Law," which some commentators argue to be the case; cf. E. Käsemann, *Commentary on Romans* (Grand Rapids: Eerdmans, 1980) and (even) E.P. Sanders, *Paul, the Law, and the Jewish People* (Philadelphia: Fortress Press, 1983). If circumcision stands for the Torah, Paul is arguing that a person must practice the Torah lawfully (לשמה; *lishmah*), or for its own sake. This is confirmed in verse 27, where Paul repeats the thought, but identifies the Gentiles as those who are "physically uncircumcised."

52 The text in CDC 16.4-6 understands Abraham's circumcision as his entrance into the community through the "exorcism" of the "evil inclination." This "apotropaic" idea (deliverance from or the warding off of evil spirits) is directly linked to the doctrine of the Two Ways (Spirits) or masters, since it was by the "exorcism" of the evil inclination (Spirit of Perversity) that a person was known to be of the "Spirit of Truth;" cf. 1QS 4.1ff.

53 This idea is clearly based upon the biblical passages which speak of Israel circumcising the foreskin of their heart as well as performing the physical rite; cf. Dt.10.16, 30.6, Jer.4.4.

54 The discussion in the Gemara concerns setting aside the portion from the dough designated for the priest (cf. Num.15.19-21). R. Eliezer's first point demonstrates that something stolen cannot be consecrated to God (by giving it to the priest). He similarly claims that if the man subsequently blessed the rest of the bread before he ate it, in accordance with the commandment, his blessing would in fact be a profanation of God's name, since in spite of all of the changes undergone by the wheat, it was still stolen and thus not fit to be blessed; cf. also Ber.35a-b.

55 Cf. the context of the prophetic verses; see also Ezek.37.14, 39.29, Joel 2.28. Paul connects this theme with the midrash of the "two masters" in chapter 6, and more immediately, in the following verses, with the motif of the "sons of Abraham," an internal Jewish debate which discusses the grounds which constitute a "true" Jew. He also makes the point here that Jews and Gentiles are equal before God in their need for His righteousness, which He bestows by circumcising their hearts through His Spirit. He specifically develops this theme only later, however, in chapter 4,

having also established in chapter 3 that "all men" are also equally sinful; and further in chapters 8ff.

56 In San.59a, R. Meir's dictum is interpreted to make the contrary point: that it is meritorious for Benei Noah to study only their own laws, but not laws which do not pertain to them—i.e., to engage in Torah-study. Although the concept of circumcision and "uncircumcision" is also characteristic of the Qumran texts, the idea that a Gentile, as a Gentile, could become part of the "sons of light" was unacceptable to that community. For the idea of "angering" one's evil inclination, see Ruth R.3.1 and 8.1, and the midrash on Job 3.19, whose principles guide Paul's thought through most of his letter; see especially the comments on chapter 6.

57 Cf. also PRK 3.2. The sayings about the "sons of Abraham" concern Israel, and do not compare Israel with the other nations. The debate was therefore an internal Jewish issue, over what qualities a Jew had to possess in order to be a true "son of Abraham."

58 This is reflected in the names given to "Scripture" in both Hebrew and Greek (as well as in English). For the Hebrew terms, see the comments on 1.2; in Greek the terms include: ἡ γραφη (*he graphe*, the written); ἁι (ἱεραι) γραφαι (*hai [hierai] graphai*, the [sacred] Writings); γραφαι αγιαι (*graphai hagiai*, Holy Writings), and ἱερα γραμματα (*hiera grammata*, the Sacred Letters). See M. Mulder, *Mikra*, 39, 653.

59 The strongest evidence against this view lies in the fact that Paul is following the tradition of an internal Jewish debate. He strengthens his argument further in this respect by conjoining two motifs, one concerning the qualities of the "sons of Abraham," the other the principle of לפנים משורת הדין (*lifnim mi-shurat ha-din*). The first tradition specifically appeals to God's gift of His Spirit through which He circumcises man's heart; the second discusses whether this "spirit" is already implicit within the Torah or is over and above it. Both motifs, however, refer to the "letter" of the Torah in terms of the Spirit, not as something which annuls the Torah or makes it obsolete.

60 These two positions are represented respectively on the one hand by the Babylonian Talmud, which perceived the principle as a legal command contained within the Torah, and by the Jerusalem Talmud, which argued that the principle was over and above the written injunctions of the Torah. Paul reflects the view of the Jerusalem Talmud here, and elaborates it in relation to the principle that God renders to every man according to his deeds (cf. verse 6), as well as in connection with the motif of the "sons of Abraham." The Rabbis also subjected this motif to the principle of the "spirit" of sonship (cf. verses 28-29).

61 The "instruction" in this case is "legal-moral" advice, which R. Hiyya was expected to seek but which behavior was apparently not expected from money changers! R. Hiyya was not legally responsible for a mistake in judgment (his advice is presumed to be honest), yet according to the "strict letter of the law" (its rigorous interpretation) he should have made restitution to the woman for the bad coin. Paul returns to this principle in chapter 14 (cf. chapters 12-15.13), since it promotes love of one's brothers and fellow-man; see especially the comments on 14.5, where Paul's argument which recalls the difference in principle between *Beit Shammai* (one Pharisaic school), whose insistence on honoring the *Shabbat* (Sabbath) alone can be viewed as a "literal" observation of the "letter" of the Torah, whereas *Beit Hillel*, a rival school, applied the "spirit" of *Shabbat* to the rest of the days of the week as well.

62 The prooftext from Prov.2.20 represents the principle of לפנים משורת הדין (*lifim mi-shurat ha-din*) (cf. Dt.6.18), since in fact the porters were responsible for the damage. Nevertheless, Rab told Rabbah that in such a case one should not insist on the "letter of the law," but should act according to its spirit.

63 The phrase to "nullify the covenant" [מפר הברית; *mepher ha-berit*] originally meant nullifying the covenant in general, and R. Eleazar specifically applied it to the covenant of circumcision. In PSan.11, 27c, the phrase is explained as "stretching the foreskin" in order to disguise circumcision (*epiplasm*) and thus avoid being identified as a Jew.

64 Cf. Paul's circumcision of Timothy (Acts 16.3), and Philo's denunciation of quick ethical or allegorical interpretations of the Torah, including the commandment of circumcision (*De Migr.Abr.*89-93).

65 See also the comments on verses 27 and 29.

66 See also 8.27, where God "searches the hearts" in order to know the "mind of the spirit" of man through the intercession of His Spirit (cf. Prov.20.27).

67 Cf. also 2 Cor.3.2-3, 1QS 3.6-12, 4.20-21. The translation "spiritual and not literal" for the Greek ἐν πνευματι οὐ γραμματι (*en pneumati ou grammati*) is both misleading and incorrect. Paul refers to the "heart of flesh" in contrast to the "heart of stone" which the prophets promise God will give to the people of Israel (cf. Jer.31.31f, Ezek.11.19, 36.26, Zech.7.12). Neither does Paul mean "allegorically and not literally." The relationship between the outward act (the "letter of the law") and its inner motivation (being "led by the Spirit") is directly associated with the issue of libertinism. Paul picks up this theme in chapter 3, where he warns against the dangers of (gnostic) libertinism and antinomianism,

and again in chapters 6 and 7, where he speaks of the "inner man" (cf. 6.6. and 7.22). See also the comments on 8.27.

68 See the comments on chapter 14.

69 See the comments on 2.2-3 and 8.15f.

70 Paul may also be playing on the similarity in Hebrew between the two roots הלל (*hallel*), "to praise," and חלל (*challel*), "to profane." "Praise" may easily turn into profaning God's name (cf. verse 24), since hypocritical behavior is itself a profanation of God's name; cf. Mid.Ps.10.4. Man's praise can come only from God, because it is He who renders to every man according to his deeds. Paul picks up this theme in chapter 14, where he rejects the possibility of judging because each person stands accountable before God alone, and because Yeshua died for each individual person, whose redemption no other man can take away.

ROMANS

3

Introduction

Paul meets an anticipated objection from his readers that his claim that the people of Israel are those who possess the qualities of Abraham (2.25-29) may lead to depreciation of Israel's election (verse 1). He begins to defend Israel's election (verses 2-3), and is then diverted into a discussion of whether man's unrighteousness (as exemplified by Israel's unfaithfulness) can be used to provide an opportunity for God's justification to increase (verses 3-8) (a libertine argument). He introduces this section (verses 3-4) with a talmudic formula which he uses frequently throughout the letter in order to refute an erroneous conclusion. He returns to the theme of Israel's election in verse 9, but again immediately diverges into a series of biblical quotes (verses 10-18) which prove that both Israel and the Gentiles are sinful. He then introduces the theme of God's righteousness in Yeshua (verses 21-26). Since God's righteousness is a gift and is received through faithfulness, Israel cannot claim superiority over the Gentiles, who stand equally before God who is One (verses 27-30). Paul then returns (cf. verse 1) to the possible denial of Israel's election, if faithfulness precedes the Torah, and states that faithfulness in fact establishes the Torah (verse 31).

Verse 1:
"What advantage . . . ?": cf. Dt.4.7f, Ps.103.6-7, 147.19-20, Rom.3.9, 9.4f; PA 3.14, PRK 12.23, Tanh.B.Va'era 9, TBE p.174, Cant.R.2.16.1, 3.11.2.

Chapter 3 follows directly from 2.25-29, since Paul anticipates that his Jewish readers will object to the implications of his argument that the "sons of Abraham" are those who behave as his "disciples" (cf. 2.25-29), and argue that if God renders to "every man" (both Jew and Gentile) according to his works then the people of Israel have no claim to any privileged standing before God. If they possess no advantage in this respect, they are then likely to protest, why should God have chosen them to be His people and sealed His covenant with them by circumcision at all?[1]

Verse 2:

"Great in every respect . . . ": cf. Ex.4.22, 19.5-6, Dt.7.6f, 10.15, 14.2, 26.18, 2 Sam.16.23, Ps.149.2, Rom.9.1-4, 11.28-29, Gal.2.7, 1 Thess.2.4, 1 Tim.1.11, Tit.1.3; 2 Bar.21.21, 48.20ff, 77.3, Sir.33.3, 36.14, 4 Ez.3.19, 9.29, Ps.Sol.7.8, 9.8-10, 11.7, 14.5, Let.Arist.177; Jos.*Contra Ap.*1.38-42; PA 1.1, 2, 3.14, Sifre Dt.Va'etchanan 36, TBE p.31, p.89, [EZ] p.187, [S] p.20, p.40, Tanh.Noah 8, Beshall.20, Ki Tissa 8, PRK 5.5, 12.23, Tanh.B.Va'era 9, Gen.R.12.2, Ex.R.27.9, 47.3, Num.R.14.10, Ber.6a; Philo, *De Vit.Cont.*25, *Hypothetica* 9.

Paul firmly defends God's (continuing) election of Israel. He begins with the general statement (כלל; *kelal*), that their "advantages"—God's choosing them as His people—are to be found in every possible area. He then begins to detail (particularize—פרט; *prat*) the elements which constitute their election.[2] The Torah stands at the center of Israel's election, since it represents God's covenant with His people—among many other things:

> Beloved are Israel in that they were called children of the All-Present. [It was a mark of] superabundant love [that] it was made known to them that they were called children of the All-Present, as it is said: Ye are children of the Lord your God (Dt.14.1). Beloved are Israel in that a desirable instrument was given to them. [It was a mark of] superabundant love [that] it was made known to them that the desirable instrument, wherewith the world had been created, was given to them, as it is said: For I give you good doctrine, forsake not My teaching (Prov.4.2). (PA 3.14)[3]

Verses 3-4:

"What then? . . . ": cf. Dt.7.9, 32.4, Ps.89.1, 119.86, 143, Isa.11.5, Jn.5.47, Rom.3.9, 4.1, 6.1, 15, 7.7, 9.14, 30, 10.16, 11.1, 7, 1 Cor.1.9, 10.13, 2 Tim.2.13, Heb.4.2, 10.23; 1QH 4.10-22; Sifre Num.Naso 1, Maa'sei 161, TBE p.4, p.31, p.83, p.89, Sifre Dt.He'azinu 307, 308, Pes.Rab.27.4, PRK 24.16, Ex.R.24.1, Num.R.16.27.

Having indicated that he is about to enumerate the "list" of Israel's "advantages," Paul in fact breaks off after the first item.[4] This first "advantage" alone causes him to anticipate an immediate objection.[5] The phrase "what then?" reflects a technical talmudic formula which raises a "difficulty" (קושיה; *kushiah*) whose resolution is regarded as untenable. The rejection of the resolution is indicated by the phrase "may it never be" (חס וחלילה; *chas ve-chalilah*; may it never be!), which normally follows the introductory formula.[6] Paul's "difficulty" here arises from the fact that while God has elected Israel, the people have not always been faithful to God.[7] The erroneous conclusion (resolution), which Paul immediately rejects, is that Israel's disobedience has caused God to reject His people, a much discussed issue in Jewish literature:

> My Masters, in the time-to-come, the Holy One, blessed be He, will sit in the great academy with the world's righteous men sitting before Him. He will say to them: My children, though you are no more than flesh-and-blood, you are still My children. Now when a man weds a good and extraordinarily beautiful woman, he rejoices in her and desires her. But when her beauty changes, he seeks to wed another woman beside her. But you are not to be so treated. From the beginning you have been and will be Mine—[beloved]—for ever and ever and ever, as is said, *The Lord said unto me: "Go yet, love a woman beloved of her friend and an adulteress, even as the Lord loveth the children of Israel, though they turn unto other gods." . . . Afterward shall the children of Israel return; and seek the Lord their God* (Hos.3.1, 5); and *Saying: If a man put away his wife, and she go from him, and become another man's, may he return to her? But thou hast played the harlot with many lovers. . . . Didst thou not just now cry unto Me: "My father, Thou art the friend of my youth. Will He bear a grudge for ever? Will He keep it to the end?" Behold,* God replies to Israel, *since thou spakest thus, though thou hast done evil, thou, nevertheless, prevailest [in retaining My love of thee]* (Jer.3.1, 4-5). (TBE p.52)[8]

Verse 4:

"Let God be found true . . . ": cf. Num.23.19, Dt.32.4, Ps.51.4 (6), 116.11, Eccl.7.29, Mic.2.11, Rom.1.25, 3.4, Jas.3.14, 1 Jn.2.22, 4.20, 5.10; CDC 8.13, CDC[b] 1.22f, 1QH 1.26-27, 30, 2.24, 4.7ff, 7.28-29, 9.15f, 12.27-31, 13.13-19; Ps.Sol.2.15f, 3.3, 5, 4.8, 8.7f, 23, 10.5; Sifre Dt.He'azinu 308, Tanh.Va'era 21, Shemot 14, Mekh.Beshall.6, Ta'anit 11a.

Paul establishes that God will never be "unfaithful" to Israel as His people, although they may have been unfaithful to Him. His faithfulness to Israel confirms His promise to Abraham and His covenant with Israel. All mankind may be evil and transgress God's ordinances, but God's words and promises remain true and firm, as the Sages clearly formulated:

> *The Rock* (*ha-Tzur*)—the Artist *(tzayyer)*, for He first designed (*tzar*) the world, and then formed man in it., as it is said, *Then the Lord God formed man (way-yitzar) man* (Gen.2.7)—*His work is perfect* (Dt.32.4): His workmanship in regard to all creatures of the world is

> perfect; there can be no complaint whatsoever about His work. . . . Hence the verse goes on to say, *For all His works are justice*—sits in judgment on everyone and dispenses to each that which is appropriate form—*a God of faithfulness*—who believed in the world and created it—*and without iniquity*—for men were created not in order to be wicked but in order to be righteous, as it is said, *Behold, this only have I found, that God made man upright, but they have sought out many inventions* (Eccl.7.29)—*just and righteous is He*—He conducts himself uprightly with all the creatures of the world. (Sifre Dt. He'azinu 307)

Paul appeals to Psalm 51.4 (6) as a prooftext to support his claim that God is faithful and without iniquity:

> *For Thee, Thee only, have I sinned . . . That Thou mayest be justified when Thou speakest* (Ps.51.4). To whom may David be likened? To a man who broke a limb, and came to a physician. The physician marveled and said to him, "How great is thy break; I am much distressed on your account." The man with the broken limb said: "Art thou distressed on my account? Was not my limb broken for thy sake, since the fee is to be thine?" Just so David said to the Holy One, blessed be He: *For Thee, Thee only, have I sinned.* Shouldst Thou receive me, then if Thou sayest, "Wherefore have ye not repented?" all transgressors will submit to Thee, for all of them will behold me, and I surely bear witness that Thou receivest the penitent. (Mid.Ps.51.6)[9]

Verse 5:
"Our unrighteousness demonstrates . . . ": cf. Job 22.4-5, Ps.71.2, Isa.45.24, 53.11, Jer.23.6 (7), 33.16, Rom.1.17, 6.1, 15, 1 Cor.1.30, 2 Cor.5.21, Gal.2.17-18, Phil.3.9, Jas.1.20; 1QS 10.25, 11.5, 12, 1QH 11.18, 12.31, 14.15-16, 16.9, 11, 18.20; Lev.R.2.12, Hag.16a, BK 38a.

Although David makes it clear that he is guilty and that God is just, the prooftext lends itself to a misinterpretation which Paul immediately addresses. The Hebrew and Greek texts of Psalm 51.4 can both be read literally to say, "I have sinned against you only *so that* you may be justified. . . . " Paul acknowledges that this interpretation may be made, and proceeds to "disprove" the case that man's unrighteousness can "prove" God right or justify His actions.[10]

"The God who . . . is not unrighteous, is He?": cf. Dt.32.4, Isa.63.17, Jer.18.6, 20.7; 1QH 1.25-27, 4.13, 18, 29-33, 40, 7.16, 28-29, 9.15-17, 33, 11.8, 18, 12.14-21, 24-35, 14.15-16, 24-27, 15.19-25; Mid.Ps.52.3, Gen.R.18.20, 22.9, Eruv.22a.

Paul elaborates the wrong idea which people may draw from Psalm 51.4 (namely that they may sin *in order that* God may have an opportunity to demonstrate His righteousness), since he understands that such a claim is based on the misapprehension that if men's evil deeds "justify" God, God's judgment and punishment of man cannot be righteous, as other Jewish texts of the same period also make clear in discussing biblical passages which, taken literally, indicate that God may in fact be responsible for man's evil inclination:

> *O Lord, Thou hast enticed me, and I was enticed; Thou hast shown me strength and hast prevailed over me* (Jer.20.7). The congregation of Israel said to the Holy One, blessed be He: Master of the universe, Thou didst entice me before Thou gavest the Torah to me, so I set the yoke of the commandments upon my neck and was punished because of my violation of them. Had I not accepted the Torah, I would have been like one of the nations, getting neither reward nor punishment. (Pes.Rab.21.16)

> "Master of the world, if I [Cain] have killed Abel, it is thou who has created in me the evil inclination. Thou watchest me and the whole world. Why didst Thou permit me to kill him? It is Thou who hast killed him . . . for if Thou hadst received my sacrifice, as thou didst receive his sacrifice, I would not have become jealous of him." (MHG Gen.4.9; cf. Ex.R.46.4)

If man's evil deeds were to "prove" that God was right—since he Himself has declared all men to be sinful—then God would not be able to declare his deeds to be evil or to punish man for them. God's judgment of man can only be righteous if man's deeds are in fact worthy of punishment. There are people, however, who blame God for their evil actions, accounting Him responsible for having created the "evil inclination" which led them to perform their deeds. Paul's parenthesis, "I am speaking in human terms," reflects a number of rabbinic term designed to disclaim the literal meaning of what might otherwise be considered anthropomorphic or otherwise blasphemous statements:

> *Then the Lord said unto Satan, Hast thou considered My servant Job, for there is none like him in the earth . . . and he still holdeth fast his integrity, although thou movedst me against him to destroy him without cause* [(Job 1.3). Said R. Johanan: Were it not expressly stated in the Scripture, we would not dare to say it. [God is made to appear] like a man who allows himself to be persuaded against his better judgment. A Tanna taught: [Satan] comes down to earth, and seduces, then ascends to heaven and awakens wrath; permission is granted to him and he takes away the soul. (BB 16a)[11]

Verse 6:
" . . . otherwise how will God judge the world?": cf. Gen.18.25, Job 5.15-16, Jn.3.17, 12.47, 1 Cor.6.2; 1QS 10.18; Jub.5.15-16, 4 Ez.7.33f, Ps.Sol.2.15, 32, 9.2-5, 15.8; ARN[a] 32, Gen.R.26.6.

Paul immediately refutes the idea that man's iniquity could ever form the basis for justifying God's righteousness, on the grounds that it precludes God's right to judge the world.[12] Because he accepts the basic biblical and Jewish premise that God "renders to every man according to his deeds" (cf. 2.6), he knows that if God was partial, or took bribes, or distorted the distinction between good and evil in any other way, He would not be fit to judge the world.[13] Since righteous judgment means to reward man's good deeds and to punish his evil deeds, God must punish the wicked, whose evil deeds cannot therefore "prove" His righteousness. God judges the world because He is righteous and because man's actions are in fact unrighteous and deserving of punishment:

> He [R. Eleazar ha-Kappar] used to say: The born [are destined] to die, the dead to be brought to life, and the living to be judged; [it is, therefore, for them] to know and to make known, so that it become known, that He is God, He the Fashioner, He the Creator, He the Discerner, He the Judge, He the Witness, He the Complainant, and that He is of a certainty to judge, blessed be He, before whom there is no unrighteousness, nor forgetting, nor respect of persons, nor taking of bribes, for all is His . . . and without thy will art thou of a certainty to give an account and reckoning before the King of the Kings of Kings, the Holy One, blessed be He. (PA 4.22)

Verse 7:
"If through my lie . . . judged as a sinner": cf. Jn.1.14, Rom.1.25, 2 Cor.3.7f, 4.15, Eph.1.6, 12, 14; 1QH 2.24, 10.22.

Paul takes himself as personal proof of the fact that God judges the world. He knows that he both commits sin and is punished for it. It therefore cannot be true that God's righteousness is demonstrated or proved by (his) sin.[14]

Verse 8:

"And why not (say) . . . ": cf. 6.1, Gal.2.17-21; Philo, *De.Mig.Abr.*89-93.

Paul returns to the argument that man's unrighteousness "proves" God's righteousness (verse 5), since his own example reminds him of the fact that he has been personally accused of reducing the argument to its absurd libertine conclusion—"let us do evil that good will come."[15] This verse virtually acts as some sort of sarcastic extension of verse 5, as if Paul himself picks up the libertine attitude in order to demonstrate its absurdity. He thus makes the suggestion, "Well, why not go ahead and advocate doing evil so that good may come (seeing that we are being accused of such an attitude in any case), if it is indeed true that man's unrighteousness is the presupposition of God's righteousness."[16] He raises the same issue of libertinism again in 6.1, following his *a fortiori* (קו"ח) קל וחומר (*kal ve-chomer*) argument over the relationship between sin and "grace," and again in Galatians 2.17-21.[17] In both these texts, Paul refutes the logical conclusions of sinning so that grace may abound, an attitude of moral dissolution promoted most prominently amongst certain gnostic sects, although the Sages also warned against such tendencies:

> . . . one ought not to celebrate the mystery of the ineffable and invisible power by means of visible and corruptible created things, the inconceivable and incorporeal by means of what is sensually tangible and corporeal. The perfect redemption is said to be knowledge of the ineffable "Greatness". From ignorance both deficiency and passion derived; through knowledge will the entire substance derived from ignorance be destroyed. Therefore this knowledge is redemption of the inner man. And this is not corporeal, since the body perishes, nor psychic, because the soul also derives from the deficiency and is like a habitation of the spirit. The redemption must therefore be spiritual. The inner spiritual man is redeemed through knowledge. Sufficient for them is the knowledge of all things. This is the true redemption. (Irenaeus, *Against Heresies* 1.21.4)[18]

> Now R. Johanan was astonished thereat [at R. Oshaia's explanation that a consecrated object can be deliberately converted into a secular one]: is then a man bidden, 'Arise and sin, that you may achieve merit!' . . . R. Bibi b. Abaye propounded: If one places a loaf of bread

> in an oven, do they permit him to remove it before he incurs the liability of a sin offering or not? . . . R. Shesheth demurred: Is then a person told, 'Sin, in order that your neighbour may gain thereby?' [Can one be told to infringe the minor injunction of removing bread from an oven in order to save his neighbour from the greater transgression of baking on the Sabbath?] (Kid.55b, Shab.4a)

"Their condemnation is just"

Paul virtually curses those who advocate and promote such morally dissolute (libertine) behavior. Not only, however, are they justly punished by God, but their punishment also proves their ideas and conduct to be wrong.

Verse 9:

"What then? . . . ": cf. 3.3, 6.1, 15, 7.7, 9.14, 30, 10.16, 11.1, 7.

Having rejected the spurious arguments of his opponents, Paul returns to his justification of God's election of Israel and His gift of the Torah.[19] In verse 1, he defends Israel's election (their "advantage"), even though they have not always been faithful to God's covenant, on the grounds that God is faithful despite man's unfaithfulness. Now in this verse Paul negates the reverse side of Israel's "advantage," when they claim superiority over the Gentiles because of their election. If Israel have been chosen to be God's people, despite their unfaithfulness, this does not make them superior to the other nations, since he has demonstrated that God renders to "every man" (cf. 2.1, 3) according to his deeds. God can therefore call anyone who does His will to be His son.[20]

"We have already charged . . . ": cf. 2.12-16, 3.4-8.

Paul refers back to the argument in verses 5-8, in which he demonstrates that God is the Judge of the whole world, whose iniquities He justly punishes. Here Paul adopts the legal terminology employed by those who accuse him of libertine views.[21] The prooftexts which he brings in verses 10-18 serve in this context as "witnesses" to the "charge." The phrase "both Jews and Greeks" emphasizes the "Jews" (rather than the Gentiles, as modern English idiom would suggest), since Paul is stressing the fact that although Israel's election is not in question, God will nevertheless punish the unfaithfulness of His people.

"Under sin": cf. Gen.4.7, 6.5, 8.21, Ps.51.5, Jn.8.34, Rom.3.23, 5.12f, 19, 6.12ff, 7.11f, 8.2, 11.32, Gal.3.22f; 1QS 2.13ff, 4.9ff, CDC 5.12-14, 8.9, 1QH 1.21-23, 27, 4.29-30, 9.15-16, 13.14-16; Test.Jud.18.6, Test.Dan 4.7, 5.5,

Test.Asher 1.9; ARN[b] 16, 30, Mid.Ps.9.5, PRK S3.2, SER 31, Pes.Rab.9.2, Gen.R.22.6, Ruth R.3.1, Eccl.R.4.9.1-14, 9.15.6, Ned.32b, Kid.30b, Suk.52b, San.91b, Ber.61a.

Paul speaks of sin as a "master" whom a man serves, in a manner consistent with the doctrine of the Two Ways or Spirits prevalent in many contemporary Jewish texts:

> [But what is] he, the spirit of flesh, to understand all these things and to comprehend [Thy] great secret of truth? And what is he that is born of woman amid all [Thy] mighty [works]? He is but a fabric of dust and a thing kneaded with water, [who]se counsel is nothing but [uncleann]ess ignominious shame and [. . .] and over whom the perverse spirit rules. (1QH 13.13-15)[22]

Verses 10-18:
"As it is written": cf. Ps.5.9, 10.7, 14 (13).1-3, 36.1 (2), 53.1-4, 140 (139).3, 10.7, Isa.59.7.

Paul brings biblical "evidence" for the universality of "every man's" iniquity, appealing to prooftexts from the Prophets and Writings, similar to texts which are used in the Qumran scrolls:

> And in all those years Belial shall be unleashed against Israel . . . . Moreover, they have defiled their Holy Spirit, and with a blaspheming tongue have opened their mouth against the precepts of the Covenant of God, saying, They are not true! But it is an abominable thing they utter concerning them. They are kindlers of fire and lighters of brands; their webs are spider webs and their eggs are adder eggs. . . . That will be the day when God will visit; < as He said >, *The princes of Judah were < like those who remove the bound >, upon whom Anger shall pour* {Hos.5.10}. For they shall be sick < without > any healing and all the < chastisings shall crush > them because they did not depart from the way of traitors, and because they defiled themselves in the ways of lust and in the riches of iniquity . . . and because each man did what was good in his eyes, and because each man chose the stubbornness of his heart, and because they kept themselves not from the people but lived in license deliberately, walking in the way of the wicked, of whom God said, *Their wine is the poison of serpents and the head of asps is cruel* {Dt.32.3}. (CDC 4.12-13, 5.11-14, 8.2-10)[23]

Verse 19:

"Now we know . . . to God": cf. Job 5.16, Ps.63.11, 107.42, 143.2, Isa.57.4, Ezek.16.62-63, Gal.4.4; 1QS 5.10-13, 10.10-13, 11.21f, 22, 1QH 1.25 26, 4.16-20, 7.11-13; 1 En.81.5, 4 Ez.7.[46]-[48], [62]-[74], [105], Test.Asher 5.3, 2 Bar.15.5-6; PA 3.7, 8; Ep.Barn.5.4.

Paul personifies the Torah as "speaking" itself the verses which he has just quoted.[24] The Torah first addresses those who agreed "to do and to hear" it (cf. 2.13), so that both those who agreed to observe God's commandments and those who refused to accept them (the Gentile nations) are brought before God's judgment (cf. verse 6). Paul combines two Jewish traditions in verses 19 and 20, however, concerning the role of the Torah (Scripture). In this verse he reflects the view that the Torah's righteousness emphasizes man's sinfulness, which is condemned by God's righteous judgments:

> These things I have known because of Thine understanding; for Thou hast uncovered my ear to marvellous Mysteries. Yet am I but a creature of clay and a thing kneaded with water, a foundation of shame and a fount of defilement, a crucible of iniquity and fabric of sin, a spirit of straying, and perverse, void of understanding, whom the judgments of righteousness terrify. . . . But how can a man count up his sins, and what can he answer concerning his iniquities? And how can he, perverse, reply to the judgment of righteousness? (1QH 1.21-26)[25]

Verse 20:

"Because . . . the knowledge of sin": cf. Rom.2.12, 4.2, 6, 15, 5.13, 20, 7.1, 9.11, 10.5, 11.6, 2 Cor.3.6ff, Gal.2.16-21, 3.11, 5.4, Phil.3.9; 1 En.81.5, 2 Bar.15.5-6, 4 Ez.7.[62]-[74]; Kid.21b; Ep.Barn.5.4.

Having demonstrated that the Torah passes judgment on those to whom it is given to "do and to hear," Paul refers to the view that the Torah's role is to bring man to the knowledge of his sin. According to this tradition, the Torah "condescends" to the level of the human inclination and "accommodates" it. Because the Torah is "holy and righteous and good" (cf. 7.12), it is so closely bound to human weaknesses that it cannot overcome them:

> The scholars propounded: May a priest take '*a woman of goodly form*'? Is it an anomaly [lit., 'a new,' unexpected law], and so there is no difference between priests and Israelites [who are permitted to marry proselytes]: or perhaps, priests are different, since the Writ imposes additional precepts upon them?—Rab said, He is permitted; while

> Samuel maintained, He is forbidden. With respect to the first intercourse there is universal agreement that it is permitted, since the Torah provided for [lit. "spoke to"] man's evil passions [inclination] [דלא דברה תורה אלא כנגד יצר הרע]. (Kid.21b)[26]

Verse 21:

"But now": Paul now begins (verses 21-31) to answer substantively the "libertine" arguments which he countered scripturally in verses 9-20. Yeshua is in himself God's righteousness, and his death and resurrection atone for man's transgressions when he repents and becomes faithful to God in Yeshua. Although the Torah is the first of Israel's possessions as God's chosen people, if it brings man knowledge of his sinfulness, which will be punished by God who renders to every man according to his deeds, then he will not be justified by "works of the Torah." "Now," however, God has displayed His righteousness "apart from" the Torah, in Yeshua who is "the Lord our righteousness" (Jer.23.6). The gospel concerning God's son, the Messiah, is the "power of God for salvation to every one who believes, to the Jew first and also to the Greek" (1.16).[27]

"Apart from the Torah . . . ": cf. Dan.9.16, Ps.71.2, 15, 19, 24, Isa.45.24, 51.5, 8, Jer.33.16, Rom.1.17, 10.3, Phil.3.9.

Paul returns to the theme of 2.12-15, where he discusses the source of righteousness, and contrasts the "hearers of the Torah" (among Israel) with the Gentiles who are "a law to themselves." Since the Gentiles do not have the Torah, and since not all of Israel obey the Torah, which itself "speaks" to—and does not overcome—man's evil inclination, God has provided another source of righteousness, independent of the Torah but not contrary to it. When God renders to "every man" according to his deeds, He is then able to base their "deeds" on their faithfulness to Yeshua, who is called "the Lord our righteousness":

> What is the name of King Messiah? R. Abba b. Kahana said: His name is 'the Lord'; as it is stated, *And this is the name whereby he shall be called, 'The Lord is our righteousness'* (Jer.23.6). For R. Levi said: It is good for a province when its name is identical with that of its king, and the name of its king identical with that of its God. 'It is good for a province when its name is identical with that of its king,' as it is written, *And the name of the city from that day shall be the Lord is there* (Ezek.48.35). 'And the name of its king identical with that of its God' as it is stated, '*And this is the name whereby he shall be*

> *called, The Lord is our righteousness.'* . . . God will call the king Messiah after His own name, for it is said of the king Messiah *This is his name whereby he shall be called: The Lord our righteousness* (Jer.23.6). (Lam.R.1.16.51, Mid.Ps.21.2)[28]

Paul builds here upon the continuation of Jeremiah 23.6-7, which speaks of the righteous reign of the Messiah. The Targumim (the Aramaic translations of the Tanakh) understand the reference to "He will reign as king and act wisely and do justice and righteousness in the land" in terms of "a righteous and meritorious law" (Targum Jonathan to Jer.23.5-6).[29]

"Witnessed by . . . ": cf. Ps.72.2, Isa.4.2, 9.7, 11.1-5, 42.3-4, 53.2, Jer.23.6-7, 30.9, 33.15-16, Zech.3.8, 6.12-13, Lk.24.27, Jn.5.39-47, Acts 10.43, Rom.1.2, 17, 1 Jn.1.2.

Paul explains the role of the Torah as being a "witness" to God's righteousness, since its writings testify to His plan to bestow His righteousness upon man in His Messiah:

> "Behold, (the) days are coming," declares the Lord, "When I shall raise up for David a righteous Branch; and He will reign as king and act wisely and do justice and righteousness in the land. In His days Judah will be saved, and Israel will dwell securely; and this is His name by which He shall be called, 'The Lord our righteousness.'" (Jer.23.5-6)[30]

Many of the same messianic prooftexts were adopted by the "Teacher of Righteousness" at Qumran:

> . . . I have been a snare for sinners, but healing for all those that are converted from sin, prudence for the simple and the firm inclination of all whose heart is troubled. And Thou hast made of me an object of shame and mockery for traitors, (but) the foundation of truth and understanding for them whose way is straight. . . . Thou hast made me a banner for the elect of righteousness and an interpreter of Knowledge concerning the marvellous Mysteries, to test [the men] of truth and to try them that love instruction. And I was a man of dispute for the interpreters of straying, [but a man] [of pea]ce for all who see true things . . . by whose mouth Thou hast established the teaching and within whose heart Thou hast set understanding that he might open the fountain of Knowledge to all the

> understanding. . . . And [Thou hast] created [me] for Thy sake to [ful]fil the Law, and [to te]a[ch by] my mouth the men of Thy council in the midst of the sons of men, that Thy marvels may be told to everlasting generations and [Thy] mighty deeds be [contemp]lated without end. And all the nations shall know Thy truth and all the peoples, Thy glory. (1QH 2.8-18, 6.10-12)[31]

Verse 22:
" . . . through faith in Yeshua ha-Mashiach": cf. Gen.15.6, Ex.14.31, Hab.2.4, Lk.2.34-35, Jn.2.11, 11.45, 12.11, Acts 3.16, 20.21, 24, Rom.1.17, 3.26, 4.5, 9, 11, 13, 9.30, 10.6, Gal.2.16f, 3.22, 26, 5.5, Eph.1.15, Phil.3.9, Col.1.4, 1 Tim.1.14, 3.13, 2 Tim.1.13, 3.15, Phlm.5, Heb.11.7, 12.2, 2 Pet.1.1; 1QH 2.8-10, 7.12, 1QpHab 8.1-3; 1 En.39.6, 43.4.

Most commentators interpret the phrase " . . . faith in Yeshua" as referring to the believer's "faith in" Yeshua, in the same way as the Qumran community had "faith in" the Teacher of Righteousness:

> [*But the righteous shall live by his faith* (Hab.2.4).] The explanation of this concerns all those who observe the Law in the House of Judah. God will deliver them from the House of Judgment because of their affliction and their faith in the Teacher of Righteousness [בעבור עמלם ואמנתם במורה הצדק]. (1QpHab 8.1-2)

Both the Greek and the Hebrew syntax, however, more correctly require the translation "through the faithfulness of Yeshua" (i.e., Yeshua's own faithfulness to God).[32] Since Paul is speaking of Yeshua here as "the Lord our righteousness," he is speaking of Yeshua's faithfulness to God.[33] Yeshua is the "end (τελος; *telos*) of the Torah for righteousness" (10.4)—the "goal" or "purpose" towards which the Torah is directed. His faithfulness expresses and manifests his righteousness, which God gives in His grace to those who are faithful to Him (in baptism; cf. chapter 6).

"For all those who believe . . . ": cf. 1.5, 16, 2.10-11, 3.20, 23, 27-30, 4.24, 5.12-21, 8.14, 10.11-12, 11.32, Gal.3.8, 14, 22.

Paul repeats the theme of equality (cf. verses 9f), this time from the perspective of man's faithfulness. God's faithfulness is to His promise to Abraham's "seed," His Messiah, in whom all the nations of the world will be blessed.[34] Yeshua's faithfulness to God establishes his righteousness, which God bestows upon all those who are faithful in turn to Yeshua. Paul develops this theme in the following verses, explaining how Yeshua is faithful to God, how his faithfulness establishes his righteousness, and how God makes His righteousness available to "every man," both to the Jews (first) and (then) to the Greeks (cf. 1.16-17). All men can be faithful to God in Yeshua, "the Lord our righteousness."

Verse 23:

"All have sinned": cf. 1 Kings 8.46, Job 14.1-4, Ps.14.1, 143.2, Eccl.7.20, 1 Jn.1.8; 1QH 9.13, 12.25, 13.15, 16.11, 18.12ff; 4 Ez.8.35-36.

Paul shifts back to the perspective of man's equality because of his sinfulness (cf. verse 9).[35] Since "every man," both Jew and Greek, transgresses, all men are in need of Yeshua's faithfulness and righteousness, as was commonly acknowledged in Second Temple Jewish texts:

> For Thou hast established my spirit and knowest my meditation. And Thou has comforted me in my confusion and in pardon I delight; and I was comforted for the original sin [על פשע ראשון]. . . . For no man is just in Thy ju[dg]ment nor [innocent in] Thy trial. Can human born of human be righteous, and can man born of man have understanding? And can flesh born of the gui[lty] inclination be glorious, and spirit born of spirit be mighty? (1QH 9.12-16)

> And now I see that the world to come will bring delight to few, but torments to many. For an evil heart has grown up in us, which has alienated us from God, and has brought us into corruption and the ways of death, and has shown us the paths of perdition and removed us far from life—and that not just a few of us but almost all who have been created. (4 Ez.7.[47]-[48])

> Another exposition: IF A WOMAN PRODUCE OFFSPRING, etc. (Lev.12.2) This is alluded to in what is written, *Behold I was brought forth in iniquity* (Ps.51.5). R. Aha said: Even if one be the most pious of the pious, it is impossible that he should have no streak of iniquity in him. (Lev.R.14.5)

"Fall short of the glory of God": cf. Isa.60.19-20, Jn.17.22, 24, 1 Cor.1.7, 8.8 (Greek), 12.24, 2 Cor.3.6-18, 4.4-6, Heb.4.1, 12.15, Rev.21.23, 22.5; 3 Bar.6.16 (Greek).

The Greek verb ὑστερεω (*hustereo*), "to fall short," means "to be behind" or "to be in want" (cf. Mt.19.20, Mk.10.21), and closely corresponds to the Hebrew root חטא (*chata'*) whose original reference was to "missing the mark" or target (cf. Judg.20.16).[36] In 1.23f, Paul speaks of man exchanging God's "glory" for his own image, based on Psalm 106.20 (cf. Jer.2.11). Here, however, he may be referring to a midrashic theme based on the phrase מצמיח קרן ישוע (*matzmiach keren yeshua'*), "who causest salvation to spring forth" (cf. 2 Sam.22.3, Ps.18.3, 89.24). The word קרן (*keren*) is used in Exodus 34.29-35 of the "shining" or "glory" of Moses' face which gave off "rays" ("horns") of light (cf. 2 Sam.22.3, Ps.18.2, Lk.1.69, 2 Cor.3.18). In the original biblical context, the whole phrase alluded to the royal Davidic line. In the *Amidah* or the Eighteen Benedictions in the Prayer Book, where it seals (ends) the prayer for the messianic king, it may have already been specifically referred to Yeshua, as David's royal scion:

> Speedily cause the offspring of David, thy servant, to flourish, and lift up his glory [תרום קרנו] by thy divine help because we wait for thy salvation all the day. Blessed art thou, O Lord, who causest the strength of salvation to flourish [קרן ישועת מצמיח]. (PB, Amidah, p.147)[37]

Paul's suggestion that God's "glory" is His Messiah is further associated with the motif of the "Branch of David" in Jeremiah 23.5-7 (צמח; *tzemach*; cf. Zech.6.12 [Isa.11.1, 10]) in one of the blessings recited after the reading of the *haftarah* (the prophetic passage read following the weekly Torah portion):

> 'Gladden us, O Lord our God, with Elijah the prophet, Thy servant, and with the kingdom of the house of David, Thine anointed. Soon may he come and rejoice our hearts. Suffer not a stranger to sit upon his throne, nor let others any longer inherit his glory; for by Thy holy name Thou didst swear unto him, that his light should not be quenched for ever. In his days Judah shall be saved, and Israel shall dwell safely; and this is his name whereby he shall be called: The Lord is our righteousness. Blessed art Thou, O Lord, Who causest the horn of salvation to flourish for Thy people Israel. (Sof.40b)[38]

> All mankind "falls short" of the "glory of the Messiah" (cf. 2 Cor.4.4-6) who is "the Lord our righteousness," because they transgress and possess no righteousness before God, who renders to every man according to his deeds (cf. verses 8f).[39]

Verse 24:

"Being justified as a gift": cf. Ps.51.4, Jn.4.10, Acts 11.17, Rom.3.28, 4.25, 5.1, 9, 16, 6.23, 8.33, Eph.1.7, Tit.3.7; 1QS 1.8, 11.3f, 10, 14, 1QH 2.25, 31,

4.31-33, 37, 5.15, 22, 7.6-7, 17f, 9.16-18, 10.15-16, 11.29f, 13.16-17, 16.16; Mekh.Shirata 9, Mid.Ps.71.2, 89.2, 119.55.

Paul describes the idea of "falling short" as a stumbling or falling, and therefore as a lack of righteousness. God's righteousness is a "gift" which He gives freely to man, who has not "earned" it on account of his deeds. Paul depicts God's grace which "justifies" man (makes him "right") in terms very similar to those used in the Qumran literature, which repeatedly reiterates that righteousness is "denied to the assembly of flesh" and comes as a direct gift from God in His grace:

> For to God belongs my justification [משפט] and the perfection of my way, and the uprightness of my heart are in His hand: by His righteousness are my rebellions blotted out. . . . For God's truth is the rock of my steps and His power, the stay of my right hand, and from the fount of His Righteousness comes my justification. . . . The fountain of righteousness, the reservoir of power, and the dwelling-place of glory are denied to the assembly of flesh; but God has given them as an everlasting possession to those whom He has chosen. . . . For is man master of his way? No, men cannot establish their steps, for their justification belongs to God, and from His hand comes perfection of way. . . . And I, if I stagger, God's mercies are my salvation for ever; and if I stumble because of the sin of the flesh, my justification is in the righteousness of God which exists for ever. . . . He has caused me to approach by His Mercy and by His favours He will bring my justification. He has justified me by His true justice and by His immense goodness He will pardon all my iniquities . . . Who then shall contain Thy Glory? And what is the son of man himself amidst all Thy marvellous works? And he that is born of woman, what is his worth before Thee? Truly, this man is a mere frail image in potter's clay and inclines to the dust. What shall clay reply, the thing which the hand fashions? What thought can it apprehend? (1QS 11.2-22).[40]

"Redemption": cf. Ps.111.9, 130.7, Lk.1.68, 2.38, 8.23, Acts 26.18, Rom.7.1-6, 24-25, 1 Cor.1.30, Gal.1.4, Eph.1.7, 5.8, Col.1.12f, Tit.2.14, Heb.9.15, 1 Pet.2.9; 1QH 2.23, 32, 9.33.

The root meaning of the Greek noun ἀπολυτρωσις (*apolutrosis*), "redemption," implies a "price paid in ransom;" in Hellenistic Greek, the word was regularly used to refer to the purchase paid to liberate a slave.[41] Paul describes man's sinfulness in terms of being bound to an oppressive master—just as

Israel were bound to slavery under Pharaoh in Egypt. He therefore understands redemption and atonement in the sense of deliverance from bondage. The idea of a person ransoming or releasing one who is bound is also found in the biblical ceremony of חליצה (*chalitzah*) which is related to יבום (*yibbum*) or levirate marriage (cf. Dt.25.5-6).[42] The Torah commands that a man whose brother dies childless is required to marry his brother's widow in order to continue the family's name (cf. Ruth). If a man does not wish to marry his sister-in-law, he must submit to a public ceremony known as חליצה, in which the widow removes his shoe and spits in his presence, thus gaining for himself the name of "the house of him whose sandal is removed" (Dt.25.10). Paul speaks of Yeshua undergoing this ceremony, as it were, in order to redeem man from his slavery, in that Yeshua's death and resurrection redeems or "releases" man (in baptism; cf. chapter 6) from the mastery of his evil inclination. Yeshua's death and resurrection frees man from the realm of darkness and the spirit of perversity into the Kingdom of light and the Spirit of Truth, according to similar Qumran descriptions:

> For what is flesh? [Behold, it was in Thy counsel to] do wonders and in Thy thought to manifest Thy might and establish all things for Thy glory. [And Thou hast created all] the host of Knowledge to recount mighty deeds unto flesh and the true precepts unto him that is born [of woman]. [And] Thou hast caused [Thine elect] to en[ter] the Covenant with Thee and hast uncovered the heart of dust that they be kept [from all evil] [and escape] from the snares of judgment unto Thy mercy. And I, a creature [of clay], [receptacle of dus]t and heart of stone, for what am I accounted that Thou shouldst [pl]ace in an ear of dust [all Thy words of truth] and engrave the everlasting happenings in a [corrupted] heart, [and] that Thou shouldst convert [him that is born of woman] and cause him to enter the Covenant with Thee, and that he should stand [before Thee always] in the everlasting place where shines the eternal light of the dawn wi[thout any] darkness . . . For with Thee is the light [. . .] and Thou hast uncovered the ear of dust [. . .] because of the design which [. . .] and they have been confirmed by [the hands] of Thy servant for ever. (1QH 18.21-29, 3-5)[43]

Verse 25:

"Whom God displayed publicly": cf. Num.21.9, Jn.3.14-15, Rom.8.28, 9.11, Col.2.15.

Paul refers to God's redemption in Yeshua whom God "displayed publicly."

Although this can be taken as an obvious reference to the crucifixion (cf. Num.21.9, Ps.22.16-17, Isa.11.10, Jn.3.14-15), Paul may also reflect here customs developed in the Second Temple Judaism, and reflected in talmudic sources.[44] Rabbinic sources illustrate the fact that during the Second Temple period, God was regarded as indicating His acceptance of Israel's sin-offering and their forgiveness by means of the scarlet thread (לשון של זהורית; *lashon shel zehorit*) which became part of the ritual of *Yom ha-Kippurim*, the Day of Atonement. A *mishnah* in the Talmudic tractate *Yoma*, which describes the procedures connected with Yom Kippur, describes the ritual performed by the High Priest:

> What did he do? He divided the thread of crimson wool, and tied one half to the rock [the peak of the mountain from which the scapegoat was to be cast], the other half between its horns, and pushed it from behind. And it went rolling down and before it had reached half its way down it was dashed to pieces. (Yoma 6.6)[45]

Since the distance from Jerusalem to *Beit Hararo* (one of the names for the place from which the scapegoat was cast down) was three miles, it took time for the news to arrive that the scapegoat had in fact reached the wilderness (cf. Lev. 16.22). The thread of crimson wool, or scarlet thread, was therefore also used for a second purpose:

> R. Ishmael says: Had they not another sign also?—a thread of crimson wool was tied to the door of the Sanctuary (Temple) and when the he-goat reached the wilderness the thread turned white; for it is written, *Though your sins be as scarlet they shall be as white as snow* (Isa.1.18). (Yoma 6.8)

A second talmudic passage gives a further report concerning the historical circumstances which occurred during the last forty years before the destruction of the Temple (70 C.E.). This talmudic passage disputes the text of the *mishnah* in Yoma 6:6f, the Rabbis (*Amoraim*) involved claiming that:

> 'Originally they used to fasten the thread of scarlet on the door of the [Temple] court on the outside [after the High Priest had performed the service on the Day of Atonement]. If it turned white the people used to rejoice, and if it did not turn white they were sad. They therefore made a rule that it should be fastened to the door of the court on the inside. People, however, still peeped in and saw, and

> if it turned white they rejoiced and if it did not turn white they were sad. They therefore made a rule that half of it should be fastened to the rock and half between the horns of the goat that was sent [to the wilderness].' (RH 31b)[46]

The theological significance of this passage clearly indicates that God demonstrated His forgiveness and the atonement of the people's sin by turning the scarlet thread white. This discussion occurs, however, in the middle of a debate concerning the identity of nine regulations laid down by Rabban Johanan b. Zaccai.[47] In the continuation of the same section, the text gives the following report:

> If you assume that it was R. Johanan b. Zaccai [who made the rule], was there in the days of R. Johanan b. Zaccai a thread of scarlet [which turned white]? Has it not been taught: 'R. Johanan b. Zaccai lived altogether a hundred and twenty years. For forty years he was in business, forty years he studied, and forty years he taught', and it has further been taught: 'For forty years before the destruction of the Temple the thread of scarlet never turned white but it remained red. (RH 31b)

Paul's text thus converges with the talmudic evidence. Yeshua's crucifixion "publicly displays" God's forgiveness, and occurred at the time when, according to rabbinic sources, the efficacy of the traditional symbol of God's forgiveness, the scarlet thread, ceased to function. Thus the *baraitha* (Mishnaic or early Tannaitic source) quoted here witnesses to the fact that the year in which Yeshua was crucified the thread remained red for the first time, indicating that God no longer accepted the sacrifice of the scapegoat to atone for Israel's sin.[48]

"As a propitiation": cf. Ex.25.17f, Lev.16.13-15, Heb.7.26-28, 9.15f, 10.10, 19-22, 1 Jn.2.2.

The language and the syntax of this sentence are difficult. The Greek term ἱλαστηριον (*hilasterion*; "propitiation") can be understood in two ways: as an adjective ("atoning") which modifies an absent noun (e.g., atoning sacrifice); or as a neuter noun, meaning "propitiation." As a (masculine accusative) adjective, the word agrees with the pronoun ὃν (*hon;* "*whom* God displayed as a propitiation"); as a substantive noun, it is frequently taken to refer to the כפרת (*kaporet*) or "mercy seat" which covered the ark and was sprinkled with sacrificial blood by the High Priest on the Day of Atonement (cf. Ex.25.17ff, Lev.16.14f).[49] The blood of the bull and of the scapegoat effected atonement for the High Priest and for Israel. Paul therefore describes Yeshua here as both the means (the scapegoat) and the place (the mercy seat) of atonement, since his blood was poured out to atone for those who are faithful to him (cf. Ps.32.1, 85.2, Heb.9.12, 13.12).

"In his blood through faith": cf. Acts 20.28, Rom.4.16, 5.1, 9, 9.30f, 10.6ff, 1 Cor.11.25, Gal.2.20, 3.7f, 22f, Eph.1.7, Heb.9.14, 10.19, 12.24, 13.12, 1 Pet.1.19, Rev.12.11; Test.Ben.3.8.

The reference to the scarlet thread, whose turning white indicated the forgiveness of Israel's sins, clarifies the textual difficulty in this verse. As it stands, the text refers "faithfulness" to Yeshua's blood ("through faith in his blood"), and translators and commentators have frequently felt justified in changing the word order to give the verse the meaning "whom God displayed publicly as a propitiation in His blood through faith." Although this does not break the rules of Greek syntax, it involves a deliberate alteration of the original word order (in violation of the exegetical principle which holds that the more difficult reading [*lectio difficilior*] should be retained). When the word "faithfulness" is taken to refer to Yeshua's faithfulness to God, as in verse 22, Paul's meaning becomes clear. Yeshua is faithful to God in becoming "obedient to death" and in "pouring out" (shedding) his blood in order to cleanse, redeem, and sanctify mankind, as a text from the Testament of the Twelve Patriarchs, influenced here by Christian tradition, clearly describes:

> Joseph also urged our father to pray for his brothers, that the Lord would not hold them accountable for their sin which they so wickedly committed against him. And Jacob cried out, 'O noble child, you have crushed the inner of feelings of Jacob your father.' He embraced him and kept kissing him for two hours, saying, 'Through you will be fulfilled the heavenly prophecy concerning the Lamb of God, the Savior of the world, because the unspotted one will be betrayed by lawless men, and the sinless one will die for impious men by the blood of the covenant for the salvation of the gentiles and of Israel and the destruction of Beliar and his servants.' (Test.Ben.3.8, version c.)

" . . . to demonstrate . . . previously committed": cf. Ex.34.6, Ps.51.4, Joel 2.13, Acts 14.16, 17.30, Rom.2.4, 3.5, 5.8; 1QH 14.15-16; 4 Ez.3.8, 7.62f, Test.Gad 4.7, Sir.17.21; PA 5.2, Mid.Ps.77.1, PRK 24.11.

Paul directly associates God's "forbearance" (cf. 2.4f) with His gift of righteousness in Yeshua.[50] God's forbearance expresses His mercy on mankind, whose sins he does not immediately punish, as they deserve. It suspends the due punishment until the time when Yeshua's sacrifice atones for man's sinfulness.[51] Yeshua's faithfulness in "obedience unto death" (cf. Phil.2.8) is in fact the true proof or "demonstration" of God's righteousness—not man's indulgence in sin in order to magnify God's grace (cf. 3.5f). God's "passing over" man's sins is also based on the blood painted on the door-lintels of Israel in Egypt when they escaped the plague of the Egyptian first-born ("Passover") (cf. Ex.12). Yeshua, "the Lord our righteousness," is also the "Passover lamb" (cf. 1 Cor.5.7).

Verse 26:
"For the demonstration . . . faith in Yeshua"

Paul repeats the thought of verse 25 in order to emphasize the embodiment of God's righteousness in Yeshua. The phrase "at the present time" refers back to the "now" of verse 21, in which Paul first introduces God's righteousness in Yeshua "apart from the Torah." God judges every man, both Jew and Gentile, according to his faithfulness to Yeshua's death and resurrection. He can therefore be the Judge of the world (cf. verse 6) because He righteously justifies every man, both Jew and Gentile.

Verses 27-28:
"Where then is boasting?": cf. Jer.9.23, Rom.2.17, 23, 4.2, 15.17-18, 1 Cor.1.29f, Eph.2.9.

Paul returns to the question which he asks in verse 9. Despite Israel's election, God still renders to every man according to his deeds, and God's gift of righteousness in Yeshua is given impartially to every man who is faithful to God in him. As a nation, Israel therefore have no grounds for boasting, because righteousness is based on faithfulness, and is not a reward for the observance of a commandment but a "voluntary conversion" to serve God from the heart:

> What being of flesh can do this, and what creature of clay has the power to do such marvellous things, whereas he is in iniquity from his mother's womb and in the sin of unfaithfulness until his old age? And I, I know that righteousness is not of man, nor of the sons of men perfection of way; to the Most High God belong all the works of righteousness, whereas the way of man is not firm unless it be by the Spirit which God has created for him. . . . What can I say unless Thou open my mouth, and how can I understand unless Thou give understanding to me? And what thou[ght] can I have unless Thou

> uncover my heart, and how can I make my way straight unless [Thou es]tablish [it]? [And how] can [my] foo[tstep] be sure [unless Thou] give strength and might. . . . (1QH 4.29-31, 12.32-35)

Verse 27:

"It is excluded . . . by a law of faith": Paul unambiguously refutes the argument that Israel's election gives them a claim to superiority over the nations (cf. verse 9). He then explains how boasting is impermissible. The expression "by what kind of law?" plays on several levels. Since the Torah is Israel's first "advantage" or proof of their election, Paul hints that the "Law"—the Torah itself -excludes boasting of righteousness over the Gentiles. In 2.14, the "law" is that which the Gentiles observe in faithfulness to God, without having been given direct commandments or knowledge of His will. Paul also uses the term in the more general sense of "principle": on what grounds or what basis is boasting excluded? In answering "by a law of faithfulness," he also adds the possibility that the Torah itself can be a matter of faithfulness. He thus builds on his argument in chapter 2, where he demonstrates that the "sons of Abraham" are those who are Abraham's "disciples" and who behave according to his qualities. The "law of faithfulness" is based on Yeshua's faithfulness on the cross and on man's faithfulness to God in Yeshua. This faithfulness brings God's righteousness to every man, based on God's promise to Abraham, that in his seed all the nations of the world will be blessed (cf. Gen.12.3).[52]

Verse 28:

"A man is justified . . . works of (the) Law": cf. 3.20, Gal.2.16-21; 1QS 11.2-22, 1QH 1.21-27, 4.29-33, 9.10-18, 12.32-35, 13.13-18, 16.11-19; Mid.Ps.44.1, 71.2, 72.1, 119.55, PPe'ah 1.1, PSan.10.1, Dt.R.2.1.

Paul states what he truly believes, and not what is slanderously attributed to him and other believers (cf. verse 8), although at this point he is more concerned with the source of righteousness in regard to the relationship between Israel and the Gentiles than with libertine issues. He again picks up the theme of "every man" (cf. 2.1, 3, 9, 10, 3.9, [19-20]), since a person may or may not have "good works," but God redeems him because of His mercy, a trait which contemporary Jewish sources frequently emphasize:

> . . . of all these designations of prayer Moses made use only of *tahanunim*. R. Johanan said: Hence you learn that no creature has any claim on his Creator, because Moses, the teacher of all the prophets, made use only of *tahanunim*. . . . God said to Moses: 'To

him who has any claim on Me *I will show mercy* (Ex.33.19), that is, I will deal with him according to My attribute of Mercy; and as for him who has no claim upon Me, to him "*I will be gracious*," that is, I will grant [his prayer] as an act of grace'. (Dt.R.2.1)[53]

As for me, I belong to wicked humanity, to the assembly of perverse flesh; my iniquities and rebellion and sin together with the iniquity of my heart (belong to) the assembly doomed to worms, (the assembly) of men who walk in darkness. . . . And I, if I stagger, God's mercies are my salvation for ever; and if I stumble because of the sin of the flesh, my justification is in the righteousness of God which exists for ever. . . . He has caused me to approach by His Mercy and by His favours He will bring my justification. He has justified me by His true justice and by His immense goodness He will pardon my iniquities. And by His justice He will cleanse me of the defilement of man and of the sin of the sons of men, that I may acknowledge His righteousness unto God and His majesty unto the Most High. (1QS 11.9-15)

Verses 29-30:

"God of Jews . . . of Gentiles also": cf. Jer.10.7; Mid.Ps.93.1.

Paul gives the reason for his "Law" or "Torah" of faithfulness (cf. the rabbinic term מה נפקא מנה; *mah nafka' minah*; lit. "what comes out of [this argument]?"). Israel's boasting is excluded, not because they possess the Torah but because possessing it leads, according to God's plan, to the "election" also of the Gentiles. Since God is One, He cannot be the "just and the justifier" of Israel alone out of the whole world (cf. verse 6). He must also demonstrate His righteousness to the Gentiles, a fact which the Rabbis acknowledged as well:

A land which the Lord thy God careth for (Dt.11.12). Is this the only land that He cares for? Does He not care for all lands, as it is said, *To cause it to rain on a land where no man is . . . to satisfy the desolate and waste ground* (Job 38.26-27)? What then does Scripture mean by *A land which the Lord thy God cares for*? It is as if it were possible to say that He cares for it alone, but because of His care of it, He cares for all the other lands along with it. Similarly you might ask, *Behold, He that keepeth Israel doth neither slumber nor sleep* (Ps.121.4)—does He keep only Israel? Does He not keep all the nations, as it is said, *In whose hand is the soul of every living thing, and the breath of all mankind*

> (Job 12.10). What then does *He keepeth Israel* mean? It is as if it were possible to say that He keeps only Israel, but because He keeps them He keeps every other nation with them. (Sifre Dt.Ekev 40)[54]

Verse 30:

"Since . . . is one": cf. Dt.4.39, 6.4, Isa.45.21-24, 46.5, 9, Zech.14.9, Rom.10.12, 1 Cor.8.6, Gal.3.20, Eph.4.6, 1 Tim.2.5; Tanh.B.Vayera 21, Sifre Dt.He'azinu 329, Gen.R.8.9.

The theme of God's unity was often used in rabbinic texts as an expression of His sovereignty.[55] God will reign when all the nations acknowledge His name:

> We therefore hope in thee, O Lord our God, that we may speedily behold the glory of thy might, when thou wilt remove the abominations from the earth, and heathendom will be utterly destroyed, when the world will be perfected under the kingdom of the Almighty, and all the children of flesh will call upon thy name, when thou wilt turn unto thyself all the evil-doers upon earth. Let all the inhabitants of the world perceive and know that unto thee every knee must bow, every tongue must swear allegiance. Before thee, O Lord our God, let them bow and worship; and unto thy glorious Name let them give honour; let them all accept the yoke of thy kingdom, and do Thou reign over them speedily, and for ever and ever. For the kingdom is Thine, and to all eternity thou wilt reign in glory; as it is written in thy Torah, THE LORD SHALL REIGN FOR EVER AND EVER (Ex.15.18). And it is said, AND THE LORD SHALL BE KING OVER ALL THE EARTH: AND IN THAT DAY SHALL THE LORD BE ONE, AND HIS NAME ONE (Zech.14.9). (PB, Aleinu prayer, p.553)

Although God justifies both Israel and the Gentiles according to Yeshua's faithfulness, each group receives His righteousness independently. Paul does not reject the Torah, but says that Israel ("the circumcised") receive Yeshua's righteousness "by" (ἐκ; *ek*) faithfulness to the Torah's witness to God's righteousness (just as they are witnesses to God's name). The Gentiles, on the other hand, who do not "have the Torah" (cf. 2.14) find God's righteousness "through" (δια; *dia*) Yeshua's faithfulness, "apart from" the Torah.

Verse 31:

"Do we then nullify Torah through faith? . . . ": cf. Mt.5.17, Gal.2.17-21, 3.2, 17-19.

Paul now raises a separate objection, with the formula familiar from verses 3-4, 5-6, and 9, which he immediately counters. Faithfulness to God in Yeshua does not nullify the Torah. If Israel cannot boast because of their possession of the Torah (verse 27), neither can the Gentiles, on the other hand, claim that Yeshua's faithfulness annuls the Torah (and thus Israel's election). God's faithfulness and righteousness are "witnessed to" by the Torah (3.21) and are the grounds of Israel's election. Paul describes this "witness" in Galatians 3.8 as the "preaching of the gospel aforehand to Abraham." The Torah itself "preaches" the "good news" of God's promise to Abraham, that in his seed all the nations of the earth will be blessed. The "sons of Abraham" are those who are faithful to God's promise to Abraham, to whom God imputed righteousness because of his faithfulness to God. Thus the Torah confirms ("establishes") that the "sons of Abraham" are those who walk according to his faithfulness to God's promises. Paul assures his Jewish readers that faithfulness to Yeshua does not "annul" the Torah, but makes it stand as the τελος (*telos;* "goal") of God's righteousness (cf. 10.4) to all men, both Jews and Gentiles. He develops this theme in chapter 4.

Endnotes on Chapter 3

1 For the use of "circumcision" to represent the covenant, and thus Israel's election, see the comments on 2.25f.

2 For the principle of כלל ופרט (*kelal u-frat*), see the introduction to chapter 2 and the comments on 2.1.

3 The "desirable instrument" is the Torah; cf. PRK 10.2.

4 Paul's defense of Israel's election (verses 1-2) raises the question of how they can remain God's people when they rebel against Him. This leads Paul to address the issue of God's righteousness, which is based (so to speak) on human unrighteousness. All men are unrighteous before God, and therefore their redemption must come directly from Him (verses 8ff). Paul concludes from this argument the fact that God's promises were given to Abraham (the forefather of Israel) before he was circumcised and entered the covenant of the Torah (chapter 4). As the "sons of Abraham," all men are therefore justified on the basis of faithfulness, and through Yeshua's own faithfulness to God (cf. verse 22). God's grace (chapters 5-6) does not allow men to sin in order to give it opportunity to abound (another libertine claim). On the contrary, everyone must in fact die to sin and put his evil inclination to death (chapters 6-8) in walking before God and serving Him in Yeshua. Paul's discussion of walking

in the Spirit of God (chapter 8) finally leads him back to the defense of Israel's election which he begins here, since he knows that everything will work towards good because God has declared His love for His people from the beginning (cf. 8.26ff).

5 Paul begins the chapter by answering the Jewish objection that his argument compromises, if not actually negates, Israel's election. In assertively affirming that God has unequivocally chosen Israel as His people, he then has to counter the objection that throughout their history (and not only in their recent rejection of Yeshua as God's Messiah), the nation has been unfaithful to God and to His covenant. Although he might have chosen to discuss whether this fact confirms the precarious nature of Israel's election, he instead follows up the issue of God's faithfulness. This leads him into an extended discourse concerning the relationship between God and man, and he only returns to his main theme in chapter 9, where he details the full list of Israel's "advantages;" (for the argument that he begins to return to this theme already in 8.27, see the summary and comments there).

6 The talmudic formula runs as follows: אילמה . . . תלמוד לומר (*'ilemah . . . talmud lomar*): "you might say . . . but the inference teaches us actually. . . ." It is normally based upon two or more conflicting opinions, according to which a resolution is offered, immediately refuted, and the proper answer then provided; cf. also the term איתימא (*'itema'*), "if you want to say . . . ; " see A. Steinsaltz, *Talmud*. Paul's pressing concern here is with the implications of Israel's irresponsibility having once received the Torah (cf. verses 3f). This issue leads him to raise and reject various possible aspects of libertinism (moral dissolution) in chapters 3-8, until he resumes the advantages of Israel's election in 9.1-4.

7 Paul picks up this argument again in chapter 9, where in verses 30-33 he again asks the question whether God has not in fact rejected Israel (and replaced them with the Gentiles) because they have stumbled over the "rock of offense," i.e., Yeshua. While Paul may be referring to Israel's rejection of Yeshua in chapter 3, Israel's unfaithfulness to God and the Torah was constantly pointed out and denounced by all the biblical prophets.

8 The description of Israel's idolatry as "adultery" is a common biblical motif. Paul picks up the reference to adultery/idolatry again in chapter 7, based on Jeremiah 3 (one of the prooftexts in the midrash from *Tanna debe Eliyyahu*). Paul plays with the thought-content of the prooftexts reflected in this midrash, emphasizing God's faithfulness through His tolerance of the people's idolatry/adultery. This "tolerance" raises the issue of whether man can "prove God right," as it were, by sinning and

thus allowing Him to repent (cf. verses 5f). In chapter 7, Paul turns back God's doubtful willingness to "remarry" Israel to the people's adultery/idolatry and their willingness to serve God instead of other "masters." He then addresses the issue raised by the midrashic reading of Jer.3.4 ("Behold, you have spoken and have done evil things, and you have had your way [lit. been able]"), which may be taken to mean that Israel's evil deeds have caused God to retain His love of them. Chapters 3 and 7 of Romans are further closely related in content, since Paul elaborates his statement in 3.7 in 7.14-25 .

9 The translation follows the Hebrew verse numbering; in the English versions of the Psalms, the verse is verse 4.

10 It is not only wrong to think that God will forsake His people when they turn away from Him; it is also wrong to justify man's evil deeds because they prove God's judgment of man to be right. See the comments on verse 3 for the use of the phrase, "what shall we say?" The following question ("the God who . . . ") is part of Paul's elaboration of the erroneous conclusion that man's evil can justify God's grace; for a similar structure of the phrase, see the discussion on 9.30ff.

11 See, for example, the phrase כביכול (*ki-ve-yakol*), "as it were;" cf. Rom.6.19, 1 Cor.9.8, 15.32, Gal.3.15, 1 Pet.4.11, PRK 12.6, 24.13, Mekh.Bachodesh 7, Shirata 4, Eruv.22a, Git.58a, BK 79b, BB 10a. Cf. also the rabbinic hermeneutic principle, דברה תורה בלשון בני אדם (*dibrah Torah be-lashon benei 'adam*), "the Torah speaks in the language of men." This latter principle was later used to support the view that the Torah "accommodates" its commandments to human nature; cf. Sifre Num.111, Ber.31b, Ket.67b, Yev.71a. Paul appeals to this principle in order to emphasize the mistaken view that man's sin can increase God's righteousness; see also 6.19.

12 For the formula "May it never be!," see the comments on verse 3. God's judgment or His role as Judge of the world, is one of the most fundamental tenets of biblical and Jewish thought. To deny that there is either Judge or judgment means to deny that God has dominion or providence over the earth.

13 See also the references on 2.2-3 and 2.5.

14 This verse becomes the basis of Paul's discourse in 7.7-25. Paul is bold here, since although he acknowledges that people have been slandering him (verse 8), he is still willing to use his own example to prove his point. The sentence is therefore not a real but a rhetorical question: there is no sense to the claim that God does not judge the world, because Paul is being judged for his transgressions.

15 See also the attitude expressed in the Testament of Asher, where the author soundly condemns the "two-faced," by whom he means those who are willing to mix evil with the good: "The soul, they say, may in words express good for the sake of evil, but the outcome of the action leads to evil. . . . Although indeed love is there, yet in wickedness is evil concealed; in name it is as though it were good, but the outcome of the act is to bring evil" (Test.Asher 2.1, 4); cf. also Mid.Prov.34b.

16 It is difficult to determine whether Paul is making a distinction between slanderous reports and the "affirmation" of others, or whether the two clauses describe the same activity. The repetition appears redundant, but the meaning of the distinction between "slanderously report" and "affirm" is hard to discern. Acts 21.21 indicates that Paul was said to "teach all the Jews who are among the Gentiles [i.e., in the Diaspora] to forsake Moses, telling them not to circumcise their children nor to walk according to the customs;" in Acts 21.28, non-believing Jews claim that Paul "preaches to all men everywhere against our people, and the Law, and this place [i.e., the Temple]." It is apparent that Paul was understood as teaching a form of "freedom from the Torah," probably primarily amongst the "Judaizing" believers sensitive to any denigration of Torah observance (cf. Acts 13.38, Gal.3.1ff). He himself firmly denied this, and his own actions proved it (cf. Acts 18.18, 20.16, 21.26, 24.10f, 17, Rom.15.25, 1 Cor.16.1-8).

17 The ק"ו argument is the talmudic equivalent of the Latin *a fortiori* or *ad maius* argument, and is one of the basic rabbinic principles of interpreting Scripture: "In essence, this is a rule of logical argumentation by means of which a comparison is drawn between two cases, one lenient and the other stringent. ק"ו asserts that if a law is stringent in a case where we are usually lenient, then it will certainly be stringent in a more serious case; likewise, if the law is lenient in a case where we are usually not lenient, then it will certainly be lenient in a less serious case. *A fortiori* argumentation is already found in the Bible, and lists of biblical verses containing *a fortiori* arguments were compiled by the Talmudic Rabbis. For example, 'If you have run with foot-soldiers, and they have wearied you, how can you contend with horses?' (Jer.12.5). This is one of the most commonly encountered exegetical principles, since *a fortiori* inferences can be drawn even without support from tradition (as opposed to *gezerah shavah*, for example). Sometimes, the Sages referred to *a fortiori* inferences as דין [*din*]—'logical argumentation.'"

A. Steinsaltz, *Talmud*, 153. Paul makes frequent use of this principle; see especially chapter 5.

18 Irenaeus (one of the great Church Fathers) describes here in his work "against heresies" a form of Valentinian gnosticism, whose logic of genuine theological (and political) dualism demanded that true perfection has no need of any external ceremony. Paul obviously refers to such tendencies (antinomian and libertine, if not specifically gnostic) not only here but also at the end of chapter 2. The term "inner man" occurs in gnostic texts, but Paul's usage of the term is closer to the theology of Qumran than to that of Gnostic thought in this regard, which, far from being antinomian (against the law), was far stricter than even the Pharisees in its emphasis on observance of the Torah. ["Gnosticism" is a notoriously difficult phenomenon to define, although the name itself derives from the word for "knowledge" (*gnosis*). Filoramo (following Hans Jonas) describes the gnostic as "the Stranger *par excellence*, the 'alien' propelled to exist in a cosmos that is strange to him, to live a life that does not belong to him, because it is rooted in illusion. His is an anxious search for *gnosis*, for a knowledge that will save him; this will be revealed to him as a call from above, a cry that will arouse him from his existence of sleep and shadows to remind him of his true origins, which know nothing of becoming and of death, and to show him the true road to salvation." G. Filoramo, *A History of Gnosticism* (Oxford: Basil Blackwell, 1990), 13. The doctrine of deliberately sinning was promoted most prominently and disastrously in the Sabbatian movement in the Seventeenth Century; see G. Scholem, *Sabbatai Sevi: The Mystical Messiah, 1626-1676* (Princeton: Princeton University Press, 1973).]

19 The formula "what then . . . not at all" anticipates an objection which will immediately be refuted, and normally arises from the preceding thought. Here, however, Paul returns to his argument in verse 3, since he identifies as Jews and Gentiles respectively the "we" who are no better then "they" in the same verse. Verse 9 thus breaks off from the issue of libertine attitudes in verses 5-8 and picks up another objection arising from verses 1-2.

20 This argument, in chapter 2, has led Paul at the beginning of chapter 3 to defend Israel's election despite their unfaithfulness, so that he now closes the circle.

21 His "charge" in 2.12-16 does not reflect the same legal tenor. However, his language in 3.4ff, which introduces this section, is "forensic" (relates to a court of law); cf. also 8.33f.

22 See also the comments on 7.14ff.

23 Cf. also 1QH 4.6ff, 4 Ez.7.22-24.

24 Paul's prooftexts in verses 10-18 are in fact from the Writings rather than from the Torah (Pentateuch), but since the Prophets and the Writings both depend on the Torah, which possesses the highest degree of sanctity, "Torah" often stands for the whole canon of Scripture; cf. Jn.5.39-47, 1 Cor.14.21, Test.Naph.8.7-8, Tanh.B.Re'eh 1, Mid.Ps.78.1, Ex.R.29.4, BM 83a, San.91b, Pes.77a, 120a, Philo, *De Vit.Cont.*78. Paul says that the Torah preaches the gospel beforehand (Gal.3.8), and shuts mankind up under sin (Gal.3.22; cf. Rom.11.32); see also the comments on 1.2 and 2.27.

25 See also the passage in Ezek.16.53-63, in which God establishes His covenant with Israel and Judah "'*in order that* you may remember and be ashamed, and never open your mouth any more because of your humiliation, when I have forgiven you for all that you have done,' the Lord God declares" (16.63). Paul may represent the Torah in similar fashion in verse 19, in that God "shuts up" (cf. 11.32, Gal.3.22) Israel (this time their mouth) by making them ashamed through the goodness of His covenant. He also gives them His righteousness "apart" from the Torah (covenant), which enables the Gentiles to be made part of his people as well (cf. verses 21ff).

26 Cf. Dt.21.11ff, Mt.19.8, Sifre Num.111, Ber.31b, Ket.67b, Yev.71a. The question of what sort of wife a priest may marry arises from the fact that a priest may not normally marry a proselyte. For the doctrine of "divine condescendence" or "accommodation" (συνκαταβασις; *sunkatabasis*), see F. Dreyfus, "Divine Condescendence (SYNKATABASIS) as a Hermeneutic Principle of the Old Testament in Jewish and Christian Tradition," *Immanuel* 19 (1984/85), 74-86.

27 Paul thus picks up the "every man" of 2.1 and 3, which includes both Jews and Gentiles. The Gentiles may be included in God's election because of Yeshua's righteousness and faithfulness, and the Jews may not be excluded, as it were, on the grounds that they cannot be justified through the works of the Torah.

28 See also the comments on 1.17.

29 Cf. also the reference to Elijah (Mal.3.23 [4.5]) in relation to Jer.23.6-7 in Sof.40b; see verse 23. Elijah is not only the precursor of the Messiah (cf. Mt.11.14, 17.10-13, Mk.9.11-13, Lk.1.17, Jn.1.21) but also the prophet who will restore the Torah's lost meanings in the messianic age (cf. Men.45a, Pes.34a). Some of the midrashim also speak of the "teaching" of the Messiah; cf. Gen.R.98.9.

30 See 1.16 for the midrashim on Jer.23.5-6, and 1.2 and 3.19 for the use of the "Torah and the Prophets" to designate Scripture.

31 The same biblical texts, therefore, were regarded as Messianic by similar Jewish circles in the Second Temple period, although the figures to whom the prophecies were attributed (such as the Teacher of Righteousness by the Qumran community, or Bar Khokhba by R. Akiba) did not prove their messiahship through their resurrection from the dead. See D. Flusser, "Two Notes on the Midrash on 2 Sam. VII," in *Judaism*, 93-98.

32 See G. Howard, "Romans 3.21-31 and the Inclusion of the Gentiles," *Harvard Theological Review* 63 (1970), 223-33. Grammatically, the genitive case (indicating ownership or association) may be either "objective" (where the "of" refers to the object as belonging to someone else), or "subjective" (where the "of" refers to something belonging to oneself, one's own). The biblical concept of "faith," moreover, is always "faithfulness" and not "(doctrinal) belief;" cf. Gen.15.6, Dt.28.66, 32.4, Judg.11.20, Job 4.18, 12.20, 15.15, 31, Ps.33.4, 96.13, 98.3, 100.5, 119.30, Prov.12.17, Mic.7.5, Hab.2.4.

33 Cf. Mt.20.28, 26.39, Phil.2.7, 1 Tim.2.6, Heb.2.10, 17-18, 3.6.

34 Cf. Gen.12.3, 22.18, Jer.4.2, Acts 3.25, Gal.3.16.

35 See the comments and references on verse 9, and the comments on 5.12f.

36 The root חטא (*chata'*) is one of the most common words for "sin" in the Tanakh, which has, however, a broad range of terms to cover the different aspects of transgression, iniquity, disobedience, rebellion, etc.

37 See Y. Libes, "Mazmiah Qeren Yeshu'ah," *Jerusalem Studies in Jewish Thought* 3.3 (1983/84), 313-48 [Hebrew]. Libes bases his argument on the fact that, as it stands, the phrase is syntactically difficult: instead of referring to a proper name (e.g., "David"), it speaks of "salvation." Libes therefore suggests that the Amidah incorporated the phrase after it had already been associated with Yeshua himself, and that the Sages suppressed the reference to Yeshua, replacing his (proper) name (ישוע) with the noun "salvation" (ישועה; *yeshu'ah*). Since the expression to "lift up" one's horn is used biblically in the sense of "to prosper" (cf. Num.6.24-26, Ps.4.6, 80.3, 7, 19), and the verbs "to fall" and "to stumble" are also closely associated with the idea of sinning, Paul may have linked the idea of "falling short" with the "signal" of the Messiah in Isa.11.10, where his resting place is said to be "glory." Luke associates this "signal" or "sign" (cf. Isa.7.14) with Yeshua, who is "appointed for the fall and rise of many in Israel" (Lk.2.34-35). The passage in Luke is also based on Prov.20.27, a verse which Paul picks up in 8.27 (cf. also 2.16), having described the "glorification" of the creation and the "sons of God;" see the comments on 8.27-28. The sign of the Messiah is "to be opposed," according to Lk.2.34, according to the tradition of the "testing-" or "stumbling-stone" in Isa.8.14 and 28.16, and Israel will either stumble over it

or "not be disappointed (ashamed)" and "rise" (be resurrected); see the comments on 9.33ff. The motif thus also has direct reference to Israel's election; cf. Amos 9.11: "In that day I will raise up the fallen tabernacle of David, and wall up its breaches; I will also raise up its ruins and rebuild it as in the days of old;" see the comments on 11.11. For the term "seal," see the comments on 15.28.

38 The tractate Soferim is one of the Minor or External Tractates, which was written during the Gaonic period (C8). It deals with the correct functioning of the scribes, their professional and religious duties, and guidance in the selection of the right materials for the sacred work. In this text the reference of the phrase has again been altered, here from "the horn of David" to "for Thy people Israel," which may be a direct response to the allusion to Yeshua. The version which is presently read (in accordance with Pes.117b) differs yet again: "Blessed art Thou, O Lord, the Shield of David."

39 Cf. also Lk.2.32 and 1QH 7.22-25. The phrase "has raised up a horn of salvation for us" also appears in Zecharias' prophecy in Lk.1.69 concerning John the Baptist (whom Yeshua links with Elijah in Mt.11.14).

40 For Paul's extended discourse on grace, see chapter 5, although the motif runs through the whole letter; for "grace" as a technical term indicating (apostolic) authority, see the comments on 12.3.

41 See TDNT 4:351-56. The Hebrew root פדה (*padah*) carries the same meaning of ransom; cf. Ex.13.13, 15, Lev.27.27f, Num.3.11f, 40ff, Ps.34.22, 44.26, 71.23, Mt.20.28, 1 Tim.2.6; see also the comments on 2.4-5.

42 Cf. Dt.25.5-6. The English word "levirate" comes directly from the Latin term *levir*, meaning a husband's brother.

43 See the comments on chapter 6 for the midrash on Job 3.19, on which Paul bases the idea of serving two masters, and the comments on 7.1ff, where Paul uses the same motif (see also Gal.1.4).

44 These are also a source of external historical evidence for the events described by the New Testament, although it must be remembered that they are literary texts as well.

45 Although the talmudic text identifies the source of the scarlet thread with the passage from Isa.1.18, it is actually mentioned in the biblical story of Rahab, where it performed the same function of deliverance for her household during the Israelite conquest of Canaan, after she had sheltered the spies (cf. Joshua 2).

46 These two reports seem contradictory, although they are apparently interpreting the same mishnaic source. The Sages in Yoma, in apparent contrast to those in Rosh Hashanah, were concerned with the risks of

the non-visibility of the scarlet thread. They argued that the thread had to be transferred from the rock and horns of the scapegoat to the Temple (rather than the reverse practice) because the High Priest might either himself be too pleased at seeing the thread turn white to remember to pass the information on to the people, or that, if the thread turned white very quickly, he might even forget to hurl the scapegoat off the mountain, thus failing to fulfil the commandments. If the two sources are not referring to two different texts, the passage in Yoma seems to carry more authenticity in light of the fact that the purpose of the scarlet thread was to be a visible sign of God's forgiveness to the people.

47 This Rabbi was one of the prominent (and very few) survivors of the destruction of Jerusalem in 70 C.E., who laid the foundations for establishment of pharisaic (rabbinic) Judaism following the collapse of the Temple and its sacrificial system. It thus precisely dates the events during the last years of the Temple, and concerns the years immediately following Yeshua's atonement in his death and resurrection (c. 27-30 C.E.).

48 The question being asked is when R. Johanan could have had an opportunity to make this rule concerning the scarlet thread. The Sages give various explanations, all of which affirm that he could reasonably have done so, thus also rejecting the possibility that the thread turned white during his lifetime. A parallel account in Yoma 39b, on the other hand, suggests that following the forty years of Simon the Righteous' high priesthood (c. 219-199 B.C.E.), during which the thread stayed white, the thread sometimes became white and at other times remained red.

49 See also 8.3.

50 For the idea of God's "forbearance," see also the comments on 2.4.

51 Although Paul does not explicitly say that God will forgive the unrighteous, this is the plain meaning of the text. He obviously considers Yeshua's public display as a propitiation to be a proof of God's righteous judgment, and he places emphasis on this rather than on the serious theological questions that lie behind his statement. Therefore at the same time as he allows for the conclusion that those before Yeshua were not condemned he also quite clearly declares that God's righteousness is also based on man's acceptance of Yeshua's atonement (cf. 'the justifier of the one who is faithful to Yeshua'). God is not merely merciful—and "winks at" at evil—but He is also just. Yeshua's obedience even to death is the means by which God can be both merciful and righteous at the same time.

52 Cf. also Gal.3.6ff. Paul picks up the theme of the blessing of the nations through Abraham's seed not only in chapter 4, but also in chapter 11,

since the root ברך (*barakh*) was also used in post-biblical Hebrew to refer to "engrafting" a plant. This is the metaphor which Paul uses in chapter 11 to describe how the Gentile believers have been "grafted into" the commonwealth of Israel, and thus made part of His chosen people.

53 The term "tachanunim" (תחנונים), supplications, is connected with חן (*chen*), "grace," and thus implies that Moses prayed not as one who demands his rights but as one who asks for grace.

54 Although Israel is the cause for God's sustenance of the whole world, according to this midrash, the text affirms God's universality; for similar midrashim on the same theme, see the comments on 11.12 and 15.

55 The recitation of the Shema, "Hear O Israel, the Lord thy God, the Lord is One" (Dt.6.4), for example, is described as receiving the "yoke of the Kingdom" upon oneself; cf. Ber.2.1, Dt.R.2.31.

ROMANS

4

Introduction

Paul justifies his statement that faithfulness establishes the Torah (and sustains Israel's election) by appealing to Abraham. Abraham is the prime exemplar, since he was both faithful to God's promises (verses 2-9) and was circumcised (verses 10-12). Paul clarifies the precedence of faithfulness over the Torah (verses 10-16), through an interpretative analogy between Genesis 15.6 and Psalm 32.1-2, and confirms that Abraham is the father of all those who possess his qualities—both Jews and Gentiles. He demonstrates that through Abraham God created a way to make the Gentiles a part of His people (verses 11-22). He then applies the principle of faithfulness through Yeshua to his own generation.

Verse 1:
"What then shall we say? . . . "

Paul turns the interrogative "what then shall we say?" (which resembles the formula in 3.3, 5 and 9) into a formal question here, in order to explain the relationship between the Torah and "faithfulness" (cf. 3.31).[1] Since Paul appeals to Abraham straightaway, Abraham has probably been the model behind his discussion of "faithfulness" in chapter 3. The phrase "Abraham, our forefather according to flesh" delineates circumcision as the symbol of God's covenant with Israel. Abraham is the "forefather" of Israel because he was the first to be circumcised and the first to make a covenant with God (cf. Gen.17.9-14).[2] He is also the "father of the proselytes," however, because he was the first "convert," and because God "imputed" righteousness to him as a result of his "faithfulness." Paul therefore asks what circumcision has "done" for Abraham, or what he has "obtained" (found) "according to the flesh."[3] The verb ἑυρισκω (*heurisko*), "to find," also reflects the Hebrew root זכה (*zakhah*), "to gain," the verbal root underlying the common rabbinic concept of the "merit of the fathers":

> R. Nehemiah said: The Israelites were privileged [זכו] to sing the Song by the sea because of their faith [זכות], for it says, *'And the people believed'* (Ex.4.31), and also *'And they believed in the Lord'* (Ex.14.31). R. Isaac said: Should they not have also believed after witnessing all the miracles performed for them? No, said R. Simeon b. Abba. It was because of Abraham's faith [זכות] in God, as it says, *'And he believed in the Lord,'* that Israel was privileged to sing the Song by the sea. . . . (Ex.R.23.5)[4]

Verse 2:

"For if . . . ": cf. Jer.9.23-24, Rom.2.17, 3.20, 23, 27.

Paul picks up the theme of 3.27, where he addresses the relationship between "boasting" and the "laws" (principles) of Torah and faithfulness. Abraham, Paul says, might have "boasted" in his circumcision—in the covenant which God made with him—but only for his own sake and not "before God," since the only "boast" which God accepts is man's acknowledgment of God's true character:

> Thus says the Lord, "Let not a wise man boast of his wisdom, and let not the mighty man boast of his might, let not a rich man boast of his riches; but let him who boasts boast of this, that he understands and knows Me, that I am the Lord who exercises lovingkindness, justice and righteousness on earth; for I delight in these things," declares the Lord. (Jer.9.23-24)[5]

Verse 3:

"For what does the Scripture say?": cf. Gen.15.6.

Paul appeals to Genesis 15.6 in order to demonstrate why Abraham could not "boast" before God. As in chapters 2 and 3, boasting takes on the specific connotation of Israel's election, since Paul wants to show how "faithfulness" (leading to righteousness) establishes the Torah even though Israel's possession of the Torah does not automatically "impute" righteousness to the people. The prooftext (Gen.15.6) (כמו שנאמר; *kemo she-ne'amar*; "as it is written") is part of the "witness" of the Torah (and the prophets) to God's righteousness apart from the Torah (cf. 3.21).

Verse 4:

"To the one who works": cf. PA 2.14, 15, 16, 3.15; 1 Macc.2.52.

Paul addresses the standard Jewish textual difficulty in Genesis 15.6, which concerns the precise meaning of the verb ויחשבה (*vay-yachshevehah*).

The standard Christian interpretation of this verse understands the root חשב (*chashav*) to refer to God's "favor," according to which He gives His gift of righteousness to someone (Abraham) who does not deserve it. God thus "imputes" righteousness to Abraham without Abraham having "earned" righteousness by "works" of his own doing. The theological "imputations" given to the verse, however, have often gone far beyond proper textual and linguistic bounds, and established a dichotomous relationship between "faith" and "works" which most of the contemporary Jewish sources do not support. Although "(good) works" are at times contrasted with "merit" (faithfulness), as Paul contrasts them here, the concept of "mitzvot" as "good deeds" or "works" which make up a person's "merit" is a later idea. Paul needs to divide them somewhat artificially for his purposes, in interpreting Genesis 15.6 in a similar manner to a midrash on Psalm 119.123:

> *Mine eyes fail for Thy salvation, and for Thy promise of mercy* (Ps.119.123). What promise? The promise Thou didst make to Israel: *When thou walkest through the fire, thou shalt not be burned, neither shall the flame kindle upon thee* (Isa.43.2). Why not? *Because I am the Lord thy God, the Holy One of Israel, thy savior* (ibid. 43.3), and because I have said: *Therefore will I save My flock* (Ezek.34.22). Then save us as Thou hast promised: *Mine eyes fail while I wait for my God* (Ps.69.3). Wouldst Thou take delight in our good works? We have neither merit nor works. But deal mercifully with us, as is said *Deal with Thy servant according to Thy mercy* (Ps.119.124). The men of old whom Thou didst redeem, Thou didst redeem not because of their works. Thou didst deal mercifully with them and thus Thou didst redeem them. (Mid.Ps.119.55)

"His wage . . . what is due": cf. Lev.19.13, Mt.10.10, Lk.10.7, Rom.11.6, 13.8, 1 Cor.9.7-10, 2 Thess.3.7-10, 1 Tim.5.18.

The difficulty in the text lies in the meaning of "imputation." Paul understands that a person who "works" deserves (is owed) his "wage." A wage cannot be "reckoned as a favor" (i.e., "imputed") because it lacks the element of something freely given ("grace"):

> R. Eleazer said: Be eager to study the Torah; and know what answer thou shouldst give to the Epicurean, and know before Whom thou toilest, and Who is thine employer Who will pay thee the reward of thy labour. . . . R. Tarfon said: The day is short, and the work [to be performed] is much; and the workmen are indolent, but the reward

> is much; and the master of the house is insistent. He used to say: It is not [incumbent] upon thee to finish the work, but neither art thou a free man so as to [be entitled to] refrain therefrom; if thou hast studied much Torah, they [i.e., God] give thee much reward, and faithful is thine employer to pay thee the reward of thy labour; and know that the grant of reward unto the righteous is in the time to come. . . . He [R. Akiba] [also] used to say: Everything is given against a pledge, and a net is spread out over all the living; the store is open, and the storekeeper allows credit, but the ledger is open, and the hand writes, and whoever wishes to borrow may come and borrow; but the collectors go round regularly every day and exact dues from man, either with his consent or without his consent, and they have that on which they [can] rely [in their claims], seeing that the judgment is a righteous judgment, and everything is prepared for the banquet. (PA 2.14-16, 3.16)

Verse 5:

"The one who does not work . . . ": cf. 2 Thess.3.10; Mid.Ps.71.2, 72.1, 119.55.

Paul differentiates the "wages" which are earned from "work" from the "favor" which is given (by God) in reward for "faithfulness" to His promises, reflecting the rabbinic concept of the "merit of the fathers" in which the "reward" comes from the "merits" of the actions committed by previous generations. The Sages specifically associated such merit with Abraham, on the basis of Genesis 15.6:

> The sages say: For the sake of His name He acted thus towards them [Israel], as it is said: "For Mine own sake, for mine own sake will I do it" (Isa.48.11). And it is written: "That divided the water before them" (Isa.63.12). What for? "To make Thyself a glorious name" (ibid., 14). Rabbi says: "That faith with which they believed in Me is deserving that I should divide the sea for them." For it is said: "That they turn back and encamp," etc. (Ex.14.2). R. Eleazer the son of Azariah says: "For the sake of their father Abraham I will divide the sea for them," as it is said, "For He remembered His holy word unto Abraham His servant" (Ps.105.42). . . . Shema'yah says: "The faith with which their father Abraham believed in Me is deserving that I should divide the sea for them." For it is said: "And he believed the Lord" (Gen.15.6). (Mekh.Beshall.4)

The "ungodly" are those who have no "merit" of their own and possess no righteousness before God, yet God "reckons" (imputes) righteousness to them notwithstanding their lack of merit:

> To whom will you be good, O God, except to those who call upon the Lord? He will cleanse from sins the soul in confessing, in restoring, so that for all these things the shame is on us, and (it shows) on our faces. And whose sins will he forgive except those who have sinned? You bless the righteous, and do not accuse them for what they sinned. And your goodness is upon those that sin, when they repent. (Ps.Sol.9.6-7)

Verses 6-8:

"Just as David also speaks . . . ": cf. Ps.32.1-2.

Paul employs the classical rabbinic principle of גזרה שוה (*gezerah shavah*; verbal analogy) to resolve the meaning of ויחשבה (*vay-yachshevehah*), "and it was reckoned to him," in Genesis 15.6. The same verb is used in Psalm 32.1-2, and Paul transfers its meaning there to the verse in Genesis 15.6 by using the principle of verbal analogy. In Psalm 32.1-2, God's righteousness is explicitly given to those who have sinned, and who therefore do not "merit" (deserve) forgiveness. "Reckoning" therefore becomes God's gift of righteousness. The same method of verbal analogy links righteousness with "blessing" (cf. Ps.32.2), which Paul associates with Abraham's blessing (cf. Gen.12.3) (cf. also Gal.3.8-9).

Verse 9:

"Is this blessing . . . upon the uncircumcised also?": cf. Gen.15.6, 27.7ff, 27ff, 35ff, 39.5, 48.9, 15, 20, 49.1ff, Dt.11.27, 23.5, Job 29.13, Ps.32.1-2, Prov.10.22, 28.20, Mal.3.10, Rom.15.29.

Paul applies the "blessing" mentioned in Psalm 32.1-2 to Genesis 15.6. Since the blessing (righteousness) in Psalm 32 relates to the period after the giving of the Torah, however, Paul further asks concerning the basis on which the blessing is obtained. Does it belong only to Israel (the circumcised), or also to the Gentiles (who are not circumcised)? Abraham's blessing in Genesis 15.6 specifically speaks of the "nations of the world," which indicates that God's righteousness is not dependent upon the Torah, and that the Gentiles can also obtain righteousness through Abraham.

Verse 10:

"How then was it reckoned . . . "

Paul repeats the question of Abraham's righteousness, putting it in terms of Abraham's personal life. Did God "reckon" (consider) Abraham as a "Jew" (as circumcised) when He reckoned his faithfulness as righteousness; or did He consider him to be a Gentile (uncircumcised)? Historically, Abraham was uncircumcised, and he expressed his faithfulness to God in leaving Haran, his ancestral home and in believing that God would fulfil His promises concerning the giving of the Land and of the blessing of all nations in his seed who would be as numerous as the stars.

Verse 11:

"Sign of circumcision": cf. Gen.17.11; Jub.15.11f, Ps.-Philo 9.15.

Abraham demonstrated his faithfulness to God by obeying His command to leave his home. Paul describes his circumcision as both a "sign" and a "seal" of that faithfulness and trust in God's promises.

"A seal": cf. Jn.3.33, 6.27, 1 Cor.9.2, 2 Cor.1.22, Eph.1.13, 4.30, Col.2.11f, 2 Tim.2.19, Rev.7.3-8; Gen.R.48.2, PB, Birkhat ha-Mazon, p.969; Ep.Barn.9.6.

Circumcision was commonly regarded as the "seal" of the covenant Israel made with God on Mount Sinai (cf. Jub.15.31f, TBE p.124). In the earliest "apotropaic" understanding of circumcision, the rite was believed to possess the power to ward off evil, a belief reflected in the blessing recited during the circumcision ceremony until today, which states that Abraham was "sanctified in his mother's womb":

> Our Rabbis taught: He who circumcises must recite: ' . . . Who hast sanctified us with Thy commandments, and hast commanded us concerning circumcision.' The father of the infant recites, ' . . . Who has sanctified us with Thy commandments and has commanded us to lead him into the covenant of our father Abraham.' . . . And he who pronounces the benediction recites: ' . . . Who hast sanctified the beloved one from the womb; He set a statute in his flesh, and his offsprings he sealed with the sign of the holy covenant. (Shab.137b)[6]
>
> The phrase "sealed . . . for a covenant of sanctity" reflects the guarantee ("promise") of "righteousness." Paul uses the same motif as in the Prayer Book, and emphasizes that Abraham's blessing (his righteousness) is "sealed" by his circumcision.[7] Paul connects all three motifs, blessing (promise), faithfulness and the "pledge" of the Spirit, in Galatians 3.14: "In order that in Messiah Yeshua the blessing of Abraham might come to the Gentiles, so that we might receive the promise of the Spirit through faith."[8]

"That he might be the father of all . . . ": cf. Gen.17.4-5, 1 Chron.1.27, Isa.51.2; Sir.44.19, 2 Bar.78.4; Tanh.B.Lech Lecha 32a, ARN[a] 12, PBik.1.4, 64a, Shab.105a.

The biblical text makes explicit Abraham's fatherhood of the nations which are his descendants when God changes his name from "Abram" to "Abraham," as other rabbinic texts make clear:

> *Abram the same is Abraham* (1 Chron.1.27). At first he became a father to Aram [*Ab-Aram*] only, but in the end he became a father to the whole world [as it says, Behold I have made thee a father of a multitude of nations (Gen.17.5)]. (Ber.13a)[9]

" . . . without being circumcised"

Paul does not mean "all those who are faithful even though they are not circumcised." This was an attitude held by the so-called "Judaizers" within the early community (as well as the Pharisees), who insisted that the Gentile believers be circumcised and observe the Torah (cf. Acts 15.5, Gal.2.3, 12f). Paul, on the contrary, repeats the fact that Abraham is the father of "all who are faithful" because his righteousness was reckoned to him on account of his own faithfulness.[10] Circumcision, like uncircumcision, is the "seal" of a person's righteousness, which God "reckons" to him because of his faithfulness to God in Yeshua's death and resurrection, which fulfils God's promise to Abraham's "seed" (cf. Gal.3.16).

Verse 12:

"The father of circumcision . . . "

All the patriarchs, including Abraham, are referred to as "our father" (אבינו; *'avinu*) in rabbinic literature (cf. PA 5.3, 19). Paul first describes Abraham as "the father of all who are faithful . . . " (in relation to the Gentiles), and then as "the father of circumcision" (in relation to Israel). The phrase "father of circumcision" therefore does not only refer to Abraham's "inheritance" of circumcision as the sign of God's covenant with Israel (Abraham being the "forefather" of the nation of Israel), but also—and first of all—to his inheritance of righteousness on the basis of faithfulness, prior to his "conversion." The force of the "not only" ("to those who not only are of the circumcision, but who also follow . . . ") reads in three complementary directions: it includes the Gentiles who, not having the Torah may still observe its commandments "instinctively" (cf. 2.14); it demonstrates that Israel are not excluded from the promise of faithfulness, since Abraham was both circumcised and righteous because of his faithfulness; and yet as the "sons of Abraham" they must also possess his qualities and follow in his "steps of his faithfulness which he had while uncircumcised."

"Follow in the steps of": cf. 2 Cor.12.18, 1 Pet.2.21.

Paul picks up the metaphor suggested by Genesis 13.14-17, where God tells Abraham that he will make his descendants as innumerable as the dust of the earth, over which he is to "lift up your eyes . . . northward and southward and eastward and westward . . . Arise and walk about the land through its length and breadth; for I will give it to you." Those who "follow in Abraham's footsteps" follow in the steps in which he himself walked in obedience to God's voice (cf. Gen.22.18), and his circumcision "followed" his faithfulness:

> For from the beginning of our forefather Abraham's laying claim to the way of truth, you led (him) by a vision, having taught him what at any time this world is. And his faith traveled ahead of his knowledge, but the covenant was the follower of his faith. (Hell.Syn.Pray.2.14-15)

Verse 13:

"Promise to Abraham or to his descendants": cf. Gen.12.2-3, 7, 13.15-17, 17.1-8, 18.18, 22.17-18, Dt.1.8-11, 35, 4.31, Josh.23.4, Ps.105.8-11, 42, Lk.1.55, 73, Acts 2.39, 3.25, 26.6-7, Rom.9.4, 8, 15.8, Gal.3.16ff, 29, 4.28, Eph.2.12, 3.6, Heb.6.13-17, 7.6, 11.9ff; Sir.44.21, Jub.19.21, Odes Sol.31.13, Test.Mos.1.8-9, 3.9; Hell.Syn.Pray.12.67.

God promised Abraham that He would: establish His covenant with him and with his descendants, and "sealed" the promise with circumcision; that He would bless him and multiply him exceedingly, and make him the father of many nations, who would be blessed through him; that He would make him exceedingly fruitful and give him many offspring from whom kings would come forth; and that He would give him and his descendants the land of Canaan as an inheritance (see references). Although Paul uses the more unusual phrase "or to his descendants" instead of the more normal "and his descendants," he obviously means both Abraham and his descendants.

"Heir of the world": cf. Gen.12.1-3, 15.3-5, 17.2-8, 18.18, 22.17-18, Ex.32.13, Ps.37.11, Mt.5.5, 25.34, Lk.10.25, 1 Cor.6.9, 15.50, Heb.6.12, 11.8, 9, Rev.21.7; Sir.44.21, 4 Ez.6.59, Jub.17.3, 19.21, 22.14, 32.19, Ps.Sol.14.9-10, 1 En.5.7; ARN[b] 26, Pes.Rab.11; Philo, *Vit.Mos.*1.155.

Paul repeats the claim that the grounds of God's promise to Abraham are his faithfulness rather than circumcision, which "seals" what his faithfulness has already obtained for him. God's promise that Abraham would inherit the land became a central tenet in Jewish thought and history.[11] Some of the midrashim link possession and inheritance both with the creation of the world and with the world to come:

> WHEN THEY WERE CREATED—BEHIBBARAM. R. Joshua b. Karhah said: BEHIBBARAM is identical in lettering with *beabraham*: i.e., for the sake of Abraham, whom He was one day to raise up. R. 'Azariah quoted on this statement of R. Joshua b. Karhah's the verse: Thou art the Lord, even Thou alone; Thou hast made heaven [. . . the earth and all that is on it . . .] (Neh.9.6,7). . . . (Gen.R.12.9)[12]

> And a certain ruler questioned him, saying, "Good Teacher, what shall I do to inherit eternal life?" (Lk.18.18)

> R. Johanan said: Three are of those who will inherit the world to come, viz.: he who dwells in Eretz Israel; and he who brings up his sons to the study of Torah; and he who recites *habdalah* over wine over the termination of the Sabbath. (Pes.113a)

> Whosoever possesses these three things is of the disciples of Abraham, our father; and [whoever possesses] three other things, he is of the disciples of Balaam, the wicked. . . . What is [the difference] between the disciples of Abraham, our father, and the disciples of Balaam, the wicked? The disciples of Abraham, our father, enjoy [their share] in this world, and inherit the world to come . . . But the disciples of Balaam, the wicked, inherit Gehinnom and descend to the nethermost pit, as it is said: But Thou, O God, wilt bring them down to the nethermost pit; men of blood and deceit shall not live out half their days; but as for me, I will trust in Thee (Ps.55.23). (PA 5.19)

Verse 14:

"For if those who are of the Law are heirs . . . ": cf. Ps.37.11, Isa.60.21, Jer.49.1, Mt.5.5, 17, 19.29, Mk.10.17, Lk.18.18, Rom.3.3, 31, 7.2, Gal.3.17f, 29, 4.1, 7, 30, 5.4, Eph.3.6, Heb.6.17, 7.28, 11.7, 9, Jas.2.5, 1 Pet.3.7; 1QS 11.6-8; Odes Sol.31.13; PA 2.12, 3.14, 5.19, San.11.1, Pes.113a.

The phrase "those who are of the Law" refers to the people of Israel, with whom God has made a covenant (the Torah) and sealed it in circumcision.

In Aboth (the talmudic tractate called "The Sayings of the Fathers"), the idea of "inheritance" is directly linked to the motif of בני אברהם *(benei 'Avraham)* (cf. PA 5.19; see above).[13] According to this saying, and others like it, being part of the covenant community does not (automatically) make a person a true "son of Abraham." His actions must prove him worthy to inherit the world to come. Paul explains that if the Torah and circumcision are used as a "boast" (cf. 2.17, 3.27, 4.2,) this usage "nullifies" the promise and therefore the faithfulness according to which God "reckons" righteousness, an idea which a text in the (Christianized) Odes of Solomon also expresses:

> Come forth, you who have been afflicted, and receive joy. And possess yourselves through grace, and take unto you immortal life. And they condemned me when I stood up, me who had not been condemned. . . . And I [Christ] bore their bitterness because of humility; that I might save my nation and instruct it. And that I might not nullify the promises to the patriarchs, to whom I was promised for the salvation of their offspring. (Odes Sol.31.6-13)[14]

Verse 15:

"For the Law brings about wrath . . . ": cf. Num.1.53, 25.11, Dt.29.28, Rom.2.12, 25, 3.19-20, 5.13, 20, 7.7f, 1 Cor.15.56, Gal.3.19, 1 Tim.1.8-11; Shab.88b, Yoma 72b.

The Torah is based upon the principle of "reward and punishment," in that it not only establishes right and wrong (good and evil) but also determines the scheme according to which moral action is judged.[15] Where the motif of the "sons of Abraham" and the doctrine of the "Two Ways" converge, as here, "wrath" as the punishment wielded by the Torah, and "eternal life" as the righteousness bestowed upon faithfulness, symbolize the "Two Spirits" which rule in the world:

> From His wondrous Mysteries is the light in my heart, in the everlasting Being has my eye beheld Wisdom: because Knowledge is hidden from men and the counsel of Prudence from the sons of men. The fountain of righteousness, the reservoir of power, and the dwelling-place of glory are denied to the assembly of flesh; but God has given them as an everlasting possession {inheritance} to those whom He has chosen. . . . As for me, I belong to wicked humanity, to the assembly of perverse flesh . . . And as for the Visitation of all who walk in this (Spirit), it consists of an abundance of blows administered by all the Angels of destruction in the everlasting Pit

> by the furious wrath of the God of vengeance, of unending dread and shame without end. . . . (1QS 11.5-9, 4.11-13)

"No law, neither is there violation": cf. 2.12, 25, 3.19, 5.13, 7.7f.

Paul indicates that God's promises cannot be based on the Torah, since where this is law there also exists punishment for its violation. This negates the promise of righteousness and eternal life.[16] Moreover, Paul knows that God's commands may "cause" people to violate His ordinances because of their prohibitions:

> The evil inclination desires only that which is forbidden. R. Mena [on the Day of Atonement] went to visit R. Haggai who was ill. R. Haggai said, "I am thirsty." R. Mena said, "Drink." Then he left him. After an hour he came again, and said, "How about your thirst?" He said, "No sooner had you permitted me to drink than the desire left me." (PYoma 6.4, 43d)[17]

Verse 16:

"For this reason"

Paul recapitulates and sums up the argument of verses 1-15. Righteousness is "reckoned" according to a person's faithfulness, since this demonstrates God's free gift of righteousness to all men, "apart from" circumcision which (only) "sealed" Abraham's faithfulness and from the Torah, which "witnesses" God's "blessing" of the nations through Abraham's faithfulness. The promise of righteousness is therefore made "certain to all" those who are faithful, Jews and Gentiles equally.

Verse 17:

" . . . God, who gives life to the dead . . . ": cf. Gen.22.17, Dt.32.39, 1 Sam.2.6, 2 Kings 4.32-34, Ps.30.3, Isa.26.19 (LXX), 43.1, 7, 15, 44.2, 21, 48.13, Ezek.37.1-10, Hos.1.10, 2.23, 6.2, Mt.9.25, Mk.5.42, Lk.7.15, 8.55, Jn.11.44, Acts 23.6, 26.8, Rom.9.25-26, 1 Cor.1.28, Eph.2.12, 1 Pet.2.10; 1QH 3.19-24; 2 Bar.21.4, 48.8, Sib.Or.1.355, 2.221-24, 4.182; Mekh.Amalek 1, PB p.133, p.135, p.1077.

In this verse, Paul summarizes his whole argument concerning God's "election" also of the Gentiles, by linking God's choice of Abraham as the "father of many nations" in whom they will all be "blessed" with the "creation" of the Gentiles (cf. Hos.1.10). God calls the Gentiles "into being" (those who were once "not-My-people") by making them part of the "commonwealth" of Israel, His people, chosen with His name.[18]

Verse 18:

"In hope against hope": cf. Gen.15.5, 17.17, Ps.31.24, 71.5, Rom.5.5, 8.24f, 1 Cor.13.13, Gal.5.5, Col.1.5, 1 Thess.5.8, Heb.6.19, 11.1, 1 Pet.3.15.

Abraham's hope was to be the "father of many nations," and it was both founded on and fulfilled in God's promise. His hope that his physical impotence could be overcome and made "fruitful" is paralleled by the "hopelessness" of the Gentiles who are "not-My-people," "strangers to the covenants of promise, having no hope and without God in the world" (cf. Eph.2.12).

Verse 19:

"Weak in faith": cf. Mt.6.30, 8.26, 14.31, 17.20, Mk.6.6, 16.14, Lk.12.28, Rom.3.3, 14.1-2, 15.1, 1 Cor.8.9; Tanh.Beshall.20, Sifre Dt.He'azinu 330, Sot.48b, Ber.24b.

Abraham's physical weakness did not limit his faithfulness to God. His faithfulness was not to his flesh but to God's promises. The Rabbis often characterized people who only trust in what they see as "small in faith" (קטני אמונה; *ketanei 'emunah*) and having little "hope" (cf. Heb.11.1) in God's creative power and provision:

> "A day's portion every day" (Ex.16.4). He who created the day created the substance thereof. R. Eleazar of Modi'im said: If a man has food for the day, but says, "What shall I eat tomorrow?" such a one is deficient in faith. R. Eliezer the Great said: He who yet has bread in his basket, and says, "What shall I eat tomorrow?" belongs to those who are small in faith. (Tanh.Beshall.20)

In the same way, Paul says, both Jews and Gentiles ought to respect God's promises that He will include "all flesh" in His salvation.[19]

"As good as dead": cf. Gen.17.17, 18.11f, Heb.11.12.

Although Abraham's body was "weak," he still hoped to receive God's promised offspring. His physical infirmity corresponds to the "non-existence" of a (Gentile) people who were once "not My-people" but whom God has promised to "call into being" (cf. Hos.1.10, 2.23).

Verse 20:

"Grew strong in faith": cf. Gen.21.8 (Isaac), Ps.27.14, 31.24, Lk.1.80, 2.40, 52, 1 Cor.16.13, Eph.3.16.

The source of Abraham's hope was his faithfulness to the promises of the God "who gives life to the dead and calls into being that which does not exist" (verse 17).

"Giving glory to God": cf. Mt.5.16, 9.8, 15.31, Lk.17.15, 18, Jn.9.24, 15.8, Acts 4.21, 11.18, 21.20, Rom.15.9, 2 Cor.9.13, Gal.1.24.
To "give glory" to God acknowledges His sovereignty (cf. 1.21-23), just as Paul claims that the Gentiles refuse to do when they do not honor Him or give Him thanks, but exchange His truth for their own speculations (cf. 1.18ff). It also expresses a person's "hope" in God's ability to provide what is lacking, to cleanse man from his "spirit of flesh," and to "create" out of nothing that which will inherit eternal life:

> I give Thee thanks, O Adonai, for Thou hast redeemed my soul from the Pit and from Sheol of Abaddon Thou hast made me rise to everlasting heights, and I have walked in an infinite plain! And I knew there was hope for him whom Thou hast shaped from the dust for the everlasting assembly. Thou hast cleansed the perverse spirit from great sin that he might watch with the army of the Saints and enter into communion with the congregation of the Sons of Heaven. And Thou hast cast an everlasting destiny for man in the company of the Spirits of Knowledge, that he might praise Thy name in joy[ful] concord and recount Thy marvels before all Thy works . . . they shall recount Thy glory in all Thy dominion. For Thou hast caused them to see what they had not known [by bringing to an end the] former [things] and by creating things that are new. . . . (1QH 3.19-23, 13.11-12)

Verse 21:
"Fully assured": cf. 14.5, Heb.3.14, 11.1.
Faithfulness is bound to knowledge through trust and hope:

> *The Lord preserveth those who affirm the faith* (Ps.31.23)—that is, preserves even those sinners in Israel who reluctantly yet regularly say "Blessed art Thou, O Lord, who quickenest the dead. . . . Another comment: *The Lord preserveth those who affirm the faith*—that is, preserves children of Israel who say "Blessed art Thou, O Lord, who quickenest the dead," although the quickening of the dead has not yet come to pass; who say, "Blessed art Thou, O Lord, Redeemer of Israel," although they have not yet been redeemed; and who say, "Blessed art Thou, O Lord, who rebuildest Jerusalem," although Jerusalem has not yet been rebuilt. Of them, the Holy One, blessed be He, declares: "Only for a little time were the children of Israel redeemed, and then again they were enslaved, but still they affirm their faith in Me, that I shall redeem them." (Mid.Ps.31.8)

"Able also to perform"

God's great power is to raise from the dead, to create something out of what had previously not existed—both in cleansing man from his sin and making him a "new creation," and in making a new people from those who had once been "not-My-people":

> A child [of R. Hiyyah, the son of Abba] died. The first day he [Resh Lakish] did not go to him. The next day he took with him Judah the son of Nahmani, his *meturgeman*, [and] said to him [Judah the son of Nahmani]: Rise [and] say something with regard to the death of the child . . . He [Resh Lakish] [then] said to him: Rise [and] say something with regard to the praise [glory] of the Holy One, blessed be He. He spoke and said: The God, who is great in the abundance of His greatness, mighty and strong in the multitude of awe-inspiring deeds, who reviveth the dead with his word, who does great things that are unsearchable and wondrous works without number. Blessed art Thou, O Lord, who revivest the dead. (Ket.8b)[20]

Verses 23-24:

"Not for his sake only was it written . . . ": cf. 15.4, 1 Cor.9.9f, 10.6, 11, 2 Tim.3.16, 1 Pet.1.10-12.

God did not write His promise only for the sake of Abraham, just as He did not give the Torah only to those who received it on Mount Sinai. His promise was for all the future generations of Israel, and for all the descendants of Abraham in whose seed they would be blessed:

> "On this day Israel came to Mount Sinai" (Ex.19.1). Why on this day? Because, when thou learnest Torah, let not its commands seem old to thee, but regard them as though the Torah were given this day. Hence, it says, 'On this day', and not, 'On that day' . . . [A]ccording to R. Eleazer, matters of Torah should not look to you like an antiquated decree, but like a decree freshly issued which all rush to read. With regard to looking upon matters of Torah as though they had just been decreed, Scripture says, "This day the Lord thy God commanded thee to do" (Dt.26.16). (Tanh.B.Yitro 13, PRK 12.5)[21]

Those who "believe in Him who raised Yeshua our Lord from the dead" make themselves part of those to whom God "reckons" righteousness, in a way similar, in reverse, to that in which the "wicked son" excludes himself from Israel's deliverance from Egypt according to the Passover *Haggadah*:

> The wicked son asks: "What is this service to you?" To you and not to him! And because he has excluded himself from the community, he has disowned the essentials. And you shall blunt his teeth and say to him: "Because of this, the Eternal did to me when I came forth from Egypt!" For me and not for him. If he had been there, he would not have been redeemed. (Passover *Haggadah*; cf. Mekh.Nezikin [Bo]18)

Verse 24:

"Him who raised Yeshua . . . ": cf. Acts 2.24, Rom.4.25, 10.9, 1 Cor.15.13-17, Heb.13.20.

The power (cf. 1.16) with which God creates something out of nothing provides Abraham with an offspring beyond his physical capability, and which also creates the Gentiles out of "not-My people," is the same power with which He gives life to the dead and raised Yeshua to life. Yeshua is "the Lord our righteousness," in whom righteousness is "reckoned" to all who are faithful to him, and whose power to bestow righteousness is guaranteed by God's ability to create, elect, and draw all people to Himself.

Verse 25:

"Delivered up": cf. Isa.53.5, 12, Mt.20.18-19, Mk.10.33, Rom.5.6, 8, 8.32, 1 Cor.15.3, Eph.5.2.

Paul concludes this section of his letter with a traditional liturgical phrase, which functions almost as a benediction (cf. also 1 Cor.11.23f). The phrase "because of" our transgressions means "on account of" them, although Paul has already warned that man's unrighteousness cannot "justify" God's grace (cf. 3.5f):

> As for me, I belong to wicked humanity, to the assembly of perverse flesh; my iniquities and rebellion and sin together with the iniquity of my heart (belong to) the assembly doomed to worms, (the assembly) of men who walk in darkness. For is man master of his way? No, men cannot establish their steps, for their justification belongs to God, and from His hand comes perfection of way. By His understanding all things are brought into being, by His thought every being established, and without Him nothing is made. . . . He has caused me to approach by His Mercy and by His favours He will

bring my justification. He has justified me by His true justice and by His immense goodness He will pardon all my iniquities. And by His justice He will cleanse me of the defilement of man and of the sins of the sons of men, that I may acknowledge His true righteousness unto God and His majesty unto the Most High. (1QS 11.9-15)

"Raised because of our justification": cf. Rom.5.16, 18, 8.1, 33; 1QS 11.2-5, 10, 13-15.

The clause "because of" is a variation on the expression "for the sake of" (cf. verses 23-24) or "in order that we might be justified." God "imputed" righteousness to Abraham "because of" his faithfulness, "so that" (cf. Gal.3.14) the Gentiles, who were without hope and without God in the world (cf. Eph.2.12), might also be "raised" to the righteousness of eternal life according to the same faithfulness. Yeshua is the first-born among these many brethren who are raised from the dead and "called into being" (cf. 1 Cor.15.20, 23, Col.1.18). The Messiah was thus delivered up and raised from the dead by the Father in order to obtain the justification of all those, Jew and Gentile, who are faithful to Yeshua's faithfulness to God.

Endnotes on Chapter 4

1 For this technical formula, which Paul frequently uses, see the comments on 3.3, as well as the extended discussion on 9.30f.

2 Cf. the interesting midrash on 1 Sam.2.8, which interprets the patriarchs as the "pillars" or "rocks" on which God built the world: "Thus it is written: *For from the tops of the rocks I see him* (Num.23.9) -this refers to the patriarchs, for . . . We find that God long desired to establish the world, but found no suitable means of doing so before the patriarchs arose. . . . When the patriarchs arose and showed themselves righteous, God said: 'On these will I establish My world'; as it says: *For the pillars of the earth are the Lord's, and He hath set the world upon them*[. *He will keep the feet of His holy ones.*] (1 Sam.2.8)" (Ex.R.15.7); cf. also Yalkut 766. (The "holy ones" are synonymous with the "pillars, and the "pillars" with the "rocks" in Num.23.9 [cf. Ex.R.17.3]). Several passages in the New Testament reflect this idea, including Yeshua's designation of Peter as the "rock" (*petra/Petros*; *Keifas*) upon whom he will build his church (cf. Mt.6.18, Jn.1.42), as well as John the Baptist's wordplay on stones and sons (אבנים; *'avanim*, and בנים; *banim*; cf. Mt.3.9), which is directly

connected to the theme of the "sons of Abraham" which Paul uses in 2.25f and further develops throughout the letter.

3 The motif of "obtaining" is directly linked to God's "creation" also of the Gentiles as His people, the theme around which Paul builds chapter 4; cf. Hos.2.23, Rom.11.7, 30, 1 Pet.2.10.

4 The Hebrew root for "faith" (אמונה; *'emunah*) normally means "faithfulness" or "trust," not doctrinal "belief;" see the comments on 3.22. For the doctrine of merit, see S. Schecter, *Aspects of Rabbinic Theology* (NY: Schocken, 1961), 170-198.

5 The next verse (Jer.9.25) directly addresses the issue of physical and "spiritual" circumcision; see also the comments on 3.19-20 and 25f.

6 Cf. Tos.Ber.6.13, PBer.9.4. The infant is named "the beloved one" after Abraham according to the *Tosafot* (medieval Jewish commentators), although the appellation is normally attributed to Isaac (cf. Gen.22.2). The blessing is early, since it appears here in the *Gemara* as a *baraitha*, a *tannaitic* saying ("Our Rabbis taught"), as well as in the *Tosefta*. The "apotropaic" belief that circumcision "wards off" evil is also reflected in the sentence which follows: "Therefore . . . give command to save the beloved of our flesh from the pit . . .". See D. Flusser, "Who Sanctified the Beloved in the Womb," *Immanuel* 11 (1980), 46-55. For the various other meanings of the word "seal," see the comments on 15.28.

7 See the lists of biblical figures whom the Sages claimed were born circumcised as a "sign" and a "seal" of their righteousness, which they possessed before they were even born; cf. ARN[a] 2, Gen.R.43.6, Eccl.R.9.2.1, Sot.12a. The term "sign" is applied to both circumcision and baptism in intertestamental literature and in the New Testament; cf. Odes Sol.11.1-3, 2 Cor.1.22, 5.5, Eph.1.13-14, 4.30, Col.2.11f.

8 See also the comments on 8.23.

9 The Hebrew terms for "father" and "son" both carry many of the same "categorical" connotations. בן (*ben*; son) not merely designates a familial relationship, but also reflects a common classification. People who possess similar characteristics are . . . בני (*benei* . . .), sons of . . .; cf. Benei Noach (the sons of Noah). For the motif of the "sons of Abraham," see the comments on 2.25f and 9.7f.

10 Similarly, the phrase "without being circumcised" does not exclude those who are circumcised (Israel).

11 Cf. Dt.1.8, 38, 4.1, 26, 38, 7.1-8.1, Neh.1.5-10, Ps.44.1-4, 105.8-11, Isa.2.1-4, 60.1ff, 62.4f, 66.20f, Jer.27.22, 29.14, Zech.14.9-19, (Rom.11.29).

12 This midrash plays on the fact that in Hebrew both words contain the same letters, though in different order: בהבראם (when they were created)

and באברהם (*be-'avraham*; lit. 'for Abraham'). Paul also plays on the dual meaning of עולם (*'olam*), "world," which also meant "eternity" in Second Temple Jewish thought. The phrase "to inherit the world" thus referred to inheriting eternity—the world to come; cf. TBE p.69, p.126.

13 The phrase בני תורה (*benei Torah*), the "sons of Torah," parallels בני אמונה (*benei 'emunah*), "sons of faithfulness."

14 Paul demonstrates in 3.30-31 that the reverse is not true, however: "faithfulness" does not "nullify" the Torah but "establishes" it, since the Torah confirms God's command of faithfulness. According to this argument, the Torah cannot be the source of God's righteousness if it excludes the Gentiles (although in the broad sense the Torah [the Tanakh] itself promises that God will also "elect" them). Paul does not mention this here, however, but chooses to emphasize the fact that the Torah "brings about wrath."

15 See the comments on 3.19-20 and 25f.

16 It is not textually justifiable to interpret νομος (*nomos*; law) here as "law in general" rather than the Torah. Paul's argument rests upon the relationship between Abraham as the person with whom God made a covenant sealed by circumcision, and as the person who "obeyed God's voice" in faithfulness.

17 Paul develops this theme in 7.7ff.

18 Paul picks up, develops, and elaborates on this theme throughout the whole letter.

19 Paul returns to this theme in chapter 14, where he describes the person who is "weak in faith" as someone who is unable to think that God can take care of Himself, as it were, and therefore feels that he must obey God's commandments to the "letter" (cf. 2.29) instead of possessing the confidence to stand (cf. 5.2) before Him according to his own convictions. Chapter 14 is thus a practical outcome of chapter 4. Here Paul demonstrates that "hope" makes both Jews and Gentiles equal before God; in chapter 14 the distinction between "weak" and "strong" faith is not divided between Jew and Gentile but according to the principle of "sanctifying" God's commandments by holding to one's understanding of their "spirit," enabling acceptance and respect for the divergent views of one's brethren.

20 The Talmudic section deals with mourning, and contains several phrases from the evening service prayer, as well as recalling the benedictions of the *Amidah* prayer. In the *Aleinu* prayer, all the nations are said finally to acknowledge God's sovereignty, bowing their knee, swearing allegiance with their tongue, and thus accepting the yoke of God's kingdom (PB, p. 210).

21 Cf. Sifre Dt.Va'etchanan 33. All future generations are said to have been present at Sinai, and those present pledged themselves for the conduct of future generation (cf. Tanh.Yitro 11); cf. also the "merit of the children" as well as of the fathers (cf. Lev.R.36.4, Tanh.Vayigash 2).

ROMANS 5

Introduction

Paul draws the implications of God's imputation of righteousness to man on the basis of faithfulness. Israel's election is not endangered by tribulation (verses 2-5) because it is based on God's grace (verses 6-11). He appeals to a קל וחומר *(kal ve-chomer)* or *a fortiori* argument (if this, how much more that . . .) throughout the chapter, based on the analogy of the two Adams. In verses 12-14, he discusses the relation between sin, death, and the Torah, in order to demonstrate that God's grace is given freely to all mankind: Israel may be redeemed from their sins because God's grace overcomes transgressions against the Torah; and therefore the Gentiles can also be redeemed from their sins, even though sin is determined through the Torah. Paul then develops these motifs more fully in chapter 8.

Verse 1:

"Therefore . . . by faith": cf. 3.24; Jub.5.12.

Paul begins to develop the theme of God's "imputing righteousness" to Abraham on the basis of Abraham's faithfulness to God's promises. God gives His righteousness as a gift to "every man," both Jew and Gentile, thereby justifying them "apart from" the Torah in Yeshua, "the Lord our righteousness" (cf. Jer.23.6, Rom.3.21-22).

"We have peace": cf. Ex.24.5-11, Num.6.26, 25.12, Dt.27.1-8, 2 Chron.33.16, Ps.85.10, Prov.3.17, Isa.27.5, 32.17, 48.22, 52.7, 54.10, 57.2, 19, Ezek.34.25, 37.26, 45.15, Jn.14.27, Rom.5.16, 8.1, Eph.2.14, 6.15, Col.3.15, 1 Jn.3.21; Test.Asher 6.4-6, Jub.25.20, 1 En.1.8, 58.4, Wis.Sol.4.15; Tanh.Yitro 17, Pes.Rab.50, Lev.R.9.9, Num.R.21.1, PB pp.155-57.

Paul understands "peace" as being the direct result of "justification." Since justification is God's free gift of righteousness to man, even when he does not acknowledge, honor, or give thanks to God (cf. 1.21), peace corresponds to righteousness in the sense of reconciliation.[1] Paul thus returns to the theme of 3.23-26, where he identifies Yeshua as the scapegoat (השעיר לעזאזל; *ha-sa'ir la-'aza'zel*) which was sacrificed on the Day of Atonement to atone for the sins of the people of Israel and the High Priest (cf. Lev.16.5-34), and the כפרת (*kaporet*) or "mercy seat" (cf. Ex.25.17ff). The biblical "peace-offering" (שלמים; *shelamim*) was a general offering, not peculiar to the service of the Day of Atonement, but peace-offerings also importantly accompanied the people's renewal of the covenant.[2] The purpose of all the sacrifices was to make atonement (להשלים; *le-hashlim*; lit. "to make peace") between man and God.[3] "Peace" as "righteousness" therefore relates to the "reconciliation" (at-one-ment) between God and man, as numerous Jewish documents of the period illustrate:

> Behold, Thou hast undertaken to fi[ll Thy servant] with grace and hast favoured me with Thy Spirit of mercy and with the [brightness] of Thy glory. Thine, Thine, is righteousness! . . . And I know that none is righteous beside Thee; and I have appeased Thy face because of the Spirit which Thou hast put [in me] to accomplish [להשלים] Thy [fav]ours towards [Thy] servant for [ever] by cleansing me by Thy holy Spirit and by causing me to go forward in Thy will according to the greatness of Thy favours. . . . [. . . for Thou art . . .] and merciful, lo[ng-suffer]ing [and rich] in grace and truth, who pardonest the sin [. . .] and compassionate towards [all the sons of righteousness], [they that love Thee] and keep [Thy] command[ments] [and] are converted to Thee with faith and a perfect heart [. . .] to serve Thee [and to do what is] good in Thine eyes. (1QH 16.8-18)

Paul emphasizes, however, that it is Yeshua's death and resurrection which effects atonement between God and those who are "faithful" to him in baptism, an act which was also attributed to the Messiah in certain Jewish texts:

> R. Joshua said: Great is peace, for the name of the Holy One, blessed be He, is called 'peace', as it is stated, *And he called it* [*the altar erected by Gideon*] *'Adonai-shalom'*. R. Hiyya b. Abba said: Hence it can be deduced that a person may not extend a greeting of peace to his fellow in a place of filth, because it is stated, *And Gideon built an altar there unto the Lord and called it 'Adonai-shalom'*. Now if an altar which does not eat, drink or smell and was erected only to make atonement for [the sins of] Israel is called 'peace', he who loves peace and pursues peace, who welcomes people with the greeting of peace

> and responds with peace, and who maintains peace between Israel and their Father in heaven, how much more so! R. Jose the Galilean said: Even the name is called 'peace', [as it is stated,] *And his name is called . . . Abi-ad-sar-shalom.* (Perek HaShalom 59b)[4]

Verse 2:

"Obtained our introduction": cf. Eph.2.18, 3.12, Heb.6.19-20, 9.6ff, 10.19f; 1QS 11.13f.

The Greek verb προσαγω (*prosago*), "to bring near," translated here as "to obtain an introduction," corresponds to two Hebrew roots: קרב (*karav*), "to offer" (which covers a range of sacrificial functions); and בוא (*bo'*), "to come."[5] The believer is given access to God's presence in the Holy of Holies "through the veil" (cf. Lev.16.2, Heb.6.19-20) and through Yeshua's blood which "seals" God's "new covenant" with man:

> He has caused me to approach [הגישני] by His mercy and by His favours He will bring my justification [משפטי]. He has justified me by His true justice and by His immense goodness He will pardon [יכפר] all my iniquities. And by His justice He will cleanse me of the defilement of man and of the sin of the sons of men, that I may acknowledge His righteousness unto God and His majesty unto the Most High. (1QS 11.13-15)[6]

"Into this grace . . . stand": cf. Prov.3.18, 4.4f, Isa.56.4, 6, Jn.1.16, Rom.1.5, 11.20, 1 Cor.15.1, 2 Cor.9.8, 12.9, 14.4, Eph.1.6, 3.2, 7, Heb.4.16, 1 Pet.5.12; 1QH 5.22, 7.20; Mekh.Shirata 9, PPe'ah 1.1, 16b, Mid.Ps.71.2, 72.1, 119.55, Gen.R.60.2, Dt.R.2.1.

Paul knows, as did the Sages of his time, that God is the only source of grace, mercy, compassion, and lovingkindness [חסד; *chesed*]:

> Wouldst Thou take delight in our good works? We have neither merit nor works, as is said, *Deal with Thy servant according to Thy mercy* [חסד] (Ps.119.124). The men of old whom Thou didst redeem, Thou didst redeem not because of their works. Thou didst deal mercifully with them and thus didst Thou redeem them. Even as Thou didst deal with the men of old, deal Thou with us. (Mid.Ps.119.55)

> For no man is just in Thy ju[dg]ment nor [innocent in] Thy trial. Can human born of human be righteous, and can man born of man have understanding? And can flesh born of the gui[lty] inclination

> be glorious, and can spirit born of spirit be mighty? Truly, nothing is strong like Thy strength and Thy glory is [price]less and Thy wisdom is measureless. . . . And it is because of Thee that I [. . .] [and because of Thy grace that] I stand. . . . (1QH 9.14-19)

For Paul, however, God's grace is specifically expressed (cf. "this grace") in Yeshua, who is the personification of God's "grace," and the free gift of His righteousness (cf. Jer.23.6; Rom.3.21, 5.15-21) to man in his faithfulness to God (cf. 3.22).[7]

"Exult in hope of the glory of God": cf. Rom.3.23, 4.18, 8.18, 24, 30, 12.12, 15.13, 1 Cor.13.13, 2 Cor.3.12, Gal.5.5, Eph.1.12, 4.4, Col.1.27, 1 Thess.2.19, 1 Tim.1.1, 4.10, Tit.2.13, 3.7, Heb.6.19, 11.1, 1 Pet.1.3; 1QH 6.12, 7.24, 8.5, 11.9-14, 26, 10.12, 27f.

Paul returns to the theme of glory (cf. 3.23) and hope (cf. 4.18f), both of which play an important part in the letter as a whole.[8] The "hope" is for "access" to God (for the Gentiles; cf. Eph.2.12f) so that the "glory" of God might be seen in the Messiah (cf. 3.23) by both Jews and Gentiles, according to God's promise of righteousness on the basis of faithfulness, as the Qumran community also understood:

> Thy mercy is obtained by all the sons of Thy loving-kindness; for Thou hast made known to them Thy secret of truth and given them understanding of all Thy marvellous Mysteries. And Thou hast cleansed man of sin because of Thy glory that he may be made holy for Thee from all unclean abomination and from (every) transgression of unfaithfulness, that he may be joined wi[th] Thy sons of truth and with the lot of Thy Saints; that this vermin that is man may be raised from the dust to [Thy] secret [of truth] and from the spirit of perversity to [Thine] understanding; and that he may watch before Thee with the everlasting host and together with [Thy] spirits [of holiness], that he may be renewed with all [that is] [and] shall be and with them that know, in a common rejoicing. (1QH 11.9-14)

Verse 3:

"Not only this . . . ": cf. Mt.5.12, Rom.11, 8.23, 2 Cor.4.17, 12.12.9, 2 Tim.3.12, Jas.1.2-4, 1 Pet.1.6, 2.21, Rev.1.9; PA 2.7; Did.3.1-10.

Paul understands that "tribulation" and "suffering" are not necessarily a sign of God's displeasure but may also be a sign of His care. "Exultation" is not only related to receiving God's righteousness as an undeserved and free gift, but it also belongs to "tribulation," since suffering and difficulties can be used in order to test and prove one's character.[9] Tribulations "create" the same hope which is the inheritance of "eternal life" (cf. 4.13f), according to several rabbinic texts:

> Furthermore, one should rejoice more in chastisement than in prosperity. For if one is prosperous all his life, no sin of his will be forgiven. What brings him forgiveness of sins: Suffering. R. Eliezer ben Jacob says: Scripture says, *For whom the Lord loveth He correcteth, even as a father the son in whom he delighteth* (Prov.3.12). What causes the son to be delighted in by his father? Suffering. R. Meir says, Scripture says, *And thou shalt consider in thy heart, that as a man chastens his son, so the Lord, thy God, chasteneth thee* (Dt.8.5). You and your heart know the deeds that you have committed, and that whatever sufferings I have brought upon you do not outweigh your deeds. R. Jose b. Judah says: Precious are chastisements, for the name of the Omnipresent One rests upon him who suffers them. (Sifre Dt.32)

> R. Phineas b. Yair says: Heedfulness leads to cleanliness, and cleanliness leads to purity, and purity leads to humility, and humility leads to the shunning of sin, and the shunning of sin leads to saintliness, and saintliness leads to [the gift of] the Holy Spirit, and the Holy Spirit leads to the resurrection of the dead. And the resurrection of the dead shall come through Elijah of blessed memory. Amen. (Sot.9.15)[10]

Paul's specific reference to "us" ("we [or: let us] exult in our tribulations") seems to reflect an actual situation, in which the early community was oppressed and persecuted, rather than simply being a "theological" argument. Yeshua himself predicted the oppression that the early believers would undergo (cf. Mt.10.16-23). The early communities suffered persecution and tribulation from both Jewish and Roman sources, from the Jewish community because of their acceptance of Yeshua; and from the Roman authorities because in the early years, although both Jews and Christians were accused of withdrawal from the surrounding pagan societies and yet at the beginning shared Roman legal protection, Christianity was also considered to be an evil and "deadly superstition" by the Roman aristocracy, paradoxically regarded as an atheist movement which broke up the order of society by abandoning the traditional gods, and refused to help fight the enemies of the Empire. It thus gradually lost its protected status. Tacitus' account of Nero's persecution is the first record of official Roman persecution, which was local and sporadic until 250 C.E., when Decius' *supplicatio*, which compelled all residents of the empire to sacrifice to the Roman pantheon, turned Christianity into a proscribed religion.[11]

"Perseverance": cf. Mt.10.22, 24.13, Rom.2.7, 12.12, 2 Cor.12.9, Heb.6.11, 10.32f, 1 Pet.1.6; Test.Jos.10.1-3, 4 Macc.17.12-18.

Paul, like Phineas b. Yair in Sotah 9.15, associates perseverance (in doing good) with God's kindness which leads to repentance and righteousness (cf. 2.7). Perseverance expresses a form of endurance, and thus also of faithfulness and hope (towards which it leads), in "unpromising" situations.

Verse 4:

"Proven character": cf. Isa.48.10, Jer.9.7, 11.20, 17.10, Rom.12.2, 14.18, 16.10, 1 Cor.16.3, 2 Cor.8.22, 9.13, Heb.3.9, Jas.1.2, 1 Pet.1.6; Test.Jos.10.1-3.

The Greek term δοκιμη (*dokime*), "proven character," comes from the verb δοκιμαζω (*dokimadzo*), "to try" or "to judge," which refers to testing something with the expectation of discovering its worth.[12] God "tries the kidneys and the heart" in order to "refine" the character of those who are faithful to Him (cf. Ps.7.9, Jer.17.10, Rom.8.27).[13] Their deeds and actions both "prove" His will (cf. 3.3f, 12.2) and are "approved" by and "acceptable" to God (cf. 14.18). This verse reflects a chain of character traits very close to Phineas b. Yair's saying in Sotah 9.15 (cf. also 2 Pet.1.5-7), indicating that "character" in Second Temple Judaism was frequently described in terms of a "step-ladder," with one trait developing another, higher trait. Character is therefore not perceived biologically or genetically, but as something which may be controlled and improved through God's spirit. The early believers, like the community at Qumran, understood themselves to be those who "keep the Covenant and seek (cf. δοκιμαζοντες; *dokimadzontes*) God's will" in terms of having been "tested" and themselves being the "testing-stone" of Isaiah 28.16 (cf. 1 Pet.2.6f):

> In the Council of the Community (there shall be) twelve men and three priests, perfect in all that is revealed of all the Law, to practice truth, righteousness, justice, loving charity, and modesty one towards the other, to guard the faith upon earth with a firm inclination and a contrite spirit, and to expiate iniquity among those that practice justice and undergo distress of affliction, and to behave towards all

men according to the measure of truth and the norm of the time. When these things come to pass in Israel, the Council of the Community shall be established in truth as an everlasting planting . . . appointed to offer expiation for the earth and to bring down punishment upon the wicked. It is the tried wall, the precious corner-stone; its foundations shall not tremble nor flee from their place. . . . [*But the righteous will live by his faith* (Hab.2.4).] The explanation of this concerns all those who observe the Law in the House of Judah. God will deliver them from the house of Judgment because of their affliction and their faith in the Teacher of Righteousness. (1QS 8.1-8, 1QpHab 8.1-2; cf. 5.2-6, CDC 7.5-6, 4QpPs.37 1.4-10)

Verse 5:

"Hope does not disappoint": cf. Ps. 22.6, 25.20, 119.116, Isa.28.16, Hab.2.3, Rom.9.32-33, 10.11, Heb.6.18, 1 Pet.2.6-12; 1QpHab 7.9-14.

Paul notes that hope, being the completion of the "chain" of character traits, brings to fruition the process which begins with tribulation. He affirms that "affliction" and "faithfulness" play a major role in the deliverance of the community from God's judgment. These concepts were also used by the Qumran community, which described itself as "a tried wall," the precious "corner-stone" (cf. Isa.28.16). Paul and Peter both share this tradition, and the New Testament applies the biblical passages common to this tradition to Yeshua, who is the "corner-stone" and the "testing-stone" (Ps.118.22, Isa.26.18, 1 Cor.1.23), through whom "expiation" (cf. 3.25) is offered for the "earth," and faithfulness towards whom brings deliverance and salvation for all mankind.[14] Just as the Messiah is "the Lord our righteousness" (cf. Jer.23.6, 1 Cor.1.30), the "glory of God" (cf. 3.23), God's "power" (and wisdom) (cf. Rom.1.16, 1 Cor.1.24), "sanctification and redemption" (cf. 1 Cor.1.30), so he is also "our hope" for salvation (cf. 1 Tim.1.1).

"Because the love of God . . . Spirit": cf. Ps.141.8, Isa.32.15, 44.3, 53.12, Jer.31.31, Joel 2.28-32, Zech.12.10, Jn.3.16, 16.7, Acts 2.17, 38, 10.45, 1 Cor.13.13, 2 Cor.1.22, 5.5, Eph.2.4, 7-8, 5.25-26, Tit.3.4-7, 1 Pet.1.3-9, 3.21, 1 Jn.3.1, 4.7ff; 1QS 3.5-9, 4.1ff, 21, 1QH 4.30ff, 7.6-7, 11.10-14, 13.17f, 16.1f, 17.26; Sir.18.11; PA 3.14, Mekh.Beshall.7; Ep.Barn.1.2-3, 1 Clem.46.6.

Man's hope is based on a historical event: the Messiah died for mankind "while we were still helpless," and his death and resurrection are proof of God's faithfulness to man. Paul refers to the tradition of Yeshua's crucifixion when he was "delivered up because of our transgressions" (cf. 4.25, 8.17). God's love (cf. חסד; *chesed*, or "grace") is the gift of His son, "the Lord our righteousness," who "justifies the ungodly"—in a way similar to the function assumed by the Teacher of Righteousness who led the community at Qumran:

> . . . I know that none is righteous beside Thee; and I have appeased Thy face because of the Spirit which Thou hast put [in me] to accomplish Thy [fav]ours towards [Thy] servant for [ever] by cleansing me by Thy holy Spirit and by causing me to go forward in Thy will according to the greatness of Thy favours [. . .] [. . . in] the place of [Thy] loving[-kindness] which [Thou hast] cho[sen] for them that love Thee and for them that keep [Thy] com[mandme]nts [that they may stand] before Thee [for e]ver [. . . to] mingle with the spirit of Thy servant and in every wor[k . . .] . . . [for Thou art . . .] and merciful, lo[ngsuffer]ing [and rich] in grace and truth, who pardonest the sin [. . .] and compassionate towards [all the sons of righteousness], [they that love Thee] and keep [Thy] command[ments] [and] are converted to Thee with faith and a perfect heart . . . and Thou [hast instructed me in] Thy Covenant and my tongue has been as the tongue of Thy disciples, whereas the spirit of calamities was without mouth and all the sons of transgression without reply of the tongue. For the lips < > of falsehood shall be dumb; for at the time of Judgment Thou will declare all of them guilty that attack me, distinguishing through me between the just and the guilty. (1QH 16.11-17, 7.10-12)[15]

Verse 6:
"For while we were still helpless": cf. Mt.26.41, Rom.3.5, 25, 6.19, 8.26, 1 Cor.1.27, 2 Cor.12.9, 13.4, Eph.2.12, Heb.2.10, 4.15, 5.2, 7.28; 1QS 11.2-21, 1QH 1.21ff, 4.29f, 9.15ff, 10.1ff, 11.11f, 12.24-35.

Paul uses the terms "helpless," "ungodly," "sinners," and "enemies" interchangeably in verses 6-8, reflecting his insistence that if a man serves his own (evil) inclination, he thereby "angers" God, and vice versa.[16] When man thus exchanges God's truth for his own image (cf. 1.21ff), he is "helpless" because he is "hopeless," and "hopeless" because he is "without God in the world" (Eph.2.12).[17] As many of the Qumran texts also do, Paul emphasizes God's grace in His free gift of love to mankind in describing man's "helpless" (or "hopeless") condition as one of enmity towards God because he has chosen to obey his own will instead of that of his Creator:

> As for me, I belong to wicked humanity, to the assembly of perverse flesh; my iniquities and rebellion and sin together with the iniquity

> of my heart (belong to) the assembly doomed to worms, (the assembly) of men who walk in darkness. For is man master of his way? No, men cannot establish their steps, for their justification belongs to God, and from His hand comes perfection of way. By His understanding all things are brought into being, by His thought every being is established, and without Him nothing is made . . . to the Most High God belong all the works of righteousness, whereas the way of man is not firm unless it be by the Spirit which God has created for him to make perfect a way for the sons of men, that all His works may know the might of His power and the greatness of His mercy to all the sons of His loving-kindness. (1QS 11.9-11, 1QH 4.30-33)[18]

"At the right time": cf. Isa.61.2, Mk.1.15, Acts 14.16, 17.30, Rom.8.18, Gal.4.4, Eph.1.10, 1 Tim.2.6, Tit.1.3; 1QS 8.4, 12, 9.3, 21, CDC 4.9-11.

The phrase "at the right time" is literally "according to the time," which corresponds to Yeshua's declaration that "the time is fulfilled."[19] This appears to reflect the passage in Isaiah 61.2, where God declares the "favorable year of the Lord" or the "year of the Lord's favor" (cf. goodwill or grace):

> And I, because of Thine understanding I know that [the righteousness of man] is not in the hand of flesh [and] that man [is not] master of his way and that mankind cannot strengthen its step. And I know that the inclination of every spirit is in Thy hand [and that] Thou hast ordained [the way of every man] [together with his visitation] before ever creating him. And how can any man change Thy words? Thou alone hast [created] the just and established him from his mother's womb until the time of good will that he may be preserved in Thy Covenant and walk in all < Thy way > , and that he [may go forward] upon it because of the immensity of Thy mercy, to (possess) eternal salvation and perpetual unfailing peace. (1QH 15.12-16)[20]

"Messiah died for the ungodly": cf. Gen.22.1ff, Num.25.10-13, Isa.53.1-12, Zech.12.10, Mt.20.28, Mk.10.45, Jn.3.16, Rom.4.25, 1 Cor.15.3, Gal.1.4, Eph.5.2, 25, 1 Tim.2.6, Tit.2.14, Heb.9.11f, 28, 10.10, 20, 1 Pet.2.24, Rev.1.5; 1QS 5.6, 8.3, 10, 9.4, 1QM 13.11, 14.9; Test.Ben.3.8, 4 Macc.6.27-29, 17.20-22; Tanh.Vayigash 1, Tanh.B.Acharei Mot 10, Sifre Num.131, Mekh.Pischa 1, Mak.3.15, Lev.R.20.12, Shab.33b, MK 28a, Yoma 43b, Sot.14a.

The biblical function of atonement was effected through the sacrificial system, whereby the offering of an animal or other sacrifice substituted for the death of the man who had violated the Torah. Paul associates Yeshua with the scapegoat in 3.24-25, as well as the "passover" who has been sacrificed (1 Cor.5.7).[21] He passes on this "tradition" which he received (from the Apostles) to the congregation at Rome, "that the Messiah died for our sins . . . was buried, and . . . was raised on the third day according to the Scriptures" (1 Cor.15.3-4). This is his gospel "concerning [God's] son" (cf. 1.3), in which the believer "stands" in God's grace and righteousness (cf. verse 2):

> 'In you will be fulfilled the heavenly prophecy which says that the spotless one will be defiled by lawless men and the sinless one will die for the sake of impious men.' (Test.Ben.3.8, Armenian version)[22]

The biblical idea of the Messiah as the Suffering Servant (cf. Isaiah 49-53) was developed in several different ways in Second Temple Jewish texts. The Teacher of Righteousness at Qumran perceived himself as carrying the same role, and the community which he led regarded themselves as "living sacrifices" which replaced the Temple which had been corrupted by a wicked and unrighteous priesthood:

> But to the uncir[cumcision] of my lips Thou hast given a reply of the tongue and hast upheld my soul with strength of loins and strong endurance; and Thou hast confirmed my steps in the realm of ungodliness. And I have been a snare for sinners, but healing for all those that are converted from sin, prudence for the simple and the firm inclination of all those whose heart is troubled. And Thou hast made of me an object of shame and mockery for traitors, (but) the foundation of truth and understanding for them whose way is straight. . . . But Thou hast made of me a banner for the elect of righteousness and an interpreter of Knowledge concerning the marvellous Mysteries, to test [the men] of truth and to try them that love instruction. And I was a man of dispute for the interpreters of straying, [but a man] [of pea]ce for all who see true things . . . Yah[w]eh [will reign (there) for] ever; He will appear above it constantly, and strangers will lay it waste no more as they formerly laid waste the sanctua[ry of I]srael because of their sin. And He has commanded a sanctuary (made by the hands) of man to be built for Himself, that there may be some in this sanctuary to send up the smoke of sacrifice in His honour before Him among those who observe the law. (1QH 2.7-15, 4QFlor.1.5-7)[23]

In a similar manner to the Qumran expectation of two messiahs, rabbinic texts also speak of the Messiah son of David and the Messiah son of Joseph, the latter to precede the former by his death:

> What is the cause of the mourning [mentioned in the last cited verse (Zech.12.12)]?—R. Dosa and the Rabbis disagree on the point. One explained, The cause is the slaying of Messiah, son of Joseph, and the other explained, The cause is the slaying of the Evil Inclination. It is well according to him who explains that the cause is the slaying of Messiah son of Joseph, since that well agrees with the Scriptural verse, *And they shall look upon me because they have thrust him through, and they shall mourn for him as one mourneth for his only son* (Zech.12.10). . . . (Suk.52a)[24]

Man can "rejoice" (exult) because his hope is founded upon God's love, which he Has proved through the death and resurrection of His only beloved son (cf. Gen.22.2) on behalf of those who had rebelled against His will, suppressed His truth, and exchanged His glory for their own.[25] Man's hope cannot be disappointed because it has been fulfilled in Yeshua's vicarious sacrifice on his behalf, so that humanity is no longer "hopeless," but has been granted the possibility of walking in "new life" in the Spirit of holiness:

> And thou hast cleansed man of sin because of Thy glory that he may be made holy for Thee from all unclean abomination and from (every) transgression of unfaithfulness, that he may be joined wi[th] Thy sons of truth and with the lot of Thy Saints; that this vermin that is man may be raised from the dust to [Thy] secret [of truth] and from the spirit of perversity to [Thine] understanding; and that he may watch before Thee with the everlasting host and together with [Thy] spirits [of holiness], that he may be renewed with all [that is] [and] shall be and with them that know, in a common rejoicing. (1QH 11.10-14; cf. 17.26-28)

Verse 7:
"For one will hardly die . . . ": cf. Ex.32.32, Mt.20.28, 26.28, Jn.11.50, Gal.1.4, 2.20, 1 Tim.2.6, Tit.2.14, Heb.9.28; Pes.25b.

Paul interjects his own response to the likelihood of someone dying on behalf of someone else. "One"—someone or anyone—functions here in the same informal manner as in modern English idiom, and the verse stands out as a personal reflection ("one" may be "I . . . ") in contrast to the biblical and traditional literary texts which underlie most of the rest of the letter. Whereas hatred kills (cf. Mt.5.21-26), love brings to life, as a text from the Testament of the Twelve Patriarchs beautifully describes:

> Just as love wants to bring the dead back to life and to recall those under sentence of death, so hate wants to kill the living and does not wish to preserve alive those who have committed the slightest sin. For among all men the spirit of hatred works by Satan through human frailty for the death of mankind; but the spirit of love works by the Law of God through forbearance for the salvation of mankind. (Test.Gad 4.6-7)

Verse 8:
" . . . His own love": cf. Jn.3.16, 15.13, Rom.8.39.

Paul returns to his more "formal" argument, contrasting God's love for "us" against the willingness of a mere human being to die on behalf of his fellow-man. There are numerous examples of vicarious suffering in the Tanakh and in later Jewish literature: Abraham interceded on behalf of the inhabitants of Sodom (cf. Gen.18.22f); Moses interceded on behalf of the people of Israel (cf. Ex.32.7ff); Gideon is described as interceding on Israel's behalf (cf. Tanh.Shoftim 4); the Torah is said to intercede on behalf of the people (cf. Ex.R.29.4); the Holy Spirit intercedes for Israel (cf. Lev.R.6.1); and according to the Rabbis, Miriam's death (as Aaron's also) is narrated immediately following the Red Heifer, in order to teach that as the red heifer expiates sins, so too does the death of the righteous (cf. Tanh.B.Acharei 10).[26] Paul interjects this personal statement in order to demonstrate that the Messiah's death is not only on behalf of the people of Israel, God's elect, but is also a "cosmic" act which atones for the sin of Adam and thus of all mankind. Once Paul establishes that "we" (the people of Israel) have been reconciled with God through Yeshua's death and resurrection, he can then draw the implications of Adam's sin for all mankind (cf. verse 12). If by one man, Adam, sin came into the world it follows that through one man, Yeshua, the "Second Adam," sin can be extirpated from the world.[27] God's love in giving His Messiah saves man from the wrath to come, because man's participation in Yeshua's death and resurrection through baptism enables him to put his evil inclination to death. Where before Yeshua he was hopeless and helpless, the hope which he possesses in Yeshua's vicarious suffering does not disappoint him but provides him with redemption, since it is fulfilled in God's love and his own "proven character" through the Holy Spirit (verses 3-5).

Verses 9-11:
"Much more then . . . ": cf. Rom.8.7, 11.28, 2 Cor.5.18f, Eph.2.3f, Col.1.21f, 1 Thess.1.10, Jas.4.4.

Paul picks up the theme of "justification" from the beginning of the chapter, and uses the same קל וחומר *(kal ve-chomer)* argument (cf. verse 3) to recapitulate his thought by presenting several variations on the same theme. Thus in verse 6, he describes man's justification in terms of the "hope" given to the "helpless;" in verse 8, he speaks of it as God's love which accepts the "sinner;" in verse 9, he focuses upon the atoning function of Yeshua's "blood" which averts God's "wrath;" and in verse 10, he presents justification as the instrument of "reconciliation" between two "enemies," man and God.[28] In verse 12, he sums up all his various descriptions of justification.[29]

Verse 12:
"Just as through one man": cf. Gen.2.17, Rom.8.17-25, 29-30, 1 Cor.15.21ff, Phil.2.6-11, 3.21; PRE 7.

Paul establishes in verses 1-11 that Yeshua's death has brought "hope" by justifying "us"—the people of Israel—while they were still helpless and hostile to God. He now draws out the implications of Israel's justification for the whole world by appealing to the analogy from Adam. God's act of salvation does not apply only to Israel (cf. "we"), but Yeshua's death and resurrection bring justification to the whole human (Adamic) race. The phrase "just as . . . (so . . .)" is a variant of the קו"ח *(kal ve-chomer)* argument, which Paul employs variously throughout the chapter, and which he links in verses 12-21 to the theme of the "two Adams." His use of "one man" ("just as through one man . . . ") contrasts strongly here with the phrase "one will hardly die" in verse 7.[30] The "one man" in this verse is specifically Adam, who is the first, as well as being the only, man at the beginning of creation. His significance lies, moreover, in his responsibility for "sin," rather than for his willingness (and fitness) to die on behalf of others. The verse implies a comparison between the first Adam and the second or "last" Adam (the Messiah): if "by one man" . . . how much the more "by one man." Paul digresses, however, immediately following the first clause ("just as through one man sin entered the world"), in order to counter the objection that the Gentiles cannot be accused of sin because they do not observe the Torah; and that Yeshua's atonement cannot justify them unless they do observe the Torah. Paul answers this charge, and then (indirectly) resumes his original thought in verse 15.[31]

"Sin entered the world": cf. Gen.2.17, 3.19, 4.7, 1 Tim.2.14; Wis.Sol.2.23f, Sir.25.24, 4 Ez.3.7-9, 21-23, 7.48, 2 Bar.54.15; Gen.R.8.4, 12.6.

It was the commonly-held view within Second Temple Jewish thought that sin "entered the world" because of Adam's first transgression of God's specific command not to eat of the tree of knowledge of good and evil (Gen.2.17, 3.11-24); (although the first time sin is explicitly mentioned in the biblical record is in Genesis 4.9, where Cain is warned of the consequences of Abel's murder):

> R. Berekiah said in the name of R. Samuel b. Nahman: Though these things were created in their fulness, yet when Adam sinned they were spoiled, and they will not again return to their perfection until the son of Perez [viz. Messiah] comes; [for in the verse] '*These are the toledoth* (generations) *of Peretz*' {Ruth 4.18}, *toledoth* is spelled fully, with a *waw*. These are they: his lustre, his immortality, his height, the fruit of the earth and the fruit of trees, and the luminaries. (Gen.R.12.6)[32]

"Death through sin": cf. Gen.2.17, Dt.24.16, 2 Kings 14.6, Jer.31.30, Ezek.18.4, 20, Rom.3.23, 1 Cor.15.21; 2 Bar.17.3, 23.4, 54.15, 4 Ez.3.21f, Wis.Sol.2.24; Sifre Dt.339, Gen.R.8.2, Ex.R.32.1, MK 28a, Shab.55a-b, Kid.30b.

The biblical text in Genesis 2-3 speaks in terms not of sin but of death: "And the Lord God commanded the man saying, 'From any tree of the garden you may eat freely; but from the tree of the knowledge of good and evil you shall not eat, for in the day that you eat from it you shall surely die'" (2.16-17). The textual connection between sin (transgression) and death is thus clearly established, as a rabbinic midrashic text describes:

> They asked Adam: "Who brought death to thee? He replied: "I brought it upon myself." They asked him: "Was it not the Holy One, blessed be He, who caused Thee to die?" He replied: Nay! Say not thus. I am like the sick man who was confined to his bed. When the physician came and looked at him, he enjoined him: "Thou mayest eat such and such a thing, but do not eat such and such a thing, which will be bad for thee and dangerous even unto death." But the sick man ate and was about to die. The people asked him: Was it perhaps the physician who is causing thee to die? He replied: "I myself have caused my death. If I had given heed to what the physician enjoined me, I would not be dying." (Mid.Ps.92.14)

Paul picks up this idea, but almost as a digression from his main argument ("just as through one man sin entered the world [so, too, grace entered the world through one man]." His statement(s) here reflect the debate over the "source" of sin recorded in the talmudic tractate Sabbath, in which the Rabbis juxtapose the well-known passage in Ezekiel 18, which clearly states (in contrast to Ex.20.5-6) that each man receives punishment for his own deeds with the fact that even the righteous die:

> R. Ammi said: There is no death without sin, and there is no suffering without iniquity. There is no death without sin, for it is written, *The soul that sinneth, it shall die: the son shall not bear the iniquity of the father, neither shall the father bear the iniquity of the son, the righteousness of the righteous shall be upon him, and the wickedness of the wicked shall be upon him*, etc. (Ezek.18.20). There is no suffering without iniquity, for it is written, *Then will I visit their transgression with the rod, and their iniquity with stripes* (Ps.89.33). An objection is raised: The ministering angels asked the Holy One, blessed be He: 'Sovereign of the Universe! Why didst Thou impose the penalty of death upon Adam?' Said He to them, 'I gave him an easy command, yet he violated it'. 'But Moses and Aaron fulfilled the whole Torah,' they pursued, 'yet they died'. *There is one event to the righteous and to the wicked; to the good*, etc. (Eccl.9.2), He replied [showing that death may come without sin]. (Shab.55a-b)

R. Ammi's dictum is refuted in the subsequent talmudic discussion, since it is shown that the same Sage who taught that Moses and Aaron died because of their sins as well, also taught that "four died through the serpent's machinations" (because the serpent caused Adam and Eve to sin and not because of the sin of each of the four). The discussion therefore concludes that death does in fact occur without sin (as well as suffering without iniquity). Paul appears to support R. Ammi's opinion. Like that of the Sages', however, his argument is ambiguous, since the objection to R. Ammi's claim that the serpent was the cause of death the serpent admits a causal relationship between Adam's sin and the death of later generations. Paul's appeal to Moses' death is similarly indecisive, because he makes the existence of sin dependent on the presence of the Torah (cf. verse 13). Death and sin are frequently thus associated in rabbinic literature, without the establishment of any direct causal relationship between them:

R. Jose said: If you wish to know of the reward of the righteous in the world to come, consider the case of Adam. One single negative command was given him. This he violated, and see how many deaths have been decreed for him and for all his generations unto the end of time. Now which is greater, the attribute of reward [lit. of goodness] or that of punishment? Surely the attribute of reward. If, then, the attribute of punishment, which is less, caused all those deaths, of him who repents from sin, and fasts on the Day of Atonement, how much more will he bring blessing to himself [lit. cause merit (*zekut*)], and to all his generations to the end of time. (Sifra 27a)

Resh Lakish said: Satan, the evil prompter [יצר הרע], and the Angel of Death are all one. He is called Satan, as it is written, *And Satan went forth from the presence of the Lord* (Job 1.7). He is called the evil prompter: [we know this because] it is written in another place, [*Every imagination of the thoughts of his heart*] *was* only *evil continually* (Gen.6.5), and it is written here [in connection with Satan], Only *upon himself put not forth thine hand* (Job 1.12). The same is also the Angel of Death, since it says, *Only spare his life* (Job 2.6), which shows that Job's life belonged to him. (BB 16a)

"So death . . . because all sinned": cf. 3.9, 23; 2 En.30.16.

Paul, like the Rabbis, struggles with the implications of the statement that "death [came] through sin." Verses 12-14 thus contain some of his most complex thought, in which he abruptly strings clauses one onto another, with little or no conjunctive force or further explanatory details; and in which some of the clauses appear to contradict one another, or are left hanging in midair. His argument against the "predestination" of death is countered by the fact that all men die "naturally", and by his modification of the Adamic analogy. He states both that sin entered the world "by one man" (Adam), and that all men die because all men sin/have sinned. It is clear, however, that his discussion of the relation between sin and death is secondary to the analogy between sin and grace, since it constitutes a digression: he is apparently anticipating an objection whose details are obscure. Thus he inserts a seemingly emphatic "so" (οὕτως; *outos*; "and so death spread . . . ") after "and death through sin," as if to claim that (Adam's) sin "caused" human mortality, but he holds this thought together with the following clause, which "because all sinned," seems to indicate that all men are responsible for their *own* sin.[33] He therefore appears to suggest that death is both a direct consequence of Adam's disobedience and a natural consequence of human sinfulness, a view which is reflected in several other contemporary Jewish texts:

> I answered and said, "This is my first and last word: It would have been better if the earth had not produced Adam, or else, when it had produced him, had restrained him from sinning. For what good is it to all that they live in sorrow now and expect punishment after death? O Adam, what have you done? For though it was you who sinned, the fall was not yours alone, but ours also who are your descendants. For what good is it, if an eternal age has been promised to us, but we have done deeds that bring death? And what good is it to us that an everlasting hope has been promised us, but we have miserably failed?. . . (4 Ez.7.46-51 [116]-[121])

> For, although Adam sinned first and has brought death upon all who were not in his own time, yet each of them who has been born from him has prepared for himself the coming torment. . . . Adam is, therefore, not the cause, except only for himself, but each of us has become our own Adam. (2 Bar.54.15-19)

Verse 13:

"For until the Law . . . ": cf. Ps.32.1, Rom.3.20, 4.8f, 15, 5.20, 11.32, 2 Cor.5.19, Gal.3.22; Shab.88b, Yoma 72b, San.46b, 101a.

Paul seems to sense that his statement "because all sinned . . . " might be misleading in the light of what he has said in the previous verse, and therefore attempts to explain the tension between the two thoughts. His appeal to the Torah, in saying that sin is defined in relation to the violation of a commandment, suggests that the phrase "because all sinned" carries the sense of the "transgression of a commandment" (cf. 3.19, 4.15 and 5.20). If so, Paul needs to explain that sin existed before the Torah in order to demonstrate that God's justification through Yeshua is based on faithfulness rather than simply on Torah-observance (cf. 4.10f). If he relates sin to violation of the Torah, he excludes the Gentiles from God's justification, since the Torah was given only to Abraham, generations later. Verse 13 thus emphasizes the presence of sin prior to the Torah—since Paul originally claims that sin entered the world with Adam, and then adds that the formal framework of reward and punishment was instituted only with the giving of the Torah (מתן תורה; *mattan Torah*).[34] It seems most likely that Paul is sidetracked by the relation between sin and death, which then introduces the theme of the Torah. Despite the anomaly which this relationship between sin/death and the Torah raises, death "nevertheless" (verse 14) was present even before the Torah was given. Verse 13 thus states that sin *was* in the world before the Torah, even though it had no legal framework. Although Adam and Eve violated a direct commandment, Paul says that sin is subsequently defined, determined, and punished within the framework of the Torah.[35]

Verse 14:

"Nevertheless, death reigned": cf. 1 Cor.15.21-22, 42f.

Paul returns to the digression in his argument concerning the relation between death and sin. The adversative "nevertheless" seems to admit that verse 13 has not adequately resolved the confusion regarding the source and/or cause of death (and may even have increased it). Despite the fact that death is causally linked to sin, and (yet) sin is not formally accounted for outside the legal framework of the Torah, Paul acknowledges that death still existed in the period between creation and מתן תורה (*mattan Torah*), the giving of the Torah to Moses on Mount Sinai.

"Even over . . . ": cf. Hos.6.7, Rom.1.23, Phil.2.7.

Paul makes the previous statement ("death reigned") inclusive, apparently indicating that Adam's sin is generic or particular (whether it creates human "sinfulness" or whether it represents a person's own "sin").[36] Paul may mean "even over . . . " as inclusive, and thus want to say that Adam's sin was generic because it covers all kinds of sins, even those which are "independent" of the specific sin committed by Adam; or he may be referring not to sin *per se*, but once again to the relation between death and sin.[37] The phrase "in the likeness" of Adam's sin suggests that Paul is referring to "generic sinfulness," rather than to the chronological problem of the death of those who sinned after Adam (until the giving of the Torah). Adam's sin becomes a type for Israel in some rabbinic midrashim:

> R. Abbahu said in the name of R. Jose b. R. Hanina: It is written, *But they are like a man* (Adam), *they have transgressed the covenant* (Hos.6.7). *They are like a man* (Adam) means like Adam: just as I led Adam into the Garden of Eden and commanded him, and he transgressed My commandment, whereupon I punished him by dismissal and expulsion, and bewailed him with *ekah* (how)! . . . so also did I bring his descendants into Eretz Israel and command them, and they transgressed My commandment, and I punished them by sending them away and expelling them, and I bewailed them with *ekah*!. . . (Gen.R.19.9)

The clause "even over . . . " may represent a digression within the "nevertheless . . . " of verse 14, and thus relate to the problem of sin as the cause of death before the giving of the Torah. On the other hand, Paul returns to the original analogy in referring to the term "likeness."[38]

"Who is a type . . . ": cf. Acts 7.44, Rom.1.23-32, 1 Cor.15.45, Heb.8.5.

Adam's uniqueness as the first man (who sinned) is the model for the Messiah's uniqueness as the redeemer of all mankind. Adam was created in the "image" of God; Yeshua is the "image" and "representation" of God (cf. Heb.1.3).[39] The Greek term τυπος (*tupos*), "type," translates the terms צלם (*tzelem*; image) and תבנית (*tavnit*; model), but both Hebrew words are also translated in Greek by παραδειγμα (*paradeigma*; example/pattern) and ὅμοιωμα/ὁμοιωσις (*homoioma/homoiosis*; likeness) in the LXX.[40] The "imagery" corresponds here to 1 Corinthians 15, where Paul details the antitheses between the earthly and heavenly images: "The first man, Adam, became a living soul. The last Adam (became) a life-giving spirit" (cf. 1 Cor.15.22 and 45), just as the second Adam is said to restore those things which the first Adam lost through his transgression:

> R. Bibi in the name of R. Reuben said: The numerical value of *waw* is six, corresponding to the six things which were taken from Adam and which are to be restored through the son of Nahshon, that is, the Messiah. The following are the things that were taken from Adam: His lustre, his life [immortality], his stature, the fruit of the earth, the fruit of the tree, and the lights. (Num.R.13.12)[41]

As Adam was the head of a race of physical beings, subject to corruption and death, so Yeshua, as the last Adam, is the first of a transformed race or genus of heavenly beings, immortal and glorified. Yeshua's human nature (his mortality) corresponds to Adam's earthly nature, and his glorification (cf. 8.17) not only demonstrates his status as the second Adam (cf. 1.4), but also glorifies the "sons of God" who are faithful to God in him.[42] Thus numerous other midrashim compare the first and second redeemers: what the first did, so did the second:

> R. Berekiah said in the name of R. Isaac: As the first redeemer was, so shall the latter Redeemer be. What is stated of the former redeemer? *And Moses took his wife and his sons, and set them upon an ass* (Ex.4.20). Similarly will it be with the latter Redeemer, as it is stated, *Lowly and riding upon an ass* (Zech.9.9). As the former redeemer

> caused manna to descend, as it is stated, *Behold, I will cause to rain bread from heaven for you* (Ex.16.4), so will the latter Redeemer cause manna to descend, as it is stated, *May he be as a rich cornfield in the land* (Ps.72.16). As the former redeemer made a well to rise {cf. Num.21.17f}, so will the latter Redeemer bring up water, as it is stated, *And a fountain shall come forth of the house of the Lord, and shall water the valley of Shittim* (Joel 4.18). . . . R. Berekiah said in the name of R. Levi: The future Redeemer will be like the former Redeemer. Just as the former Redeemer revealed himself and later was hidden from them (and how long was he hidden? Three months, as it is said, *And they met Moses and Aaron* [Ex.5.20]), so the future Redeemer will be revealed to them, and then be hidden from them. How long will he be hidden? R. Tanhuma, in the name of the Rabbis, said: Forty-five days, as it is said, *And from the time that the continual burnt-offering shall be taken away . . . there shall be a thousand two hundred and ninety days. Happy is he that waiteth, and cometh to the thousand three hundred and five and thirty days* (Dan.12.11-12). . . . . He who believes in him will live, and he who does not believe will depart to the Gentile nations and they will put him to death. R. Isaac b. Marion said: Finally the Holy One, blessed be He, will rain down manna upon them, *And there is nothing new under the sun* (Eccl.1.9). (Eccl.R.1.9.1, Ruth R.5.6)[43]

Verse 15:

"But the free gift . . . ": cf. Ex.34.6, Isa.53.11, Jn.1.14, 17, 4.10, Acts 2.38, 11.17, Rom.6.23, 1 Tim.1.14, 2.5; 1QS 11.7.

Here Paul resumes his original thought from the beginning of verse 12, and completes the second half of the analogy which he left hanging there. Following the digression in verses 12-14, he also inverts the ק״ו (*ad maius*) argument by contrasting the negative (Adam's sin) with the positive (God's grace). He thus also emphasizes the "how much more . . . " aspect conveyed by the principle, however: God's grace is far greater (in its power) than Adam's transgression, because whereas Adam's sin led to human mortality, God's grace leads to eternal life. This is a typical argument made in the Qumran texts:

> And [Thou hast] drawn [me] from the dust and [out of clay] I was sh[aped] as a fount of defilement and ignominious shame, a container of dust, a thing knea[ded with water] [. . .] and a dwelling-place of darkness. And the law of the creature of clay is return unto dust; at

the time of [death the being] of dust will return to that from which he was taken. . . . And I, I know that righteousness is not of man, nor of the sons of men perfection of way; to the Most High God belong all the works of righteousness, whereas the way of man is not firm unless it be by the Spirit which God has created for him to make perfect a way for the sons of men, that all His works may know the might of His power and the greatness of His mercy to all the sons of His loving kindness. . . . And Thou hast cleansed men of sin because of Thy glory that he may be made holy for Thee from all unclean abomination and from (every) transgression of unfaithfulness . . . that this vermin that is man may be raised from the dust to [Thy] secret [of truth] and from the spirit of perversity to [Thine] understanding; and that he may watch before Thee with the everlasting host and together with [Thy] spirits [of holiness], that he may be renewed with all [that is] [and] shall be and with them that know, in a common rejoicing. (1QH 12.24-27, 4.30-33, 11.12-14)[44]

Verses 16-19:

"Free gift . . . from many transgressions": cf. 2 Cor.9.5, 2 Tim.2.12, Rev.3.21, 5.10, 20.4, 6.

Paul reiterates the negative comparison between sin and grace. Here he qualifies the analogy by contrasting "one transgression," leading to condemnation, with "many transgressions," leading to justification.[45] Although a typological relation exists between the first Adam and the second Adam, Paul also points to a difference. The "free gift of grace" does not lead, as does Adam's (one) sin, to the *condemnation* of many but to the *justification* of many, although grace is normally given to those who are condemned. Paul states that God's gift in Yeshua justifies the condemned (cf. verses 6f). He expands this idea in verse 17, where the analogy between "one [first] Adam" and "one [second] Adam" is maintained, even though the opposite result is obtained. Yeshua bestows eternal life on those who were condemned through Adam's transgression.[46]

Verse 19:

"Disobedience . . . obedience": cf. Acts 6.7, Rom.1.5, 6.16, 16.19, 2 Cor.10.5, Phil.2.8, Heb.5.8.

Yeshua's "obedience" corresponds to Adam's disobedience: Yeshua gave up in his obedience the things which Adam reached for in his disobedience (cf. Phil.2.8) in his faithfulness to God's will.[47]

Verses 20-21:

"Transgression might increase": cf. 3.20, 4.15, 6.16, 23, 7.7f, (11.32), Gal.3.19, Jas.1.14-15; PA 4.2, PRK 4.8, Gen.R.19.1, Shab.88b, Ta'anit 7a.

Paul returns to the discussion of the function of the Torah in God's justification of man (cf. verse 13), and includes it in the ק״ו (*ad maius*) analogy. Since sin is closely associated to the Torah (cf. 3.19, 4.15, 7.1, 7-9, 13, 18f, 8.3), when the Torah is given sin "increases," both because the evil inclination desires what is prohibited, and because the Torah regulates the principle of reward and punishment.[48] The Torah was also given, however, *because* sin increased, so that God's grace might abound:

> R. Adda son of R. Hanina said: Had not Israel sinned, only the Pentateuch and the Book of Joshua would have been given them, [the latter] because it records the disposition of Palestine [among the tribes]. Whence is this known? *For much wisdom proceedeth from much anger* (Eccl.1.18). (Ned.22b; cf. Eccl.R.1.13.1)

R. Adda's point is clearly that the other books of the Tanakh, especially the rebukings contained in the prophets, would have been unnecessary. He bases his argument upon the prooftext from Ecclesiastes 1.18, which he interprets as demonstrating that the prophets were sent with their "wise teachings" because of God's anger with His people. In this way, because man learns by error, sin becomes the occasion for God's giving of His Torah, or His instructions as to how to observe His will. The second clause of the verse ("where sin increased . . . ") once again reinforces the ק״ו analogy: where sin increases grace increases even more—not merely to Israel but to all mankind.[49]

Endnotes on Chapter 5

1 Paul elaborates on man's hostility to God in verses 8-10.

2 Cf. Ex.24.5, Dt.27.6-7, 2 Chron.29.31. Peace-offerings were also part of the renewal of the Noachide covenant; cf. Jub.6.4-14. See also the "covenant of peace" made by the priests for atonement; cf. Num.25.12, Isa.54.10, Ezek.34.25, 37.26.

3 The Hebrew root שלם (*shalem*) is made the basis in many midrashic texts for a series of wordplays which connect "peace" (שלום; *shalom*) with שלם (*shalem*), "complete" or "whole;" להשלים (*lehashlim*), "to make perfect" or "to reconcile;" and לשלם (*leshalem*), "to pay" or "to reward." Paul's thought of Rom.5.1-2 is very similar to the passage in Eph.2.12ff, and thus to many

of the motifs of justification, righteousness, and grace in the Qumran texts; see K. Kuhn, "The Epistle to the Ephesians in the light of the Qumran texts," and F. Mussner, "Contributions made by Qumran to the understanding of the Epistle to the Ephesians," both in *Paul and Qumran*, ed. J. Murphy-O'Connor (London: Geoffrey Chapman, 1968), 115-131 and 159-178. The English word "atonement" itself is a notarikon (a word composed of several words), literally meaning "at-one-ment" (being in harmony).

4 Perek HaShalom (lit. "Chapter on Peace") is part of the Minor Tractates, and appears in the Vilna edition of the Talmud as the final chapter of *Derekh Eretz Zuta*. It was originally an independent collection of sayings on the theme of peace, and was presumably appended to the tractate either because it concludes with a description of the degeneracy of the world prior to the advent of the Messiah or because *Derekh Eretz Zuta* concludes with a chapter on the blessings of peace (or for both reasons). This particular section is based on Judg.6.24, where the Hebrew text may be read to say either that Gideon called the altar "The Lord is Peace," or that he called God Himself "Lord, Peace;" cf. Lev.R.9.9 and Shab.10b. The author of this midrash obviously prefers the latter reading since he then applies the messianic titles "Everlasting Father, Prince of Peace" in Isa.9.6 to the person who acts as the altar whose name is "Adonai-Shalom."

5 See BDB: 897. In his Hebrew translation of the New Testament, Delitzsch translates προσαγωγη (*prosagoge*) as מבוא (*mavo'*), "access" or "introduction" (cf. Eph.2.18) into God's presence through the atonement of one's sins.

6 The verb הגישני (*hagisheni*), "He has caused me to approach," carries a similar meaning to Paul's use of the Greek προσαγω (*prosago*). The Qumran text also associates "approaching" or being "brought near" to God with man's "justification" and "atonement." Paul returns to this theme also in chapter 12, where the believer offers his own body as a "living and holy sacrifice" (12.1).

7 See also the comments on 14.4, where Paul develops the idea of "standing" in grace as God's acceptance of a person's "sanctification" of what is otherwise "profane" (or "secular"). God's grace not only makes a person "stand" before Him but also makes him "stand" before his fellow-man (cf. PA 3.10, 4.6) in his understanding of God's commandments and his convictions before God.

8 See the comments on 3.23 and 4.18f. Paul further develops the theme of glory in chapter 8.

9 The phrase "not only this" is a variation on a קל וחומר (*kal ve-chomer*) argument: "not only this but also . . . " corresponds to "if this then how much more. . . . "

10 Cf. also DEZ 3.6, 6.5, Ned.20a.

11 For the relation of Roman society to the early church, see E. Ferguson, *Backgrounds*, 472ff.

12 The verb δοκιμαζω corresponds in this sense to the biblical image of smelting and refining precious metal; cf. Ps.17.3, 66.10, Isa.48.10, Jer.12.3, Zech.13.9, Mal.3.2-3, Heb.11.17, Jas.1.12, 1 Pet.1.7. Paul returns to this theme again in 12.2f, where the "living and holy sacrifice" which the believer offers "proves" the will of God as that which is "good and acceptable and perfect," all of which terms also reflect the idea of "peace" (שלם; *shalem*); see above on verse 1. "Proven character" again relates not only to man's acceptability to God but also to his acceptability before his fellow-man; see the comments on 14.18.

13 Paul associates the "proven character" of the "inner man" (cf. 7.22) and the "mind of [his] spirit" with the intercession of the Holy Spirit in 8.27; see the comments on 8.26-27.

14 Cf. 1 Pet.2.4-10 and 1QS 8.4-10; see the comments on 9.24ff for the influence of many of the Qumran texts on the book of Romans; see also D. Flusser, *Pre-Pauline*, for the idea that Qumran-influenced ideas formed a stratum within pre-Pauline Christianity.

15 The author of the Thanksgiving Scroll (the Teacher of Righteousness in at least some of the psalms) frequently describes humanity as the "men of vermin," literally in Hebrew תולעת מתים (*tol'at metim*), or the "worm of the dead," whom God raises from the dust (i.e., death) by His grace and through the outpouring of His Holy Spirit; cf. 1QH 6.34, 11.12. Sin and death therefore become virtually synonymous terms. The allusion to Isa.50.4 ("the tongue of the disciples;" cf. also 1QH 8.36) reflects the Teacher of Righteousness' self-association with the Suffering Servant, reinforced by the other allusion to Mal.3.18 ("distinguishing through me . . . "), which reflects the "touch-" or "testing-stone" of Isa.28.16 (cf. also 1QH 2.13-14).

16 This idea is based on the doctrine of the Two Ways or Two Spirits, which he uses as a basic theme throughout the letter; see the midrash on the two masters in chapter 6.

17 See the comments on 1.28.

18 The contrast between man's helplessness, which shows the greatness of God's love, clearly illustrates the libertine argument against which Paul argues in 3.5f, where he negates the claim that man's unrighteousness proves God's righteousness.

19 Cf. Mk.1.15. This statement also relates to John's pronouncement that "the Kingdom of heaven is at hand" (cf. Mt.3.2, 10.7). The Greek verbal

form ἤγγικεν (*engiken*) means "has come" or "has arrived," and in the LXX regularly translates the Hebrew root קרב (*karav*). Paul thus returns to the thought of verses 1-2, and man's "introduction" into God's grace or favor; see also the comments on 8.18, 12.11, and 13.11f.

20 Cf. Lk.4.16-22, 1QS 11.10, 1QH 18.12-15. Although Paul does not share the ideas of "double predestination" which is characteristic of the Qumran community, Yeshua "fulfils" for him the task of the Servant in Isa.61.2f in the same way that the Teacher of Righteousness perceived his calling; see also the comments on 8.26-28, where Paul uses the same motif of good will in conjunction with the intercession of the Holy Spirit and Yeshua's defense of Israel's election.

21 Paul explicitly bases the idea of the Messiah as "our passover who has also been sacrificed" on the leaven in this passage. Since at Passover, God commanded the people to eat *matza* because there was no time for the leaven to work in order to make bread (Ex.12.14ff, 34, 39), leaven took on a negative connotation (cf. Lev.2.11, 6.17), and was later associated with the evil inclination; cf. Mt.16.6, Gal.5.9, Gen.R.34.10, Yalkut 601, Ber.17a; (however in Mt.13.33/Lk.13.21 Yeshua uses it in a positive sense); see also the comments on 11.16. The biblical text also allows "the passover" to be understood as the lamb which was sacrificed, in which case it symbolizes the blood of the animal sacrificed, as well as the blood sprinkled on the door lintels, by which sign God "passed over" those households and did not kill their first-born. In later tradition, following the destruction of the Temple, the *afikoman*, the middle piece of *matza* broken in two and hidden to be found at the end of the seder, replaced the animal sacrifice which it was no longer possible to offer (cf. Ber.55a). These two concepts combine the idea of putting one's evil inclination to death, or dying to sin, in order to serve the Creator in newness of life through the Spirit of holiness, which Paul develops in chapters 6ff, having established that Yeshua was "delivered up because of our transgressions, and was raised because of our justification" (4.25); see the midrash below from Suk.52a, whose differing interpretations of Zech.12.12 relate on the one hand to the evil inclination, and on the other to the Messiah ben Joseph.

22 Cf. Rashi's commentary on Lev.17.11: "The soul of every creature is in the blood. Therefore I gave it [the blood] as an atonement for the souls of men, that one soul should come and atone for others." Paul subsequently transfers the idea of a "human" sacrifice (in place of an animal or other offering) to the "living sacrifice" of man's own body (cf. 12.1).

23 Cf. 1QH 3.7-18, 4.8-9, 23, 5.5, 22-25, 7.23-25, 8.4-15, 26ff, 9.10, 24-26. The interpretation of the text from the Florilegium (מקדש אדם; *mikdash 'adam*) is uncertain. Dupont-Sommer translates it as "a sanctuary (made by the hands) of man," but comments in the note that it may also be taken to mean "a sanctuary of men," i.e., a spiritual sanctuary. This view is supported by the "spiritual sacrifices" which the community offered; cf. 1QS 9.3-5; see D. Flusser, *Two Notes*.

24 In the Jerusalem Talmud, the same passage appears without the designation "son of Joseph." It is therefore apparent that the concept of the "Messiah son of Joseph" developed between the recension of the Jerusalem and Babylonian Talmuds. For the tradition of the death of the Messiah ben Joseph, see J. Klausner, *Messianic*, 483-501, and the comments on 1.4; for the messianic expectations of the Qumran community, see the *Patriarchal Blessings* and *Testimonia* (Dupont-Sommer, *Essene*, 314ff).

25 Paul includes all mankind in the designation of ungodly, a term ("ungodliness") which in 1.18 he attributes to the Gentiles as the representatives of pagan society. In chapters 2 and 3, he emphasizes that *all* men have sinned, the Gentiles because they have suppressed God's truth and are therefore without hope (cf. Eph.2.12), and Israel because they have transgressed His covenant. This section of chapter 5 prefaces the theme of suffering and glorification in chapters 6-8.

26 Cf. also 4 Macc.6.27-29, PYoma 1.1, 38b, Tanh.Vayigash 1, MK 28a, Shab.33b; see also the comments on 8.27 and 34.

27 Paul consistently refers to the Jewish believers as "we" and to the Gentile believers as "they" in his letters. He strongly emphasizes Israel's role at the beginning of this chapter, using the pronouns "we," "us," and "ours" twenty times. In verses 11f, however, he switches to an impersonal style, demonstrating the transition of his focus in verses 11-12 from God's particular dealings with the people of Israel to the universal implications of Yeshua's death and resurrection for all mankind in the rest of the chapter.

28 Paul adopts this style of argument throughout the chapter in comparing the "two Adams," and again in 11.12-16, in reference to Israel's role in the redemption of the world.

29 Verse 11 is awkward, since although the first half of the קו"ח analogy ("not only this") is present, Paul leaves out the comparison ("but also . . . "). Since the concepts which he is discussing all derive from the preceding verses, however, verse 11 can be seen as a repetition of the previous verses rather than as beginning a new thought. The "therefore" in the following verse further indicates that verse 12 begins a new section.

30 See also Paul's use of the "one man"—Isaac—in 9.10, from whose fathering of twins Paul once again brings proof of God's election of the Gentiles as well as of Israel, because of His free gift of grace in Yeshua's righteousness; see the comments on 9.10f.

31 Verses 12b-14 are therefore subsidiary and dependent upon the first clause of verse 12. Consequently, they should not be made to carry the theological weight of the doctrine of "original sin" attributed to them by many commentators.

32 R. Berekiah's midrash uses a similar comparison between Adam and the Messiah as Paul also employs here. He bases his analogy on the fact that in Gen.5.1, the word תלדות (*toledot*; "this is the book of the *generations* of Adam") is spelled without a ו (*waw*), which he interprets as representing the loss of Adam's (descendants') full potential. Since, however, the same word is written fully in Ruth 4.18 (תולדות), "these are the generations of Perez," who is the ancestor of king David and thus of the Messiah, Adam's full glory will be restored when the Messiah comes. The midrash thus directly links sin with Adam, and its abolishment with the Messiah; see also the comments on 8.17f.

33 The sequence of verse 12 thus appears to run as follows: Paul begins his argument with an analogy between Adam and Yeshua, the first Adam and the last Adam. Adam is the prototype for sin (12a). This thought introduces the subject of human mortality (12b), a theme which verse 12c may either continue or from which it may begin to digress. The causal nexus between the spread of death and universal sin seems to indicate that 12d is dependent upon 12c, and therefore forms part of the digression rather than of the main argument. If so, the digression encompasses verses 12c-14. Paul is deflected from the analogy of "through the one man (the first Adam) came sin and through the one man (the second Adam) came righteousness" into a discussion of the connection between sin/death and the Torah.

34 The Sages at times attributed full Torah-observance to Adam and at other times claimed that Adam and the patriarchs observed only the six Noachide commandments; cf. Gen.R.24.5, Dt.R.2.25; see also L. Ginzberg, *Legends*, V:187, 259. Paul is forced into the reverse position, since he needs to demonstrate that God's justification is based on His promise to Abraham rather than on His covenant with Israel. Since he cannot hold, however, that sin did not exist before the giving of the Torah, he must explain why the Torah was given later. He takes up this theme in chapter 7.

35 This idea corresponds to the majority of Paul's statements concerning the relation of the Torah to sin; cf. Rom.5.20, 7.1, 7-9, 13, 18f, 8.3.

36 Traditional Christian doctrine has frequently understood Adam's sin to be generic (or genetic) and to "infect" all future generations with sinfulness: human beings sin because they are descended from Adam, and are genetically "sinful" in that his sinful nature was passed on also to them. This clause is the closest support in the text for this doctrine of "original sin," since here Paul directly addresses the issue of those whose sins differ in nature from Adam's. Since the passage remains within the sphere of a digression still, however, its "doctrinal" status should be very cautiously established.

37 The conjunctive και (*kai*), "and," at times carries the force of "even." Here it possesses no meaning as "and."

38 Paul uses the expression דמות צלם אדם (*demut tzelem 'adam*), "the figure of the image of man (Adam)" in 1.23, closely anticipating 5.14; he uses the term "likeness" again in 6.5, where the likeness of Yeshua's death is mirrored in a person's baptism, and in 8.3, where he emphasizes the fleshly aspect of sin.

39 Since Adam was created by God without a normal birth and lived in the Garden of Eden in God's presence, a wide body of Jewish, gnostic, and Christian literature arose which gave a messianic interpretation to these biblical texts. See R. Scroggs, *The Last Adam: A Study in Pauline Anthropology* (Philadelphia: Fortress Press, 1966); K. Rudolf, *The Nature and History of Gnosticism* (San Francisco: Harper and Row, 1985); G. Scholem, *Jewish Gnosticism, Merkabah Mysticism and the Talmudic Tradition* (NY: Jewish Theological Seminary of America, 1960).

40 Cf. Ex.25.8 (9), 1 Kings 6.5, 1 Chron.28.11, 12, 18, 19, Ezek.8.10.

41 The letter *waw* [ו] carries the numerical value of six. The midrash plays on the fact that the word "generations" (תולדות) is spelt first without a *waw* and then with a *waw*, indicating that what was "lost" will be restored; cf. Gen.R.12.6.

42 Paul makes this clear in 1 Cor.15.21: "For since by a man [Adam] (came) death, by a man also (came) the resurrection of the dead." See J. Tabor, *Unutterable*, 17, and the comments on 8.17.

43 Here the prototype of the Messiah is Moses and not Adam. The prooftext from Eccl.1.9 is used to mean that whatever is destined to take place in the future Redemption took place in the first. R. Berkeiah's midrash in the name of R. Levi is apparently a response to Christian claims, although precisely how is not clear. The Soncino edition of Ruth Rabbah in fact notes concerning the statement that the Jew who does not believe in the future Redeemer will be put to death is perhaps meant "in a religious sense. There he will die to Judaism." This indictment can certainly be

historically corroborated in the fact that only until recently, those Jews who "converted" became Christians and no longer Jews, in the eyes of the Jewish people, the Church, and frequently their own eyes.

44 This hymn from the Thanksgiving Scroll could be entitled "the redemption of Adam," and demonstrates how Adam's nature and his sin preoccupied circles within (sectarian) Jewish thought. According to this text, Adam's sin is cleansed because of God's glory, an idea which corresponds to Paul's thought in chapter 8.

45 Paul interchangeably uses several terms for justification and condemnation: justification, righteousness, and free gift/grace; transgressions, condemnation, and judgment.

46 Paul enlarges on the theme of "universalism" here, which he introduces in chapter 4 in discussing Abraham's faithfulness. Although the shift from Abraham to Adam (chapter 5) is a chronological anachronism, it is a theological progression. Paul replaces the argument that God's favor is dependent upon or affected by human behavior with the analogy of the "one and the many," whose paradigm is the creaturehood of all mankind. He maintains the theme of justification throughout the argument, however, since God's "free gift" brings righteousness to all men indiscriminately, as a result of their sinfulness. Paul then returns to the dialectic of chapter 3 in chapter 6.

47 See also 1.5, 15.3, 18 and 16.26, where Paul uses the example of Yeshua's obedience (cf. Phil.2.8, Heb.5.8) as the basis for the "obedience of faith" among the Gentiles.

48 See the comments on 3.19-20 (cf. 3.8), which link this concept with the principle of "divine condescendence" or accommodation to human weakness.

49 Paul once again anticipates the libertine argument here, (cf. 3.5ff), and immediately deals with the issue of whether sin may increase because it causes grace to abound, in chapter 6.

ROMANS

6

Introduction

Paul again counters (cf. chapter 3) the libertine argument raised in chapter 5, that man's unrighteousness gives God's grace the opportu nity to abound. In response, he appeals to the motif of the "two masters," based on a midrash on Job 3.19. This midrash reflects the doctrine of the Two Ways or Two Spirits characteristic of certain Jewish (sectarian) theologies. This doctrine emphasizes the fact that each individual must choose to serve either his own, evil inclination, or his Creator, God. In order to serve one master, he must "anger" the other, and in serving God he angers his evil inclination by putting it to death or "dying to sin" (verses 2-23). Paul identifies this "death" with baptism into Yeshua's death and resurrection (verses 3-11). This motif underlies the rest of the letter, and Paul later re-combines it with the theme of the "sons of Abraham" from chapter 2 (cf. chapters 8 and 12).

Verse 1:
"What then shall we say? . . . ": cf. 3.3, 5-6, 9, 31, 4.1, 6.15, 7.7, 9.14, 30, 11.1; BK 38a.

Paul again takes up the issue of libertinism (cf. 3.8 and 19-20), this time in consequence of his argument at the end of the previous chapter which suggests that people may engage in sinful deeds in order to give God's grace an opportunity to "increase."[1] Paul uses the same talmudic formula as in 3.3f, raising an erroneous conclusion in order to immediately refute it.[2] The question is whether, if grace increases where sin abounds, a person may not in fact sin in order to give God the opportunity to bestow His grace in abundance.[3] Paul emphatically rejects this possibility—may it never be!—in a similar fashion to other rabbinic formulations:

> What is the meaning of the verse: *Trust ye not in a friend, put ye not confidence in a familiar friend* (Mic.7.5). If the evil inclination say to thee: Sin and the Holy One, blessed be He, will pardon, believe it

> not, for it is said: *Trust ye not in a friend* and *friend* [*re'a*] means none other than one's evil inclination, for it is said: *For the inclination of man's heart is evil* [*ra'*] (Gen.8.21).... Perhaps thou wilt say: Who testifies against me? ... the Sages say: A man's limbs testify against him [to his own sins], for it is said: *Therefore ye are My witnesses, saith the Lord, and I am God* (Isa.43.12). (Hag.16a)

Verse 2:

"May it never be!": cf. Lk.20.16, Rom.3.4, 6, 31, 6.15; Ber.22a, 63b, Shab.138b, Hag.4b.

Paul emphatically refutes the premise that sin can be justified because it "increases" God's grace. Every man must serve God pure-heartedly and with a single mind, as Jewish literature of the period frequently derived from biblical texts:

> 'And thou shalt love the Lord thy God' (Deut.6.5). Act from love. The verse makes a distinction between him who acts from love and him who acts from fear. ... But do you act from love, for there is no love where there is fear, or fear where there is love, except in relation to God. ... 'With all thy heart': that is with both the good and the evil inclination. 'With all thy heart': let not your heart be divided—i.e. not wholly one—as regards your love for God. 'And with all thy soul': even if He takes your soul. So it says, 'For thy sake we are slain every day' (Ps.44.22). R. Simeon b. Menasya said: Can a man be killed every day? But God accounts it to the righteous as if they were killed every day. R. Simeon b. Azzai said: 'With all thy soul': that is, love Him to the pressing out of the last drop of your life.' ... (Sifre Dt.Va'etchanan 32)

The same idea is frequently expressed in the *Derekh Eretz* literature, which encourages the ideal of "denying oneself" in ethical and ascetic conduct in the world:

> RABBI JUDAH THE PRINCE SAYS: DO HIS WILL AS THOUGH IT WERE YOUR WILL SO THAT HE MAY DO YOUR WILL AS THOUGH IT WERE HIS WILL; UNDO YOUR WILL FOR THE SAKE OF HIS WILL SO THAT HE MAY UNDO THE WILL OF OTHERS FOR THE SAKE OF YOUR WILL. He used to say: If you have done His will as though it were your will, you have not yet done His will as He wills it. But if you have done His will as though

> it were not your will, then you have done His will as He wills it. Is it your wish not to die? Die, so that you will not need to die. Is it your wish to live? Do not live, so that you may live. It is better for you to die in this world, where you will die against your will, than to die in the age to come, where, if you wish, you need not die. (ARN[b] 32)[4]

> He [Alexander of Macedon] said to them [the Rabbis]: . . . What shall a man do to live? They replied: Let him mortify himself [lit. 'kill himself,' with study and hard work]. What should a man do to kill himself? They replied: Let him keep himself alive [i.e. indulge in luxuries]. (Tamid 32a)[5]

"How shall we who died to sin still live in it": cf. 4.12, 6.6, 7, 11, 18, 7.6, 8.4-5, 13, 2 Cor.5.1, Gal.2.19-20, Eph.2.2, 4.17-19, Col.2.6, 20, 3.3-5, 7, 1 Pet.2.24, 1 Jn.1.7, 2.6, 3.24, 4.13, 2 Jn.6, 3 Jn.3; 1QS 1.1-11, 3.13-4.26, 5.4f, 9.17-20, CDC 16.5; Test.Iss.4.6, Test.Dan 5.1, Test.Asher 1.3-7, Test.Naph.2.10; Ruth R.3.1, 8.1, Tamid 32b.

Paul does not follow the path of ascetic practice advocated in the Derekh Eretz literature. Instead he chooses to follow another rabbinic tradition, which he combines with the doctrine of the "Two Ways" or the Two Spirits (cf. 1QS 3.18-4.26). His argument is apparently founded upon a midrashic tradition based on Job 3.19 and Psalm 88.5 (6), a tradition already known by Yeshua (cf. Mt.6.24, Lk.16.13), and reported in rabbinic literature in the name of R. Simeon ben Pazzi:

> This [i.e., the idea that it is too late to repent after death] is the meaning of the Scriptural verse, *The small and great are there alike; and the servant is free from his master* (Job 3.19). R. Simon said: This is one of four similar Scriptural verses. '*The small and the great are there alike.*' In this world he who is small can become great and he who is great can be rendered small, but in the world to come he who is small cannot become great nor he who is great small. '*And the servant is free from his master,*' he who performs the will of his creator (*yozer*) angers his evil inclination (*yezer*), but once he is dead he emerges into freedom, as it is said, '*And the servant is free from his master.*' (Ruth R.3.1; cf. 8.1)

It is clear from this account that R. Simeon's midrash originally also included an explanation of Genesis 2.7, since it is based upon the textual anomaly found there. The irregular spelling of the Hebrew root יצר (*yatzar*) as וייצר (*vay-yitzer* [with a double *yod*]), was interpreted to mean that man is in subjection to two masters: to his Creator (*yotzer*), and to his (evil) inclination (*yetzer*):

> . . . R. Simeon b. Pazzi said: Woe is me because of my Creator, woe is me because of my evil inclination. (Ber.61a; cf. Eruv.18a)

Since it makes no sense to regret the good inclination ("woe is to me because of my Creator"), R. Simeon obviously intended his saying to mean that man is obliged to serve either his own inclination or his Creator; the two masters cannot be served simultaneously. If a man serves his evil inclination, then his Creator indeed brings him into woe; if, on the other hand, he serves his Creator, then he must "anger" his evil inclination.[6] Paul describes man's freedom from the mastery of his evil inclination in terms of "dying to sin." To "live" in sin is to "walk" according to the "spirit of perversity" or the "spirit of flesh" and thus to "anger" the Creator and the Spirit of truth, in the language used in many of the Qumran texts:

> . . . For [the man of understanding that he may instruct the sai]nts to li[ve according to the ru]le of the Community; to seek God with [all their heart] and [all their soul] [and] do what is good and right before Him, as He commanded by the hand of Moses and all His servants the Prophets; and to love all that He has chosen and hate all that He has despised; and to depart from evil and cling to all good works; and to practice truth and righteousness and justice on earth, and to walk no more in the stubbornness of a guilty heart, nor with lustful eyes committing every kind of evil. . . . And He allotted unto man two Spirits that he should walk in them until the time of His Visitation; they are the Spirits of truth and perversity. The origin of Truth is in a fountain of light, and the origin of Perversity is from a fountain of darkness. Dominion over all the sons of righteousness is in the hand of the Prince of light; they walk in the ways of light. All dominion over the sons of perversity is in the hand of the Angel of darkness. (1QS 1.1-7, 3.18-21)

Verse 3:

"Or do you not know . . . ": cf. Jn.3.10, Rom.7.1.

Paul emphasizes the untenability of the libertine attitude, explaining that the believer cannot use sin as an excuse to engender God's grace because in order to serve God (the Creator) a man must "anger" his evil inclination which leads him to sin. He then illustrates the idea of "dying to sin" in terms of baptism into the death and resurrection of Yeshua.

"Baptized into . . . his death": cf. Jer.17.13, Ezek.36.25, Mt.3.15, Mk.10.38, Lk.12.49-50, Acts 8.16, 19.5, 1 Cor.1.13, 15, 10.2, 12.13, Gal.3.27, Eph.5.25-26, Col.2.12, 3.3, 1 Pet.3.21; 1QS 3.4ff, 4.20-21, 5.13; Yoma 8.9, Yev.46a-b.

Since Paul assumes the practice of baptism, and expects that his readers will also understand the connection of baptism to "dying to sin," the rite of baptism had apparently already acquired that significance in the early believing community. The primary meaning of the Greek verb βαπτιζω (*baptidzo*) is "to dye," in the sense of immersing something in liquid.[7] To "baptize" a person is literally to immerse them bodily, normally in water. In the immersion of cloth into fluid, the cloth "takes on" the color of the dye, so that a person can be said to "put on" Yeshua when they are "dyed" (cf. Rom.13.14, Gal.3.27). Baptism represents a person's symbolic death, burial, and resurrection with Yeshua, and brings him near (cf. 5.2) to God through Yeshua's purifying blood.[8] Baptism as a rite of purification was one of the means of the "conversion" of the members of the Qumran community, and thus constituted an integral element of the doctrine of the Two Spirits:

> . . . whoever scorns to enter the ways of God in order to walk in the stubbornness of his heart . . . he shall not be absolved by atonement, nor purified by lustral waters, nor sanctified by seas and rivers, nor cleansed by all the waters of washing. Unclean, unclean shall he be for as long as he scorns the ordinances of God and allows not himself to be taught by the Community of His Council. For by the Spirit of true counsel concerning the ways of man shall all his sins be atoned when he beholds the light of life. By the Holy Spirit of the Community, in His truth, shall he be cleansed of all his sins; and by the Spirit of uprightness and humility shall his iniquity be atoned. By his soul's humility towards all the precepts of God shall his flesh be cleansed when sprinkled with lustral water and sanctified in flowing water. (1QS 2.25-3.9)[9]

"Sanctification" or purification is clearly related here to the (*apotropaic*) "warding off" of evil and the gift of God's grace which "justifies" man and makes him righteous in His sight. Paul conveys the same idea in relating to baptism into Yeshua's "death," in stating that Yeshua was "delivered up because of our transgressions" and "raised because of our justification" (4.25), an idea that is reflected in certain rabbinic texts concerning the process which the proselyte underwent in becoming part of God's covenant people:

> ... all [the Sages] agree that ritual ablution [immersion for a proselyte] without circumcision is effective; and they differ only on circumcision without ablution. R. Eliezer infers from the forefathers [whom, he claims, did not perform any ritual ablution upon conversion], while R. Joshua [maintains that] in the case of the forefathers also ritual ablution was performed. Whence does he [R. Joshua] deduce it? If it be suggested, 'From that which is written, *Go unto the people, and sanctify them today and to-morrow, and let them wash their garments* (Ex.19.10), if where washing of the garments is not required ablution is required, how much more should ablution be required where the washing of the garments is required' [when Israel received the Torah and were thus admitted into Judaism], [it may be retorted that] that [i.e., the washing of the garments] might have been a mere matter of cleanliness.—It is rather from here: *And Moses took the blood, and sprinkled it on the people* (Ex.24.8), and we have a tradition that there must be no sprinkling without ritual ablution. (Yev.46b)

Through the contortions of the rabbinic argument, the conclusion reached states that even circumcision must be accompanied by ritual ablution (the *mikveh*). The appeal to the text in Exodus 19.10, which is derived from a קו״ח (*kal ve-chomer*) argument, is rejected because it does not prove that the purpose of the ablution (washing) was merely for cleanliness. The determining text from Exodus 24.8 is therefore all the more forceful in the circumstances, because it is based upon an interpretive tradition. This tradition (cf. Ker.9a) states that "there must be no sprinkling without ritual ablution." The Sages applied this principle to Exodus 24.8, which speaks only of sprinkling the blood and not of ritual ablution, and thus "prove" that sprinkling of blood and ritual ablution (here, baptism) are equivalent acts.[10]

Verses 4-5:

"Buried with him": cf. 1 Cor.15.4, Col.2.12; Eccl.R.8.10.1, San.46b.

The motif of burial is naturally associated with death, and Paul may have Yeshua's physical burial in mind here. The Rabbis also discussed the symbolic function of burial in a similar sense, however:

> The scholars propounded: Is burial [intended to avert] disgrace [since decomposition and putrefaction make the dead loathesome, burial

might be intended to spare their relatives that disgrace], or a means of atonement? What is the practical difference? If a man said, 'I do not wish myself to be buried.' If you say that it is to prevent disgrace, then it does not depend entirely on him [because his relatives are humiliated along with him]; but if it is for atonement, then in effect he has declared, 'I do not desire atonement.' What [then is its purpose]? -Come and hear! 'From the fact that the righteous were buried.' If then you say that it is for atonement—are the righteous in need thereof?—Even so, for it is written, *For there is no righteous man upon earth who doeth good and sinneth not* (Eccl.7.20). . . . The decay of the flesh too is necessary [for forgiveness]. This follows from what he [the Tanna] teaches: WHEN THE FLESH WAS COMPLETELY DECOMPOSED, THE BONES WERE GATHERED AND BURIED IN THEIR PROPER PLACE [proving that only then is the crime fully expiated]. This proves it. (San.46a, 47b)[11]

AND SO I SAW THE WICKED BURIED, AND THEY ENTERED INTO THEIR REST (Eccl.8.10). . . . R. Levi said: [BURIED refers to the wicked who are accounted dead even when they are alive, as it is written], *The wicked man travaileth with pain* [mitholel] *all his days* (Job 15.20), i.e., he is dead and slain (*meth wehalal*), as in the verse, *And thou, O wicked one, art slain* (Ezek.21.29) [addressed to a living person]. (Eccl.R.8.10.1)[12]

Verse 4:

"In order that . . . newness of life": cf. Gen.5.24, Lev.26.3, 1 Sam.2.30, Ps.1.1, Mic.6.8, Jn.3.3, 17.22-24, Rom.4.25, 5.14, 17, 18, 21, 7.6, 1 Cor.3.3, 15.17, 20, 23, 2 Cor.3.18, 4.4, 6, 10f, 5.7, 17, Gal.5.16, 6.15, Eph.4.1, 23f, 5.2ff, Col.2.6, 3.3-4, 10, 1 Thess.2.12, Heb.2.10, 1 Pet.1.3, 23, 2 Pet.1.3, 1 Jn.2.6, 29, 3.9, 4.7, 5.1, 4; 1QS 3.9, 4.6-8, 20-21, 1QH 9.17-18, 12.15, 15.16-17, 16.9, 17.14-16; Ps.Sol.16.1-4; P RH 4.8, 59c, Ex.R.15.6, Mid.Ps.102.3, Yev.46a-b, 62a, Bek.47a, Tamid 32a.

Paul develops the idea of "dying to sin" in connection with "being dead in one's sins" (cf. Eph.2.1, 5). If death atones for man's sins, together with his repentance, he can be made into a "new creature" according to many Jewish texts of the period:

I give Thee thanks, O Adonai, for Thou hast redeemed my soul from the Pit and from Sheol of Abaddon Thou hast made me rise to everlasting heights, and I have walked in an infinite plain!

> And I knew there was hope for him whom Thou hast shaped from the dust for the everlasting assembly. Thou hast cleansed the perverse spirit from great sin that he might watch with the army of the Saints and enter into communion with the congregation of the Sons of Heaven . . . that he may be renewed with all [that is] [and] shall be . . . And Thou hast cast an everlasting destiny for man in the company of the Spirits of Knowledge, that he might praise Thy name in joy[ful] concord and recount Thy marvels before all Thy works. . . . Thou alone hast [created] the just . . . that he may . . . walk in all < Thy way >, and that he [may go forward] upon it because of the immensity of Thy mercy, and that he may unloose all the distress of his soul to (possess) eternal salvation and perpetual unfailing peace. And Thou hast raised up his glory from among flesh. . . . (1QS 3.19-23, 11.13-14, 15.14-17)

> The angels renew themselves each day, praise the Lord, and then return to the river of fire from which they emerged, and the Lord renews them and restores them to their former condition; for it says: *They are new every morning* (Lam.3.23). So also Israel is sunk in iniquity on account of the evil impulse which is within them, but they do penitence, and God each year pardons their iniquities and renews their heart to fear him; for it says: *A new heart also will I give you* (Ezek.36.26). (Ex.R.15.6)

Paul emphasizes, however, that it is Yeshua's death and resurrection, as an act of atonement, which bring eternal life to those who are "baptized into" him as the "first fruits of those who are asleep" (1 Cor.15.20, 23).[13]

Verse 5:

" . . . united . . . resurrection": cf. Rom.8.10-11, 17, 2 Cor.4.10, Phil.3.10f, Col.2.12; Odes Sol.3.7.

Paul knows that Yeshua's example binds together those whom he redeems both with him and with one another, when they die to sin, put their evil inclination to death, and are baptized into his death in order to rise in him in the newness of eternal life, as other Jewish texts interpreted the commandment to "circumcise your hearts":

> Moses said to Israel: "Remove the evil inclination from your heart, and be united in one fear of God and in one counsel to minister before Him; as He is unique in the world, so let your service be unique before Him, as it says, *Circumcise your hearts* (Dt.10.16). (Sifra 43d)

Paul may be influenced here by the well-known text in Isaiah 53.5, which speaks of the Messiah's atonement for man's sins. This verse is normally translated in English as " . . . by his scourging (בחבורתו; *be-chavurato*) we are healed," and the root word חבר (*chavar*) correctly means a "bruise" or "stripe."[14] In Isaiah 53.5, however, the vocalization of the word (which lacks a *dagesh* in the *bet*) differs from most of its other uses in the Tanakh, but it is similarly vocalized in Hosea 4.17 ("Ephraim is joined to [חבור; *chavur*] idols"). Since one of the root meanings of the verb is also "to be joined," Paul is possibly referring here to Isaiah 53.5, in the sense that the believer is "healed" (redeemed) by being "joined to" the Messiah in his death and resurrection.[15]

Verse 6:

"Our old self": cf. 2 Cor.5.17, Eph.2.15, 4.22, 24, Col.3.9; 1QH 3.19-21, 11.10-14, 17.19f, 25-26; PRK S3.2.

Paul refers to several Jewish traditions in the idea of man's "old self." He picks up the theme of the two Adams from chapter 5, turning its "cosmic" elements into the personal life of the individual.[16] Proselytes were frequently described within various streams of Jewish thought during the Second Temple period as "like a new-born child," whose familial relations were considered to be made void on conversion and who were *halakhically* permitted to re-marry, for example, if they wished (cf. Yev.48a). Israel were likewise described as innocent infants upon repentance:

> . . . the disciples of Hillel said: The phrase *kebasim bene sanah*, "he-lambs of the first year" (Num.28.3), is to be understood as though written *kabbasim bene sanah*, "they that cleanse the things which are of many a year." That is, the daily offerings cleanse the sins of Israel, as it is said *Though your sins be as of many a year, they shall be as white as snow* (Isa.1.18). And Ben Azzai said: The phrase *kebasim bene sanah* means that they cleanse the sins of the people of Israel and make them as innocent as an infant in its first year. (PRK 6.4)[17]

This idea assumed a pronounced "apotropaic" function in the Qumran texts, where sin is personified as the "spirit of flesh" and is "exorcised" (warded off or driven out) through the "circumcision of the foreskin of the (evil) inclination and disobedience" and the purification ("baptism") of the

Spirit of holiness which "renews" the body and the spirit of those who "volunteer together for His truth and to walk in His way":

> . . . God will cleanse by His Truth all the works of every man, and will purify for Himself the (bodily) fabric of every man, to banish all Spirit of perversity from his members, and purify him of all wicked deeds by the Spirit of holiness; and He will cause the Spirit of Truth to gush forth upon him like lustral water . . . that this vermin that is man [תולעת מתים] might be raised from the dust . . . and from the spirit of perversity to [Thine] understanding; and that he may watch before Thee with the everlasting host and together with [Thy] spirits [of holiness], that he may be renewed with all [that is] [and] shall be and with them that know, in a common rejoicing. (1QS 4.20-21, 1QH 11.12-14)

"Crucified . . . done away with": cf. Mt.26.2, 28.5, Rom.7.24, 1 Cor.1.13, 17, 23, 2 Cor.13.4, Gal.2.20, 5.24, 6.14, Eph.2.16, Phil.2.8, 3.18, 21, Col.2.11-15, Heb.6.6, 12.2; 1QS 3.6-9, 4.20-21, 1QH 11.10-14, 13.13, 18.25-30; PA 2.4, ARN[b] 32, Sifra 93d, Tamid 32a.

Paul takes up the idea of Yeshua's physical crucifixion on the cross, and begins to turn it into a symbolic metaphor (cf. Gal.2.19).[18] He describes those who "volunteer to be converted from all evil" as being willing to "die to themselves" (to their "body of sin" or "spirit of perversity") in order to serve their Creator when they unite themselves with Yeshua in his death and resurrection, in language similar to that of the Qumran texts:

> And this is the rule for the members of the Community, for those who volunteer to be converted from all evil and to cling to all His commands according to His will . . . When they join the Community, let . . . him undertake by oath of obligation to be converted to the Law of Moses according to all His commands, with all his heart and all his soul, following all that is revealed of it to the sons of Zadok the priests who keep the Covenant and seek His will, and to the majority of the members of their Covenant, they who volunteer together for His truth and to walk in His will. And let him undertake by the Covenant to be separated from all perverse men who walk in the way of wickedness. . . . Let no man walk in the stubbornness of his heart to stray by following his heart and eyes and the thoughts of his evil inclination. But in the Community they shall circumcise the

> foreskin of the (evil) inclination and disobedience in order to lay a foundation of truth for Israel. . . . (1QS 5.1, 7-11, 4-5)

" . . . no longer slaves to sin": cf. Jn.8.33-35, Rom.6.12, 13, 14, 16, 17, 19, 20, 8.15, Gal.4.3, 5.1, Heb.2.15, 2 Pet.2.19; 1QS 10.8, 11, 1QH 9.16, 11.12, 17.25; Test.Jud.18.6, Test.Dan.4.7, Test.Asher 3.2, 6.5, 4 Macc.7.16-23; ARN[a] 16, ARN[b] 16, TBE [S] p.1, MHG Gen.4.9, Gen.R.22.6, 34.10, Ruth R.3.1, Eccl.R.9.4.1, Hag.16a, AZ 5b, BB 17a; Did.1.1f, 2 Clem.6.1-6.

Paul understands that in baptism, the believer puts to death his "spirit of flesh" by "angering" his evil inclination so that he may make God his sole master in uniting with Yeshua, in line with R. Simeon b. Pazzi's midrash on Job 3.19, which was elaborated upon by other Sages:

> '*And the servant is free from his master*,' he who performs the will of his creator (*yotzer*) angers his evil inclination (*yetzer*), but once he is dead he emerges into freedom, as it is said, '*And the servant is free from his master*.' . . . *Tremble, and sin not* (Ps.4.4). . . . R. Jacob b. Ahijah said: [The meaning of this verse is]: Fight against your [Evil] Inclination, and sin not. The Rabbis explain: Anger your Inclination [by refusing to do his bidding] and sin not. (Ruth R.3.1, 8.1)[19]

This same idea also lies behind the doctrine of the "Two Ways" in the Didache, and the "Two Spirits" in Qumran, where the "spirits of Belial" (cf. CDC 12.2) "possess" the "members" of a person's body:

> These things I have known because of Thine understanding; for Thou hast uncovered my ear to marvellous Mysteries. Yet am I but a creature of clay [יצר החמר] and a thing kneaded with water, a foundation of shame and a fount of defilement, a crucible of iniquity [כור העוון] and fabric of sin [מבנה החטאה], a spirit of straying, and perverse, void of understanding, whom the judgments of righteousness terrify. . . . [But what is] he, the spirit of flesh, to understand all these things and to comprehend [Thy] great secret of truth? And what is he that is born of woman amid all [Thy] mighty [works]? He is but a fabric of dust [מבנה עפר] and a thing kneaded with water, [who]se counsel is nothing but [uncleann]ess, ignominious shame and [. . .] and over whom the perverse spirit rules. . . . [O my God, prevent] Thy servant from sinning against Thee and from stumbling aside from all the ways of Thy will. Strengthen [his] l[oins] [that he may re]sist the spirits [of Belial]

> [and w]alk in all that Thou lovest, and that he may despise all that Thou hatest [and do] what is good in Thine eyes! [Banish] from my members [all] their [domi]nion, for Thy servant [possesses] a spirit of fl[esh]. (1QH 1.21-23, 13.13-15, 17.23-25)

Verse 7:

"Freed from sin": cf. Jn.8.31-36, Acts 13.38-39, Rom.6.14, 18, 7.4-6, 24-25, 8.2, Gal.4.5, 31, 5.13; 4 Macc.7.16-23; PA 6.2, Ex.R.51.8, Shab.30a, 151b.

Paul, like R. Simeon's midrash which interprets Job 3.19 and Psalm 88.6 to say that a man is freed from the "mastery" of sin (cf. Gen.4.7) by his "death," knows that since a man cannot serve both God and his evil inclination, he must free himself from one master in order to serve the other. When he puts his evil inclination to death in baptism (and in circumcising the "foreskin of his heart"), he is then freed to serve his Creator:

> And on the day on which a man undertakes to be converted to the Law of Moses, the Angel of Hostility will depart from him if he fulfils his promises. For this reason Abraham circumcised himself on the day on which he knew. (CDC 16.4-6)[20]

Verses 8-10:

"If we have died . . . live with him": cf. 6.4, 1 Cor.15.12ff, 20f, 42f, 2 Cor.4.10-14, Col.1.18, 1 Thess.5.10, 2 Tim.2.11.

Using the rabbinic principle of הקש (*hekesh*), Paul again refers to "creation" as the basis for God's gift of righteousness to those who are "faithful" to Him (cf. 4.17f): if a person dies to his evil inclination with Yeshua, so also ought he to be raised with him to serve his Creator.[21] Yeshua is "the Lord our righteousness" (cf. Jer.23.6), whose own "faithfulness" to God (cf. Rom.3.21) is honored through his resurrection as the "first fruits of those who are asleep" (cf. 1 Cor.15.20), and through whom God's "grace" to men "reigns through righteousness to eternal life" (cf. 5.21). Yeshua's resurrection confirms God's "mastery" over sin, and the person who is faithful to Yeshua is not only faithful to the Creator by "angering" his evil inclination (putting it to death in baptism), but is also "renewed" in "newness of life" (resurrected) together with Yeshua.

Verse 9:

"Raised . . . never to die again": cf. Acts 2.24, 32, 13.34, 37, Rom.4.24, 6.10, 8.11, 10.9, 1 Cor.6.14, 15.15, 2 Cor.4.14, Phil.3.8-11, Col.2.12, 3.3-5, Heb.9.26, 28, 1 Pet.3.18.

Yeshua's example is the example for all those who are faithful to him in baptism.[22] Just as Yeshua was "obedient to death" (Phil.2.11), so too the believer who refuses to do the bidding of his evil inclination and let sin be master over him (cf. Gen.4.7) becomes obedient in service to God. The God who raised Yeshua from the dead is also faithful to raise those who are faithful to Yeshua, together with him. God's "power" and "mastery" in Yeshua is therefore His "good news (gospel) concerning His son . . . who was declared the son of God with power by the resurrection from the dead" (1.3-4; cf. 1 Cor.1.18). Yeshua was raised "because of our transgressions" (cf. 4.25), in order to "justify" the unrighteous, and his "redemption" (cf. 3.24-25)—"once and for all," instead of year by year (cf. Heb.7.27, 9.12, 28, 10.10)—delivers those who are faithful to him from the kingdom of darkness into the Kingdom of God (cf. Acts 26.18), calling into being (cf. 4.17) a people who were "not-My-people" (cf. 1 Pet.2.9-10):

> And Thou hast cleansed man of sin because of Thy glory that he may be made holy for Thee from all unclean abomination and from (every) transgression of unfaithfulness, that he may be joined wi[th] Thy sons of truth and with the lot of Thy Saints; that this vermin that is man may be raised from the dust to [Thy] secret [of truth] and from the spirit of perversity to [Thine] understanding; and that he may watch before Thee with the everlasting host and together with [Thy] spirits [of holiness], that he may be renewed with all [that is] [and] shall be and with them that know, in a common rejoicing. (1QH 11.10-14)

Verses 9-10:
"Death . . . lives to God": cf. Gen.4.7, Rom.6.14, 1 Cor.15.12-16, Gal.2.19, 4.4, Phil.2.6-9, Heb.2.14-15, Rev.1.18; 4 Macc.7.18-19.

Since death came because of (through) sin (cf. 5.12), once Yeshua became obedient to God through his death and resurrection, he was freed from the power of death (cf. 1 Cor.15.54-57). Although Yeshua was born "under the Torah" (cf. Gal.4.4), and he mastered his own inclination by dying to the Torah through being obedient to its commandments (cf. Gal.2.19), even to the point of death, God raised him to life.[23] He has thus made God "Master" of the whole world, of the living and of the dead (cf. 14.9), and now "lives to God" (cf. 2 Cor.5.14, Gal.2.19-20, Eph.5.2), in other words, to obediently serve the Creator who has put all things under his feet (cf. Eph.1.22, Col.1.16ff).[24]

Verses 12-13:

"Therefore . . . righteousness to God": cf. Lk.2.22, 15.24, 16.9-11, Jn.18.3, Acts 1.3, 20.12, Rom.3.19, 27, 4.13f, 5.20-21, 6.16, 7.4ff, 8.6, 10-13, 11.15, 12.1, 13.11-14, 1 Cor.15.22, 2 Cor.6.7, 10.4, Gal.4.4 5, 21, 5.16ff, Eph.2.1ff, 4.17ff, 5.1-27, Col.1.21-22, 2.13, 3.7, 2 Tim.2.15, Rev.1.18, 2.8; 1QS 8.4-10, 9.3-4, 11.8, 1QH 3.19f, 13.13, 17.25, 4QFlor.1.6f; ARN[a] 16, ARN [b] 16, Eccl.R.4.13.1, 4.14.1, Ned.32b.

Although Paul usually uses "therefore" to introduce either the implications or the practical application of a particular thought, here the "theological" and the "practical" aspects are hardly distinguishable, and Paul is recapitulating the same theme on which he has been elaborating throughout the whole chapter. Many rabbinic midrashim associate the number of the commandments (negative and positive) with the number of man's limbs, and describe how his limbs may obey the commandments or transgress against them:

> When a man's passions are stirred and he is about to commit an act of lewdness, all his limbs are ready to obey him, because the evil inclination is king over the two hundred and forty-eight limbs of man. On the other hand, when a man is about to perform an act of piety, all his limbs become sluggish, because the evil inclination which is within him bears sway over the two hundred and forty-eight limbs of his body, whereas the good inclination is like one confined in prison, as it is stated, *For out of prison he came forth to be king* (Eccl.4.14). . . . (ARN[a] 16; cf. PRK S3.2)

> Another interpretation of NOW THERE WAS A LITTLE CITY: i.e., the body, AND FEW MEN WITHIN IT: i.e., the limbs. AND THERE CAME A GREAT KING AGAINST IT: i.e., the Evil Inclination. (Why is it called GREAT? Because it is thirteen years older than the Good Inclination). AND BESEIGED IT: i.e., tortuous paths and concealed spots. NOW THERE WAS FOUND IN IT A MAN POOR AND WISE: i.e., the Good Inclination. (Why is it called POOR? Because it is not found in all persons, nor do most of them obey it.) AND HE BY HIS WISDOM DELIVERED THE CITY: for whoever obeys the Good Inclination escapes [punishment]. David said: Happy is he who obeys it, as it is written, *Happy is he that considereth the poor* (Ps.41.1). YET NO MAN REMEMBERED THAT SAME POOR MAN: the Holy One, blessed be He, said: 'You have not remembered it, but I will

remember it,' as it is written, *I will take away the stony heart out of your flesh, and I will give you a heart of flesh* (Ezek.36.26). (Eccl.R.9.15.8)

Verse 14:

"For sin . . . under grace": cf. Jn.1.17, Rom.3.28, 4.14, 5.15f, 7.4, 6, 8.2, Gal.4.21; Mid.Ps.71.2, 72.1, 119.55.

Paul explains how the doctrine of the Two Spirits, the Two Ways, or the two masters, enables man to serve God in righteousness instead of being in slavery to his evil inclination, which "angers" God and causes His wrath to bring punishment on all mankind. The verb "shall (not)" means "will not," in the sense that the believer who has been baptized into Yeshua's death and resurrection has been freed from sin's "law" (cf. 8.2). Paul does not make Torah and grace contradictory here, but demonstrates how when the believer frees himself from the punishment of the Torah (cf. 4.15, 5.13) in baptism, in which he puts his evil inclination to death, he is enabled to obey God's commandments.[25]

Verse 15:

"What then? . . .": cf. Jn.1.17, Rom.3.23-4, 5.17, 11.5, Eph.2.5, 8, 2 Tim.1.9, 1 Pet.1.10, 13, 3.7; 1QS 1.8, 1QH 7.20.

Paul again addresses the dangers of libertine attitudes amongst some believers (cf. 3.8, 19-20, 5.20-6.1), and repeats his refutation of the erroneous conclusion that people may sin more in order to give God's grace an opportunity to abound. God's free gift of righteousness in Yeshua does not give men the license to sin in order to give God further opportunity to bestow His grace.[26] Grace is not a warrant for antinomianism but a guarantee for faithful observance of God's will freely and out of a sincere heart.

Verses 16-19:

"Slaves . . . ": cf. Mt.6.24, Lk.16.13, Jn.8.33-35, Rom.6.12, 13, 14, 16, 17, 20, 22, 8.15, Gal.4.3, 5.1, Heb.2.15, 2 Pet.2.19; 1QS 1.6, 2.13-14, 3.3, 10.8, 11, 24, 1QH 9.16, 11.12, 17.25; Test.Jud.18.6, Test.Dan 4.7, Test.Asher 3.2, 6.5; ARN[a] 16, ARN[b] 16, TBE [S] p.1, MHG Gen.4.9, PRK S3.2, Gen.R.22.6, 34.10, Ruth R.3.1, Eccl.R.9.4.1, Hag.16a, AZ 5b, BB 17a.

Paul once again recapitulates the theme of verses 4-14, elaborating the incompatibility of serving two masters, one's evil inclination and the Creator:

R. Simeon [ben Yohai] said: *Wisdom strengtheneth [the heart] of a wise man more than ten rulers which are in the city* (Eccl.7.19). Does a

> city have ten rulers? Does it not, in fact, have only one ruler? What then does Scripture mean by *ten rulers*? When a disciple of the wise reads Scripture, recites Mishnah, occupies himself with Torah, and resolves on repentance and good deeds, he is delivered from ten harsh masters, namely, his two eyes, his two ears, his two hands, his two feet, his mouth and his male member: from his two eyes with which he looks upon money that is not his, for, as the Sages taught in a Mishnah, Do not set your eyes longingly upon money which is not yours . . .; from his two ears with which he hears idle words, since ears catch fire, so to speak, [from evil] before all other organs; from his two hands with which he steals from, robs, and assaults people . . . < . . .; from his two feet with which he runs to [sexual] transgression . . .; and from the mouth with which he speaks slander, since the mouth is first [of the body's organs] to be brought to judgment. Even > if a man reads Scripture, recites Mishnah, gives all kinds of charity during all his days, feeding the hungry, giving drink to the thirsty, clothing the naked, redeeming the captives, his deeds of charity will not for one moment make up for the noxious breath [of slander] which comes out of his mouth. . . . Finally, [in occupying himself with Torah], he is delivered from the male member's mastery of him, the member with which he sins to excess. (TBE [Pirkei Derek Eretz 16] S p.1)

Verse 17:

"Obedient . . . committed": cf. Dt. 6.5-6, 10.16, 30.6, Ps.51.10, Jer.4.4, 17.9, Mt.15.19, 22.36-40, Lk.24.25, Rom.1.5, 2.20, 10.10, 11.25, 16.17, 25, 1 Cor.2.7, Eph.3.3ff, Phil.1.9, Col.1.9, 2 Tim.1.13, Tit.1.9, Heb.10.22; 1QS 1.6ff, 2.13-14, 3.3, 15, 5.1f, 8f, 6.14f, 9.12f, 10.24, CDC 15.7, 16.9; Test.Asher 1.3ff, 2.1-10, 3.1-2, 4.1-15, 6.1-5; Sifre ARN[b] 32, Dt.Va'etchanan 32.

Putting one's evil inclination to death enables a person to commit himself to obedience to his Creator, since he cannot serve two masters simultaneously, as the Qumran texts describe:

> And this is the rule for the members of the Community, for those who volunteer to be converted from all evil and to cling to all His commands according to His will . . . They shall practice truth in common, and humility, and righteousness and justice and loving charity, and modesty in all their ways. Let no man walk in the stubbornness of his heart to stray by following his heart and eyes and the thought of his (evil) inclination. But in the Community they

shall circumcise the foreskin of the (evil) inclination and disobedience in order to lay a foundation of truth for Israel, for the Community of the everlasting Covenant . . . and let him undertake by oath of obligation to be converted to the Law of Moses according to all His commands, with all his heart and all his soul. . . . (1QS 5.1-10)

Verse 19:

"I am speaking in human terms . . . ": cf. 3.5, 8.3, 1 Cor.9.8, Gal.3.15; Kid.21b.

Paul directly addresses the issue of libertinism, and counters any possible misunderstanding of his own words in such a manner by "making a fence" around his statement.[27] He makes it clear that he is not making an absolute statement but is speaking so that he will be understood by his human readers, a device frequently found in rabbinic literature, for various purposes, including that of precluding blasphemous statements:

> *Then the Lord said unto Satan, Hast thou considered My servant Job, for there is none like him in the earth . . . and he still holdeth fast his integrity, although thou movedst me against him to destroy him without cause* (Job 1.3). Said R. Johanan: Were it not expressly stated in the Scripture, we would not dare to say it. [God is made to appear] like a man who allows himself to be persuaded against his better judgment. A Tanna taught: [Satan] comes down to earth, and seduces, then ascends to heaven and awakens wrath; permission is granted to him and he takes away the soul. (BB 16a)[28]

Paul clearly states that people should not take his words as הלכה למשה מסיני (*halakhah le-Mosheh mi-Sinai*), as it were, and use them to support libertine attitudes. On the contrary, the principle that דברה תורה בלשון בני אדם (*dibrah Torah be-lashon benei 'adam*), "the Torah speaks in the language of men," which Paul hints at here, does not enable a person to "master" his evil inclination and serve God in "newness of life" and according to the Spirit of Truth, since דלא תורה אלא כנגד יצר הרע (*de-lo' Torah 'ela' ke-neged yetzer ha-ra'*), "the Torah only provided for man's evil human passions" (Kid.21b).[29]

"Lawlessness, resulting in (further) lawlessness": cf. 8.2, 2 Thess.2.1-12; PA 4.2.

Slavery binds a person to a course of action and a pattern of conduct, just as in rabbinic thought one transgression was regarded as leading to another, and was "punished" by a further transgression:

> Ben 'Azzai said: Run to [perform] an easy precept as [you would] in [case of] a difficult one, and flee from transgression; for [one] precept draws another [in its train], and [one] transgression draws [in its train] another transgression; for the recompense for performing a precept is a precept, and the recompense for [committing] a transgression is a transgression. (PA 4.2)

Some of the Qumran texts speak of "the mystery of lawlessness" in parallel with the "mysteries of iniquity" and thus with the "spirit of perversity" and the "spirit of flesh" (cf. 1QS 3.23, 1QM 3.9, 14.9, 1QH 5.36, 1Q27 1.2). The "man of lawlessness" in 2 Thessalonians 2.7, identified in Christian exegesis with the "Antichrist," may well be linked to Belial (Satan) in Qumran, who is the "master" of the spirit of perversity.[30]

Verse 20:
" . . . free in regard to righteousness": cf. 7, 7.2-6; Pa 2. 9, 3.5, 6.2.

Paul plays on the "freedom from" sin and the "freedom to" obey God. Since a man cannot serve two masters at once, the commitment to obey one both gives him "freedom" from the mastery of the other and leaves him free to serve the other. If he chooses to let his evil inclination master him, he is not responsible to God's commandments, nor does he benefit from their reward. If he serves God, on the other hand, he is "free" from obedience to his evil inclination:

> . . . it says, And the tables were the work of God, graven upon the tables (Ex.32.16). Read not *haruth* [which means 'graven'] but *heruth* [which means 'freedom'], for there is free man for thee but he that occupies himself with the study of the Torah; and whoever regularly occupies himself with the study of the Torah, lo, he is exalted. . . . (PA 6.2)

Verse 21:
"Benefit": cf. Jer.12.13, Jn.4.36, Rom.7.5, 1 Cor.3.12-14, 9.17f; 1QS 4.6f, 15-16, 25, 1QH 8.11-12; PA 2.14, 15, 16, 4.2, Pe'ah 1.1, Lev.R.27.1.

Paul speaks of benefit in terms similar to R. Johanan's interpretation of Psalm 88.6, which is closely linked to R. Simeon's midrash on Job 3.19, according to which the dead do not have "praise" from God because they cannot observe any of the commandments and do not receive any merit stored up from good deeds in the world to come:

. . . as to what David said: '*The dead praise not the Lord*' (Ps.115.17), this is what he meant: Let a man always engage in Torah and good deeds before he dies, for as soon as he dies he is restrained from [the practice of] Torah and good deeds, and the Holy One, blessed be He, finds nought to praise in him. And thus R. Johanan said, What is meant by the verse, *Among the dead [I am] free* (Ps.88.6)? Once a man dies, he becomes free of the Torah and good deeds. . . . (Shab.30a; cf. Shab.115b)

Paul refers to a similar idea in using the Greek word καρπος (*karpos*), "fruit," which is translated here as "benefit." "Fruit" is a form of "merit," or good deeds which are "stored up" (cf. 2.5) to be given to future generations, and thus corresponds to "reward" (and/or "wages") and "inheritance" (cf. 4.4, 13-17, 5.23) as in other Jewish texts:

What is [the difference] between the disciples of Abraham, our father, and the disciples of Balaam, the wicked. The disciples of Abraham, our father, enjoy [lit. 'eat'] [their share] in this world, and inherit the world to come, as it is said: That I may cause those that love me to inherit substance and that I may fill their treasuries (Prov.8.21), but the disciples of Balaam, the wicked, inherit Gehinnom, and descend into the nethermost pit, as it is said: But Thou, O God, wilt bring them down to the nethermost pit; men of blood and deceit shall not live out half their days; but as for me, I will trust in Thee (Ps.55.24). (PA 5.19)

"Now ashamed": cf. Ezek.16.54, 63, Mk.8.36-38, Lk.9.25-6, Rom.1.16, 3.19, Eph.2.1ff, Col.3.1ff, 2 Tim.1.8, 12, Heb.2.11, 12.24; Ned.20a.

Paul speaks here, in contrast to 1.16 (where he is proud of the power of the gospel), of being "ashamed" in the biblical and rabbinic sense of "repentance":

Raba b. Hinena the elder further said in the name of Rab: If one commits a sin and is ashamed of it (מתביש), all his sins are forgiven him, as it says, *"That thou mayest remember and be confounded, and never open thy mouth any more, because of thy shame, when I have forgiven thee all that thou hast done," saith the Lord God* (Ezek.16.63). (Ber.12b)

Repentance and confession are the means whereby a person "angers" his evil inclination and puts it to death so that he may serve God instead according to the doctrine of the Two Ways:

> And I, I know that righteousness is not of man, nor of the sons of men perfection of way; to the Most High God belong all the works of righteousness, whereas the way of man is not firm unless it be by the Spirit which God has created for him to make perfect a way for the sons of men, that all His works may know the might of His power and the greatness of His mercy to all the sons of His loving-kindness. And shaking and trembling seized me and all my bones cracked, and my heart melted like wax before fire and my knees slipped like water descending a slope; for I remembered my faults and the unfaithfulness of my fathers when the wicked arose against Thy Covenant and the wretched against Thy word. And I said, It is because of my sins that I am abandoned far from Thy Covenant. But when I remembered the might of Thy hand together with the greatness of Thy mercy I rose up and stood . . . For [I] leaned on Thy favours and on the greatness of Thy mercy. For Thou pardonest iniquity and clean[sest m]an of sin by Thy righteousness . . . for Thou art Truth and all [Thy works] are righteousness. (1QH 4.30-40)

Verses 22-23:
"But now . . . Yeshua our Lord": Paul sums up his whole argument through chapters 4-6 within the framework of R. Simeon's midrash on Job 3.19, combined with the doctrine of the "Two Spirits" or "Two Ways," and defined through Yeshua's death and resurrection. Every man (cf. 2.1, 3) must choose which master he will serve—either his Creator, or his own evil inclination. When he puts his evil inclination to death by refusing to do its bidding, he makes God his master and is thus freed from the mastery of his inclination. When he dies to sin through his baptism into Yeshua's death and resurrection, God gives him His free gift of grace, and cleanses him from his evil inclination through His Spirit of holiness, and grants him newness of life to perform deeds of righteousness which are the "fruit" worthy of the repentance whose inheritance (cf. 4.13f) is eternal life. The man who makes his evil inclination his master, on the other hand, "angers" God, and inherits death and destruction:

> The Lord is faithful to those who truly love him, to those who endure his discipline, to those who live in the righteousness of his commandments, in the Law, which he has commanded for our life. The Lord's devout shall live by it forever; the Lord's paradise, the trees of life, are his devout ones. Their planting is firmly rooted forever; they shall not be uprooted as long as the heavens shall last,

> for Israel is the portion and inheritance of God. But not so are sinners and criminals, who love (to spend) the day in sharing their sin. Their inheritance is brief and decaying, and they do not remember God. . . . Therefore their inheritance is Hades, and darkness and destruction; and they will not be found on the day of mercy for the righteous. But the devout of the Lord will inherit life in happiness. . . . And the inheritance of sinners is destruction and darkness, and their lawless actions shall pursue them below into Hades. Their inheritance shall not be found for their children, for lawless actions shall devastate the homes of sinners. And sinners shall perish forever in the day of the Lord's judgment, when God oversees the earth at his judgment, but those who fear the Lord shall find mercy in it and shall live by their God's mercy; but sinners shall perish for all time. (Ps.Sol.14.1-10, 15.10-13)

Here Paul concludes the section which he begins in 5.12, based on the principle of כלל ופרט (*kelal ufrat*) "general principle and particular."[31] His "general principle" there states that through one man death came into the world, and through one man life eternal was given to mankind. In 5.17-6.23, he then "details" how this is effected, including the relation of God's justification of all mankind to the Torah, grace, works, faithfulness, and righteousness. In chapter 7, he returns to the objections of his Jewish readers, and takes up the concept of freedom from one's evil inclination in death (cf. Ps.88.6 and Ps.115.17) in relation to the Torah (cf. Ps.88.6), taking up R. Johanan's side of R. Simeon b. Pazzi's midrash on Job 3.19, where the dead do not earn "praise" from God because they can no longer gain merit from Torah-observance, using the biblical comparison of idolatry as adultery to describe how the believer must be released from the Torah-framework of reward and punishment in order to become free to be God's bride.

Endnotes on Chapter 6

1 Paul faces opposition from two quarters on this issue. The group of "Judaizers" among the early Jewish believers claimed that Gentiles could only become "fellow-heirs" in the commonwealth of Israel if they converted to Judaism and fully observed the Torah. Many of the Hellenistic Jewish believers, on the other hand, held an antinomian attitude and claimed that neither Jews nor Gentiles were any longer "under the Law." Paul takes up the implications of this latter view in chapter 6.

2 Cf. also the terms פשיטא (*peshita'*!), in which a statement whose apparently obvious meaning is in fact demonstrated to be more complicated than at first glance; and מהו דתימא (*mahu de-teima'*), "lest you say erroneously" (that we shall continue in sin) . . ., קא משמע לן (*ka' mishma' lan*), "it tells us in fact" (how can we live in sin who died to it?); see A. Steinsaltz, *Talmud*, 129, 137. See also verse 15, and the comments on 7.1.

3 See the comments on 3.5-8.

4 The capitalized section quotes the Mishnah from PA 2.4, on which saying the author or editor of Abot de Rabbi Nathan proceeds to comment.

5 Cf. Mt.16.25, Lk.17.33, Jn.12.25-26, Sifra 93d, Ber.61b. Self-abstinence and asceticism were often practiced as a way of life by the *Tannaitic Chasidim*, the "pious ones," who were largely responsible for the production of the Derekh Eretz literature; see M. Lerner, "The External Tractates," in *The Literature of the Sages*, ed. S. Safrai (Philadelphia: Fortress Press, 1987), 1:379-89.

6 Cf. Ruth R.8.1 for the same concept. For the textual history and understanding of this midrashic tradition, see D. Flusser and S. Safrai, "The Slave of Two Masters," in *Judaism*, 169-72.

7 Cf. TDNT 1:538ff.

8 See the comments on 3.25. The textual variants which add "into the Messiah" or "into the name of . . . " reflect some of the historical and doctrinal development of baptismal practices. 1 Cor.1.13 indicates that "baptism into the name" had already become a formula in the early community, approaching the sacramental usage in Mt.28.16. This usage is clearly based upon an earlier conception which associates baptism into Yeshua with Moses when Israel crossed the Red Sea: the people "believed Me and followed Moses" (cf. Ex.R.21.8), and were thus delivered from the slaughter of the Egyptians when they passed through the water. Moses, who was regarded as God's שליח (*shaliach*; "agent"), is the prototype for baptism "into Yeshua"—"having faith in the shepherd of Israel is the same as having faith in Him who spoke and the world came into being" (Mekh.Beshall.7); cf. also 2 Cor.12.13 and Gal.3.27.

9 This aspect was the original element of baptism within the early community, which baptized "for the remission of sins." Paul's integration of baptism within the context of the "two masters" further serves to strengthen the idea that as an act which puts sin to death, or in which the believer "dies to sin," baptism is an integral part of the faithfulness which leads to new birth and the inheritance of eternal life in Yeshua.

10 The talmudic discussion in Yebamot relates to the necessity or otherwise of ritual immersion for the proselyte, on the presupposition that

proselytes are subject to the same conditions "as your forefathers [i.e., Israel] entered into the Covenant only by circumcision, immersion and the sprinkling of the blood" (Ker.9a). The appeal to Ex.24.8 and the Mishnaic "tradition," however, indicates not only that the Rabbis understood the "sprinking of the blood" (i.e., a sacrifice) as an act parallel in significance to immersion in water (ritual ablution), but considered immersion to be even more important than circumcision, at least for the proselyte.

11 This text establishes the fact that even the righteous are in need of atonement, and that burial is a part of the process of atonement. Several other rabbinic texts say that death itself atones; cf. Ber.60a, Tos.San.9.5. The baptism that Paul speaks of in Col.2.12 is synonymous with the circumcision of the Messiah, "made without hands," the same phrase which he applies in Eph.2.11 to circumcision (cf. Dt.10.16, 30.6, Jer.4.4, 9.25-26; 1QS 5.5), and uses in 2 Cor.5.1 to describe the "spiritual" body. Circumcision and baptism are further linked, according to the passage in Kerithoth quoted above, through the "sprinkling of blood," and in several other texts through the cleansing presence of the Holy Spirit; see the comments on 2.29. It is possible, however, that Paul derives the idea of burial from the context of Job 3.19, in which Job laments over his birth and wishes to be in his grave rather than among the living.

12 The symbolic death and burial represented in baptism may also be associated with a tradition linked to Adam. Adam symbolizes both pristine and sinful man. He therefore stands as a central baptismal image, embodying the "old" and "new" man. Having broken God's commandment not to eat of the fruit of the tree of the knowledge of good and evil, his sense of shame gave rise to the need for an outer covering, and he used fig leaves to cover their nakedness. God replaced these with "garments of skin," which are identified in several midrashim with the physical or earthly body of man: by a wordplay on the Hebrew text in Gen.3.21, the idea is generated that Adam was originally created out of "garments of light" (אור; *'or*), but when he sinned, he received garments of skin (עור; *'or*); cf. Gen.R.20.12, Zohar 1, 36b, Philo, *De Virt.*76, *Quaest.*(Gen.)1.53, 2.69; see also G. Scholem, *The Messianic Idea in Judaism* (NY: Schocken, 1975), 303. Death and burial here become more than linguistic metaphors. According to Gal.3.27, baptism is a "putting on" at the same time as a "burial" or "putting off." It thus represents the act of putting off the body of death in the putting on of Yeshua; cf. Ezek.44.19, Job.29.14, Rom.6.6, 7.6, 13.14, Gal.3.27, Eph.4.22-24, Col.3.9-10. The contrast between the "garments of cotton" (the body) and "garments of light" (the

soul) is maybe a variant on the theme of the body as the temple built with human hands or by God Himself. Adamic typology is also a link in the association between "newness of life" and "new birth," since "the little child is a standard metaphor of innocence and sinlessness like that of Adam and Eve before the Fall." See J.Z. Smith, "The Garments of Shame," *History of Religion* 5 (1966), 217-38; cf. Mt.18.3, Shep.Herm.Sim.9.29.1-3.

13 Paul thus builds on his argument in 3.21-4.25, and anticipates the themes of chapter 8.

14 Cf. Gen.4.23, Ex.21.25, Ps.38.5, Prov.20.30, Isa.1.6.

15 The connection between healing and the forgiveness of sin is found in biblical texts such as Ps.103.3, and Yeshua also links the two concepts in Mt.9.2ff. Numerous rabbinic texts suggest that sufferings atone for man's sins (cf. Mid.Ps.106.9, Gen.R.65.9), although, in keeping with Paul's statement here, the most effective form of atonement is death, at times said to be dependent also on repentance (cf. PYoma 5.9, San.6.2, Tos.San.9.5, Ber.60a), just as the death of the righteous man is also claimed to atone for sin (cf. PYoma 1.1, 38b, Lev.R.20.12, MK 28a).

16 The first Adam represents the "old man" through whom sin entered the world; the Second or Last Adam—the Messiah—is the "new man" who is righteous before God; cf. esp. 1 Cor.15.20-23, 39-49. It is possible that this idea reflects a "proto-gnostic" concept grounded in two creations and two Adams; cf. 1QS 4.23; see also the comments on 8.17.

17 This midrash plays on two words: Beit Hillel interpret the noun *kevasim* ("he-lambs") from the root "to wash" or "to cleanse" (כבס; *kavas*), and refer the noun שנה (*shanah*; "a year old") to the adjective שנים (*shanim*; "scarlet" but also "years") in Isa.1.18. The offering (the lamb) thus "washes" the people's sins away (cf. in baptism), and makes them like "new-born" children. [*Beit Shammai*, on the other hand, derive the word for "he-lambs" from the root כבש (*kavash*), and thus read the verse as "they that put out of sight," as in Mic.7.19: "He will turn again and have compassion on us; He will put our iniquities out of sight [*yikbosh*]." Beit Shammai therefore consider that the offerings "suppress" Israel's sins, while Beit Hillel regard them as "washing the sins clean."]

18 Yeshua also spoke of crucifixion metaphorically as "taking up your cross," in the sense of a person's willingness to accept the consequence of discipleship and to "renounce" everything in order to follow him; cf. Mt.10.38, 16.24-26, Mk.8.34-37, Lk.9.23-25.

19 R. Jeremiah gives another interpretation of Job 3.19, which closely corresponds to Yeshua's words in Mt.10.39, 16.25 and parallels:

> R. Jeremiah questioned R. Zera: What is meant by, *The small and great are there* [sc. the next world]; *and the servant is free from his master*? Do we then not know that '*the small and great are there*'—But [it means that] he who humbles himself for the sake of Torah in this world is magnified in the next; and he who makes himself a servant to the [study of the] Torah in this world becomes free in the next. (BM 85b)

20 See also the comments on 2.25.

21 הקש or analogy is one of the important rabbinic exegetical principles according to which, when two cases are mentioned together in the same verse(s) they are assumed to be analogous and legal inferences may be drawn from comparing them; cf. Dt.22.26; see A. Steinsaltz, *Talmud*, 151-52. Paul applies the analogy here to life and death: if a person dies to sin in baptism into Yeshua's death, he is also raised to new life in Yeshua's resurrection.

22 Although the Tanakh gives examples of physical resurrection, the people who were raised subsequently died again; cf. 1 Kings 17.17-24, 2 Kings 4.18-37.

23 Paul picks up the theme of sin in relation to obedience to the Torah in chapter 7.

24 The verse in Mk.12.26, which quotes Ex.3.6 ("I am the God of Abraham, and the God of Isaac, and the God of Jacob"), which implies God is "living," is also brought by Yeshua as a prooftext for the resurrection, in which Yeshua masters death.

25 See also the comments on 8.2.

26 Developments in Christian theology have proven Paul's fears justified in this regard, since he is frequently described by both Christian and Jewish scholars as being antinomian and rejecting the legitimacy of observing the Torah. Even in his own lifetime, Paul was falsely accused of teaching against the Law of Moses (cf. Acts 21.21).

27 See also the comments on 3.5 and 7.7 (making a fence).

28 See also the comments on 3.5.

29 See the comments on 3.19-20 and 8.3.

30 Yeshua also refers to Israel's "father" (or "master") as Satan, the "father of lies," a title similar to the "Preacher of Lies" in 1QpHab 10.9 and the "prophet of lies" in the Oracle of Hystaspes. These texts all refer to a figure who will call himself, or be called, God and the Son of God in the wicked times at the End of Days. See D. Flusser, "The Hubris of the Antichrist in a Fragment from Qumran," in *Judaism*, 207-213.

31 See the comments on 2.1.

ROMANS

7

Introduction

Paul continues to refute certain libertine arguments. In chapters 5-6 he primarily deals with the issue of God's justification of the Gentiles through faithfulness. He now takes up the claim (verse 1) that Jewish believers are, by the same token, either no longer responsible to the Torah or able to overcome their evil inclination through Torah-observance alone. Based on the biblical depiction of Israel's idolatry as adultery (especially in Jeremiah 3), he describes the "master" which Israel serves as her "husband," to whom she may be faithful or with whom she may play the harlot. He appeals to a rabbinic *halakhah* (ruling) concerning marriage, according to which a woman may remarry following either divorce from her husband or his death (verses 1-3); and demonstrates that the believer is freed to serve God (to remarry) when he is released from the marriage framework (the Torah) (verses 4-6). He then counters the objection that his argument proposes that the Torah itself is "sinful" (verses 7-14), and describes the true role of the Torah in the life of the believer, which, because it determines and defines the nature of sin (verses 7-8), causes each person (and he takes himself as a personal example) to acknowledge that if he lets his evil inclination master him (instead of putting it to death or dying to sin in baptism; cf. chapter 6), he both affirms the righteousness of the Torah and his inability to keep its commandments (verses 14-23). It is therefore only by joining himself to Yeshua's death and resurrection in baptism that God releases him from his former master (his evil inclination) to serve God with a whole and clean heart, and to receive the free gift of God's grace in Yeshua through which he inherits eternal life.

Verse 1:

"Or do you not know, brethren . . . ": cf. 2.4, 6.3, 16, 7.4.

Paul repeats his claim (cf. 6.3, 16) that his readers should "know" what he is teaching them. This time, however, he specifically refers to his "brethren," a word which he then explains as "those who know the Torah."

He immediately makes it clear, therefore, that he is addressing the Jewish believers in the Roman congregation.[1] Paul directly appeals to his "kinsmen" in order to bring out the biblical basis of his argument, which here has specific relevance to Israel. God's covenant in the Torah demands the people's faithfulness and obedience to God. When they disobeyed and worshipped other gods, God regarded their idolatry as adultery.[2] Paul's expression "or do you not know . . . " further reflects the talmudic term קא משמע לן (*ka' mashma' lan*), "it tells us," since he is confronting several possible erroneous conclusions to his argument in chapters 5 and 6, and now wants to counter certain specifically Jewish objections which his readers might raise.[3] What he "comes to tell" his readers is that he is not justifying a libertine attitude: they are not to understand from his analogy of the two Adams (in chapter 5) that they are "free from the Torah" and its commandments because God has given His grace to them through Yeshua. His argument until this point, however, might allow his Jewish readers to understand that they can overcome their evil inclination simply through observing the Torah.[4]

"The law has jurisdiction . . . ": cf. 3.19-20, 4.15, 5.20.

Paul takes up his argument from 3.19-20 (cf. 4.15 and 5.20), intending to clarify the relation of the Torah to the theme of serving two masters which he introduces in chapter 6.[5] There, in the same way as R. Simeon b. Pazzi interprets the verse "and the servant is free from his master" in Job 3.19, Paul explains that "angering" one's evil inclination in order to serve God is accomplished through "dying" to it, in terms of "dying to sin" or putting one's inclination to death.[6] Now he takes up the issue raised by another midrash, given in the name of R. Johanan, and based on Psalms 88.5 and 115.17:

> As to what David said: '*The dead praise not the Lord*' (Ps.115.17), this is what he meant: Let a man always engage in Torah and good deeds before he dies, for as soon as he dies he is restrained from [the practice of] Torah and good deeds, and the Holy One, blessed be He, finds nought to praise in him. And thus R. Johanan said, What is meant by the verse, *Among the dead [I am] free* (Ps.88.6 [E.V. vs.5: cast off among the dead])? Once a man dies, he becomes free of the Torah and good deeds. (Shab.30a)[7]

Paul "comes to tell" his Jewish readers here that Torah-observance does not free a man from his evil inclination, despite the fact that according to the normative Jewish view expressed here by R. Johanan, it brings him "praise" (credit) from God. Paul thus comes to a similar conclusion to R. Simeon, rather than to R. Johanan's view.[8] When a man dies to his evil inclination he is free to obey the Torah in obeying his Creator (cf. 6.17f), just as when the people Israel stop playing the harlot with idols and obey God as their husband or master.[9]

Verses 2-3:
"Married woman . . . ": cf. Ex.22.16, Lev.21.7, Num.5.11ff, Dt.21.10f, 24.1-5, Jer.3.1ff, Jn.15.19, Rom.8.7-8, 1 Cor.6.16-17, 7.39.

In the biblical and rabbinic world, marriage was a legal contract which contained binding conditions. Paul appeals to current *halakhic* ordinances governing the rules of marriage, divorce, and adultery, which explained that a woman might remarry without being regarded as an adulteress not only through divorce (a biblical provision), but also through the death of her husband:

> A WOMAN IS ACQUIRED [IN MARRIAGE] IN THREE WAYS AND ACQUIRES HER FREEDOM IN TWO. . . . SHE ACQUIRES HER FREEDOM BY DIVORCE OR BY HER HUSBAND'S DEATH. As for divorce, it is well, since it is written, *then he shall write her a bill of divorcement* (Dt.24.1); but whence do we know [that she is freed by] her husband's death?—It is logic: he [the husband] bound her; hence he frees her . . . thus death is compared to divorce: just as divorce completely frees [lit. 'permits'] her, so does death completely free her. (Kid.1.1 [Mishnah] and 13b)[10]

According to the Torah, a married woman is forbidden to remarry under pain of death (cf. Lev.18.20, 20.10, Dt.22.22). The Sages made a *halakhic* ruling, however, that a woman who remarries following the death of her husband is not guilty of adultery, even though the Torah only permits remarriage if her husband has given her a bill of divorce:

> If her husband's death has effect, let her be entirely free; and if not, let her remain in her original status! Why not? It [her husband's death] withdraws her from [the penalty of] death and places her under [the interdict of] an affirmative precept [as a married woman she is forbidden to others by a negative precept under pain of death]. (Kid.13b)

The *halakhah* thus adds to the biblical regulation the legal possibility of a woman being "freed" from her husband and from her marriage not only if he gives her a bill of divorce but also if he dies. Since his death is thus as legally effective as divorce, a married woman is also thereby freed from the penalties for committing adultery. The woman is in fact considered by the Rabbis to be unmarried, and thus free to marry (to "join herself") to another man (another "master").[11]

Verse 4:

"Therefore . . . ": cf. 6.2, 7.1, 6.

Paul now explains the implications of what his argument comes to "tell us" (cf. verse 1). Having warned his Gentile readers against misinterpreting his argument in chapters 5-6 as encouraging libertinism, he now warns his Jewish readers ("my brethren") against misinterpreting the same argument to exclude God's righteousness in Yeshua's death and resurrection. A person may only "live to God" by dying to the Torah through the Torah. Paul exploits the *halakhic* emendation of the biblical ordinance which permits a woman to remarry if her husband dies. He then conflates the position of the married woman and her husband. The woman "dies to" her husband at the same time as his death enables her to be "free" to remarry. The believer may therefore "join himself" to his Creator by "dying to" or putting to death his evil inclination. At the same time, he is also freed from the marital framework (i.e., the Torah) which imposes the death penalty for adultery (idolatry)—for serving two "masters," God and "Ba'al" or "Belial." Since the Torah regulates rewards and punishments, it "determines" what sin and transgression is (cf. 3.20, 4.15, 5.13, 20).[12] The Torah itself does not "die" or become obsolete, but its penalties are annulled when a person commits himself to serving his Creator and puts his own inclination to death. He is free to obey its ordinances in obedience to his Creator when he "dies to sin" through his baptism into Yeshua's death and resurrection. Paul explains this by interpreting verses such as Job 3.19 in the light of the halakhot of marriage, divorce, and adultery. A person ("woman") cannot have relations with two men: either she is married to her husband, or she commits adultery by "joining herself" to another man. Just as a person cannot serve two masters, his evil inclination or God, at one and the same time, so Israel also cannot simultaneously serve God and their own inclination. Moreover, Torah-observance does not gain a man merit in the world to come, to which death puts an end. Contrary to R. Johanan's view, since the Torah regulates the conditions of marriage—and therefore also of adultery—it can only be obeyed once a person has been taken out from under its jurisdiction.

"Through the body of the Messiah . . . ": cf. 4.24-25, 6.3ff, 23, 1 Cor.10.16, 15.12ff, Eph.2.15, Col.1.22, Heb.2.14, 10.10, 5, 19-22.

Paul describes Yeshua's redemption as delivering men from "this present evil age" (cf. Gal.1.4) in the additional marital regulations concerning יבום (*yibbum*) and חליצה (*chalitzah*).[13] In this context the Torah represents the evil inclination's enmity to God, since the commandments of the Torah govern human passions (cf. Kid.21b). In dying to his evil inclination, a person also dies to the regulations which govern it in the Torah: "For through the Torah I died to the Torah that I might live to God" (Gal.2.19).[14]

" . . . bear fruit for God": cf. Mt.3.8f, 7.16f, 12.33, 21.19, 33-43, Lk.6.43f, Jn.12.24, Rom.6.21, 8.23, 2 Cor.5.15, Gal.5.19-23, Eph.5.8-11, Col.1.10, Tit.3.14, Jas.3.12; 1QS 4.2-14, 1QH 8.11-13, 18; 4 Ez.3.20, 6.27-28, 1 En.91.1ff, Sir.27.6, 2 Bar.32.1; PA 4.11, Gen.R.16.3, 30.6, Lev.R.27.1, Shab.127a.

The essence of "fruit" is that it is the natural product of the tree which bears it. As in 6.21, Paul speaks of "fruit" as "wages" or "benefit" in the sense of "meriting the world to come."[15] The fruit which the believer bears is the product of God's gift of righteousness, which he receives in his baptism into Yeshua's death and resurrection. Having put his evil inclination to death and died to sin, the believer is enabled to perform God's will in keeping his commandments, and so to serve God in the "newness of (eternal) life." Righteousness and salvation are thus also the "fruit" which God gives to His sons as the inheritance of eternal life according to several contemporary Jewish texts:

> The fountain of righteousness, the reservoir of power, and the dwelling-place of glory are denied to the assembly of flesh; but God has given them as an everlasting possession to those whom He has chosen. He has granted them a share in the lot of the Saints, and has united their assembly, the Council of the Community, with the Sons of Heaven. And the assembly of the holy Fabric shall belong to an eternal planting for all time to come. (1QS 11.6-9)

> Our Rabbis taught: It is related of King Monobaz that he dissipated all his own hoards and the hoards of his fathers in years of scarcity. His brothers and his father's household came in a deputation to him and said to him, 'Your father saved money and added to the treasures of his fathers, and you are squandering them.' He replied: 'My fathers stored up below and I am storing above, as it says, *Truth springeth*

> *out of the earth and righteousness looketh down from heaven* (Ps.85.11). My fathers stored in a place which can be tampered with, but I have stored in a place which cannot be tampered with, as it says, *Righteousness and judgement are the foundations of his throne* (Ps.97.2). My fathers stored something which does not produce fruits, but I have stored something which does produce fruits, as it is written, *Say of the righteous [tzaddik] that it shall be well with them, for they shall eat of the fruit of their doings* (Isa.3.10). My fathers gathered treasures of money, but I have gathered treasures of souls, as it is written, *The fruit of the righteous [tzaddik] is a tree of life, and he that is wise winneth souls* (Prov.11.30). My fathers gathered for others and I have gathered for myself, as it says, *And for thee it shall be righteousness [tzedakah]* (Dt.24.13). My fathers gathered for this world, but I have gathered for the future world, as it says, *Thy righteousness [tzedakah] shall go before thee, and the glory of the Lord shall be thy rearward* (Isa.58.8).' (BB 11a)

Verse 5:

"Sinful passions . . . fruit for death": cf. 3.19-20, 4.15, 5.13, 20, 6.12ff, 7.7f, 8.8, 2 Cor.10.3; 1QS 4.20-22, 11.12-15, 1QH 10.23, 13.13-14, 17.25; 4 Ez.3.20, 15.5-7, 20f, 1 En.91.1ff, Ps.Sol.15.7f, Test.Gad 4.7; PA 2.9, 5.19.

A person chooses to serve either his "evil inclination" (יצר הרע; *yetzer ha-ra'*) or the "spirit of the flesh" ("the spirit of perversity"), or his Creator, since his "flesh" or body (human appetites and attitudes) is subject to his will. A person must therefore "present his members"—his body—either to God or to the "spirits of Belial." The effect of the Torah, although its commandments are "holy and righteous and good," is to activate those passions which serve ("belong to") the evil inclination. Paul appeals here to the language of "divine condescendence" in which the Torah "provided for [spoke to] man's evil passions" (cf. Kid.21b). The Torah does not change human nature but "accommodates" itself to man's weaknesses and limitations. The "fruit" (cf. "reward") of sinful deeds is death and destruction, whereas the righteous "inherit" eternal life:

> Whoever possesses these three things, he is of the disciples of Abraham, our father; and [whoever possesses] three other things, he is of the disciples of Balaam, the wicked. The disciples of Abraham, our father, [possess] a good eye, an humble spirit and a lowly soul. The disciples of Balaam, the wicked, [possess] an evil eye, a haughty spirit and an overambitious soul. What is [the difference] between the disciples of

> Abraham, our father, and the disciples of Balaam, the wicked. The disciples of Abraham, our father, enjoy [lit. 'eat'] [their share] in this world, and inherit the world to come, as it is said: That I may cause those that love Me to inherit substance and that I may fill their treasuries (Prov.8.21), but the disciples of Balaam, the wicked, inherit Gehinnom, and descend into the nethermost pit, as it is said: But Thou, O God, wilt bring them down to the nethermost pit; men of blood and deceit shall not live out half their days . . . (Ps.55.24). (PA 5.19)[16]

Verse 6:
" . . . released from the Law . . . ": cf. 6.22, 7.2, 24, Heb.8.1ff, 10.1ff.

Paul recapitulates his argument from chapter 6 and the preceding verses, and clearly states that "release from the Torah" (cf. חליצה; *chalitzah*) corresponds to "dying to sin." He also picks up the theme of the "Spirit" and the "letter" (cf. 2.29), integrating it here into the motif of serving two masters.[17] A person must be "free" to serve one master or the other. He is either "bound," in the "oldness of the letter," to serve his evil inclination ("that by which we were bound"), or he is "freed" from his inclination to serve his Creator. Serving God by putting the evil inclination to death leads to the "inheritance" of eternal life by walking according to the Spirit of Truth (cf. 6.4-5), just as the Qumran literature describes man's total dependence on God's grace as the only way to be justified:

> And I, I know that righteousness is not of man, nor of the sons of men perfection of way; to the Most High God belong all the works of righteousness, whereas the way of man is not firm unless it be by the Spirit which God has created for him to make perfect a way for the sons of men . . . For it is Thou who hast established them from before eternity and the work [. . .] they shall recount Thy glory in all Thy dominion. For Thou hast caused them to see what they had not known [by bringing to an end the] former [things] and by creating things that are new, by setting aside the former covenants and by [set]ting up that which shall remain for ever. . . . And Thou hast cleansed man of sin because of Thy glory that he may be made holy for Thee from all unclean abomination and from (every) transgression of unfaithfulness . . . that this vermin that is man may be raised from the dust to [Thy] secret [of truth] and from the spirit of perversity to [Thine] understanding . . . that he may be renewed with all [that is] [and] shall be and with them that know, in a common rejoicing. (1QH 4.30-32, 13.10-12, 11.10-14)

Verse 7:

"What shall we say then?": cf. 3.3, 5, 9, 4.1, 6.1f, 15f, 9.30, 11.1, 7, 11, Gal.2.18f.

Paul immediately stops to counter yet another possible erroneous conclusion which people might draw from his statements.[18] In linking the Torah so closely to human passions (cf. the principle of "divine accommodation"), he lays his argument open to the charge that the Torah is itself "sin"(ful).[19] Paul unequivocally denies that its "divine condescendence," in which God "accommodates" Himself to man's weaknesses, implicates the Torah in the "spirit of the flesh," and reiterates his claim (cf. 3.20) that the Torah "brings knowledge" of sin. The knowledge (consciousness) of sin intervenes between the Torah and sin, so that the Torah is an "agent" given to "provide" for man's sinful passions but is not a part of those passions. The rabbinic dictum which states that "an agent is as the one who sent him" (cf. Ber.5.5) indicates that the Torah is as "holy and righteous and good" as the God who gave it. As in the book of 4 Ezra, Paul recognizes that while the Torah is holy, it does not have the power to remove man's evil inclination from within him:

> Yet you did not take away from them their evil heart, so that your Law might bring forth fruit in them. For the first Adam, burdened with an evil heart, transgressed and was overcome, as were also all who were descended from him. Thus the disease became permanent; the law was in the people's heart along with the evil root, but what was good departed, and the evil remained. (4 Ez.3.20-23; cf. 9.32-37)

" . . . known about coveting": cf. Ex.18.21, 20.17, Dt.5.21, 7.25, Ps.119.36, Ezek.33.31, Mt.19.16-26, Mk.7.22, 10.17-30, Lk.12.15ff, 18.18-30, Rom.13.9, 1 Cor.5.11, 6.10, Eph.5.5, Col.3.5; CDC 4.14-ff; Test.Reub.3.3, 6.4, Test.Sim.3.1-5.3, Test.Jud.18.2-6, 4 Macc.2.6, Sir.23.5-6; Pes.Rab.21.17, PYoma 6.4, 43d.

At first sight, Paul's appeal to "coveting" seems to be an example of the way in which the Torah brings about the knowledge of sin. However, several streams of Jewish thought emphasize the fact that the injunction against coveting is equal to the Torah in its entirety. Thus a passage in the Damascus Document from Qumran, for example, associates lust (sexual covetousness) with wealth as one of the "snares" of Belial:

> And in all those years Belial shall be unleashed against Israel; as God said by the hand of the prophet Isaiah son of Amoz, *Terror and pit and snare are upon thee, O inhabitant of the land* {Isa.24.17}. The explanation of this (is that) these are Belial's three nets, of which Levi son of Jacob spoke, by which he (Belial) ensnared Israel, and which he set [be]fore them as three sorts of righteousness: the first is lust, the second is riches, (and) the third is defilement of the sanctuary. . . . The builders of the wall . . . have been caught by lust in two things: by marrying two women during their lifetime, whereas nature's principle is *Male and female created He them* {Gen.1.27}. (CDC 4.13-21)[20]

The link between covetousness, lust, and divorce reflects the themes which Paul describes in the immediately preceding verses (1-3) in terms of the motif of the "two masters." The renunciation of wealth and covetousness in the form of material possessions is explicitly connected with the motif of slavery in a passage in the Manual of Discipline:

> And these are the norms of conduct for the man of understanding in these times, concerning what he must love and how he must hate. Everlasting hatred for all the men of the Pit because of their spirit of hoarding [כרוח הסתר]. He shall surrender his property to them and the wages of the work of his hands [עמל כפיים], as a slave to his master [כעבד למושל בו] and as a poor man in the presence of his overlord. But he shall be a man full of zeal for the Precept, whose time is for the Day of Vengeance. (1QS 9.22-23)[21]

Paul, like some of the writers of the Qumran literature, therefore seems to regard "coveting" as a direct manifestation of the "spirit of the flesh."[22] He may therefore have chosen coveting not merely as an example of one of the Torah's commandments, but as representative of the whole Torah, especially since the commandment specifically refers to coveting your neighbor's wife (cf. Ex.20.17, Dt.5.20), which carries the connotations of adultery as idolatry (cf. Dt.7.25).[23] Coveting is not simply one example of the Torah's injunction (even of one of the "Ten Commandments") but represents the principle of the whole Torah itself, according to rabbinic literature:

> R. Jakum said: He who violates the command *Thou shalt not covet* is as one transgressing all Ten Commandments. . . . (Pes.Rab.21.17; cf. Col.3.5)

Verse 8:

"Sin, taking opportunity": cf. 11, Gal.5.13, Jas.1.14; ARN[b] 1, PRE 13, Ber.R.19.3.

The Torah, by prohibiting covetousness, makes people aware of coveting, and prompts the evil inclination's desire to covet. The idea that the Torah "arouses" sin is reflected in a series of rabbinic midrashim based on the concept of "making a fence round the Law." The idea of a "hedge" was most frequently employed as a safeguard against violating biblical commandments, in that the Sages added non-biblical injunctions to those explicitly stated in order to protect ("hedge") the ordinances which the Torah itself commands (cf. PA 1.1, 3.13, ARN[a] 26, Nid.4b). Here, however, the adding of prohibitions is instead perceived as leading to violation of the heart of the Torah:

> Where are we told that Adam made a hedge about his words? When the Holy One, blessed be He, said to him: "You may eat freely of every tree of the garden; but of the tree of the knowledge of good and evil you shall not eat" (Gen.2.16-17). Now, from the words of Eve we learn that Adam hedged her in. The serpent debated with himself, saying: If I go to Adam and speak to him, I know that he will not listen to me. Instead, I will go to Eve because I know that women are influenced by everyone. He went and said to her: "Did God say, 'You shall not eat of any tree of the garden (Gen.3.1)." She said to him: "No, we may eat of the fruit of the trees of the garden; but God said, 'You shall not eat of the fruit of the tree which is in the midst of the garden, neither shall you touch it, lest you die' (Gen.3.2-3)." As soon as the serpent heard Eve's words, he found the weak spot in her argument [מצא פתח להכנס בה; lit., he found an opening through which to enter]. (ARN[b] 1)[24]

Right at the beginning of creation, the sin of Adam and Eve reflects the association which coveting reflects between idolatry and adultery:

> The serpent went and spake to the woman: Is it (true that) you also have been commanded concerning the fruit of the tree [garden]? She said (to him): Yes, as it is said, "Of the fruit of the tree which is in the midst of the garden" (Gen.3.3). And when the serpent heard the words of Eve, he found a way [lit. 'opening'] through which he could enter (to approach her), so he said to her: This precept is nought except the evil eye, for in the hour when ye eat thereof, ye will be like Him, a God. Just as He creates worlds and destroys worlds, so

> will ye be able to create worlds and destroy worlds. Just as He slays and brings to life, so also will ye be able to kill and to bring to life, as it is said, "For God doth know that in the day ye eat thereof, then your eyes shall be opened" (ibid.. 5). (PRE 13)[25]

Verse 9:

"I was once alive . . . ": cf. ARN[a] 16.2, ARN[b] 16, Eccl.R.4.13.1, BM 85b.

Paul's statement, which he picks up from 3.7-8, reflects both autobiographical and "temporal" elements, although there he infers from his own example to "man" in general.[26] According to Jewish custom, a boy becomes responsible for his transgressions when he becomes bar mitzvah—when he becomes a "son of the commandment."[27] Until then he is not obligated ("bound") to observe the Torah, nor is he "bound" by its commandments and punished for their transgression. Before his bar mitzvah he is "free of" (from) the commandments and exempt from their penalties. Once he enters into God's covenant, however, he loses his independence and must either die to sin by putting his evil inclination to death or accept the wages of sin which are death (cf. 6.23):

> It is written, *God made man upright* (Eccl.7.29) and that *Man is become like one of us* (Gen.3.22). God, who is righteous and upright, created man in order that he should be upright and righteous like Himself. But if you say, "Why did God create the *yetzer*?" or, "No man can keep himself (from the power of the *yetzer*)," the reply is: "Why does a child of five, six, seven, eight or nine years not sin, but only at ten years and upwards? He himself makes his *yetzer* big. *You* make your *yetzer* bad. Why did you, when you were a child, not sin? But when you grew up you sinned. There are many things in the world harder and bitterer than the *yetzer*, such as lupin, mustard and capers, but by soaking them in water etc. you know how to make them soft and sweet. If the bitter things, which I have created, you can make sweet, to meet your own needs, how much more the *yetzer*, which has been delivered into your hand." (Tanh.Ber.7)

"When the commandment came, sin became alive": cf. 3.19-20, 4.15, 5.12, 7.5, Jas.1.14-15; ARN[a] 16.2, ARN[b] 16, Eccl.R.4.13.1.

Paul builds here on the material of 5.12 and 7.5 (cf. 3.19-20, 4.15), "for until Torah, sin was in the world; but sin is not imputed when there is no Torah." Sin was present before the Torah was given, but paradoxically sin achieves its "power" through the Torah (cf. 1 Cor.15.56). The power ("wages") of sin is death (cf. 6.23), and Paul says that when sin "became alive, I died." Although this death appears to be involuntary (and thus recalls Paul's discussion in chapter 5), it is also directly linked to the necessity of serving two masters. Prior to his bar mitzvah, Paul was alive because he was not "bound" to put his evil inclination to death. When he entered the covenant of the Torah, however, he had to choose which master he would serve. In order to serve God he had to "anger" his inclination by putting it to death—and thus he died. He must "die" to his evil inclination (under whose mastery he cannot obey God) in order to "become alive" to serve God in righteousness:

> The inclination to evil, as the Sages tell us, is thirteen years older than the Inclination to good. Since a man's Inclination to evil is born as he leaves his mother's womb, it keeps growing even as he grows. Accordingly, if he proceeds to violate the Sabbath [before he has reached the age of thirteen], there is nothing to stay his hand. And if he proceeds to commit an act of unchastity [before the age of thirteen], there is nothing to stay his hand. Only when a man reaches the age of thirteen is the Inclination to good born within him. Then, if he would profane the Sabbath, it says to him, "Wretch! Scripture declares, *Everyone that profaneth it, shall surely be put to death*" (Ex.31.14). If he would take a life, it says to him, "Scripture declares *Whoso sheddeth man's blood, by man shall his blood be shed*" (Gen.9.6). When a man, his imagination heated, proceeds to commit an act of unchastity, all the parts of his body obey him. But when he sets out to fulfill a religious obligation, all the parts of his body protest from deep within him because the Inclination to evil in his innermost being is king over the two hundred and forty-eight parts that make up a man; the Inclination to good, however, may be likened to a king who is shut up in prison, as is said *For out of prison he comes forth to rule* (Eccl.4.14), that is, the Inclination to good [finally comes out in a man and rules his conduct]. (PRK S3.2)

The commandments, in other words, not only "bring knowledge" (cf. 3.20) of sin (which, especially in relation to a prohibition, arouses the temptation to engage in what is forbidden) but also carry punishment for their transgression.

Verse 10:

"Was to result in life . . . death": cf. Lev.18.5, Dt.4.1, 28.15-20, Prov.3.18, 4.4, 13, 22, Ezek.20.11, Lk.10.28, Rom.10.5, Gal.3.12, 1 Tim.1.8f; Sir.17.11, 32.24, 45.5, Ap. Bar.4.1, 2 Bar.38.2, Wis.Sol.6.18, 7.14, Ps.Sol.14.2, 4 Ez.7.45;

Jos.*Ant*.4.210; Sifre Dt.Ekev 45, He'azinu 306, Ex.R.41.4, Ta'anit 7a, Num.R.17.6, Suk.52b, Kid.30b.

Paul affirms that although the purpose of the Torah is to give life (cf. Lev.18.5, Dt.28.15-20, Prov.3.18, 4.4, 13, Ezek.20.11), the desire of the evil inclination is only for what is forbidden, and the punishment attendant on transgression means that its injunctions can also bear fruit for death instead of the inheritance of eternal life:

> The evil inclination desires only what is forbidden. R. Mena [on the Day of Atonement] went to visit R. Haggai who was ill. R. Haggai said, "I am thirsty." R. Mena said, "Drink." After an hour he came again, and said, "How about your thirst?" He said, "No sooner had you permitted me to drink than the desire left me." (PYoma 6.4, 43d)

> R. Hananel b. Papa said: What is meant by, *Hear, for I will speak princely things* (Prov.8.6): why are the words of the Torah compared to a prince? To tell you: just as a prince has power of life and death, so have the words of the Torah [potentialities] of life and death. Thus Raba said: To those who go to the right hand thereof it is a medicine of life; to those who go to the left hand thereof it is a deadly poison. (Shab.88b)

Since God "condescends" to human limitations in the commandments of the Torah, the Torah cannot make man live, despite (or even because of) the fact that it is "holy and righteous and good." The Torah "witnesses" to God's righteousness "apart from" or outside the framework of its principles of reward and punishment, and brings men to the realization ("knowledge") that they must put their evil inclination to death in order to serve God in the "newness" of life and righteousness (cf. "for through the Torah I died to the Torah that I might live to God" [Gal.2.19]).

Verse 11:

"Deceived . . . killed me": cf. Gen.3.13, Dt.11.16, Jer.20.7, Rom.5.12f, 2 Cor.11.3, 1 Tim.2.14; TBE p.62, Hag.16a.

Paul recalls the serpent's (Satan's) deception of Eve in Genesis 3.13, and the dangers of adding commandments to the Torah.[28] Sin "takes opportunity through the commandment," and instead of the Torah being a friend whose love wills him to live (cf. Rom.5.6-8, Test.Gad 4.6-7), it deceives man through his evil inclination, and turns into an enemy who attempts to kill him, as several rabbinic midrashim interpret through biblical texts:

> If the evil inclination say to thee: Sin and the Holy One, blessed be He, will pardon, believe it not, for it is said: *'Trust not in a friend'* (Mic.7.5), and *'friend'* [*re'a*] means none other than one's evil inclination, for it is said: *For the inclination of man's heart is evil* [*ra'*]. (Hag.16a)

> R. Samuel bar Nahman construed the words *When a man's ways please the Lord* (Prov.16.7) to refer to the impulse to good, and the words *He maketh even his enemies to be at peace with him* (*ibid.*.) to the impulse to evil. Generally, if a man is brought up with another in the same city, if only for two or three years, he binds himself in friendship to the other. But as to this side of man—the Impulse to evil -though it grow up with a man from his youth to his old age, its enmity is such that if it finds occasion to bring him down when he is twenty, it will bring him down; when he is sixty, it will bring him down; even when he is eighty, it will bring him down. . . . With regard to the Impulse to evil, David said: All my bones shall say, *Lord, who is like Thee, who deliverest the poor from him that is too strong for him* (Ps.35.10)—deliverest the weak Impulse to good from the strong Impulse to evil. David went on: *Deliverest . . . the poor and the needy from him that spoileth him* (*ibid.*): what despoiler is there stronger than the Impulse to evil? (PRK 11.1)

Verse 12:

"Holy . . . righteous and good": cf. Ps.19.7-10, 119.7, 137, 160, Prov.4.2, Rom.7.16, 1 Tim.1.8, 2 Tim.3.15-16; Test.Levi 14.4, Ps.Sol.7.22ff, Sib.Or.3.257, 580, 600, 4 Ez.3.20-23, 9.36-37, Sir.Prologue; Jos.*Contra Ap.*1.38-42; PRK 15.5, Mekh.Beshall.1, Mid.Ps.24.31, 119.7, AZ 19b, Men.53b; Philo, *De Vit.Cont.*1f, 25, 28f.

Paul reiterates his constant and emphatic affirmation that, although the Torah is implicated in man's sin because it stirs up his evil inclination, it in itself remains righteous. Verse 12 forms Paul's definitive refutation of the erroneous conclusion that the Torah might be sin (cf. verse 7), and thus forms another part of his argument against "libertinism" (cf. 3.5ff). The fact that the Torah "arouses" sin cannot be used as a basis on which to claim that the Torah is sinful, in the same way the author of 4 Ezra explains that the "vessel" which bears the "goods" is at fault for not being able to contain them safely and bring them to fruition rather than the goods themselves being faulty:

> But though our fathers received the Law, they did not keep it, and did not observe the statutes; yet the fruit of the Law did not perish—for it could not, because it was yours. Yet those who received it perished, because they did not keep what had been sown in them. And behold, it is the rule that, when the ground has received seed, or the sea a ship, or any dish food or drink, and when it happens that what was sown or what was launched or what was put in is destroyed, they are destroyed, but the things that held them remain; yet with us it has not been so. For we who have received the Law and sinned will perish, as well as our heart which received it; the Law, however, does not perish but remains in its glory. (4 Ez.9.32-37; cf. 3.20-23)[29]

Verse 13:
"Therefore . . . ": Paul repeats his claim that because the Torah gives man an opportunity to give in to temptation the Torah itself does not become part of "sin." He clearly identifies sin with death by interchanging the two words (cf. verses 7 and 24), and reiterating "rather it was sin . . . " in order that "sin might become utterly sinful."[30] It is sin, deceiving man through stirring up his evil inclination through the Torah—and not the Torah—which leads to death. By using the Torah, which is "good," to achieve its purposes, sin clearly demonstrates its "sinful" nature, since its opposition to what is good makes its evil character stand out in greater contrast. Sin thus "increases" (cf. 5.20), one transgression drawing another in its wake, the second a punishment for the first—just as good (observing the commandments) "increases" the good by providing the opportunity to perform more commandments:

> Ben 'Azzai said: Run to [perform] an easy precept, as [you would] in [the case of] a difficult one, and flee from transgression; for [one] precept draws [in its train another] precept, and [one] transgression draws [in its train another] transgression; for the recompense for [performing] a precept is a precept, and the recompense for [committing] a transgression is a transgression. (PA 4.2)

Verse 14:
"The Law is spiritual": cf. Ex.18.20, Dt.6.18, Prov.2.20, Rom.2.25-29, 3.19; 4 Ez.3.23, 9.37.

Paul now feels confident to claim that everyone "knows" that the truth is that God's law is holy, righteous, and good, and that man's human inclination is evil. Just as God's faithfulness is not impugned by Israel's unfaithfulness (cf. 3.3ff), the Torah is not contaminated because man does not fulfil its commandments. Although God intended the Torah to give life, because its commandments also hold the "power of sin" it is also a means of death for the "sons of darkness," or those who use it unlawfully (cf. 1 Tim.1.8f, Shab.88b). Paul conceives this dual role to be part of the Torah's basic function—so that sin will be shown as sin (verse 13). He considers that the Torah contains legal ethical principles (שורת הדין; *shurat ha-din*) and also demands a "higher" moral principle, external to its own ethical code (לפנים משורת הדין; *lifnim mi-shurat ha-din*).[31] The holiness, righteousness, and goodness of the Torah is "that which is right and good" (cf. Dt.6.18, Prov.2.20) according to the Spirit (cf. 2.25-29). To "do what is right and good in the sight of God" means serving the Creator by dying to sin and putting one's evil inclination to death.

"But I am of flesh . . . sin": cf. Dt.32.30, Judg.2.14, 3.8, 1 Kings 21.20, Ps.44.12, Jer.21.8-14, Jn.3.6, Rom.6.6, 8.8, 15, 1 Cor.3.1-3, 6.20, 7.22-23, 2 Cor.1.12, Gal.4.3, 8, 1 Pet.2.11; 1QS 3.13-4.26, 11.9-10, 21-22, 1QH 1.21-27, 3.23ff, 4.30-31, 9.13-16, 10.23, 11.10-12, 12.24ff, 13.13-16, 17.23-25; Test.Jud.18.1-6, 20.1-3, Test.Asher 1.1-9, Sir.15.11-17, 2 En.30.15; Suk.52b (R. Huna).

Man's "flesh" consists of his two hundred and forty-eight limbs, as Paul describes in chapter 6, which he must present either to the slavery of righteousness of his Creator, or to unrighteousness and his evil inclination. When a man serves his evil inclination, he is bound to his "spirit of flesh," which the Qumran texts describe as a spirit of defilement and perversity, an idea reflected in other intertestamental literature:

> And [Thou hast] divi[ded] all these things in the Mysteries of Thine understanding to make Thine glory known. [But what is] he, the spirit of flesh, to understand all these things and to comprehend [Thy] great secret of truth? And what is he that is born of woman amid all [Thy] mighty [works]? He is but a fabric of dust and a thing kneaded with water, [who]se counsel is nothing but [uncleann]ess ignominious shame and [. . .] over whom the perverse spirit rules. . . . [O my God, prevent] Thy servant from sinning against Thee and from stumbling aside from all the ways of Thy will! Strengthen [his] l[oins] [that he may res]ist the spirits [of Belial] [and w]alk in all that Thou lovest, and that he may despise all that Thou hatest [and do] what is good in Thine eyes! [Banish] from my members [all] their [domi]nion, for Thy servant [possesses] a spirit of fl[esh]. (1QH 13.13-15, 17.23-25)

> For what man is he that can know the counsel of God? or who can think what the will of the Lord is? For the thoughts of mortal men are miserable, and our devices are but uncertain. For the corruptible body presseth down the soul, and the earthy tabernacle weigheth down the mind that museth upon many things. And hardly do we guess aright at things that are upon earth, and with labor do we find the things that are before us: but the things that are in heaven who hath searched out? And thy counsel who hath known, except thou give wisdom, and send thy Holy Spirit from above? For so the ways of them which lived on the earth were reformed, and men were taught the things that are pleasing unto thee, and were saved through wisdom. (Wis.Sol.9.13-18)[32]

Verse 15:

"That which I am doing, I do not understand . . . ": cf. Gal.5.17; 1QH 1.21f, 5.25-26, 7.26-27, 9.15f, 10.3-7, 20-22, 27-30, 11.3-4, 14.8-16, 23-27, 15.12-14; Kid.30b.

Paul again takes his own life as an example of having to choose between serving two masters (cf. 3.7, 7.8f), and associates the mastery of his evil inclination over his will with a lack of understanding. He does not know *why* he does what he does as much as he does not understand what he does, since he does the opposite of what he intends to do.[33] He thus emphasizes how dependent he is upon God's grace, and follows the theology expressed in the Qumran scrolls, which affirm God's gift of "wisdom" as the source of man's justification. God's grace gives man the knowledge of His truth (His "Mysteries") by which the "sons of light" may walk according to the Spirit of holiness and do what is "right and good":

> All the judgments of chastisement are in Thy wrath and abundance of pardon in Thy goodness. And Thy mercy is obtained by all the sons of Thy loving-kindness; for Thou hast made known to them Thy secret of truth and given them understanding of all Thy marvellous Mysteries. And Thou hast cleansed man of sin because of Thy glory that he may be made holy for Thee from all unclean abomination and from (every) transgression of unfaithfulness, that he may be . . . raised from the dust to [Thy] secret [of truth] and from the spirit of perversity to [Thine] understanding. . . . But what is he that is flesh to understand Thy works? [And] can he that is dust establish his steps? It is Thou who hast formed the spirit and established its activity [. . .] and it is from Thee that the way of all

> the living proceeds. . . . From His wondrous Mysteries is the light in my heart, in the everlasting Being has my eye beheld Wisdom: because Knowledge is hidden from men and the counsel of Prudence from the sons of men. The fountain of righteousness, the reservoir of power, and the dwelling-place of glory are denied to the assembly of flesh; but God has given them as an everlasting possession to those whom He has chosen. . . . And the assembly of the holy Fabric shall belong to an eternal planting for all time to come. . . . Blessed be Thou, O my God, who hast opened unto Knowledge the heart of Thy servant! (1QH 11.8-12, 15.21-22, 1QS 11.5-9, 15-16)[34]

"Like . . . hate": cf. Ps.36.2, 45.7, 97.10, 101.3, 119.104, 113, 128, 163, Prov.8.13, 36, 13.5, Amos 5.15, Mt.6.24, Lk.16.13, Rom.12.9; Test.Jud.18.6, 20.1-2, Test.Asher 1.5; PA 2.9, PRE 15, Gen.R.21.5; Ap.Const.7.1. Ep.Barn.17-20, Shep.Herm.Mand.6.2.

Paul describes his struggle between the "Two Ways," illustrating how he must constantly "anger" his evil inclination, which wants to enslave him to death, in order to present his members as "slaves for obedience . . . resulting in righteousness" (cf. 6.16). The terms "like" and "hate" correspond to "good" and "evil" and the conflict between the Spirit of Truth and the Spirit of Perversity. The struggle, which is a consequence of the fact that man cannot serve two masters, is mediated through the "spirit of knowledge" which enables each person to choose which master he will serve, as a text from the Testament of the Twelve Patriarchs clearly describes:

> God has granted two ways to the sons of men, two mind-sets, two lines of action, two models, and two goals. Accordingly, everything is in pairs, the one over against the other. The two ways are good and evil; concerning them there are two dispositions within our breasts that choose between them. If the soul wants to follow the good way, all of its deeds are done in righteousness and every sin is immediately repented. Contemplating the just deeds and rejecting wickedness, the soul overcomes evil and uproots sin. But if the mind is disposed toward evil, all of its deeds are wicked; driving out the good, it accepts the evil and is overmastered by Beliar, who, even when good is undertaken, presses the struggle so as to make the aim of his action into evil, since the devil's storehouse is filled with the venom of the evil spirit. . . . So understand, my children, that two spirits await an opportunity with humanity: the spirit of truth and

> the spirit of error. In between is the conscience of the mind which inclines as it wills. (Test.Asher 1.3-9, Test.Jud.20.1-2)

Only God's gift of "knowledge," given through His grace through the Spirit of holiness, enables man to escape from the "dominion" of the "spirits of Belial" which "possess" his members, and thus to "love all that He has chosen and hate all that He has despised":

> And all the volunteers that cling to His truth shall bring all their understanding and powers and possessions into the Community of God, to purify their understanding in the truth of the precepts of God, and to order their powers according to the perfection of His ways . . . And they shall not depart from His precepts of truth to walk either to right or to left. And all who decide to enter the rule of the Community shall pass into the Covenant in the presence of God, (undertaking) to act according to all His commands and not to turn back from Him on account of fear, or fright, or any affliction whatever, if tempted by the dominion of Belial. (1QS 1.11-18)

Verse 16:
"Do the very thing I do not wish . . . good": cf. 12, 13, 22; Gal.2.18.

Paul's desire to emphasize the fact that the Torah is "holy and righteous and good" leads him to risk further dangers of libertine claims (cf. 3.3, 5ff). He almost confirms the "slanderous reports" about him, which assert that his human nature and sinfulness prove God's righteousness, when he argues that he "agrees with" (confesses) the Torah's righteousness when he acts against his will to serve God.[35] If he wants to do what is right, and his inclination prevents him from doing it, then he knows that observing the Torah's commandments is to do what is "right and good." Despite these theological risks, however, Paul insists that man's "flesh" is weak and cannot be overcome simply through Torah-observance. A man can only serve God by "angering" his "evil" inclination through refusing to do its bidding, by putting his evil inclination to death, and by dying to sin through his baptism into Yeshua's death and resurrection (cf. chapter 6). He is totally dependent upon God's grace in Yeshua (cf. chapter 5.15f), and the cleansing of his "bodily fabric" through the Spirit of holiness:

> What being of flesh can do this, and what creature of clay has power to do such marvellous things, whereas he is in iniquity from his mother's womb and in the sin of unfaithfulness till his old age? And I, I know that righteousness is not of man, nor of the sons of men

> perfection of way; to the Most High belong all the works of righteousness, whereas the way of man is not firm unless it be by the Spirit which God has created for him to make perfect a way for the sons of men, that all His works may know the might of His power and the greatness of His mercy to all the sons of His loving-kindness. . . . For Thou pardonest iniquity and clean[sest m]an of sin by Thy righteousness; and [the wor]ld [which] Thou hast made belongs not to man. For it is Thou who hast created the just and the wicked [. . .] [. . .] I wish to cling to Thy Covenant for[ever . . .] [. . .] for Thou art Truth and all [Thy works] are righteousness. (1QH 4.29-40)

Verse 17:

"No longer am I . . . me": cf. vs.9; 1QS 3.18-4.26, 11.9-10, 21-22, 1QH 1.21-27, 3.23ff, 4.30-32, 9.13-16, 11.10-14, 12.24ff, 13.13-16, 17.23-25; Test.Jud.18.6, Test.Dan 4.7, Test.Asher 3.2, 6.5, 4 Ez.3.23; ARN[a] 16.2, ARN[b] 16, PRK 11.1, S3.2, Sifre Dt.45, 343, MHG Gen.4.9, Gen.R.22.6, 34.10, Ruth R.3.1, Eccl.R.9.4.1, BB 17a, AZ 5b, Suk.52a-b, Shab.105b.

Paul extricates himself from the difficulty of labelling himself with the same "libertine" attitudes which he claims people have slanderously attributed to him (cf. 3.8) by distinguishing between his own "self" and "sin" as a force which dwells in his "flesh."[36] The evil inclination is frequently personified in a similar way in Jewish texts of the period, reflecting the view which Paul adopts here, that sin is not merely an *act* but that it dwells within man and must be replaced by God's Spirit:

> [But what is] he, the spirit of flesh, to understand all these things and to comprehend [Thy] great secret of truth? And what is he that is born of woman amid all [Thy] mighty works? He is but a fabric of dust and a thing kneaded with water, [who]se counsel is nothing but [uncleann]ess ignominious shame and [. . .] and over whom the perverse spirit rules. . . . All dominion over the sons of perversity is in the hand of the Angel of Darkness; they walk in the ways of darkness. And because of the Angel of darkness all the sons of righteousness go astray; and all their sin and iniquities and faults, and all the rebellion of their deeds are because of his dominion . . . [O my God, prevent] Thy servant from sinning against Thee and from stumbling aside from all the ways of Thy will! Strengthen [his] l[oins] [that he may res]ist the spirits [of Belial] [and w]alk in all that Thou lovest, and that he may despise all that Thou hatest [and

do] what is good in Thine eyes! [Banish] from my members [all] their [domi]nion, for Thy servant [possesses] a spirit of fl[esh]. (1QH 13.13-15, 1QS 3.20-22, 1QH 17.23-25)

R. Isaac stated, The [Evil] Inclination of a man grows stronger within him from day to day, as it is said, *Only evil all the day* [as the days go on] (Gen.6.5). R. Simeon b. Lakish stated, The Evil Inclination of a man grows in strength from day to day and seeks to kill him, as it is said, *The wicked watcheth the righteous and seeketh to slay him* (Ps.37.32); and were it not that the Holy One, blessed be He, is his help, he would not be able to withstand it, as it is said, *The Lord will not leave him in his hand, nor suffer him to be condemned when he is judged* (Ps.37.33) . . . R. Huna pointed out an incongruity: It is written, *For the spirit of harlotry hath caused them to err* (Hos.4.12), but is it not also written, [*For the spirit of harlotry*] *is within them?* (Hos.5.4). First it only causes them to err, but ultimately it enters into them. Raba observed, First he [the evil inclination] is called a passer-by, then he is called a guest, and finally he is called a man, for it is said, *And there came a* passer-by *to the rich man, and he spared to take of his own flock and of his own herd, to dress him for the* guest and then it is written, *but took the poor man's lamb and dressed it for the* man *that was come to him* (2 Sam.12.4). (Suk.52b)

Verses 18-20:

"Nothing good dwells in me . . . flesh": cf. Dt.32.30, Judg.2.14, 3.8, 1 Kings 21.20, Ps.44.12, Jer.21.8-14, Jn.3.6, Rom.6.6, 8.8, 15, 1 Cor.3.1-3, 6.20, 7.22-23, 2 Cor.1.12, 4.7-12, Gal.4.3, 8, 1 Pet.2.11; 1QS 3.13-4.26, 11.9-10, 21-22, 1QH 1.21-27, 3.23ff, 4.30-31, 9.13-16, 10.23, 11.10-12, 12.24ff, 13.13-16, 17.23-25; Test.Jud.18.1-6, 20.1-3, Test.Asher 1.1-9, Sir.15.11-17, 2 En.30.15; Suk.52b.

In Second Temple Jewish thought, "flesh" became a theological term opposed to "spirit," especially under the influence of the doctrine of "election-by-grace" prevalent within Qumran and the New Testament, where it took on the meaning of humanity without the ennobling gift of God's divine grace:

For no man is just in Thy ju[dg]ment nor [innocent in] Thy trial. Can human born of human be righteous, and can man born of man have understanding? And can flesh born of the gui[lty] inclination be glorious, and can spirit born of spirit {i.e., the carnal spirit} be

> mighty? . . . the inclinations of men and the return of mankind {is} [to dust] [and their inclination] {is} to sin and to the sorrow of transgression. (1QH 9.14-16, 11.20-21)

Verse 18:

"Wishing . . . doing": cf. 15f; Test.Jud.18.6, 19.3-4; MHG Gen.4.9.

The conflict between the Two Spirits (Two Ways) in the texts associated with the Qumran literature is based on a strict dualism which divides mankind into the "sons of light" and the "sons of darkness," whose "lot" and destiny is predetermined and unalterable. Although some of the texts express a concept of non-retaliation which allowed the members of the community to tolerate the wickedness of the "sons of darkness" (an idea which Paul picks up in chapters 12 and 13), the theology of these circles was not sympathetic to any discrepancy between thought and actions. A broader attitude generally prevailed in rabbinic literature, on the other hand, one which allowed that a person's intention to perform a commandment is sufficient for God to judge the person as though he had fulfilled it. Sin, however, was often said not to be imputed to a person until he actually committed the deed:

> Raba expounded: What is the meaning of the verse, *Good and upright is the Lord therefore and doth He instruct sinners in the way?* (Ps.25.8). Come and see the righteousness of the Holy One, blessed be He. Whoever has the intention in his heart to perform a precept but under duress fails to perform it, Scripture accounts it to him as if he had fulfilled it; and whoever has the intention to commit a sin is not regarded as guilty until the time of its commission; as it is written, *If I had regarded iniquity in my heart, the Lord would not hear* (Ps.66.18). (Kall.Rab.1)

Although Paul acknowledges that his intention (his "wish") to do good is important, he does not consider that by itself this intention is sufficient to accomplish good deeds. If his intention to do good is not realized in actual deeds, he remains under the mastery of his evil inclination. Similarly, Paul also disclaims the *Shammaite* view that observance of God's commandments is an end in itself, so that a man's intention is irrelevant since he responds purely to the command to perform the deed.[37] Paul knows that God does not look for rote observance, or reward a man for observance of His ordinances simply because He has commanded them, or count a person's intention as fulfilment of the deed. He wishes for man to serve Him out of love and a whole and pure heart. Paul's dilemma is therefore that while he wishes to do what is good and right, his inclination prevents him from fulfilling his desire. He is engaged in a constant struggle to master his evil inclination instead of letting it master him.

Verses 21-23:
"Principle . . . to do good": cf. 23, 25, 8.2.

Although Paul usually uses the Greek term νομος (*nomos*; "law") in reference to the Torah (cf. verse 22, where he speaks of the "law of God"), in this chapter it corresponds very closely to the principle of the Two Spirits or Ways.[38] Every man is constantly presented with the choice between obeying his evil inclination or letting it master him. Moreover, whenever he chooses to obey His Creator, he is confronted with the opposite desires of his inclination to evil, which is also personified as the "principle" of evil—Belial or Satan:

> When a man, his imagination heated, proceeds to commit an act of unchastity, all the parts of his body obey him. But when he sets out to fulfil an act of religious obligation, all the parts of his body protest from deep within him because the Inclination to evil in his innermost being is king over the two hundred and forty-eight parts that make up a man. . . . (PRK S3.2)

> . . . such are the wiles of the Tempter: Today he says to him, 'Do this'; to-morrow he tells him, 'Do that,' until he bids him, 'Go and serve idols,' and he goes and serves [them]. R. Abin observed: What verse [intimates this]? *There shall be no strange god in thee; neither shall thou worship any strange god* (Ps.81.9): who is the strange god that resides in man himself? Say, that is the Tempter! (Shab.105b)

Verse 22:
"Joyfully concur . . . inner man": cf. 16, 2 Cor.4.16, Eph.3.16, 4.24; Test.Zev.5.3, 7.3.

Paul understands that when a man is baptized into Yeshua's death and resurrection, the "inclination to evil" is no longer "king" in his "innermost being"—over his fleshly desires—but has been mastered by the Spirit of truth and holiness in the newness of life (cf. chapter 6).[39] The "inner man" represents the will or spirit of the man who has "angered" his evil inclination by putting it to death in baptism and banished the "spirit of flesh" from his members so that he may "agree with" the Torah, proving through his observance of its commands that it is "holy and righteous and good" (cf. verses 12 and 16):

> "Now listen to me, children, and live in integrity of heart, for in it I have observed everything that is well-pleasing to the Lord. The genuine man does not desire gold, he does not defraud his neighbor, he does not long for fancy foods, nor does he want fine clothes. He does not make plans to live a long life, but awaits only the will of God. And the spirits of error have no power over him . . . For he lives by the integrity of his soul, and perceives all things by the rectitude of his heart, making no place for an outlook made evil by this world's error, in order that he might envision no turning aside from any of the Lord's commands." (Test.Iss.4.1-6)

> He shall do the will of God in every enterprise of his hands, that he may reign over all things according to His command; and he shall gladly delight in all that He has made, and beyond the will of God he shall desire nothing. [And] he shall delight [in all] the words of His mouth, and shall covet nothing of that which He has not command[ed] . . . and shall bless Him [with the offering] of the lips. (1QS 9.23-26)

Verse 23:

"A different law": cf. 1 Cor.3.11, 2 Cor.11.4, Gal.1.6-9.

Paul again uses the term νομος (*nomos*) in the sense of "principle," although here he clearly refers it to the "evil inclination" whose bidding "angers" the inclination of the Creator (cf. Ruth R.3.1). The Qumran texts describe this principle as the "spirit of flesh" or "spirit of perversity," which is the יצר הרע (*yetzer ha-ra'*) the evil inclination which entices a man to sin and then sin again, and again (cf. Jas.1.14-15). This principle wages war against the Creator, and the "wages" of its sin are death and destruction (cf. 6.23 and 8.2):

> Another comment: The Inclination to evil dwells at the very entrance of the heart [and is like a fly, an enemy to fly from]. As Scripture says, *Flies of death cause the ointment of the perfumer to stink and putrefy* (Eccl.10.1). Thus, when an infant still in his cradle puts his hand on glowing coals, what is the cause of his doing so? Is it not the Inclination to evil, [an enemy to the person it dwells in]? So, too, when one goes up to a rooftop and falls off, what brought the fall about? Is it not the inclination to evil which flings him headlong? (PRK S3.2)[40]

> [O my God, prevent] Thy servant from sinning against Thee and from stumbling aside from all the ways of Thy will! Strengthen [his] l[oins] [that he may re]sist the spirits [of Belial] [and w]alk in all that Thou lovest, and that he may despise all that Thou hatest [and do] what is good in Thine eyes! [Banish] from my members [all] their [domi]nion, for Thy servant [possesses] a spirit of fl[esh]. (1QH 17.23-25)[41]

"Waging war": cf. Gal.5.17, Jas.4.1, 1 Pet.2.11-12; 1QS 4.16-18, 23-25, 1QM 1.1ff; Kid.30b, Suk.52b.

Paul emphasizes the conflict between the Two Spirits or Two Ways, and the choice which a man must constantly cling to between serving either his own evil inclination or his Creator. The battle between good and evil in the world is mirrored in each individual person's decision to obey God or the desires of his flesh:

> Another comment: The words *Who deliverest the persecuted from him that is too strong for him* (Ps.35.10) refer, as R. Aha stated, to the deliverance of David from Saul; and the words which follow *the poor and needy from him that spoils him* (ibid.) refer to the deliverance of the good man from the evil Impulse. Can there be any greater despoiler? How greatly the evil Impulse labors that a man should not do a good deed! How often does the evil Impulse succeed in offsetting a good deed! Can there be a greater despoiler? Hence the words *Who deliverest. . . . the poor and needy from him that spoileth him* mean "deliverest the good man from the evil Impulse. (Pes.Rab.9.2)

"The law of my mind": cf. 25, 8.5-7, 12.2.

Paul contrasts the "members of my body" with "the law of my mind," since it is man's will which makes the choice between serving his evil inclination or his Creator. Man's "flesh," the limbs of his body and its appetites, can serve either master. Once a person lets his evil inclination become master over him, however, his mind and will are "taken captive" (cf. 2 Cor.10.5) by his fleshly desires.[42] A man can only be "freed" from his "spirit of flesh" when God "enlightens" his heart and his eyes (his "inner man") with His Knowledge and Truth according to the Qumran texts:

> For to God belongs my justification, and the perfection of my way, and the uprightness of my heart are in His hand: by His righteousness

> are my rebellions blotted out. For He has poured forth from the fount of His Knowledge the light that enlightens me, and my eye has beheld His marvels and the light of my heart pierces the Mystery to come. The everlasting Being is the stay of my right hand; the way of my steps is on a stout rock, nothing shall be fearsome before me. For God's truth is the rock of my steps and His power, the stay of my right hand, and from the fount of His Righteousness comes my justification. From His wondrous Mysteries is the light in my heart, in the everlasting Being has my eye beheld Wisdom: because Knowledge is hidden from men and the counsel of Prudence from the sons of men. The fountain of righteousness, the reservoir of power, and the dwelling-place of glory are denied to the assembly of flesh; but God has given them as an everlasting possession to those whom He has chosen. (1QS 11.2-7)

Verse 24:

"Wretched man that I am . . . ": cf. Gen.18.27, Dt.32.30, Judg.2.14, 3.8, 1 Kings 21.20, Job 6.11-13, 7.1-21, 17.13-14, 25.6, Ps.22.6, 44.12, Isa.41.14, Jer.21.8-14, Jn.3.6, Rom.6.6, 8.8, 15, 1 Cor.3.1-3, 6.20, 7.22-23, 2 Cor.1.12, Gal.4.3, 8, Jas.4.9, 5.11, 1 Pet.2.11; 1QS 3.13-4.26, 11.9-10, 21-22, 1QH 1.21-27, 3.23ff, 4.30-31, 5.28-39, 8.26-35, 9.4f, 13-16, 10.23, 11.10-12, 12.24ff, 13.13-16, 17.23-25; Test.Jud.18.1-6, 20.1-3, Test.Asher 1.1-9, Sir.15.11-17, 2 En.30.15, Tob.3.1-6; PA 3.1, ARN[a] 19.2, DER 3.1-2, Suk.52b (R. Huna).

Without God's gift of righteousness no man is able to "master" his evil inclination and free himself from the "slavery" and "imprisonment" of his body to the desires of the "spirits of Belial" and the "wages of sin." Paul describes his miserable inability to please God by his own will, since whenever he wishes to observe God's will, his body either entices him away from doing so or puts obstacles in his way. At the same time, however, he also acknowledges his dependence upon God's grace, so that admitting his wretched state is also a confession that leads to repentance, a very common theme in contemporary Jewish literature:

> Akabiah b. Mahalaleel said: Apply thy mind to three things and thou wilt not come into the power of sin: Know whence thou camest, and whither thou art going, and before Whom thou art destined to give an account and reckoning. Whence camest thou?—From a fetid drop. Whither art Thou going?—To a place of dust, of worm and of maggot. Before Whom art thou destined to give an account and reckoning?—Before the King of the Kings of Kings, blessed be He. (PA 3.1)[43]

> For Thou hast established my spirit and knowest my meditation. And Thou hast comforted me in my confusion and in pardon I delight; and I was comforted for the original sin. And I knew there was hope in Thy [fav]ours and expectation in the greatness of Thy might. For no man is just in Thy ju[dg]ment nor [innocent in] Thy trial. Can human born of human be righteous, and can man born of man have understanding? And can flesh born of the gui[lty] inclination be glorious, and can spirit born of spirit be mighty? Truly, nothing is strong like Thy strength and Thy glory is [price]less and Thy wisdom is measureless. And [life] belongs to the me[n of Thy Covenant], but [death] to all them that have departed from it. . . . And [Thou hast] drawn [me] from the dust and [out of clay] I was sh[aped] as a fount of defilement and ignominious shame, a container of dust, a thing knea[ded with water], [. . .] and a dwelling-place of darkness. . . . And I was silent; what could I say? It is according to my Knowledge that I speak: the creature of clay is without righteousness. What can I say unless Thou open my mouth, and how can I understand unless Thou give understanding to me? And what thou[ght] can I have unless Thou uncover my heart, and how can I make my way straight unless [Thou es]tablish [it]? [And how] can [my] foo[tstep] be sure [unless Thou] give strength and might. . . . (1QH 9.12-18, 12.24-26, 32-35)[44]

Verse 25:
"Thanks be to God . . .": cf. 8.36-37, 1 Cor.15.57, 2 Cor.2.14, Heb.2.14f, 1 Jn.5.4.

Paul confesses his inability to please God, which leaves him the power of his evil inclination, and confesses that only God's gift of righteousness in Yeshua can deliver him from his human limitations and the desires of his evil inclination. In thanking God for His grace, he recites, as it were, the blessing said on deliverance from evil or unfortunate circumstances ברכת הגומל (*birkat ha-gomel*): "Blessed is He who bestows lovingkindnesses" ברוך גומל חסדים טובים; *barukh gomel chasadim tovim*):

> Rab Judah said in the name of Rab: There are four [classes of people] who have to offer thanksgiving: those who have crossed the sea, those who have traversed the wilderness, one who has recovered from an illness, and a prisoner who has been set free. . . . Whence for a prisoner who was set free?—Because it is written: *Such as sat in darkness and in the shadow of death. . . . Because they rebelled against*

> *the words of God. . . . Therefore He humbled them with travail. . . . They cried unto the Lord in their trouble. . . . He brought them out of darkness and the shadow of death. . . . Let them give thanks unto the Lord for His mercy* (Ps.107.10-15). What blessing should he say? Rab Judah said: 'Blessed is He who bestows lovingkindnesses'. (Ber.54b)

The Gemara (talmudic passage) here associates imprisonment with rebellion, and thus also with death, since the psalm understands that death is the "wages of sin." The man who gives thanks to God for being delivered from "slavery to sin" gives Him thanks for His "lovingkindnesses"—for His merciful grace and His gift of righteousness which makes him inherit "eternal life" in the world to come:

> I give Thee thanks, O Adonai, for Thou hast redeemed my soul from the Pit and from Sheol of Abaddon Thou hast made me rise to everlasting heights, and I have walked in an infinite plain! And I knew there was hope for him whom Thou hast shaped from the dust for the everlasting assembly. Thou hast cleansed the perverse spirit from great sin that he might watch with the army of the Saints and enter into communion with the congregation of the Sons of Heaven. And Thou hast cast an everlasting destiny for man in the company of the Spirits of Knowledge, that he might praise Thy Name in joy[ful] concord and recount Thy marvels before all Thy works. (1QH 3.19-23)

"So then . . . ": Paul sums up his conflict between desiring to serve God yet constantly being enticed by his inclination to evil, and again describes how while his "mind" or will wants to obey God, his "flesh" constantly inclines towards the impulse to unrighteousness. He must continue to "anger" his evil inclination and "die to sin" because the "members" of his body are still open to the desires and passions of the "spirit of perversity." Paul acknowledges this weakness of man's flesh, and gives God thanks that He has "delivered" (cf. חליצה; *chalitzah* [cf. verse 4]) him from bondage to his evil inclination through the gift of His righteousness in Yeshua ("the Lord our righteousness") so that he may walk according to the Spirit of truth and holiness, putting to death the "spirit of flesh."[45] He is able to die to sin and live to God because God's understanding and truth have enlightened his heart and eyes and mind, and have given him "the fountain of righteousness, the reservoir of power, and the dwelling-place of glory" (cf. 1QS 11.6-7).

Endnotes on Chapter 7

1 The mixed Jewish and Gentile congregation at Rome is evident from 1.5-6, 13-15, 15.18f, and from the people to whom Paul sends greetings in chapter 16 (cf. "kinsmen," in verses 16.7, 11, and 21).

2 Cf. Ex.34.15-16, Lev.20.5, Num.25.1, Dt.31.16, Judg.2.17, 8.27f, 1 Chron.5.25, Isa.1.21, Jer.2.20, Jer.3.1ff, Ezek.6.9, 16.23ff, Hos.1.2ff, 2.1ff, 3.1f, 4.10ff, 5.10, 7.4ff, 9.1f. God's "marriage" with the people of Israel ("you shall be My people and I shall be your God") is contracted through the Torah or covenant, so that idolatry is also adultery (cf. Dt.7.25). The community of believers who are the "body of the Messiah" (cf. 1 Cor.12.27, Eph.1.23) are therefore also described as the "bride" of Yeshua (cf. Eph.5.22ff, Rev.21.2, 9).

3 The phrase משמע לן קא is used to introduce the conclusion of a צריכותא [necessity]: the Talmud explains that an apparently unnecessary source was cited in order to avoid mistaken conclusions; in such cases it states that the superfluous source "tells us" not to arrive at such conclusions. The term צריכותא is used to explain a "seemingly unnecessary repetition of an idea in a Mishnah by arguing that each statement was meant to teach us something which we would otherwise not have known, or to prevent us from reaching erroneous conclusions." A. Steinsaltz, *Talmud*, 138.

4 Some scholars have suggested that the term νομος (*nomos*), "law," does not refer here to the Torah but to "the general nature of law" (cf. Cranfield, ICC). Although the Greek text says "know law" rather than "know the law," the anarthrous (unarticled) use of νομος does not preclude reference to the Torah since the Torah was conceived as an independent entity already in the Prophets (cf. Isa.2.3, Hag.2.11, Mal.2.6) and in the intertestamental Wisdom literature (cf. Sir.24.23f, Wis.Sol.2.12, 6.4). The libertine argument may have been raised most frequently by Gentile believers being pressured by "Judaizing" believers to keep the "whole Torah." Paul now addresses the objections raised in consequence by Jewish believers, and says that his argument concerning "angering" one's evil inclination must not be understood as saying that justification only comes through Torah-observance. (He may also possibly be referring to a Hebrew wordplay here in reference to Ps.94.8, which juxtaposes כסיל [*kesil*], fool [i.e., one who is ignorant] with משכיל [*maskil*], the wise or understanding person. Those who should be wise and "know the Torah" maybe are in fact foolish since they do not appear to "understand" his argument.)

5 See the comments on 6.2ff.

6 See the comments on 6.3ff. The verses in Rom.7.1-7 are frequently regarded by commentators as an allegory, in which the Torah is explained as "dying" (becoming obsolete) so that the wife (the believer in Yeshua) is freed from its jurisdiction to serve God in the "Spirit." Paul is appealing here, however, to a specific *halakhah* regarding marriage and divorce as a legal precedent. He establishes that the *halakhah* regulates that the death of a husband carries the same legal force as divorce does in freeing a woman from the penalty of adultery if she remarries (whereas the biblical text only rules concerning divorce). Just as a woman commits adultery as long as she is married (bound) to her husband, and is free to remarry only when he divorces her or when he dies, so the people of Israel commit adultery when they serve other gods and "go whoring after" their idols. As a legal precedent and not an allegory, the Torah does not represent the husband (and thus "die"). It rather represents the legal framework which institutes the marriage. If the woman is not married—or if no institution of marriage exists—she is not "bound" to one master. Paul thus understands the Torah, as he demonstrates in 3.19-20 (cf. 4.15, 5.20), as the legal system which administrates reward and punishment and which therefore determines what is "sin." When a person "dies" to the ordinances which regulate transgression, he is no longer bound to his inclination to sin and is free to serve God in His righteousness; cf. also 3.30-31.

7 Cf. Shab.151b, Ned.61b.

8 Although some commentators cite this passage as a parallel to Paul's thought, they frequently dismiss it as irrelevant since it in fact makes the opposite point to that which Paul makes. R. Johanan alludes to death as a restraint on Torah-observance and thus as an end to man's praise from God, whereas Paul regards death in a positive light. Flusser resolves the disparity between these two views by connecting R. Johanan's dictum with R. Simeon b. Pazzi's midrash on Job 3.19: "It is possible that Rabbi Simeon combined a similar idea [to that of R. Johanan and the majority view] with an older saying, and came to the conclusion that, in death, man is freed from one master, his inclination, and belongs only to the other master, to God." D. Flusser, *Slave*, 170.

9 The Tanakh plays on the Hebrew associations between בעל (*ba'al*) as the name for Ba'al, the chief Canaanite god, and בעל as the term for "husband" and/or "master;" cf. Hosea 2, where God accuses Israel of taking "Ba'alim" as their (her) lovers and wishing to return to them as her "first husband." He also promises, however, that Israel will

no longer call Him בעלי (*Ba'ali*) ("my master—my Ba'al") but אישי (*'Ishi*)—"my Husband." One of the names for Satan in Second Temple Jewish thought was also "Belial" or "Beliar" (cf. also בעל זבול [*Ba'al-zevul*], "the master of the house," in Mt.12.24-27 and Lk.11.15-19). "Belial" is a נוטריקון (*notarikon*), or a term composed of two words. It appears in the Tanakh as בלי יעל (*beli ya'al*), meaning "without profit" or "worthless(ness)" (cf. Dt.13.14, Ps.101.3); the Rabbis also sometimes interpreted the name as two words, בלי עול (*beli 'ol*), referring to the wicked people who "remove the yoke" (of the Torah) (cf. San.111b).

10 The *halakhah* is based on a סברא (*sevara'*) or "logical deduction" from the biblical text. It is thus a rabbinic regulation (מדרבנן; *mi-de-rabbanan*) and not a biblical commandment (דאריתא; *de-'oraita'*) which makes the husband's death, which is not explicitly denoted by the biblical text, equally binding as divorce, which is a biblical ordinance.

11 Adultery is a form of idolatry in which Israel serves another master instead of being faithful to their "Maker," in the same way as every believer "angers" the Creator by serving their own evil inclination; cf. Jas.4.4: "You adulteresses, do you not know that friendship with the world is hostility toward God? Therefore whoever wishes to be a friend of the world makes himself an enemy of God." Yeshua also refers to his generation as an "adulterous" generation (cf. Mt.12.39, 16.4, Mk.8.38), a saying which Paul might have in mind; see Jn.8.38-42, and the comments on 8.15.

12 The Torah also constitutes the legal framework of marriage, divorce, and the penalty for adultery. To escape the penalties which the law imposes one must either annul the law or remove oneself from its authority.

13 The motif of חליצה (*chalitzah*) is common to the motif of the two masters and to the motif of marriage and divorce. It represents the means through which a woman is "released" from an obligatory marriage to her brother-in-law by undergoing the humiliating ceremony in which the widow removes his shoe and spits in his presence before the elders of the city to free him from his levirate obligation (cf. Dt.25.7-10). This ceremony frees the woman to marry whomever she wishes. She is not "bound" either to one husband or to one master, but may marry or serve another man with no legal consequences; (cf. also Gen.38.26, Ruth 4, Gen.R.85.5); see the comments on 3.24. In Gal.1.4, Paul describes Yeshua as performing this redemption on behalf of mankind, delivering man from bondage to "this present evil age." A similar idea appears in a talmudic passage where the Sages interpret Dt.25.9 ("pull his sandal off his foot") in the light of Ps.34.8:

> What, however, is the explanation of the Scriptural text, *The angel of the Lord encampeth round about them that fear Him, and He girds them* [ויחלצם; *vay-chaltzem*]—[The meaning is that] as a reward for those who fear him, He will deliver them [יחלצם; *ye-chaltzam*] from the judgment of Gehenna (Yev.102b)?

The same Gemara reports that R. Gamaliel (probably of Yavneh, after the destruction of the Temple in 70 C.E.) refuted a "Min" (heretic) who interpreted Hos.5.6, "They will go with their flocks and herds to seek the Lord, but they will not find (Him); He has withdrawn [חלץ] (*chalatz*); drawn off the shoe] from them," to mean that "you [Israel] are a people with whom its God has performed *chalitzah*" by arguing that since it is the sister-in-law who performs the ceremony, God cannot be said to have performed it, and thus further cannot be said to have rejected His people (Yev.102b).

14 It should be clear that Paul does not intend to disparage the Torah here, as he makes evident in the subsequent verses. His objective is to demonstrate the need of both Jewish and Gentile believers to be faithful to God in Yeshua, through whom God has given righteousness to all mankind. Paul wants all mankind to keep God's commandments, those commandments which are given specifically to each person, whether they are male or female, Jew or Gentile (cf. 1 Cor.7.17f).

15 See the comments on 6.21-22 ("benefit" and "wages").

16 The fruit which Balaam's disciples produce "removes a man from the world," while the fruit which Abraham's disciples bring gives them the inheritance of eternal life. It is interesting that the saying in Aboth refers to the "disciples of Abraham" rather than the "disciples of Moses," since Moses would have been a more natural (contemporary) parallel to Balaam. The author of the Mishnah chose Abraham as his paradigm, however, as Paul does in chapter 4, because Abraham gained his "inheritance" by his faithfulness to God's promises and before God gave the Torah on Mt. Sinai. Abraham is thus not only the "father" of Israel but of all the nations of the world.

17 See verse 4. The verb κατειχομεθα (*kateichometha*), "we were bound," expresses the bondage of men by the Torah which is linked to the human inclination. Paul uses the same verb, in the active voice, in 1.18, where man's evil inclination keeps God's truth in bondage ("men who suppress the truth in unrighteousness").

18 For the use of the talmudic formula, "what shall we say then . . .," see the comments on 3.3.

19 The question whether the Torah is itself "sinful" forms another perspective of the problem of "libertinism," of whether a person can sin in order to give God further opportunity to demonstrate His grace. It can also be understood as a question concerning Israel's election, of whether, if God "condescends" to human limitations the election of Israel is "spiritually" effective. Paul asks the same question regarding Yeshua in Gal.2.17-21, and answers it in very similar terms to the argument he evinces in 7.7ff.

20 The reference to "Levi son of Jacob" is probably to the Testament of Levi. Although the passage does not appear in the present text, the basic ideas are found in various passages in the Testaments of the Twelve Patriarchs. The dictum that "the love of money ["mammon"] is a root of all sorts of evil" was a commonplace in the circles to which the Qumran literature and the Testament of the Twelve Patriarchs belonged; cf. Test.Jud.18.3, 19.1f, 1 Tim.6.10, Pes.Rab.21.17 (R. Judah).

21 Cf. 1QS 10.19ff, Test.Levi 14.5-8, PA 5.10. The translation of "hoarding" is uncertain and may signify either the concealment of doctrine or of treasure, since in the next sentence the writer recommends abandonment of wealth. The piling up of riches characterizes the "men of the Pit," just as disdain for wealth is an essential virtue of the "sons of light." The reference to "zeal" as the complement to the "poor in spirit" suggests covetousness in its verbal proximity to "jealousy." Paul picks up the ideas of "non-retaliation," which this passage also reflects, in chapters 12f.

22 Cf. 1QS 3.18-4.26, 1QH 3.21, 11.10-14, 13.13-15, 17.23-25. Although the Qumran documents do not speak of God's "accommodation" (condescendence) to man's weaknesses, they do emphasize the limitations of the flesh and the need for God's grace for justification (cf. 1QS 11.2-22, 1QH 4.30-33). Their observance of the Torah which is "holy and righteous and good" was perhaps even stricter sense than that of the Pharisees, but it was filtered through the cleansing of man's "(bodily) fabric" by the Spirit of holiness, and its esoteric interpretation by the Teacher of Righteousness (cf. 1QH 2.10ff, 4.27-28, 7.26-27, 8.16, 18.10-12, 1QpHab 2.8-9, 7.4-5). It is interesting that the clearest example of the principle of "divine condescendence" in the New Testament (cf. Mt.19.8) is related to divorce, and Yeshua himself states, "I say to you, whoever divorces his wife, except for immorality, and marries another commits [or makes her commit] adultery" (Mt.19.9).

23 See the introduction, and the comments on verses 1ff.

24 Cf. also PRE 13, Ber.Rab.19.3, Mid.Ps.1.9. The "hedge" is the addition of the prohibition against "touching" the tree (as well as not "eating" from it). Adam's precaution in adding the commandment against touching in fact gave the serpent an opportunity to tempt Eve to sin; "when the hedge fell down," says the midrash in ARN[b] 1, "it cut down the plants"—i.e., it opened the way for the breaking of the actual commandment. Of a list of eight individuals and groups who "make a hedge about their words" according to this series of midrashim, at least five of the hedges relate to some form of sexual immorality.

25 This chapter in Pirke de Rabbi Eliezer opens with the Mishnah from PA 4.21 which speaks of covetousness: "Envy [הקנאה], (and) cupidity [התאוה] and ambition take a man [Adam] out of the world." "Making a hedge" is thus immediately associated with sexual lust and covetousness. Eve's covetousness of the fruit causes her to transgress God's command, exchanging the truth of the Creator for that of the creature (cf. Rom.1.21ff); several of these midrashim claim that one of Eve's fears once she had touched the tree was that she would die and that God would make another woman and give her to Adam. She thus gave the fruit to Adam so that he would also die; cf. aso PRE 13, Ber.Rab.19.5.

26 Personal autobiographical references are frequent in the Tanakh, rabbinic literature, and in the Qumran psalms; cf. PA 1.14, Lev.R.1.5, Suk.53a, 1QH 2.6-19, 7.12, 9.23-25, Jn.8.12, 57, 10.7, 14, 14.6. See also D. Flusser, *Hillel's*, and the comments on 2.1-3 ("every man [of you]," "O man").

27 Cf. PA 5.21, Gen.R.63.10. The יצר הרע (*yetzer ha-ra'*) is said to be present from birth (cf. San.91b), while the יצר הטוב *(yetzer ha-tov)*, the good inclination, begins to function only at the age of bar mitzvah (cf. ARN[a] 16.2, ARN[b] 16, Eccl.R.4.13.1).

28 Cf. the "hedge" referred to in the midrashim in the comments on 7.8.

29 Cf. 2 Cor.4.7, as well as the comments on 6.21-22, 7.4, and 9.20-23.

30 For the talmudic formula, see the comments on 3.3.

31 For this principle of "within the strict line of justice," see the comments on 2.27-28.

32 See the comments on 6.3f.

33 For the equation of Adam's sin with his ignorance, however (and his death with his sin), cf. 2 En.30.16.

34 Cf. 1QH 1.21-27, 2.8-9, 13-14, 5.25-26, 7.26-27, 10.27-29, 11.15-18, 27-31, 12.11-15, 32-35, 15.12-14, 17.9-12. It is not clear here whether Paul's statements reflect a (proto-) gnostic view or whether he is denying such

views. Qumran theology shared a common dualism with gnostic thought, but restrained from the excesses of the gnostic opposition between evil matter (the body) and the spiritual γνωσις (*gnosis*) or "Knowledge" which liberated man from his "flesh." Since the community remained within the framework of Torah-observance, it laid emphasis on the esoteric interpretation of the Torah revealed only to the members of the community, through the Teacher of Righteousness; see D. Flusser and S. Safrai, *Essene*, and the comments on 6.17. Paul equates his lack of knowledge here with his inability to keep the Torah because of his evil inclination. However, he quite clearly does not see his "release" (cf. verses 2, 6, and 24) from the mastery of his own desires either as a form of γνωσις or of esoteric interpretation, but through baptism into Yeshua's death and resurrection and the cleansing of the Holy Spirit (cf. chapter 6). For some of the ideas characteristic of gnosticism, see the comments on 3.8.

35 A similar argument against "libertine" views is found in the Testament of Asher, where the author addresses the issue of whether evil can be used as a means to achieve a good end. The principle of "single-mindedness" which the author espouses counters a hypocritical attitude (cf. 3.8) which Paul does not focus upon here but which is related to his argument, since it regards the conflict between wanting to do the right and the good but actually doing the opposite:

> The soul, they say, may in words express good for the sake of evil, but the outcome of the action leads to evil. . . . For those who are two-faced are not of God, but they are enslaved to their evil desires, so that they might be pleasing to Beliar and to persons like themselves. . . . You therefore, my children, keep the Law of the Lord; do not pay attention to evil as to good, but have regard for what is really good and keep it thoroughly in all the Lord's commandments, taking it as your way of life and finding rest in it. (Test.Asher 2.1, 3.2, 6.3)

36 The "person" who is his "master" when he is enslaved by sin is thus replaced by the Spirit of Yeshua (cf. 8.9), and his "body of death" (verse 24) is replaced by an imperishable, spiritual body (cf. 1 Cor.15.40-49) through his baptism into Yeshua's death and resurrection (cf. chapter 6).

37 Cf. Tos.Maksh.1.1-4, Maksh.1.2-4, AZ 3a (R. Hanina), Kid.31a.

38 See the Hebrew term כלל (*kelal*), however, which means "principle or general rule, but in conjunction with a preposition is also used to describe the "influence" of something; cf. "because he was under the influence (בכלל; *bi-kelal*) of anger, he came under the influence (בא לכלל; *ba' le-kelal*)

of mistaken judgment" (Sifre Num.157). The "principle" is quite easily mistaken here as man's actual "inclination" (to evil or to good), and the term יצר (*yetzer*) could bear this meaning without difficulty. Thus although in this verse Paul specifically identifies the "principle" as the "fleshly" frustration of his desire to obey God's commandments, he uses the same expression ("a different law") in verse 23 to refer to the evil inclination.

39 Paul consistently lays his argument open to the claims which he counters so emphatically in 3.5ff, that his sin "justifies" God because it demonstrates His righteousness in the face of the evil inclination in man. He takes this risk, however, in order to emphasize that a person cannot serve two masters and must choose to serve either God or his evil inclination. This argument then leads him also to emphasize the "possession" (mastery) of the members of the body by the "spirit of flesh" (cf. 1QH 13.13).

40 The editors of Pesikta de-Rab Kahana note that the commentator may be playing here on the Aramaic words *dibaba'* (fly), and *debaba'* (enmity) ("[and is like a fly, an enemy to fly from]"); cf. Ber.61a.

41 Although this particular text is fragmentary, the reconstructions reflect phrases used in other passages in the Scrolls; cf. CDC 12.2, 1QH 1.22, 11.12, 13.13. Since the context of verse 23 relates to the motif of the two masters, it is unlikely that this verse parallels the "law" observed by the Gentiles in 2.12f, although it may be the reverse of Paul's statement there that the Gentiles do "do the law," i.e., they do fulfil God's will (their "conscience," as it were, representing their "inner man").

42 See also the comments on 12.1f.

43 Akabiah's saying is based on verses from Gen.3.19, Job 25.6, and Eccl.11.9. Consideration of the first point is designed to induce humility; of the second, to prevent too strong a craving for worldly pleasures; and of the third, to lead to a fuller appreciation of the majesty and power of God. Paul also recognizes that sin and the mastery of the evil inclination inevitably leads to death (cf. 5.12, 6.23, 7.9, 13, PA 4.22).

44 See also the midrash in PRK which plays on Job 13.12, and is directly connected to the theme of the "sons of Abraham," which Paul introduces in 2.25f and picks up again in chapters 8f:

> [In comment on God's command to remember Amalek], R. Tanhum bar Hanila'i began his discourse by citing the following verse: *Your acts of remembering [Amalek, followed by repentance for your sins], will be like "ashes"; but when you deserve visitation [for sin], visitation in "clay" shall be your punishment* (Job 13.12).

> The Holy One said to Israel: My children, I inscribed in Torah two references to Amalek that you are to remember—heed them: *Thou shalt blot out the remembrance of Amalek* (Dt.25.19); *I will utterly blot out the remembrance of Amalek* (Ex.17.14). But let *your acts of remembering [be followed by repentance for your sins so that you] will be like "ashes"*—that is, if through repentance you gain merit, you will be true children of Abraham who spoke of himself as "ashes," saying "I am . . . but dust and ashes" (Gen.18.27). (PRK 3.2)

The literal translation of Job 13.12, "your memorials shall be like unto ashes, your eminences to eminences of clay," can be interpreted to construe the word גב (*gav*; eminence) as a form of גבה (*gavah*), "to collect, impose, or visit punishment for sin;" the commentator then seems to interpret the word זכרוניכם (*zikhroneikhem*), "your acts of remembering," to contain the verb as זכיתם (*zekhitem*), "you gain merit."

45 The apparent anomaly between Paul's two statements in verse 25, where he first states that God has delivered him from his "body of death," and then describes how he continues to struggle against evil inclination, is resolved by the fact that Paul is not only repeating what he has illustrated throughout the chapter, but also emphasizing the fact that a man is not "free" from his evil inclination unless he dies. As long as he lives, he must continually put his evil inclination to death. In Yeshua's death and resurrection, however, he has been freed from the "law" or the inevitable mastery of "sin and death."

ROMANS
8

Introduction

Paul argues for the sake of his Jewish brethren in chapter 7 that Torah observance alone does not free a man from his evil inclination. Only Yeshua's death and resurrection redeems all men, both Jews and Gentiles, to live faithfully before God in the righteousness of the Spirit. In chapter 8, Paul continues to demonstrate that the Torah's association with human limitations is overcome through putting one's evil inclination to death, and describes the doctrine of the Two Ways or Spirits (or the "two masters") in terms of walking either in the flesh (the "spirit of flesh" or "perversity") or in the Spirit (verses 1-13). He combines the doctrine of the Two Spirits with the motif of the "sons of Abraham" (cf. chapter 2), together with the idea of creation and resurrection (cf. chapter 4), and identifies the "son" as the believer who serves God from love and not from fear (verses 14-17). He picks up the theme of hope, reconciliation, and glorification from chapter 5 (verses 17-25), and the hope for creation's ultimate purpose leads him to the idea of God's intercession through His Spirit on behalf of man's weakness (verses 26-27). He develops this thought in regard to Israel's election (verses 28-39), and thus returns to his interrupted argument from 3.1-3. Since God has foreknown, predestined, called, justified, and glorified His people, no one can claim that He has rejected them (verses 31-33). If Yeshua himself is the ultimate proof of God's love, he will justify Israel and not present an obstacle to separate them from God.

Verse 1:
" . . . therefore now"

Paul begins expanding some of the implications of the theme of the two masters from chapters 6 and 7. Both the "therefore" and the "now" emphasize the conclusion which he draws from the argument in chapter 7—namely, that there is "now no condemnation" for those who have been baptized into Yeshua's death and resurrection (cf. chapter 6). His claim that man is not "condemned" when he chooses to serve God by putting to death his evil inclination gains its force in contrast to 7.25, where he admits that he must continually fight to master his evil inclination.[1] Paul acknowledges that even though the believer has put his inclination to death and died to sin, he still struggles against serving his inclination. Despite the fact, therefore, that he may be accused of serving both God and his evil inclination, Paul concludes that in dying to sin in baptism, a person has been "freed" from the "mastery" of his evil inclination, and is therefore "free" to serve God. His release (cf. חליצה; *chalitzah* [cf. 7.4]) from slavery to sin provides him with the freedom and the righteousness in which to serve God. As a direct result, he is under "no condemnation" in Yeshua.

"No condemnation in the Messiah, Yeshua": cf. Job 34.29, Isa.50.9, Jn.5.24, 14.20, 17.21-23, Acts 13.38, Rom.2.16, 5.16, 18, 6.11, 23, 8.34-35, 1 Cor.1.2, 30, 15.22, 2 Cor.3.6-18, 5.17, 19, Eph.1.13, 2.10, 13, 2 Tim.1.1, 2.10, Heb.3.14, 10.18, 1 Pet.5.14.

Paul returns to the theme of chapter 5 (cf. the "Adamic" typology), and the midrash of the two masters (cf. chapter 6), both of which motifs confirm the claim that "there is therefore no condemnation in the Messiah" to be the "freedom" to serve God while still living in the "flesh."[2] The root of the Greek word κατακριμα (*katakrima*), "condemnation," is the verb κρινω (*krino*), "to judge." Κατακριμα means "judgment" or "sentence." The person who has been baptized into Yeshua's death and resurrection has been "freed" from serving his inclination by God's gift of righteousness ("justification") in Yeshua.[3] This means that although he may still be confronted by the "spirit of flesh" or "perversity" he no longer faces God's wrath and judgment ("condemnation") because he has committed himself to serving God in "newness of (eternal) life" (cf. 6.4), as the Qumran texts describe:

> I give Thee thanks, O Adonai, for Thou hast redeemed my soul from the Pit and from Sheol of Abaddon Thou hast made me rise to everlasting heights, and I have walked in an infinite plain! And I knew there was hope for him whom Thou hast shaped from the dust for the everlasting assembly. Thou hast cleansed the perverse spirit from great sin that he might watch with the army of the Saints and enter into communion with the congregation of the Sons of Heaven. And Thou hast cast an everlasting destiny for man in the company of the Spirits of Knowledge, that he might praise Thy Name in joy[ful] concord and recount Thy marvels before all Thy works. (1QH 3.19-23)

Verse 2:

"Law of . . . life . . . death": cf. cf. Ex.24.16-17, 32.16, Dt. 30.15, 19, Josh.24.15, Prov.3.18, Isa.43.19, 48.6-7, Jer.31.31f, Ezek.36.26f, Rom.3.27, 7.21-23, 1 Cor.15.45, 2 Cor.3.3ff, 17, Gal.3.21, Jas.1.25; 1QS 4.25, 1QH 13.11-12; Ap.Bar.4.1, Wis.Sol.6.18, 7.14, Ps.Sol.14.2, 4 Ez.7.45; PA 6.2.

In making very clear his conclusion, Paul presents the doctrine of the "Two Ways" or the "Two Spirits" in its classic terms.[4] In this context, "law" can mean either "principle" (cf. 7.21, 23), or the Torah itself. The Sages refer to the death-bringing as well as the life-giving properties of the Torah (cf. Deuteronomy 28-30), in numerous midrashim which speak of the Torah as a "drug for life" or a "drug for death."[5] Since it is impossible to serve "two masters," a man must choose whether to present his members for righteousness through the Torah, which brings him life, or present his body to unrighteousness, and thus be condemned to death through his violation of the Torah (cf. chapter 6). Paul holds a similar attitude to the idea expressed in these midrashim, in that he sees in the Torah the possibilities for both life and death. For him, however, in contrast to the esoteric interpretation of the Teacher of Righteousness or the Torah-study and observance of rabbinic Judaism, the choice of life is found in baptism into Yeshua's death and resurrection, in which a person dies to his sin and puts his evil inclination to death:

> O you sons of men, return, and you their daughters, come. And abandon the ways of that Corrupter, and approach me. And I will enter into you, and bring you forth from destruction, and make you wise in the ways of truth. Be not corrupted nor perish. Hear me and be saved, for I am proclaiming to you the grace of God. And through me you will be saved and become blessed. I am your judge; and they who have put me on will not be rejected, but they will possess incorruption in the new world. My elect ones have walked with me, and my ways I shall make known to them who seek me; and I shall promise them my name. . . . For the Most High circumcised me by his Holy Spirit, then he uncovered my inward being toward him, and filled me with his love. And his circumcising became my salvation, and I ran in the Way in his peace, in the way of Truth. (Odes Sol.33.6-13, 11.1-3)[6]

Verse 3:

"What the Law could not do . . . ": cf. Jn.8.31-47, Acts 13.39, Rom.3.19-20, 4.15, 5.20, 7.5, 13, Heb.7.18-19, 10.1f; Test.Jud.19.3-4.

As in chapter 3, Paul again directly associates the Torah with the weakness of human nature. His claim is that the Torah cannot free a man from sin because in its commandments God "accommodates" Himself to man's sinfulness.[7] The power of the Torah thus brings man to the knowledge of sin, but it does not free him from it, as Maimonides expresses in a very clear but contrary perspective, in his *Guide for the Perplexed*:

> What was there to prevent Him [God] from causing the inclination to accomplish acts of obedience willed by Him . . . to be a natural disposition fixed in us? God does not change at all the nature of human individuals by means of miracles . . . It is because of this that there are commandments and prohibitions, rewards and punishments. . . . We do not say this because we believe that the changing of the nature of any individual is difficult for Him. . . . Rather it is possible and fully within His capacity. But according to the foundations of the Law, of the Torah, He has never willed it, nor shall He ever will it. For if it were His will that the nature of any human individual be changed because of what He wills from that individual, the sending of prophets and all giving of the Law would have been useless. (Maimonides, *Guide for the Perplexed*, 3.31)[8]

Maimonides states exactly the opposite view to Paul's claim that God has given His righteousness to all men "apart from" the Torah (cf. 3.21). The "sending of prophets and all giving of the Law" is not sufficient, according to Paul, precisely because it does not change "the nature of any human individual." The "weakness" of the Torah is the same "weakness" of human nature under the mastery of the evil inclination. Paul states, however, that God condemned man's "spirit of flesh" (cf. 1QH 13.13) through Yeshua's sacrifice in his death and resurrection. He juxtaposes the Torah which is "weakened through" the flesh with Yeshua who came "in the likeness" of human flesh. As the "righteousness of God" (cf. Jer.23.5, Rom.1.16-17), Yeshua is the "goal" (*telos*; τελος) of the Torah (cf. 10.4), and the righteousness "apart from" the Torah to which the Torah witnesses (cf. 3.21-22) and which God promised through His prophets (cf. Jer.31.27f, Ezek.36.2f). The gift of his righteousness is thus the "law" (Torah) according to which the person who is faithful to God in Yeshua walks in the Spirit of truth and holiness.

"Likeness . . . in the flesh": cf. 1.3, 3.24, 5.8ff, Gal.4.4-5, Eph.2.15, Phil.2.7, Col.1.22, Heb.2.14-18; 1QS 3.18-24, 4.9-26, 11.9-11, 17, 21-22, 1QH 1.21-27, 3.23ff, 4.21, 29-31, 7.16-17, 9.13-16, 11.10-12, 12.25-35, 13.13-16, 17.23-25; Test.Levi 3.5-6, Odes Sol.7.4.

Paul emphasizes Yeshua's identification with humanity in man's weaknesses and limitations. Yeshua (the Last Adam) would have possessed no power to redeem man and to give him life had he not become subject to the same weaknesses and limitations (cf. Heb.2.18, 4.15). Paul then contrasts this fact with the "weakness" of the Torah "through the flesh," which disables the Torah from setting man free from "the law of sin and death." He resolves the paradox by appealing to Yeshua's sacrificial offering, in which he gave himself (the "members" of his own body) "as (an offering) for sin."[9] In the same way as the חטאת (*chata't*) represented both the sin and the sin offering, God sent Yeshua "in the likeness" of sinful flesh (as "sin") and as a sin offering to atone for man's sins.[10] Paul also plays on the meanings of "condemnation" (κατακριμα) in verse 1, where the word refers to God's gift of His righteousness to man, and here, where God's wrath and judgment (κριμα comes from the root verb κρινω, "to judge") is unleashed upon sin. The man who in his faithfulness to God in Yeshua is freed from "the law of sin and of death" is freed first of all because Yeshua has "condemned" (judged) sin in his own death to sin and his subsequent resurrection to God. Since he put his own will to death in dying on the cross, God therefore raised him to new life so that he might become the "first-born of many brethren" (cf. 1 Cor.15.23, Col.1.15). The phrase "in the flesh," in similar fashion to the double meaning of the phrase "(as an offering) for sin," refers to Yeshua's being "born of woman" (cf. 1QH 13.14, 18.12-13, 16, 23-24, Gal.4.4) and to his condemnation of sin in human beings ("in the flesh"). Yeshua "sentenced" sin to death in his own body ("flesh") on the cross; he also sentenced it to death in the people who put their own "flesh" to death in baptism, as the Qumran community similarly trusted in the Teacher of Righteousness:

> And Thou hast opened [his] {the Teacher of Righteousness'} fount[ain] to reprove the deeds of the creature of clay and the transgression of him that is born of woman, in conformity with his works; and to open Thy l[aws] of truth to the creature whom Thou hast upheld by Thy might, that according to Thy truth [he may be] the one who announces good tidings [in the ti]me of Thy goodness, preaching the gospel to the humble according to the abundance of Thy mercy, [giving them to drink] from the fountain of h[oliness] [and consoling the co]ntrite of spirit and the afflicted to (bring them)

> everlasting joy. . . . For what is flesh? [Behold, it was in Thy counsel] to do wonders and in Thy thought to manifest Thy might and establish all things for Thy glory. [And Thou hast created all] the host of Knowledge to recount mighty deeds unto flesh and the true precepts unto him that is born [of woman]. [And] Thou hast caused [Thine elect] to en[ter] the Covenant with Thee and hast uncovered the heart of dust that they be kept [from all evil] [and escape] from the snares of judgment unto Thy mercy. (1QH 18.12-25)

Verses 4-8:

"In order that . . . ": cf. Mt.5.17, Lk.1.6, Rom.2.26, 7.6, Gal.2.19, 3.13-14; 2 Bar.32.1.

Paul builds on his argument from 2.25f, and now makes explicit the Torah's function. Although the Torah "speaks in the language of men" or "only provides for human passions" (cf. Kid.21b), and thus makes man "aware" (knowledgeable) of their sin, that purpose itself is subject to a further goal. The "knowledge of sin" (cf. "understanding," in the Qumran texts) which comes through the Torah (cf. 7.7ff) frees (releases) man from service to his evil inclination to serve of God in righteousness. Paul is clearly still addressing "Israel" in this verse (cf. 7.1, "for I am speaking to those who know the Torah"), although God's gift of righteousness in Yeshua specifically brings both Jews and Gentiles into His kingdom. The "requirement (δικαιωμα; *dikaioma*) of the Torah" refers to God's "statutes and ordinances and laws" which God "established between Himself and the sons of Israel through Moses at Mount Sinai" (Lev.26.46; cf. Lev.7.37-38, Dt.4.8). Yeshua accomplished its "fulfillment" (cf. Mt.5.17), because he is "the Lord our righteousness" (Jer.23.6, Rom.3.21). Paul states this in the passive tense, in order to emphasize the fact that the Torah brings man "knowledge of (his) sin" (cf. 3.20, 7.7), and that God gives His righteousness to man in his baptism into Yeshua's death and resurrection, whereby he is empowered to fulfil the Torah's requirements through the cleansing of the Spirit of holiness (cf., "so shall you keep My statutes and My judgments, by which a man may live if he does them; I am the Lord" [Lev.18.5]).[11] The person who is "filled" with the Spirit is able to "fulfil" the principles of the Torah and to serve God because he has "died" to his evil inclination and is "walking according to the Spirit of holiness."

Verses 4-6:

"Walk . . . life and peace": cf. Lev.18.5, Dt.4.1, 28.15-20, 30.15-20, Prov.3.18, 4.4, 13, 22, Ezek.20.11, 37.26, Mal.2.5, Lk.10.28, Jn.3.6, Rom.5.1-5, 12, 6.16,

21, 23, 8.10, 10.5, 12.18, 13.10, 17, 15.13, 1 Cor.15.42, 50, Gal.5.16f, 25, 6.8, Eph.2.14, 1 Tim.1.8f, 4.8; 1QS 1.1-8, 2.1, 14, 3.9, 18, 4.1ff; 1QS[a] 1.2, 1QH 11.12, 20, 13.13, 17.25; Sir.17.11, 32.24, 45.5, Ap.Bar.4.1, 2 Bar.38.2, Wis.Sol.6.18, 7.14, Ps.Sol.14.2, 4 Ez.7.45; Jos.*Ant*.4.210; Sifre Dt.Ekev 45, He'azinu 306, Ex.R.41.4, Num.R.17.6, Suk.52b, Kid.30b, Ta'anit 7a.

Paul restates the doctrine of the Two Spirits (Two Ways, or masters), which he introduces in chapter 6 and develops in the subsequent chapters. In these verses, he once again describes the "sons of light" who belong to the Spirit of Truth on the one hand, and on the other hand the "sons of darkness" who belong to the Spirit of Perversity and are the "assembly of flesh," as well as the "Visitation" (cf. "reward" or "wages") which God bestows upon those who walk according to each Spirit:

> And these are the ways of these (Spirits) in the world. It is < of the Spirit of trut h > to enlighten the heart of man, and to level before him the ways of true righteousness, and to set fear in his heart of the judgment of God . . . And as for the Visitation of all who walk in this (Spirit), it consists of healing and abundance of bliss, with length of days and fruitfulness, and all blessings without end, and eternal joy in perpetual life, and the glorious crown and garment of honour in everlasting light. But to the Spirit of perversity belong cupidity, and slackness in the service of righteousness, impiety and falsehood, pride and haughtiness, falsity and deceit, cruelty and abundant wickedness, impatience and much folly, and burning insolence . . . causing a man to walk in all the ways of darkness, and malignant cunning. And as for the Visitation of all who walk in this (Spirit), it consists of an abundance of blows administered by all the Angels of destruction in the everlasting Pit by the furious wrath of the God of vengeance, of unending dread and shame without end. . . . (1QS 4.2-13)[12]

Verse 7:

"Mind . . . hostile toward God": cf. Dt.32.30, Judg.2.14, 3.8, 1 Kings 21.20, Ps.44.12, Jer.21.8-14, Jn.3.6, Rom.5.6-8, 6.6, 8.8, 15, 1 Cor.3.1-3, 6.20, 7.22-23, 2 Cor.1.12, Gal.4.3, 8, Eph.2.14, Jas.4.4, 1 Pet.2.11, 1 Jn.2.15; 1QS 3.13-4.26, 11.9-10, 21-22, 1QM 13.11, 1QH 1.21-27, 3.23ff, 4.30-31, 9.13-16, 10.23, 11.10-12, 12.24ff, 13.13-16, 17.23-25; Test.Jud.18.1-6, 20.1-3, Test.Asher 1.1-9, Sir.15.11-17, 4 Ez.7.[62]-[69], 2 En.30.15; Suk.52b (R. Huna).

Paul expands the themes of chapters 5 and 6 on the basis of the motif of the two masters (Two Spirits or Ways), which expresses the idea that "everlasting hatred" exists between the two Spirits because God delights in the

Spirit of Truth and hates the Spirit of Perversity. A man therefore cannot serve both God and his evil inclination, but must be "freed" from one master in order to be able to obey the other:

> Truly, the Spirits of light and darkness were made by Him; upon these (Spirits) He has founded every work, upon their [counsels] every service, and upon their ways [every Visit]ation. The one, God loves everlastingly, and delights in all his deeds forever, but the counsel of the other He loathes, and He hates all his ways for ever. . . . For God has allotted these (Two Spirits) in equal parts until the final end, and has set between their divisions eternal hatred [איבת עולם]. An abomination to Truth are the deeds of Perversity, and an abomination to Perversity are all the ways of Truth. And a fighting ardour (sets one against the other) on the subject of all their ordinances, for they walk not together. (1QS 3.25-4.1, 16-18)

The "hostility" which God has set between "Perversity" and "Truth"—between the "sons of light" and the "sons of darkness"—is at work in each person's individual life.[13] Man's "mind" must constantly "will" to obey God, since his "members" (cf. the "spirit of flesh") are continually being tempted to present themselves to unrighteousness (cf. 6.12ff). Paul further speaks of this hostility as the "enmity" (cf. איבת עולם; *'eivat 'olam*, "eternal hatred") which divides Israel from the Gentile nations (cf. Eph.2.12f). Yeshua is the true "peace" (reconciliation) (cf. Isa.9.6, 57.19) which makes the two into "one new man."[14] Since the Torah's requirements are fulfilled by Yeshua, who also takes upon himself the curse attendant upon the violation of its commandments (cf. Gal.13-14), in their faithfulness to him both Jews and Gentiles are "built together into a dwelling of God in the Spirit" (cf. Eph.2.22).[15]

Verses 7-8:

"Not even able . . . please God": cf. Jn.8.34-47, Rom.7.5, 14, 1 Cor.7.32-35, 2 Cor.5.9, Gal.1.10, 1 Thess.2.4, 15, 4.1, 2 Tim.2.4; 1QS 3.18-24, 4.9-26, 11.9-11, 17, 21-22, 1QH 1.21-27, 3.23ff, 4.21, 29-31, 7.16-17, 9.13-16, 11.10-12, 12.25-35, 13.13-16, 17.23-25.

Paul describes here the impossibility of serving two masters. The Greek verb ἀρεσκω (*aresko*), "to please," carries the sense of "making peace" or "reconciling." In the LXX one of its synonyms, εὐαρεστεω (*euaresteo*), "to be pleasing," is also used, however, to translate the Hebrew verb התהלך (*hithalekh*), "to walk (before God)."[16] This means that when a man "pleases"

God he makes Him his "master" and serves Him instead of serving his own inclination, since the Spirit of truth does not "walk together" with the "spirit of flesh, as the Qumran texts repeatedly emphasize:

> What being of flesh can do this, and what creature of clay has power to do such marvellous things, whereas he is in iniquity from his mother's womb and in the sin of unfaithfulness till his old age? And I, I know that righteousness is not of man, nor of the sons of men perfection of way; to the Most High God belong all the works of righteousness, whereas the way of man is not firm unless it be by the Spirit which God has created for him to make perfect a way for the sons of men, that all His works may know the might of His power and the greatness of His mercy to all the sons of His loving-kindness. . . . And he shall establish his steps to walk perfectly in all the ways of God, according to His command . . . and he shall step aside neither to right nor to left, and shall make no single step from all His words. Then will he please God with agreeable expiation, and it will obtain for him the Covenant of the eternal Community. (1QH 4.29-33, 1QS 3.9-12)[17]

Verse 9:

"Not in the flesh . . . belong to Him": cf. Gen.41.38, Ex.31.3, 33.14, 40.34, Num.11.25-29, 1 Sam.10.10, 19.20, 2 Chron.15.1, 24.20, Neh.9.20, Ps.51.11, Isa.44.3, 59.21, 63.10-11, Ezek.39.29, Joel 2.28-29, Hag.2.5, Mt.3.16, Jn.1.14, 14.23, Rom.8.11, 1 Cor.3.16, 23, 12.3, 2 Cor.6.16, Gal.5.24, Eph.4.30, 2 Tim.1.14, 1 Pet.4.14, 1 Jn.4.2; 1QS 3.1-5.7, 1QH 4.29-33, 12.11ff, 14.12-14, 16.9-12, 17.26.

According to Paul, man's conflict between serving two masters lies in choosing to "please" God by "angering" his own evil inclination (cf. Ruth R.3.1, 8.1). In order to serve God as his only master, a person must "belong" to the Spirit of Truth and walk according to the Spirit of holiness. As the Qumran texts clearly state, man's "flesh," which contains the "spirit of perversity" or the "spirit of defilement," must be cleansed through the Spirit of holiness.[18] This gift of the Holy Spirit parallels the "dwelling" of God's Spirit (cf. His glory or Presence [שכינה; *Shekhinah*]) in the Tabernacle (cf. Ex.33.14) and the Temple (cf. 1 Kings 8.10-11, Isa.6.1f). Paul first extrapolates this dwelling of God's Presence in the Temple to Yeshua (in whom the "fullness of the Godhead dwells" [שוכן; *shokhen*; cf. Col.1.19, 2.9]), and then to the community of believers, whose bodies become the "temple of the living God" (cf. 1 Cor.3.16, 2 Cor.6.16-18), their "heart of stone" having been replaced with the Spirit of holiness as rabbinic texts interpret biblical passages to say:

> God said: 'In this world, because there are amongst you slanderers, I have withdrawn My Divine Presence [שכינה] from amongst you,' as it is said, *Be Thou exalted, O God, above the heavens* (Ps.57.12). 'But in the time to come, when I will uproot the Evil Inclination from amongst you,' as it is said, *And I will take away the stony heart out of your flesh* (Ezek.36.26), 'I will restore My Divine Presence amongst you.' Whence this? For it is said, *And it shall come to pass afterward, that I will pour out My spirit upon all flesh*, etc. (Joel 3.1 [2.28]); 'and because I will cause My Divine Presence to rest upon you, all of you will merit [זכין] the Torah, and you will dwell in peace in the world,' as it is said, *And all thy children shall be taught of the Lord; and great shall be the peace of thy children* (Isa.54.13). (Dt.R.6.14)[19]

Another midrash, in the name of Rabbi Simeon ben Lakish, identifies God's "Presence" with the "spirit of the Messiah" which "was moving over the face of the waters" when God created the world:

> AND THE SPIRIT OF GOD HOVERED (Gen.1.2): this alludes to the spirit of Messiah, as you read, *And the spirit of the Lord shall rest upon him* (Isa.11.2). (Gen.R.2.4)[20]

These rabbinic midrashim express the expectation of the Sages in the Second Temple period for a change in man's relationship with God, represented by the "new covenant" which He promised to write on man's heart through His Spirit. Paul knows that God has poured out His spirit of righteousness and holiness through Yeshua, and that man is cleansed from the defilement of his "spirit of flesh" through his baptism into Yeshua's death and resurrection (cf. chapter 6).

Verses 10-11:

"If Yeshua is in you": cf. Jn.17.23, Rom.6.5, Gal.2.20.

In these verses, Paul reverses his normal expression of the two masters (cf. a person serves God by walking according to the Spirit of holiness) by referring to Yeshua's "dwelling" or "presence" (both of these words are covered in the term שכינה [*Shekhina*]) in the bodies (lives) of those who are faithful to Yeshua in his death and resurrection. This usage reflects the biblical description of the "outpouring" of God's Spirit on His prophets, through whom He also promised to pour out His Spirit on "all flesh" (cf. Isa.32.15, 44.3, Ezek.39.29, Joel 2.28). As God's שליח (*shaliach*) or "agent" (cf. "apostle"), Yeshua has been "anointed" (cf. משיח; *Mashiach*, Messiah) by God, who has put His Spirit on him in order that he might bring deliverance—life and healing—to his people (cf. Isa.49.8, 61.2f). The Teacher of Righteousness ascribed the same role to himself, on the basis of the same biblical texts:

> Behold, Thou hast undertaken to fi[ll Thy servant] with grace and hast favoured me with Thy Spirit of mercy and with the [brightness] of Thy glory . . . because of the Spirit which Thou hast put [in me] to accomplish Thy favours towards [Thy] servant for [ever] by cleansing me by Thy holy Spirit and by causing me to go forward in Thy will according to the greatness of Thy favours . . . [For] Thou hast opened a [fount]ain in the mouth of Thy servant and upon his tongue Thou hast graven [Thy precepts] on a measuring-cord, [that he] may proclaim them unto creatures because of his understanding and be an interpreter of these things unto that which is dust like myself. And Thou hast opened [his] fount[ain] to reprove the deeds of the creature of clay and the transgressions of him that is born of woman, in conformity with his works; and to open Thy l[aws] of truth to the creature whom Thou hast upheld by Thy might, that according to Thy truth [he may be] the one who announces good tidings [in the ti]me of Thy goodness, preaching the gospel to the humble according to the abundance of Thy mercy, [giving them to drink] from the fountain of h[oliness] [and consoling the co]ntrite of spirit and the afflicted to (bring them) everlasting joy. (1QH 16.8-12, 18.10-15)[21]

" . . . the body is dead . . . give life . . . ": cf. Jn.6.39f, Acts 2.24, Rom.4.19, 24, 6.4, 7.9-13, 10.9, 1 Cor.6.14, 15.13-17, 36-58, 2 Cor.4.14-16, Col.2.12, 3.10, Tit.3.5, Heb.11.12, 1 Pet.1.21.

Paul picks up both the relationship between sin and death (cf. 5.12ff, 7.10f) within the theme of the two masters (cf. chapter 6) and the idea of election (creation-resurrection) from chapter 4. Abraham's body was "as good as dead" (cf. 4.19) because it was past the age of creating offspring. God, however, gave "life to the dead" and called "into being that which does not exist" (4.17). The "deadness" (infertility) of Abraham's "body" formally corresponds to the "unfruitfulness" (impotence) of the "dead" who cannot "praise God" and store up good works and merit before Him (cf. Ps.115.17).[22] Paul identifies Yeshua with Abraham's "seed" (cf. Gal.3.16): Yeshua was "raised . . . from the dead" (verse 11) just as Isaac was (metaphorically and typologically; cf. Gen.R.56.9).[23] Abraham, moreover, became the "father" of a nation which God created from "not-My-people," so that the Gentile nations, as well as Israel, have become "sons of God." Abraham's "fatherhood" becomes God's work in creating (resurrecting) "sons" through the gift of His Spirit in Yeshua (the "spirit of the Messiah").[24]

Verses 12-13:

"Under obligation . . . ": cf. 13.7-8, Gal.5.3.

Paul here describes the doctrine of the Two Spirits (Ways) and two masters in terms of being in "debt," since the verb "to be under obligation" (ὀφειλω; *opheilo*) corresponds to "service" (cf. "bond servant" [1.1]) and being "bound" to a master (cf. 6.2ff).[25] Paul makes this very clear when he replaces the phrase "under obligation" (to living "according to the Spirit") with the clause, "if by the Spirit you are putting to death the deeds of the body."[26] A person "pleases" (serves) God when he chooses to "anger" (put to death; die to) the "spirit of flesh" as his "master," being cleansed and released from the "spirit of defilement" through the Spirit of holiness in order to serve his Creator:

> For by the Spirit of true counsel concerning the ways of man shall all his sins be atoned when he beholds the light of life. By the Holy Spirit of the Community, in His truth, shall he be cleansed of all his sins; and by the Spirit of uprightness and humility shall his iniquity be atoned. By his soul's humility towards all the precepts of God shall his flesh be cleansed when sprinkled with lustral water and sanctified in flowing water. . . . Then God will cleanse by His truth all the works of every man, and will purify for Himself the (bodily) fabric of every man, to banish all Spirit of perversity from his members, and purify him of all wicked deeds by the Spirit of holiness; and He will cause the Spirit of Truth to gush forth upon him like lustral water. All lying abominations shall come to an end, (and) defilement by the Spirit of defilement. The just will comprehend the Knowledge of the Most High, and the perfect of way will have understanding of the wisdom of the Sons of Heaven. For God has chosen them for an everlasting Covenant and all the glory of the Man is theirs. (1QS 3.6-9, 4.20-23)

> Hence, say the sages, "Whoever has never glanced at another woman, his evil inclination does not rule over him, and in the world to come God will remove it from him altogether, and put in his heart His Holy Spirit" (Ezek.36.26). (Tanh.B.Chuk.1.1, supplement)

Verse 14:
"All who are . . . sons of God": cf. Ex.4.22, Dt.14.1, 32.5, 19-21, Isa.43.6, 63.16, 64.8, Jer.31.8-9, Hos.1.10, 11.1, Mt.5.9, 45, Jn.1.12, Gal.3.26, 1 Jn.3.1; 1QH 7.20-21, 9.35-36; Sir.4.10, Test.Jud.24.3, Odes Sol.3.7, Ps.Sol.17.27, Jub.1.22-25; Pes.Rab.27.3, Ex.R.24.1, 46.4, 5, Ber.8a.

Paul recalls the motif of the "sons of Abraham" (cf. 2.25-29), integrated into the two masters (cf. 6.2ff), and develops the complex of ideas in relation to another common idea in the Jewish thought of the period. This is the discussion over the various merits of a son over a servant. In the Tanakh, the people of Israel are called both "sons" (cf. Dt.14.1) and "servants" (cf. Lev.25.55), but the status of the son was normally considered to be higher than that of the servant:

> He [R. Akiba] said to him: 'You are called both sons and servants. When you carry out the desires of the Omnipresent you are called "sons", and when you do not carry out the desires of the Omnipresent, you are called "servants."' (BB 10a)[27]

Paul broadens this series of motifs and themes which derive from Israel's election to include the Gentiles as well.[28] As he makes clear from his argument in chapter 2, "every man" who "does God's will"—both Jew and Gentile—is "led" to obey the Creator through the circumcision of man's heart by the Spirit of holiness:

> "O Lord, let your mercy be lifted up upon your people, and create for them an upright spirit. And do not let the spirit of Beliar rule over them to accuse them before you and ensnare them from every path of righteousness so that they might be destroyed from before your face. But they are your people and your inheritance, whom you saved by your great might from the hand of the Egyptians. Create a pure heart and a holy spirit for them. And do not let them be ensnared by their sin henceforth and forever." And the Lord said to Moses, "I know their contrariness and their thoughts and their stubbornness. And they will not obey until they acknowledge their sin and the sins of their fathers. But after this they will return to me in all uprightness and with all of (their) heart and soul. I shall cut off the foreskin of their heart and the foreskin of the heart of their descendants. And I shall create for them a holy spirit, and I shall purify them so that they will not turn away from following me from that day and forever. And their souls will cleave to me and to all my commandments. And they will do

> my commandments. And I shall be a father to them, and they will be sons to me. And they will all be called 'sons of the living God.' And every angel and spirit will know and acknowledge that they are my sons and I am their father in uprightness and righteousness. And I shall love them." (Jub.1.20-25; cf. 1QH 7.21, 9.35-36, 10.27)[29]

Verse 15:

"Not received a spirit of slavery": cf. Gen.4.7, Jn.8.31-44, Heb.2.15; 1QS 3.18-4.26, 11.9ff, 21-22, 1QH 1.21-27, 3.23ff, 4.21, 29-31, 7.16-17, 9.13-16, 11.10-12, 12.25-35, 13.13-16, 17.23-25; Test.Jud.18.6, Test.Dan 4.7, Test.Asher 3.2, 6.5; MHG Gen.4.9, Gen.R.22.6, 34.10, Ruth R.3.1, Ecc.R.9.4.1, AZ 5b, BB 17a.

Here Paul explicitly denotes the theme of the "two masters" (cf. "slavery").[30] He further picks up the ideas of "grace" (cf. 5.5, 15-21) as God's "gift" of righteousness in which those who are faithful to God in Yeshua's death and resurrection "stand" (cf. 5.2), thus freeing them from the "spirit of slavery" under the "dominion of Belial," as the Qumran texts describe:

> Thou hast appeared unto me from my youth (giving) understanding of Thy judgment (to me) and hast upheld me by certain truth, and in Thy holy Spirit Thou hast set my delight. And [Thy hand] has [gui]ded me until this day and Thy righteous punishment accompanies my [si]ns. But Thy loving keeping is for the saving of my soul and over my steps is abundance of pardon and when Thou judgest me, greatness of [mer]cy; and until I am old Thou wilt care for me. For my father knew me not and my mother abandoned me to Thee; for Thou art a father to all Thy [sons] of truth and hast put Thy joy within them as her that loves her babe, and as a foster father (bearing the child) in his breast so carest Thou for all Thy creatures. . . . And unto Thy sons of truth Thou hast given under[standing] [and they shall know Thee for ever and] ever [and] shall be glorified according to their knowledge. . . . (1QH 9.31-36, 10.27)[31]

Without God's "adoption" (cf. Gal.4.5) man is an orphan, "having no hope and without God in the world" (Eph.2.12). When man acknowledges God as his Father (and God acknowledges men as His sons), however, man inherits God's understanding and His truth.

"Leading to fear again": cf. Rom.5.1-9, Gal.4.1f, 9, Eph.4.17ff, 2 Tim.1.7, Heb.2.15, 1 Jn.4.7-21.

Paul describes "slavery" as "fear," in the tradition of a series of rabbinic midrashim which address the relative merits between serving God out of love—as sons—and serving Him out of fear—like slaves:

> What parable illustrates how, in the sight of their heavenly Father, the house of Israel in this world [is instructed in all of Scripture]? The parable of a mortal king who had many sons and servants. He took and built many houses and many palaces with extensive—indeed limitless—open ground. Then an idea struck him. He said: I will test my sons and my servants [to find out] who loves me and who stands in awe of me. Whereupon he proceeded to build a courtyard four by four cubits wide. At its entrance he made an opening four by four handbreadths wide, and in it set a wicket facing the open ground where people might come to pay their respects to the king. Then, when his sons and servants came and stationed themselves either in the courtyard or in the lane leading to it, the king was able to discern those who loved him and stood in awe of him and those who stood in awe of him but did not love him. He who both loved and stood in awe of the king suffered discomfort as he squeezed his way through the wicket facing the open ground beyond it to pay his respects to the king. And he who merely stood in awe of him but did not love him remained standing in the courtyard or in the lane. How does the parable apply? The Holy One said to those of Israel [who remained standing in His courtyard and lane]: My children, why though I came to pay My respects to you, do you not come to pay your respects to Me? Even though, *Some of you choose to dwell in courtyards* [*outside the open ground before My palace*], *nevertheless, just as companions* [*who, having made their way into the open ground before Me*], *hearken eagerly for your utterance* [*of regard for Me*], *I, too, would have you make Me hear such utterance* (Song 8.13). (TBE p.82)[32]

Paul integrates this midrashic tradition with the theme of the two masters. Those who serve God (and not their evil inclination) are God's sons because they serve Him out of love.[33] The distinction between love and fear as the criterion for serving God developed, according to Flusser, from the "new sensitivity" relating to the doctrine of reward and punishment in Second Temple Jewish thought.[34] Intertestamental, Qumran, and early rabbinic Jewish texts began to claim, based on an innovative interpretation of Leviticus 19.18, that love for God was more important than awe of Him.[35] "True" worship should be based on love for God, not on fear of His retribution. The fear of punishment is a fear of death, and death is the true "master" of the evil inclination (cf. 4.15, 5.12-14, 20-21, 1 Cor.15.56, Heb.2.15). The "true" "sons of Abraham" are therefore not only those who serve God out of love (rather than out of fear of His wrath and judgment), but those who have become "sons" by "dying to sin" and death in baptism into Yeshua's death and who have been "freed" from sin and death by being raised (resurrected) with him into the "newness of (eternal) life" (cf. 6.3ff, 7.1ff, 8.1ff).

"Spirit of adoption as sons . . . ": cf. Ex.4.22, Dt.14.1, 32.5, 19-21, Ps.27.10, Isa.63.16, 64.8, Mal.1.6, 2.10, Mk.14.36, Jn.8.38-42, Rom.8.23, 9.4, Gal.4.1-7, Eph.1.5; 1QH 7.20-22, 9.35-36; Sir.4.10, Test.Jud.24.3, Test.Job 33.3; Pes.Rab.21.5, TBE p.11, Gen.R.1.1, Ex.R.24.1, 30.9, 46.4, Cant.R.8.1, Ber.10b, 35b.

Paul now parallels the phrase "the spirit of slavery" with the "spirit of adoption," on the basis that a son serves God out of love, whereas a servant (slave) serves Him out of fear. Since God has adopted those who serve Him in love through the cleansing of His Spirit, the "spirit of flesh" has been replaced by God's Spirit of holiness, just as the Qumran texts describe:

> Thou hast appeared unto me from my youth (giving) understanding of Thy judgment (to me) and hast upheld me by certain truth, and in Thy holy Spirit Thou hast set my delight. And [Thy hand] has [gui]ded me until this day and Thy righteous punishment accompanies my [si]ns. But Thy loving keeping is for the saving of my soul and over my steps is abundance of pardon and when Thou judgest me, greatness of [mer]cy; and until I am old Thou wilt care for me. For my father knew me not and my mother abandoned me to Thee; for Thou art a father to all Thy [sons] of truth and hast put Thy joy within them as her that loves her babe, and as a foster father [כאומן] (bearing the child) in his breast so carest Thou for all Thy creatures. (1QH 9.31-36)[36]

It is possible that Paul (as well as the author of the Qumran psalm) is here interpreting Psalm 27.10, a psalm in which David conquers his fear (verse 1) by knowing that although his natural parents may have abandoned him the Lord would "adopt" him and make him His son. The idea of a "foster father" or "guardian" appears in several other biblical texts (cf. Num.11.12, Ruth 4.16, 2 Kings 10.1, Isa.49.23), just as Yeshua also says he will not leave his disciples as "orphans," and implies that the Holy Spirit will act as a "guardian" to them (cf. Jn.14.16-18) in similar fashion to other Jewish midrashim:

> Another explanation of '*But now, O Lord, Thou art our Father*' (Isa.64.8). The Holy One, blessed be He, said: 'You have ignored your own fathers, Abraham, Isaac and Jacob, and Me do you call father?' To which they [Israel] replied: 'Thee do we recognize as our Father.' It can be compared to an orphan who was brought up with a guardian [אפוטרופוס] that was a good and trustworthy man, and brought her up and looked after her most carefully. Later he wished to marry her, and when the scribe came to write the marriage document he asked her: 'What is your name?' to which she replied: 'So-and-so'; but when he asked her: 'What is the name of your father?' she was silent. Whereupon her guardian asked her: 'Why are you silent?' and she replied: 'Because I know of no other father save you, for he that brings up a child is called a father, and not he that gives birth' . . . Similarly, the orphan is Israel, as it says, *We are become orphans and fatherless* (Lam.5.3). The good and faithful guardian is the Holy One, blessed be He, whom Israel began to call 'Our father', as it says, '*But now, O Lord, Thou art our father*' (Isa.64.8). God said: 'You have ignored your own father, and now call Me your father'; as it says, *Look unto Abraham your father*, etc. (Isa.51.2). They replied: 'Lord of the Universe! He who brings up children is called the father, not he who gives birth,' as it says, *For Thou art our father; for Abraham knoweth us not* (Isa.63.16). (Ex.R.46.5)[37]

Verse 16:

"The Spirit bears witness": cf. Lk.24.48, Jn.15.26, Acts 5.32, Rom.2.15, 8.26, 1 Cor.12.3, Heb.10.15, 1 Jn.5.7-8, 3.21, 5.6-12; Test.Jud.20.5; Lev.R.6.1.

The normal function of a witness is to attest or confirm the truth of a statement or an act. Biblical (and *halakhic*) law usually requires two attesting witnesses (cf. Dt.19.15, Mt.18.16, 2 Cor.13.1, 1 Tim.5.19, Heb.10.28, Sifre Dt.188, Sot.2b, San.30a), although the testimony of a single witness is sufficient in matters of ritual, and in the particular case of a woman who wishes to remarry (cf. Rom.7.1-7), where the testimony of a single witness that her husband is dead is also sufficient (cf. Git.2b-3a). The "Spirit of Truth," together with "our spirit" (the spirit of man) (as two witnesses) attests and confirms that the "children of God" are those whom the Spirit of God "leads" (cf. verse 14), since the indwelling of the Spirit is the testimony of man's sonship:

> I give [Thee thanks, O Adonai], for Thou hast given me understanding of Thy truth . . . because of the Spirit that Thou hast put in me; and I have heard what is certain according to Thy

> marvellous secret because of Thy holy Spirit. Thou hast [o]pened Knowledge in the midst of me . . . and hast made me know Thy marvellous Mysteries and Thy favours to [sinful] man [and] the abundance of Thy mercy toward the perverse heart! Who among the gods is like Thee, O Adonai, and who is like Thy truth? And when he is judged, who will be ju[s]t before Thee, since there is no answer to Thy reproof? All majesty is but wind and none can brave Thy fury. But Thou causest all Thy sons of Truth to enter into pardon before Thee, [to puri]fy them of their sins through the abundance of Thy goodness and the greatness of Thy me[r]cy, to set them before Thee for ever and ever. (1QH 7.26, 12.11-13, 7.27-31)[38]

Verse 17:

"If children . . . heirs of God": cf. Acts 20.32, 26.18, Rom.4.13ff, Gal.3.29, 4.7, Eph.1.14, 3.6, 5.5, Col.1.12, 3.24, Heb.9.15, 1 Pet.1.4, Rev.21.7.

Paul begins his discussion of the theme of inheritance ("heirs") in chapter 4, in relation to Abraham.[39] Abraham is the "father of many nations"—both Israel and the Gentiles—because God's promise to him (the inheritance of righteousness) was based on his faithfulness, prior to מתן תורה (*mattan Torah*), the giving of the Torah at Sinai. Paul first appeals to the motif of the "sons of Abraham" in 2.25f, and here he brings the two themes together (sons, [children], heirs).[40] The person who is an heir is also a "son," because the "qualities" of heirs are the same as those who are sons, and because both sons and heirs are "free" from the evil inclination to serve God in the righteousness of eternal life. The "true "sons of Abraham," according to rabbinic sources, are those who walk in his steps and are not disciples of Balaam, the wicked:

> Whoever possesses these three things, he is of the disciples of Abraham, our father; and [whoever possesses] three other things, he is of the disciples of Balaam, the wicked. The disciples of Abraham, our father, [possess] a good eye, an humble spirit and a lowly soul. The disciples of Balaam, the wicked, [possess] an evil eye, a haughty spirit and an over-ambitious soul. What is [the difference] between the disciples of Abraham, our father, and the disciples of Balaam, the wicked. The disciples of Abraham, our father, enjoy [lit. 'eat'] [their share] in this world, and inherit the world to come, as it is said: That I may cause those that love Me to inherit substance and that I may fill their treasuries (Prov.8.21), but the disciples of Balaam, the wicked, inherit Gehinnom, and descend into the nethermost pit,

as it is said: But Thou, O God, wilt bring them down to the nethermost pit; men of blood and deceit shall not live out half their days . . . (Ps.55.24). (PA 5.19)[41]

"Fellow-heirs with the Messiah": cf. Mk.12.7, Rom.4.13f, Gal.3.29, 4.1, 7, Eph.3.6, Heb.1.2, 2.8.

Paul's immediate model for inheritance (an heir) is Abraham (cf. 4.13). Abraham becomes a prototype for the Messiah not only because God "imputed righteousness to him" because he was faithful to God's voice but also because God's promise of righteousness was made to his "seed" (cf. Gen.22.17). Paul interprets this promise to refer specifically to the Messiah (cf. Gal.3.16), who is both Abraham's descendant and his "heir." God's promise of the righteousness of eternal life was inherited and "incarnated" in Yeshua (cf. Heb.1.2), "the Lord our righteousness" (Jer.23.6). Abraham inherited the "(nations of the) world" (cf. 4.13), and the Messiah inherits both the nations and the "(very) ends of the earth" (cf. Ps.2.8) when, according to God's "decree" (Ps.2.7), he is "declared the Son of God with power by the resurrection of the dead" (Rom.1.4).[42] Those who are faithful to God by making Him their "master" through baptism into Yeshua's death and resurrection (cf. 6.3f) become God's heirs as His sons. Yeshua's death and resurrection made him the "first-born among many brethren" (cf. Acts 26.23, 1 Cor.15.20, 23, Col.1.18, Rev.1.5), and gave him the right of inheritance, which he then passes on to those who are baptized into his name.[43]

"If indeed we suffer with (him)": cf. Mt.16.21, Mk.8.31, Lk.9.22, 24.26, 46, Acts 3.18, 17.3, Rom.6.3ff, 2 Cor.4.10, 17, Col.1.24, 2 Tim.2.3, 12, Heb.2.18, 5.8, 9.26, 13.12, 1 Pet.2.21, 23, 4.13; 1QH 2.8-9, 3.6-18, 1QpHab 8.2-3; Sifre Dt.32, Ber.5a.

Paul describes Yeshua's death and resurrection in the language of the early tradition: "The Son of Man must suffer many things, and be rejected by the elders and chief priests and scribes, and be killed, and be raised up on the third day" (Lk.9.22).[44] He restates the theme of chapter 6 (cf. 5.1-11), in which the baptism and burial of the believer into Yeshua's death (his suffering) lead to his sharing in Yeshua's resurrection in newness of life.[45]

"Glorified with (him)": cf. Ps.8.5, 106.20, Ezek.1.28, Dan.7.13f, Lk.9.26, 21.27, Rom.3.23, 5.1-2, 6.4, 8.21, 30, 1 Cor.2.7, 11.7, 15.35ff, 2 Cor.3.7-18, 4.4-6, Phil.2.5-11, 3.21, 2 Thess.1.7-10, 1 Tim.3.16, Heb.1.2-3, 2.9-10, Jas.1.12, 1 Pet.1.11, 18f, 21, 5.4, 2 Pet.1.17, Rev.2.10; 1QS 9.11-13, 11.5-7, 1QM 1.8-9,

1QH 7.23-25, 9.16, 24-26, 10.27-29; Odes Sol.38.17-21, 41.4, 1 En.108.11-14, 4 Ez.7.[98], 2 Bar.51.3, Test.Levi 18.8.

Paul continues the "Son of man" tradition here, which is associated not only with the suffering of the Messiah but also with his "coming on the clouds of the sky with power and great glory" (cf. Ps.80.18, Dan.7.13f).[46] The "Son of man" is given God's glory and power, and establishes the Kingdom of God overcoming all iniquity and wickedness. The "Saints of the Highest One (Most High)" inherit this kingdom and possess it forever (cf. Dan.7.18). This tradition is easily combined midrashically with Israel's election as God's "son" and the "sons of Abraham." This association can be further applied to Adam, the first (son of) "man," who is a prototype of the Messiah, the Second (Last) Adam, who will restore Adam's lost glory (cf. Gen.R.12.6):

> For without Thee no way is perfect, and without Thy will nothing is done. . . . Who then shall contain Thy Glory? And what is the son of man himself amidst all Thy marvellous works? And he that is born of woman, what is his worth before Thee? . . . But in His Mysteries of understanding and in His glorious Wisdom God has set an end for the existence of Perversity . . . All lying abominations shall come to an end, (and) defilement by the Spirit of defilement. The just will comprehend the Knowledge of the Most High, and the perfect of way will have understanding of the wisdom of the Sons of Heaven. For God has chosen them for an everlasting Covenant and all the glory of the Man [Adam] is theirs . . . and He built for them a sure House in Israel . . . They who cling to it are (destined) for everlasting life and theirs shall be all the glory of the Man . . . they that ho[pe] in Thy laws [Thou wilt deliver], [and bring aid] to them that serve thee with faith [that] their seed [may] be before Thee for ever. And [Thou] wilt forg[ive them and] raise up [a Saviour (?)] [to redeem them from s]in and to cast away all their in[iquities] and to give them a share of the glory of man [and] abundance of days . . . [and to them will belong all the glory] of the man and to their seed for ever. (1QS 11.17-20, 4.18-23, CDC 3.20, 1QH 17.13-16, 4QpPs.37 2.1-2)[47]

Verse 18:
"Sufferings . . . to be revealed to us": cf. Mt.12.32, Mk.10.30, Lk.16.8, 18.30, 20.34, Rom.5.6, 8.1, 12.11 (mss), 1 Cor.2.6-10, 2 Cor.1.4-10, 3.7-18, 4.4ff, Eph.1.21, 2.1-7, Col.3.4, 1 Tim.6.17, 2 Tim.4.10, Tit.2.12, Heb.2.9-18; 1QS 8.4, 12, 9.3, 5, 1QM 1.8-12, 1QH 3.6-18, 1QpHab 7.2, 4QpPs.37 1.9-19, 2.3; 1 En.91.14, 104.1-5, 4 Ez.6.11-28, 7.10-14, 2 Bar.15.8, 32.1-6.

Paul's concept of "glorification" is based on the idea that man's inheritance of the world to come rests upon his endurance of persecution for his faithfulness to God in Yeshua (cf. Mt.5.10). The self-designations of the Qumran community, such as the "contrite of spirit" (cf. 1QH 18.15), "poor of spirit" (cf. 1QM 14.7, 1QH 14.3), "paupers of grace" (cf. 1QH 5.22), "paupers of Thy redemption" (1QM 11.9), and "desperate of justification" (cf. 1QH 5.22), reflect a similar sense of persecution by those who had strayed from God's commandments. Flusser suggests that these combinatory phrases are deliberately paradoxical (although their construction is facilitated by the Hebrew syntax), and are meant to contrast "the abject state of the Sect in the present with a second one, which proclaims triumphantly the plenty of God's grace bestowed upon His elect. This paradoxical contrast between the present plight and persecution of the blessed and their future glory in the kingdom of heaven is also the main burden of the Beatitudes."[48] Thus the Qumran commentary on Psalm 37 associates glorification with inheritance:

> *But the humble will possess the earth and taste the delights of perfect bliss* {Ps.37.11}. The explanation of this verse concerns [the Congregation of the] Poor who accept the time of affliction and will be delivered from all the snares [of the Pit . . .] all the [. . .] of the earth [. . .] all the deli[ghts] . . . [*Yahweh knows the days of the perfect and their inheritance will abide for ever. They will not be ashamed on the day of misfortune* (ibid. 18-19a).] [The explanation of this concerns] the converts of the desert who will live for a thousand generations . . . [. . . and to them will belong all the glory] of the man and to their seed forever. (4QpPs.37 1.8-2.2)

Verse 19:

"Anxious longing of the creation": cf. Gen.3.17-9, Isa.11.6 9, 51.6, 65.17, 66.22, Rom.1.21-32, 8.23, Phil.1.20, 2 Pet.3.13, Rev.21.1; 2 Bar.32.1-6; Gen.R.12.6, Num.R.13.12.

The Greek noun ἀποκαραδοκια (*apokaradokia*), "earnest expectation," is rarely found in Greek writings prior to 200 B.C., and is absent from the LXX. Delitzsch appropriately translates it back into Hebrew as תערוג (*ta'arog*) from a root which is used only in Psalm 42.1 ("my soul pants for Thee, O God") and Joel 1.20. The passage in Joel speaks of the coming of the "Day of the Lord" as "destruction from the Almighty," and it is clear that Paul understands the "panting," in parallel with "glorification," as an eschatological event (cf. 1 Cor.1.7, [Heb.9.28]). The pristine purity of God's creation was "cursed" as a result of Adam's disobedience (cf. Gen.3.17), and would only be restored in the messianic age, which would also restore Adam's glory to the "sons of man":

> R. Berekiah said in the name of R. Samuel b. Nahman: Though these things were created in their fullness, yet when Adam sinned they were spoiled, and they will not again return to their perfection until the son of Perez [viz. Messiah] comes; [for the verse] '*These are the toledoth* (generations) *of Peretz*', *toledoth* is spelled fully, with a *waw* {intimating that they were created with their full power}. These are they {the six things whose restoration is symbolized by the inclusion of the *waw*}: his lustre [cf. Jud.5.31], his immortality [cf. Isa.65.22], his height [cf. Lev.26.13], the fruit of the earth and the fruit of trees [cf. Zech.8.12], and the luminaries [cf. Isa.30.26]. (Gen.R.12.6)[49]

"Revealing of the sons of God": cf. Lk.20.36, Rom.8.14, 1 Cor.15.38ff, Phil.3.20-21, Col.3.4, 1 Jn.3.2; 1QS 4.7-8, 8.5-10, 1QH 11.10-14, 13.11-12; Jub.1.20-25, 4 Ez.7.28-[44], 2 Bar.30.1-5; Gen.R.1.6.

Paul speaks of the "glorification" of men when they become the "sons of God" in a specifically eschatological context. The "revelation" of their glory takes place when God destroys the spirits of Belial and darkness in the final, awful Day of Judgment when the whole earth is liberated and illuminated by the "sons of light," as described in the Qumran texts:

> This shall be the time of salvation for the people of God, the hour of dominion for all the men of his lot and of final destruction for all the lot of Belial. And there shall be im[mense] confusion [for] the sons of Japheth and Asshur shall fall without help from any man, and the dominion of the Kittim shall vanish that wickedness may be crushed without a remnant and without any survivor for [all the son]s of darkness. The [the sons of righteou]sness shall lighten all the ends of the world progressively, until all the moments of darkness are consumed. Then in the time of God His sublime greatness shall shine for all the times [of the ages] unto gladness and blessing; glory and joy and length of days (shall be given) to all the sons of light. (1QM 1.5-9)

God "shows forth" the glory of His sons to the whole creation. Paul follows the Jewish tradition which sees men as being "crowned with glory" and "clothed with the garments of honour" (cf. 13.14). God's garments of glory are given to man through the victory of His Messiah, and man's earthly, physical body is then transformed into an imperishable "spiritual" body through the resurrection of Yeshua, after he is seated at the right hand of Power (God):

> The Elect One stands before the Lord of the Spirits; his glory is forever and ever and his power is unto all generations. In him dwells the spirit of wisdom, the spirit which gives thoughtfulness, the spirit of knowledge and strength, and the spirit of those who have fallen asleep in righteousness. . . . In those days, there will be a change for the holy and righteous ones and the light of days shall rest on them; and glory and honor shall be given back to them on the day of weariness. . . . For the Son of Man was concealed from the beginning, and the Most High One preserved him in the presence of his power; then he revealed him to the holy and the elect ones. The congregation of the holy ones shall be planted, and all the elect ones shall stand before him . . . and from henceforth they shall never see the faces of the sinners and the oppressors. The Lord of the Spirits will abide over them; they shall eat and rise with that Son of Man forever and ever. The righteous and elect ones shall rise from the earth and shall cease being of downcast face. They shall wear the garments of glory. These garments of yours shall become the garments of life from the Lord of Spirits. Neither shall your garments wear out, nor your glory come to an end before the Lord of the Spirits. (1 En.49.2-3, 50.1, 62.7-8, 13-16)[50]

Verse 20:
"Creation . . . subjected it": cf. Gen.6.7-8, Acts 14.15, Rom.1.18ff, Eph.4.17; DEZ 10, Mekh.Shirata 1, San.97a ff.

Paul describes nature's "bondage" to man in the same two senses in which he describes man's "subjection" to his evil inclination when he exchanged God's truth for his own image (cf. 1.21ff) and the "futility" of man's idolatrous and pagan worship when he himself is "bound" by the "ruler of this world."[51] God has "subjected" ("cursed") nature because of man's (Adam's and Eve's) disobedience, and as a result it as it were "idolizes" itself, since the "images" which man makes from its products are objectified and reified parts of its own nature. Yet God is still the cause of nature's subjection, in the same way that He has "shut up all in disobedience"—so that He might "show mercy to all" of His creation (11.32), both man and nature.

Verses 20-21:
"In hope that . . . ": cf. 4.17, 11.32, Gal.3.22; Ps.Sol.17.26-43.

Paul includes the whole of creation in the "hope" for re-birth and resurrection (cf. 4.17f). The function of this phrase as a "purpose clause" ("in hope that" = "in order that") is thus strengthened by the "hope" that "gives life to the dead and calls into being that which does not exist" (cf. 4.17). God has "promised" that He will create a "new heaven and earth" (cf. Isa.65.17, 66.22). Jewish apocalyptic literature in particular adopted and adapted the language and imagery of Genesis 1-3 to describe this Eschaton. Thus the "birthpangs of the Messiah" and the "messianic tribulations" describe the physical and spiritual suffering of the creation before the advent of the Messiah:

> And Thou hast cleansed man of sin because of Thy glory that he may be made holy for Thee from all unclean abomination and from (every) transgression of unfaithfulness, that he may be joined wi[th] Thy sons of truth and with the lot of Thy Saints; that this vermin that is man may be raised from the dust to [Thy] secret [of truth] and from the spirit of perversity to [Thine] understanding; and that he may watch before Thee with the everlasting host and together with [Thy] spirits [of holiness], that he may be renewed with all [that is] [and] shall be and with them that know, in a common rejoicing. . . . For it is Thou who hast established them from before eternity and the work [. . .] they shall recount Thy glory in all Thy dominion. For Thou hast caused them to see what they had not known [by bringing to an end the] former [things] and by creating things that are new . . . and by [set]ting up that which shall remain for ever. For Th[ou art a God of eternity . . .] and shalt be for ages without end. (1QH 11.10-14, 13.10-13)[52]

Verse 21:

"The freedom of . . . the children of God": cf. Jn.8.31-51, Acts 13.38, Gal.4.3ff, 31, 5.1; 4 Ez.6.17-28, 7.10-14, 13.26, 2 Bar.23.6, 39.7.

Paul now extends the human "freedom from bondage" to sin and the fear of death to the whole of creation. All those who are faithful to God in Yeshua are "freed" to serve God in the "newness of life," which is "crowned with glory" because of the cleansing presence of the Spirit of truth and holiness. Man's "mastery" over his evil inclination (the "spirits of Belial," the "spirit of perversity" or the "spirit of flesh") is finally joined with the "Renewal" of the whole world when the "dominion of Belial" (cf. 1QS 1.18) or the "ruler of this world" (cf. Jn.14.31, 2 Cor.4.4, Gal.1.4, Eph.2.2, 6.12) is finally destroyed by God at the End of the Times:

> Till now the Spirits of truth and perversity battle in the hearts of every man; (they) walk in Wisdom and Folly. . . . For God has allotted these (Spirits) in equal parts until the final end, the time of Renewal. . . . All lying abomination shall come to an end, (and) defilement by the Spirit of defilement. The just will comprehend the Knowledge of the Most High, and the perfect of way will have understanding of the wisdom of the Sons of Heaven. For God has chosen them for an everlasting Covenant and all the glory of the man is theirs. Perversity will exist no more: shame upon all the works of deceit! (1QS 4.24-25, 21-23)

Verse 22:

"The whole creation groans . . . ": cf. Isa.19.8 (LXX), 21.2-3, Lam.1.8, Jer.4.31, 12.4, 11, 13.21, 30.6, Mk.13.8, Jn.16.21, 2 Cor.5.2-4.

Paul explicitly associates the "suffering" of creation with the "birthpangs" of the messianic age, since the metaphor of childbirth was frequently used to describe the suffering preceding and bringing the advent of the Messiah or the messianic age.[53] The "groaning" of creation is, as it were, the audible expression of the "sufferings of this present time" (verse 18), which a messianic text from Qumran clearly describes:

> [And] I was confused like the Woman about to bring forth at the time of her first child bearing. For terrors and fearful pains have unfurled on its billows that She who is with child might bring into the world (her) first born. For the children have reached as far as the billows of Death . . . and the billows of the Pit (are unleashed) unto all the works of terror . . . and the clouds roar in a noise of roaring . . . because of the boiling of the deeps upon the fountains of the waters. [And] the waves [are turb]ulent (rearing) into the air and the billows resound with the roaring of their voice. (1QH 3.7-16)

Verse 23:

"Also we ourselves . . . ": cf. Ezek.21.6-7, 2 Cor.5.1-8; 1QH 5.30-31, 11.22ff; Tob.3.1.

Paul uses the same style and thought as in 5.11, based on the principle of קו״ח *(kal ve-chomer)*, where if one thing is true (here, that if the whole of creation is waiting for redemption), how much the more so is another thing linked with it—here, that the "sons of men" are also awaiting adoption as sons and physical redemption. In 2 Corinthians 5.1-10, Paul links man's "groaning" with the hope for physical redemption, and uses the metaphor of the "house" or "building" also common to the Qumran texts, which he picks up again in chapter 12.[54] The groaning of mankind and the whole creation are expressions of the "birthpangs of the Messiah," who brings forth his "church," and "glorifies" the members of the community with an imperishable, spiritual body:

> She who is big with the man of distress (?) is in her pains. For She shall give birth to a man-child in the billows of Death, and in the bonds of Sheol there shall spring from the crucible of the Pregnant one a Marvellous Counsellor with his might; and he shall deliver every man from the billows because of Her who is big with him. Every womb suffers pain and terrible anguish at the time of child-bearing, and terror seizes them that conceived these children; and at the time of the bearing of her first-born every terror unfurls over the crucible of Her who is with child. (1QH 3.9-12)[55]

"Having the first-fruits of the Spirit": cf. Ex.23.16-19, Lev.2.12-14, Num.28.26, Neh.10.35-37, Ezek.44.30, Rom.15.16, 16.5, 1 Cor.15.20, 23, 16.15, 2 Cor.1.22, 5.5, Gal.5.22f, Eph.1.13-14, Jas.1.18, Rev.14.4; 1QH 3.7-12; Odes Sol.11.1-3; Bik.3.1.

Man's redemption (glorification) and resurrection are a form of "new birth" (a new creation), since God's gift of His Spirit cleanses man from the "spirit of flesh" and makes him "inherit" eternal life (cf. verses 14f, Eph.1.13-14). Men themselves become "spiritual offerings"—"living sacrifices" who manifest the "fruit of the Spirit" (cf. Gal.5.22f) in their "voluntary conversion" and service of God according to the Spirit of holiness and truth.[56] The "first fruits" (בכורים; *bikkurim*) are the produce offered at *Shavuot* (Pentecost), the "Feast of the Harvest of the first fruits of your labor" (cf. Ex.23.16, 34.22, Lev.23.15f, Num.28.26f):

> How do they set apart the First-fruits? When a man goes down to his field and sees [for the first time] a ripe fig or a ripe cluster of grapes or a ripe pomegranate, he binds it round with reed-grass and says, 'Lo, these are First-fruits'. (Bik.3.1)

Paul describes the Spirit as the "first fruits" or the first signs of the "ripeness" or fullness (fulfillment) of glorification and resurrection; they represent the "pledge" or guarantee (cf. "hope") of eternal life.[57] Shavuot was also associated during the Second Temple period with the festival of the "giving of the Torah" (מתן תורה; *mattan Torah*; cf. Acts 2.1ff), and Paul's thought here reflects a midrashic tradition according to which the "tongues as of fire" which the author of Acts describes as falling on the heads of those gathered together in Jerusalem are interpreted from the flashes or torches of God's "voices" which the people "saw" at Sinai (Ex.20.18):

> The word that went out from the mouth of the Holy One, may His Name be blessed, was like shooting stars and lightnings and like flames and torches of fire. . . . (Targ.Pseudo-Jonathan on Ex.20.18)[58]

The division of "flames" into "tongues" is rooted in a further midrashic tradition which teaches that each of God's words at Sinai was divided into seventy "tongues," the languages of the nations of the world:

> The school of Rabbi Ishmael taught: [*Behold My word is like fire, declares the Lord,*] *And like a hammer that breaks the rock in pieces* (Jer.23.29): just as a hammer is divided into many sparks, so every single word that went forth from the Holy One, blessed be He, split up into seventy languages. (Shab.88b)[59]

Shavuot or "the day of Pentecost" (Acts 2) thus becomes the writing of God's law on people's hearts, according to Jeremiah 31.31 and Joel 2.28, through the "outpouring" of the Holy Spirit on "all flesh," both Jews and Gentiles. A passage in the Odes of Solomon further describes God's "circumcision of the hearts" of the people in relation to the "planting" of God's "trees of righteousness" (cf. Isa.61.3):

> My heart was pruned and its flower appeared, then grace sprang up in it, and it produced fruits for the Lord. For the Most High circumcised me by his Holy Spirit, then he uncovered my inward being toward him, and filled me with his love. . . . And the Lord renewed me with his garment, and possessed me by his light. And from far above he gave me immortal rest; and I became like the land which blossoms and rejoices in its fruits. . . . Then I adored the Lord because of his magnificence. And I said, blessed, O Lord, are they who are planted in your land, and who have a place in your Paradise; and who grow in the growth of your trees, and have passed from darkness into light. Behold, all your laborers are fair, they who work good works, and turn from wickedness to your kindness. For they turned away from themselves the bitterness of the trees, when they were planted in your land. And everyone was like your remnant.

> (Blessed are the workers of your water), and the eternal memorial of your faithful servants. Indeed, there is much room in your Paradise. And there is nothing in it which is barren, but everything is filled with fruit. (Odes Sol.11.1-3, 11-12, 17-23)[60]

Verses 24-25:

"For in hope have we been saved": cf. 4.17f, 5.1-5, 8.20, 1 Cor.13.12-13, 2 Cor.4.18, 5.7, Gal.5.5, Heb.3.6, 11.1, 7, 13; Test.Jud.24.1-6, Ps.Sol.17.34.

Those who have "died to sin" and become "sons" and "fellow-heirs" of God through Yeshua have been "called into being" (cf. 4.17f) and resurrected.[61] They have been "shut up" and "sealed" for the "world to come." Paul uses the metaphor of planting which was common in Second Temple Jewish literature, based on various biblical texts:

> [Thou hast plant]ed unto Thy glory a planting of cypress and elm mixed with box. Trees of life are hidden among all the trees by the waters in a mysterious realm, and they shall send out a Shoot for the everlasting planting. . . . And he who causes the Shoot of ho[li]ness to grow into the planting of truth has remained hidden with none to consider him, and his Mystery has been sealed with none to know it. And Tho[u, O G]od, has shut up his fruit in the mystery of the strong Valiant Ones and of the Spirit of holiness and of the Flame of whirling fire. . . . And Thou, O my God, hast put in my mouth as it were an autumn rain for all [the sons of men] and a spring of living waters which shall not run dry. . . . They that were hidden in secret shall suddenly gush forth [and shall flow like rivers of ever-run]ning [waters] . . . the fruitful planting [shall prosper], [and it shall become an] everlasting [fount]ain for the glorious Eden and shall bear fr[uit for ever]. (1QH 8.5-20)[62]

Verse 26:

"In the same way . . . words": cf. Gen.20.7, Num.21.7, 1 Sam.2.25, 7.5, 1 Kings 8.22-53, Job 5.1, 33.23, 42.8-10, Ps.106.30, Isa.53.12, Jer.7.16, 11.14, 37.3, Dan.10.13, 21, 12.1, Rom.6.19, 8.16, 34, (11.2), 1 Tim.2.1, Tit.2.5, Heb.7.25, 9.8-15, 24, 12.22-24, Rev.12.7; Tob.12.12, 15, 1 En.40.6, Test.Mos.10.2, Test.Levi 5.6, Test.Dan 6.2; PA 4.11, Lev.R.6.1.

Paul elaborates on man's "groaning" (verse 23), and identifies it with a form of praying.[63] In verse 23, the "groan[ing] within ourselves" appears to correspond to the "groaning of creation," and suggests a mute, inchoate expression. Here, however, Paul ascribes it to the Spirit, the result of man's inability ("weakness") to "pray as we ought" ("according to [the will of] God"—verse 27). This weakness is an outcome of the mastery of the evil inclination over the members of a person's body (cf. 6.19), which is overcome by "dying to sin" and obeying God through the Spirit of holiness and truth.[64] The Spirit of truth "intercedes" for men by giving them utterance to praise God according to Knowledge:

> From His wondrous Mysteries is the light in my heart, in the everlasting Being has my eye beheld Wisdom . . . The fountain of righteousness, the reservoir of power, and the dwelling-place of glory are denied to the assembly of flesh; but God has given them as an everlasting possession to those whom He has chosen. He has granted them a share in the lot of the Saints . . . And I, [I know] because of the ho[ly] Spirit [which Thou hast pu]t in m[e] that [. . .] and that m[an] cannot [. . .] . . . Because I know all these things [I] will utter a reply of the tongue [מענה לשון], praying and [entreating] [and turning back from al]l my sins, and searching [Thy] Spirit [לבקש רוח] [of Knowledge] and clinging fast to [Thy] ho[ly] Spirit, and adhering to the truth of Thy Covenant and serving Thee in truth and with a perfect heart, and loving [Thy truth]. . . . Who among all Thy creatures can recount [the multitude] of Thy [wonders]? By the mouth of them all may Thy name be praised for everlasting ages! May they bless Thee by the mouth of the humbl[e of spirit] [and may the Sons of Heave]n utter also a voice of rejoicing and let there be no more sorrow nor groaning nor perversity [. . .] And may Thy truth shine out unto everlasting glory and happiness without end! (1QS 11.5-8, 1QH 16.1-7, 11.24-27)[65]

Verse 27:
"He who searches . . . God": cf. 1 Sam.16.7, Ps.7.9, 139.1, Prov.20.27, Jer.11.20, 17.10, 20.12, Mt.11.27, Lk.2.35, Rom.2.16, 8.6-7, 16, 1 Cor.2.10-11, 4.5, Heb.4.12, Rev.2.23; 1QH 7.13-19, 9.12-18, 12.27-35; 4 Ez.16.54-67; 1 Clem.21.1-2, 9.

The expression "He who searches the hearts" is frequently found in the Tanakh, and normally describes God's sovereign power to judge man because He knows his innermost thoughts and attitudes. Here, however, Paul appears to be following a tradition based on Proverbs 20.27, in which God's Spirit is the one who divines man's intentions.[66] This tradition is reflected in a passage from Clement of Alexandria's First Letter to the Corinthians, in which he interprets the original text of Proverbs 20.27 ("The spirit of man is the lamp of the Lord, searching all the innermost parts of his body") as though the "lamp of the Lord" is the "Spirit of the Lord" rather than the "spirit of man." This transposition is easily made, since it is through God's light that man's spirit is disclosed:

> Take heed, beloved, lest his [the Messiah's] many good works become towards us a judgment [κριμα] on us, if we do not good and virtuous deeds before him in concord, and be citizens worthy of him. For he says in one place:—"The Spirit of the Lord is a lamp searching the inward parts." . . . For he is a searcher of thoughts and desires; his breath is in us, and when he will he shall take it away. (1 Clem.21.1-2, 9)[67]

Flusser suggests that this tradition based on Proverbs 20.27 also lies behind the words in Luke 2.35, which speak of the "sword" (Yeshua) which will "pierce Israel's soul" so that the "thoughts of many hearts may be revealed," as well as in Hebrews 4.12, where as the "word of God" it "pierces as far as the division of soul and spirit, of both joints and marrow, and [is] able to judge [κριτικος; *kritikos*] the thoughts and intentions of the heart."[68] The interpretation of Proverbs 20.27 reflected in 1 Clement understands man's "thoughts and intentions" as pertaining to his "soul," "spirit," and "flesh" (cf. "bones and marrow").[69] In the preceding verse, Paul says that "he who searches the hearts" knows the "mind of the spirit."[70] The "Spirit of the Lord," as both the "candle" and the "sword," searches men's thoughts and intentions. The Spirit of God thus "searches" and "knows" man's thoughts, according to Paul, because (ὅτι; *hoti*) he intercedes on their behalf, cleansing them from their evil inclination and enlightening their eyes with "knowledge" "according to God's will":

> For Thou has established my spirit and knowest my meditation. And Thou has comforted me in my confusion and in pardon I delight; and I was comforted for the original sin. And I knew there was hope in Thy [fav]ours and expectation in the greatness of Thy might. For no man is just in Thy ju[dg]ment nor [innocent in] Thy trial. Can human born of human be righteous, and can man born of man have understanding? And can flesh born of the gui[lty] inclination be glorious, and can spirit born of spirit be mighty? . . . And I was silent; what could I say? It is according to Knowledge that I speak: the creature of clay is without righteousness. What can I say unless Thou open my mouth, and how can I understand unless Thou give

> understanding to me? And what thou[ght] can I have unless Thou uncover my heart, and how can I make my way straight unless [Thou es]tablish it? . . . And I know that none is righteous beside Thee; and I have appeased Thy face because of the Spirit which Thou hast put [in me] to accomplish Thy [fav]ours towards [Thy] servant for [ever] by cleansing me by Thy holy Spirit and by causing me to go forward in Thy will according to the greatness of Thy favours. (1QH 9.12-16, 12.32-34, 16.11-12)[71]

Verse 28:

"And we know . . . purpose": cf. Isa.40.9, 52.6-10, 61.1-2, Jer.24.6-7, 29.10-11, Rom.9.23, Eph.1.9; 1QM 3.2, 1QH 15.14-17, 18.14-15; Ps.Sol.4.25; PA 3.14, Ber.60b, Men.53b.

Paul elaborates the theme of "intercession" from verse 27, and associates it with the "working together" of everything "for good." Here he develops the theme of redemption and God's grace also found in Luke 2.34-35, which reflects the tradition of the Qumran thanksgiving hymns of victory.[72] The "saints," who are frequently identified as those who "love God" (cf. 1 Cor.2.9, 8.3, Ps.Sol.6.6, 10.3, 14.1) and are "called" by Him (cf. 1.1, 6 and 7), are also designated in Qumran as the "paupers of Your redemption" (1QM 11.9), "the people of His redemption" (1QM 1.12), and "the lot whom He has [re]deemed" (1QM 17.6):

> [O God of] our [fath]ers, the eternal people is Thine, and Thou hast caused us to fall in the lot of light unto Thy truth. And Thou didst appoint the Prince of Light in former times to bring us help, and [all the angels of justi]ce [are] in [his lot] and all the spirits of truth are in his empire. . . . And we in the lot of Thy truth shall rejoice because of Thy mighty Hand, and we shall be glad because of Thy salvation. And we shall rejoice with joy because of [Thy] succou[r and because of] Thy [p]eace! O God of Israel, who is strong like Thee? Truly, Thy mighty Hand is with the Poor! . . . From former times Thou didst appoint unto Thyself the Day of grea[t] battle [against dark]ness, [to save the li]ght in truth and to destroy among the guilty, to strike down darkness and to raise up light [. . .] to wipe out all the sons of darkness; whereas joy (shall be) the [lo]t of the [sons of light . . .]. (1QM 13.9-16)[73]

The phrase "for good" reflects God's purpose to "favor" Israel and to fulfil His "good word" to them to return them to the Land (cf. Jer.29.10-11). He anoints His Messiah "to bring good news to the afflicted . . . to bind up the brokenhearted, to proclaim liberty to captives, and freedom to prisoners; to proclaim the favorable year of the Lord" (Isa.61.2)—the "year of His goodwill." Paul thus directly associates "intercession" with God's election and redemption of Israel:

> Withdraw not Thy [great] hand [from Thy people] that it may have one that clings firm to Thy Covenant and stands before Thee i[n perfection]. [For] Thou hast opened a [fount]ain in the mouth of Thy servant and upon his tongue Thou hast graven [Thy precepts] on a measuring-cord, [that he] may proclaim them unto creatures because of his understanding and be an interpreter of these things unto that which is dust like myself . . . and to open Thy l[aws] of truth to the creature whom Thou hast upheld by Thy might, that according to Thy truth [he may be] the one who announces good tidings [in the ti]me of Thy goodness, preaching the gospel to the humble according to the abundance of Thy mercy, [giving them to drink] from the fountain of h[oliness] [and consoling the co]ntrite of spirit and the afflicted to (bring them) everlasting joy . . . they that ho[pe] in Thy laws [Thou wilt deliver], [and bring aid] to them that serve Thee with faith [that] their seed [may] be before Thee for ever. And [Thou] wilt forg[ive them and] raise up [a Saviour (?)] [to redeem them from s]in and to cast away all their in[iquities] and to give them a share in the glory of man [and] abundance of days. (1QH 18.9-15, 17.13-15)

In verses 28-30, Paul returns to his original discussion of Israel's unconditional election (cf. 3.1f). His starting point in 1.16-17 is that God has proclaimed His "good news" of salvation not only to Israel but to the Gentile nations as well. He proceeds to illustrate how the pagan nations are immersed in idolatry (1.18-32), and then to charge Israel with similar practices (2.1ff). He thus establishes that God's election is based on His rendering to each man according to his deeds (2.12-16, 25-29). This raises possible doubts that God's covenant with Israel is unconditional and unbreakable (3.1f). Paul begins to answer these objections, demonstrating first of all that all men are equal before God since they all sin (3.9f). This equality also forms the ground, secondly, for the equality of both Jews and Gentiles in faithfulness to Yeshua's righteousness (3.21-5.21). In the course of this argument Paul engages in a series of refutations against various forms of "libertinism" (cf. 3.8, 6.1ff, 7.7f), in which he also lays out the doctrine of the Two Ways or Spirits (masters) upon which chapters 6-8 are based. Now, his thought returns to the discussion of the "advantages" and unconditionality of Israel's election which he left uncompleted in 3.1-3. The "good" towards which "all things work" is first of all God's "good will" in His promises to Israel:

> Let the good come and receive the good from the Good for the good. 'Let the good come' -that is, Moses, as it is written, *And she saw that he was good* (Ex.2.2). 'And receive the good'—that is, the Torah, as it is written, *For I give you good doctrine* (Prov.4.2). 'From the Good'—that is, the Holy One, blessed be He, as it is written, *The Lord is good to all* (Ps.145.9). 'For the good'—that is, Israel, as it is written, *Do good, O Lord, unto the good* (Ps.125.4). (Men.53b)[74]

God has called His people by his name, and established His covenant with them and has not rejected them. Contrary to forsaking Israel, He has assured them of the "year of His good will" when He will cleanse them and circumcise their hearts through His Spirit.[75]

Verses 29-30:
"For . . . ": cf. Isa.43.1, 7, 44.1-5, 24, 45.3-4, Rom.4.25, 5.1-2, 11.2, 1 Cor.2.7, 15.42-52, 2 Cor.3.18, 4.7-12, Eph.1.5, 11, 1 Thess.2.12, 1 Pet.1.2; 1QS 3.18-4.26, 11.13-20, 1QH 7.24, 9.16, 26, 10.27-29, 15.14-16; 1 En.108.11-13, 2 En.23.5, 49.3, Odes Sol.8.12-19.

Paul sums up all the elements of his thought from the previous verses. The plethora of verbs ("foreknew," "predestined," "called," "justified" and "glorified") are all directly associated with the concept of election, and therefore with Israel.[76] Paul describes the various elements of election in ascending order, as it were, using compound verbs whose prefix ("pro-") suggests a succession of acts: first knowledge, then designation, then calling, followed by justification. Finally, God glorifies His people in the Glory of Yeshua, who gives God's gift of righteousness to all those, Jew and Gentile, who are faithful to God in him:

> Thou alone hast [created] the just and established him from his mother's womb unto the time of good-will that he may be preserved in Thy Covenant and walk in all < Thy way >, and that he [may go forward] upon it because of the immensity of Thy mercy, and that he may unloose all the distress of his soul to (possess) eternal salvation and perpetual unfailing peace. (1QH 15.14-16)

Verse 31:

"What then shall we say . . . ": Paul indicates that he is picking up an earlier theme by returning to the technical formula ("what then shall we say . . . " [cf. 3.3]).[77] The answer, "If God (is) for us, who (is) against us?" suggests that the rather vague phrase "these things" refers to objections which people are leveling against Israel's election; the formula then becomes a response: "what shall we answer to these objections?"[78] Paul firmly counters that Israel's election is assured because God is "for" them—that He has foreknown, predestined, called, justified and glorified them. Although people may therefore say what they like, God is both more powerful and has undisputedly demonstrated His choice of His people and His love for them.[79]

"If God (is) for us . . . ": cf. Ex.6.7, 29.13, Ps.41.11, 56.9, 118.6, Mt.1.23, Heb.13.6, 1 Pet.3.13; Jub.15.31-32; Mid.Ps.118.10, TBE p.31, p.127, Tanh.Toledot 8, Sifre Num.Behe'al.84, Mekh.Beshall.4, Ex.R.15.29, 33.2, 49.1.

The objection of "these things" (verse 31) resembles the claims and arguments against God's love for His people: "Why should the Egyptians speak saying, 'With evil (intent) He brought them out to kill them in the mountains and to destroy them from the face of the earth" (Ex.32.12; cf. Num.14.15-16, Dt.9.28). Paul directly counters such claims: since God is "for us" He obviously has not and will not reject His people. He then develops this theme in the following verses, in which he introduces the legal metaphor, and demonstrates in the subsequent chapters (9-11) that even the most telling objection possible—that God has rejected His people because Israel have rejected His Messiah (Yeshua)—carries no force, because Israel's election is irrevocable:

> . . . the Holy One went on to swear to His people that He would never exchange them for another nation, never give them up or substitute another people for them. And with regard to Israel alone, God asserted, *I will not execute the fierceness of Mine anger* (Hos.11.9). (TBE p.127; cf. p.191)

Verse 32:

"He who did not spare His own Son . . . ": cf. Gen.18.24, 22.16, Jn.3.16, Rom.4.25, 11.21, Heb.11.17, 2 Pet.2.4-5, 1 Jn.4.9.

The ultimate proof of God's unconditional love for Israel is the gift of His son, Yeshua. Just as Abraham was willing "not to spare" Isaac yet God "spared" him in order to fulfil His promise of a "seed" to Abraham (cf. 4.1ff, Gal.3.16f), so God has confirmed the election of Israel as His people by "not sparing" His only son (cf. 2 Cor.1.20). Paul returns to the "proofs" of Israel's election which he invokes in verses 28-30, by repeating that God will demonstrate His "good will" (cf. verse 28) by "freely giving us all things" (cf. 5.15-21, Eph.4.7-8) with Yeshua (cf. verse 17). Yeshua's suffering, in which Israel and the church share, is "crowned" with his glorification, in which Israel and the church also share. Israel's election, furthermore, guarantees the salvation of the whole world through God's gift of righteousness to "all those" who are faithful to Him in Yeshua. Paul develops this argument in chapters 9-11.

Verse 33:
"Who will bring a charge . . . justifies": cf. Job 10.2, 33.13, 34.29, 40.1-5, Isa.50.8; 1QS 10.26-11.9, 1QH 9.17-26, 15.12-25; Test.Zev.9.7-9.

Paul uses the "forensic" language (cf. 3.8) of the law court to formalize his "defense" of God's election of Israel.[80] No one can "bring charges" against the people of Israel because the "Judge of all flesh" is their Father. God's "free gifts" demonstrate His grace and favor in bestowing Yeshua's righteousness on man so that he can walk according to the Spirit of holiness. Paul thus speaks of "intercession" in the forensic or legal sense of "justification." God will be proved just (cf. 3.4-5) by those who walk justly before Him; and they will be proved just by their election by God:

> Therefore when you turn back to the Lord, you will receive mercy, and he will lead you into his holy place, proclaiming peace to you. And there shall arise for you from the tribe of Judah and (the tribe of) Levi the Lord's salvation. He will make war against Beliar; he will grant the vengeance of victory as our goal. And he shall take from Beliar the captives, the souls of the saints; and he shall turn the hearts of the disobedient ones to the Lord, and grant eternal peace to those who call upon him. And the saints shall refresh themselves in Eden; and the righteous shall rejoice in the New Jerusalem, which shall be eternally for the glorification of God. And Jerusalem shall no longer undergo desolation, nor shall Israel be led into captivity, because the Lord will be in her midst [living among human beings]. The Holy One of Israel will rule over them in humility and poverty, and he who trusts in him shall reign in truth in the heavens. And now fear the Lord, my children, be on guard against Satan and his spirits. Draw near to God and to the angel who intercedes for you, because he is the mediator between God and men for the peace of Israel. He shall stand in opposition to the kingdom of the enemy. Therefore the enemy is eager to trip up all who call on the Lord,

> because he knows that on the day in which Israel trusts, the enemy's kingdom will be brought to an end. This angel of peace will strengthen Israel so that it will not succumb to an evil destiny. But in Israel's period of lawlessness it will be the Lord who will not depart from her and therefore she will seek to do his will, for none of the angels is like him. His name shall be everywhere throughout Israel; [and the Savior will be known among the nations]. (Test.Dan 5.9-6.7)[81]

Verse 34:

"Who is the one who condemns?": cf. 5.16, 8.1.

Paul reiterates the more than rhetorical question, "who will bring a charge?" (verse 33), and thus links the end of the chapter to its beginning ("there is therefore no condemnation . . . "). Here he asserts that Yeshua's justification of those who are faithful to God in him not merely "makes peace" between them and God, but that this reconciliation is based upon Israel's election, using a sophisticated form of paradox to counter the claim that God has rejected Israel because they have rejected His Messiah. He appeals to the source of the objection itself, the sending of the Messiah, to prove God's love for His people instead of His abandonment of them. Yeshua is the person whose death and resurrection bring life to Israel—not rejection. There is "*no* condemnation" for those who are in Yeshua; on the contrary, the gift of his righteousness brings newness of eternal life. Yeshua does not "condemn" but "intercedes" on behalf of God's people (cf. Jn.3.16-18). God has not rejected His people because they have rejected His Messiah, nor can Yeshua's crucifixion, which has in fact proved to be a stumbling block to many of his own people, be seen as proof of God's rejection and condemnation of Israel as a whole.[82]

"At the right hand of God . . . ": cf. Ps.80.17, 110.1, Isa.9.6, Dan.7.13-14, Mt.19.28, 25.31, 26.64, Mk.14.62, 16.19, Lk.12.8, 22.69, Acts 7.55f, Rom.2.16, Eph.1.20, Col.3.1, Heb.1.3, 7.25, 8.1, 10.12, 12.2; 1QH 3.10; 1 En.49.1-4, 61.8-9, 69.29, Test.Job 33.3, Odes Sol.7.6, 25.2.

Paul follows a midrashic tradition based on a complex of messianic texts (cf. Ps.80.18, 110.1, Isa.9.6) which speak of the Messiah as God's "counselor." The original text in Isaiah 9.6 speaks of the messianic figure as "Wonderful Counselor, Mighty God." Later Jewish thought found difficulty in attributing God's own name to a human being, and found a textual resolution to the problem. A description of the Messiah in 1QH 3.10 reads the text in Isaiah 9.6 as "Wonderful Counselor with his Might." This text implies that the Messiah is (or shall be) God's "counselor," or that his task as a counselor will be together with God's Might. The author possibly understood the words "with God's might" in the light of Psalm 110.1, and believed that the Messiah's place as God's Counselor would be "at the right hand of the Power."[83] Paul is apparently cognizant of this tradition, and directly associates it with Yeshua's intercession (cf. "Counselor"), further reflecting the link made between the Son of man in Daniel 7.13-14 and the high-priestly and royal figure of Melchizedek.[84] He then builds on this complex tradition which conceives of the Messiah as judging and interceding before God at the End of Days on behalf of Israel. Since Yeshua is the very person who intercedes for Israel's continued existence, he cannot condemn Israel for their rejection of him when he has ascended to sit at God's right hand to intercede on their behalf.

Verse 35:
"Who shall separate us from the love of the Messiah?": cf. Mt.5.11, Mk.13.8-9, Rom.2.9, 5.5-8, 1 Cor.4.11-13, 12.10.

Paul speaks of Yeshua as the intercessor in verse 34, and as the "stumbling block" over which Israel, temporarily, falls and are then restored, bringing life and resurrection to the whole world.[85] Nothing, either on earth or in heaven, can break God's covenant with His people. God expresses His love for His people in Yeshua, and even their temporary rejection of him breaks neither His covenant nor His promises. Israel's tribulation and distress therefore cannot be described as a sign of His rejection, although they may signify His הסתר פנים (*hester panim*), the "hiding of His face" from them; persecution is not a sign of His abandonment; famine is not a sign of His withdrawal ("separation"); nakedness is not a sign of shame; peril is not a sign of His unconcern; nor is the sword a sign of God's destruction of His people.

Verse 36:
"Just as it is written . . . ": cf. Ps.44.22; Sifre Dt.Va'etchanan 32, Berekah 343, Mekh.Shirata 3, Cant.R.1.15.2, Lam.R.1.16.45.

Paul appeals to Psalm 44.22 to describe the principle of קידוש ה' (*kiddush ha-Shem*), the "sanctification of God's name." Although the biblical verse depicts Israel's martyrdom, when the people have been faithful and yet are killed for His sake, Paul's use of it clearly expresses the midrashic interpretation of the biblical text. In arguing that nothing can separate the people of Israel from God's love in Yeshua, he appeals to a verse which speaks of Israel as "sheep to be slaughtered," raising the question directed at God in other texts as well: if You love us so much, how come You kill us? Paul understands this text in similar fashion to that of R. Akiba, whose own martyrdom was a reflection of the way in which he interpreted the biblical text. Both Paul and R. Akiba stress the fact that the only way to truly live is to die in fulfillment of the commandment to "love the Lord with all your soul":

> *This is My God and I Will Glorify Him* (Ex.15.2). R. Akiba says: I shall speak of the prophecies and praises of Him by whose word the world came into being, before all the nations of the world. For all the nations of the world ask Israel, saying: "What is thy beloved more than another beloved, that thou dost so adjure us" (Cant.5.9), that you are so ready to die for Him, and so ready to let yourselves be killed for Him?—For it is said: "Therefore do the maidens [עלמות] love Thee" (ibid. 1.3), meaning, they love thee unto death [עד מות]. And it is also written: "Nay but for Thy sake are we killed all the day" (Ps.44.22).—"You are handsome, you are mighty, come and intermingle with us." But the Israelites say to the nations of the world: "Do you know Him? Let us but tell you some of His praise: 'My beloved is white and ruddy,'" etc. (Cant.5.10). As soon as the nations of the world hear some of his praise, they say to the Israelites, "We will join you," as it is said: "Whither is thy beloved gone, O thou fairest among women? Whither hath thy beloved turned him, that we might seek him with Thee" (ibid. 6.1). The Israelites, however, say to the nations of the world: "You can have no share in Him, but 'My beloved is mine and I am his' (Cant.2.16), 'I am my beloved's and my beloved is mine,' etc. (ibid. 6.3)." (Mekh.Shirata 3)[86]

Paul appeals to the same prooftext in Psalm 44.23, in the face of a similar challenge by the nations to Israel's election. Like R. Akiba, he too insists that Israel are God's chosen people and that nothing can separate them from God's love, especially when the people themselves are willing to fulfil God's commandment in return, by loving Him with all their soul—unto death. Instead of being rejected by God, Israel (as the "church" will also be) is persecuted for bearing God's name and observing His covenant:

> Another interpretation of IT IS BECAUSE OF THE SONS OF MEN (Eccl.3.18): because of the manner in which the righteous conduct themselves in this world, with privation, fastings, and sufferings. For what purpose? THAT GOD MAY SIFT THEM (ibid.): to make manifest to them the quality of their righteousness. AND THAT THEY MAY SEE THAT THEY THEMSELVES ARE BUT AS BEASTS (ibid.): that they should recognise and demonstrate to the peoples of the world how Israel is drawn after Him like a beast [which follows its owner], as it is said, *And ye My sheep, the sheep of My pasture, are men, and I am your God* (Ezek.34.31).

> Furthermore, just as a beast stretches forth its neck for slaughter, so it is with the righteous, as it is said, *Nay, but for Thy sake are we killed all the day, we are accounted as sheep for the slaughter* (Ps.44.22). (Eccl.R.3.18.1)

Verse 37:
"Conquer": cf. Lk.10.19, Jn.16.33, Rom.12.21, 1 Jn.2.13, 4.4, 5.4, Rev.12.11, 15.2, 17.14; PA 4.1.

The phrase "all these things" refers to the list of tribulations and persecutions in verse 35, which Paul repeats in verses 38-39. It also recalls the "these things" in verse 31, which are possible objections to Israel's election. The link with the theme of 3.1f, where Paul begins to discuss the purpose of Israel's election, may be reinforced through his choice of verbs in this verse.[87] The Greek verb ὑπερνικαω (*hupernikao*), "to conquer," is a rarely used and strengthened (compound) form of the verb νικαω (*nikao*), "to be victorious." The LXX uses this verb to translate the phrase תזכה בשפטך (*tizkeh beshoftekha*) in Psalm 51.6, which Paul uses as a prooftext in 3.4ff. The Hebrew text, "You shall be made blameless (be justified) in your judgments" is then rendered by the Greek, "You shall be victorious in Your judgments," a theme to which the Psalms of Solomon repeatedly appeals:

> The righteous remember the Lord all the time, by acknowledging and proving the Lord's judgments right. . . . The righteous stumbles and proves the Lord right; he falls and watches for what God will do about him; he looks to where his salvation comes from. The confidence of the righteous (comes) from God their savior; sin after sin does not visit the house of the righteous. The righteous constantly searches his house, to remove his unintentional sins. He atones for (sins of) ignorance by fasting and humbling his soul, and the Lord will cleanse every devout person and his house. . . . [T]hose that fear the Lord shall rise up to eternal life, and their life shall be in the Lord's light, and it shall never end. (Ps.Sol.3.3, 5-12)

"Conquering" in this context means "to be proved right," or to be "justified" by God (cf. "through him who loved us"), so that there is indeed "no condemnation" in Yeshua the Messiah. Yeshua intercedes on Israel's behalf, and for all those who are faithful to God in him, so that they are made righteous in dying to sin and in proving God righteous by obeying Him. The "sons of God" conquer their own evil inclination as they also overcome those who rebel against God and those who claim that God has rejected His people.

Verses 38-39:

"For I am convinced . . . in the Messiah, Yeshua our Lord": cf. 8.35, 14.14, 15.14, 1 Cor.3.22, 15.24-26, Eph.1.21.

Paul reiterates his conviction that God has not rejected His people but has chosen them eternally through His Messiah, Yeshua, through whom the whole world is also "called (into being)" by God (cf. 4.17). "Separation" is a rabbinic synonym for election and holiness: God chose Israel to be "set apart" as His holy people.[88] The "love of God," from which nothing can separate Israel, is "unseverable" because it constitutes Israel's very election. Paul sets down a further list of examples of those things which might—but cannot in fact—cut Israel, and the "church," off from God's love, based on Deuteronomy 30.11-4: "This commandment which I command you today is not too difficult for you, nor is it out of reach. . . . "[89] The "angels" resemble the evil angels of the nations, who are their "guardian spirits":

> And you command the sons of Israel and let them keep this sign of the covenant for their generations for an eternal ordinance. And they will not be uprooted from the land because the command was ordained for the covenant so that they might keep it forever for all the children of Israel. . . . For . . . [the Lord] chose Israel that they might be a people for himself. And he sanctified them and gathered them from all the sons of men because (there are) many nations and many peoples, and they all belong to him, but over all of them he caused spirits to rule so that they might lead them astray from following him. But over Israel he did not cause any angel or spirit to rule, because he alone is their ruler and he will protect them at the hand of his spirits and at the hand of all his authorities so that he might guard them and bless them and they might be his and he might be theirs henceforth and forever. (Jub.15.31-32; cf. Sir.17.17-21)

Paul similarly speaks of the "principalities" (ἀρχαι; *archai*) and "powers" (δυναμεις; *dunameis*), those forces of evil which in dualist thought such as in Qumran are personified and hypostasized (cf. CDC 16.4-6). The Gentile nations are each assigned their own "Prince" (שר; *sar*); in other texts, the people of Israel are said to have twelve "princes," one for each of the tribes, but are also said to have been given a Guardian Angel after Moses' death.[90] The doctrine of the "Two Powers" which is associated in rabbinic literature with מנות (*minut*) or "heresy," reflects gnostic elements of the Demiurge, as well as a possible reference to embryonic trinitarian formulations.[91] Paul concludes and sums up the list of possible but powerless hindrances to God's love for Israel with the comprehensive phrase, οὔτε τις κτισις ἑτερα (*oute tis ktisis hetera*), "or in any other created thing," which covers any potential power other than God. "Things present or things to come" represent here the history of God's dealings with Israel, both their faithfulness and their rebellion and punishment: history cannot be called upon to prove God's rejection of His people whenever He has punished them, nor can it be appealed to as God's postponement of their rejection. "Height nor depth" reflect the power of the stars and probably refer to astrological terms denoting a star's greatest proximity to, or distance from, its zenith; Paul is possibly referring to personified sidereal powers.[92] In all "these things," it is impossible to claim that Israel have been rejected by God because they have rejected His Messiah. Yeshua embodies God's love for His people, a love which is, as are His gifts and calling, irrevocable (cf. 11.29), and which includes not only Israel but the whole world as well.

Endnotes on Chapter 8.

1 For the motif of the "two masters," see the comments on 6.2ff.

2 For the idea of being "in Yeshua," see the comments on 6.2ff, where Paul describes how baptism unites the believer with Yeshua's resurrection in his baptism into Yeshua's death.

3 Paul speaks of the same idea in terms of "reconciliation" in Rom.5.10-11, as well as in 2 Corinthians 3, where he contrasts the "ministry of condemnation" with the "ministry of righteousness." (There, he also deals with the theme of righteousness as "glory" [cf. Rom.3.23], and describes the role of the Torah in justifying man [cf. Rom.7.1ff]). He further picks up the themes of "no condemnation" and "peace" in chapter 14, in regard to loving one's neighbor as a way of being approved by God.

4 See the comments on 6.2ff.

5 Cf. Yalkut 934, Yoma 72b, Shab.88b, Ta'anit 7a.

6 The Odes of Solomon are an apocryphal collection of very early hymns whose Jewish expression conveys the author's thanksgiving for the advent of the Messiah, Yeshua. Although the author does not quote either from the Tanakh or the New Testament, the odes reflect many of Paul's themes in Romans, especially the ideas of baptism as both the putting on of Yeshua (cf. Rom.13.14) and as circumcision by the Holy Spirit (cf. Romans 6); of being united with the Messiah (cf. Rom.6.5); and of sonship (cf. Romans 8).

7 See the comments on 3.19-20.

8 Although Maimonides' formulation is much later (c. 1190 C.E.) than the New Testament texts, and therefore cannot be invoked as a contemporary influence on Paul's thought, several of his ideas are derived from rabbinic concepts already present in Second Temple Judaism; see F. Dreyfus, *Divine*.

9 The Greek phrase περι ἁμαρτιας (*peri hamartias*), "as (an offering) for sin," regularly translates the Hebrew term חטאת (*chata't*) or "sin offering;" cf. Lev.4.1f, 6.25f. The guilt offering (אשם; *'asham*; cf. Lev.5.1ff, 7.1f) is distinguished from the sin offering in name, but the "law" (תורה; *torah*) or regulations are the same for both offerings, and they were frequently offered together. See R. de Vaux, *Ancient Israel: Religious Institutions* (NY: McGraw-Hill, 1965), 418-21.

10 This corresponds to Paul's description of Yeshua as the כפרת (*kaporet*) or "mercy seat" in 3.25. It is possible that the και (*kai*), "and" (" . . . sending His son in the likeness of sinful flesh *and* [as an offering] for sin") intensifies the first clause. It can then mean "namely": Yeshua came "in the likeness of sinful flesh"—namely, as a sin offering (both the victim offered and the means of atonement).

11 Paul's perception of the Torah's function here again corresponds to the rabbinic principle of לפנים משורת הדין (*lifnim mi-shurat ha-din*), or "within the strict line of justice." The Torah is both שורת הדין (*shurat ha-din*), the repository of ethical laws and principles, and לפנים משורת הדין (*lifnim mi-shurat ha-din*), a body of laws which points to a "higher" moral law ("and you shall do what is right and good in the sight of the Lord" [Dt.6.18]); see the comments on 2.29 and 7.10ff.

12 Although this passage does not directly speak of reconciliation, which is one of the basic meanings of "peace" (see the comments on 5.1), the idea that the community brings atonement for the world is clearly stated in 1QS 5.6, 8.5-10, 9.3-5; (cf. also Rom.11.12-15).

13 See the comments on 5.6-10 and 7.14-25.

14 Paul speaks of Israel's possession of the Torah as a source of the hostility between Jews and Gentiles in Ephesians 2, since it is a sign of God's covenant with His people.

15 Paul alludes to the overcoming of the hostility between Jews and Gentiles in the following verses, where he describes the final redemption of the whole creation (verses 18-25), but he only really fully develops the theme in chapters 9-11. There he explains how Israel's temporary rejection of Yeshua opens God's kingdom to the Gentiles, as part of God's prophetic promises, and how those Gentiles who believe then turn Israel back to their own God through jealousy that He is being worshipped by a foreign people.

16 Cf. Gen.5.22, 24, 6.9, 17.1, Ps.26.3, 56.13, Sir.44.16; see TDNT 1:455; see also the comments on 12.1 and 14.18, where Paul expresses different aspects of the same idea.

17 These passages from the Hymn Scroll and the Scroll of the Rule reflect the association between "walking" and "pleasing" God, as well as the connection between pleasing and reconciliation (cf. "agreeable expiation").

18 Cf. 1QS 3.1-12, 4.18-26, 1QH 11.10-14, 13.13, 17.25; see the comments on the midrash on Job 3.19 in chapter 6.

19 Cf. Pes.Rab.4.3, Lam.R.Proems 24.

20 In Gen.R.8.1, Simeon b. Lakish identifies Adam's spirit with that of the Messiah: "*And the spirit of God hovered* (Gen.1.2) refers to the soul of Adam, as you read, *And the spirit of the Lord shall rest upon him* (Isa.11.2)." This dictum is associated with the motif of the two Adams; (cf. verse 17).

21 See also the comments on verses 26ff.

22 Psalm 115.7 underlies Paul's thought in 7.1ff in a similar fashion to R. Johanan's midrash on Ps.115.7, which is directly linked to R. Simeon's midrash of the "two masters" on Job 3.19; see the comments on 6.2ff and 7.1f.

23 God's creation (resurrection) of man as His "sons" and the "brethren" of the "first-born" (Yeshua) is a form of מידה כנגד מידה (*middah ke-neged middah*), or "measure for measure": the Spirit gives life to the believer in the measure that God gave life to Yeshua in his resurrection; cf. Jn.14.19.

24 Paul returns to this theme (and the prooftexts from Hos.1.10 and 2.23) in 9.24ff, where he addresses the relationship between Israel and the Gentiles; cf. 1 Pet.2.9-10.

25 The Greek verb ὀφειλω (*opheilo*; "to owe") means either to owe a debt (of money) or to owe in the sense of "duty." It thus very closely corresponds to the Hebrew root חוב (*chuv*), which expresses both obligation and guilt. Both the Greek and Hebrew roots refer to "debt" in the sense of "sin": the "debtor" is a "sinner" (cf. Mt.6.12) and/or someone bound to a duty (cf. Gal.5.3); cf. a similar sense in PA 4.22. The English idiom, on the other hand, captures the double meaning of being "bound"—in the sense of being held captive and of being "obliged" to do something.

26 Paul picks up the idea of "obligation" in 13.7-8 (cf. 12.9f), where he says that the only "debt" men should owe is to "love one another." This is the כלל גדול בתורה (*kelal gadol be-Torah*), the "essential principle" or "greatest commandment" of the Torah, based on Lev.19.18; cf. Mt.7.12, 22.36-40, Jas.2.8, Test.Zev.8.3, Wis.Sol.6.18, ARN[a] 15.1, 16.4, ARN[b] 23, 26, 32, Sifra Ked.39b, Gen.R.24.7, Shab.31a. This "principle" underlies Paul's

statement in verse 4 and his discussion of physical and "spiritual" circumcision in 2.25f (cf. Gal.5.3).

27 Cf. Sifre Dt.96, Pes.Rab.27.3, Ex.R.24.1, 46.4, 5; a similar tradition is found in Gal.4.1ff and Heb.3.1ff (cf. 12.7-8 and Mk.12.1-12). A further link between the motifs of the two masters and the sons of Abraham is formally provided through the idea of "obligation" (verse 12). Lev.19.18 serves as the "greatest commandment of the Torah," and is frequently associated with the love of God (Dt.6.5) (cf. Mt.22.36-40, Jub.36.4ff), which is also the "essential principle" for serving God as "true" "sons of Abraham."

28 As Paul's argument in chapter 2 indicates, this was a common theme in Second Temple Jewish thought. Paul more fully explains the biblical, prophetic basis for the inclusion of the Gentiles in God's election in chapters 9-11.

29 Paul's statement on the "sons of God" gathers together most of the strands of his argument in Romans. He introduces the motif of the "sons of Abraham" in chapter 2, where he establishes that Israel's election must be accompanied by the "qualities" of Abraham. In chapter 4, he applies this motif to the "creation" of the Gentiles as part of God's people, which he grounds in chapters 6-7 on the theme of the two masters. Here he integrates the various elements which he has dealt with previously, all of which are interdependent: if Israel's election is ignored (or denied), God's Kingdom becomes meaningless (without a people to serve Him, God cannot reign as King); if the inclusion of the Gentiles is denied, God's power to raise from the dead is annulled; and if the Spirit does not make men "sons" when they die to sin, then neither Israel nor the Gentiles can please God.

30 The "spirit of slavery" was frequently attributed to the mentality of the "generation of the wilderness," who wanted to return to Egypt; cf. Ex.16.3, Num.14.2-3, 20.5, Sifre Dt.319.

31 This text is clearly influenced by Isa.49.14ff; cf. also Isa.54.4f.

32 Cf. Mal.3.16-18, Mt.25.14-27, Lk.19.12-26, PA 1.3, ARN[a] 37, TBE p.63, p.69, p.141, Sifre Dt.32, PBer.9.7, 14b, PSot.5.5, 20c. The parable describes those who stay within the "four cubits of *Halakhah*" (cf. Ber.8a) as those who fear God but do not seek Him out of love and who (in the continuation) may know God's words but are "imprisoned" as the blind and deaf (cf. Isa.42.7) in its "courtyard."

33 Among the seven types of Pharisees distinguished in the Talmud, for example, the two "positive" types, the Pharisee of awe and the Pharisee of love, were respectively modeled on Job and Abraham (cf. PBer.9.5, 14b).

34 See D. Flusser, *New*.

35 This interpretation also underlies the principle of judging one another, to which Paul appeals in 2.1f, leading on to the principle of לפנים משורת הדין (*lifnim mi-shurat ha-din*) in 2.25f, which he uses in order both to integrate the "spirit" (higher principles) of the Torah with its regular ordinances and to demonstrate that to love and respect one's brethren is to love God Himself; see the comments on 2.2-3 and 27-29.

36 Paul seems to speak interchangeably of Israel's election both as sons and as adoption (cf. 8.23, 9.4, Gal.4.5, Eph.1.5), possibly based on the play between "sons" and "servants" (cf. verse 14).

37 Paul here describes the theme of the two masters in familial terms. Abraham (man's earthly father) corresponds, as it were, to the mastery of the evil inclination; God as Father corresponds to His role as Creator. The gift of God's Holy Spirit enables man to acknowledge God as master instead of his own inclination; cf. 1 Cor.12.3, 1 Jn.4.2f. This is especially clear in Jn.8.38-42, where Yeshua's statement that "every one who commits sin is the slave of sin" leads to an exchange in which the "son" (Yeshua himself in this case), in contrast to those who are in slavery, sets man free. Yeshua accuses the people of Israel of being the children of their "father" (Satan), a claim which his audience rejects on the grounds that "we were not born of fornication; we have one Father, God (Himself)." He sets them "free," however, by releasing them from their "slavery" to the kingdom of darkness and the rule of Satan (cf. 7.1ff) and "adopting" them (both from their physical father, Abraham, and from their "spiritual" father, Belial); cf. Gal.3.23-4.11. "Abba" is the Aramaic word for "father," but was also frequently used in Hebrew to mean "my father" (cf. San.3.2, BB 9.3), as well as being a title given to scholars (cf. Abba Saul, Abba Yudan). It then sometimes became a name instead of a person's given name (cf. Abba bar Abbahu, father of Samuel; Abba Mari); cf. Ber.18b.

38 This verse anticipates verse 27, although in the latter verse Paul is already turning his argument back to pick up his interrupted thought from 3.1ff, so that in verse 27 he is specifically referring to Israel's election, whereas here he is addressing the universal sonship of all those who are faithful to God in Yeshua, both Jew and Gentile; see the comments on verses 26-28.

39 See the comments on 4.13f.

40 The intervening chapters (5-7) deal with the relationship between sin and death (chapter 5), which grounds the theme of the "two masters" upon which chapters 6, 7, and 8 are based. Chapter 8 thus integrates all three themes.

41 As the prooftext from Ps.55.24 indicates, the Sages equated the unrighteous within Israel in terms of the Gentile Balaam. The idea of being a "disciple" of Abraham thus clearly refers to walking in his ways. The Mishnah does not mean to say that such people are to be considered Gentiles but to point out that the inheritance of the ungodly is Sheol.

42 Abraham is also linked to the Messiah through the Melchizedek tradition; cf. Heb.6.13-7.28.

43 All of the terms and phrases Paul employs here are based on Israel's election. His use of the term "fellow-heirs" in Eph.3.6 clearly marks this, when he declares that the Gentiles have become "fellow-citizens" in the "commonwealth of Israel" (cf. Eph.2.12ff). This idea of inheritance as election underlies the idea of inheritance in the Messiah (as here), since nearly all of Paul's themes are originally biblical and Jewish concepts which contain God's plan of salvation for the whole "world."

44 See also the parallels. Yeshua's crucifixion and resurrection is frequently referred to as the "Passion" in Christian theology, from the Latin *passio*, and often held, through false etymology, to derive from the Greek πασχω (*pascho*), "to suffer;" the Greek noun πασχα (*pascha*) was also used by the New Testament writers to refer to the "Passover" so that Yeshua is also known as the "Paschal lamb" (cf. Jn.1.29, 1 Cor.5.7). The early tradition is based on Yeshua's own words, which derive from passages in "the Scriptures" (cf. Lk.24.44-45) such as Isaiah 53 and Zech.12.10 (cf. also Ps.34.19). Yeshua defines "the Scriptures" ("the Law of Moses and the Prophets and the Psalms") as containing "those things which are written about me," indicating that messianic passages are found in all three sections of the Tanakh (cf. Paul's similar statement in Acts 26.23).

45 For the suffering of creation as part of the "birthpangs of the Messiah," see verse 22; cf. also the comments on verse 19.

46 Cf. Mt.16.21, 27-28, 24.27-31, Mk.8.31, 13.26, Lk.9.22, 26, 21.27. Yeshua identifies the "Son of man" with the Messiah (cf. Mk.13.24ff, Lk.9.20f) according to midrashic tradition (cf. Mid.Ps.2.9, 72.5). Paul refers to the same tradition in 2.16, where he emphasizes the role of judgment. For the Messiah as God's "Glory," see the comments on 3.23.

47 This complex of passages is based on a series of biblical texts. The motif of the "house" refers to 1 Sam.2.35, which then recalls 2 Sam.7.11-14 (" . . . He shall build a house for My name, and I will establish the throne of his kingdom forever. I will be a father tc him and he will be a son to Me . . ."). This text alludes to Num.12.7, which is associated midrashically with Isa.52.13, according to which the Messiah "shall be exalted above Abraham, and lifted up above Moses . . . " (cf. Heb.1.2-3, 3.1f,

Tanh.Toledot 14, Yalkut 476). The passage from 4QpPs.37 is an interpretation of Ps.37.18 ("The Lord knows the days of the perfect; and their inheritance will be for ever"), which the Qumran community applied to the "House of Truth" whose members are "the perfect of way," but which is also one of Abraham's appellations (cf. Gen.17.1). For the whole discussion, see D. Flusser, "Messianology and Christology," in *Judaism*, 246-79.

48 D. Flusser, "Blessed are the Poor in Spirit," in *Judaism*, 102-14.

49 For the structure of the midrash, see the comments on 5.12.

50 See the comments on 2.16 for the (Enochic) association of the "Son of man" with the eschatological Day of Judgment, a theme which Paul develops in the subsequent verses of chapter 8. Paul describes the believers' "glorification" when they "put on" God's glory in Yeshua (cf. 3.23) in 13.14; see the comments there.

51 The Greek term ματαιοτης (*mataiotes*), "futility," translates the various Hebrew terms for "vanities" in the LXX, which are various forms of idols; cf. Dt.32.21, 1 Kings 16.13, 26, Ps.31.6, Jer.8.19, 14.22, 18.15, 25; cf. also the comments on 1.21.

52 For the idea of the "birthpangs of the Messiah," cf. Mk.13.8, 1QH 3.7-12, 4 Ez.4.52-5.13, 2 Bar.26.1-30.5, Apoc.Ab.30.1-32.8, PRE 30, DEZ 10.1, Ruth R.5.6, Sot.9.15, San.97a and following, Ket.111a. George Foot Moore claims, however, that the phrase חבלי המשיח (*chevlei ha-mashiach*), although frequently found "in modern Christian books," is fictitious, and should in fact read חבליה דמשיח (*chavlei de-Mashiach*), the "travail" or "sufferings" preceding the Messiah's coming; see G.F. Moore, *Judaism in the First Centuries of the Christian Era* (Cambridge: Harvard University Press, 1927), 2:361 n.2.

53 See the references and comments on verse 20.

54 See also the comments on verse 17, and on 12.2ff. The imagery of the "house" is directly linked to the "sure House in Israel" in CDC 3.19-20: those who cling to it are destined for "everlasting life and theirs shall be all the glory of the Man." For the use of the Qumran metaphor of the "house" as a "temple," see B. Gärtner, *The Temple of the Community in Qumran and the New Testament* (Cambridge: Cambridge University Press, 1965).

55 In this hymn, the Psalmist (the Teacher of Righteousness) combines verses from Jer.30.6, which speaks about the pains of childbirth, with references to the Messiah in Isa.9.5-6, in a passage which reflects traces of a myth concerning the "Mother of the Messiah" (cf. Isa.7.14, Mic.5.2, Revelation 12). The Messiah who is about to be born must be tried and

purified by suffering: the crucible (the womb) is the crucible of suffering. The Hebrew noun כור (*kur*), a "smelting-pot," is always used metaphorically in the Tanakh of human sufferings in punishment or discipline, and several texts refer to Egypt as the "iron furnace" from which the people of Israel were delivered from the bondage under which they "groaned" to God (cf. Ex.2.23-24, 3.7-9, Dt.4.20, Isa.48.10, Jer.11.4, Ezek.22.18-22). The Messiah is the "first-born" (cf. Col.1.18, Heb.12.23) who delivers the community of the Saints from the persecution of Belial and from the "billows" of death, Sheol, and perdition, upon whose destruction they receive "all the glory of the Man."

56 Cf. Rom.12.1, Heb.13.15-16, 1 Pet.2.5, 1QS 8.4-10, 9.3-5, 4QFlor.1.6f.

57 Cf. 2 Cor.1.22, 5.5, Eph.1.13-14. The term "seal" also comes from the tradition of Shavuot, when the "first fruits" were "sealed" by being exchanged for Temple currency; see the comments on 15.16.

58 See M. Weinfeld, "Pentecost as a Festival of the Giving of the Law," *Immanuel* 8 (1978), 7-18.

59 Cf. Tanh.Shemot 25, PRE 24, (Ex.R.13.16), San.34a.

60 Cf. Ps.Sol.14.1-5, 15.3, 1 En.10.16, 93.2-5. Moshe Weinfeld suggests that "the fiery tongues which rested on each of them [the disciples] (Acts 2.3) are reminiscent of the divine glory of the divine diadems which were put on the head of the Israelites when they proclaimed 'we will do and obey' (Shab.88a)" (idem, 15; cf. Mid.Ps.92.3). The divine glory (הדר/זיו/כבוד; *hadar/ziv/kavod*) constitutes a "halo"—being "crowned with glory."

61 See the comments on 4.17f.

62 The "Shoot" (cf. Isa.11.1, 53.2, 60.21, Jer.23.5, 33.15, Zech.3.8, 6.12 ["Branch"]) is the Teacher of Righteousness and the "church" which he has founded. The Teacher describes himself in terms of the Suffering Servant in the Servant Songs (cf. Isa.42.1-9, 49.1ff, 50.4-7, 52.13-53.12). The "flame of whirling fire" alludes to the Garden of Eden guarded by the Cherubim (Gen.3.24), but also recalls the midrashic "tongues of fire" of Ex.20.2: the "autumn rain" (יורה; *yoreh*) which God has put in the mouth of the Teacher of Righteousness may mean either the "early rain" (cf. Joel 2.23) or "teaching" (cf. "Torah"); the theme of rain/teaching (cf. "spring of living waters" and the "fountain") is part of a tradition which associates "teaching" with the life-giving Spirit (cf. Jn.4.14 [which alludes directly to the "tradition"], 1QS 3.19, 1QH 2.17-18, Sir.24.30-31, PA 2.8, 6.1), glory, and power (1QS 11.5f). The Teacher's "fruit" (or "merit") has been kept and "put in reserve," as it were, by God in the "glorious Eden" (cf. the "sealing" of his "Mystery"), alluding to his resurrection ("salvation") in the world

to come in eternal life—the "everlasting fruit." (For the idea of "perseverance," see the comments on 2.4f and 5.3.)

63 This is the force of the phrase "And in the same way," which otherwise appears to be a *non sequitur* and to lack correspondence with that which it allegedly parallels in the preceding verses.

64 See the comments on chapters 6-8.

65 Cf. 1QH 11.33-34. 1QH 11.26 may be inspired by Isa.35.10 (cf. Isa.51.11, 60.19-21, 61.7); see also Isa.35.6, which speaks of the "tongue of the dumb" shouting for joy. These passages are all related to the End Days, when Israel will be redeemed together with the Gentile nations.

66 Heb.4.12 speaks directly of the revealing of the "thoughts and intentions of the heart" in the context of Yeshua's intercession as the great high priest who has passed through the heavens, which is connected to his role in Lk.2.34-35.

67 Clement plays on the Hebrew text of Prov.20.27, which literally reads, the "breath of man," which God may "take away" if the good works of the believers instead become a judgment and condemnation (cf. Rom.8.1) on them. Although 1 Clement is later than the Pauline text, the tradition which he transmits apparently reflects an earlier source; see the comments below.

68 D. Flusser, "The Magnificat, the Benedictus and the War Scroll," in *Judaism*, 128 n.10. Flusser proposes that although Luke understood the "sword" to pierce Mary, the words were originally intended to refer to Israel, Yeshua being "set for the fall and rising of many in Israel." Flusser's argument in the article is designed to demonstrate that the Magnificat (Lk.1.46-55) and the Benedictus (Lk.1.68-79) are both drawn from a "[John the] Baptist militant hymn" in the Qumran tradition of thanksgiving hymns for eschatological victory (cf. 1QM 14.4-15). Paul picks up this motif in chapter 11, based on a midrash on Jer.11.15-16, in which Prov.20.27 is also interpreted as the "the lamp of the Lord is the spirit of man," as well as being linked to the same passage(s) in Isaiah regarding the light of the Messiah to which Lk.2.32 refers; see the comments on 11.18.

69 This threefold division of man is reflected in the Qumran texts (see below); cf. also 1 Thess.5.23 and Test.Jud.20.2, texts which are both similar to the theology of the Qumran literature.

70 The Tanakh usually ascribes the knowledge of man's mind to God Himself (see the references). Those commentators who consider that Paul might be referring to the Holy Spirit here mostly reject the identification on the grounds that the text then becomes tautological: the Holy Spirit

does not need to discover his own mind. The difficulty is removed, however, if the second clause is understood as the "mind of the spirit (of man);" see the comments below.

71 The "spirit born of spirit" refers to man's "carnal" spirit, so that the three elements can all be subsumed under such phrases as "born of woman" (cf. 1QH 13.14, 18.12-13), the "spirit of perversity" (cf. 1QS 4.9, 20, 23), the "spirit of flesh" (cf. 1QH 13.13, 17.25), and the "spirit of defilement" (cf. 1QS 4.22).

72 See the comments on verse 27.

73 The "Prince of Light" is the "Spirit of Good" (cf. 1QS 3.20), who is called "Prince of lights" in CDC 5.18.

74 This talmudic passage reflects a similar thought pattern to Paul's argument in Romans, since it continues to ask why Israel is likened to an olive tree, the same image which Paul uses in chapter 11, and concludes that although "Israel returns to the right way only after suffering," they shall "never be lost either in this world or in the world to come."

75 See also the midrashim which speak of the advent of the Messiah following upon *Israel's* travail; cf. TBE p.13, Pes.Rab.15.14/15. The principle of "good will" which applies to all those who are faithful to God in Yeshua is a direct consequence of Israel's election. Verse 28 therefore refers first to Israel and only secondly (but no less certainly) to all those who are faithful to God in Yeshua. Paul's thought carried a further specific significance to the community in Rome, which was suffering persecution as well as facing internal problems. Paul's defense of Israel's election was therefore also an encouragement to them to persevere in faithfulness, knowing that even tribulation is a part of God's plan for the final good to come.

76 God formed the people of Israel in the womb (cf. Isa.43.1, 44.2, 24); He called them by name (cf. Isa.43.1, 7, 45.4); He proclaimed to them the year of His good will (Isa.61.2); and He created them for His glory and glorified them (cf. Isa.43.7, 44.23, 46.13).

77 See the comments on 3.3.

78 "These things" are therefore what other people are saying as well as what Paul has said in the course of his argument not only in the immediately preceding verses but possibly also back to 3.5 where he left the original discussion in mid-thought.

79 This argument stands also for the "church," but only because it is first true of Israel. The argument can also be made that, beginning in verse 28, Paul brings a series of proofs of how "all things work together for good for those who love God," both Jews and Gentiles. The first proof is

the fact that He sent His son to die on behalf of man; and the second is that He has elected Israel as a "guarantee" of the redemption of all mankind.

80 Cf. Job 40.1ff, Isa.5.3, 41.1, 21, 43.26. See also 3.3f, where Paul, having begun to appeal to the "advantages" of Israel's election, then appeals to Ps.51.4, according to which God is "justified" in His words (His judgment of man's unrighteousness); see also the comments on verse 37.

81 The Testament of Dan comes from the same circles as the Qumran literature. Although the editors of the text suspect that the bracketed sentences may be a later Christian interpolation they also note that the last statement "stands in poetic parallel to verse 7a, and that its universalism can be documented elsewhere" in the Testament of the Twelve Patriarchs as a whole.

82 Paul discusses the effects of Israel's rebellious behavior on their status as "God's elect" and His chosen people in chapters 9-11. Here, however, he anticipates his conclusion, that God has not rejected His people, nor will He ever in the future.

83 The biblical expression "right hand" in itself indicates power; cf. Dt.33.2, Ps.18.35, Isa.48.13; Paul uses the same epithet for Yeshua in 1.16. Yeshua himself quotes the Son of man tradition in response to the question concerning whether he is the Messiah (cf. Lk.22.69), and thus also associates it with Ps.110.1 and Ps.80.18, both of which mention a messianic figure sitting at God's right hand, as well as with Dan.13.14. See D. Flusser, "At the Right Hand of Power," in *Judaism*, 301-5. For "Power" as one of God's epithets, see the comments on 1.16.

84 Flusser comments that, "It is . . . plausible that the Son of Man influenced the representation of Melchizedek as judge of the Latter Days. At the same time, attention must be paid to the fact that, but for two sayings of Jesus in the NT, no tradition mentions the Son of Man as sitting at the right hand of the Lord (as in Psalm 110.1); the seat is on the throne of glory. It is, therefore, possible that a contamination occurred between the two personages, Melchizedek as a mythical figure and as the Son of Man, but the material available does not allow any definite inferences." D. Flusser, *Melchizedek*, 191.

85 The alternative manuscript reading of this verse, "who shall separate us from the love of God" (in place of "the love of the Messiah"), represents an accommodation to the more normal phrase ("love of God"). The "love of the Messiah" is the more difficult text, and should be retained.

86 R. Akiba explains the text in Ex.15.2 through Israel's glorification of God by being ready to die for His name. In a well-known midrashic tradition, he interprets the events of the Exodus through texts from the

Song of Songs. Here, he makes his point—which he illustrated in his own death—by playing on the ambiguity of the word עלמות (*'alamot*; maidens), which he reads as two words (על מות; *'al mavet*) and understands as עד מות (*'ad mavet*), "unto death." For this whole discussion, see the excellent exposition of the nature of midrash in D. Boyarin, *Intertexuality and the Reading of Midrash* (Bloomington: Indiana University Press, 1990); he specifically deals with this passage from the *Mekhilta* in chapter 8.

87 See the comments on verse 28. Paul resumes his enumeration of Israel's "advantages" (cf. the list of tribulations in 8.35, 38-39) which he leaves uncompleted in 3.1, in 9.4-5.

88 Cf. Lev.11.47, 20.24, 26, 1 Kings 8.53, Ezek.22.20, 26, Ezra 10.11, Sifra Ked.93d, Pes.Rab.15.5, Cant.R.5.16.5, and Lev.R.24.4, where פרוש (*parush*; separated) translates the biblical קדוש (*kadosh*), holy. In the Second Temple period, for example, the "Pharisees" (פרושים; *Perushim*) further "set themselves apart" from the עמי הארץ (*'ammei ha-'aretz*), the common people, in respect to the laws of purity.

89 This text is also the basis for the midrash in Rom.10.5f, upon which Paul builds his own midrash concerning Yeshua's gift of righteousness. "Death" probably specifically refers in this context to martyrdom, and "life" is living in bondage to the "spirit of flesh" and the "fear of death;" see the comments on the doctrine of the Two Ways or Two Spirits in chapters 6-8.

90 Some texts speak of this Angel as being שר שלום (*sar shalom*), after the Prince of Peace in Isa.9.6; cf. Sir.17.17, Tanh.Mishp.17, 18, PRE 24, Ex.R.21.5, 32.2, 3, 7, Lev.R.29.2.

91 Cf. 1QM, Jub.15.32, Sifre Dt.He'azinu 329, San.38b, Orig.*Con.Cel.*5.25-30.

92 See E. Käsemann, *Romans*, 251, for this whole section.

ROMANS 9

Introduction

Paul's defense of Israel's election (in 8.28-39) leads him to pick up his interrupted argument from 3.1-3, and resume the list of "advantages" which prove God's election of Israel (verses 1-5). He repeats his claim (cf. 3.3f) that God's word has not failed because some of Israel have rejected Yeshua as God's Messiah (verse 6), and develops it in further reference to the "sons of Abraham" (cf. 2.25-29 and 8.14-17) (verses 7-13). He picks up the theme of God's promise and Abraham's blessing (cf. chapter 4) in the example of Esau and Jacob (verses 9-13), and deals with the objection that God's election is arbitrary (verses 14-24). In claiming that God has the sovereign power to elect whom He will, whenever He will, and for whatever purpose He chooses, Paul demonstrates that Israel's temporary rejection of Yeshua fulfills God's prophetic plan to elect the Gentiles also (verses 25-29). In verse 30, he raises once again the erroneous conclusion that God has replaced Israel, who have stumbled over Yeshua, with the Gentiles, who have achieved His righteousness. He discusses this issue through chapter 10, and finally answers the objection in 11.11, clearly stating that all Israel will be saved.

Verses 1-3:

"I am telling the truth . . . ": cf. Gen.3.14, 17, 4.11, Ex.32.32, Dt.5.29, Ps.37.22, 81.13, 119.21, Isa.40.3, 48.18, Jer.3.19, Mk.1.1f, Rom.1.9, 1 Cor.12.3, 16.22, Gal.1.8; 1QS 2.15-18, CDC 3.1, 9.1, 12.21-22, CDC[b] 1.33-35.

Paul picks up the theme of 3.1f, where he begins but never finishes the list of Israel's "advantages" and the purpose of their election in God's plan of redemption for the world.[1] This section also directly follows 8.28ff, where Paul has actually returned to his defense of Israel's election.[2] He prefaces the resumption of the list with his own personal conviction (cf. 8.38) and his willingness to "intercede" for his people (cf. 8.34, 11.2-4). He emphasizes the verity of his claim (cf. also the legal and forensic language he uses in 8.31-39) not only by appealing to witnesses (his conscience in the Holy Spirit) but also by stating in talmudic fashion that what he is saying comes directly from God: the "real" truth is that God has indeed not rejected His people.[3] The "truthfulness" of his words also proves the sincerity of his grief over Israel's rejection of Yeshua, but his statement also confirms God's will and proves God to be righteous.[4] Despite his assurance that God has not rejected His people even when they have rejected His Messiah (cf. 8.28-39), Paul also knows that his people risk being "accursed" and "separated" ("cut off") from God. In the manner of the Biblical prophets, Paul takes upon himself the punishment which is due to fall upon Israel (cf. Ex.32.31-32, Jn.10.11-17):

> And the Levites shall curse the men of the lot of Belial, and shall speak and say: Be thou cursed in all the works of thy guilty ungodliness! May God make of thee an object of dread by the hand of all the Avengers of vengeance! . . . May God not favour thee when thou callest upon Him, and may He be without forgiveness to expiate thy sins. . . . May the Wrath of God and the Zeal of His judgment burn him in eternal destruction! May there cling to him all the curses of this Covenant! May God set him apart for evil, and may he be cut off from the midst of the sons of light because he has turned away from God. . . . (1QS 2.5-18)[5]

Verses 4-5:

"Israelites . . . fathers": cf. Gen.12.2, 15.5, 17.1f, 28.14, Ex.4.22-3, 25.8, 29.45, 33.18, 40.24, Dt.1.31, 14.1-2, 28.47, 32.5, 1 Kings 8.11, Ps.100.2, Isa.6.1-3, Jer.31.31, Ezek.37.26, 43.1-5, Zech.2.5, 8.3, Lk.22.20, Jn.1.47, Acts 9.15, 1 Cor.11.25, 2 Cor.3.6, Heb.9.1, 6; CDC 6.19; Sir.24.8f, 23, Ps.Sol.7.2, 9.8-10, 14.5, Sib.Or.3.254-58, 573-80, Wis.Sol.9.9; PA 1.1, 2, 3.14, PRK 2.7, 15.5, Sifre Dt.He'azinu 308, Pes.Rab.35., Tanh.B.Terumah 8, DEZ 1.16.

Paul continues his enumeration of the "advantages" of Israel's election (cf. 3.1f). God "contemplated" the creation of "Israel" (Paul's "kinsmen according to the flesh") even before the creation of the world, and redeemed them so that they would be the "tribe of His inheritance" (cf. Ps.74.2):

> Six things preceded the creation of the world; some of them were actually created, while the creation of the others was already contemplated. The Torah and the Throne of Glory were created. The Torah, for it is written, *The Lord made me as the beginning of His way, prior to His works of old* (Prov.8.22). *The Throne of Glory, as it is written, Thy throne is established of old*, etc. (Ps.93.2). The creation of the Patriarchs was contemplated, for it is written, *I saw your fathers*

> *as the first-ripe in the fig-tree at her first season* (Hos.9.10). [The creation of] Israel was contemplated, as it is written, *Remember Thy congregation, which Thou hast gotten aforetime* (Ps.74.2). [The creation of] the Temple was contemplated, as it is written, *Thou throne of glory, on high from the beginning, the place of our sanctuary* (Jer.17.12). The name of Messiah was contemplated, *His name existed ere the sun* (Jer.17.12). R. Ahabah b. R. Ze'ira said: Repentance too, as it is written, *Before the mountains were brought forth*, etc. (Ps.90.2). . . . (Gen.R.1.4)[6]

God's "inheritance" includes those other "possessions" which belonged to Israel before the creation of the world—the Temple, the (Throne of) Glory, the (name of the) Messiah, the Patriarchs, and repentance.[7] The "Fathers" (אבות; *'Avot*) are all of the illustrious forefathers of Israel, whose merit often stands on behalf of later generations.[8] They are the "forefathers" of Israel's "spiritual genealogy." The "covenants" (cf. Sir.44.12, 18, 45.17, Wis.18.22, 2 Macc.8.15) are those of circumcision (Gen.17.2); מתן תורה (*mattan Torah*), the giving of the Torah (Dt.4.13f, Ps.147.19; CDC 1.4-5, 6.2-3; Heb.9.15), which Paul lists separately here; and the "new covenant" (cf. Jer.31.31, Ezek.37.26, Lk.22.20, 1 Cor.11.25, 2 Cor.3.6, CDC 6.19, 8.21). "Service" (λατρεια; *latreia*) refers to the Temple worship (עבודת ה'; *'avodat ha-Shem*), "the work of the Lord" (cf. Dt.28.47, Ps.100.2, Heb.9.1, 6, PA 1.2). The "promises" are those God gave to Abraham, that his descendants would be as the sand and the stars (cf. Gen.12.2, 15.5, 17.1f, 28.14); of the land (cf. Gen.15.7, 17.8, 28.13, Ex.12.25, 13.5, Dt.1.11, 6.3, 19.8, Neh.9.8, Rom.11.29, Heb.11.11-3, 17); to the House of David and his messianic offspring (cf. 1 Kings 2.24, 8.20, 2 Kings 8.19, Isa.7.13-6, 9.6-7, 11.1-5, Rom.1.3, 2 Cor.1.20, Gal.3.16-22, 1 Pet.1.10 12); of the Spirit and the new covenant (cf. Jer.31.31, Ezek.37.26, Joel 2.28, Acts 2.16-21, 39, Gal.3.8, 15f, 4.24-8, Eph.1.13, 2.12); and of life itself (cf. Dt.8.3, 30.15-6, 32.39, Prov.3.16, 8.35, Hab.2.4, 1 Tim.4.8, 2 Tim.1.1, 2 Pet.1.4).

Verse 5:

"From whom is the Messiah . . . forever": cf. 2 Sam.7.14, Ps.2.2, 89.20-29, 110.1-7, Isa.7.14, 11.1-5, 49.5-13, 52.13 53.12, Mt.1.1-16, Jn.3.31, Rom.1.3, Col.1.16-17; PRE 3, DEZ 1.18, Pes.Rab.33.6, 36.1, Mid.Ps.2.9f, 72.6, Gen.R.1.4, 85.1, Pes.54a, Ned.39a; 1 Clem.32.2.

Paul places the Messiah as the head of those things which God contemplated before the creation of the world.[9] At the same time, he is one of Israel's "possessions," which Paul emphasizes by the phrase "according to the flesh."[10]

The Patristic tradition (the Church Fathers) almost unanimously ascribes the whole of this verse to Yeshua.[11] Paul in fact quotes almost verbatim here the continuation of the messianic prooftext in Psalm 72.17(-19): "And let (men) bless themselves by him; let all nations call him blessed. Blessed be the Lord God, the God of Israel . . . and blessed be His glorious name forever; and may the whole earth be filled with His glory. Amen, and amen." If Paul has in mind the midrashic tradition on Psalm 72.17, he hints here at the Messiah's pre-existence in the same way as the Psalm understands the name of the Messiah to have been contemplated before the creation of the world (cf. Jer.23.6). Paul's "doxology" seems to reflect this tradition, and understands Yeshua as he "by [whom] all things were created, (both) in the heavens and on earth, visible and invisible . . . all things have been created by him and for him" (Col.1.16).[12]

Verse 6:

"But (it is) not . . . failed": cf. Num.23.19, Isa.40.8, 55.11, Rom.3.3-4; 1QH 4.13, 15.14.

Paul refers directly back to the theme of 3.3ff. Here, however, he continues the argument that Israel's rebellious behavior does not make God a liar and thus nullify His promises (cf. verses 4-5) to Israel.[13] The questioning of God's truthfulness and His faithfulness to His promises which Paul anticipates raises doubts concerning Israel's continued election (cf. also 8.33-39), which he counters by building on the theme of the "sons of Abraham" in a similar fashion to texts from Qumran:

> It is by Thy goodness alone that man is justified, and by the immensity of Thy mer[cy]. [For] Thou wilt adorn him with Thy brightness and fi[ll] him [with abun]dance of pleasure, with everlasting bliss and length of days. For [Thou hast sworn it] [and] Thy word shall not turn back. . . . And unto Thy sons of truth Thou hast given under[standing] [and they shall know Thee for ever and] ever [and] shall be glorified according to their knowledge . . . And likewise, unto the son of ma[n . . .] Thou hast given an abundant portion of the knowledge of Thy truth and he shall be [gl]ori[fied] according to his knowledge . . . . (1QH 13.16-18, 10.27-28)

"For . . . ": cf. Jn.8.33-47, Rom.2.28, 11.21, 24-26.

Paul appeals to the motif of the "sons of Abraham," this time (cf. 2.28-29) in order to demonstrate that even though Israel's election is sure, those who inherit God's promise to Abraham as the people (sons) of "Israel" themselves are only those who are in fact Abraham's disciples and exhibit his "qualities."[14]

Verses 7-9:
"But: 'Through Isaac . . . ' ": cf. Gen.13.15-6, 16.10, 18.10, 21.12, 22.17-8, Ex.32.13, Josh.24.3, 2 Chron.20.7, Neh.9.8, Ps.105.6, Isa.41.8, 45.19, Jer.31.36, 33.26.

Paul returns to the distinction between the "wages" of righteousness and God's "promise," emphasizing once again that Israel's election is based, as he proceeds to demonstrate in the following verses, on their faithfulness to His word and not on the physical rite of circumcision which "seals" their faithfulness to the covenant in the Torah.[15] Here he specifically names Isaac as the "heir of the promise" (cf. Gen.17.19-21).[16] God's "promise(s)" to Abraham establish Israel as the "sons of Abraham," through whose "seed" (according to the flesh) the Messiah bestows God's righteousness on all those who are "faithful" to God like Abraham.[17] Israel's election, is therefore at once assured and the basis for the "election" also of the Gentiles. Moreover, Israel's temporary rejection of God's Messiah also leads to the "creation-resurrection" of the nations of the world. The faithfulness of the Gentiles to the God of Abraham, Isaac and Jacob finally provokes Israel to jealousy for their own God, so that the whole world receives "life from the dead" (cf. 11.15).

Verse 10:
"One man . . . ": cf. 5.12, 15, 17.

Paul uses the theme of twins (two sons) who were born to "one man" to highlight the theme of the "one man" through whom "sin entered the world" (cf. 5.12) and the "one man" through whom God gives his "free gift of righteousness" (5.15f). Paul appeals to the story of Esau and (Jacob and) Isaac as an analogy both for the "sons of Abraham" and for the "two masters" (Two Ways or Spirits). Jacob and Esau are Abraham's two "seeds," one of who represents Israel (Jacob), and the other the Gentile nations (Esau).[18]

Verses 11-13:
" . . . had not yet done anything . . . ": cf. 4.2.

Paul develops the distinction between "wages" and "imputation" from chapter 4 in relation to the allegations of God's "arbitrary" choice of Jacob over Esau. "Works" corresponds in this context to the genealogical "right" whereby the birthright is "owed" to the first son. God's "calling" (of Jacob instead of what was rightfully Esau's inheritance) parallels His "imputation" of righteousness to Abraham (who did not "deserve" righteousness on the basis of his "deeds"). The purpose clause ("in order that God's purpose . . . ") further demonstrates God's "imputation" of righteousness: God announces ("promises") (even before the twins are born and have had opportunity to do "good or bad") that Esau will "serve" Jacob in order to indicate that His righteousness is not "earned" but "reckoned."

Verse 14:

"What shall we say then? . . . ": cf. 2.11, 3.5, 9, 29-30, 6.1, 7.7, 9.30, 11.1, 11.

Paul anticipates the obvious objection, that God's choice of Jacob over Esau is arbitrary and unjust. This objection carries the further implication that God's choice (election) of Israel is also arbitrary and unjust. Paul deals with this issue in 3.5f, but there he develops a counter-argument against the possibility that Israel's rebellious behavior might in fact "prove" God to be right. The following verses (3.9ff) recapitulate the thought of 2.11f, where Paul appeals to God's impartiality in order to demonstrate that when God renders to each person according to his deeds He retains the freedom to condemn each man and to "justify" him as He wills. Israel and the Gentiles are thus "equal" before Him.[19]

Verses 15-16:

"For He says to Moses . . . ": cf. Ex.33.19, Tit.3.5; 1QS 11.9-11, 1QH 4.29-33, 5.2-4, 7.30-33, 10.1-12; Wis.Sol.11.21-25.

Paul rebuts the claim that God's choice(s) are unjust by appealing to Exodus 33.19, a verse which may be read quite literally to prove that God's actions are arbitrary.[20] Paul uses the verse, however, to demonstrate that God is completely sovereign and may choose to "justify" those who possess no "merit" or "good works" (cf. 2.11f). Similar midrashim deal with the same problem of theodicy:

> AND I SHALL BE GRACIOUS TO WHOM I WILL BE GRACIOUS (Ex.33.19). Then it was that God showed him all the treasures in which the rewards of the righteous are stored away. Moses asked: 'To whom does all this treasure belong?' and He replied: 'To those who fulfil My commandments.' 'And to whom does this treasure belong?' 'To those who bring up orphans.' So it was with every treasure. Later he saw a huge treasure and inquired: 'Whose is this great treasure?' The Divine rejoinder was: 'Unto him that hath [such things to his credit] I give of his reward, but unto him who hath not, I have to supply freely and I help him from this great pile,' as it says, AND I WILL BE GRACIOUS TO WHOM I WILL BE GRACIOUS,

> namely, unto him to whom I wish to be gracious [even if he has not earnt it]. Similarly, AND I WILL SHOW MERCY ON WHOM I SHALL SHOW MERCY. (Ex.R.45.6)[21]

This midrash verges on the edge of declaring salvation for all mankind without the need to observe the Torah. Paul makes the same argument, but knows that since Yeshua is the τελος (*telos*) or "goal" (10.4) of the Torah, man's salvation comes about through his faithfulness to God in Yeshua.

Verse 16:
"So then . . . ": cf. Ex.33.19, 34.6, Ps.111.4, Isa.49.10, Neh.9.31, 1 Cor.9.24, Gal.2.2, Eph.1.7, 2.4, Tit.3.5; 1QH 16.16-17, 17.11-12, 1QpHab 7.1-4; Ps.Sol.2.15f, 32, 36, 5.1-2, 9-15, 9.2-3, 11, 10.5.

Paul explains the prooftext from Exodus 33.19 in countering the charge of God's arbitrary actions. Man's "will" may be his "running" to observe the commandments (cf. PA 4.2) or to raise orphans (cf. 8.15).[22] God's mercy and compassion express His "favor" and "good will," to which Paul appeals in 8.28 in "proof" of God's unconditional election of Israel:

> And I know that the inclination of every spirit is in Thy hand [and that] Thou hast ordained [the way of every man] [together with his visitation] before ever creating him. And how can any man change Thy words? Thou alone hast [created] the just and established him from his mother's womb unto the time of good will. . . . (1QH 15.13-15)

In the Qumran texts, what appears arbitrary action on God's part is explained as the right of the Creator over what He has created. God's right to elect Israel as His people is based on His being the Creator of all. Paul modifies the "predestination" of this attitude by demonstrating in the subsequent verses that Israel may in fact be "vessels of wrath" in God's plan to make the Gentiles part of His people as well, who once themselves had once been destined for wrath, without hope and without God in the world (cf. Eph.2.12).

Verses 17-18:
"For the Scripture says to Pharaoh . . . ": cf. Ex.4.21, 7.3, 9.12, 16, Dt.2.30, Josh.11.20, Isa.6.10, Rom.2.4-8, 3.19, 11.7, 25, 32, Gal.3.2; 1QS 3.18-25, 1QM 13.9-11, 1QH 1.7f, 10.9f, 14.11f, 15.13-19; Sir.16.15-16; Ex.R.13.2, 3.

Paul brings a second prooftext to refute the claim that God's actions are arbitrary and unjust. Exodus 9.16 parallels Exodus 33.19, but where the latter text speaks of God's mercy and compassion the former verse speaks of God's "hardening" of Pharaoh's heart. The two texts together demonstrate God's complete sovereignty, to reward as He wills and to punish as He wills (verse 18): although what might seem to man to be God's arbitrary action works both towards mercy and towards punishment, the prooftext from God's hardening of Pharaoh's heart indicates that God possesses considerations which are both hidden from man and which are independent of human merit.[23]

Verse 19:

"You will say to me then . . . ": cf. 2 Chron.20.6, Job 9.12, Dan.4.35, Rom.3.5-7, 19.14, 11.19, 1 Cor.15.35; 1QS 11.22, 1QH 7.28-29, 10.3-12, 12.24-35; Wis.Sol.12.12, Sir.15.11-12; PA 3.15, TBE p.62.

Paul preempts the anticipated objection and modifies the traditional talmudic formula, "what shall we say then?" into a response.[24] He returns to his argument in 3.7 ("why I am still being judged a sinner?"), this time from the opposite perspective (cf. also verse 14). Since God is totally sovereign, according to this view it does not matter at all whether man obeys God out of love or out of fear (cf. 8.15), because God has already determined the motive according to which each person will serve Him.[25] He appeals to a motif common to the biblical and prophetic texts, namely that of the potter and his clay. This theme, which clearly expresses the right of the Creator over what He creates, was frequently discussed in various midrashic treatments of this theme:

> What is the meaning of *We are the clay, and Thou our potter*? Israel said: 'Lord of the Universe! Thou hast caused it to be written for us: *Behold, as the clay in the potter's hand, so are ye in My hand, O house of Israel* (Jer.18.6); for this reason, do not depart from us though we sin and provoke Thee, for we are but the clay and Thou art our potter.' See now, If the potter makes a jar and leaves therein a pebble, then when it comes out of the furnace it will leak from the hole left by the pebble and lose any liquid poured into it. Now what caused the jar to leak and thus to lose any liquid placed therein? The potter who left the pebble therein. This was how Israel pleaded before God: 'Lord of the Universe! Thou has created in us an Evil Inclination from our youth, for it says, *For the imagination of man's heart is evil from his youth* (Gen.8.21), and it is that which has caused us now to sin, for Thou hast not removed from us the instigator to sin. (Ex.R.46.4)[26]

Verses 20-21:
"On the contrary . . . ": cf. Job 4.19, 10.9, 33.6, Lam.4.2, 0Isa.29.16, 45.9, 64.8, Jer.18.4-6, Rom.2.1, 3, 2 Cor.4.7, 2 Tim.2.20; 1QS 11.22, 1QH 1.21-27, 10.3-7, 12.24-35, 15.12ff; Sir.33.10-13, Test.Ben.10.8-9, Ps.Sol.17.21-25, Wis.Sol.12.12, 15.7-8; PA 4.22, Ex.R.46.4.

Paul's indignant rejoinder underlines man's status as a human being ("O man") created by God according to His will and not his own:

> Akabiah b. Mahaleleel said: Apply thy mind to three things and thou wilt not come into the power of sin: Know whence thou camest, and wither thou art going, and before whom thou art destined to give an account and reckoning. Whence camest thou?—From a fetid drop. Wither art thou going?—To a place of dust, of worm and of maggot. Before whom art thou destined to give an account and reckoning? -Before the King of the Kings of Kings, the Holy One, blessed be He. (PA 3.1).[27]

Paul will not admit any validity to man's complaint that God is responsible for His bad workmanship. "On the contrary," he rebuts the charge against God in line with another biblical "clay" motif, according to which God made man out of the clay to be the glory of His creation:

> For without Thee no way is perfect, and without Thy will nothing is done. It is Thou who hast taught all Knowledge, and all that is brought into being exists by Thy will. And there is none other beside Thee to dispute Thy decision and to comprehend all Thy holy Thought and to contemplate the depths of Thy mysteries and to understand all Thy Marvels and the power of Thy Might. Who then shall contain Thy Glory? And what is the son of man himself amidst all Thy marvellous works? And he that is born of woman, what is his worth before Thee? Truly, this man was shaped from dust and his end is to become the prey of worms. Truly, this man is a mere frail image in potter's clay and inclines to the dust. What shall clay reply, the thing which the hand fashions? What thought can it comprehend? (1QS 11.17-22)

Although God makes man perfect, he must also remember that he came out of the dust of the earth which God subjected to futility until the "freedom of the glory of the children of God" (cf. 8.20).[28]

Verses 22-23:

"What if God . . . ": cf. Prov.16.4, Isa.45.9, Lam.4.2, Acts 9.15, Rom.1.16, 2.4, 8.29f, 10.12, 11.33, Eph.1.4-9, 18, 2.7, 3.16, Phil.4.19, Col.1.27, 1 Pet.2.8; 1QH 15.14-17; 2 Bar.59.6, Test.Naph.2.2ff.

Although Paul phrases the sentence as a hypothetical question, he takes up the hypothesis as true in verse 23.[29] The terms "vessels of wrath" and "vessels of mercy" correspond to the terms "honorable use" and "common use" in verse 21:

> And all men are from the ground, and Adam was created of earth. In much knowledge the Lord hath divided them, and made their ways diverse. Some of them hath he blessed and exalted, some of them hath he sanctified, and set near himself: but some of them hath he cursed and brought low, and turned out of their places. As the clay is in the potter's hand, to fashion it at his pleasure: so man is in the hand of him that made him, to render to them as liketh him best. (Sir.33.10-13)[30]

Verse 22:

"Endured . . . vessels of wrath": cf. Ex.34.6, Ps.2.9, Isa.29.15-16, 45.7, Jer.18.6, Lam.4.2, Joel 2.13, Rom.2.4-10, 3.25, 11.32, Gal.3.22; 1QS 11.21-22, 1QH 1.21f, 4.29, 10.3f, 12.24f, 13.13f; Wis.Sol.11.23, 15.7, 1 En.60.5, 25, Test.Gad 4.7, Test.Abr.10.14f, 4 Ez.3.8, 7.62f, 8.36, Test.Gad 4.7, Sir.17.21, 18.11-12, 33.12; PA 5.2, Mid.Ps.77.1, Pes.Rab.11.2, PRK 24.11, 25.1, TBE p.62, p.189, Tanh.Shemot 20, Gen.R.49.8, Ex.R.46.4, Eccl.R.8.11.1, Ber.7a, San.111a; Philo, *Leg.All.*3.106.

Paul turns his hypothetical question into a real one, and asks the question whether it is not in fact true that although God has "endured" Israel's rebellious and sinful ways, He should actually have destroyed them as His people due to their transgressions and iniquities (cf. Ex.32.9-10, Num.14.11-12, Dt.9.13-14). Almost imperceptibly, his argument has therefore turned around (cf. 2.1f), so that Israel now stand in the place of "vessels of wrath" (vessels deserving of wrath).[31] Although Paul uses the same terminology as found in the Qumran ideas of predestination as in Qumran, according to which " . . . Thou hast ordained [the way of every man] [together with his visitation] before ever creating him. And how can any man change Thy words? Thou alone hast [created] the just and established him from his mother's womb unto the time of good-will . . . And Thou has raised up his glory from among flesh, whereas Thou hast created the wicked [for the time of] Thy [wr]ath and hast set them apart from their mother's womb for the

Day of Massacre. . . . " (1QH 15.13-17), he interprets them according to the biblical pattern.[32] As in Ezekiel 16 and 20, for example, he declares that God's wrath is indeed poured out upon His people, but that He will not destroy them for His name's sake, i.e., for His reputation among the nations. Moreover, His wrath in fact expresses His sovereignty and thus also His mercy, since it brings about Israel's repentance and obedience:

> "As I live," declares the Lord God, "surely with a mighty hand and with an outstretched arm and with wrath poured out, I shall be king over you. . . . And you will know that I am the Lord, when I bring you into the land of Israel, into the land which I swore to give to your forefathers. And there you will remember your ways and all your deeds, with which you have defiled yourselves; and you will loath yourselves in your own sight for all the evil things that you have done. Then you will know that I am the Lord when I have dealt with you for My name's sake, not according to your evil ways or according to your corrupt deeds, O house of Israel," declares the Lord God. (Ezek.20.33-34, 42-44)

"Vessels of wrath" are therefore vessels which are deserving of punishment. If they do not repent, all attempts to escape judgment prove futile, but God will have mercy on them if they repent:

> R. Abba bar Yudan said: What God regards as unfit [for sacrifice] in an animal, He holds fit in a human being. In an animal He regards as unfit one that is *blind, or broken, or maimed, or having a wen* (Lev.22.22); but in a human being He holds *a broken and contrite heart* (Ps.51.17) to be fit for an offering to Him. R. Alexandri said: If an ordinary person makes use of a broken vessel, it is taken as a reflection upon him. But the Holy One is unconcerned about the use of broken vessels—indeed His entire use is broken vessels: *The Lord is nigh to them that are of a broken heart* (Ps.34.18); *Who healeth the broken in heart* (Ps.147..3); *A broken and contrite heart, O God, Thou wilt not despise* (Ps.51.17). Hence, admonishing Israel, Hosea says to them: *Return, O Israel* (Hos.14.1). . . . When the Holy One is asked, "The sinner—what is to be his punishment?" the Holy One replies: In penitence let him mend his ways, and his sins shall be forgiven him. Hence it is written, [*At one and the same time*] *kind and strict in judgment is the Lord* (Ps.25.8). R. Phinehas commented: How can He who is strict in judgment be called kind? And how can

> He who is kind be called strict in judgment? *Because He doth instruct sinners in the way* (*ibid.*)—that is, He teaches sinners the way to act in penitence. Therefore Hosea, admonishing Israel, said to them: *Return, O Israel* (Hos.14.1). (PRK 24.5, 7)

At the beginning of chapter 9, Paul defends Israel's election by appealing to the motif of the "sons of Abraham." The "sons" of Israel are those who are Abraham's disciples and possess his qualities (cf. PA 5.19). God's sovereignty and power guarantee Israel's election to show compassion to those who have no merit. He may also rightfully punish Israel's sins, however. He has in fact chosen to "endure" those sins "with much patience"—*in order to* bestow His "glory" (cf. 8.17f) upon vessels destined for mercy, the Gentiles who were once "not-My-people," to whom God was "uncompassionate" (cf. Hos.2.23).[33]

Verse 23:

" . . . in order that . . . ": cf. Acts 9.15, Rom.2.4, 8.29f, 11.7 15, 25, Eph.1.5-12, 18, 2.4, 3.8-10, 16; 1QH 4.27f, 11.9-10, 12.13, 13.7-21, 15.15f.

The "purpose" of God's sovereignty is to demonstrate, in His forbearance of Israel's disobedience, His compassion also for the Gentiles (cf. Hos.2.23). Through Israel's partial and temporary rejection of God's Messiah He calls the Gentiles "into being" (cf. 4.17) who, in their "glory," thus provoke Israel back to jealousy for their own God:

> And these things [which Thou hast] est[ablished . . .] all Thy works before Thou createdst them with the host of Thy spirits and the congregation [of Thy Saints] . . . an everlasting Visitation. For it is Thou who hast established them from before eternity and the work [. . .] they shall recount Thy glory in all Thy dominion. . . . And [Thou hast] divi[ded] all these things in the Mysteries of Thine understanding to make Thy glory known. . . . It is by Thy goodness alone that man is justified, and by the immensity of Thy mer[cy]. [For] Thou wilt adorn him with Thy brightness and [fi]ll him [with abun]dance of pleasure, with everlasting bliss and length of days. For [Thou hast sworn it] [and] Thy wo[rd] shall not turn back. (1QH 13.7-18)

Verse 24:

" . . . among Jews . . . Gentiles": cf. Hos.11.1, Rom.4.17, 9.8, 1 Pet.2.10; Jub.2.10; 1QS 8.4-10, 1QH 6.10-14.

Paul now draws the conclusions of his argument, in which, having started out (re-)defending Israel's election, he demonstrates that the people's disobedience performed the purpose of bringing also the Gentiles into God's Kingdom. Although God made His covenantal "calling" first with the nation of Israel, whose God He would be and who would be his people (cf. 8.28ff), not all of Israel have accepted Yeshua.[34] God's purpose from the beginning was to "create" the Gentiles as well, and Israel's (partial) rejection of Yeshua is part of the way He planned to make those who were once "not-My-people," without God and without hope in the world (cf. Eph.2.12) part of His people, through their joint faithfulness to God in Yeshua.

Verses 25-26:
"As he also says in Hosea . . . ": cf. Hos.1.10, 2.23, 1 Pet.2.10, 1QS 8.4-10.

Paul turned to Hosea 1.10 and 2.23 as prooftexts of his claim that in electing the people of Israel God has also made a way to bring hope to the nations of the world as well.[35] These prooftexts were possibly adapted from their original reference to Israel in circles influenced by Qumran ideology and applied to the Gentiles, and Paul follows this tradition here.[36] God's "calling" is based upon His election of Israel, through which the Gentiles also may enter the "household of God" as "sons of the living God" (cf. 8.14f, Eph.2.19).[37]

Verses 27-29:
"And Isaiah cries out . . . ": cf. Gen.22.17, Dt.29.23, Isa.1.9, 10.22-23, 13.19, Jer.49.18, 50.40, Hos.1.10, Amos 4.11, Mt.10.15, Rom.11.5.

Paul now brings prooftexts (Isa.1.9, 10.22-23) concerning God's election of *Israel*, which speak specifically about the "remnant" of Israel which will be saved.[38] Paul demonstrates in verses 14-23 that God's rejection and election is not dependent upon man's will or exertion, but upon God's mercy alone (9.16). According to verse 24, one of the consequences of God's free election is that not only Jews but also Gentiles can belong to the "elect." Thus verse 24 is not only the conclusion of the preceding homily, but also a transition to the following one. The main theme of this homily itself is to demonstrate from Scriptural prooftexts that the "elect" are now composed of Gentiles, and of only a remnant of the Jews; the "Jewish Christians" are therefore saved together with the Gentile Christians. He concludes saying that, "By the way, this does not naturally exclude the final salvation of all of Israel, which Paul announces later on in the famous chapter 11 of the epistle."[39] Paul thus begins defending Israel's election by dealing with the issue of theodicy.[40] God's election of

Israel is not for the purpose of excluding but of *including* all the nations of the world in the redemption of the whole earth.

Verse 30:

"What shall we say then?": cf. 3.3, 9, [4.1], 6.1, 15, 7.7, 8.31, 9.14, 11.1, 7, 11.

Paul anticipates a further objection (cf. verses 14 and 19) which his argument raises.[41] It is important to note that his use of the talmudic formula here determines the understanding of chapters 10-11. The question he raises (verses 30b-31), whose erroneous conclusion he intends to refute, is: Shall we say that the Gentiles, who did not pursue righteousness, attained righteousness . . . by faith but that Israel, pursuing a law of righteousness, did not arrive at (that) law.[42] Paul repeats the question almost verbatim in 11.7, where again he leaves out the negation. His final summary therefore appears in 11.11: "I say then, they [Israel] did not stumble so as to fall, did they? May it never be! But by their transgression salvation (has come) to the Gentiles, to make them [Israel] jealous."

"Gentiles . . . attained righteousness": Paul establishes in verses 24-29 that God has, in Yeshua, "called (into being)" the Gentiles, as well as the people of Israel. His "people" ("sons") are the Gentile believers and a "remnant" of Israel (cf. 11.5).[43] He here anticipates the potential objection that the Gentile believers have taken Israel's place in God's favor.[44] The verse does not stand as a statement but as a question (see above). Paul describes the reality that God has given His righteousness to the Gentiles through Yeshua, but refutes the erroneous conclusion that "therefore" Israel, who also pursued but did not "arrive at," God's righteousness, have "stumbled so as to fall" (cf. 11.11) and been rejected by God in favor of the Gentiles.

Verses 31-33:

"Israel . . . did not arrive at (that) law": cf. Isa.51.1, Rom.2.17f, 10.2.

Paul continues his question of verse 30.[45] Although it is true that Israel did not "arrive at" God's righteousness but "stumbled over the stumbling stone," they have not stumbled "so as to fall" completely (cf. 11.11) from God's grace. Their stumbling opens the way for the election also of the Gentiles, but it does not mean that God has replaced them with another people. Paul's comparison between Israel and the Gentile believers is not between righteousness as faithfulness and righteousness through the Torah. Most commentators have normally expanded the elliptical phrase "did not arrive at law," in an attempt to describe "what" or "which" law Israel did not "arrive at." However, Paul is actually arguing here that Israel "did not arrive at (the goal of the) Torah"—Yeshua.[46] He draws this claim out in verse 32, where the direct question, "Why?" refers to the reason for Israel's failure to achieve the "goal" of the Torah. He appeals first to the distinction between faithfulness and works (cf. chapter 4). The "goal" of faithfulness, however, is Yeshua, and Israel "stumbled" because they were "unfaithful" to God in not accepting His Messiah. The "testing-stone" in the prooftext from Isaiah 28.16 (verse 33) is part of the tradition common to 1 Peter 2.3-9, 1QS 8.4-10 and Romans 9.24-33. Flusser (*Romans*, 77) notes that the Hebrew אבן בחן (*'even bochan*; "tested-stone) in Isaiah 28.16 stands grammatically for a "stone which tests" and thus for stone to "trip over" ("strike") and a rock to "stumble over" (Isa.8.14).[47]

Endnotes on Chapter 9

1 Paul begins to enumerate these "advantages," in response to an anticipated objection that if a Gentile (believer) exhibits the "qualities" of Abraham he is considered to be "Jewish" (circumcised). If a non-Jew may please God in this way, then what purpose did God have in electing Israel and setting them apart to be His holy people?

2 See the comments on 8.28.

3 The use of the phrase "I am telling you the truth" (דברי אמת אני מדבר עמך; *divrei 'emet 'ani medaber 'imkha*) in rabbinic literature often implies that what is being stated carries the weight of a revelation or of a (divine) conclusion, bringing the definitive point of an argument; cf. Ex.R.3.7. Paul establishes this point as the climax of argument throughout chapters 9-11.

4 This is the theme of verses 6ff, where God is "true to His word" (His promises).

5 Cf. also 1QH 2.6-19, 7.12, 1QpHab 8.1-3.

6 Cf. Pes.R.33.6, PRE 3, TBE p.187, Pes.54a, Ned.39a, Zohar Lev.34b. The prooftext for Israel's election (Ps.74.2) is in fact a reply to the "charge" of God's rejection in Ps.74.1.

7 For Israel as God's (adopted) "sons," see the comments on 8.14f; for "glory" as the name of God's Messiah, see the comments on 3.23, as well as the "glorification" of those who suffer with him in 8.17f.

8 Cf. Acts 3.13, 7.32, Rom.11.28, PSan.10.1, 27d, Tanh.B.Vayera 9, Mekh.Beshall.4, Ex.R.44.3, 6, 9.

9 Flusser states in his discussion of Melchizedek that, "Pre-existence—as we learn from the New Testament—is not necessarily incompatible with nativity; and, indeed, in the Slavonic 'Book of the Secrets

of Enoch', a miraculous nativity of Melchizedek is reported." D. Flusser, *Melchizedek*, 189.

10 Cf. the rabbinic expression [מלך] בשר ודם ([*melekh*] *basar ve-dam*), "(king of) flesh and blood," which distinguishes God from human figures in many rabbinic parables; cf. Tanh.Vayere 8, Nisa 30, Gen.R.1.3, Ex.R.28.3, AZ 11a.

11 The long last clause of the verse causes several problems, due to the lack of commas and full stops in the Greek text. A major theological difficulty is consequently raised by the phrase, "over all." If a comma is placed after "flesh," the verse may refer the phrase to Yeshua as God ("who is God over all . . . "). If, alternatively, the verse is divided by a colon or full stop, several translations are possible: either, "He who is God over all be blessed forever;" or, "He who is over all is God blessed forever." The final possibility treats the end of the clause as a doxology, and reads the verse either as: "Yeshua who is over all, (God) be blessed forever;" or, "God who is over all, be blessed forever." Paul nowhere refers to Yeshua as God. (The possible exceptions are Phil.2.6 and Rom.10.9-10; see the comments there. The issue rests on whether Yeshua is identified as God Himself or partakes of His "divinity.") The strictness with which the ascription "God" is restricted to no other person than God Himself, including His Messiah, is reflected in the use of Isa.9.6 in 1QH 3.9-10, for example, where the appellation "Mighty God" is understood as the "Mighty Counselor of God;" (see the comments on 8.34.) The Messiah's possession of divine attributes such as pre-existence, sonship, God's name, redeemer, righteous, etc., are never confused with God's Oneness; cf. 2 Sam.7.14, Isa.9.6, Jer.23.5-6, Ps.72.17, 93.2, 110.1, Prov.30.4, 1QH 3.9-10, 1 En.48.3, Mid.Ps.21.2, 72.6, 93.3, Pes.Rab.33.6, Num.R.18.21, Lam.R.1.16.51, Sof.13.13, San.96b.

12 Paul develops the messianic theme of Abraham's blessing to the nations through his "seed" (cf. Rom.4.13f, Gal.2.8, 3.16) in the immediately following discussion (chapters 9-11).

13 See 8.28 for an outline of the argument of 3.1-8.28. Paul picks up the theme of the "sons of Abraham" from 2.25f-3.1f.

14 In chapter 2, Paul's concern is to demonstrate that the Gentiles can also possess Abraham's qualities. Israel are no "better" than those Gentiles, therefore, if they do not prove themselves to be Abraham's disciples.

15 See the comments on 2.26-29 and 4.9-16.

16 Paul assumes the "genealogy" of Isaac in chapter 4 but does not refer directly either to Isaac or to Ishmael; nor does he mention Isaac in Gal.3.16f, although he bases the allegory in 4.21-31 directly upon Hagar and Ishmael, and Sarah and Isaac.

17 The "children of the flesh" are not only the nation ("sons") of Israel but also reflect "those who are according to the flesh" (8.5), who are slaves to their own inclination and to death and who, in order to become "sons of God," must "die to sin" and "anger" their "spirit of flesh" by putting it to death; see the midrash on the "two masters" in chapters 6f.

18 Isaac also corresponds, as it were, to the One God in 3.30, and Esau and Jacob to the Gentiles and Israel (3.29). "Esau" was used as a code-name for the Gentile nations from the Mishnaic period. Since he was characterized as a "sinner" and because Esau was associated with Edom (cf. Gen.25.30, 36.1), the name was adopted as a symbol in rabbinic literature first for Rome (cf. also the Idumean Herod's alliance with Rome) and then for Christianity when the Roman Empire was Christianized; cf. Tanh.B.Tol.14, TBE p.126, Eccles.R.11.1.1. This historical development lies behind the substitution of the term ארמי (*'Arami*), Aramean, in later censored editions of the Talmud; cf. Pes.87b, San.12a.

19 For the formula "what shall we say then . . .," which introduces an erroneous conclusion (here, that God is unjust), see the comments on 3.3; cf. also Mt.20.1-16.

20 The verse is obviously intended to be an answer to the objection, however, since Paul both explains and applies its meaning in verse 16.

21 The prooftexts in verses 12-13 (Gen.25.23, Mal.1.2) and verse 17 (Ex.9.16) function similarly to this prooftext.

22 The expression "to run" is also used in the context of false prophets (cf. Jer.23.21) who do not listen for God's word but "run with" their own words; in Qumran, "to run" designates the community's esoteric prophetic interpretation of Scripture (cf. Hab.2.2, 1QpHab 7.1-4).

23 Paul is aware that God's sovereignty may still be construed as arbitrary action, and counters the objection in the following verses. This verse also anticipates 11.7 and 22, and the issue of the hardening of Israel's heart towards Yeshua (God's severity), which leads to the "grafting in" of the Gentiles and Israel's final salvation (God's compassion). See also the comments on 2.4f, where Paul warns Israel against "taking lightly" their election in the sense of being sure of God's goodness towards them.

24 See verse 14, and the comments on 3.3.

25 God's arbitrary actions are the basis of the classic arguments concerning theodicy, or the "justification" of God. If God Himself hardens men's hearts, how then can He still hold them responsible for their evil actions? The question, "for who resists His will?" acts as a quasi-answer and is somewhat ambiguous. To resist God's will in this context could mean to deny that God has created man's evil inclination! Alternatively,

Paul may be noting God's *force majeur*, in the face of which who has the strength to "unharden" the heart which God has hardened? Paul addresses the issue of "double predestination"—of those who do not obey God at all—in the following verses.

26 Cf. Gen.R.34.10, Num.R.13.4, Suk.52b, Kid.30b. The midrash plays here between the meanings of יוצרינו (*yotzrenu*), "our potter" (the One who makes us), and יצרנו (*yitzrenu*), "our [evil] inclination; cf. R. Simon's similar play on the same words (יצר/יוצר; *yotzer/yetzer* [the Creator/the (evil) inclination]), in his midrash on Job 3.19 (cf. Ruth R.3.1); see the comments on chapter 6.2ff.

27 Consideration of the first point induces humility; of the second, avoidance of craving for worldly pleasures; and of the third, a fuller appreciation of God's majesty and power; cf. 11.33-36. Paul's argument here also indicates, however, that the contention over God's election of Israel contains within it God's purpose for the Gentiles as well; see verses 22f.

28 It should be clear, however, that Paul is speaking in these chapters of the collective election of Israel and not primarily of the personal salvation of the individual.

29 The phrase is a Hebraism (מה אם!), and is therefore not a true conditional sentence. It implies: "So what; what business is it of yours?"

30 The phrase "vessels of wrath" may reflect a play of words in Hebrew. The term כלי חרש (*klei cheres*) may be the "earthenware" jars created by God for "common use" (cf. 2 Cor.4.7). The word חרש (earthenware), however, is homophonically identical to חרס (*cheres*; a "devoted thing" [to the Lord]); (the letters *samekh* and *sin* are also often interchangeable in the Tanakh). The word חרס, because of its use for those things which are "banned," came to describe the destruction attendant upon the ban. Thus חרש/ס can linguistically represent "vessels for destruction"—which the biblical verses already hint at; cf. Isa.45.9, Jer.18.6, Lam.4.2.

31 The same idea is found in 1 Peter 2.8, a text which Flusser associates with a common tradition including Rom.9.24-10.3 and 1QS 8.4-10. See D. Flusser, "Romans 9.24-33," in *Judaism*, 75-87.

32 Cf. 1QS 3.13-4.26, 11.10, 17-22, 1QM 13.9-12. The idea is also implicit in 1QS 8.4-10, which Flusser identifies as the common source of Rom.9.24f and 1 Pet.2.3-9.

33 The purpose clause is very important, since Paul is not arguing (may it never be!) that God has rejected His people but that, as he demonstrates in the following chapters, Israel's "falling away" is only temporary and is destined to bring the Gentiles to God (whose own "election" will finally provoke Israel back to jealousy for their own God). In this respect,

Paul makes a very similar point to that of the parable of the laborers in the vineyard (Mt.20.1-16): they cannot complain about God's election also of the Gentiles although He had chosen Israel from the beginning. Moreover, they must recognize that God's patience in enduring their unfaithfulness forms part of His plan to bring all people into His kingdom.

34 This does not mean, of course, that God has rejected His people of Israel in favor of those Gentiles who have become faithful to him in Yeshua.

35 Paul distinguishes the prooftexts in verse 27, where he specifies that Isaiah "cries out concerning Israel."

36 " . . . it is not a community within the Jewish people to whom he [the author of 1 Peter] speaks but the gentile Church. The pagan past of its members becomes clear from 1 Pet.2.9b-10, and it is even very probable that once similar arguments were addressed to proselytes of Judaism." D. Flusser, *Romans*, 79.

37 The prooftexts function also as "proof" that God purposed in Scripture and made known through the "servants His prophets" His intention to save the whole world. As he continually demonstrates throughout chapters 9-11, Paul understands that universal redemption is based on God's covenant with a particular people, Israel.

38 Flusser notes that these prooftexts are not part of the tradition common to 1 Pet.2.3-9 and Rom.9.24-33, and argues that the homily in Romans 9.24-36 comes after another homiletic unit, namely Rom.9.14-23.

39 See D. Flusser, *Romans*, 85, 82.

40 The classic issue of theodicy is concerned with reconciling the presence of evil in the world with God's goodness. Here, however, it takes the form of reconciling God's choice of one nation to the exclusion of all others in the matter of human redemption.

41 For the technical use of the phrase "what shall we say then?" which counters an erroneous conclusion, see 3.3.

42 This is an unusual example of the talmudic formula (cf. 3.3), in that the anticipated negation ("May it never be!") does not appear immediately but only in 11.1 (cf. also verses 7 and 11); (cf. 3.9f and verse 19). This means that although Paul articulates the question in verses 30-31 his answer includes the extended passage from 9.32-10.21. This structure leads to a different interpretation than the majority view, which understands verse 31 as the answer to verse 30 rather than as part of the question itself.

43 See the comments on verses 27-29.

44 This may be understood both as an "outnumbering" of the Jewish believers by those among the Gentiles and in the later sense that the

"church" has *replaced* Israel as the "People of God." Paul's question has itself been interpreted to mean precisely that the Gentiles, who have attained to God's righteousness ("the righteousness which is by faith"), have replaced Israel, who did not obtain that righteousness ("law"), as God's people.

45 For the structure of verses 30-31, see the comments on verse 30.

46 Israel's downfall was their failure to achieve the τελος (*telos*; goal) of the Torah (cf. 10.4)—to accept Yeshua—rather than to stumble over the stumbling stone (cf. Ps.118.22, Isa.8.14, 28.1). This is further confirmed by verse 33; see below.

47 Paul is working with a homiletic collection of passages which speak of "stones." Flusser suggests that Paul's conflation of Isa.8.14 and 28.16 is influenced by the (Essene) source of 1 Peter, out of which he created a non-existent Scriptural quotation, and which he adapted to his own purpose of explaining Israel's rejection of Yeshua (ibid., 84). Flusser himself, however, is ambiguous about the reason for Israel's stumbling. Although he suggests that if Paul had intended to state that Israel in fact stumbled over Yeshua it would have been sufficient to refer to Isa.8.14, he also treats the conflated quotation (including Isa.28.16) as if it came only from Isa.8.14. We would want to support the view that Paul *does* in fact introduce at the end of the homily "the additional element that Israel did not attain righteousness, because they fell over the stone of stumbling and lacked faith in Christ." See D. Flusser, *Romans*, 84-85.

ROMANS

10

Introduction

Paul continues to address the issue of Israel's unrighteousness and their continued election. After repeating[1] his earnest desire for Israel's re demption (verses 1-3) he goes on to describe the relationship between righteousness gained through Torah-observance and righteousness based on Yeshua's faithfulness (verses 3-4). He does this by using a variant of a rabbinic principle called בנין אב משני כתובים or analogy based on two biblical verses (Lev.18.5 and Dt.30.11-14) which speak of differing grounds of "life." The combination of these two verses allows him to establish a new principle, that "faith (comes) from hearing, and hearing comes by the word of the Messiah," which he then backs up with a third verse (Isa.28.16) (verses 5-11). He interprets the "commandment" in Deuteronomy 30.11-14 which is "near you" in the light of a midrash on Job which connects this passage with a search for Moses following his "disappearance." He thus understands these verses as the search for Wisdom and thus for the goal of the Torah itself—Yeshua—through an identification of the Torah with Wisdom. He thus once again establishes that since the basis of God's righteousness is faithfulness, it is available to all men who call on God's name (verses 11-13). This once more leads him back to whether the Gentiles have been given the opportunity to be obedient (verses 14 and 16), and to the objection that Israel's rebellion has caused God to reject them (verses 15-16 and 19-21).

Verses 1-3:

"My heart's desire . . . knowledge": cf. Jer.23.6, Dan.9.13-19, Lk.16.15, 18.9, Acts 21.20, 22.3, Rom.1.17, 2.1-10, 17-20, 3.21, 9.1-4, 1 Cor.1.30, Gal.1.14, Eph.1.17, 3.16-17, 4.13, Col.1.9-11; 1QS 1.1-10, 9.12-16, 21-26, 10.20-25, 1QH 1.21f, 12.11-14, 13.18-20; PA 1.17, 2.2, 3.9, 17, 5.14, 6.1, 5, San.99b.

Paul argues in chapter 9 that God's sovereignty is completely justifiable. This is true even and especially regarding Israel's election. He takes the bold interpretive step of claiming that God can endure the people of Israel as "vessels of wrath" in order that He might make known the riches of His glory upon the "vessels of mercy."[2] These he immediately identifies as being both Jews and Gentiles. He then needs to explain how Israel are "vessels of wrath" when in all other respects they are and always have been God's chosen people. He quotes two passages from Isaiah. Although the first determines that God has always kept a remnant for Himself among the people (9.27), the second demonstrates that the majority of the people have in fact consistently disobeyed His Torah. Paul then addresses the paradox which this situation creates: the fact that God has indeed "endured" the disobedience of His people in order to show mercy to those who were once "not-My-people"—the Gentiles; and the ways in which God has brought about this situation. He thus raises an answer which his readers might be anticipated to bring but which he proceeds to reject: that the Gentiles received God's righteousness through Yeshua's faithfulness but that Israel did not receive either Yeshua or his righteousness and were consequently rejected by God.

As in 9.1-4, Paul again pours out his heartfelt desire for Israel's salvation. He himself is a witness that God has not rejected them, since he knows that they are zealous for the Torah (cf. 2.17-20).[3] He also knows, however, that they have been disobedient, as the prophets constantly lamented, and have missed the τελος (*telos*) of the Torah. Not only were they rebellious, however; they were also ignorant of the fact that God's plan included "shutting them up in disobedience" in order that He might have mercy on *all* people, both Jews and Gentiles (cf. 11.30-32). They disregarded the witness of the Torah to God's righteousness "apart from the Torah" (3.21) in Yeshua, which is available to all mankind.[4] Their failure to "arrive" at God's righteousness came from a lack of "knowledge" that this was the goal (τελος) of the Torah (cf. verse 4). Due to this ignorance they sought a righteousness which, as the Teacher of Righteousness interpreted to his community, was not to be found only through their observance of the Torah but specifically through their faithfulness to God's chosen figure, a righteousness which would also encompass the Gentiles:

> . . . Thou hast made me a banner for the elect of righteousness and an interpreter of knowledge concerning the marvellous Mysteries, to test [the men] of truth and to try them that love instruction. . . . {F} or at the time of Judgment Thou wilt declare all of them guilty that attack me, distinguishing through me between the just and the guilty. . . . And Thou knowest the inclination of Thy servant, that right[eousness] is not [of man]. [But] I have l[e]aned [upon Thee]

that Thou should lift up [my] hea[rt] [and] give (me) strength and vigour. And I have no fleshly refuge; [and man has no righteousness o]r virtue to be delivered from si[n] [and wi]n forgiveness. But I, I have leaned on Thy abun[dant mercy] [and on the greatness of] Thy grace. . . . And [Thou hast] created [me] for Thy sake to [ful]fil the Law, and [to te]a[ch by] my mouth the men of Thy council in the midst of the sons of men, that Thy marvels may be told to everlasting generations and [Thy] mighty deeds be [contemp]lated without end. And all the nations shall know Thy truth and all the peoples, Thy glory. For Thou hast caused [them] to enter Thy [glo]rious [Covenant] with all the men of Thy council and into a common lot with the Angels of the Face; . . . [. . .] and they shall be converted by Thy glorious mouth and shall be Thy princes in the lo[t of light]. . . . (1QH 2.13-14, 7.12, 16-18, 6.10-14)[5]

Verse 4:
"Messiah is the end of the law . . . ": cf. Jn.1.17, Rom.3.22, 9.31, Gal.3.24.

The Greek noun τελος (*telos*; "end") refers to the "aim" or "goal" of a purpose as well as to its "termination."[6] Paul states in 3.21 that the Torah "witnesses" to the righteousness of God. This "witness" is the "goal" of the Torah; i.e., God's gift of righteousness in the Messiah not only to the people of Israel but also to the Gentiles. Verse 4 therefore sums up Paul's argument from 9.19ff, in which he argues that although Israel have been disobedient they have also transgressed God's word by not accepting His declaration in the Torah and the prophets that He would also make the Gentiles part of His people, and through them provoke His own people back to Him through jealousy. Israel have "stumbled" over this goal, because they have not believed in the "stone of stumbling" and not accepted God's righteousness in Yeshua.[7]

Verses 5-13:
"For Moses writes . . . ": cf. Lev.18.5, Dt.30.11-14, Neh.9.29, Isa.28.16, Ezek.20.11, 13, 20, Hab.2.4, Rom.2.13, 9.30; Test.Jud.24.6, Ap.Bar.3.29, 4 Ez.4.7ff, 1 En.48.1-7, Sir.24.3-9, 23, 4 Macc.1.17, 7.21-23, 8.7; Sifre Dt.305.

To prove his point that faithfulness to God in Yeshua is the goal of the Torah Paul uses a familiar rabbinic exegetical technique. He cites two biblical verses (Lev.18.5 and Dt.30.11-14) which attribute different grounds to the finding of "life" to establish a new principle—that eternal life is found through faithfulness to Yeshua's death and resurrection and is therefore open to all who call on the name of the Lord (cf. Isa.28.16, Joel 2.32).[8] Leviticus 18.5 suggests that life is gained through observing all the commandments, while Deuteronomy 30.11-14 says that "life" is gained through faithfulness (an attitude of heart which motivates one's deeds) rather than by an external act. This tension is also reflected in other rabbinic sources. Although the majority Jewish view emphasized the life-giving nature of the Torah (cf. 7.10), some of the Sages openly lamented the fact they were unable to perform the commandments of the Torah so as to obtain the promise of life in the world to come. In a passage in which several of the Rabbis discuss the "essence" or "guiding principle" (כלל גדול; *kelal gadol*) of the Torah, R. Gamaliel laments his inability to "stand firm" and be made completely righteous:

> [THEREFORE GAVE HE THEM TORAH (TEACHINGS) AND MANY COMMANDMENTS . . .]. R. Simlai when preaching said: Six hundred and thirteen precepts were communicated to Moses . . . David came and reduced them to eleven [principles], as it is written, *A Psalm of David. Lord who shall sojourn in Thy tabernacle? . . . He that doeth these things shall never be moved* (Ps.15.1-5). Whenever R. Gamaliel came to this passage he used to weep, saying [Only] one who practised all these shall be moved; but anyone falling short in any of these [virtues] would be moved! (Mak.24a)[9]

The passage in Makkot is well-known, since it culminates with R. Nahman b. Isaac's statement, that " . . . it is Habakkuk who came and based them all on one [principle], as it said, *But the righteous shall live by his faith*" (Hab.2.4; see below).[10] Paul reaches the same conclusion (cf. he makes this his key verse in 1.16-17), that the essence of the Torah is summed up in the "righteousness of faithfulness." He knows that Yeshua's faithfulness to God makes God's righteousness available to all those who have faith (i.e., trust) in Yeshua. Paul recognizes that the Torah specifies (Lev.18.5) that righteousness is based on observance ("the man who *practices* the righteousness which is based on law"). However, in Deuteronomy 30.11-14, the Torah gives an alternative ground, referring to God's word being "in your heart." Paul's terminology ("but the righteousness based on faith") naturally reflects the verse in Habakkuk (cf. 1.17), but he is aware that the context of the passage in Deuteronomy itself also emphasizes the element of faithfulness. Moses profoundly focuses on the need for love towards God as the source of obedience (cf. Dt.6.4ff). The "words" (דברים; *devarim*) which God commanded Israel to be "on your heart" (Dt.6.6) are the words that proceed out of the mouth of the Lord by which man lives (Dt.8.3). Paul associates these texts with the **Λογος** (*Logos*), the Messiah who is God's son (cf. Jn.1.1, Heb.1.2, 1 Jn.1.1). This interpretation is strengthened by an extant midrashic tradition concerning Moses' death.[11] The biblical text records that Moses died but makes no mention of the place of his burial (cf. Dt.34.6). This textual enigma forms the basis for a midrashic tradition about Moses' "disappearance."[12] Although Moses is buried, it is suggested that he did not really die, and the midrash expands on the search thus made for him by the angel of death. (If the angel of death cannot find him, then surely he cannot be dead.) The midrashic author further associates Moses, the author of the Torah, with Wisdom, according to a current Jewish tradition (cf. Sir.24.23). He moves quite naturally from passages directly connected to events in Moses' life to a series of verses from Job 28 in which Wisdom is personified:

> The angel of death began again seeking the soul of Moses; he said: I know that God said to him: "Come up to me on the mountain . . . (Ex.24.12)." He went to Mount Sinai and said: Is the soul of Moses perhaps here? The mountain said to him: He captured from me Torah, which refreshes the soul, as Scripture says: "The law of the Lord is perfect, reviving the soul . . . (Ps.19.8)." He said: I know that the Holy One, blessed be He, said to him: "Lift up your rod, and stretch out your hand over the sea and divide it . . . (Ex.14.16)." He went to the sea and said: Is the soul of Moses perhaps here[?] It said to him: No, because Scripture says: "He divided the sea and let them pass through it . . . (Ps.78.13)." He said: I know that he is standing and beseeching to enter the land of Israel, because Scripture says: "And I besought the Lord . . . (Dt.3.23)." "Let me go over, I pray, and see the good land beyond the Jordan, that goodly hill country, and the Lebanon (Dt.3.25)." . . . The angel of death went to the land of Israel and said to it: Is the soul of Moses perhaps here? It answered him: No, because Scripture says: "It is not found in the land of the living (Job 28.13)." He went to the clouds of glory and said to them: Is the soul of Moses perhaps here? They answered him: "It is hid from the eyes of all living . . . (Job 28.21)." He went to the ministering angels. They said to him: No, because Scripture says: "It is concealed from the birds of the air (Job 28.21)." He went to the deep. It said to him: No, because Scripture says: "The deep says, 'It is not in me . . . ' (Job 28.14)." He went to Sheol and Abaddon and said to them: Is the soul of Moses perhaps here? They said to him: No. Abba used to interpret in the name of Rabbi Simeon ben Jose and say: "Abaddon and Death say, 'We have heard a rumor of it with our ears' (Job 28.22)." With our ears we heard, but we did not see. (ARN[b] 25)[13]

This "Job midrash" interprets the quest for the commandment—which is left unspecified in Deuteronomy 30.11-14—in terms of wisdom (although Moses' "disappearance" and the angel of death's search for him hint at his resurrection).[14] The search for wisdom and the Torah, according to Paul, is to be found specifically in Yeshua, who is the "goal" of the Torah, the Word of God himself, and "the Lord our righteousness" (Jer.23.6). Paul thus reaches the same conclusion as R. Nachman in the Rabbis' discussion of the essence and goal of the Torah, although the Sages did not recognize Yeshua as the τελος (*telos*) of the Torah:

> Again came Isaiah and reduced them to two [principles], as it is said, *Thus saith the Lord,* [*i*] *Keep ye justice and* [*ii*] *do righteousness* [etc.] (Isa.56.1). Amos came and reduced them to one [principle], as it is said, *For thus saith the Lord unto the house of Israel, Seek Me and live* (Amos 5.4). To this R. Nahman b. Isaac demurred, saying: [Might it not be taken as,] Seek Me by observing the whole Torah and live?—But it is Habakkuk who came and based them all on one [principle], as it is said, *But the righteous shall live by his faith* (Hab.2.4) (Mak.24a)[15]

Verses 9-10:

"If you confess . . . salvation": cf. Ex.14.31, Lev.5.5, 16.21, 26.40, Num.5.7, 1 Kings 8.33, 2 Chron.6.24, Neh.1.6, Ps.32.5, Mt.10.32, Mk.16.16, Lk.12.8, Jn.3.18, 9.22, Acts 2.24, 32, 16.31, Rom.3.21f, 4.24, 6.4, 7.4, 8.11, 14.9, 11, 15.9, 1 Cor.12.3, 15.21ff, 2 Cor.4.14, Gal.1.1, 2.15-21, Eph.1.20, Phil.2.11, Col.2.12, 1 Thess.1.10, Heb.13.20, 1 Pet.1.21, 1 Jn.1.9, 4.15, Rev.3.5; 1QH 2.8-14, 7.12, 1QpHab 8.1-3; Mekh.Beshall.7, Tanh.Beshall.10, Mid.Ps.27.1-3, Sifra 86b, BK 38a, AZ 3a, San.43b, 59a, Ta'anit 16a, Mak.34a.

Paul begins to draw out his conclusion or new principle, aided by the midrashic interpretation of Deuteronomy 30.11-14. The "commandment" refers to faithfulness to Yeshua's resurrection, since faithfulness to the "word" (commandment) or λογος (*logos*) "in your mouth" (בפיך; *be-fikha*) is a verbal expression of repentance. The man who "angers" his evil inclination by refusing to do its bidding (cf. chapter 6), repents of the desires of his flesh (cf. chapter 7) and acknowledges allegiance to God as his master. R. Joshua ben Levi speaks of salvation in the same way, equating eternal life with the "sacrifice of confession" taken from the cultus (cf. Lev.5.5, 16.21, Num.5.6-7):

> R. Joshua b. Levi said: He who sacrifices his [evil] inclination and confesses [his sin] over it, Scripture imputes it to him as though he had honoured the Holy One, blessed be He, in both worlds, this world and the next; for it is written, *Whoso offereth the sacrifice of confession honoureth me* (Ps.50.23) (San.43b)[16]

Jewish tradition understood the verse, "So it shall be when he becomes guilty in one of these [sins], that he shall confess that in which he sinned" (Lev.5.5) to mean that those required to bring sin- or guilt-offerings are not forgiven through these offerings for sins committed either intentionally or unintentionally unless they make verbal repentance and confession.[17] Confession acknowledges God's sovereignty and righteousness in the face of man's sin, which is part of the reason why it is included in the ceremony of sacrifice.[18] Paul directly connects verbal confession and repentance with Yeshua's resurrection, which parallels Moses' "disappearance" according to the midrashic interpretation of Deuteronomy 30.11-14. Yeshua is the "word" whom God has brought back to life and who is therefore in the land of the living, close to man, who therefore does not need to search him out. At the same time man's repentance demonstrates his willingness to "anger" his evil inclination and to make God his master. In his baptism into Yeshua's death and resurrection (cf. chapter 6) he makes all his members slaves to righteousness, circumcises his heart, and inherits eternal life, an attitude characteristic of the community at Qumran:

> And this is the rule for the members of the Community, for those who volunteer to be converted from all evil and to cling to all His commands according to His will . . . They shall practice truth in common, and humility, and righteousness and justice and loving charity, and modesty in all their ways. Let no man walk in the stubbornness of his heart to stray by following his heart and eyes and the thoughts of his (evil) inclination. But in the Community they shall circumcise the foreskin of the (evil) inclination and disobedience in order to lay a foundation of truth for Israel, for the Community of the everlasting Covenant . . . . (1QS 5.1, 3-6)

Verse 11:
"For the Scripture says . . . ": cf. Isa.28.16, Rom.9.33.

Paul brings the third verse which supports his new principle of faithfulness to Yeshua as the grounds of inheriting "life" (between what a man practices—his deeds and his inner motivation—in his heart). Not only does the verse from Isaiah 28.16 speak of faithfulness as the means of salvation; it also states that this salvation is available to "whoever believes." It therefore strengthens Paul's view that Yeshua is the goal of the Torah because in him both Jews and Gentiles receive God's righteousness. The "word of faith" is first of all God's word of promise to Abraham whose "goal" (τελος; *telos*) is fulfilled in Yeshua's resurrection ("re-creation").[19] Yeshua's resurrection, as the "first-born from the dead" (cf. 1 Cor.15.20, 23) makes him the "creator" of the "sons of God" (the "sons of Abraham"), both Israel and the Gentiles who were once "not-My-people." God's raising Yeshua from the dead "calls into being" His "new creation" since faithfulness to Yeshua, "the Lord our righteousness," is both the goal of the Torah and the gift of righteousness to the Gentiles. Paul uses Joel 2.32 (3.5) as a supporting verse for Isaiah 28.16, which also draws out the universalist implications of Leviticus 18.5 and Isaiah 28.16: the man (= "whoever") who observes the "commandment" is the person who demonstrates his faithfulness to the God who raised His Messiah, Yeshua, from the dead and who, in his baptism into Yeshua's death and resurrection, presents his members to God as servants of righteousness (cf. chapter 6). As Paul states in 2.12-16 and 26-29, both Jews and Gentiles can be pleasing to God by circumcising their hearts:

> What was the special character of Deborah that she, too, judged Israel and prophesied concerning them? In regard to her deeds, I call heaven and earth to witness that whether it be a heathen or a Jew, whether it be a man or a woman, a manservant or a maidservant, the holy spirit will suffuse each of them in keeping with the deeds he or she performs." (TBE p.48)[20]

Verses 12-13:

"For there is no distinction . . . ": cf. Lev.19.15f, Dt.10.17, 2 Chron.19.7, Job 34.19, Ps.36.6, 145.9, Isa.19.19-25, 26.2, Mal.2.9, Acts 10.34-36, Rom.3.22, 29, Gal.2.6, 3.28, Eph.2.11-22, Col.3.11, 25, 1 Pet.1.17; Ps.Sol.5.15, Wis.Sol.6.7, 1 En.63.8, Test.Jud.24.6; TBE p.8, p.48, p.65, DER 3.1, Tanh.B.Vayetzei 16, Sifra Achare Mot 86b, Mekh.Bechodesh 1, Amalek 3, Pes.Rab.48.4, Yalkut 76, 429, AZ 2b, San.59a, BK 38a, 50b.

Paul draws out the point of Yeshua's righteousness as the goal of the Torah, namely that it brings the Gentiles into His salvation. He thus returns to the theme of 2.11-16, 25-29, and 3.21-31, where he addresses the issue of the equality of those who are faithful to God through Yeshua (cf. chapter 4). The "abundance of (God's) riches" extends God's grace towards *all* men. His election ("calling into being") of men is universal and is not exclusive to Israel.

Verses 14-15:
"Call upon him in whom they have not believed?": cf. Isa.28.16; Test.Jud.24.1-6, Test.Dan 5.10-11.

Paul returns to the objection that Israel cannot be saved (although they may call on the Lord's name) because in the main they have rejected His Messiah. If Israel have not "believed" in Yeshua but have stumbled over the stone, how will they be saved?[21] None of the common explanations of the following section are quite satisfactory; it is a far more complex passage than is generally perceived. Two main possibilities exist: a) that the whole section (14-21) refers to Israel; and b) that Paul refers now to the Gentile nations.[22]

Verse 14:
"And how . . . without a preacher?": cf. Ps.95.7, Isa.2.2-4, 9.1-7, 11.10, 42.6-7, 51.4-5, 57.19, Acts 15.7, Rom.2.13-16, Eph.2.17.

On the other hand, how can the Gentiles who walk in darkness, without hope and God in the world (cf. Isa.9.1-2, Eph.2.12, 1 Pet.2.9), "believe" without a "witness" to enlighten them (cf. Isa.43.10, 52.7)? The Gentiles have not "heard" God's "good news" because Israel have not lifted up God's name and the name of His Messiah and have not understood that God's plan, which He announced to His prophets, was also to include the Gentiles.[23] God's Messiah preaches and brings peace "to him who is far [the Gentile nations] and to him who is near [Israel]" (cf. Isa.57.19, Eph.2.17, Test.Naph.4.5), as a passage from the apocryphal book of the Testament of the Twelve Patriarchs clearly describes:

> "And after this there shall arise for you a Star from Jacob in peace: And a man shall arise from my posterity like the Sun of righteousness, walking with the sons of men in gentleness and righteousness, and in him will be found no sin. And the heavens will be opened to him to pour out the spirit as a blessing of the Holy Father. And he will pour the spirit of grace on you. And you shall be sons in truth, and you will walk in his first and final decrees. This is the Shoot of God Most High; this is the fountain for the life of all humanity. Then he will illumine the scepter of my kingdom, and from your root will arise the Shoot, and through it will arise the rod of righteousness for the nations, to judge and to save all that call on the Lord." (Test.Jud.24.1-6)[24]

Verse 15:
"How shall they preach . . . ": cf. Isa.43.10, 12, 44.8, 55.4, 57.19, 61.1, Nah.1.15, Mt.10.18, Mk.16.15, Acts 1.8, 22, 2.32, 13.31, 22.15.

This verse gives the strongest grounds for the "apostolic commission" of the church. Paul chooses to use neither the masoretic nor the LXX text of Isaiah 52.7 (cf. Nah.1.15), both of which speak of the bringer of good tidings in the singular. Paul's change to the plural therefore cannot be accidental. Neither can he refer to the "kerygma" or preaching of the church, however, since he is clearly giving a historical review. He thus seems to be referring to Israel's biblical task of being God's witnesses to the nations of the world.[25]

Verse 16:

"They did not all heed . . . report": cf. Isa.53.1, Jn.12.38.

Paul once again claims that Israel did not understand that the goal of the Torah is to bring Yeshua's righteousness to all mankind. The quotation from Isaiah 53.1 directly relates to Yeshua whom, despite being God's people, Israel did not recognize as His Messiah. His word (λογος; *logos*), which Paul interprets from the "commandment" in Deuteronomy 30.11-14, must be "heard" by Israel and obeyed by proclaiming it to the Gentiles. Yeshua's "commandment" (word) brings righteousness to all those who are faithful to God in him:

> "I say these things, my children, because I have read in the writing of the holy Enoch that you also will stray from the Lord, living in accord with every wickedness of the gentiles and committing every lawlessness of Sodom. The Lord will impose captivity upon you; you shall serve your enemies there and you will be engulfed in hardship and difficulty until the Lord will wear you all out. And after you have been decimated and reduced in number, you will return and acknowledge the Lord your God. And it shall happen that when they come into the land of their fathers, they will again neglect the Lord and act impiously, and the Lord will disperse them over the face of the whole earth until the mercy of the Lord comes, a man who effects righteousness, and he will work mercy on all who are far and near." (Test.Naph.4.1-5)

Verse 17:

"So faith . . . the word of the Messiah": cf. Gen.1.1-2, Ex.24.7, Dt.5.27, 6.4, 8.3, 18.18, 30.10, Isa.52.6-10, 61.1-3, Mk.12.28-34, Jn.1.1, 14, 3.18, 5.24, 38, 6.26-58, 63, 68-69, 8.31-32, 43, 51, 10.27-28, 12.44-50, 17.8, Eph.2.17, Heb.1.1-2, 3.14-15, 4.2-3, 1 Jn.1.1-3, Rev.19.13; 1QH 2.13-15, 6.10-19, 7.10-25, 8.16ff; Tar.Ps-Jon. to Dt.30.8, Tar.Jon. to Isa.9.6, 42.1 and Hab.3.1.

Paul summarizes his argument from verses 5-15, namely the meaning of the biblical passages from Deuteronomy 30.11-14, Isaiah 28.16, and Joel 2.32. He explains how Yeshua is first of all the Word in which all the commandments are summed up, who preaches the "good tidings" of salvation to the whole world, who carries God's name, image, and character, and whom God raised from the dead in order to bring righteousness to all mankind through his faithfulness in obedience to God. "Hearing" becomes synonymous with "obedience" and no longer a contrast to "doing" (cf. 2.13). It is the observance ("doing") of God's word in faithfulness to Yeshua's death and resurrection.[26] The λογος (*telos*) of the Torah is Yeshua himself, the light through which man inherits eternal life:

> Open your ears, and I shall speak to you. Give me yourself, so that I may also give you myself; the word of the Lord and his desires, the holy thought which he has thought concerning his Messiah. For the will of the Lord is your life, and his purpose is eternal life, and your perfection is incorruptible. Be enriched in God the Father; and receive the purpose of the Most High. Be strong and saved by his grace. For I announce peace to you, his holy ones, so that none of those who hear will fall in the war. And also that those who have known him may not perish, and so that those who receive (him) may not be ashamed. . . . We live in the Lord by his grace, and life we receive by his Messiah. . . . And his Word is with us in all our way, the Savior who gives life and does not reject ourselves. The man who humbled himself, but was raised because of his own righteousness. The Son of the Most High appeared in the perfection of his Father. And light dawned from the Word that was before time in him. The Messiah in truth is one. And he was known before the foundations of the world, that he might give life to persons forever by the truth of his name. (Ps.Sol.9.1-7, 41.3, 11-15)

Verse 18:

"But I say . . . ": Paul again returns to the anticipated objection to his claim that righteousness is based on Yeshua's faithfulness. The subject of this verse is difficult to establish. If Paul intends to argue that the Gentiles have not been faithful, as suggested by the quotation from Psalm 19.4, he runs the risk of negating his argument that Yeshua's resurrection has included them in God's kingdom as well. If, however, he is claiming that Israel have not heard, he is using Psalm 19 to prove that Israel must have heard because the proclamation has reached the "ends of the world," and to re-emphasize Israel's ignorance which he recalls in the following verse where he specifies them by name. The quotation itself is of no direct assistance since it speaks of a nonverbal declaration of God's mighty works through nature. The solution therefore again seems to be that Paul is referring to Israel's failure to understand and fulfil their task as God's witnesses to the nations.[27]

Verses 19-21:

"But I say . . . ": cf. Dt.32.21, Isa.55.4, Hos.1.10, 2.23, Rom.11.11, 14.

Paul returns yet again to the possibility that Israel did not know what was the τελος (*telos*) or goal of the Torah.[28] In place of the normal refutation of the erroneous conclusion ("may it never be!"), he brings a quotation from Deuteronomy 32.21 which specifically states that God will make Israel jealous by the worship of the Gentile nations.[29] He strengthens this claim with a quotation from Isaiah 65.1. On the one hand, therefore, he demonstrates that Israel did not recognize God's plan to "create" the Gentiles (once "not-My-people") by including them as part of the "commonwealth of Israel" (Eph.2.19). Paul understands Israel's "knowledge" in the light of what he says in 10.4, that God's righteousness is a gift in Yeshua to both Jews and Gentiles because it is based on faithfulness. God's purpose (τελος; *telos*) or goal, to which the Torah witnesses from the beginning (cf. 3.21), is to make also the Gentiles righteous. On the other hand, however, part of this plan also includes the fact that the people of Israel have proved themselves disobedient to God. It is (partially) through this disobedience, which contains the element of not knowing or understanding the goal of the Torah, that opens the way for the Gentiles to be included in God's kingdom. Finally, the Gentile believers will then "provoke Israel to jealousy" for their own God. God has revealed in Scripture, through Moses and His prophets, that He would "call into being" a people who did not know Him, whom He had not chosen, nor with whom had He entered into a covenant relationship. His righteousness is not confined to Israel, His chosen people, nor to the revelation of His will in the Torah. Because it was also His will that the Gentiles receive His righteousness through faithfulness in Yeshua, He chose Israel to be His own people in order to include the Gentile nations as well, through Israel's temporary hardness of heart and their (partial) rejection of God's Messiah (cf. Isa.65.1-2). This hardness, however, is proof of Israel's election, not proof of their rejection by God. Israel will finally prove their election by being provoked to jealousy by those who formerly were not part of God's people but have now been "grafted in" to the commonwealth of Israel. This is the argument which Paul raises as the proper answer to the erroneous conclusion that God has in fact rejected Israel as His chosen people and replaced them with the Gentiles (or the "Church").

Endnotes for Chapter 10

1 See Romans 9.1-4.

2 This argument is based on prophetic passages in the Tanakh, and is also substantiated by Paul's remarks in 11.30-36, which parallel 9.18ff.

3 Paul's language here also closely resembles 2.4-10, where he establishes that the "true" "sons of Abraham" are those who possess his qualities and are his disciples; as well as 4.1ff where he develops the relationship between "wages" and "reckoning."

4 See the comments on 3.21f.

5 Cf. 1QH 2.8-9, 1QpHab 8.2-3. The psalmist, whom most commentators identify here with the Teacher of Righteousness, refers here to Isa.11.10, a messianic passage in which the shoot of the root of Jesse—the Messiah—serves as a rallying sign for the elect. The Teacher interprets this text as relating to a messianic figure (himself) whose teaching constitutes a decisive test whereby those who believe in him will be saved and those who do not will be judged. It is obvious that faithfulness to him is also dependent upon the special measure of righteousness which God has bestowed upon him, as in the similar messianic passage from Jer.23.6-7 where the Messiah is called "the Lord our righteousness." It is difficult to know on the basis of this one passage precisely how the community at Qumran regarded the position of the Gentiles. Paul certainly makes their inclusion in the election of God far more central than the extant texts would indicate.

6 See TDNT 8:49-57.

7 Israel have also been "disappointed" (καταισχυνθησεται, *kataischunthesetai*; יחיש, *yachish*) in that they have not "arrived at" the purpose of the Torah (cf. Isa.28.16).

8 This argument is a variation of the hermeneutic principle known as בנין אב משני כתובים (*binyan 'av mi-shnei ketuvim*): "This type of בנין אב is used when . . . two cases being compared are not fully analogous, and so an objection is raised to the comparison. In such instances, the Talmud cites an additional case (C), which, together with the first case (A), may serve as the basis of viable comparison. . . . Then case C is introduced, and hence we may infer that just as law X applies in cases A and C, so too it should apply in case B, which is similar to both A and C." A. Steinsaltz, *Talmud*, 149-150. Paul's two cases of "life" are not strictly comparable, since one is based on observance, the other on faithfulness. From the verses in Isa.28.16 and Joel 2.32, however, he establishes the principle that life is found through faithfulness to Yeshua

as the Word of God; cf. the same principle in Gal.3.10-14. (Paul takes up Isa.28.16 from 9.33.)

9 Cf. Hag.4b, as well as many the other texts which speak of the "essence" of the Torah: Mt.7.12, 22.36-40, Rom.13.9, Shab.31a, Sifre Ked.4.12, ARN[b] 26. The eleven "principles" to which David reduced the Torah are taken from the verses of Psalm 15: a) he who walks with integrity; b) and works righteousness; c) and speaks truth in his heart; d) does not slander with his tongue; e) nor does evil to his neighbor; f) nor takes up a reproach against his friend; g) in whose eyes a reprobate is despised [but]; h) but who honors those who fear the Lord; i) he swears to his own hurt, and does not change; j) he does not put out his money at interest; k) nor does he take a bribe against the innocent. He who does these things shall never be shaken. It is clear that R. Gamaliel understands being "moved" as referring to redemption and the inheritance of eternal life. (It is possible, though unlikely, that this R. Gamaliel was the Elder [10-80 CE], the grandson of Hillel, who was Paul's teacher; cf. Acts 22.3. Although this passage is from the Gemara, and thus mostly records Amoraic statements, there is no way of knowing whether the reference to R. Gamaliel is contemporary with the other figures mentioned, or relates to a tradition preserved concerning R. Gamaliel the Elder).

10 Cf. also the same usage in the Talmud of referring to the biblical writings by the name of the author attributed to the passage as Paul adopts here ("For Moses writes . . . ").

11 See D. Flusser, *Yehadut umekorot vaNotzrut* [Jewish Sources in Early Christianity] (Jsm: Sifriat Poalim, 1979), 308-11. Flusser appeals to a midrash on Job 28 in order to explain Paul's argument, and apparently assumes that the midrash is applicable to Dt.30.11-14, which is not used as a prooftext in the Job midrash. The same motifs of height and depth are common to both the midrash and Dt.30.11-14, however. It is also possible that Paul is using the midrash polemically, against the view that Torah-observance is designed as the means whereby the people of Israel inherit eternal life in the world to come. By focusing on Moses' disappearance, the midrash de-emphasizes the centrality of Torah-observance in favor of something more ephemeral or mysterious, which Paul identifies with the "mystery of the Messiah" (cf. Rom.16.25-26, Eph.3.4f, Col.1.27).

12 See J. Tabor, *Returning*.

13 Cf. Mid.Tannaim, pp.224-25, ARN[a] 12, Shab.89a. This passage relates to the time after God has taken Moses' soul. The point of the midrash is thus that Moses is not in Sheol, and even the Angel of Death has only

heard a rumor of his death. Flusser notes that the replacement of Moses by the search for the Torah in Shab.89a is a later alteration of the original midrash on Job 28 (ibid., 309). The replacement of "abyss" for "sea" in the Masoretic (Hebrew) text is already reflected in Ps.106.26, but Paul also follows the ordering (heaven, *sheol*) of the midrash on Job (which itself alters the original sequence of verses in Job 28), as well as interpolating the references to Yeshua (verses 6 and 7). For the explanation of the various prooftexts cited in the midrash (which in this version are mainly taken from Job), see A. Saldarini, *The Fathers According to Rabbi Nathan* (Leiden: Brill, 1974), 151-52; and for the identification of Torah and Wisdom, see the references and comments on 1.16-17.

14 Like Dt.30.11-14, the *midrash* on Job does not refer to a specific commandment. Paul, however, directly associates it with "faithfulness." For further links between the *Logos* and faithfulness based on Moses' example, see Jn.5.46-47, Mekh.Beshall.7 (on Ex.14.31).

15 R. Nahman argues against taking the verse from Amos 5.4 as the essence of the Torah because he understands that it might be interpreted to mean that by observing all the commandments a man inherits the world to come (eternal life). Both R. Gamaliel (cf. San.43b; see above) and Paul adopt the same view. Paul makes the same argument in relation to Lev.18.5 ("So shall you keep My statutes and My judgments, by which a man may live if he does them . . . "), and resolves the contradiction between that verse and Dt.30.14 (which indicates an inner attitude rather than an external act) by appealing in 1.16-17, like R. Nahman, to Hab.2.4, "But the righteous will live by his faith," and here to Isa.28.16. Inheriting "life" is therefore based not only on the righteousness of observing the commandments but on faithfulness.

16 When a man is induced to sin, he may resist and conquer his inclination and acknowledge the temptation it posed to him before God. R. Joshua interprets the phrase זבח תודה (*zevach todah*) in Ps.50.23 ("He who offers a sacrifice of thanksgiving honors me") in the second sense of the verb ידה (*yadah*), "to confess;" cf. 1 Kings 8.33-35, 2 Chron.6.24-27, Ps.32.5, Prov.28.13.

17 See Yad, Hil.Teshuva 1.1, 2.2; cf. Hil.Edut 12.4-10.The *halakhah* in fact posits two separate principles with reference to repentance: verbal repentance may a) serve to divest the sinner of his status as a wicked man (רשע; *rasha'*) ; and b) serve as a means of atonement like the other means of atonement—sacrifices, the Day of Atonement, afflictions, death, and such. The lack of verbal repentance, therefore, does not prevent repentance from divesting a sinner of his status as a sinner, which is inde-

pendent of receiving atonement. "Repentance per se does not require verbal confession. Only the second aspect of repentance, which has as its aim the obtaining of atonement, requires verbal confession, for, as the Talmud states, 'And he shall make atonement for himself, and for his house' (Lev. 16:6): the Torah speaks of atonement through words' [Yoma 36b]." J.B. Soloveitchik, *Halakhic Man* (NY: Jewish Publication Society, 1983), 110-12. Paul's view is that repentance and atonement are not two separate principles but one and the same, which he emphasizes by combining verbal confession with belief from the heart. According to the *halakhah*, this is the element of repentance which obtains atonement.

18 The idea of "confessing God's name" is a further expression of repentance in the Tanakh; cf. Josh.7.19, 1 Kings 8.33-35, 2 Chron.6.24-26.

19 See the comments on 4.17f.

20 See the comments on 2.12-16 and 25-29.

21 Paul interprets Joel 2.32 here in terms of the "salvation" of Isa.28.16: how can those who stumble over the stone be "saved"?

22 The textual difficulty stems from Paul's neglect in specifying the subject of most of the sentences in this passage, using the vague third person plural without a referent, save in verse 19. The thesis (cf. Käsemann) that the subject is "naturally" the apostolic commission cannot be justified except as an unwarranted interpolation into a biblical context. The other two possibilities both possess textual difficulties. The claim that the section refers to Israel's guilt does not satisfactorily explain their being called to preach (presumably to the Gentile nations) (verse 15); the quotation in verse 18 implies a Gentile audience; and Paul's specific reference to Israel in verse 19 suggests that previously he has been referring to someone else. The other possibility suffers from a rapid succession of subject changes—from Israel to the Gentiles and back—within a single sentence. It seems, however, to carry stronger weight for several reasons: it resolves the difficulties of the first thesis and it also addresses the issue of universal salvation which is Paul's main point in the preceding section. The subject of "How shall they hear . . ." can thus, for example, be the Gentiles, while the sentence, "And how shall they preach . . ." may refer back to Israel, making a chiastic pattern, A B B A, characteristic of biblical poetry.

23 Cf. Isa56.6-7, 60.1-3, 66.19-23.

24 The affinities of this verse with Acts 10.34-36 suggest that Paul is referring to an early tradition which associated Yeshua's lordship with the unity of those who are faithful to him among both Jews and Gentiles. The tradition is clearly reflected in Eph.2.11-22, which relates to

Rom.4.13-25 and 8.24-25 in the "hope" of life. Paul anticipates this argument in 2.13-16, where he establishes the principle that "hearing" is based on "the work of the Torah written in their [the Gentiles'] hearts;" see the comments and references there. For the "Shoot," see the references and comments on 8.24-25. The possibility that Israel are the subject here requires reading the verb "heard" as "accepted" or "obeyed." Although this is certainly a biblical usage (cf. Ex.24.7, Josh.1.17, Jer.42.6), Paul obviously means the verb in its literal sense here, of hearing the word of faithfulness in Yeshua proclaimed.

25 Cf. Isa.43.10. Although the plural "the feet of those . . ." is attested in other midrashim (cf. Mid.Ps.147.2) it does not seem to suit Paul's purpose here, since his emphasis lies on Yeshua's role as the "word of faithfulness." On the other hand, Paul wants to demonstrate that although the people of Israel were called to be a witness to the nations they did not fully understand that this was meant to result also in their inclusion in God's kingdom.

26 Paul refers back here to 1.16-17, where he introduces his thesis that the gospel which concerns God's son is the "power of God for salvation to everyone who believes, to the Jew first and also to the Greek. For in it the righteousness of God is revealed from faith to faith; as it is written, 'But the righteous (man) shall live by faith.'" See also the comments on 2.13-16.

27 This appears to be the one real exception in Paul's use of the technical formula, "what then shall we say?" which raises a proposition which will immediately be refuted; (verse 19 is another variation on the same theme, since Paul brings a quotation from Dt.32.21 as the continuation); see the comments on 3.3. Here he clearly endorses the statement rather than rebutting it. If it is thus demonstrated that Paul's use of the formula is not consistent, it may be suggested that the present proposed interpretation of 9.30-11.11 is itself erroneous. Since, however, 9.30 is also an unusual usage and the whole context of chapters 9-11 corroborates Paul's claim that God has not rejected His people, argued according to the same formula, it is possible to maintain the validity of the exegesis given here.

28 For the structure of Rom.9.30-11.11, see the comments on 9.30-33.

29 The meaning of the phrase "at the first Moses" seems merely to be an indication of textual priority: first Moses, then Isaiah, and then Isaiah again relate to Israel's understanding of the τελος (*telos*) of the Torah. Once again, Paul is not arguing that Israel did not know but that their ignorance and disobedience did not lead to their rejection by God and replacement by the Gentiles.

ROMANS 11

Introduction

Paul begins the climax to the argument which he begins in 9.30 and will finally resolve in 11.11-36: that far from God having rejected His people because of their unfaithfulness, their transgression is in fact part of God's purpose to include all mankind in His kingdom. Although the text from Isaiah 65.2 raises once again the possibility that God has rejected His people, Paul continues to counter this claim, reviewing his argument of 9.30-10.21 in verses 1-6. He appeals to his ancestor Elijah (cf. his personal desire for his people's redemption in 9.1-3, 10.1 and 11.14) in order to demonstrate how God has always kept for Himself a remnant of faithful people (verses 2-5). He recapitulates verses 1-6 (and 9.30-10.21) once more in verse 11, where he finally brings his definitive refutation of the erroneous conclusion that God has replaced Israel with the Gentiles. He interprets the "mystery" of God, clearly stating that God's plan was for the Gentiles to be "resurrected" (cf. 4.17) as a result of Israel's temporary rejection of God's Messiah (verses 12 and 15), and that their inclusion will in turn make Israel jealous for their own God and thus return to Him in faithfulness (verses 12-27). Paul appeals midrashically to Jeremiah 11.14-17, combined with verses from Job 14.7-9 and Isaiah 6.13, passages which speak of the regrowth of a tree-stump, in order to show how God's choice of Israel will be fulfilled once the Gentiles have (also) become obedient in Yeshua (cf. 1.5) (verses 16-24). Moreover, he uses the metaphor of "grafting in" to graphically demonstrate God's plan to bless all the nations of the world through Abraham through the dual meaning of the Hebrew root ברך (*barakh*), "to bless" "to graft." He thus brings the argument to its climax in verses 28-32, showing through the disobedience of both Jews and Gentiles He justifies all mankind through His righteousness in Yeshua. Paul then concludes with a doxology praising God for the wisdom of these mysteries of His universal salvation (verses 33-36).

Verse 1:

"I say then . . . ": cf. 1 Sam.12.22, Ps.94.14, Jer.31.37, 33.24-26.

Paul repeats the objection originally raised in 9.30-31, that the Gentiles have replaced Israel as God's people because Israel have refused to discern the purpose (τελος; *telos*) of the Torah and to accept the fact that God has demonstrated His righteousness in Yeshua's death and resurrection, thus enabling also the Gentiles to become faithful to God. Now he refutes the charge, citing the traditional refutation, "May it never be!" which is missing in 9.31 (cf. also verses 7 and 11).[1] In verses 1-10 he recapitulates the argument of chapter 10 in brief and rebuts the erroneous conclusion that God has rejected His people (verses 11-36).

"For I too am an Israelite . . . ": cf. Num.1.37, Josh.18.11, Lk.3.8, 13.16, 19.9, Jn.8.33, Rom.4.13-16, 9.4, 7, 2 Cor.11.22, Gal.3.7, 6.16, Phil.3.5, Rev.7.8.

Paul's first proof of Israel's election is his own personal example. He is "living proof" of the fact that God has not rejected His people because he himself is part of the nation of Israel, whose are the fathers, the covenants, and the promises etc. (cf. 9.1-3). If God has called him, as an Israelite, then He cannot have forsaken all of His people.[2]

Verses 2-6:

"God . . . foreknew": cf. 8.29-30.

Israel's election is based most securely, however, not on Paul's own example, but on God's promises to the forefathers. Paul appeals directly to the fact that those "whom He foreknew, He also predestined . . . and whom He predestined, these also He called; and whom he called, these also He justified; and whom He justified, these He also glorified" (8.29-30). God's foreknowledge (His promises to the forefathers) is inseparably linked to His "glorification" of Israel: Israel's original election irrevocably leads to their resurrection (cf. verses 12 and 15), not only because God so purposed but also because having purposed it He could not renege on His promise without compromising His own nature.[3] God knew Israel first and chose them as His people from the beginning. He further chose Israel so that the nations could then become part of the commonwealth of Israel. Paul's appeal to God's "foreknowledge" thus sets his argument concerning the "remnant" in the context of his defense of Israel's election in chapter 8. Since "nothing can separate us from the love of God . . . in Yeshua," all Israel will ultimately be saved (cf. verse 26).

Verses 2-4:

"Or do you not know . . . ": cf. 1 Kings 19.10f, Mt.2.12, 22, Acts 10.22, 11.26, Rom.6.6, 16, 7.3, 9.11, 16, 1 Cor.3.16, 5.6, 6.2, 19, 9.13, Heb.8.5, 11.7, 12.25.

Paul juxtaposes God's "foreknowledge" with the people's ignorance: although God chose His people from the beginning his (Gentile) readers seem to be unaware of this fact and to want to deny it. In countering this view Paul appeals to the Scriptures as his first proof because in them God has made clear His promises to Israel. To say that God had rejected his people is tantamount to claiming that His words are untrustworthy.[4] He turns to the example of Elijah, who claimed that he alone among the people of Israel was faithful to God. Paul understands Elijah's claim of faithfulness as his protest against Israel's election: Elijah's "pleading with God against Israel" reflects Elijah's belief that Israel's unfaithfulness had brought God's punishment upon them. God reproves Elijah, however, and proves that He has kept a remnant (including Elijah) for Himself.[5]

Verse 5:
"In the same way . . . choice": cf. Gen.14.10, Num.21.35, Dt.2.20, 34, Josh.8.22, 2 Kings 10.11, 19.4, 25.22, 1 Chron.4.43, Ezra 9.14, Isa.1.8-9, 4.3, 6.1-8.22, 10.20, 37.22, Jer.6.9, 8.3, 40.6, Amos 5.15, Hag.1.12, 2.2, Zech.8.6-12, 14.16; 1QM 4.2, 13.8, 14.8-12, 1QH 6.8; 4 Ez.9.7f, 12.34, 13.48, 2 Bar.40.2, Sib.Or.5.384-85.

Paul appeals to Elijah's example as a paradigm for his own generation (and for future generations). Elijah believes himself to be the only one faithful to God in Israel—a single "remnant" out of a nation all of whom are disobedient. God, however, disproves the fact that Elijah alone is faithful, and in fact tells him that the "remnant" numbers seven thousand. "In the same way," says Paul, God has (also) kept a remnant among the people faithful to Himself in Yeshua in Paul's generation.[6] In the Tanakh, the idea of the remnant frequently refers to a part of Israel which is "saved" out of the whole people, often following God's judgment.[7] It represents the whole people or may also be the whole people who are left after God's punishment.[8] God thus judges His people and saves them from destruction. Paul thus again emphasizes (cf. chapter 9) that God's election of Israel is based upon "His choice of grace," in the term found in the Qumran literature to express the way in which God bestows His righteousness on man: not according to man's (or Israel's) deeds but according to those whom He wills. He thus creates a remnant out of His grace of those whom He has cleansed from transgression and their evil inclination to serve Him in purity of heart:

> And I was comforted for the roaring of the crowd and for the tumult of ki[ngd]oms when they assemble, [for] I [kn]ow Thou wilt soon raise up survivors among Thy people and a remnant in the midst of

> Thy inheritance, and that Thou hast purified them that they may be cleansed of (all) sin. For all their deeds are in Thy Truth and Thou wilt judge them with abundant mercy and pardon because of Thy favours, and Thou wilt teach them according to (the words of) Thy mouth and wilt establish them in Thy Council unto Thy glory according to the uprightness of Thy truth. (1QH 6.7-10)[9]

Verse 6:

"If it is by grace . . . ": cf. 3.28, 4.4, 5.2, 9.16, 23, Gal.2.16, 3.18.

Paul relates the idea of the "remnant" back to the argument in chapter 4 over "wages" and "imputation;" to chapter 8 and his defense of Israel's election in the face of their rejection of Yeshua; and to chapter 9 where he discusses God's sovereignty in extending "mercy" (giving grace) to whom He wills.[10] Now he explicitly identifies the remnant of Israel with the "true" "sons of Abraham":

> Whoever possesses these three things, he is of the disciples of Abraham, our father . . . : a good eye, an humble spirit and a lowly soul. . . . The disciples of Abraham, our father, enjoy [their share] in this world, and inherit the world to come, as it is said: That I may cause those that love Me to inherit substance and that I may fill their treasuries (Prov.8.21). (PA 5.19)

The "remnant" numbers those who exhibit Abraham's qualities through being faithful to God. Paul's argument emphasizes two complementary facts: that God's grace in keeping a faithful remnant for Himself not only proves that He has not and never will abandon His people because Israel's election is based on God's gracious gift; and also that no one else can take it away from them.[11] Just as God had kept a remnant of those faithful to him of whom Elijah was unaware, so too Paul claims that even though they might not be presently visible he is not the only one who has remained faithful to God by accepting Yeshua's righteousness as the goal of the Torah. God can therefore certainly not be said to have rejected His people.

Verses 7-10:

"What then? . . . ": cf. Dt.29.4, Ps.69.22f, Isa.29.10, Mt.13.13f, Rom.3.3, 9, 6.1, 7.7, 14, 9.30, 11.1, 11.

Paul repeats for the third time, and almost verbatim here, the question which he raises in 9.30-31 and which he has just recapitulated in verses 1-6. Verses 7-10 are therefore a question not a statement.[12] Here the erroneous conclusion, which Paul finally rejects in verse 11, lies in a fine distinction between the "remnant" which God has kept for Himself and the "all Israel" which shall be saved (cf. verse 26). The prooftexts which Paul brings describe the hardening of Israel's heart, a theme to which he appeals to in 9.18f in order to indicate that God has also included the Gentiles, and to which he returns in verse 25 in demonstration of the same principle of God's mercy. Israel's hardness of heart (in rejecting God's Messiah) is both "partial" and functions to bring the Gentiles into the commonwealth of Israel (cf. Eph.2.12). The "remnant" are those who accept Yeshua; "all Israel" are those whose rejection of Yeshua brings about God's inclusion ("creation" or "resurrection;" cf. 4.17) of the Gentiles. The faithfulness of the Gentile believers subsequently provokes this second "remnant" to jealousy, breaking their hardness of heart and bringing salvation to "all Israel" through God's grace in Yeshua.[13]

Verse 11:

"I say then . . . ": cf. Dt.7.25, Lk.2.34-35, Acts 28.28, Rom.11.14, Jas.2.10, 3.2, 2 Pet.1.10; 1QH 6.26-27, 9.25, 17.7; Ps.Sol.3.9-10; Tanh.B.Bechuk.3.

Paul repeats, and finally answers, the question which he raises in 9.30-31, of whether God has in fact rejected His people in favor of the Gentiles. Although it is true that some of the people of Israel may have "stumbled" over the "corner-stone" and not arrived at the "goal" (τελος; *telos*) of the Torah, which is God's righteousness in Yeshua, this fact does not substantiate the conclusion that Israel have "fallen" and been replaced by the Gentiles as God's people.[14] When the "fullness of the (times of the) Gentiles" has "come in," Israel will be provoked back to jealousy of their own God and will all be saved.

"Make them jealous": cf. Dt.32.21, Rom.10.2, 19, 11.14, Gal.1.14, Phil.3.6; 1QH 2.15.

Paul returns to the prooftext of Deuteronomy 32.21 which he brings in 10.19. He uses a verbal analogy (גזרה שווה; *gezerah shavah*) which enables him to apply the common motif "that which is not a nation" and "those who sought Me not" in Deuteronomy 32.21 and Isaiah 65.1 to state the principle that God had plainly foretold His plan to include the Gentiles in His kingdom in His word (cf. also Hos.1.10, 2.23). He then brings the quote from Isaiah 65.2 to demonstrate that despite knowing the Torah, Israel were disobedient and refused to acknowledge God's purposes.[15] Now, however, he brings the final refutation of the erroneous conclusion raised in 9.30. He states the precise claim: that Israel stumbled so as to fall (from God's "grace" and be replaced as His people with the Gentiles) and gives the traditional unambiguous refutation ("May it never be!"). He then gives what he considers to be the true interpretation of Israel's history. Contrary to the people's" obstinacy" and transgression being the cause of their rejection and replacement with the Gentiles, God's original promise to Abraham was to bless all the nations of the world. The fact that Israel were stiff-necked and did not understand God's plan gave Him the opportunity to provide all mankind with His righteousness through Yeshua's faithfulness. The "obedience of faith" of the Gentiles then becomes a source of "jealousy" for the people of Israel, for whom God Himself is "jealous," and in this way they return in faithfulness to their own God.[16]

Verse 12:

"Transgression . . . fulfillment be!": cf. Zech.8.13, 20-23, Rom.9.23, 11.15, Eph.1.9-10, Col.1.27; Sifre Dt.Ekev 40, TBE p.174, Pes.Rab.15.5, Tanh.B.Toledot 14, Terumah 8, Bechuk.3, Lev.R.23.3, Num.R.1.3, Cant.R.5.16.5.

Paul employs the classic ק"ו (*kal ve-chomer*) formula (cf. chapter 5) in verses 12-15 to demonstrate how he maintains his argument concerning God's plan that the Gentiles would provoke Israel to jealousy for their own God and return to Him for their salvation. This reinforces his claim that Israel have always been God's chosen people: if even Israel's transgression brought goodness (Yeshua's righteousness) to the world—how much more will their fulfillment of God's will mean for all mankind. Paul uses the same terms of "transgression" and "reconciliation" (verse 15) in chapter 5, where he makes God's righteousness ("justification") "accessible" (cf. "introduction" [5.2]) also to the Gentiles (verses 12f). Here he reiterates God promises to give the "riches of His glory" (9.23) to the Gentiles which are found in Yeshua's righteousness—their "reconciliation" according to verse 15, where Paul repeats the idea of Israel being the salvation of the whole world in line with other rabbinic midrashim:

> R. Azariah in the name of R. Judah son of R. Simon says: The matter may be compared to the case of a king who had an orchard planted with one row of fig-trees, one of vines, one of pomegranates, and one of apples. He entrusted it to a tenant and went away. After a time the king came and looked in the orchard to ascertain what it had yielded. He found it full of thorns and briars, so he brought wood-cutters to raze it. He looked closely at the thorns and noticed among them a single rose-coloured flower. He smelled it and his spirits calmed down. The king said: 'The whole orchard shall be saved

because of this flower.' In a similar manner the whole world was created only for the sake of the Torah. After twenty-six generations the Holy One, blessed be He, looked closely at His world to ascertain what it had yielded, and found it full of water in water {wicked people in a wicked environment} . . . . So He brought cutters to cut it down; as it says, *The Lord sat enthroned at the flood* (Ps.29.10). He saw a single rose-coloured flower, to wit, Israel. He took it and smelled it when He gave them the Ten Commandments and His spirits were calmed when they said, *We will do, and we will hear* (Ex.24.7). Said the Holy One, blessed be He: 'The orchard shall be saved on account of this flower. For the sake of the Torah and of Israel the world shall be saved.' . . . In fact, were it not for Israel no rain would fall nor would the sun shine {cf. Jer.31.35f} . For it is due to their merit that the Holy One, blessed be He, brings relief to this world of His. In the World to Come when the idolators behold how the Holy One, blessed be He, is with Israel they will come to join them; as it is said, *In those days it shall come to pass, that ten men shall take hold out of all the languages of the Nations, shall even take hold of the skirt of him that is a Jew, saying, We will go with you, for we have heard that God is with you* (Zech.8.23). (Lev.R.23.3, Num.R.1.3)[17]

Verses 13-14:

"Speaking to . . . save some of them"

Paul now turns directly to the Gentile believers among the Roman congregations (cf. 1.5, 13-15, 15.15-16), identifying them with the source of the sort of objections he is countering against Israel's election and salvation.[18] He appeals to his "commission" (שליחות; *shelichut*) to the Gentiles as giving him the right, as it were, to act as a Gentile believer and himself provoke his "fellow-countrymen" to jealousy. He wishes at least to serve as an example to the Gentile believers to encourage them to fulfil their calling to provoke Israel to jealousy. This is his (only) justification for "magnifying" his ministry, which he otherwise diminishes as God's working through him (cf. 15.17-18).[19] Although he emphasizes his lineage (cf. 9.1-2, 11.1), he becomes, as it were, a Gentile to the Jews (cf. 1 Cor.9.20). His "ministry to the Gentiles" is thus finally a means to another end, the salvation of his own people.[20]

Verse 15:

"If their rejection . . . life from the dead": cf. Zech.8.13, 20-23, Rom.11.15, Eph.1.9-10, Col.1.27; Pes.Rab.15.5, Tanh.B.Toledot 14, Terumah 8, Bechuk.3, TBE p.174, Sifre Dt.40, Lev.R.23.3, Num.R.1.3, Cant.R.5.16.5.

Paul brings out the full implications of God's purpose to bless all the nations of the world through Abraham. Not only did He choose a people for Himself from Abraham's seed but He also made that people jealous when they forsook their own God and saw those who formerly had not been a nation (Dt.32.21)—not merely not part of Israel but without hope and without God in the world (cf. Eph.2.12)—become part of God's kingdom, and thus returned to Him in faithfulness. The life which God gave to the Gentile nations thus becomes eternal life for both Israel and the Gentile believers; Israel's partial rejection of God's Messiah brings God's reconciliation to the Gentile nations (cf. 5.10-11). Although Israel have "transgressed," "failed," and "rejected" God's righteousness in Yeshua their (partial) rejection leads to "riches for the world," "riches for the Gentiles," "fulfillment," "reconciliation," and "life from the dead."[21] Israel's "fulfillment"—their redemption in Yeshua—brings the Gentiles an even greater blessing.[22] Not only will God reconcile them to Himself (cf. 5.10-11), but He who "gives life to the dead" will also "call into being" (cf. 4.17) a people who did not exist. Paul's analogy, moreover, suggests how the Gentiles' obedience will provoke Israel to jealousy for their own God and bring their "fulfillment" and salvation. He interprets the verse in Genesis 12.3 (cf. 18.18), "'And in you [Abraham] all the families of the earth shall be blessed'" (ונברכו בך; *ve-nivrekhu be-kha)* by playing on the meaning given to the root ברך (*barakh*) in Second Temple literature. Through the influence of the Aramaic form, one part of the verb was used to refer to the process of "engrafting" or "sinking" of a plant, especially that of a vine, by drawing it into the ground and thus making it grow forth as an independent plant.[23] Paul interprets the blessing in Genesis as the "engrafting" of the Gentiles, in a similar fashion to R. Eleazar's interpretation of the same verse, in which the blessing returns upon the people of Israel:

> R. Eleazar further stated: What is meant by the text, *And in thee shall the families of the earth be blessed* (Gen.12.3)? The Holy One, blessed be He, said to Abraham, 'I have two goodly shoots [ברכות; lit. 'blessings'] to engraft [להבריך; lit. 'make blessing'] on you: Ruth the Moabitess and Naamah the Ammonitess'. *All the families of the earth*, even the other families who live on the earth are blessed only for Israel's sake. *All the nations of the earth* (Gen.18.18), even the ships that go from Gaul to Spain are blessed only for Israel's sake. (Yev.63a)[24]

Verse 16:

"If the first piece . . . branches are too": cf. Num.15.18f, Lev.6.17, Neh.10.37, Job 14.7-9, Isa.6.13, Jer.11.15-17, Ezek.44.30, Mt.13.33, 16.6, Mk.8.15, Lk.13.20-21, 1 Cor.5.6-8, Gal.5.9; PRK 21.4.

The second part of God's promise to Abraham was to inherit the Land (cf. Gen.13.14-18, 17.8). Paul remembers the commandment God gave to Israel when they entered the Land, "that it shall be, that when you eat of the bread of the land, you shall lift up a heave offering to the Lord. . . . From the first of your dough you shall give to the Lord a heave offering throughout your generations" (Num.15.19, 21). according to Leviticus 6, these offerings, were holy so that "whoever touches them shall become consecrated" (Lev.6.18). Paul uses this theme to develop the ideas of rejection, reconciliation, acceptance, and life from the dead (verse 15). He further connects them with texts from Jeremiah 11.14-17, Job 14.7-9, and Isaiah 6.13. Creating a גזרה שווה (*gezerah shavah*; verbal analogy) between the biblical description of Israel as an (olive)-tree and the "tenth portion" (עשיריה; *'asiriyah*) he creates a midrash on the theme of a "holy stump":

> The Lord called your name, "A green olive-tree, beautiful in fruit and form"; with the noise of a great tumult He has kindled fire on it, and its branches are worthless . . . "For there is hope for a tree, when it is cut down, that it will sprout again, and its shoots will not fail [lit. cease]. Though its roots grow old in the ground, and its stump dies in the dry soil, at the scent of water it will flourish and put forth sprigs like a plant." . . . "Yet there will be a tenth portion in it [the land] and it will again be (subject) to burning, like a terebinth or oak whose stump remains when it is felled. The holy seed is its stump." (Jer.11.16, Job 14.7-9, Isa.6.13)[25]

In Isaiah 6.13, the stump of the terebinth or oak is associated with the olive tree. Paul connects the stump of the tree with the "tenth of the . . . seed of the land or of the fruit of the tree" which is "holy to the Lord" (Num.27.30).[26] He thus describes Israel as a "holy seed" (זרע קדוש; *zera' kadosh*). Although the root is indeed holy, the tree may be felled (cf. "fallen" in 11.11) if its members (branches) do not obey the commandment to be holy as the Lord is holy (cf. Lev.19.2). In several rabbinic midrashim, man's evil inclination is compared to just such a plant, together with the idea of the "leaven" which permeates man's evil heart (cf. Gen.6.5 and Jer.11.15-17) and prevents him from observing God's will:

> FOR THE IMAGINATION OF MAN'S HEART IS EVIL (Gen.6.5). R. Hiyya the Elder said: How wretched must be the dough when the baker himself testifies it to be poor! [Thus man's Creator says] FOR THE IMAGINATION OF MAN'S HEART IS EVIL. Abba Jose the potter said: How poor must be the leaven when he who kneaded it testifies that it is bad! Thus: *For he knoweth our* [evil] *passions, He remembereth that we are dust* (Ps.103.14). The Rabbis said: How inferior must be the plant when he that planted it testifies that it is bad; thus, *For the Lord of hosts, that planted thee, hath spoken evil of thee*' (Jer.11.17). (Gen.R.34.10)[27]

Paul turns this midrashic denial of man's responsibility for the "evil inclination" into an explanation of Israel's "transgression" and a justification of their election, drawing upon the sacrificial offerings and the "dough" which constituted the "holy" grain, sin, and guilt offerings (cf. Num.15.18f, Lev.6.14ff). In analogy with Isaiah 6.13, these sacrifices become the "first piece" (a lump or the stump) of the "remnant" which guarantees the holiness of the whole root.[28] The branches which are broken off the tree thus represent the "leaven" of the evil inclination, or the disobedience of His people, Israel, whom God punished by kindling fire upon and making them "worthless."[29]

Verse 17:
"If some of the branches were broken off": cf. Isa.27.1-13, Jer.11.15, Mt.3.10, 7.16-20, Lk.3.9, 6.43-44, Jn.15.1-11; PRK 21.4, Lam.R.1.1.20.

Paul uses the idea of pruning to describe God's punishment of Israel's transgression. As the passage in Jeremiah 11.16 indicates (cf. Isa.6.13, 27.1-13), although the breaking off of the branches is a sign of God's wrath, expressed in the people's exile from the Land, the act of pruning represents a time of trouble and suffering which leads to a direct improvement in the growth of the tree. Israel's punishment and exile are therefore only for a temporary period and will be replaced when God forgives them and brings them redemption "at the end of time," an idea beautifully portrayed in a midrash in the name of R. Isaac:

> R. Isaac said, At the time of the destruction of the Temple the Holy One, blessed be He, found Abraham standing in the Temple. Said He, *What hath My beloved to do in My house?* (Jer.11.15). Abraham replied, 'I have come concerning the fate of my children'. Said He, 'Thy children sinned and have gone into exile'. 'Perhaps',

> said Abraham, 'they only sinned in error?' And He answered, *She hath wrought lewdness* (Ps.139.20). 'Perhaps only a few sinned?' *With many* (ibid.), came the reply. 'Still', he pleaded, 'Thou shouldst have remembered unto them the covenant of circumcision'. And He replied, *The hallowed flesh is passed from thee* (Jer.11.15). 'Perhaps hadst Thou waited for them they would have repented', he pleaded. And He replied, *When thou doest evil, then thou rejoicest!* (ibid.). Thereupon he put his hands on his head and wept bitterly, and cried, 'Perhaps, Heaven forfend, there is no hope for them'. Then came forth a Heavenly Voice and said, *The Lord called thy name a leafy olive-tree, fair with goodly fruit* (Jer.11.16): as the olive-tree produces its best only at the very end, so Israel will flourish at the end of time. R. Joshua b. Levi said, Why is Israel likened to an olive-tree? To tell you that as the olive-tree loses not its leaves either in summer or in winter, so Israel shall never be lost in this world or in the world to come. (Men.53b)[30]

"You, being a wild olive tree . . . ": cf. Prov.3.19, Ps.128.1 2, Ezek.31.6, 14, Dan.4.10-27, Eph.2.11f; 1QH 8.25-26; Wis.Sol.16.11, Ps.Sol.14.3-4, Odes Sol.11.1ff.

Paul describes the Gentiles, who were not God's people (cf. Hos.1.10), and were without hope and without God in the world(cf. Eph.2.12f), as an "uncultivated" olive tree.[31] Although they are therefore not of the original stock—part of God's covenant with Abraham—they are still capable of bearing fruit in God's kingdom. They are "wild" branches in the sense of being "strangers and aliens" to the "covenants of promise" (cf. Eph.2.23f). However, God has turned them from being "not-My-people" and as it were "naturalized" them into being "fellow-citizens," "fellow-heirs," and "fellow-members" of the "commonwealth of Israel" (cf. Eph.2.12, 3.6). Their "partaking of the rich root of the olive tree" makes them "fellow-partakers of the promise in Yeshua through the gospel" (Eph.3.6):

> And I said, blessed, O Lord, are they who are planted in your land, and who have a place in your Paradise; and who grow in the growth of your trees, and have passed from darkness into light. Behold, all your laborers are fair, they who work good works, and turn from wickedness to your kindness. For they turned away from themselves the bitterness of the trees, when they were planted in your land. And everyone was like your remnant. (Odes Sol.11.18-22)[32]

Verse 18:

"Arrogant . . . root (supports) you": cf. Jn.15.4-6, Jas.3.14.

Paul clearly knows of Gentile believers in the community at Rome who are acting arrogantly or expressing such views, towards Israel, and behaving as though they were the root instead of its branches. He thus addresses his argument directly to them (cf. verse 13).[33] The root and its (original) branches are Israel. Moreover, the root has not been cut off. The stump remains, and only from its root may new branches—even those which have been "grafted in"—receive life (cf. "life from the dead" [verse 15]):

> R. Hoshaia said in the name of R. Aphes: Jerusalem is destined to become a beacon for the nations of the earth, and they will walk in its light. And the proof? The verse *And nations shall walk at thy light*, etc. (Isa.60.3). R. Aha said: Israel is likened to an olive tree—*A leafy olive tree, fair with goodly fruit* (Jer.11.16). And the Holy One is likened to a lamp—*The lamp of the Lord is the spirit of man* (Prov.20.27). What use is made of oil? It is put into a lamp, and then the two together give light, as though they were one. Hence the Holy One, blessed be He, will say to Israel: My children, since My light is your light, and your light is My light, let us go together—you and I—and give light to Zion: *Arise, give light, for thy light has come* (Isa.60.1). (PRK 21.4)[34]

Verses 19-20:

"You will say then . . . but fear": cf. Rom.12.16, 1 Cor.10.12, 15.1-2, 16.13, 2 Cor.1.24, Phil.2.12; Wis.Sol.4.5.

Paul quotes the argument of those Gentile believers who believe that they have replaced Israel as God's people and arrogantly express their feelings by assuming that the branches which God broke off deserved such punishment (cf. 9.19). Paul does not dispute this claim but objects to the "erroneous conclusion" that this gives the Gentile believers any right to be proud. The original (natural) branches might indeed have been cut off, as a punishment—but not in order that they might be *replaced*. The Gentiles must be thankful for God's grace in "grafting them in" to His kingdom but they must also remember that God will use their salvation as a means to provoke Israel to jealousy for Himself. Since they have been grafted in according to their faithfulness to Yeshua ("you stand by your faithfulness") they cannot therefore use their inclusion against Israel, either to prove themselves superior to Israel or to claim that God has replaced them as His people. Their inclusion is as dependent upon God's grace as is Israel's, and they too may be broken off if they become unfaithful. Paul further implies ("you stand [only] by your faithfulness") that Israel still stand on firmer ground than the Gentiles because they are the root on which God's promises to Abraham stand (cf. verses 28-29). The Gentile believers therefore have no grounds upon which to boast. On the contrary, they need to fear God because they are dependent upon His favor. It is only because God promised His grace to all peoples that the Gentile believers have access to His righteousness in Yeshua.

Verses 21-24:
"Did not spare the natural branches": cf. Isa.9.18-19, 27.1-13, Jer.11.16-17, 21.14, Mal.3.16-18, Mt.3.7-12, 7.16-27, Lk.3.7-9, Rom.8.32, 9.21-22, 1 Cor.10.12, 2 Cor.13.2, 2 Pet.2.4-9; Mid.Ps.92.11, Ex.R.29.9.

Paul picks up the theme of God's sovereignty from 9.14f, where he demonstrates that God shows mercy to whom He will, and combines it with the midrashic tradition based on Jeremiah 11.15-16 (cf. Job 14.7-9 and Isa.6.13).[35] God's justification of both Israel and the Gentile nations is based upon His free gift of righteousness based on Yeshua's faithfulness. If He is willing to cast away branches from the original tree, those who have been grafted in (as possessing the "qualities of our father, Abraham") must also know that He is able to cut them off as well:

> . . . [Thou hast plant]ed unto Thy glory a planting of cypress and elm mingled with box. Trees of life are hidden among all the trees by the waters in a mysterious realm, and they shall send out a Shoot for the everlasting planting. . . . And Thou hast opened their fountain by my hand among the [water] courses . . . If I move my hand to dig its ditches, its roots sink even to the rock of flint and [estab]lish their stock [securely] within the earth, and in the season of heat it retains (its) strength. But if I take away my hand, it shall be like a juni[per in the wilderness] [and] its stock like nettles in a salt-marsh, and in its ditches shall grow prickles and thorns and it [shall be delivered up] to thickets and thistles [and all its] border [trees] shall change into trees of wild fruits; before the heat its leaves shall wither. (1QH 8.5-6, 21-26)[36]

Verse 22:
"Kindness and severity of God . . . ": cf. Jn.15.2, Rom.2.4f, 1 Cor.1.18, 15.2, 2 Cor.2.15, Heb.3.6, 14; 1QS 4.1, 12, 22-23, 1QH 1.31-32, 4.18-20, 26-29, 6.9, 7.30, 9.14, 30-34, 11.8-9, 13.16-18, 14.15-16, 15.13-25, 16.16-18.

Paul continues the theme of 9.21-23, changing the metaphor of the potter and the clay to that of the natural and wild olive trees. God's "severity" corresponds to His creation of "vessels of wrath" (9.22) and His "kindness" to His preparation of "vessels of mercy" (9.23).[37] In chapter 9, he emphasizes the grafting in of the Gentiles together with Israel; here he warns the Gentile believers that God may "harden" whom He will, as well as have mercy on whom He will. Since His kindness is meant to lead to repentance (cf. 2.4), where it does not, He withdraws it from man. Thus only when the Gentile believers remain faithful to Yeshua and stand in God's grace are they themselves assured of not falling and being punished as those who have fallen within Israel have been "cut off."[38] Conversely, when Israel become faithful to Yeshua they will be "grafted in" to God's righteousness once again. Thus Paul reconfirms the fact that Israel's stumbling has not led them to utterly fall from God grace. God's sovereign will operates both in severity (wrath) and kindness (mercy), and He will graft back the people of Israel back into their natural root when the Gentiles are faithful to their own calling to provoke Israel to jealousy for their own God.

Verse 23:

"And they also . . . again"

When Israel "bring forth fruit in keeping with repentance" (cf. Mt.3.8), God's "kindness" will once again make them "vessels of mercy" (9.23). God never intended to utterly destroy His people, but "endured with patience" their transgression so that He might also make the Gentiles a part of His kingdom.

Verse 24:

"By nature": cf. Mt.15.21-26, Rom.2.14, Gal.2.15; 1QH 8.25.

Israel are the "natural" branches; the Gentiles are "naturally" a wild olive tree.[39] This "naturalness" relates to the pagan ("wild" or "uncultivated") nature of the Gentiles, who were once "not-My-people" (cf. Hos.1.10), without "hope and without God in the world" (cf. Eph.2.12), in contrast to Israel who have been chosen by God to be His people: "We (are) Jews by nature, and not sinners from among the Gentiles" (Gal.2.15).[40]

"How much more . . . ": cf. 5.15, 17, 11.12, 15.

Paul picks up the קו"ח (*kal ve-chomer*) argument of verses 12 and 15 and repeats the greater "advantages" (cf. 3.1) and benefit to the world which Israel's redemption brings. Here he describes Israel's "natural rights" as the tree of God's planting (cf. Isa.5.1ff, 61.3). It is far easier, in fact, for natural branches to be re-grafted than for different branches to be grafted into the original stock.

Verses 25-27:
"For I do not want . . . ": cf. Job 15.17-18, Isa.55.4-13, Jer.50.2f, Rom.1.13, 12.3, 16, 1 Cor.10.1, 12.1, 2 Cor.1.8, 1 Thess.4.13; Test.Ben.10.11.

Paul indicates that his point is of the greatest importance—just as he writes the congregation of his eagerness to visit them (cf. 1.13). Here he indicates that the Gentiles must understand that what he is telling them now is a revelation of God's plan—His "mystery"—of salvation for both Israel and the Gentile nations. The gravity of the Gentiles' arrogant attitude towards the people of Israel can only be countered by the weight of divine revelation; no one can be left unaware ("uninformed") of God's true intentions, both towards Israel and the Gentiles.

Verse 25:
"This mystery": cf. 16.25, 1 Cor.2.7-10, Eph.1.9-10, 3.3-5, 9, 6.19, Col.1.26-27; 1QH 2.13, 4.27f, 7.27, 11.10, 12.12, 20, 1QpHab 7.5, 13; 4 Ez.4.35f, 14.5, Test.Zev.9.5-9, 2 Bar.81.4.

Paul describes God's "mystery" in terms of His sovereign will as His prerogative to show mercy to whom He will, specifically regarding bringing about "the obedience of faith among the Gentiles" (1.5, 16.25).[41] The "mystery" is directly related to the "fullness of (the times of) the Gentiles because it marks the period when He includes them in His kingdom, the conclusion of which will end the time of God's הסתר פנים (*hester panim*) or the hiding of His face from Israel (cf. Ezek.39.23-29). Because Yeshua died for the ungodly "at the right time" (cf. 5.6) the "mystery of the Messiah" was revealed, namely that "the Gentiles are fellow-heirs and fellow-members of the body [Israel], and fellow-partakers of the promise in the Messiah, Yeshua, through the gospel" (Eph.3.6). Picking up the subject of God's "hardening" of Israel's heart from 9.18 (cf. 11.22), whose τελος (*telos*) or "goal" (cf. 10.4) is to lead first also to the inclusion of the Gentiles in God's kingdom and then to Israel's full salvation, Paul demonstrates that all Israel will finally be saved:

> "In the writings of the fathers I came to know that in the last days you shall defect from the Lord, and you shall be divided in Israel, and you shall follow two kings; you shall commit every abomination and worship every idol. Your enemies will take you captive and you shall reside among the gentiles with all sorts of sickness and tribulation and oppression of soul. And thereafter you will remember

> the Lord and repent, and he will turn you around because he is merciful and compassionate; he does not bring a charge at wickedness against the sons of men, since they are flesh and the spirits of deceit lead them astray in all their actions. And thereafter the Lord himself will arise upon you, the light of righteousness with healing and compassion in his wings. He will liberate every captive of the sons of men from Belial, and every spirit of error will be trampled down. He will turn all nations to being zealous for him. And you shall see [God in a human form], he whom the Lord will choose: Jerusalem is his name. You will provoke him to wrath by the wickedness of your works, and you will be rejected until the end of the time" . . . "And after this there shall arise for you a Star from Jacob in peace: And a man shall arise from my [Judah's] posterity like the Sun of righteousness, walking with the sons of men in gentleness and righteousness, and in him will be found no sin. And the heavens will be opened upon him to pour out the spirit as a blessing of the Holy Father. And he will pour the spirit of grace upon you. And you shall be sons in truth, and you will walk in his first and final decrees. This is the Shoot of God Most High; this is the fountain for the life of all humanity. Then he will illumine the scepter of my kingdom, and from your root will arise the Shoot, and through it will arise the rod of righteousness for the nations, to judge and to save all that call on the Lord." (Test.Jud.24.1-6, Test.Zev.9.5-9)[42]

"Fullness of the Gentiles": cf. Mt.24.15-36, Mk.13.1ff, Lk.21.24, Jn.1.16, Acts 1.6-8, Gal.4.4, Eph.1.10; 4 Ez.4.35f, Test.Zev.9.5-9.

The Greek noun πληρωμα (*pleroma*), "fullness," normally indicates the "completion" or "wholeness" of an object or period of time.[43] It may also mean "whole" in the sense of "all," and thus corresponds both to the "obedience of faith among *all* the Gentiles" (1.5) and to the "times of the Gentiles" (cf. Lk.21.24, Acts 1.6-8).[44] Descriptions of the "fullness of the time" (cf. Gal.4.4), an expression which combines both of these meanings, are numerous in the Qumran literature, and are frequently related to the revelation of God's "Mysteries" in the consummation (fulfillment) of His "purposes" in history.[45] Flusser suggests that Paul is here theologically interpreting Yeshua's statement in Luke 21.24, where he speaks about the fulfillment of the "times of the Gentiles."[46] Where Yeshua refers to the imminent destruction of the Second Temple and to the end of the Roman occupation of Israel, Paul changes the original expectation of the breaking of the Gentiles' "yoke" of oppression into their obedience to faithfulness.[47] Paul understands that Israel's redemption will come as a result not (merely) of the breaking of the yoke of the Gentile nations but (also) through their faithfulness to God in Yeshua. Thus Israel's redemption also becomes the redemption of the world (cf. verses 12 and 15). The "fullness of (the times of) the Gentiles" therefore refers to the period in which the Gentiles become faithful to Yeshua. In this "waiting" period, as it were, Israel's partial hardening of heart prepares the Gentile nations for mercy and their inclusion in God's kingdom. When the Gentiles become faithful they will provoke the people of Israel back to their own God through their jealousy of the Gentiles' worship of the God of Abraham, Isaac, and Jacob.

Verse 26:

"And thus all Israel will be saved . . . ": cf. Isa.27.9, 59.20-21; Yoma 86a.

Paul finally fully answers the erroneous conclusion raised in 9.30-31.[48] Israel have *not* been replaced as God's people by His inclusion of the Gentiles, although they have not all "arrived at (the τελος [*telos*] or "goal" of the) Torah"—God's righteousness in Yeshua. They have not stumbled "so as to fall" but on the contrary have erred so that they might obtain their final salvation by being provoked to jealousy by the Gentiles' participation in God's kingdom (cf. verse 11). Paul counters here the double predestination of Qumran ideology, according to which the "sons of darkness" (the "wicked" among Israel and/or the Gentiles) will be completely destroyed and the community will be the sure and true House of Judah which no one can further join (cf. CDC 4.10-12). Paul, however, states that *all* Israel will be saved together with the entry of the Gentiles into the "commonwealth of Israel" (cf. Eph.2.12f).[49] He develops the metaphor of the (olive) tree (cf. verses 16-24) from the prooftext in Isaiah 27.9, where the prophet speaks of God's deliverance of Israel as the flourishing of a vineyard to which the "scattered" of Israel will finally be restored in order to worship the Lord on the holy mountain in Jerusalem: "In the days to come Jacob will take root, Israel will blossom and sprout; and they will fill the whole world with fruit" (27.6).[50] Paul combines this text with Isaiah 59.20 which describes the covenant which God will write on Israel's heart by His Spirit, a verse which recalls Joel 2.28 and the outpouring of God's spirit on "all flesh." Israel's salvation through God's Messiah is therefore also the salvation of the whole world:

> See, Lord, and raise up for them their king, the son of David, to rule over your servant Israel in the time known to you, O God. . . . He will gather a holy people whom he will lead in righteousness; and he will judge the tribes of the people that have been made holy by the

> Lord their God. He will not tolerate unrighteousness (even) to pause among them, and any person who knows wickedness shall not live with them. For he shall know them that they are all children of their God. . . . He will judge peoples and nations in the wisdom of his righteousness. . . . And he will be a righteous king over them, taught by God. There will be no unrighteousness among them in his days, for all shall be holy, and their king shall be the Lord Messiah. . . . He shall be compassionate to all the nations (who) reverently (stand) before him. He will strike the earth with the word of his mouth forever; he will bless the Lord's people with wisdom and happiness. And he himself (will be) free from sin, (in order) to rule a great people. . . . Blessed are those who are born in those days, to see the good things of the Lord which he will do for the coming generation; (which will be) under the rod of discipline of the Lord Messiah, in the fear of his God, in wisdom of spirit, and of righteousness and of strength, to direct people in righteous acts, in the fear of God, to set them all in the fear of the Lord. A good generation (living) in the fear of God, in the days of mercy. (Ps.Sol.17.21, 26-29, 32, 34b-36a, 18.6-9)

Verse 28:

"Standpoint of the gospel . . . your sake": cf. 5.10, 8.7, 11.7, Eph.2.14-22, 4.18, Col.1.21f, Jas.4.4, 1 Jn.2.15.

Paul continues his direct address to the Gentile believers, warning them against acting arrogantly towards Israel. He clearly states that Israel have become God's enemies (cf. 5.10) "for your sake" only. Israel's transgression, stiff-neckedness and rejection of God's purpose foretold in the Torah that He would include the Gentiles in His kingdom was in fact one of the means whereby God made His righteousness available to the Gentiles in Yeshua. Israel are "hostile" to the gospel concerning God's son (cf. 1.3) which is the "power of salvation to all who are faithful, to the Jew first *and also to the Greek*" (cf. 1.16) and which embodies the mystery of the Messiah in which God makes the Gentiles fellow-heirs and fellow-citizens in the commonwealth of Israel (cf. Eph.2.12-3.12). This determines the perspective of the Gentiles, whose position derives "from the standpoint of the gospel." God has made Israel enemies *only for the sake of the inclusion of the Gentiles in His kingdom.* In relation to God's promises to the forefathers, however, Israel's election remains sure. He has chosen them because He promised their forefathers that He would multiply them and make out of them a great nation in which all the nations of the world would be blessed (cf. Gen.12.1-3, 15.5, 17.1-8,

22.17-18, 26.4, Ex.32.13).[51] Israel's election is the foundation upon which the Gentiles, who were once "not-My-people," could also be included and "called (into being)" as God's children and inherit God's promises together with Israel. Even if, therefore, the people of Israel have temporarily become "enemies" for the sake of the Gentiles, they are first God's beloved and the "sons of the Lord your God" (cf. Dt.14.1).

"Beloved for the sake of the fathers": cf. Gen.26.3, Ex.33.1, Num.32.11, Dt.1.8-11, 4.37, 7.8, 10.15, Lk.1.72-73, Rom.4.3, 11ff, 9.5, 25; Mekh.Beshall.4, PRK 17.5, 22.4, 23.7, 33.1, Gen.R.44.5, 14, Ex.R.23.5, Lev.R.36.2, 6.

Israel's election (God's "choice" [ἐκλογην; *eklogen*]) is based upon God's promises to the Patriarchs. Since it, too, is promised by God to Abraham, it stands forever. God will not annul His promise, nor recall the heritage which He has given to Israel, who are His inheritance and whose inheritance He also is:

> Why dost Thou show favor to Israel, as indicated by the verse *That which is a statute for Israel is an ordinance for the God of Jacob* (Ps.81.4)? God replied: I show them favor out of consideration for the merit of their Fathers. (PRK 33.1)

Verse 29:

"For the gifts and calling of God are irrevocable": cf. Gen.17.8, Ex.33.1, Dt.1.8, 4.31, 31.6-8, Josh.1.5, Ps.110.4, Isa.43.1, 7, 45.3-4, Rom.8.28, 9.4f, 1 Cor.1.26, Eph.1.18, 2 Tim.1.9, Heb.3.1, 7.21; Jub.15.32, TBE p.7, p.17, p.31.

Paul repeats the "proofs" of Israel's election as God's "possession" (cf. 9.4-5), knowing that although God carries out His threats of punishment if the people are disobedient the castigation can be averted, and, furthermore, that His promises for good are sure and certain. Thus God's promises to both Abraham and David are irrevocable blessings which will never be annulled:

> All Israel and Moses with them assembled, and he spoke up to God: Master of the universe, between us and the peoples of the world there is in fact no difference. *For how would it be known that I have found grace in Thy sight, I and Thy people, unless Thou goest with us that we may be distinguished, I and Thy people, from all the people that are upon the face of the earth?* (Ex.33.16). Thereupon the Holy One swore by His great name that the entire Torah [both Written and Oral] would be given to them. . . . And the Holy One went on to

swear to His people that He would never exchange them for another nation, never give them up or substitute another people for them . . . nor have them dwell in any city [other than Jerusalem], as it is said, *I will not execute the fierceness of Mine anger, I will not return to destroy Ephraim, for I am . . . the Holy One, [ever] in the midst of thee* (Hos.11.9) (TBE p.127, [EZ] p.191)[52]

Verses 30-31:

"Disobedient . . . shown mercy": cf. 6.6, Eph.2.1-3, 11-22, 4.17-22, Col.1.21, 3.9.

Paul's "commission" is to bring the Gentiles out of their "disobedience" (cf. 1.18-32) into the "obedience of faith" (cf. 1.5, 16.26). God has "shown mercy" in grafting into the natural root a people who were once "not-My-people" and left "without compassion" (cf. Hos.1.10, 2.23), and has brought them into the commonwealth of Israel through the fact that Israel themselves have not accepted God's righteousness in Yeshua. The causal link ("because of their [Israel's] disobedience") is subsumed under God's final purpose to save all Israel. Israel's transgression allows God to graft in the Gentile nations, who will then turn Israel back to their own God. Because God does not wish anyone to perish, the Gentiles' inclusion must also lead to Israel's salvation. The mercy which God shows to the Gentiles they in turn show to Israel, so that all men are saved (cf. מידה כנגד מידה; *middah ke-neged middah*—"measure for measure").

Verse 32:

"Shut up all in disobedience": cf. 3.9, 19, Gal.3.22; 1QH 8.11.

Paul picks up the theme of "shutting up" (הסגיר; *hisgir*) (cf. 1.24), in relation to God's turning away of His face (הסתר פנים; *hester panim*) and the equality of all men in sin (cf. chapter 3).[53] God has removed His presence and His favor from men and has "given them over" to serve their own evil inclination instead of their Creator (cf. 1.18-32, and chapter 6). The analogy between disobedience and mercy (which parallels Paul's analogy between grace and condemnation in 5.12f) emphasizes the fact that all men fall short of God's glory (cf. 3.9, 23) and have exchanged the glory of God's image for their own (cf. 1.23).[54] After Paul has demonstrated God's sovereignty in the mystery of the inclusion of the Gentiles in His kingdom through the gospel of the Messiah he can show that God's "shutting up" of all in disobedience expresses God's ultimate righteousness in Yeshua, given freely to all those who call on the name of the Lord (cf. 10.12-13).

Verses 33-36:

"Depth of the riches . . . ": cf. Job 5.9, 15.8, 35.7, 41.11, Ps.40.5, 92.5, Prov.3.16, 8.18, 22.4, Isa.40.13, 55.8-9, Jer.23.18, Jn.7.38, Rom.2.4, 9.23, 11.12, 1 Cor.1.24, 30, 2.10, 21, Eph.1.7, 18, 2.7, 3.16, Phil.4.19, Col.1.27, 2.2-3; 1QS 10.12, 11.3, 17-22, 1QH 2.18, 4.27-33, 5.20-21, 26, 6.14-18, 8.8, 20f, 10.31, 12.29, 1QS[b] 1.3; Wis.Sol.7.17.1f, Jub.2.3, 2 Bar.14.8f; PA 3.4.

Paul sums up the complex of motifs in the preceding chapters and repeats the "doxology" of 9.5. God's Messiah has delivered all men from their bondage to sin and death (cf. 7.25). As God's "counselor" (cf. 9.34), Yeshua intercedes on man's behalf and gives him God's righteousness and life eternal in the "riches of His grace."[55] In him all things are "summed up" and "glorified" "with a view to an administration suitable to the fullness of the times" (cf. Eph.1.3-12). Paul expresses his exuberance over the revelation of God's plan for the salvation of both Jews and Gentiles, which also vindicates his own ministry, in the psalmic tradition also continued within the Qumran community:

> I will sing in Knowledge, and my whole lyre shall throb to the Glory of God, and my lute and harp to the holy Order which He has made. I will raise the flute of my lips because of His righteous measuring-cord. . . . I will pronounce my judgment according to my iniquities, my rebellions shall be before my eyes like the graven Decree. But to God I will say, My righteousness! (and) to the Most High, Support of my goodness! Source of Knowledge! Fountain of Holiness! Infinite Glory and Might of Eternal Majesty! . . . For to God belongs my justification, and the perfection of my way, and the uprightness of my heart are in His hand: by His righteousness are my rebellions blotted out. For He has poured forth from the fount of His knowledge the light that enlightens me, and my eye has beheld His marvels and the light of my heart pierces the Mystery to come. The everlasting Being is the stay of my right hand; the way of my steps is on a stout rock, nothing shall be fearsome before me. For God's truth is the rock of my steps and His power, the stay of my right hand, and from the fount of His Righteousness comes my justification. (1QS 10.9-12, 11.2-5)[56]

Man has been "given over" (cf. 1.24, 28) into the power of his evil inclination and cannot say anything to justify himself before God (cf. 3.19-20). It is God's mercy alone which bestows upon them His righteousness in Yeshua, who "has shone in [men's] hearts to give the light of the knowledge of the glory of God" (2 Cor.4.6). Paul expresses a "hymn of thanksgiving" to God for this fact, in the tradition of the Magnificat and the Benedictus (cf. 8.27-28) also known from Qumran:

> Blessed be the God of Israel who keeps favour unto His Covenant and testimonies of salvation to the people whom He has redeemed! He has called them that staggered to [mar]vellous [salvation] but has wiped out the assembly of the nations unto destruction, leaving no remnant. He raises in righteousness the discouraged heart and opens the mouth of the dumb that it might cry out with joy because of [His] lofty [deeds]. [To] feeble [hands] He teaches battle and to them whose knees stagger He gives strength to stand . . . And we, the re[mnant of Thy people,] [shall praise] Thy name, O God of favours, who hast kept the Covenant with our fathers, and during all our generations lettest Thy favours fall upon the remn[ant of Thy people]. . . . And we, Thy holy people, shall praise Thy name because of Thy works of truth, and we shall exalt [Thy] ma[gnificence] because of Thy lofty deeds [during] the seasons and times appointed by the eternal testimonies, at the [com]ing of day and night and [when] evening and morning depart. For Thy [glori]ous [kingship] is great, together with Thy marvellous Mysteries in the heights [of heaven] . . . Be lifted up, O God of gods, be lifted up! Be praised in the c[louds of heaven . . .]. (1QM 14.4-16)

Endnotes for Chapter 11

1 Chapter 10 is an extended "discussion" which is formally part of the question in 9.30-31; for the structure of 9.30-10.21, see the comments on 9.30.

2 Paul's physical lineage is in fact impeccable: Abraham is the father of his nation and Benjamin the patriarch of his tribe. According to rabbinic tradition, Benjamin was the first to cross the Red Sea (cf. Mekh.Beshall.6, Sot.37a) and Elijah, Saul, and Jeremiah were all from the tribe of Benjamin (cf. 1 Chron.8.27, 1 Sam.9.1-2, Jer.1.1). For Elijah, see verse 2.

3 See the comments on 8.28f for Paul's defense of Israel's election.

4 It is therefore true that in order to claim that God has rejected his people one must also reject the Torah. Consequently, it is not surprising that when Paul's warning to the Gentiles, in this chapter, was completely disregarded by the later church fathers, views such as that of Marcion

surfaced, completely refuting the *Tanakh* (The Old Testament) and parts of the New Testament corpus, including Paul's own writings. For a brief but good overview of the early sources of "replacement theology," see *Mishkan* 21.2 (1994), ed. O. Chr. Kvarme.

5 Paul's appeal to Elijah is also a personal appeal to his own ancestry, since Elijah was a Benjamite (cf. 1 Chron.8.27) as he himself was (cf. Phil.3.5).

6 Paul uses the same phrase, "in the same way," in 8.26, where he also explains how God's intercession on behalf of His people, and the maintenance of their election; see the comments there.

7 Cf. Isa.1.8-9, 4.2ff, 7.3, 10.20ff, 11.11ff, 37.32, 46.3, Jer.23.3, 31.7, Joel 2.32, Mic.4.7, 5.6-7, Zeph.2.9, 3.12-13, Obad.17, Zech.14.16.

8 The idea is expressed by a number of Hebrew roots: שאר (*sha'ar*), "to leave"; פלט (*palat*), "to escape"; שרד (*sarad*), "to survive": and יתר (*yatar*), "to be left over." The most common root, both verbal and nounal, is שאר (cf. שאר [*she'ar*] and שארית [*she'arit*]); the English verb "save" expresses the same dual ideas of deliverance and "exception" (save for . . .).

9 In the continuation of this passage, the Teacher of Righteousness speaks of his task as being the "light of the nations" (cf. Isa.42.4, 6, 49.6); see the comments on verses 25-26.

10 Chapters 4 and 9 also establish the inclusion of the Gentiles together with Israel on the basis of the motif of the "sons of Abraham." See also Paul's קו"ח (*kal ve-chomer*) argument over grace in chapter 5.

11 Paul's ultimate conclusion, at which he arrives in the latter part of this chapter, is that the "sons of Abraham" are those people, among both Jews and Gentiles, upon whom God bestows His righteousness in Yeshua. Since Yeshua's faithfulness is the τελος (*telos*) or goal of the Torah (cf. 10.4), it is available only as a gift from God, and yet therefore precisely open to all mankind.

12 For the talmudic formula, "what then shall we say?," see the comments on 3.3; for the structure of 9.31-10.21, see 9.30. Paul is not arguing that Israel have not been disobedient but disputing the claim that their disobedience has led God to reject them as His people and to replace them with the Gentiles. Their fault lay in not understanding that God's plan was to gather also the Gentiles into His kingdom through the gift of His righteousness in Yeshua. In rejecting Yeshua they therefore also dismissed God's purpose both for their own redemption and that of the whole world. However, God Himself accepts this rejection and uses it, as He had foretold in His word, to bring the Gentiles into His kingdom, a fact which will then finally provoke the people of Israel back to their own God through jealousy (cf. Dt.32.21, Rom.10.19).

13 As part of his refutation of the erroneous conclusion Paul brings prooftexts (Dt.29.4, Isa.29.10, Ps.69.22f) which speak of God's punishment of the transgressors within Israel, following which He will restore them to grace; the quotation from Ps.69.22-23 appears to be a גזרה שוה (*gezerah shavah*) in which Paul associates "eyes to see not" in Dt.29.4 with "eyes . . . to see not" in Ps.69.23, although in the latter David (the psalmist) is calling down punishment upon his persecutors. For Paul, because Scripture is an example from which later generations learn (cf. 15.4) it must be read in the light of God's whole plan, so that the prooftexts (cf. also Isa.6.9-10) reflect the "dialectic" of God's purpose in hardening Israel's heart so that He can also include the Gentiles in His kingdom.

14 "Falling" frequently means "turning aside" to idolatry; cf. Dt.28.14, 31.29, Prov.40.4. Paul may also be influenced here, however, by a midrashic tradition on the "fallen tabernacle of David" (Amos 9.11-12) reflected in James' speech in Acts 15.16-17. James' (Hebrew) text of Amos either read or was interpreted to mean that Israel would "possess the remnant of אדם (*'adam*; 'mankind')" rather than אדום, in parallel to the sentence "and all the nations who are called by My name" (Amos 9.12). The fragment 11Q 27 interprets the "tent of David" in Isa.65.1, 5 in a similar manner to James, who understands that the "raising" of David's tabernacle both rests upon and brings about the repentance of the Gentiles. Paul speaks of "standing" (the opposite of "falling") in chapter 14, where he describes the grounds upon which God accepts men and makes them "stand" before Him; cf. also 5.2.

15 Paul anticipates this argument in chapter 4; cf. also 9.25-26.

16 Cf. Ex.20.5, 34.14, Dt.4.7, 24, 6.4, 7.6-8, 14.2, 12, 26.19, 32.8, Jer.31.33, 32.38, Ezek.36.28. Paul refers to Israel's jealousy of the Gentiles' worship (cf. verse 14), as the prooftext (Dt.32.21) makes clear. The Gentiles, furthermore, may be jealous of Israel's election when they are "without hope and without God in the world," but they have no further cause to be so when they are made "fellow-citizens" and "fellow-heirs" with Israel (cf. Eph.2.12-3.7).

17 See the comments on verse 15 for the "greater" side of Israel's contribution to the whole world.

18 Paul has primarily been addressing the Jewish believers ("those who know the Torah") since 7.1, and then begins dealing with Gentile objections to Israel's election in 8.28ff.

19 Cf. 1 Cor.1.26-31, 5.6, 2 Cor.16-18, 30, 12.1, 5, 9, Jas.4.16. Paul's normal cautiousness about boasting corresponds to his stern warning to the Gentiles in the directly following section against being arrogant towards the

root (Israel) which upholds them. Arrogance and boasting go hand in hand. Paul here does not so much boast of as highlight his ministry to the Gentiles since it is this ministry which will ultimately bring his people back to faithfulness to their own God.

20 This is reflected, again, in the ק״ח (*kal ve-chomer*) argument which is not a simple comparison (between Israel's "transgression" and the "riches" of the Gentiles) but a three-stage process which leads from Israel's transgression to the reconciliation of the world, and then to Israel's "fulfillment" and "life from the dead" for the whole world.

21 This passage seems to be based on Zechariah 8 (cf. the midrash on verse 12). The pronoun "their" (transgression, failure, fulfillment, rejection, and acceptance) in verses 12 and 15 refers to Israel (as a subjective genitive). Similarly, "their" rejection in verse 15 refers to Israel's rejection of Yeshua and not God's rejection of Israel.

22 The word πληρωμα (*pleroma*), "fulfillment" or "fullness," is consistently used in the New Testament to refer to Yeshua himself. In him "all the fullness of Deity dwells in bodily form" (Col.2.9; cf. Col.1.19, Eph.4.13), and he gives of that "fullness" to his body (Jn.1.16, Eph.1.23, 3.19; cf. Rom.13.10); (see also his role as the τελος [*telos*] or "goal" of the Torah [Rom.10.4; cf. Mt.5.17]). He also embodies the "fullness of the times" in which all things are "summed up" (Eph.1.10; cf. Gal.4.4). This includes the "fullness (of the times of) the Gentiles" (cf. Lk.21.24), so that Israel's "fulfillment" is also closely linked to the "fullness of the Gentiles" (verse 25) which leads to the salvation of "all Israel."

23 Cf. Shev.2.6, Kil.7.1, Tos.Shev.1.6, RH 10b. The association comes from the "knee" shape which the bending of the vine produces when it is drawn into the ground, since the root meaning of the Hebrew verb ברך (*barakh*) is "to bend the knee." Paul speaks of the grafting of the Gentiles as the scion into the original stock (Israel) rather than creating a new growth in the same way as R. Eleazar uses the verbal root in the sense of engrafting.

24 Both Ruth and Naamah belonged to idolatrous nations, and were "grafted" into the stock of Israel. Naamah was the mother of Rehoboam (cf. 1 Kings 14.31), from whom descended Asa, Jehoshaphat, and Hezekiah; and Ruth was King David's ancestress (cf. Ruth 4.13ff). R. Eleazar speaks of these two Gentile women as "blessings" whose blessing is finally for the sake of Israel. In the same way, Paul also says that Israel will be a "blessing" for the whole world, although he first speaks of the "grafting in" of the Gentile believers as a blessing for them, which will then bless Israel in their final redemption. The verse in Gen.12.3

was therefore obviously understood in a messianic context during the Second Temple period, and Paul directly connects it with Yeshua in Gal.3.8ff. For the reference to Spain, see also the comments on 15.24.

25 The "tenth portion" is not only the tenth of an *ephah* of flour offered as a sin offering by the person unable to afford two turtledoves or pigeons (cf. Lev.5.1) but also the מעשר (*ma'aser*) or "tithe of the land" which is holy to the Lord: "'Thus all the tithe of the land, of the seed of the land or of the fruit of the tree, is the Lord's; it is holy to the Lord'" (Num.27.30). This verse encompasses all the elements from which Paul draws for his midrash.

26 The Tanakh describes the people of Israel as various trees, including the vine, the cedar, the palm tree, and the olive tree; cf. Ps.92.12, Isa.5.1-7, Jer.11.16, Ex.R.36.1, Men.53b; cf. also the messianic image of the "Shoot" and the "Branch" in Isa.11.1, Jer.23.5, 33.15, Zech.3.8, 6.12, 1QH 6.10ff, 8.4ff. The olive tree is called אשר (*'asher*) and the tribe of Asher is associated in Gen.49.20 with olive oil (cf. Dt.33.24), its traditional sign or symbol being the olive tree itself; cf. Test.Jud.25.2, PRK 21.4, and the comments on verse 18. 4 Ezra also calls Israel the "holy seed (race)" (4 Ez.9.2), a phrase which recalls both Abraham's "seed" (cf. Gen.17.7f, 22.17f, Gal.3.16) and Israel's calling as a "holy nation" (cf. Ex.19.6, Dt.7.6, 14.2, 21, 26.19, 1 Pet.2.9).

27 Leaven is commonly associated with the evil inclination in rabbinic literature; cf. Tanh.B.Noach 4, PBer.4.2, 7d, Gen.R.34.10, Num.R.13.4, Ber.17a.

28 See also the idea of the "first fruits" in 8.23.

29 John the Baptist appeals to the motif of trees bearing fruit in distinguishing the "true" "sons of Abraham;" cf. Mt.3.7-10, 7.17ff, Lk.3.7-9, 13.21, Jn.15.1-6, Sir.27.6. A midrash on Job 13.12 associates the "true" sons of Abraham with the motifs of both clay (cf. 9.20-21) and bondage (service to the evil inclination; cf. chapter 6):

> [In comment on God's command to remember Amalek], R. Tanhum bar Hanila'i began his discourse by citing the following verse: *Your acts of remembering [Amalek, followed by repentance for your sins], will be like "ashes"; but when you deserve visitation [for sin], visitation in "clay" shall be your punishment* (Job 13.12). The Holy One said to Israel: My children, I inscribed in Torah two references to Amalek that you are to remember—heed them: *Thou shalt blot out the remembrance of Amalek* (Dt.25.19); *I will utterly blot out the remembrance of Amalek* (Ex.17.14). But let

> *your acts of remembering [be followed by repentance for your sins so that you] will be like "ashes"*—that is, if through repentance you gain merit, you will be true children of Abraham who spoke of himself as "ashes," saying "I am . . . but dust and ashes" (Gen.18.27). If you do not gain such merit, however, [because when you remembered Amalek you did not repent of your own sins], then a deserved *visitation, visitation in "clay" shall be your punishment* (Job 13.12): You will have to prepare yourselves for another servitude like that in Egypt. What is written of the servitude in Egypt? The Egyptians "made their lives bitter with hard service in clay," etc. (Ex.1.14). (PRK 3.2)

See also the comments on 7.25.

30 R. Isaac exploits the association of the olive tree in other places with the righteous (cf. Ps.52.8, 128.3) and thus uses it as a metaphor for pruning despite the fact that in the context of Jeremiah 11 God says that He will not even listen if the people pray and will not avert the coming disaster because they have done so many vile things.

31 Paul may be influenced here by Isaiah 60-61, chapters which speak of God's "planting" and of the glorification of Israel by the nations. Isa.60.1-3 recalls the light to (the salvation of) the Gentiles in Isa.9.2f, 42.6f, 49.6, 51.4, which is associated with Hos.1.10 in 1 Pet.2.9-10; Isa.60.21 speaks of the righteous as "the branch of My [His] planting;" Isa.61.3 refers to "oaks of righteousness, the planting of the Lord;" and in Isa.60.13, the sanctuary will be beautified by "the juniper, the box tree, and the cypress together."

32 This passage combines the motif of "planting" (which frequently describes the Qumran community) with the metaphor of light and darkness so that the "wild" tree (the Gentiles) is delivered from the kingdom of darkness into the kingdom of light; cf. Acts 26.18, 1 Pet.2.3-9, 1QS 3.13-4.26, 1QH 8.4ff, Test.Jos.19.3, 3 Bar.6.13, 2 En.30.15, Did.1.1, Ep.Barn.18.1-20.2; see the comments on 2.19.

33 In a verbal communication, Dr. David Young suggested that one of the possible reasons for the reflection of Gentile arrogance in the Roman community arose from the return of Jewish believers expelled from the city by Claudius' decree in 52 C.E (cf. Acts 18.2). The dating of Romans as 57-58 C.E. would demonstrate that those who had been banished were already returning, since Paul sends them greetings in 16.3; see Sanday and Headlam, *Romans*, 418. The return of the Jewish believers might have created some resentment on the part of the Gentile believers who would probably have filled the places left by the absence of the former.

It might even have given rise to some feelings of actual superiority, although this surmise is even more speculative seeing that attitudes of the kind expressed here normally arise in an arena of actual conflict rather than in a social vacuum. For the mixed nature of the congregation in Rome, see the comments on chapter 16 passim; for the dating of the letter, see Sanday and Headlam, *Romans*, xxxvi-vii.

34 This passage combines many of the motifs to which Paul appeals in Romans. Just like the talmudic Rabbis, he associates God's "light" with His election of Israel ("as though they were one"), based on the same verse from Prov.20.27 (cf. 8.26f). Also like the midrashic passage, he links the light of Israel's election with the redemption of the Gentiles in reference to a series of messianic prooftexts (cf. Isa.9.1ff, 42.6, 49.6, 51.4, Lk.2.32). (For the tradition of Prov.20.27, see the comments on 8.27, where in the related passage in Lk.2.32-35, Prov.20.27 and Isa.42.6 [49.6, etc.] are also combined.)

35 John the Baptist also appeals in distinguishing the "true" "sons of Abraham" in Mt.3.7-12, where he plays on the words אבנים (*'avanim*), "stones," and בנים (*banim*), "sons," although he ties this wordplay to the image of the torn-down trees. For the motif of the "sons of Abraham," see the comments on 2.25f.

36 The Teacher of Righteousness (the probable author of the psalm) describes himself here as the "gardener" who is responsible (in place of God) for the divine planting (cf. Isa.6.1-7). If he removes his tending care from the community, they will become "trees of wild fruits," and wither and die. Paul anticipates this argument, that the Gentiles can become "sons of Abraham" by doing the "work of the Torah" even without participating in the covenant, in 2.12ff.

37 For God's kindness, see also the comments on 2.4.

38 Paul combines the horticultural metaphor with the biblical punishment of כרת (*karet*), "cutting off," in the Tanakh. God "cuts off" a person either from the nation or from the earth, as punishment by death for a transgression against Himself; cf. Gen.9.11, Ex.9.15, Num.15.31, 1 Kings 2.4, Isa.48.19, Jer.33.18.

39 This "natural," uncultivated state recalls the "natural" morality of the Gentiles in 2.14. It is also possible that Paul is making a play on the word בר (*bar*) which means both "wild" and "son" (cf. Job 39.4, Ps.2.12, Prov.31.2): the זית ביתי (*zait beiti*) is not only the natural or domestic/cultivated olive tree but also literally the "home olive," while the זית בר (*zait bar*) is both the wild olive and metaphorically the "son olive." Paul can thus intimate that even the wild olive is His son and has the right to

be grafted into the original natural stock. (The word בר has the additional meaning of "pure," so that both the wild and the natural olive trees become "the generation of those who seek Him, who seek Thy face"—of those who may ascend into the hill of the Lord and stand in His holy place because they have "clean hands and a pure heart," and shall thus "receive a blessing from the Lord and righteousness from the God of [their] salvation" (Ps.24.6, 4-5).

40 Paul justifies his reproof of Peter in Galatians for his hypocritical behavior towards the Gentiles by appealing to the "naturally" sinful character of the Gentiles, which, however, is "made righteous" through their faithfulness to God in Yeshua. As the midrash in Yev.63a indicates, however, the engrafting of the "wild" Gentiles could also be perceived as a blessing to Israel.

41 For a contrary view to the link between God's "mystery" and the "obedience of the Gentiles," see J. Coppens, "'Mystery' in the theology of Saint Paul and its parallels at Qumran," in *Paul and Qumran*, ed. J. Murphy O'Connor (London: G. Chapman, 1968), 142f.

42 Cf. Test.Levi 17.1-18.14, CDC 1.7, 1QH 6.8-14; for the references on the Shoot, see verse 16. The "knowledge" of God's mysterious purpose therefore leads both to righteousness (cf. 10.3) and to humility before God's grace, a theme which Paul picks up again in 12.9ff, where he promotes a policy of "non-retaliation" and love of one's neighbor in the "service of the time" (see 12.11 for the text).

43 See TDNT 6:298ff. Paul uses the same word in verse 12 for the "fulfillment" of Israel, where "fulfillment" corresponds to (more than) "riches" in the same verse and to "life from the dead" in verse 15. Paul favors the expression, particularly in relation to Yeshua's "divinity;" cf. Eph.1.23, 3.19, 4.13, Col.1.19, 2.9.

44 In the first sense the phrase would refer to (the time when) all the Gentile nations become faithful to God in Yeshua; in the latter sense it emphasizes the time when the Gentiles became faithful. The two meanings are not necessarily exclusive of one of another.

45 Cf. the terms מועד (*mo'ed*), תיקון (*tikkun*), גמר הקץ (*gemar ha-ketz*), קצי אל (*kitzei 'El*); 1QS 3.15, 23, 4.18-19, 1QM 3.9, 1QH 3.7, 1QpHab 7.13, 1Q26 1.1, 4, 1Q27 1.6-7. The expression "fullness of the time" in Gal.4.4 refers to "the right time" (cf. 5.6) or the time which God chose in order to show His grace and favor to man in forgiving their iniquity. It is therefore connected with repentance and grace and thus also with faithfulness.

46 See D. Flusser, *Jewish*, 253-75.

[47] The throwing off of Gentile rule from the land and people of Israel was a frequent messianic expectation; cf. Lk.1.71, 74-75, Ps.Sol.17.23-51, 2 Bar.72.2-6, Ber.24b.

[48] For the structure of 9.30-11.11, see the comments on 9.30.

[49] The Greek word πας (*pas*), "all," frequently corresponds to the remnant as all those who remain, as does the Hebrew word כל (*kol*) in the Tanakh; see the comments on verse 5, where the story of Elijah proves that although "all the people" were gathered together there, seven thousand still remained faithful to God. It also corresponds to πλοῦτος (*ploutos*; "the richness") in Eph.1.7 and 2.7 and so directly to רוב (*rov*; many) and המון (*hamon*; many); cf. Eph.1.3, 4.2, 19, 31, 5.3, 6.18, 1QpHab 8.13.

[50] Isa.27.6 may also underlie verses 12 and 15. Jacob and Israel are not merely poetic parallels but represent "all" of Israel, the ten northern tribes (of Israel) and the two southern tribes (of Judah); cf. Jer.5.20, Hos.10.11, 12.2, Mic.1.5.

[51] Paul thus directly links Israel's election with Abraham's blessing and the promise of righteousness on the basis of faithfulness (cf. chapter 4). He also recalls the theme of the "two masters" (cf. chapters 6f): Israel are temporarily serving their own evil inclination and "angering" God by refusing His righteousness in Yeshua (cf. 10.3).

[52] The polemical tone of these passages is clear, and comes from exactly the same sort of sources against which Paul is fighting here. The reference to the access of the Gentile nations to the Written Torah indicates Gentile believers in Yeshua, who nevertheless claim that God has placed them in His favor instead of Israel. The claim that the Oral Torah separates and distinguishes Israel from the other nations was one of the counter-arguments to the Gentile usurpation of Israel's inheritance as God's portion; cf. Pes.Rab.5.1, PShab.12.4, 13d, Gen.R.50.9, Num.R.14.10.

[53] In Gal.3.22, Paul says that the "Torah shuts up" men, perhaps identifying the Torah as the "jailor" who guards those who are shut up ("imprisoned;" cf. "custody" in verse 23, and maybe also "tutor" in Gal.3.24).

[54] See the comments on 1.24.

[55] For the Messiah as God's Wisdom and Power, see the references and comments on 1.16-17.

[56] The term "riches" occurs frequently in Qumran, where it is often further strengthened by רוב (*rov*), "many" or "most," or המון (*hamon*), "much" or "many," which correspond to the Greek terms πλοῦτος (*ploutos*), "fullness," and πληρωμα (*pleroma*), "fulfillment" (cf. verse 12); cf. 1QS 4.3-5, 1QH 4.36, 6.9, 7.30, 9.8, 10.21, 11.28, 12.14, Eph.1.18.

ROMANS

12

Introduction

Having firmly established God's purpose to make the Gentiles fellow-citizens in the commonwealth of Israel, Paul draws out some of the major *halakhic* or practical implications of the common heritage of Jewish and Gentile believers in Yeshua the Messiah. He picks up most of the themes which he has dealt with in the course of the letter, using the metaphor of "living sacrifices," under which he addresses the relationships between the community of believers (verses 1-2). He sets out the guidelines for "walking according to the Spirit" in the community, where every member is committed to serving one another as priests serving in the Temple of God (verses 3-8). He then adapts a Qumran homily dealing with the community's relations between one another and with the society around them, based on a "new" interpretation of Leviticus 19.18. The commandment to love others as oneself is observed in fulfillment of the commandment to love God Himself (verses 9-21). He further appeals to rabbinic proselytizing dicta which advocate putting oneself in the other's place in order to persuade and convince him (verses 14-18), and integrates the Qumran principle of non-retaliation against one's enemies in order to allow them to better their own behavior and/or to let God punish them fully in His own time (verses 19-21).

Verse 1:

"I urge you . . . worship": cf. Ps.50.12-23, Prov.21.3, Isa.1.11-17, 66.19-24, Jer.7.21-23, Hos.1.10, Amos 5.21-24, Mic.6.6-8, Lk.2.22, Rom.6.13, 16, 19, 9.15, 23, 15.16, 1 Cor.3.16-17, 6.20, 2 Cor.1.3, 10, 6.14-7.1, Eph.2.18-22, 5.19, Phil.1.20, Col.3.16, 1 Tim.3.15, Heb.12.18ff, 28, 13.15, 1 Pet.2.2-6; 1QS 1.1f, 16-18, 4.2ff, 5.5f, 8.4-10, 9.3ff, 1QH 1.15-20, 15.13-16, 4QpIsa.[d] 1; Test.Levi 3.6, Test.Naph.2.2-10, Odes Sol.20.1ff, Sib.Or.8.405, 408, Corp.Herm.1.31, 13.17ff; PA 2.9, Sifre Dt.Ve'etchanan 32, Ekev 41, Mid.Ps.66.1, Lev.R.3.5, Ta'anit 2a; Philo, *De Spec.Leg.*1.277.

Paul begins to sets forth the *halakhic* or practical principles governing the community of Jews and Gentiles whom God has created to be faithful to

Himself through walking in the Spirit of truth ("I urge you *therefore*, brethren . . . ").[1] His personal example carries the weight of his apostolic authority, here, as he issues *halakhic* ordinances. The authority with which he has been invested reflects a spiritual "anointing" which enables him to instruct the community in the ways of God—in a similar fashion to the role of the Teacher of Righteousness and the halakhot laid out in the "Manual of Discipline" for the community at Qumran:

> And this is the rule for the members of the Community, for those who volunteer to be converted from all evil and to cling to all His commands according to His will; to separate themselves from the congregation of perverse men, to become a Community in the Law . . . . They shall practice truth in common, and humility, and righteousness and justice and loving charity, and modesty in all their ways. Let no man walk in the stubbornness of his heart to stray by following his heart and eyes and the thoughts of his (evil) inclination. But in the Community they shall circumcise the foreskin of the (evil) inclination and disobedience in order to lay a foundation of truth for Israel, for the Community of the everlasting Covenant; that they may atone for all who are volunteers for the holiness of Aaron and for the House of truth in Israel. . . . (1QS 5.1-6)[2]

Similarly to the Qumran texts, Paul describes this principle as a "living and holy sacrifice. . . which is your spiritual service of worship." The underlying metaphor, common to Paul and to the Qumran community, is that of the Temple or "House" which is built of "living stones."[3] God abides in people through Yeshua who, being called as His "royal priesthood," offer their own lives as a sweet-smelling offering pleasing to God (cf. Ex.29.18, 25, 2 Cor.2.14-16, Eph.5.2):

> When these things come to pass in Israel according to all the appointed times for the Institution of the Spirit of holiness (founded) in accordance with eternal Truth, they shall expiate guilty rebellion and sinful infidelity and (procure) Loving-kindness upon earth without the flesh of burnt offering and the fat of sacrifice, but the offering of the lips in accordance with the law shall be as an agreeable odour of righteousness, and perfection of way shall be as the voluntary gift of a delectable oblation. . . . *And no son of perversion [shall oppress it agai]n as formerly, from the day when [I established judges] over my people Israel* (2 Sam.10b-11a) This is the House which

> [will be built at the e]nd of days; as it is written in the Book of [Moses, *In the sanctuary, O Adonai,*] *which Thy hands have established, Yah[w]eh will reign for ever and ever* {Ex.17-18}. It is the House into which will enter [neither the ungodly nor the undefiled], ever; neither the Ammonite, nor the Moabite, ever, nor the half-breed, nor the stranger, nor the sojourner, ever, but they that are called saints. Yah[w]eh [will reign (there) for] ever; He will appear above it constantly, and strangers will lay it waste no more as they formerly laid waste the sanctua[ry of I]srael because of their sin. And He has commanded a sanctuary (made by the hands) of man to be built for Himself, that there may be some in this sanctuary to send up the smoke of sacrifice in His honour before Him among those who observe the law. (1QS 9.3-5, 4QFlor.1.2-7)[4]

This image also governs Paul's use of the word λογικος (*logikos*) or "reasonable" worship. Although the original meaning of the Greek adjective λογικος related to rational thought -reasoning—the word became a focal term in the philosophical polemic against the superstition of the "primitive" sacrificial system. For the Stoics, for example, "rational" worship meant agreeing with God's will to His praise in proper moral thought, will, and action.[5] Hellenistic and Jewish mysticism associated the same word with "heavenly praise," such as that expressed in the Odes of Solomon:

> I am a priest of the Lord, and to him I serve as a priest; and to him I offer the offering of his thought. For his thought is not like the world, nor like the flesh, nor like them who serve according to the flesh. The offering of the Lord is righteousness, and purity of heart and lips. Offer your inward being faultlessly; and do not let your compassion oppress compassion; and do not let yourself oppress anyone. (Odes Sol.20.1-5)

Paul follows the tradition also expressed in the Qumran texts which re-merges the philosophical and mystical perspectives, emphasizing that the "rational" aspect of moral conduct in a man's whole life is in effect his proper "spiritual" worship of God.[6]

Verse 2:
"Do not be conformed . . . your mind": cf. Ex.19.5-6, Dt.7.6, 26.18-19, Mt.6.24, 13.22, Jn.15.19, Rom.5.10, 7.24, 8.7, 2 Cor.4.4, 5.17, 10.5, Gal.1.4, Eph.2.2, 4.23-24, Phil.2.5, Col.1.21, 3.10, Tit.3.5, Heb.12.28, Jas.1.27,

1 Pet.1.13-16, 4.4, 1 Jn.2.15-17; 1QS 1.1-5, 17ff, 3.1-12, 19-22, 4.20-23, 5.1-20, 9.12-21, CDC 6.14, 12.23, 1QH 4.30-33, 5.7, 11.11-14, 13.11f, 16.1ff; Test.Jud.20.1-5, Test.Asher 1.5-9, 4.1f, 6.1; 2 Clem.6.1-6.

Paul once again picks up the theme of the two masters (the Two Ways or Spirits), describing here how "service" to the world, which is in the "dominion of Belial" (cf. 1QS 2.19), is "hostility" to God and "bondage" to the "spirit of flesh" or "perversity" or "defilement" (cf. 1QS 3.18-4.26). Every man must choose to whose law he will confirm, that of Belial or that of God:

> "So understand, my children, that two spirits await an opportunity with humanity: the spirit of truth and the spirit of error. In between is the conscience of the mind which inclines as it will. The things of truth and the things of error are written in the affections of man, each one of whom the Lord knows." . . . For two passions contrary to God's commands enslave him, so that he is unable to obey God: They blind his soul, and he goes about in the day as though it were night. . . . "And now, my children . . . choose for yourselves light or darkness, the Law of the Lord or the works of Beliar." . . . Till now the Spirits of truth and perversity battle in the hearts of every man; (they) walk in Wisdom and Folly. And according to each man's share of Truth and Righteousness, so does he hate Perversity. And according to his portion in the lot of Perversity, and (according to) the wickedness (which is) in him, so does he abominate Truth. For God has allotted these (Spirits) in equal parts until the final end, the time of Renewal. (Test.Jud.20.1-4, 18.6, Test.Levi 19.1, 1QS 4.23-25)

The "renewal" of man's "mind" νους (*nous*) delivers him from bondage to the "dominion of Belial" in the "spirit of flesh" (spirit of perversity or spirit of defilement) and his evil inclination, in order to serve God in Yeshua.[7] The LXX regularly uses νους for לב (*lev*; heart), as well as for רוח (*ruach*; spirit, wind or breath).[8] This passage also refers directly back to 7.16 and 22, and "inversely" to 3.5f: walking in faithfulness to Yeshua "proves" God's righteousness because His righteousness is made manifest in human life and daily conduct.

"Prove . . . perfect": cf. Ps.19.7, 119.39, 68, 137, 160, 164, 172, Prov.4.2, Rom.1.28, 2.18, 3.4-5, 19-20, 7.12, 16, 8.27, Gal.6.4, Eph.5.10, 17, Phil.1.10, 1 Thess.5.21, 1 Tim.1.8, 2 Tim.3.15-16; 1QS 9.13-15, 24-6, 11.17-22, CDC 2.14-16, 3.15-16, 7.4-6, 1QH 4.31-33, 9.9-10, 10.1-12, 4QFlor.1.6f; Test.Levi 14.4, Ps.Sol.7.22ff, Sib.Or.3.257, 580, 600, 4 Ez.3.20-23, 9.36-37; Jos.*Contra Ap.*1. 38-42;

PRK 15.5, Mekh.Beshall.1, Mid.Ps.24.31, 119.7, AZ 19b, Men.53b; Philo, *De Vit.Cont.*1f, 25, 28f.

Paul demonstrates, in contrast to the claim made in 3.5f, that the true "way" in which God is "justified" is through just actions (righteousness) (cf. 6.1ff) and not through unrighteousness (so that His grace may abound), and reinforces his argument in 7.12f that although sin deceives and thus kills man, man's inability to observe the (commandments of the) Torah "proves" the latter to be "holy and righteous and good" (cf. the "good" which God promises in 8.28) in Yeshua's deliverance of man from his "body of death," a view of God's grace reflected in many of the Qumran texts:

> When they join the Community, let whoever comes to the Council of the Community enter into the Covenant of God in the presence of all the volunteers, and let him undertake by oath of obligation to be converted to the Law of Moses according to all His commands, with all his heart and all his soul, following all that is revealed of it to the sons of Zadok the priests who keep the Covenant and seek his will . . . And let him undertake by the Covenant to be separated from all perverse men who walk in the way of wickedness. . . . Thine, Thine, is righteousness! For Thou hast made ever[y spirit] [with its strength] and understanding; for it is Thou who hast allotted the spirit to the just. And I have chosen to cleanse my hands according to [Thy] wil[l] and the soul of Thy servant has l[oath]ed every work of perversity. And I know that none is righteous beside Thee; and I have appeased Thy face because of the Spirit which Thou hast put [in me] to accomplish Thy [fav]ours towards [Thy] servant for [ever] by cleansing me by Thy holy Spirit and by causing me to go forward in Thy will according to the greatness of Thy favours . . . [. . . for Thou art . . .] and merciful, lo[ng-suffer]ing [and rich] in grace and truth, who pardonest the sin [. . .] and compassionate towards [all the sons of righteousness], [they that love Thee] and keep [Thy] command[ments] [and] are converted to Thee with faith and a perfect heart [. . .] to serve Thee [and to do what is] good in Thine eyes. (1QS 5.7-11, 1QH 16.9-18)[9]

Verse 3:

"Through the grace given to me I say . . . ": cf. Lk.2.40, Acts 14.26, 15.40, Rom.1.5, 15.15, 1 Cor.3.10, 15.10, Gal.2.9, Eph.3.2, 7f, 1 Pet.4.10; 1QH 2.13-19, 4.27-29, 6.10-14, 7.10-27, 8.16, 35-36.

Paul directly appeals to his authority as an apostle to establish *halakhic* principles for the early communities, exhorting the congregation in Rome to act in love and respect towards one another, particularly regarding their functions within the "body" of the Messiah. As he demonstrates in 1.5 and recalls in the previous verse ("I urge you therefore, brethren, by the *mercies of God*"), חסד (*chesed*; grace) was used as a technical phrase in Second Temple Jewish literature for *halakhic* authority. This usage is particularly notable in the words of the Teacher of Righteousness in support of his authoritative teachings, the mysteries of God directly revealed to him through the Holy Spirit:

> And I, gifted with understanding, I have known Thee, O my God, because of the Spirit that Thou hast put in me; and I have heard what is certain according to Thy marvellous secret because of Thy holy Spirit. Thou hast [o]pened Knowledge in the midst of me concerning the Mystery of Thine understanding, and the source of [Thy] powe[r and the fountain of] Thy [goodness] [Thou hast revealed [to me] according to the abundance of grace and destroying zeal . . . But they shall watch for Thy goodness, for in [Thy] gra[ce . . .] [. . .] and they have known Thee and at the time of Thy glory they shall rejoice. And in proportion to [their knowledge . . .] [and] according to their understanding Thou hast made them draw near, and they shall serve Thee in conformity with their authority according to the division. . . . (1QH 12.11-23; cf. 10.27-28, 1QS 5.20-24)[10]

On the basis of the apostolic authority which he has received from Yeshua, he exhorts the community to fit themselves together as "living stones" which build the royal priesthood of the "spiritual House" in the Messiah (1 Pet.2.5). He devotes the next section of the letter to different aspects of the equality of each member (cf. 6.13) of the body, and the unity which this equality promotes.

"Think too highly . . . faith": cf. 11.25, 12.16, 1 Cor.4.6, 7.17, 8.1, 12.7, 13.4, 2 Cor.10.13, Eph.4.7, 5.21, Phil.2.2-8, 1 Pet.4.7; 1QS 2.22-23, 5.20-25, 6.3-4, 8.4, CDC 13.7-16; Test.Naph.2.6; PA 1.13, PShab.1.3, 3b, Sot.5b, San.43b, Pes.25b.

Paul immediately subjects his own authority to his warning against arrogance (cf. 2.8, 11.18, 25). He plays here on the various forms of the Greek root φρονεω (*phroneo*), "to think": ὑπερφρονεω (*huperphroneo*) means "to overthink" (to boast), and σωφρονεω (*sophroneo*) "to think soberly" in the sense of "to observe the proper measure" or "not to transgress the set law(s)" (cf. 1 Pet.1.13, 4.7). This kind of humility is one of the "gifts" of the "Way" of the Spirit of truth:

> It is < of the Spirit of truth > to enlighten the heart of man, and to level before him the ways of true righteousness, and to set fear in his heart of the judgments [משפטי אל] of God. And (to it belong) the spirit of humility [רוח ענווה] and forbearance, of abundant mercy [רחמים] and eternal goodness, of understanding [שכל] and intelligence [בינה], and almighty wisdom [חכמת גבורה] with faith [מאמנת] in all the works of God and trust in His abundant grace [חסדו], and the spirit of knowledge [רוח דעת] in every design and zeal for just ordinances, and holy resolution with firm inclination and abundant affection towards all the sons of truth, and glorious purification from hatred of all the idols of defilement, and modesty with universal prudence, and discretion [חבא] concerning the truth of the Mysteries of Knowledge. Such are the counsels of the Spirit to the sons of truth in the world. (1QS 4.2-6)

Humility was also one of the traits with which the Rabbis sought to fill the gap left by the absence of actual offering of animal sacrifices following the destruction of the Temple in 70 C.E., although the basis of the prophetic critique of the cultus had already provided a precedent for emphasizing the motivation behind a person's worship:

> R. Joshua b. Levi said: He who sacrifices his [evil] inclination and confesses [his sin] over it, Scripture imputes it to him as though he had honoured the Holy One, blessed be He, in both worlds, this world and the next; for it is written, *Whoso offereth the sacrifice of confession honoureth Me* (Ps.50.23). R. Joshua b. Levi said: When the Temple was in existence, if a man brought a burnt offering, he received credit for a burnt offering; if a meal offering, he received credit for a meal offering; but he who was humble in spirit, Scripture regarded him as though he had brought all the offerings, for it is said, *The sacrifices of God are a broken spirit* (Ps.51.17). And furthermore, his prayers are not despised, for it is written, *A broken and contrite heart, O God, Thou wilt not despise* (ibid.). (San.43b)[11]

Humility, as an expression of "sound judgment," takes the form of respecting and loving one's brothers. Paul equates "sound judgment" with "faithfulness" in a manner similar to the Qumran texts, which speak, for example, of "weighing" (cf. "measure") each man's spirit in regard to their ability to discern (cf. "sound judgment") "what [they] must love and how [they] must hate" (1QS 9.21). Paul's phrase "allotted to each a measure of faith" corresponds in this sense to the Qumran expression, "spirit of faithfulness" (cf. 11QPsa.154.14-15), according to which God has made "distinctions" between the members of the community (cf. also the phrase, "weigh . . . according to their spirits" in 1QS 9.12, 14). "Faithfulness" (πιστις; *pistis*) then closely resembles the "love" which is enjoined upon the Qumran community. Paul commands that everyone should love his brother according to the love (faithfulness) which God has given to him, knowing that each member is bound to his brother through the grace which God has given to every member.[12] Just as faithfulness is a gift of God so, too, is humility amongst the brethren.[13]

Verse 4:

"Just as we have many members . . . ": cf. 1 Cor.6.15, 10.17, 12.12-31, Eph.4.4-16, Col.3.15; PRK 12.1, Mak.23b.

Paul adapts the metaphor of a person's "members" or "limbs" in chapter 6 (which illustrates the theme of the "two masters") to the whole community who "present (their) bodies a living and holy sacrifice" (verse 1). In the same way as each person must present the members of his body to God in righteousness, so every believer must also offer himself to his brethren in righteousness. As in chapters 14-15 (cf. also 1 Cor.12.4-31), Paul's primary concern here is moral and ethical. Naturally, however, as his use of the same image in other texts demonstrates (cf. 1 Cor.7.17-22, 12.13, Gal.3.28, Eph.2.13-18, Col.3.11), this cannot be distinguished from the dominant ethnic divide between Jews and Gentiles. Following his warning to the Gentile believers against acting arrogantly towards Israel, Paul wants all the "members" of Yeshua's body to love and respect one another. Since the Gentiles have become part of the "body" of the Messiah, the necessary "unity in diversity" can be maintained only by every member knowing that he has died to sin and is willing to continually offer his own body as a living sacrifice to God:

> For just as a potter knows the pot, how much it holds, and brings clay for it accordingly, so also the Lord forms the body in correspondence to the spirit, and instills the spirit corresponding to the power of the body. And from one to the other there is no discrepancy, not so much as a third of a hair, for all the creation of the Most High was according to height, measure, and standard. And just as the potter knows the use of each vessel and to what it is suited, so also the Lord knows the body to what it extent it will persist in goodness, and when it will be dominated by evil. For there is no form or conception which the Lord does not know since he created every human being according to his own image. As a person's

> strength, so also is his work; as is his mind, so also is his skill. As is his plan, so also is his achievement; as is his heart, so is his speech; as is his eye, so also is his sleep; as is his soul, so also is his thought, whether on the Law of the Lord or on the law of Beliar. As there is a distinction between light and darkness, between seeing and hearing, thus there is a distinction between man and man and between woman and woman. One cannot say they are one in appearance or in rank, for God made all things good in their order: the five senses in the head; to the head to the head he attached the neck, in addition to the hair for the enhancement of appearance; then the heart for prudence; the belly for excretion from the stomach; the windpipe for health; the liver for anger; the gallbladder for bitterness; the spleen for laughter; the kidneys for craftiness; the loins for power; the lungs for the chest; the hips for strength and so on. Thus my children you exist in accord for a good purpose in fear of God; do nothing in a disorderly manner, arrogantly, or at an inappropriate time. If you tell the eye to hear, it cannot; so you are unable to perform the light while you are in darkness. (Test.Naph.2.2-10)[14]

Verse 5:
"We, who are many . . . another": cf. 1 Cor.12.20, 27, Eph.1.22-23, 2.14-3.6, 4.1-16, Col.3.12-15; 1QS 6.8, 20, 7.3, 10, 16, 19-21, 8.26; Jos.*Bell*.2.122.

Paul's phrase, "we who are [the] Many," is recollective of one of the names used by the Qumran community in order to distinguish itself as a definitive group. The "Many" (ὸι πολλοι—*hoi polloi*; הרבים; *ha-rabim*) constituted a "house" or "body" whose members, despite their strict hierarchy (cf. 1QS 6.8-12), were obligated to "practice truth in common, and humility, and righteousness and justice and loving charity, and modesty in all their ways" (1QS 5.3-4) and to "love each man his brother as himself . . . and to seek each man the well-being of his brother" (CDC 6.21-7.1). Since each believer represents the body as a whole, if another member is injured, the whole community is affected (cf. 1 Corinthians 12). The phrase "individually members one of another" (cf. 1 Cor.12.27, Eph.4.25) also recalls the Qumran term "flesh of his flesh" (cf. CDC 7.1; cf. 8.6), and demonstrates how Yeshua has made both Jews and Gentiles into "one new man, (thus) establishing peace" (cf. Eph.2.15).[15]

Verse 6:
"Since we have gifts that differ . . . ": cf. 1 Cor.7.6, 12.4 30, Eph.4.4-16, Heb.2.4, 1 Pet.4.10; 1QS 4.2-8.

Paul continues the analogy of the "body," whose members (cf. 6.13f) are enjoined to "love one another according to the measure of [their] faithfulness." Each person must be faithful to his brethren in loving and respecting one another as equal "members" within the body. The differences between individual people, e.g., Jew and Gentile, stronger and weaker, superior and inferior, etc., are differences only in the tasks which they perform within the community.[16] Paul may here be relating to a midrashic tradition based on Psalm 68.18.[17] Paul uses Psalm 68.19 as a prooftext in Ephesians 4.8 for the "gifts" of service in the body of Yeshua and interprets "taking" (לקחת; *lakachat*) as "giving" in the midrashic tradition.[18] Yeshua's "gift," the consequence of his death and resurrection (descent and ascent), is the gifts of service (apostles, prophets, evangelists, pastors, and teachers) for the "building up of the body of the Messiah."[19] These gifts are further elaborated in reference to Psalm 68, which describes God as being victoriously seated on Mount Sinai and on Bashan. These two mountains are midrashically linked to those of Seir and Paran (cf. Dt.33.2, Hab.3.3—Teman), the mountains on which God revealed Himself to the nations of the world (cf. AZ 2b and following).[20] The gifts are therefore associated with the seventy languages of the nations of the world (cf. San.34a, Shab.88b).[21] The receipt of God's "gifts of service" make Jews and Gentiles into "one new man," and are the practical (cf. "halakhic") expression of "walking in the Spirit."

("Let each exercise them accordingly")

Paul identifies the "living sacrifice" which men give to God in Yeshua with the "service of gift" (עבודת המתנה; *'avodat ha-matanah*) offered by the Levites to make atonement for Israel (cf. Num.18.6-7).[22] Every believer is responsible to act before God and before his brothers "according to (the) faithfulness" of the gift which he has received.

"If prophecy . . . faith": cf. Acts 2.17-18, 11.27, 13.1, 15.32, 19.6, 21.9-10, 38, 1 Cor.11.4-5, 12.10, 28-31, 14.37-39, Eph.4.11; 1QS 4.18-21, 8.15-16, 1QH 2.8-13, 6.10-12, 7.6-7, 12.11-13, 13.18-19, 14.25, 17.26, 18.14-15, 1QpHab 2.8-9; Test.Dan 2.3; Jos.*Ant.*20.8.6; Sot.9.15, Tos.Pes.4.13, Ber.55b, 57b, Ned.38a, Yev.49b-50a, San.11a, 67a, 70b, 84a, Ber.34b, Meg.2b-3a, Ta'anit 28a, Sot.48b, AZ 20b, Pes.66a; Did.13.1ff, 15.2.

The New Testament writings, especially the epistles, are evidence of the continuation of biblical prophecy which was gradually and deliberately replaced in rabbinic (pharisaic) Judaism by the authority of the Sages. As early as the Tannaitic period (C3 B.C.E.—C2 C.E.), the Sages declare that prophecy had ceased, and the later Rabbis claim that the office of the prophet had been transferred to the Sages.[23] Later still, even a בת קול (*bat kol*; lit. "daughter of a voice"), or the "echo" of God's revelation, was disputed as authoritative for a *halakhic* ruling, and prophecy itself was regarded as only for fools and children.[24] The New Testament both reflects a period in which prophets were still recognized (cf. Anna [Lk.2.36]) and demonstrates a divergent trend in which prophecy continued. In the Qumran texts, which bridge the New Testament and later rabbinic literature, prophecy represents the "spiritual gift" of interpretation in Qumran. The Teacher of Righteousness was identified (and/or identified himself) with the "prophet like Moses" (cf. Dt.18.15, 1QS 9.11, 1QH 2.6-19, 7.12). This idea of prophecy as interpretation and exposition remained dominant within the New Testament community, in accordance with the transitional rabbinic view that prophecy was a matter of arising in the morning with a verse on one's mind (and/or that a dream is one sixtieth of prophecy) (cf. Ber.55b, 57b). Prophecy thus represented an aspect of one's close relationship with God. The early community also combined this aspect of prophecy, however, with the second element of prediction or divination, which was recognized by the Rabbis as well (cf. Lev.R.21.8, Tos.Pes.1.27, Eruv.64b). Paul begins his list of "services" or functions amongst the Body with prophecy, and characterizes its exercise as "according to the proportion of [the person's] faithfulness"—just as he describes the proper attribute of giving as liberality, of mercy as cheerfulness, etc. "Faithfulness" in this sense is the proper attribute of prophecy, and may be no more than the general "measure of faithfulness" which God bestows upon every believer (cf. verse 3). Paul may also want to illustrate the same idea which Phineas b. Yair expressed (cf. Sot.9.15), according to which "saintliness leads to [the gift of] the Holy Spirit," i.e., saintliness leads to the gift of prophecy.

Verse 7:

"Service": cf. Mt.25.44, Lk.4.39, Jn.12.26, Acts 6.1, Rom.15.25-31, 16.1, (1 Cor.12.5, 28), 2 Cor.3.3, 9.12, 11.8, Phil.1.1, 1 Tim.3.8-13, 1 Pet.1.12, Rev.2.9; 1QS 3.26, 4.9-10, 1QS[a] 1.13, 17-19, 1QH 6.19, 1QpHab 7.11; PA 1.2, 3, 2.2, 3.12, PRE 16, Sifre Dt.Ekev 41, Meg.3a-b, 18a; Did.14.1-2.

The term "service" (based on the Temple worship; cf. verse 1) covers such activities as prayer, financial contributions, and preaching, and is frequently characterized in rabbinic texts by the need to act without thought for personal gain:

> Antigonus (a man) of Socho received [the oral tradition] from Simeon the Righteous. He used to say: Be not like unto servants who serve the master in the expectation of receiving a gratuity, but be like unto

> servants who serve the master without the expectation of receiving a gratuity, and let the fear of heaven be upon you. . . . And all who labour with the community, let them labour with them for the [sake of the] name of heaven, for the merit of their fathers sustains them, and their righteousness endures forever. (PA 1.3, 2.2)

> The world rests upon three things: upon the Torah, upon Divine Worship, and upon the service of loving kindness. "Upon the Torah," whence do we know (this)? Because it is written, "If my covenant of *day and night* stand not" (Jer.33.25); and (another text) says, 'This book of the Torah shall not depart out of thy mouth, but thou shalt meditate therein *day and night*" (Josh.1.8). Whence do we know (that the world rests) upon the service of loving-kindness? Because it is said, "For I desired love, and not sacrifice" (Hos.6.6). Whence do we know (that the world rests) upon Divine Worship? Because it is written, "And the prayer of the upright is His delight" (Prov.15.8). [What is the Divine Worship? Prayer, for thus we find in Daniel, to whom Darius said: "Thy God whom those *servest* continually, he will deliver thee" (Dan.6.16). Was there any Divine Worship in Babylon? But this (refers to) Prayer.] (PRE 16)[25]

"Teaching": cf. Mt.28.20, Acts 5.25, 13.1, Rom.2.21, 15.16, 1 Cor.12.28, 2 Cor.12.15, Eph.4.11, Phil.2.17, 1 Tim.1.7, 4.13, 2 Tim.4.6, Tit.2.3, Heb.5.12, Jas.3.1, 2 Pet.2.1; 1QS 5.16, CDC 1.11, 3.8, 1QH 2.13-19, 6.10, 1QpHab 2.9; PA 1.6, 16, 4.5, 6.6, Kall.Rab.8.6, DEZ 4.3; Did.11.1-2.

The office of "teacher" (מורה, *moreh*; רב, *rav*) was central in the Torah-oriented society of Second Temple Judaism, and greatly increased in importance when the Sage replaced the prophet.[26] The root-meaning of the Hebrew word Torah (ירה; *yarah*) is "to teach," and God's word was given in order to teach man to walk in His ways (cf. Ex.4.15, Dt.33.10, Ps.25.12). When it was preserved in written form, Scripture became the source of "teaching, reproof . . . correction . . . [and] training in righteousness" (2 Tim.3.16). The way to know God's will was through interpreting and applying His words and commandments which had been written down:

> And this is the law concerning the overseer of the camp. He shall instruct the Many in the works of God and shall teach them His marvellous deeds and shall recount before them the happening of former times. . . . And he shall have pity on them as a father of his children and shall carry them in all their despondency as a shepherd

> his flock. . . . On their arrival, they shall gather them all together, including the children and the women, and shall read into [their] ea[rs] all the precepts of the Covenant and shall instruct them in all their ordinances lest they stray in [their] st[ray]ing. And this is the rule for all the hosts of the Congregation, concerning every native in Israel. From [his] you[th] [he shall be in]structed in the Book of Meditation and shall be taught the precepts of the Covenant in accordance with his age, and [shall receive] his [edu]cation in their ordinances for ten years [from] the time of entry into the children's [class]. (CDC 13.7-9, 1QS^a 1.4-8)[27]

In 15.15-16, Paul further describes his own teaching as the offering of a "sacrifice" (cf. 12.1) designed to bring the Gentiles as a "gift" to Israel, in words similar to those of the Teacher of Righteousness from Qumran:

> And [Thou hast] created [me] for Thy sake to [ful]fil the Law, and [to te]a[ch by] my mouth the men of Thy council in the midst of the sons of men, that Thy marvels may be told to everlasting generations and [Thy] mighty deeds be [contemp]lated without end. And all the nations shall know Thy truth and all the peoples, Thy glory. For Thou hast caused [them] to enter Thy [glo]rious [Covenant] with all the men of Thy council and into a common lot with the Angels of the Face; and none shall treat with insolence the sons [. . .] [. . .] and they shall be converted by Thy glorious mouth and shall be Thy princes in the l[ot of light]. (1QH 6.10-14)

Verse 8:
"Exhortation": cf. Acts 2.40, 11.23, 13.15, 15.32, Heb.3.13, 10.25, 13.22; Sifre Dt.49, Shab.87a, BK 60b, Ta'anit 16a.

Paul's distinction between "teaching" and "exhortation" reflects the rabbinic distinction between מדרשי הלכה (*midrashei halakhah*) and מדרשי אגדה (*midrashei 'aggadah*). In his Hebrew translation, Delitzsch correctly translates παρακλησις (*paraklesis*), "exhortation," as דבר מוסר (*davar musar*) to indicate homiletic material (אגדה; *'aggadah*). *'Aggadah* was primarily an exposition of the biblical text, but in its homiletic function it frequently also served as a peg upon which to hang expositions of the most divergent sort. The Sages used it as means of "bringing heaven nearer to the congregation" and "lifting man heavenward." On the one hand, it was a way to glorify God, and on the other a way of bringing consolation to Israel. Its chief contents consisted of religious truths, maxims of morality, colloquies on just retribution, inculcation of the laws which mark off national coherence, descriptions of Israel's greatness in past and future, scenes and legends from Jewish history, parallels drawn between the institutions of God and those of Israel, praises of the holy Land, edifying accounts, and all kinds of consolation. These homiletic addresses were delivered in the synagogue or academy, possibly at times in private dwellings or in the open, principally on Sabbaths and festivals, but also on important public or private occasions such as war, famine, circumcision, weddings, funerals, etc.[28] The most familiar of these exhortations are collected in such texts as "The Sayings of the Fathers" (*Aboth*) or in the *Derekh Eretz* literature, which are introduced with formula "[So and so] used to say . . .":

> He [Hillel] used to say: the more flesh, the more worms; the more property, anxiety; the more wives, the more witchcraft; the more bondwomen, the more lewdness; the more slaves, the more robbery; [but] the more [study of the] Torah, the more life; the more sitting down to [study and contemplate], the more wisdom; the more counsel, the more understanding; the more righteousness, the more peace. One who has acquired unto himself a good name, has acquired [it] for himself; one who has acquired unto himself words of Torah, has acquired unto himself the life of the world to come. (PA 2.7)
> Seek not greatness and covet not honour. Not learning, but doing is the more important, and do not crave for the table of kings, for your table is greater than their table and your crown than their crown. Faithful is your Employer to pay you the reward for your labour. (Kall.Rab.8.6)

"Gives . . . liberality": cf. Ex.25.2, 35.5, Mt.6.3-4, 10.8, Lk.6.38, Acts 3.6, 20.35, 2 Cor.8.2-5, 9.6-15; Jos.*Bell*.2.127, 6.134; PA 1.2, 5, ARN[a] 7, Sifre Dt.116, 118, Mid.Ps.118.17, TBE p.71, p.135, Eccl.R.7.1.4, 7.14.2, PPe'ah 1.1, 15b, 8.9, 21b, BB 9a,b, 10a, Suk.49b; Did.1.5-6, 4.5-8.

The act of "giving" includes contributions, charity and alms, as well as hospitality to strangers. In keeping with the "measure of faithfulness" with which each member of the Body exercises their particular gift (leading with diligence, mercy with cheerfulness, etc.), Paul says that he who gives should give liberally:

> *Therefore I command thee, saying—therefore* means for this reason; *I command you saying* means I am giving you advice for your own benefit—*Thou shalt surely open thy hand wide unto thy poor and needy*

> *brother* (Dt.15.11). Why are all these specified? To indicate that one should give bread to one who requires bread, dough to one who requires dough, a *meah* coin to the one who requires a *meah* coin, and even actually feed by mouth one who requires such feeding. (Sifre Dt.Re'eh 118)

> Give to everyone that asks thee, and do not refuse, for the Father's will is that we give to all from the gifts we have received. . . . Be not one who stretches out his hands to receive, but shuts them when it comes to giving. Of whatsoever thou hast gained by thy hands thou shalt give a ransom for thy sins. Thou shalt not hesitate to give, nor shalt thou grumble when thou givest, for thou shalt know who is the good Paymaster of the reward. Thou shalt not turn away the needy, but shalt share everything with thy brother, and shalt not say that it is thine own, for if you are sharers in the imperishable, how much more in the things which perish? (Did.1.5, 4.5-8)[29]

"Leads . . . diligence": cf. (Lk.8.41), 2 Cor.8.2, 1 Thess.5.12, 1 Tim.3.4-5, 12, 5.17; 1QS 1.1, 3.13, 6.14-16, 9.12-21, CDC 13.7-13, 14.8; Ber.55a.

The verb προιστημι (*proistemi*), "to lead" or "to preside over," reflects the function of the "elders" (πρεσβυτεροι; *presbuteroi*) in 1 Timothy 5.17, and corresponds to the role of the "overseer" (המבקר; *ha-mevaker*) at Qumran:

> And this is the law concerning the overseer of the camp. He shall instruct the Many in the works of God and shall teach them His marvelous deeds and shall recount before them the happening of former times. . . . And he shall have pity on them as a father of his children and shall carry them in all their despondency as a shepherd his flock. . . . And the priest who is overseer of the Many shall be aged between thirty and sixty years, learned in the Book [of Meditation] and in all the ordinances of the law, to lead them according to the Law that is theirs. And the overseer in charge of all the camps shall be aged between thirty and fifty years, having mastered all the secrets of men and all the tongues which their various clans speak. The members of the Congregation shall enter at his command, each in his turn. And for everything which a man has to say, let him say it to the overseer, concerning every dispute and judgment. (CDC 13.7-9, 14.6-8)[30]

The office of "leader" may also reflect the function of the ראש בית כנסת (*ro'sh beit knesset*; ἀρχισυναγωγος; *archisunagogos*), the synagogue president. The president conducted worship, took responsibility for those participating in the Torah reading etc., and maintained the synagogue building. The synagogue itself functioned under the administrative authority of three or seven officials (ἀρχοι; *archoi*), a "council of elders" (γερουσια; *gerousia*) co-opted or elected, who maintained order, regulated the finances, collected subscriptions, and authorized expenditure and contributions.[31]

"Shows mercy": cf. Mt.5.7, 18.33, Rom.2.4, 9.15, 11.22, 2 Cor.9.7; 1QS 4.5, 5.3-4, 10.26-11.2, CDC 6.21, CDC[b] 2.18; Test.Zev.5.1, 3, 8.1, Test.Ben.4.2, Sir.18.13; PA 1.12, ARN[a] 13.4, Sifre Dt.49, 96, TBE p.135, PMeg.4.9, 59c, PBer.5.3, 9c, P BK 8.10, 6c, Bez.32b, Shab.127b, 151b.

The "measure" of "showing mercy" is cheerfulness, just as Paul speaks of giving cheerfully (cf. 2 Cor.9.7). The showing of mercy, which dominates Paul's thought in the remainder of the chapter, is as much a character trait as the performance of an action:

> AND RECEIVE ALL MEN WITH A CHEERFUL COUNTENANCE. A parable: If a man should give his friend much money and not have a genial countenance, it is as though he gave him nothing at all. If a man did not give his friend anything at all, but does show a genial countenance, it as though he gave him much money. In the same way it is said: AND RECEIVE ALL MEN WITH A CHEERFUL COUNTENANCE. (ARN[b] 23)[32]

Paul continues this theme in the following verses (9ff), and incorporates the teaching of mercy with the doctrine of "non-retaliation." This integrates love of one's neighbor with accepting another person's point of view in order to communicate one's own to him:

> I will apportion the Precept with the measuring-cord of the times and [. . .] righteousness, full of loving charity towards the disheartened and strengthening the hands of those whose [heart] is troub[led]; [teaching] understanding to those whose spirit has gone astray, instructing in the doctrine those that murmur, answering with humility the proud of spirit, and with a contrite spirit, those that brandish a stick, that point the finger and utter wounding words and have possessions. (1QS 10.26-11.2)[33]

Verse 9:
"Love without hypocrisy": cf. Isa.1.10-17, 24.5, Jer.7.22-23, Amos 5.15, 21-24, Mic.6.6-8, Mt.5.44-48, 23.13-32, 1 Cor.13.4-8, 2 Cor.6.6, 1 Tim.1.5, 2 Tim.2.22, Jas.3.17; 1QS 1.9, 5.25-26, CDC 6.20-21, 1QH 4.13-21; Test.Asher 1.3-6.5, Test.Gad 6.1-7, Test.Ben.6.5f; ARN[a] 6.4, ARN[b] 23, 32, Mid.Ps.52.1, 101.3, Tos.BM 2.26, Gen.R.38.3, Sot.41b.

Paul describes "love" as the "measure of faithfulness" in summarizing all the various "gifts" of service in the previous verses. Although love is the opposite of hypocrisy in that sense, Paul also emphasizes the fact that "the goal of our instruction is love from a pure heart and a good conscience and a sincere faith" (1 Tim.1.5). Where in chapter 2, he reproves Israel for their hypocrisy towards the Gentiles, he is here concerned with right attitude between Jewish and Gentile believers, especially regarding what is evil (see the second half of the verse). Paul raises the issue of how to love what God hates (or what men understand God to hate): can love and respect for men overlook their evil thoughts or actions, or can a person use evil means in order to gain good results?[34] He argues that a man must be "single-minded" and pure in heart so that all his actions are good:

> "The soul, they say, may in words express the good for the sake of evil, but the outcome of the action leads to evil. There is a man who has no mercy on the one who serves him in performing an evil deed; there are two aspects of this, but the whole is wicked. And there is a man who loves the one who does the evil, as he is himself involved in evil, so that he would choose to die in evil for the evildoer's sake. There are also two aspects of this, but the whole situation is evil. Although indeed love is there, yet in wickedness is evil concealed; in name it is as though it were good, but the outcome of the act is to bring evil. Someone steals, deals unjustly, robs, cheats, but yet has pity on the poor. This also has two aspects, but is evil as a whole. . . . Such persons are hares, because although they are halfway clean, in truth they are unclean, for this is what God has said on the tables of the commandments. But you, my children, do not be two-faced like them, one good and the other evil; rather, cling only to goodness . . . do not pay attention to evil as to good, but have regard for what is really good and keep it thoroughly in all the Lord's commandments. . . . Flee from the evil tendency, destroying the devil by your good works. For those who are two-faced are not of God, but they are enslaved to their evil desires, so that they might be pleasing to Beliar and to persons like themselves." (Test.Asher 2.1-6, 9-10, 3.1, 6.3, 3.2)

"Abhor what is evil . . . good": cf. Ps.34.13-14, 37.27, 97.10, Prov.8.13, Isa.1.16, 55.7, Jer.4.1-2, 25.5, 35.15, Ezek.18.31, Amos 5.15, 1 Thess.5.21-22, 1 Tim.1.5, 2.22, Jas.4.7; 1QS 1.1-5, 11, 5.15-20, 9.16, 21-23, 10.19-22, CDC 2.15, 1QH 14.10, 15.19, 17.24; Test.Asher 1.3-6.5, Test.Ben.7.1, 8.1-3; Jos.*Bell*.2.135, 141; PA 1.7, 10, 2.9, PPe'ah 4, PBer.4.2, 7d, Ber.60b, AZ 19b; Did.4.12.

Paul develops the theme of love without hypocrisy by appealing to the concept of the "purity of heart" which underlies some versions of the Two Ways or Spirits (two masters), especially in the circles represented by the Testament of Asher. According to this latter text, a man cannot compromise God's truth and His commandments by accepting what is evil; evil cannot be made good, although good can be made evil. The author differentiates between the merciful and unjust man on the basis of discerning between the "seeming good" and the "genuine good." The man who is undivided in his love for the righteous and in his hatred for sinners follows God's will, because he does not accept the seeming good as the genuine good:

> "For persons who are good, who are single-minded—even though they are considered by the two-faced to be sinners—are righteous before God. For many who destroy the wicked perform two works—good and evil—but it is good as a whole, because evil is uprooted and destroyed. One person hates the man who, though merciful, is also unjust, or who is an adulterer, even though he fasts, and thus is two-faced. But his work is good as a whole, because he imitates the Lord, not accepting the seeming good as though it were the truly good. Another person does not want to see any pleasant days among the convivial, lest they disgrace the body and pollute the soul. This also has two aspects, but is good on the whole. For such persons are like gazelles and stags: In appearance they seem wild and unclean, but as a whole they are clean. They live by zeal for the Lord, abstaining from what God hates and has forbidden through his commandments, staving off evil by the good." (Test.Asher 4.1-5)[35]

Although Paul's thought here is similar to the Essene ideal which this text represents, and which demanded that to love truly (honestly) one must love (only) those who are true, he modifies this view in the following verses, reflecting the semi-Essene doctrine which leads to the alternative principle of "non-retaliation" against those who persecute the community:

> And these are the norms of conduct for the man of understanding in these times, concerning what he must love and how he must hate. Everlasting hatred for all the men of the Pit because of their spirit of hoarding! He shall surrender his property to them and the wages of the work of his hands, as a slave to his master and as a poor man in the presence of his overlord. But he shall be a man full of zeal for the Precept, whose time is for the Day of Vengeance.... To no man will I render the reward of evil, with goodness will I pursue each one; for judgment of all the living is with God, and He it is who will pay to each man his reward. I will not envy from a spirit of wickedness and my soul shall not covet the riches of violence. As for the multitude of the men of the Pit, I will not lay hands on them till the Day of Vengeance; but I will not withdraw my anger far from perverse men, I will not be content till He begins the Judgment. I will be without malice and wrath towards those that are converted from rebellion, but merciless to those that have turned aside from the way; I will not comfort them that are smitten until their way is perfect. And I will not keep Belial in my heart; no folly shall be heard within my mouth, and on my lips shall be found no criminal deceit or falsity or lies. But on my tongue shall be fruit of holiness and no abominations shall be found on it. I will open my mouth in thanksgiving, and my tongue shall ever recount the deeds of God, together with the unfaithfulness of men until the destruction of their rebellion. I will cause vain words to cease from my lips, and defilement and perfidy from the understanding of my heart. With wise reflection I will conceal Knowledge; with understanding prudence I will guard [it] within firm bounds, to keep the faith and the law strictly according to the righteousness of God. (1QS 9.21-23, 10.17-25)[36]

Verse 10:

"Be devoted to one another . . . ": cf. Lev.19.18, Jer.31.33f, Jn.13.34-35, 15.12, Gal.6.10, 1 Thess.4.9, Heb.13.1, 2 Pet.1.7, 1 Jn.2.7f, 3.11, 23; 1QS 2.24-25, 5.3-4, 25-26, CDC 6.20-7.1; Sir.18.13, 28.2-7, Jub.36.4, 8-11, Test.Zev.5.1, Test.Iss.5.1-2, 7.6-7, Test.Dan 5.3; PA 1.10, 12, 13, 2.4, 3.12, 4.1, 3, 7, 10, 12, 15, 21, 5.19, 6.1, 6, ARN^{a} 12, 16, ARN^{b} 26, TBE p.135, p.143, Sifra Ked.39b, PBer.4.2, 7d, Gen.R.24.7.

Paul continues to give instructions as to "how to love," based on the "Golden Rule" (do to others what you would wish them to do to you; do not do to others what you would not wish them to do to yourself) inspired by a new interpretation of Leviticus 19.18 in Second Temple Jewish circles:

> R. Hanina, the Prefect of the Priests says: An oath from Mount Sinai has been sworn on (this) saying ["Love your fellow man as yourself"] upon which the entire world depends: If (you) hate your fellowman whose deeds are evil like yours, I the Lord am judge to punish that same man and if you love your neighbor whose deeds are proper like your own, I the Lord am faithful and merciful toward you. (ARN^{b} 26)[37]

"Preference . . . in honor": cf. 13.7, 1 Pet.1.22, 2.17; 1QS 5.3-4, 25-26, 8.1-4, CDC 6.20-21; PA 2.4, 10, 12, 4.1, 3, 6.6.

The attitudes and forms of conduct which Paul lists here draw out the meaning of Leviticus 19.18, to "love your fellow-man as yourself." As Flusser suggests, this meaning comes from understanding כמוך (*kamokha*), "as yourself," to mean: what you would avoid happening to you, you should avoid doing to others because others partake of the same human nature as yourself. Love then comes to expression in making the priorities of the other your own—giving them "preference" (cf. chapters 14-15).

> R. Eliezer said: Let the honour of thy friend be as dear to thee as thine own.... Who is he that is honoured? He who honours his fellow-men, as it is said: For them that honour Me I will honour, and they that despise Me shall be lightly esteemed. (PA 2.10, 4.1)

The concept of "honor" or human dignity also lies at the root of two additional rabbinic halakhot which correspond to the concept of loving one's fellow-man:

> Things that are in themselves permissible, and yet are treated by others as forbidden, you may not treat them as permitted in order to nullify them... the dignity of human beings is a great thing, for it supersedes [even] a negative injunction of the Torah. (Ned.81b, Shab.94b)[38]

Verse 11:

"Not lagging behind in diligence": cf. 8, 2 Cor.7.11, 8.7-8, Heb.6.11, 2 Pet.1.5-11; 1QS 4.4, 5.4, 24, 7.6, 8.1-4, 22, 9.16, 23; 1QS 5.20-26, 8.21-23; PA 1.17, 2.14, 3.9, 17, 6.5, 6.

The quality of "diligence" is "leading" (cf. verse 8)—the opposite of "lagging." Paul encourages the members of the congregations to lead one another onward and to strive to outdo one another in love:

> Love him that made thee with all thy strength, and forsake not his ministers . . . stretch thine hand unto the poor, that thy blessing may be perfected. A gift hath grace in the sight of every man living; and for the dead detain it not. Fail not to be with them that weep, and mourn with them that mourn. Be not slow to visit the sick: for that shall make thee to be beloved. Whatsoever thou takest in hand, remember the end, and thou shalt never do amiss. (Sir.7.30, 32-35)

"Fervent in spirit": cf. Acts 18.25; 1QS 4.4-5, 8.1-4, 9.23, 9.24; PA 4.2.

"Diligence" in "leading" is the expression of a "fervent spirit" of love and truth towards one's brothers:

> It is < of the Spirit of truth > to enlighten the heart of man, and to level before him the ways of true righteousness, and to set fear in his heart of the judgment of God. And (to it belong) the spirit of humility and forbearance, of abundant mercy and eternal goodness, of understanding and intelligence, and almighty wisdom with faith in all the works of God and trust in His abundant grace, and the spirit of knowledge in every design and zeal for just ordinances, and holy resolution with firm inclination and abundant affection towards all the sons of truth. (1QS 4.2-5)

"Serving the Lord": cf. Acts 20.19, Rom.12.1, 1 Cor.7.22, Eph.6.7, Col.3.23-24; 1QS 3.26, 4.9-10, 9.16-23, 10.17-11.2, 1QS 1.1f, 17-18, 5.8-10, 9.12ff, 1QpHab 7.11.

The phrase "serving the Lord" should be read, according to the textual variant (and more difficult reading), as "serving the time."[39] This reading is substantiated by Paul's clear dependence on the Qumran principle of serving the "Decree of time."[40] Paul's discussion is set against the expectation of a final victory of the "sons of light" over the "sons of darkness." Until the final "Day of Vengeance" arrived, however, on which God would utterly destroy all the forces of Belial, the community had to live in a hostile world and needed to determine guidelines for its relations with the "wicked" outside the community. During this intervening period (the "dominion of Belial"), the members of the community were enjoined not to take their own revenge nor to act in hatred towards their enemies. They were to "conceal" the knowledge of the truth from their opponents and refrain from retaliating in taking violent steps against them. The phrase "serving the time" or the "age" thus meant for the Qumran community a temporary submission to those who opposed them and who had power over them:

> And these are the norms of conduct for the man of understanding in these times, concerning what he must love and how he must hate. Everlasting hatred for all the men of the Pit because of their spirit of hoarding! He shall surrender his property to them and the wages of the work of his hands, as a slave to his master and as a poor man in the presence of his overlord. But he shall be a man full of zeal for the Precept, whose time is for the Day of Vengeance. . . . And let him not rebuke the men of the Pit nor dispute with them; and let him conceal the maxims of the Law from the midst of the men of perversity. (1QS 9.21-23, 16-17)

The reading "serving the time" is clearly supported by this principle expressed by the Qumran texts.[41] It also explains Paul's use of the quotation from Prov.25.21f at the end of the chapter, according to which he urges his readers leave room for God's vengeance upon the evil doers and oppressors.

Verse 12:
"Rejoicing . . . tribulation": cf. Mt.5.12, Rom.4.18, 5.3-5, 8.24-25, 12.15, Phil.3.1, 4.4, 1 Thess.5.16, 1 Pet.1.8; 1QH 6.6, 10.30-31, 11.4-7, 23-34.

Paul enjoins the members of the community not to retaliate against those who oppose them on the grounds that submission to God's will is more important than overcoming their persecutors (cf. 5.2-3). As Yeshua's teaching does (Mt.5.12), this focuses a person's attention on God's sovereignty. He knows that all things are in His hands and that He will not allow the wicked to triumph. He can thus even rejoice during his tribulations:

> He shall do the will of God in every enterprise of his hands, that He may reign over all things according to His command; and he shall gladly delight in all that He has made, and beyond the will of God he shall desire nothing. [And] he shall delight [in all] the words of His mouth, and shall covet nothing of that which He has not command[ed]. And he shall constantly watch for the Judgment of God. [And in all that be]falls, he shall bless Him who did it, and in all that befalls, he shall tell [of His deeds] and shall bless Him [with the offering] of the lips. . . . (When) a prey to fear and dread, in the depth of distress, in full desolation, I will bless Him. I will confess Him because He is marvellous and will meditate on His might; and I will lean on His favours every

> day. I know that in His hand is judgment of all the living and that all His works are truth; when distress is unfurled I will praise Him, and when He saves me I will likewise shout with joy. (1QS 9.23-26, 10.15-17)[42]

Paul joins three specific commandments—"rejoice," "persevere," and "pray"—into a single principle. All three commandments are related to tribulation. Prayer is a natural response in a time of trouble. Constancy in prayer, which tribulation demands, also encourages perseverance, however, and, as Paul says in chapter 5, perseverance generates joy, since if God is always there to answer prayer, He will ultimately also bring salvation.

"Devoted to prayer": cf. Prov.15.8, Isa.56.7, Lk.2.25, 36-37, Acts 1.14, 2.42, Eph.6.18, Phil.4.6, Col.4.2, 1 Thess.5.17; CDC 11.20-21, 1QH 12.3-9, 17.17-18; PA 2.13, Tanh.Beshall.9, Vayera 1, Tanh.B.Tzav 8, Sifre Dt.29, 41, Mid.Ps.5.7, 61.2, PBer.1.1, 2b, Ex.R.38.4, Ber.10a, 12b, Shab.30b, AZ 7b-8a, Ta'anit 2a.

Prayer, both of thanksgiving and of supplication, was an integral part of all Jewish life. In certain "sectarian" circles, however, it was also specifically directed towards the hope that God would deliver them from their persecutors (whoever they might be). The sort of groups to whom both Simeon the Righteous and Anna the prophetess belonged (cf. Lk.2.25, 36), for example, are described in an "Apostrophe to Zion" text found at Qumran:

> Generation after generation will dwell in thee [Jerusalem], and generations of pious will be thy splendour: those who yearn for the day of Thy salvation, that they may rejoice in the greatness of Thy glory. . . . How they have hoped for Thy salvation, Thy pure ones have mourned for Thee. (11QPsa.Zion 3-4, 9)

Such communities also encouraged prayer on behalf of those who were persecuting them, in the same spirit of doing good to one's enemies:

> . . . if anyone wantonly attacks a pious man, he repents, since the pious shows mercy to the one who abused him, and maintains silence. And if anyone betrays a righteous man, the righteous man prays. Even though for a brief time he may be humbled, later he will appear far more illustrious, as happened with Joseph, my brother. (Test.Ben.5.4)[43]

Verse 13:

"Contributing to the needs of the saints": cf. Acts 11.29, 24.17, Rom.15.25-28, 1 Cor.16.1-3, 2 Cor.8.1-4, 9.12, Gal.2.10, 6.10, Heb.6.10, Jas.1.27; 1QS 5.3-4, 8.2, CDC 6.20-21; Sir.7.10, 29-32; PA 1.2.

Prayer goes together with provision for the various needs (here perhaps primarily material) of the members of the community. Looking after the needs of the community was a biblical measure of righteousness.[44] Paul has taken upon himself a personal responsibility in this regard, since he has promised to bring a special contribution from the Gentile communities in Macedonia to the "saints" in Jerusalem, in response to the dire situation in the city.[45]

"Practicing hospitality": cf. Job 31.32, Mt.25.35, 1 Tim.3.2, 5.10, Tit.1.8, Heb.13.2, 1 Pet.4.9; CDC 6.20-21; PA 1.4, 5, Suk.9.2, San.103b, Ber.10b, 63b, Shab.127a, Kid.39b, Shevu.3b.

Hospitality is a further example of loving one's neighbor as oneself, derived from Leviticus 19.18, a commandment practiced by all groups within Second Temple Judaism:

> On the arrival of any of the sect from elsewhere, all the resources of the community are put at their disposal, just as if they were their own. In all other matters, they do nothing without orders from their superiors: two things only are left to individual discretion, the rendering of assistance and compassion. Members may of their own motion help the deserving when in need, and supply food to the destitute. . . . (Jos.*Bell.*2.8.124, 134)

> Jose b. Jo'ezer used to say: Let thy house be a house of meeting for the sages and suffer thyself to be covered by the dust of their feet, and drink in their words with thirst. . . . Jose b. Johanan (a man) of Jerusalem used to say: Let thy house be wide open, and let the poor be members of thy household. . . . (PA 1.4, 5)

Verse 14:

"Bless . . . ": cf. Mt.5.43-48, Lk.6.28, 35-38, 1 Cor.4.12, Gal.6.10, 1 Thess.5.15, 1 Pet.3.9; 1QS 10.17-20; 2 En.50.1-4, Sir.28.2-7, Test.Ben.4.2ff, 5.4, 6.5, Let.Arist.227; ARN[a] 15.1, 16.4, ARN[b] 23, 26, 32, Ber.10a.

Paul repeats Yeshua's injunction to do good to those who persecute you, and combines this with the principle of non-retaliation. All men must be respected and loved, even if they are evil and disobedient to God.[46]

Verse 15:

"Rejoice . . . weep . . . ": cf. Job 30.25, Ps.35.13-14, Phil.4.14; Sir.7.34, Test.Zev.7, 8, Test.Iss.7.5; PA 2.4, 4.18, 19, DER 7.7, DEZ 5.5, Tos.Ber.2.21, 29, Ket.17a, BM 86b (R. Tanhum), Ta'anit 11a.

Paul combines the reference to blessing and cursing with the idea of rejoicing and weeping, based on a "missionary maxim" known from other Jewish sources. According to this principle, the members of the community are encouraged to respect the views and opinions of others in order to establish the grounds on which they may be brought to "the obedience of faith":

> A man should not rejoice when among people who weep or weep when among those who rejoice. He should not stay awake among people who sleep or sleep when among those who are awake. He should not be standing when all others are sitting or sit when all others are standing. This is the general rule: A man should not deviate from the custom of his companions or from society. . . . Do not appear naked, do not appear dressed, do not appear standing and do not appear sitting, do not appear laughing, do not appear weeping, as it is said, "A time to weep and a time to laugh, a time to embrace and to a time to refrain from embracing (Eccl.3.4-5)." (DER 7.7, Tos.Ber.2.21; cf. DEZ 5.5)[47]

This saying, which is attributed to Hillel in the passage in the *Tosefta*, is based on the familiar text in Ecclesiastes 3.4-5, and promotes a principle for the conduct of the community "in the world" (primarily with Gentiles). It corresponds to another rabbinic dictum, which has become an idiom in modern English: "when in Rome, do as the Romans."[48] The principle encourages respect for one's "neighbor" by "accommodating" one's own views to his:

> He [Rabban Gamaliel] used to say, Do His will as [thou wouldst do] thine own will, so that He may do thy will as [He does] His [own] will. Set aside thy will in the face of His will, so that He may set aside the will of others before thy will. Hillel said: Separate not thyself from the community, neither trust thou in thyself until the day of thy death, moreover judge not thy fellow-man until thou hast reached his place. . . . (PA 2.4)

Verse 16:

"Be of the same . . . mind": cf. Acts 2.46, Rom.15.5, 1 Cor.1.10, 2 Cor.13.11, Phil.2.2, 4.2, 1 Pet.3.8; 1QS 4.2-6, 5.3-4, 25-26, 8.2-3; PA 1.10, 13, 2.4, 3.12,

4.1, 3, 7, 10, 12, 15, 21, 5.19, 6.1, 6, DEZ 5. 5, 7.7, Ket.17a, Hor.10a, RH 17a, Yoma 6b; Ep.Barn.19.2f.

Paul continues the themes raised in Leviticus 19, which he sums up in three *halakhic* principles: do not judge another person until you have come into his place; do not think too highly of yourself; and do not separate yourself from the community. As well as warning the members of the community against behaving arrogantly towards one another (cf. 11.18, 12.3), he further enjoins upon them the need to "accommodate" other people's views in order to draw them to faithfulness to God in Yeshua. Within the community, each member should respect the opinions of those who hold to divergent convictions: "A man should not act differently from the practice of his fellow-man and the sons of men" (DEZ 5.5).[49] Paul continues to emphasize this principle in the subsequent clauses, in which he encourages the community to exhibit an attitude of service and sacrifice in humility:

> I will apportion the Precept with . . . righteousness{,} full of loving charity towards the disheartened and strengthening the hands of those whose [heart] is troub[led]; [teaching] understanding to those whose spirit has gone astray, instructing in the doctrine those that murmur, answering with humility the proud of spirit, and with a contrite spirit. . . . (1QS 10.25-11.1)[50]

"Associate with the lowly . . . ": cf. Ps.131.1-3, Isa.61.1-2, 66.2, Jer.45.5, Mt.5.3, 5, 9.11, 11.19, 23.8-12, Lk.15.2, Jas.2.1ff; 1QM 11.9-10, 14.7, 1QH 5.22, 14.3, 18.14-15; Sir.1.30, 2.17, 3.17f, 7.4f, 17, 10.26f, 13.1ff; PA 1.10, 4.4, 10, 15, DEZ 1.1, TBE [EZ] p.197, Ned.38a; Did.3.9, 4.8.

When a man "associates with the lowly," whether this refers to men of lowly estate or to humble things, he not only puts himself on their level and accepts their point of view but he also acknowledges that God accepts them and their opinions. Just as the Qumran community called themselves the "Lowly" or "Poor" to indicate their contriteness of heart before God, the term primarily indicates a humility of attitude (cf. "poor in spirit").[51] Lowliness may also, however, as demonstrated again by the Qumran community, refer to the "low" or poor as a social class (cf. Mt.26.11). The biblical identification of the poor and the outcast as those to whom God pays special attention encouraged a mistrust of wealth, elitism, and social standing based on class status:

> My child, be not a grumbler, for this leads to blasphemy, nor stubborn, nor a thinker of evil, for from all these things are blasphemies engendered, but be thou "meek, for the meek shall

> inherit the earth;" be thou long-suffering and merciful and guileless, and quiet, and good, and ever fearing the words which thou hast heard. Thou shalt not exalt thyself, nor let thy soul be presumptuous. Thy soul shall not consort with the lofty, but thou shalt walk with righteous and humble men. Receive the accidents that befall to thee as good, knowing that nothing happens without God. (Did.3.6-10)[52]

"Do not be wise . . . ": cf. Prov.3.7, 12.3, Isa.5.21, Rom.11.25, 12.3; DER 2.9, Kall.Rab.5; Did.3.9.

Paul picks up the warning against the arrogance of Gentile believers towards Israel's election as a nation in 11.25, as well as from 12.3, where he applies it to the relations within the community of believers.[53] Here he applies the exhortation to the community's relationship to society at large (the behavior of believers to non-believers). His statement might be based on Proverbs 3.7, whose injunction to "abhor evil" Paul states in verse 9: "Do not be wise in your own eyes; fear the Lord and turn away from evil." The phrase "turning away from evil" corresponds in this regard to the principle of non-retaliation towards one's fellow-man which guards against being sure of one's own judgment, standing, or status. The attitude of the believer should be to encourage right behavior in another person by not condemning what he regards, and God's word states to be, ungodly conduct. "Evil" is then defined as "non-acceptance." The goal of the believer, however, should be to "love" those who transgress God's will (yet without hypocrisy) in order to encourage right behavior in them, even when such an attitude may be at the believer's own expense. Paul elaborates this principle in the following verses.

Verse 17:

"Never pay back evil for evil": cf. Prov.20.22, 24.29, Mt.5.39, Lk.6.37-38, 17.3, Rom.12.19, 1 Cor.4.12, 1 Thess.5.15, Heb.3.13, 1 Pet.2.23, 3.9; 1QS 5.25-6.1, 9.21ff, 10.18-20, CDC 7.2, 9.2-8; Sir.27.30-28.7, Test.Gad 6.3-6, Test.Jos.18.2, Test.Ben.4.2-4, 5.1-4; Ber.10a, Yoma 23a; Did.2.7.

Paul develops the concept of non-retaliation (cf. verses 9ff) into the full-blown view that restraint and love for one's neighbor is not only proper behavior, but can also influence one's opponents towards better, more righteous behavior. Amongst certain "pietist" Jewish circles, this view was drawn from the commandment to "love your fellow as yourself" in Leviticus 19.18, which was interpreted to mean that if you overwhelm the sinner by a human approach, you can make him better. This was not strictly an Essene idea, since it contradicts the concept of "double predestination," which does not permit a moral improvement of the Sons of Darkness.[54] It is reflected in works on the fringe of Essenism; however, notably in the Testament of Benjamin:

> See then, my children, what is the goal of the good man. Be imitators of him in his goodness, because of his compassion, in order that you may wear crowns of glory. For a good man does not have a blind eye, but is merciful to all, even though they may be sinners. And even if persons plot against him for evil ends, by doing good this man conquers evil, being watched over by God. He loves those who wrong him as he loves his own life. If anyone glorifies himself, he holds no envy. If anyone becomes rich, he is not jealous. If anyone is brave, he praises him. He loves the moderate person; he shows mercy to the impoverished; to the ill he shows compassion; he fears God. He loves the person who has the gift of a good spirit as he loves his own life. If your mind is set toward good, even evil men will be at peace with you; the dissolute will respect you and will turn back to the good. The greedy will not only abstain from their passion but will give to the oppressed the things which they covetously hold. If you continue to do good, even the unclean spirits will flee from you and wild animals will fear you. For where someone has within himself respect for good works and has light in the understanding, darkness will slink away from that person. For if anyone wantonly attacks a pious man, he repents, since the pious man shows mercy to the one who abused him, and maintains silence. (Test.Ben.4.1-5.4)

Yeshua demonstrates the same principle in Matthew 18.15: "And if your brother sins, go and reprove him in private; if he listens to you, you have won your brother." The purpose of conciliating your brother in place of provoking him further, is to "win" him. This corresponds to the principle of doing good to others so that they will change their own conduct for the good:

> There were once some highwaymen in the neighbourhood of R. Meir who caused him a great deal of trouble. R. Meir accordingly prayed that they should die. His wife Beruria said to him: How do you make out [that such a prayer should be permitted]? Because it is written Let *hattaim* {sins} cease? Is it written *hotim* {sinners}? It is written *hattaim*! Further, look at the end of the verse: *and let the wicked men*

> *be no more* (Ps.104.35). Since the sins will cease, there will be no more wicked men! Rather pray for them that they should repent, and there will be no more wicked. He did pray for them, and they repented. (Ber.10a)

"Respect what is right . . . ": cf. Ps.34.14, 37.27, 2 Cor.8.21, Phil.1.10, 4.8, Heb.12.14; PA 1.6, 2.5.

Paul states the positive aspect of not repaying evil with evil.[55] This closely coincides with the "missionary" or proselytizing policy of "accommodation," according to which accepting the views of other people can be a way to bring them to good conduct in faithfulness to God.[56]

Verse 18:
"If possible . . . at peace with all men": cf. Mk.9.50, 2 Cor.13.11, 1 Thess.5.13, Heb.12.14; PA 1.12, Ber.17a.

In this statement, Paul summarizes the theme of the whole chapter, since it combines the principle of love for one's enemies with the principle of non-retaliation (cf. "peaceful co-existence"):

> Hillel used to say: Be thou of the disciples of Aaron, loving peace and pursuing peace, [be thou] one who loveth [one's fellow-] creatures and bringeth them nigh to the Torah . . . separate not thyself from the community, neither trust in thyself until the day of thy death, moreover judge not thy fellow-man until thou hast reached his place. (PA 1.12, 2.4)

Paul develops this theme fully in chapter 14, where he refers to most of the major principles concerning peace, based on love and respect for one's brothers. The letter therefore possesses a literary unity throughout its entire length, since chapters 9-11 fully answer the question Paul raises in 3.1-2 and chapters 12-15 represent the direct implications and applications of chapters 9-11. (Chapter 16, while independent in regard to the greetings Paul conveys, also forms an integral part of the letter in referring back to previous themes in verses 17-20.)

Verses 19-20:
"Your own revenge . . . head": cf. Lev.19.18, Dt.32.35, 2 Kings 6.22, Ps.94.1, Prov.20.22, 24.29, 25.21-22, Mt.5.38-48, 23.25, 1 Thess.5.15, 2 Thess.1.6-8, 1 Pet.3.9; 1QS 9.21ff, 10.17-20; Test.Gad 6.7, Test.Ben.5.1; Suk.52a.

Paul enjoins the believing community to love their enemies and to refrain from repaying evil with evil, since God Himself will punish the transgressors. This idea is subsequently developed by certain circles into the principle that another person's attitude can be changed through good behavior towards him. The prooftext from Proverbs 25.21-22 is midrashically linked with "peace" through a play on the word "reward" (ישלם; *yeshalem*) (" . . . and the Lord will reward you"), which can also be read as "to make peace" (ישלים; *yashlim*):

> R. Berechiah applied to the impulse to evil the verse *If thine enemy be hungry, give him bread to eat* (Prov.25.21)—that is, if your enemy be hungry, have him eat the bread of Torah; *if he be thirsty, give him water to drink (ibid.)*, the water of Torah. Why? Because *Thou wilt heap coals of fire upon his head, and the Lord will reward (yeshallem) thee* (Prov.25.22), by which is meant that "the Lord will make the Impulse to evil be at peace with you." (PRK 11.1)[57]

Paul's appeal to Proverbs 25.21-22 at first glance seems to contradict the principle of doing good to one's enemy instead of retaliating against him. Flusser notes the discrepancy between Romans 12.14f and 12.19f: "If you pursue your neighbor with good, you need not love him and you can even hate him, because you can explain your behavior by assuming that by acting thus you do not diminish your wicked neighbor's portion of divine punishment. This is evidently the meaning of Rom.12:19f and very probably of the last passage quoted from the Scrolls [1QS 10.17-20], but this attitude is prone to develop into a more humanistic position. In the already quoted passage of the epistle to the Romans we read also: 'Bless the persecutors, bless them and do not curse them' (Rom.12:14). There is a certain tension between these words and the end of the chapter, because if you bless the evil-doers, you cannot fail to hope that your blessings will be accepted by God. Thus Rom.12:14 is not far from Mt.5:44. When you pray for those who persecute you, you surely do not pray for divine vengeance."[58] Paul's appeal to the prooftext thus appears to specifically relate to the idea of God's vengeance, which precludes men paying back evil for evil and taking their own revenge. The insistence of the Qumran community on God's timing and divine sovereignty explains Paul's use of Proverbs 25.21. In being submissive in front of the "sons of darkness" until God destroys them in His allotted time, the community at Qumran ensured that the punishment of the evil is made by God Himself. God alone has the prerogative to punish, and He will pour out His wrath in the fulfillment of His time. Thus acting in peace towards one's enemy does not "heap burning coals upon his head" by the hands of men, but gives room for God's punishment when He visits the wicked in the Eschaton.[59] The wicked will then receive their full and due punishment at the hands of God Himself.[60]

Verse 21:
"Do not be overcome . . . good": cf. 9, 14, 17, 19.

Paul summarizes the whole chapter in enjoining the believers to win people to faithfulness to God in Yeshua through love and respect and to refrain from repaying evil with evil. The community's integrity is based upon a spirit of humility and a contrite spirit towards the brethren. By their practice of non-retaliation, the conduct of those around them is influenced so that the world as a whole is determined by good and not by evil. However, the perpetrators of disobedience and transgression will receive their punishment directly from the hands of God Himself on the "Day of Vengeance." This leads Paul to directly address the issue of government and authority in chapter 13. He exhorts the community to do good in all things and to all people because God is sovereign and will take care of human injustice. From this position the thought naturally derives that God has set human authorities in place to govern the evildoers whom He will punish at the Day of Judgment. Paul thus lays out the "division of labor" or respective responsibilities of the believer, governments, and God.

Endnotes Chapter 12

1 Although commentators frequently note that chapter 12 introduces the "halakhic" section of the epistle, dealing with the practical implications of his theological arguments, Paul here draws together the material which he has gathered from the beginning of the letter, recapitulating and building on the various themes.

2 Cf. 1QS 1.1ff, 5.7-11, 20f9.12ff, 21f. See also the function of the "man of understanding" (המשכיל; *ha-maskil*) who acknowledges that his own authority comes from God's gift of the Holy Spirit; cf. 1QH 1.21ff, 2.6f, 7.26-27, 8.16, 35-36, 12.11-15, 14.12-13, 25-26, 16.1-2, 11-12, 17.17, 26-28. Rabbinic authority, on the other hand, while it was also recognized by the "laying on of hands" (סמיכה; *semikhah*) was self-professedly independent of the work of the Holy Spirit. The prevailing view of the Sages was that they had superseded and taken over the role of the prophet; cf. Sifra Bechuk.94, BB 12a, Yev.102a, AZ 36a.

3 These themes are picked up from chapter 4 (Abraham's "sons" [בנים; *banim*] [cf. chapter 8] made from אבנים [*'avanim*; stones], a people "called into being" from "not-My-people"), and from chapters 9-11 (the "testing-stone" and "cornerstone" [cf. Isa.8.14, 28.16] of Yeshua [cf. also Heb.3.1f]). Paul builds the theme of "present[ing] your bodies . . ." on

the motif of the "two masters" which he introduces in chapter 6; see the comments on 6.2ff.

4 Cf. 1QS 5.5f, 8.3f, 9.3f, CDC 3.19, Test.Levi 3.5-6. The Temple imagery is taken from Ezekiel 44ff; cf. 1 En.90.28-29, Tob.14.5, Mt.26.61, Mk.14.58, Jn.2.19, Acts 6.14. See D. Flusser, *Two*. The phrase מקדש אדם (*mikdash 'adam*) can be read either as "a sanctuary (made by the hands) of man" ("a man-made sanctuary") or as "a sanctuary of men" or a sanctuary "built in" men: "And He has commanded a sanctuary of men to be built for Himself, that in this sanctuary may be sent up, as smoke of sacrifice in His honour before Him, the works of the Law." See A. Dupont-Sommer, *Essene*, 312 n.5. The motifs to which the phrase alludes may also include Isa.66.20 and God's turning of the Gentile believers into priests and Levites who bring Israel back to the Land as a gift to the Messiah (cf. Cant.R.4.8.2). (Alternatively, or complementarily, Paul understands Israel to bring the Gentiles to faithfulness to Yeshua as their offering to God [cf. Rom.15.16]). Both "offerings" are made in order to bring salvation to Israel and to the Gentiles. Delitzsch's Hebrew translation (גויה [*geviah*], "your corpses") reflects Ezekiel's vision of the dry bones (Ezekiel 37; cf. Ps.103.29-30), into which God breathes life to transform them from lifeless corpses into "living bodies." Delitzsch further translates νους (*nous*; mind) in verse 2 as a "new heart" (לב חדש; *lev chadash*); cf. Isa.11.9, Jer.31.31f, Ezek.36.27, Jn.3.3, Rom.6.4, 2 Cor.5.17.

5 See E. Käsemann, *Commentary*, 328-29.

6 Käsemann translates the passage in the Odes as "I offer him his spiritual sacrifice," and immediately adds that the "idea of divinely effected praise which both continues and replaces the cultic sacrifice governs the *Hodayoth* [Hymns] of Qumran . . . but it sheds less light on Paul's view than on its Jewish presuppositions" (*Commentary*, 328). While appreciating Käsemann's note that Paul stands in a tradition which is adopted in baptismal exhortation (cf. 1 Pet.2.2), we would argue that the idea sheds light on Paul's view precisely *because of* its Jewish presuppositions. The close connection between the Qumran texts and Paul is very evidently mediated in Romans 12 through 1 Peter 2, which Flusser (*Romans*) has convincingly demonstrated to be directly influenced by a Qumran tradition linked to conversion; and Paul is quite clearly building on the motifs of baptism from chapter 6.

7 See also the comments on 8.27 for the Spirit's "knowledge" of men's "minds" because He "searches their hearts" (cf. Prov.20.27).

8 Cf. Ex.7.23, Josh.14.7, Isa.10.7, 12, 40.13 (where νους represents the Spirit of the Lord), 41.22.

9 God's "good will" [רצון; *ratzon*] or favor also leads to man's "acceptability;" cf. Ps.69.13, Isa.56.7, 60.7, 61.1-3, Ezek.20.40-41, Rom.15.16, 2 Cor.2.14, Eph.1.5, 9, 5.2, Phil.2.13, Heb.13.21; see also the comments on 8.28.

10 See the comments on 1.5, although Paul describes the basis of his authority in his commission by Yeshua in verses 1-4. Paul and Silas, for example, are authorized by the Antiochian congregation to minister and evangelize (cf. Acts 14.26, 15.40). The use of the Greek verb παραδιδωμι (*paradidomi*), "to hand down," in those verses parallels the term "given" in this verse, and thus recalls the "tradition" of *halakhic* authority (מסורת; *masoret*) in PA 1.1: "Moses received [קיבל] the Law from Sinai and handed it down [מסרה] to Joshua. . . . " Paul's "pulling rank," so to speak, over those whom he is addressing, is frequently interpreted as his response to challenges to his apostolic authority. Although there is no doubt that Paul is emphasizing his authority, the paradox lies in the fact that his authority is based on God's "grace"—His free calling—of Paul, the same grace which God bestows upon everyone who is faithful to Him in Yeshua. Whereas in chapter 1, Paul asserts his authority as an apostle *to the Gentiles*, here he may be asserting it in order to counter the "charismatics" or "pneumatics," who claim authority on the basis of their "spiritual gifts." See J. Tabor, *Unutterable*.

11 Cf. Sifre Num.143, Tanh.B.Shemini 12, Gen.R.44.1, Lev.R.7.2, 13.3, 30.13. The "spiritualization" of the sacrifices is one of the common themes of Qumran, and feeds into the imagery of the house and temple; cf. 4QFlor.1.6f, 1QS 8.5-10, CDC 3.19, 1QH 6.25-27, 4QpIsa.[d]; see the comments on verse 2.

12 Cf. Jn.15.10 and 1 Jn.2.5f, which define love as faithfulness to God's commandments. In distinction to the Qumran community, however, Paul distinguishes between individual believers according to their gifts of service rather than their spiritual knowledge, so that the gift of service which each possesses does not create a hierarchy in the body of Yeshua. Paul develops this theme in chapters 14-15, where he explicitly associates faithfulness with love for one's neighbor.

13 In 15.3 Paul shows that Yeshua is the ultimate example, rather than his own personal authority which, of course, comes from his calling in Yeshua. Cf. also 1 Cor.17-22, where he speaks of the social and cultural aspect of equality (slaves and freemen), as well as the particular status of Jews and Gentiles which must be respected in the community in humility and not in arrogance. There, too, he equates the "measure of faithfulness"

allotted to each man with the "keeping of the commandments of God" in the same way in which he establishes the equality of Jews and Gentiles in 2.14ff.

14 The context of this passage from the Testament of the Twelve Patriarchs mitigates against the view that Paul is here countering the authority of pneumatics or charismatics, since the work comes from the same circles as the Qumran texts, and exhorts its readers not to act "in a disorderly manner, arrogantly, or at an inappropriate time," or to confuse their different functions, because man is unable to "perform the works of light while [they] are in darkness." Thus the motif of the serving two masters—either God or one's evil inclination—determines the principle of diversity in unity for the author, without any reference to pneumatic "spiritual gifts."

15 Here, as in chapter 14, Paul is primarily addressing the varying functions of the body of the Messiah, and only secondarily the differences between Jews and Gentiles, who together make up the body.

16 Paul's inclusion of "male and female" in his discussion of the unity in diversity of the body indicates that he is speaking of natural distinctions which should not be destroyed. If his emphasis is primarily ethical, therefore, it also includes ethnic aspects which must be respected in similar fashion.

17 Cf. Eph.4.8, 1QH 10.27-29, Ex.R.28.1, 33.2, Cant.R.8.11.2, ARN[a] 2.3, Shab.89a. Ps.68.18 is used as a prooftext in the rabbinic midrash on Job 28, which lies behind Paul's own midrash in Rom.10.6-12.

18 The text of the LXX translation (67.19) retains the verb "taking" (ἔλαβες; *elabes*), so that it is evident that Paul's text reflects a midrashic tradition on the original Hebrew text.

19 The "measure of faithfulness" in Rom.12.4 corresponds to the "measure of the Messiah's gift" in Eph.4.7 (cf. Eph.4.13).

20 The Torah itself is the greatest "gift," and corresponds to God's "free gift" in Yeshua (cf. chapter 5).

21 This interpretive tradition precedes the motif of ascension in Shab.89a (in the name of R. Johanan rather than that of R. Joshua), and also appeals to verse 12 from Psalm 68. It is therefore possible that Paul has in mind the unity of Israel and the Gentiles within the "seventy faces" of the Torah and that the "faces" correspond to the "gifts" of 12.6f and Eph.4.7f. See P. Tomson, *Paul and the Jewish Law* (Minneapolis: Fortress Press, 1990), 78 n.97, who also cites the Targum to Psalm 68, Mid.Ps.68.6, Tanh.B.Shemot 22. Tomson establishes the link between the midrashic tradition on Dt.30.11-14 and Ex.20.19 (the sight of the "voices" [קולות])

and Acts 2, the outpouring of the Spirit, in discussing the gifts of the Spirit in 1 Corinthians 12-14. Paul opens his enumeration of the "services" with the "gift" of prophecy. (For the association between the Torah and Pentecost, see M. Weinfeld, *Pentecost.*)

22 The Levites were also given as a "gift" (נתונים; *netunim*) to the sons of Aaron (the priests) who perform God's "service" (עבודה; *'avodah*) on behalf of the laity of Israel; cf. Num.8.19.

23 Cf. Tos.Sot.13.2, San.11a, BB 12a.

24 Cf. Sifra Bechuk.94b, BM 59b, Yoma 9b, Pes.114a, BB 12a-b. The transferal of authority from prophet to Sage was gradual, and occurred both on theological and epistemological levels. Prophecy came first to represent a form of exegesis, and then non-rational thought; the prophet was gradually denied the authority to enact any legal emendations (תקנות; *takkanot*) based on Scriptural interpretation, and finally considered to be like a blind man who uttered ungrounded statements. See H. Strack, *Introduction*, 8-25; E.E. Urbach, "Matay Paseqa ha-Nevu'a [When did prophecy cease?]," *Tarbiz* 17 (1946), 1-27 [Hebrew]; E. Berkovits, *Not.*

25 God's covenant in Jer.33.25 is understood as the Torah (cf. Shab.33a, Ned.32a). The bracketed material appears in the first editions of PRE. This passage provides a clear example of the principle of גזרה שוה (*gezerah shavah*) or verbal analogy, in which the phrase "day and night" in various verses is applied to their different contexts. A comparison between PA 1.2 (on which this text is based) and PA 1.18 equally clearly reflects how the "service" of the Temple was transferred to the "service of the heart" or lips, in addition to the fact that the Temple was physically destroyed in 70 C.E.; see the comments on verse 2.

26 See the comments on verse 6.

27 The role of teacher was assumed in Qumran by the מבקר (*mevaker*), which is the Hebrew equivalent of the Greek term ἐπισκοπος (*episkopos*), translated into English as "bishop;" see the comments on verse 8. The "Book of Meditation" mentioned may in fact refer to the Scroll of the Rule itself, which is presented as a collection of basic texts intended for constant reading and meditation. The rabbinic education system similarly accustomed children to education according to their age: "Five years [is the age] for [the study of] Scripture, ten—for [the study of] Mishnah, thirteen—for [becoming subject to] commandments, fifteen—for [the study of] talmud . . ." (PA 5.21).

28 See H. Strack, *Introduction*, 202-3; cf. G.F. Moore, *Judaism*, 161-204.

29 The Didache, or "teaching," is one of the earliest Christian documents and well reflects the Jewish practices of the first communities. Paul

employs the principle of mutual indebtedness in chapter 15, where he exhorts the Gentiles to repay the Jewish people in material benefits what they have received from them spiritually; cf. 1 Cor.9.11; see the comments on 15.27.

30 The Hebrew term מבקר (*mevaker*), "overseer," corresponds to the Greek term ἐπισκοπος, which is literally translated into English as "bishop;" cf. Acts 20.28, Phil.1.1, 1 Tim.3.1-2, Tit.1.7, 1 Pet.5.2. Both the Greek and Hebrew verbs (בקר; *bakar*) carry the basic meaning of "to look," which is extended to refer to the "looking after" given by the shepherd to his flock (cf. Ezek.34.11-12).

31 Cf. TDNT 7:844-47; E. Sch¸rer, *The History of the Jewish People in the Age of Jesus Christ* (Edinburgh: T&T Clark, 1973), 3:95-103.

32 This saying interprets R. Ishmael's dictum in PA 3.12, which is quoted in capitals.

33 For the idea of such "missionary maxims" as the latter principle, see D. Daube, "Missionary Maxims in Paul, in *The New Testament and Rabbinic Judaism* (NY: Arno Press, 1973), 336-51.

34 Paul develops this theme further in chapter 14, specifically in relation to the social problems between Jewish and Gentile believers in the early congregation.

35 See D. Flusser, *New*, 124. Paul addresses the same issue, from a slightly different perspective, in chapter 14, where he urges every man to love and respect his brethren and their opinions, even when they oppose his own understanding of God's will, and states that whatever a man performs without conviction ("faith"), to him that act is a sin.

36 Cf. CDC 6.20-7.4. These passages also resemble some of the Jewish "apotropaic" prayers of the period, in which people plead before God for grace in "bringing (them) near" (קירב; *kirev*, "to offer [as a sacrifice]") and "deliverance from evil." Flusser notes that such prayers are an integral part of the doctrine of the Two Ways: "Cause us to cleave to good inclination and to good works. Subdue our inclination to submit to Thy service. Grant us this day and every day to deserve grace, kindness and mercy in Thine eyes and in the eyes of all who see us. And bestow kindness upon us" (PB). See D. Flusser, "Qumran and Jewish 'Apotropaic' Prayers'," in *Judaism*, 214-205; see also the comments on 12.17f.

37 Cf. Mt.7.2, 22.36-40, Acts 15.20, 29, Gal.5.14, Jas.2.8, Shab.31a, Did.1.2. Flusser notes that R. Hanina's statement interprets the commandment (on which the whole world depends) 'Love your fellow man—like yourself' as being determined by your right and wrong deeds in solidarity with him; 'like yourself' is taken to mean: he—the fellow man—is one

like you. . . . This interpretation, which relates the Hebrew comparative pronoun *kamokha* to the subject rather than to the predicate—'your fellow man who is like yourself,' instead of 'love him like you love yourself'—is sound and legitimate exegesis. . . ." D. Flusser, *New*, 114-16.

38 Paul develops this theme fully in chapter 14, reinforcing the association between faithfulness and love; see the comments on 14.13f.

39 The Greek term καιρω (*kairo*), "time," is easily replaceable by the more normally anticipated term κυριω (*kurio*), Lord.

40 Cf. 1QS 2.19, 8.4, 12, 9.3, 12-14, 1QpHab 7.13-14; see D. Flusser, "A Jewish Source for the Attitude of the Early Church to the State," in *Jewish*, 397-401.

41 The principle of non-retaliation further fits the context since in the following verses Paul appeals to similar principles advocated in rabbinic circles regarding proselytizing: what actions a man should take to win a man over rather than call down judgment upon him.

42 See also the comments on 5.3-5.

43 The same complex of motifs appears in various passages in which rejoicing and prayer under oppression and love for the oppressor appear (cf. Mt.5.3 12, 43-48, 6.5-15, 1 Thess.5.15-22). Similarly, prayer as "a delectable oblation" (cf. 1QS 9.5, CDC 11.21) describes the "perfection of way" in which the Qumran community walked according to the Spirit of Truth. Prayer is part of the "living sacrifice" which is the "rational" or "spiritual" worship in the "Institution of the Spirit of holiness."

44 Cf. Lev.19.9f, 35f, Dt.10.12ff, 14.29, 17.19-20, 23.19, Job 31.1-40, Isa.1.17, 58.7, Ezek.18.7, 16-17, Amos 5.11ff, 8.4ff, Mt.25.31-46, Jas.1.27.

45 See the comments on 15.25f.

46 See the comments on verse 9.

47 See D. Flusser, "Introduction," in *Judaism*, xiv-xv; D. Daube, *Missionary*.

48 Cf. Gen.R.48.14. A similar dictum says, "if you come into a city, do according to their customs" (cf. Ex.R.47.5).

49 Paul develops the theme of loving and respecting one's brethren within the community in chapter 14, where he claims that the principle of "pursuing peace" must govern each individual's observance of the commandments, in conjunction with the precept that God's ordinances may be "uprooted" in the service of love.

50 The phrase "haughty in mind" recalls Ps.131.1:"Do not walk in great matters . . . " (אל תהלכו בגדולות; *'al tehalkhu bigdolot*).

51 Cf. Ps.51.17, Isa.57.15, 61.1, 66.2, Mt.5.4-5, 1QS 10.26-11.2, CDC[b] 1.9, 1QM 11.9-14, 14.7, 1QH 5.22, 18.12-15, Sir.3.20, Mekh.Bachodesh 9. See D. Flusser, *Blessed*, 102-13.

52 See D. Flusser, "The Sermon on the Mount," in *Judaism*, 503. Paul's saying here may reflect Yeshua's encouragement to his followers to mix with the "sons of this world" which countered the policy of isolation and separatism practiced by the "sons of light" at Qumran. See Flusser's interpretation of the parable of the unjust steward in Lk.16.1-9: "Jesus' Opinion about the Essenes," in *Judaism*, 162-64; cf. Rom.15.26-27, 1 Cor.9.11, 1QS 1.12-13, Did.4.8. The parable addresses the injunction to "make friends" in society, and is thus closely related to the idea of "associating." Flusser also cites John the Baptist's extension of the principle, prior to Yeshua, to include spiritual as well as material wealth in the command to share one's possessions.

53 Paul develops the theme through a further wordplay on the Greek root φρονεω (*phroneo*) which he uses in verse 3. The whole argument of chapter 12 thus revolves around the issue of being wise through loving one's neighbor—or loving one's neighbor through being wise.

54 D. Flusser, *New*, 484-85. The texts from the Testament of Benjamin recall the preceding verses; cf. "mercy" (verse 8), "prayer" (verse 12), a "good mind" (verses 3 and 16). For the "dark eye," see also PA 2.9, which is the rabbinic parallel of the "Two Ways." Daube illustrates the affinities between accommodation and non-retaliation; see D. Daube, *Missionary*.

55 The "Golden Rule" is expressed both positively and negatively: act towards others in the way in which you wish them to act towards you (cf. Mt.7.12); whatever is hateful to you do not do to others (cf. Targ.Jonathan to Lev.19.18, Shab.31a); cf. also Test.Zev.8.3, Tob.4.15, Syr.Menander 245-51, ARN[a] 15.1, 16.4, ARN[b] 23, 26, 32.

56 Delitzsch translates the Greek verb προνοεω (*pronoeo*), "to take thought for," with the verb דרש, which means to seek (and by extension, to interpret). Paul might then mean to say, after the manner of Ps.34.14, that men should seek the good of all by pursuing peace. This idea also corresponds to Paul's statements concerning "faithfulness" and sin, in which he claims that particular doctrines or acts are to be considered sinful according to the peculiar situation and circumstances of the believer; cf. 1 Cor.8.1-13; see the comments on chapter 14.

57 Cf. ARN[a] 16.3, Tanh.B.Beshall.3, Mid.Ps.25.21, Suk.52a. This midrash associates the "evil inclination" with the "enemy," but by analogy it can also mean the evil inclination *in* one's enemy which is also made to "be at peace" with you when you act well towards him. 1QS 10.17f also alludes to Prov.25.22 in establishing the principle of non-retaliation: "To no man will I render the reward of evil. . . and He it is who will pay to each man his reward."

58 D. Flusser, *New*, 485. See also K. Stendahl, "Hate, Non-Retaliation, and Love," *Harvard Theological Review* 55 (1962), 343-55.

59 This accords with the Scriptural context in which "burning coals" usually designate the pouring out of God's wrath (cf. Ps.18.8, 12, 13).

60 Cf. also the concept reflected in Prov.24.17-18: "Do not rejoice when your enemy falls, and do not let your heart be glad when he stumbles; lest the Lord see (it) and be displeased, and He turn away His anger from him." God will avert punishment from a man if another person is pleased by that man's disgrace.

ROMANS 13

Introduction

Paul develops the theme of repaying evil with love, and applies it to the community's relationship to the ruling authorities (verses 1-4). He adapts the Qumran principle of non-retaliation and claims that the community needs to honor the government not only because God has established it to keep order, but also because it gives them the opportunity to love their neighbors (verses 5-10). He repeats his justification of the injunction by appealing once again to the Qumran principle of "serving the time" (cf. 12.11), and then combines it with injunctions concerning the end of time, when the battle against darkness has been won and the community can act according to the principles of the Kingdom of light (verses 11-14).

Verse 1:

"Let every person . . . by God": cf. Job 12.21, 36.7, Prov.8.15, Ps.2.1-12, 22.27-28, 24.7-10, 47.1-9, 82.8, 86.8-10, 107.40, Isa.40.22-25, 43.14-21, 44.24-49.26, Jer.29.7, Dan.2.21, Obad.21, Zech.14.9, Jn.19.11, 1 Pet.2.13-17, 1 Tim.2.1-2, Tit.3.1; 1QS 9.21-23, 10.19-11.2, CDC 9.2-5; 2 Bar.1.11f, Wis.Sol.6.3; Jos.*Bell*.2.140; Gen.R.9.13, Ber.58a, Yoma 69a, Ned.28a, AZ 18a, BK 113a, BB 54b, Git.10b; *MT* Hilk.Gezelah 5.11ff.

Paul continues the theme of peaceful coexistence and temporary submission to those who oppose and oppress the people who are faithful to God (cf. 12.9ff). He applies the principle of non-retaliation in relation to ruling authorities or governments of the State. Just as the brethren are to respect one another in love, and the community must love those who oppose God's will, so they are also required to accept the rule of the State as ordained by God. Here Paul applies the new interpretation of Leviticus 19.18 in Second Temple Jewish thought to the political sphere, where the principle of loving one's neighbor as oneself requires the acceptance of "secular" authority. Just as all men are human and therefore sinful so the world is governed by profane principles as well as godly ones.[1] According to Flusser, this section of the letter (12.9-13.7) is based upon a Qumran homily.[2] The members of the community at Qumran were commanded to submit to those who persecuted them until God finally destroyed the "dominion of Belial" on the "Day of Vengeance." Until that day, however, God allowed the wicked to flourish and wield power in the world and the community was bound to tolerate their reign and not to take revenge into their own hands. The novitiate was required to swear "tremendous oaths" to this effect:

> . . . first that he will practice piety towards the Deity, next that he will observe justice towards all men: that he will wrong none whether of his own mind or under another's orders; that he will for ever hate the unjust and fight the battle of the just; that he will for ever keep faith will all men, especially with the powers that be, since no ruler attains his office save by the will of God. . . . (Jos.*Bell.*2.140)

The believer's obligation to obey those in authority gives him the opportunity to love his enemies, even when he may hate or disapprove of their deeds. Paul's commandment thus rests upon the particular understanding which the Qumran texts gave to Proverbs 25.21-22. When the believer obeys the ordinances of the government, he "repays" those in authority with good rather than with evil, and in doing so he actually insures their full punishment by God (if they are evil), since he does not take vengeance out of God's hands.[3] The authorities may be, and often are, wicked and evil. Yet because God reserves their punishment for Himself, He thus not only sanctions their existence but also commands people to obey their ordinances. Since God alone possesses the power and the right to repay He may raise up and maintain whatever authority He wishes, even if its officers oppose those who are faithful to Him. This means that the community and its members cannot take retribution into their own hands, but are in fact enjoined to accept and to submit to evil behavior, people, and leaders.[4]

Verse 2:

"He who resists authority . . . of God": cf. Mt.5.44, Lk.6.37-38; ARN[a] 16.4, ARN[b] 26.

Paul adapts the principle of non-retaliation within the community to the political administration of society as a whole, in which "resisting" authority corresponds to retaliating or "hating" those who are evil and opposing their edicts:

> And concerning that which He said, *Thou shalt take no revenge and shalt bear no malice against the sons of Thy people* {Lev.19.18}, any

> man from among the members of the Covenant who brings an action against his fellow without having reproved him before witnesses, or brings this action in the heat of anger, or tells (the matter) to his elders to dishonour him, is a man who takes revenge and bears malice; whereas it is written (that) only *he* (*God*) *takes vengeance on his adversaries and bears malice against his enemies* {Nah.1.2}. (CDC 9.2-5)

> Malice and wrath, even these are abominations; and the sinful man shall have them both. He that revengeth shall find vengeance from the Lord, and he will surely keep his sins [in remembrance.] Forgive thy neighbor the hurt that he hath done unto thee, so shall thy sins also be forgiven when thou prayest. One man beareth hatred against another, and doth he seek pardon from the Lord? He showeth no mercy to a man, which is like himself: and doth he ask forgiveness of his own sins? If he that is but flesh nourish hatred, who will entreat for pardon of his sins? Remember thy end, and let enmity cease; [remember] corruption and death, and abide in the commandments. Remember the commandments, and bear no malice to thy neighbor: [remember] the covenant of the Highest, and wink at ignorance. (Sir.27.30-28.7)

Paul describes the person who "resists authority" as someone who "has opposed the ordinance of God." This ordinance is first God's commandment not to take revenge (cf. Lev.19.18), as well as the "Decree of time" which establishes the principle of temporary submission to oppressive authorities (cf. 1QS 9.14ff); and perhaps also the "ordinances" (edicts) of the authority which God places in power.[5] 1 Peter 2.12-15 gives a similar reason for submitting to the authorities, and links non-retaliation (doing good) with קידוש ה' (*kiddush ha-Shem*) or the "sanctification of God's name": "keep your behaviour excellent among the Gentiles . . . that by doing right you may silence the ignorance of foolish men." "Doing right," rather than repaying evil with evil, gives those who are evil no cause to punish men.[6]

"Condemnation": cf. 5.16, 8.1, 34; Sir.27.30-28.1f; PA 3.5, 4.4, , 7, ARN[a] 16, ARN[b] 26.

The Qumran texts explicitly state the form of punishment imposed by the community for taking revenge and acting maliciously:

> That will be the day when God will visit; < as He said > , *The princes of Judah were < like those who removed the bound >* , *upon whom Anger*

> *shall pour* {Hos.5.10}. For they shall be sick < without > any healing and all the < chastisings shall crush > them because they did not depart from the way of traitors, but because they defiled themselves in the way of lust and in the riches of iniquity, and because they took revenge and bore malice each towards his brother, and because each man hated his fellow, and because they refused their help, each man to him who is flesh of his flesh. . . . (CDC 8.2 6)

Paul combines this principle of "non-resistance" with the "new" interpretation of Leviticus 19.18 (cf. 12.9ff), according to which God punishes those who do not love Him by loving their fellow-man:

> R. Hanina, the Prefect of the Priests, says: An oath from Mount Sinai has been sworn on (this) saying upon which the whole world depends: If (you) hate your fellowman whose deeds are evil like yours, I the Lord am judge to punish that same man [him who dislikes] and if you love your neighbor whose deeds are proper like [as right as] your own, I the Lord am faithful and merciful toward you. (ARN[b] 26)[7]

If men do not love their neighbors, they have no basis upon which to ask mercy from God for their own sins. The punishment in this case, however, is not only directly from God but also from the authorities which He has instituted to execute the law (cf. verses 3-4).

Verse 3:

"Rulers are not a cause of fear . . . ": cf. Jer.29.7, 1 Pet.2.13f; PA 3.2, AZ 4a.

According to the Qumran theology, rulers were considered to be agents who must be tolerated as instruments of God's will and within His timing, they are not good in themselves nor good to or for others. Paul recalls here, on the other hand, a rabbinic tradition concerning governments and authorities which appeals to Jeremiah 29.7. The same R. Hanina, the deputy (prefect) of the Priests (1 C.E.), who adapted (PA 3.2, ARN[b] 26) Simeon b. Eleazar's interpretation of Leviticus 19.18 (ARN[a] 16.4), also spoke of submission to the authorities in terms of loving one's neighbors, an attitude which claimed that governments hold in check men's own evil actions:

> Another explanation: Just as among fish of the sea, the greater swallow up the smaller ones, so with men, were it not for fear of the government, men would swallow each other alive. This is just what we learnt: R. Hanina, the Deputy High Priest, said, Pray for the

welfare of the government, for were it not for the fear thereof, men would swallow each other alive. (AZ 4a)[8]

"No fear . . . praise from the same": cf. Dt.6.18, Prov.2.20, Isa.1.17, Mt.5.44-48, 19.16, Rom.2.10, 12.9, 17, 21, Gal.6.10, 1 Pet.3.11; 1QS 10.18, 9.20f; Test.Ben.4.2f, 5.1, 6.5f.

Paul repeats the injunction to "abhor evil; cling to what is good," "respect what is right in the sight of all men," and "overcome evil with good" (cf. 12.9, 17, 21). "Good" behavior recalls the "goodness" which should replace hatred, which is a variation of the principle of "measure for measure." Fear is the natural response to punishment, just as praise is the natural complement to goodness. Fear calls forth punishment; just as goodness calls forth praise. If you do good and are praised (rewarded) for it, then those who reward you are good themselves.

Verse 4:

"Minister . . . for good": cf. Jer.29.7.

Since governments are appointed by God and represent His will, they are thus designed to promote observance of His laws:

> R. Simeon b. Lakish said: BEHOLD IT WAS VERY GOOD alludes to the kingdom of heaven; AND BEHOLD, IT WAS VERY GOOD, to the earthly kingdom. Is then the earthly kingdom very good? How strange! [It earns that title] because it exacts justice for men; [hence it is written,] *I, even I, have made the earth, and created man [adam] upon it* (Isa.45.12). (Gen.R.9.13)[9]

In the framework of "accommodation" (cf. 12.9f), the secular authorities serve the believer by giving him the opportunity to win them over through "love" and altruism. Obedience to an earthly authority encourages the habit of obedience and observance, and is a discipline which strengthens the believer's walk according to the "law of the spirit of life" (8.2).[10] This further relates to the principle of loving one's neighbor as oneself within the legal sphere (of the Torah).[11]

"Bear the sword . . . ": cf. Mt.26.52, Heb.4.12.

The condemnation or punishment which falls on those who disobey the decrees of the government comes first from God and secondly from those to whom He has appointed power. "Bearing the sword" is the means whereby order is established and maintained:

> Seven kinds of retribution come to the world for seven categories of transgressions. . . . Pestilence comes to the world for [sins] the death-penalties [for] which are pronounced in Torah, but which have not been referred to a [human] tribunal; and on account of [the transgression of the laws regarding] the produce of the Seventh year. The sword comes to the world for the retardation of judgment, and for the perversion of justice, and on account of those who interpret the Torah not in accordance with the accepted law. (PA 5.8; cf. Shab.33a)[12]

"Minister of God": cf. 1 Cor.3.5, Eph.3.7, Col.1.23, 25.

Paul describes the secular government in terms borrowed from the qualities of the Torah:

> R. Samuel bar R. Nahman read the word *slysym* to mean "captains," as in the verse "and captains (*slysym*) over all of them" (Ex.14.7), for, as R. Samuel bar Nahman used to say, words of Torah are like [captains'] weapons. Even as such weapons stand up in battle for their owners, so do words of Torah stand up for him who valorously gives them the labor they require to be understood. And the proof? The verse *The glories of God in their throat are like a sword pifiyyot in their hand* (Ps.149.6). R. Judah, R. Nehemiah, and the Rabbis differ on the interpretation of this verse . . . R. Nehemiah, considering the word *pifiyyot* as meaning "an edge that is two edges"—*peh* signifying "edge," and *fiyyot* signifying "two edges"—took it to be depicting the Torah as a blade which cuts with both edges and is therefore capable of assuring life in this world as well as in the world-to-come. The Rabbis, however, took "mouths" {*pifiyot*} to be referring to priests whose utterances showed them to be Sages, "princes of holiness and princes of godlike beings" (1 Chron.24.5), as Scripture describes them, who issue decrees for angels in heaven, which the angels obey, and decrees for Israel on earth, which Israel obey. (PRK 12.5)[13]

Paul does not identify the government with the Torah. However, since the authorities perform the same function as the Torah, Paul can equate them with the "avenger" which brings evil, in parallel to the "commandment, which was to result in life, [which] proved to result in death" (7.10). The Torah and the ruling powers are good, just as God is good. When men respond to others and to the government in "love," they imitate God's goodness and love in forgiving their sins. When they resist the law, they receive God's punishment, just as the Torah condemns those who disobey its ordinances.

Verse 5:
"Wherefore . . . also for conscience' sake": cf. Acts 23.1, 1 Cor.8.7, 1 Tim.3.9, 4.2, Heb.9.14, 10.22, 1 Pet.2.19, 3.16.

Paul adds here a second reason for submission to the authorities. Although the government punishes wrongdoing, it does not punish right actions. Paul interprets this "good behavior" as "for conscience' sake." The principle of loving one's neighbor (as oneself) is a matter of "conscience." Right or wrong behavior should not be determined by coercive force, but by the commitment a man makes to be single-minded in his love for all men. The idea of "conscience" (more Hellenistic than Semitic, in its terminology) is therefore based on purity of heart and singleness of mind. Man's love should be without "hypocrisy" (cf. 12.9): it must not make a distinction between the "seeming good" and the "genuine good" (cf. Test.Asher 4.3). His actions should express his inner intent to "do what is right and good in the sight of the Lord" (Dt.6.18).[14] Paul's invocation of "subjection for conscience' sake" removes any doubt that non-retaliation is practiced out of submission to superior force. Submission is one of the highest possible of principles, in which loving God is represented in loving first of all in order to be pure in heart, and then in the hope of changing the behavior of those who oppose His will. Paul fully develops this theme in chapter 14.

Verse 6:
"Because of this . . . very thing": cf. Mt.17.25, 22.17-21, Lk.20.22, 23.2; 1 Macc.10.33; Tanh.B.Noah 15, Tos.BK 10.8, Sem.2.9, BK 113a, Ned.28a.

The rather ambiguous phrase, "devoting themselves to this very thing," refers back to Paul's assertion that the governing authority is a "minister of God to you for good" (verse 4). Payment of taxes was (is) another opportunity to act in purity of heart in loving one's neighbor (in the form of the government). This is the specific force of the phrase, "for because of this," which relates to submission "for conscience' sake":

> *I (counsel thee), keep the king's command, and that on account of the oath of God* (Eccl.8.2): the Holy Spirit said to Israel, I adjure you that if the government imposes on you harsh decrees, you shall not rebel against it, whatever it decrees, but *I (counsel thee), keep the king's command*. But if it decrees that you shall nullify the Law and the commandments and the Sabbath, do not listen to it, but say to it, I will keep the king's command in everything necessary to you, but *on account of the oath of God . . . Do not be in a hurry to leave him. Do not stand in an evil thing* (Eccl.8.3). Why? Because they are not stopping

you from the commandments, but making you deny God; therefore, *on account of the oath of God*. This is what Hananiah, Mishael, and Azariah did when Nebuchadnezzar set up the image {Dan.3.13-18}. They said to him, whatever you impose on us, levy of produce (*arnoniot*), duties and tolls, or poll-tax, we will obey thee; but to deny the Lord, we will not obey thee. (Tanh.B.Noah 15)[15]

Verse 7:

"Render to all what is due them": cf. Mt.17.25, 22.21, Lk.20.22, 23.2; 1QS 1.10-11, 9.16, 21-22; 1 Macc.10.31; Ned.28a.

Paul first introduces the כלל (*kelal*) or general rule, to "render to all what is due them," and then gives the פרט (*prat*) or specific examples of the general rule. He repeats virtually verbatim Yeshua's statement in Matthew 22.21, and makes it a general principle.[16] Rendering what is due reflects the principle of a "measure for measure" (מידה כנגד מידה; *middah ke-neged middah*), and Paul appeals back to the "proselytizing" principle of "accommodation" once again (cf. 12.9f): "a man should not act differently from his fellow-man" (cf. DEZ 5.5).

"Tax . . . custom . . . ": cf. Mt.17.25; 1 Macc.10.31; Mid.Ps.28.1, Cant.R.2.14.1, Ned.28a.

The term τελος (*telos*), translated here as "custom," refers to the tax levied as a "tribute" in Roman colonies. The provinces were required to pay two direct taxes, one on agricultural produce (*tributum soli*) and a poll-tax (*tributum capitis*), a personal tax which included a tax on property, levied according to a person's capital valuation and a poll-tax proper, at a flat-rate for all *capita*. In Eretz Israel, tolls and other levies were known from as early as the Persian era (cf. Ezra 4.13, 20, 7.24).[17]

"Honor": cf. 12.10; PA 2.4, 10, 12, 4.1, 3, 6.6.

Paul returns to the discussion in 12.10, and applies the principle of accommodation ("be of the same mind") to submitting to the authorities and loving one's "neighbors." Honor is a positive attribute which must be paid to the authorities (in contrast to fear and custom or taxes). The ruling powers are honorable and hence must be treated also with honor.

Verse 8:

"Owe nothing . . . fulfilled (the) law": cf. Isa.1.10-17, 24.5, Jer.7.22-23, Amos 5.15, 21-24, Mic.6.6-8, Mt.5.44-48, 23.13-32, Rom.1.14, 8.12-13, 12.9f, 1 Cor.13.4-8, 2 Cor.6.6, 1 Tim.1.5, 2 Tim.2.22, Jas.3.17; 1QS 1.9, 5.25-26,

CDC 6.20-21, 1QH 4.13-21; Sir.18.13, 28.1-7, Jub.36.4, 8-11, Test.Zev.5.1, Test.Iss.5.1-2, 7.6-7, Test.Gad 6.1-7, Test.Asher 1.3-6.5, Test.Ben.6.5f; PA 1.12, 15, 2.4, 10, 3.12, 4.12, ARN[b] 23, 26, 32, Mid.Ps.52.1, 101.7, Tos.BM 2.26, Sifra Ked.39b, Gen.R.24.7, 38.3, Sot.41b.

Paul restates the "Golden Rule," playing on the association in Greek between the terms ὀφειλη (*opheile*), "due" (verse 7), and ὀφειλετε (*opheilete*), "render" (verse 8).[18] Verse 8 refers not only to the ruling authorities but also to the general conduct of believers. It recalls common Jewish ethical exhortations such as, "let the honor of thy friend be as dear to you as thine own" (PA 2.10); "be eager (or quick, easy) to . . . " (PA 2.14, 3.12); "judge all men in the scale of merit" (PA 1.6); "receive all men with a pleasant countenance . . ." (PA 1.15). The verb חייב (*chayav*), "to owe," referred to both a "debt" and "sin" in the Second Temple period.[19] Paul thus implies that the only "debt" men should incur is to love one another; by so doing they will avoid "sinning" against their brethren.[20]

Verses 8-10:
"He who loves . . . fulfillment of (the law)": cf. Mt.5.43-48, 7.12, 22.35-40, Mk.12.28-34, Lk.10.25-37, 18.18-20, Jn.13.34, 14.15, 21, Rom.5.5-8, 1 Cor.13.13, 14.1, Eph.1.10, Col.3.12 14, 1 Tim.1.5, Heb.13.1, Jas.2.11, 1 Jn.2.10, 4.7-21, 5.3; Wis.Sol.6.18, Test.Zev.5.1, 8.3, Test.Iss.5.2, 7.6, Test.Dan 5.3, Jub.36.7f; Targ.Jon. to Lev.19.18, ARN[a] 15.1, 16.4, ARN[b] 23, 26, 32, Sifra Ked.39b, Gen.R.24.7, Shab.31a; Did.1.2, Aristides, *Apology* 15.14.

Paul reiterates the Golden Rule as the כלל גדול בתורה (*kelal gadol be-Torah*), the "greatest principle" or "summary" of the Torah:

> On another occasion it happened that a certain heathen came before Shammai and said to him, 'Make me a proselyte, on condition that you teach me the whole Torah while I stand on one foot.' Thereupon he repulsed him with the builder's cubit which was in his hand. When he went before Hillel, he said to him, 'What is hateful to you, do not to your neighbor: that is the whole Torah, while the rest is the commentary thereof; go and learn it.' (Shab.31a)

Verses 8-9 indicate that the Ten Commandments (עשר הדברות; *'eser ha-dibrot*) were well established as a central element within Second Temple Judaism.[21] Paul's appeal to Deuteronomy 5.6-21 (cf. Ex.20.1-17) supports Flusser's contention that the Sages regarded Leviticus 19.18 as a commentary on (the second half of) the Decalogue.[22] The phrase "love does no wrong . . ." repeats the negative form of the Golden Rule.

Verse 11:

"This do, knowing the time . . . ": cf. Mt.13.24-30, 36-43, Rom.12.11, 1 Cor.7.29ff, Eph.5.7-21, 1 Thess.5.1-11.

The final section of chapter 13 (verses 11-14) is a literary unit based on Essene motifs. Paul picks up the injunction to "serve the time" in 12.11.[23] The expression "the time" refers both to "these times" under the "dominion of Belial" (cf. 1QS 8.13, 9.3, 12-23, 10.18-11.2), in which people are bound to submit to their oppressors and to refrain from retaliation (either to leave full judgment to God or to bring them to better conduct), and to the end of this present period. It thus combines an eschatological perspective with temporal and ethical injunctions.[24]

"Already the hour . . . sleep": cf. Mt.3.2, 10, 4.13-17, Mk.1.15, Lk.21.34-36, Jn.4.23, 5.25, Eph.5.14f, 1 Thess.5.1-11, 1 Pet.4.7, 2 Pet.3.3-13, 1 Jn.2.7-11, Rev.3.3, 16.15; 1QH 2.19f; Ps.Sol.16.1-4.

Paul's reference to "the hour" is a synecdoche, in which a part of time (an "hour") stands for the whole ("time"). The "nearness" of the hour or time is most probably based on the tradition common to Ephesians 5.14 (1-21). This is a midrash on Isaiah 26.19, in which the theme of rising from the dead in Ephesians 5.14 parallels the phrase "to awaken from sleep" in this verse.[25] "Deadness" refers to the mastery of the evil inclination under the "dominion of Belial," and man's resurrection gives him the means to serve God's will as his Creator, advancing the establishment of His kingdom on earth.[26] Paul indicates that the interim period of peaceful coexistence and non-retaliation is at the verge of coming to its end. Kuhn links verses 11-14 of this chapter with 1QS 5.25-6.1, 9.17, CDC 7.2 and 9.6-8, in which the members of the community at Qumran are enjoined to reprove one another: " . . . the proper way to act in the face of the works of darkness is to rebuke the person who commits the sin, i.e., to tell him that what he is doing is sinful. For, as we read in Eph. 5:13, everything that is revealed as sinful in this manner ('everything that is reproved') is 'made manifest by the light'. *Phaneroun* (to manifest) here beside *elenchein* [to reprimand; cf. Eph.5.11] has a parallel in CDC 20:3 [CDC^b 2.3] . . . 'when his (the evil doer's) deeds come to light'. . . . The purpose of this reprimand is that the other may regret his offence and not commit it again, that he be 'converted'. Yet if he continues to commit this sin he reveals himself as one who acts obstinately before God, who 'walks in the hardness of his heart' and who thereby earns eternal damnation from God."[27] At the time when God prepares to destroy all evil, man also must challenge and fight the forces of darkness and walk completely in the light. The "sons of light" are no longer restrained by the principle of non-retaliation towards the "sons of darkness," but are commanded to "walk in the light as he is in the light" (1 Jn.1.7).

"Now salvation . . . believed": Paul explains what he means in the phrase to "awaken from sleep." He perceives "awakening" as "salvation" or as "walking in the light," but refers to salvation eschatologically here, rather than as personal and national redemption. It corresponds to the "day" which is "at hand" which is the "Day of the Lord," the "Day of Judgment" or Vengeance.[28] The phrase "when we believed" refers to the time when the community volunteered to "be converted from all evil and to cling to all His commands according to His will; to separate themselves from the congregation of perverse men, to become a Community in the Law . . . [to] practice truth in common, and humility and righteousness and justice and loving charity, and modesty . . . [and to] circumcise the foreskin of the (evil) inclination and disobedience in order to lay a foundation of truth for Israel" (1QS 5.1-5).

Verse 12:
"Night . . . day is at hand": cf. 1 Cor.3.13, 7.29f, 1 Thess.5.1-11, Heb.10.25, 1 Pet.4.7, 1 Jn.2.8, Rev.1.3, 22.10; 1QM 7.4-5; Ps.-Philo 19.13, 2 Bar.20.1, 54.1, 83.1.

Paul refers to the common association between light and good and darkness and evil.[29] The "day" is both the "light" of good in contrast to the "darkness" of evil, as well as possibly "the Day of the Lord" or the "Day of Vengeance" on which God will destroy all the works of darkness.[30]

"Deeds of darkness": cf. Jn.1.4-5, 3.19-21, 7.7, 8.12, 12.35 36, Acts 26.18, Eph.5.8-11, Col.1.12f, 1 Jn.1.5-10, 2.8-11; 1QS 3.18-26, 1QM 1.1ff, 1QH 12.24-28.

The deeds of darkness are the works of the Spirit of darkness, performed by the "sons of darkness":

> But to the Spirit of perversity belong cupidity, and slackness in the service of righteousness, impiety and falsehood, pride and haughtiness, falsity and deceit, cruelty and abundant wickedness, impatience and much folly, and burning insolence, (and) abominable deeds committed in the spirit of lust, and the ways of defilement in the service of impurity, and a blaspheming tongue, blindness of eye and hardness of ear, stiffness of neck and heaviness of heart causing a man to walk in all the ways of darkness, and malignant cunning. (1QS 4.9-11)

"Armor of light": cf. Isa.51.9-10, 52.1, 59.17, 59.16-17, 61.10, 2 Cor.6.7, 10.4, Eph.6.11-18, 1 Thess.5.8; Wis.Sol.5.17-19; PRK 22.5, PRK S6.5, Gen.R.1.6, Dt.R.2.37, Cant.R.4.4.

The metaphor of "spiritual armour" is based on several biblical texts which speak of God as clothing Himself (cf. verse 14) with strength and righteousness appropriate to His actions:

> . . . there are ten occasions on which the Holy One clothed Himself in the garment appropriate to each occasion. The first garment, one of glory and majesty—*Thou art clothed with glory and majesty* (Ps.104.1)—the Holy One wore on the day of His creating the world. The second garment, one of overwhelming power—*The Lord reigneth, He is clothed with power* (Ps.93.1)—the Holy One wore to requite the generation of the flood. The third garment, one of strength—*The Lord is clothed, He hath girded Himself with strength* (Ps.93.1)—the Holy One wore to give Torah to Israel. The fourth garment, white—*His raiment was as white snow* (Dan.7.9)—the Holy One wore on the occasion of the requital of the kingdom of Babylon. The fifth [and sixth] garments, garments of vengeance—*He put on garments of vengeance for clothing, and was clad with zeal as a cloak* (Isa.59.17): thus it was two garments the Holy One wore to requite the kingdom of Media. The seventh [and eighth] garments, garments of righteousness and vindication—*He put on righteousness as a coat of mail, and a helmet of deliverance upon His head* (Isa.59.17): thus it was these two the Holy One wore to requite the kingdom of Greece. The ninth garment, red—*Wherefore is Thine apparel red?* (Isa.63.2)—the Holy One will wear to requite the kingdom of Edom. The tenth garment, one of glory—*This one that is the most glorious of His apparel* (Isa.63.1)—the Holy One will wear to requite Gog and Magog. (PRK 22.5)

According to the Qumran texts, in the final war between the "sons of darkness" and the "sons of the light" the Spirit of Truth will utterly destroy the Spirit of Perversity. Spiritual weapons are the "armour" of battle for those who are engaged in the fight:

> And no young boy and no woman shall enter their camps when they leave Jerusalem to go into battle until their return. And no lame man, nor blind, nor crippled, nor having in his flesh some incurable blemish, nor smitten with any impurity in his flesh, none of these

> shall go with them into battle. They shall all be volunteers for the battle and shall be perfect in spirit and body and prepared for the Day of Vengeance. (1QM 7.3-5)

Verse 13:

"Behave properly as in the day": cf. 1 Cor.6.9-11, Gal.5.19 21, Eph.5.5; 1QS 1.1ff, 13ff, 4.1ff, 5.1ff, 8.21f; PRK 22.4.

The "proper" behavior (cf. 1.28) of those who walk "in the light" contrasts with "those things which are not proper" practiced by those whom God has "given over to a depraved mind" (cf. 1.24-32). Paul gives similar injunctions to the believers as the commandments in which the Overseer (משכיל; *maskil*) instructs the community at Qumran:

> For [the man of understanding that he may instruct the sa]ints to li[ve according to the ru]le of the Community; to seek God with [all their heart] and [all their soul] [and] do what is good and right before Him . . . to love all that He has chosen and hate all that He has despised; and to depart from all evil and cling to all good works; and to practice truth and righteousness and justice on earth, and to walk no more in the stubborness of a guilty heart, nor with lustful eyes committing every kind of evil. . . . And He allotted unto man two Spirits that he should walk in them until the time of His Visitation; they are the Spirits of truth and perversity. The origin of Truth is in a fountain of light, and the origin of Perversity is from a fountain of darkness. Dominion over all the sons of righteousness is in the hand of the Prince of light; they walk in the ways of light. All dominion over the sons of perversity is in the hand of the Angel of darkness; they walk in the ways of darkness. (1QS 1.1-7, 3.18-21)

"Carousing and drunkenness": cf. Lk.21.34, 1 Cor.5.11, 6.10, Gal.5.21, Eph.4.19, Col.3.5, 1 Thess.5.6-8, 1 Pet.1.13; CDC[b] 1.21; Test.Jud.14.1f, 16.1f; PA 3.10.

Drunkenness corresponds to the stupor and insensibility which are characteristic of sleep or death ("night"). Paul regularly includes injunctions against drunken orgies in his letters, which suggests that such behavior was a serious social and moral problem in the pagan society around the early church. Jewish texts also reflect the view, however, that similar behavior amongst the Jewish community was responsible for the exile of the people into such pagan surroundings:

> "And now, my children, I tell you, Do not be drunk with wine, because wine perverts the mind from truth, arouses the impulses of desire, and leads the eyes into the paths of error. For the spirit of promiscuity has wine as its servant for the indulgence of the mind. If any one of drinks wine to the point of drunkenness, your mind is confused by sordid thoughts, and your body is kindled by pleasure to commit adultery. Thus he commits sin and is unashamed. Such is the drunkard, my children; he who is drunken has respect for no one . . . [I]f he exceeds the limit, the spirit of error invades his mind and makes the drunkard become foul-mouthed and lawless; yet rather than be ashamed, he boasts in his dishonorable action and considers it to be fine." (Test.Jud.14.1-8)

"Sexual promiscuity and sensuality": cf. Zeph.2.9, Mt.10.15, 11.23, Rom.1.18f, 1 Cor.6.9, 2 Cor.12.21, Gal.5.19, Eph.5.5, Col.3.5, 2 Pet.2.2, 6, 18, Jude 4, 7; 1QS 4.10, CDC 2.16, 4.13-5.10, 7.1-2, CDC^b 1.21; Test.Reub.3.3, Test.Jud.4.5f, 5.1-6.5, Test.Sim.5.3, Test.Levi 9.9, Jub.15.1f, 18.2; PA 2.7, 3.13, Ex.R.41.7.

Paul knows that the deeds done in darkness are sinful, and warns the congregation in Rome that, since "the day is at hand," the believer must perform acts which accord with the Torah which has illuminated their eyes:

> "And now, my children, I know from the writings of Enoch that in the endtime you will act impiously against the Lord, setting your hands to every evil deed . . . For what will the nations do if you become darkened with impiety? You will bring down a curse on our nation, because you want to destroy the light of the Law which was granted to you for the enlightenment of every man, teaching commandments which are opposed to God's just ordinances. You plunder the Lord's offerings; from his share you steal choice parts, contemptuously eating them with whores. You teach the Lord's commands out of greed for gain; married women you profane; you have intercourse with whores and adulteresses. You take gentile women for your wives and your sexual relations will become like Sodom and Gomorrah. . . . With contempt and laughter you will deride the sacred things." (Test.Levi 14.1, 4-8)

"Strife and jealousy": cf. 1 Cor.1.11, 3.3, 2 Cor.12.20, Gal.5.20; 1QS 5.24-25, 6.26, 7.3-5, 8-9, 17, 10.18-19, CDC 1.21, 7.1-4, 8.5-8, 9.1-8, 13.18-19, 14.22, CDC^b 1.18-21; Test.Reub.3.4, Test.Sim.3.1, 4.5.

Just as wine leads to promiscuity, anger leads to strife and envy:

> " . . . I say to you in truth that if you do not guard yourselves against the spirit of falsehood and anger, and love truth and forbearance, you will perish. There is blindness in anger, my children, and there is no angry person who can perceive the face of truth. For even if one is his father or mother, he treats them as enemies; if it is a brother, he does not recognize him; if it is a prophet of the Lord, he misunderstands; if it is a just man, he is unaware of him; if it is a friend, he ignores him. For the spirit of anger ensnares him in the nets of deceit, blinds his eyes literally, darkens his understanding by means of a lie, and provides him with its own peculiar perspective. By what means does it ensnare the vision? By hatred in the heart, it give him a peculiar disposition to envy his brother." (Test.Dan 2.1-5)

Verse 14:
"Put on the Lord Yeshua ha-Mashiach": cf. Job 29.14, Gal.3.27, Eph.4.24, 6.11, 1 Thess.5.8, Col.3.16; 1QS 4.8; Ps.Sol.11.7, Odes Sol.7.4, 20.7, Ap.Bar.5.1-3, Test.Levi 18.14, Sir.27.8; PRK 22.4-5, Gen.R.1.6, 20.12, Num.R.14.3, Nid.25a, Zohar 1, 36b.

The motif of "clothing" oneself with righteousness is based on several eschatological messianic passages.[31] In interpreting these texts, the Sages described God as clothing Himself in various garments throughout Israel's history, and at the end of times clothing His Messiah in robes of glory, majesty, light, and righteousness:

> The words *For He hath clothed me with the garments of salvation* (Isa.61.10) refer to the seven garments which, according to Scripture, the Holy One will have put on successively from the time the world was created until the time He requites wicked Edom. . . . When the Messiah appears, God will put on the sixth garment: He will be clothed in righteousness, as is said *He put on righteousness as a coat of mail, and a helmet of salvation upon His head* (ibid.). . . . The splendor of the garment He put on the Messiah will stream forth from world's end to world's end, as implied by the words *As a bridegroom putteth on a priestly diadem* (Isa.61.10). Israel will live in his radiance and say: Blessed is the hour in which the Messiah was created! (PRK S6.5)[32]

In this context, the motif of light (cf. verse 11) comes from an eschatological source of splendor and glory. Paul speaks in similar terms of the same messianic expectations, according to which those who are faithful to God in Yeshua will "live in his radiance" because they are clothed in his glory (cf. 8.17) and righteousness:

> . . . And then the Lord will raise up a new priest to whom all the words of the Lord will be revealed. He shall effect the judgment of truth over the earth for many days. And his star shall rise in heaven like a king; kindling the light of knowledge as day is illumined by the sun. And he shall be extolled by the whole inhabited world. This one will shine forth like the sun in the earth; he shall take away all darkness from under heaven, and there shall be peace in all the earth. The heavens shall greatly rejoice in his days and the earth shall be glad; the clouds will be filled with joy and the knowledge of the Lord will be poured out on the earth like the waters of the seas. And the angels of glory of the Lord's presence will be made glad by him. The heavens will be opened, and from the temple of glory sanctification will come upon him, with a fatherly voice, as from Abraham to Isaac. And the glory of the Most High shall burst forth upon him. And the spirit of understanding and sanctification shall rest upon him . . . For he shall give the majesty of the Lord to those who are his sons in truth forever. And there shall be no successor for him from generation to generation forever. And in his priesthood the nations shall be multiplied in knowledge on the earth, and they shall be illuminated by the grace of the Lord. . . . In his priesthood sin shall cease and lawless men shall rest from their evil deeds, and righteous men shall find rest in him . . . and he will grant to the saints to eat of the tree of life. The spirit of holiness shall be upon them. And Belial shall be bound by him. And he shall grant to his children the authority to trample on wicked spirits. And the Lord will rejoice in his children; he will be well pleased by his beloved ones forever. Then Abraham, Isaac, and Jacob will rejoice, and I shall be glad, and all the saints shall be clothed in righteousness. (Test.Levi 18.2-14)[33]

Endnotes Chapter 13

1 For the background to the "new interpretation" of Lev.19.18, see D. Flusser, *New*, and the comments on 12.9ff.

2 See D. Flusser, *Introduction*, xv; ibid., *Jewish*, 397-401.

3 A similar idea appears in rabbinic literature regarding the suffering of the righteous who, because they suffer in this world suffer less in the world to come; cf. BK 60a, Kid.39b. The idea is a further variant on the libertine theme which Paul consistently refutes throughout the letter (cf. 3.5, 8f, 6.1, 7.7f). Here Paul actually advocates the view that a person should do good so that evil will come (to those who deserve punishment). However, as Flusser (*Jewish*, 400) notes, Paul modifies the principle advocated by Qumran, by asserting that the authorities punish only those who are evil (cf. verse 4) and by combining the principle of non-retaliation with the idea of "conscience" (cf. verses 5f). "Doing good" may enable a person to "hate" his oppressors, but such behavior is also designed to improve their conduct.

4 Rabbinic literature also reflects a wariness before Roman rule in the knowledge that peaceful coexistence leads to survival; cf. PA 1.10, Pes.113a. See also the frequently cited rabbinic dictum דינא דמלכותא דינא (*dina' de-malkhuta' dina'*), "the law of the Government is law;" cf. Git.10b, BK 113b, BB 54b, Ned.28a.

5 Käsemann notes in his discussion on verse 1 that, "the phrase *exousiai tetagmenai* [authorities instituted by God] describes prominent Roman officials. *Leitourgos* [minister] carries the secular sense of the authorized representative of an administrative body, while *arche* [ruler] designates the municipal authority. . . . *ekdikos* can be the 'agent' who acts intermediately as a representative of the governor in a community. . . . As the apostle's terminology shows, he has in view very different local and regional authorities and he is not so much thinking of institutions as of organs and functions, ranging from the tax collector to the police, magistrates, and Roman officials. It deals with that circle of bearers of power with whom the common man may come in contact and behind which he sees the regional or central administration." E. Käsemann, *Commentary*, 353-54; cf. TDNT 8:29f, 43f.

6 See also the effect of the "missionary maxims" and the principle of "accommodation" in 12.9ff, which "win" people to God.

7 Cf. Lk.6.37-38, where Yeshua cites "condemnation" as an example of mutual non-judgment.

8 The passage is based on Hab.1.14. The *pesher* (interpretation) of 1QpHab 5.12-6.2 relates the prooftext of Hab.1.13 to the *Kittim* (the Romans) who gathered the community "like fish of the sea." The author of this scroll did not therefore associate this text with the tradition of non-retaliation.

9 R. Simeon b. Lakish interprets "adam" [אדם; man] as Edom [אדום], a synonym in talmudic and Midrashic literature for Rome. The surprise of the saying is generated by the association of Rome with a "very good" earthly kingdom. For Edom as a code name for Rome (and later also for Christianity) cf. Tanh.B.Tol.14, Eccles.R.11.1.1, Pes.87b, San.12a; see also the comments on 9.11-13.

10 Dt.6.18 and Prov.2.20 are also used as prooftexts for the principle of לפנים משורת הדין (*lifnim mi-shurat ha din*); see the comments on 2.29.

11 "Doing good" may be going beyond the commandments of the Torah or may represent their "essence;" cf. the versions of the Golden Rule given by R. Akiba, Hillel and Yeshua, which all describe as loving God and one's neighbor as the "essential" or "great commandment" (כלל גדול; *kelal gadol*) of the Torah; see Mt.7.12, ARN[b] 26, Shab.31a; cf. also Mt.22.36-40, Acts 15.20, 29, Gal.5.14, Jas.2.8, Did.1.2). Paul gives his own version of the rule in verses 8-10.

12 The saying associates the sword with governmental powers. The distinction between the בית דין (*Beit Din*, the "human court") and the Heavenly Court [בית דין של מעלה; *beit din shel ma'alah*] is based upon judgments which God Himself will carry out where He has made no provision for them in the Torah and no punishment occurs on earth; cf. PA 5.8, BK 47b, 56a, 59b, 91a, 98a, Git.53a, Shab.129b. The saying may thus also allow for the "doing good" which gives room for God's final judgment on the wicked.

13 Cf. also the sayings which describe the Torah as a drug which brings life or death—Sifre Dt.Ekev 45, Berakah 343, Ta'anit 7a, Kid.30b, Shab.88b, Yoma 72b. This verse may underlie Heb.4.12 (the "two-edged sword"), although the latter is also based on Prov.20.27; see the comments on 8.27.

14 This verse is one of the prooftexts for the principle of לפנים משורת הדין (*lifnim mi-shurat ha-din*), "within the strict line of justice;" see the comments on 2.29.

15 The opposite injunction occurs in PA 2.3: "Be ye circumspect [in your dealings] with the ruling authorities for they suffer not a man to be near them except it be for their own requirement; they show themselves as friends when it is to their own interest, but they do not stand by a man in the hour of his distress."

16 The general principle corresponds to the rabbinic dictum, "The law of the land is [the] law" [דינא דמלכותא דינא; *dina' de-malkhuta' dina'*]; cf. BK 113b, BB 54a, Git.10b, Ned.28a.

17 See E. Schürer, *History*, 1:401-2, 373. These regulations concern the "provinces" or Roman colonies, including Eretz Israel. Citizens of Rome would have been exempt from many of the indirect taxes, but the reference to τελος (custom) in Mt.17.25 indicates that Paul is referring to some of the same taxes.

18 See also 8.12-13.

19 See, for example, the meaning given to the word in the parable of the Unjust Steward (Lk.16.1-13), where the dishonest steward reduced the "debts of his master's debtors in order to gain their good will. Flusser notes that, "Too often one forgets that in a parable when a reference is made to a man who owes a debt to his landlord, the landlord always means God and the debt cannot refer to anything other than human obligations to God." D. Flusser, "Jesus'," 157. This is the same context in which Paul's passage comes here, influenced as it is by the Qumran doctrine of non-retaliation in the framework of the motif of the two masters.

20 This makes it possible to understand actions which in different contexts might be considered as sinful, as acts of love if they are performed out of the purity of one's heart. It might, for example, appear to be sinful to allow irresponsible and ungodly behavior go unpunished. If, however, the principle of correction through love is the motivating force behind such a course of action, love is the proper response.

21 Paul follows the order of the commandments according to the Diaspora tradition. The recital of the Ten Commandments before the Shema was later annulled outside the Temple (in the synagogue and the Diaspora), because the "minim" (heretics, usually "Christians") claimed that the Ten Commandments were the sole valid remaining part of the Torah (cf. Ber.12a).

22 See D. Flusser, "A Rabbinical Parallel to the Sermon on the Mount," in *Judaism*, 494.

23 See the comments on that verse for the correct reading.

24 Cf. Hillel's dictum of "accommodation" in Tos.Ber.2.21 ("This is the general rule: A man should not deviate from the custom of his companions or from society"), which is based upon Eccl.3.4-5 ("there is a time for everything . . . "); see the comments on 12.15. The similarity between the idea of peaceful existence with the wicked and the Parable of the Tares (Matthew 13) also supports the mediation of the idea of non-retaliation through Qumran, since the parable shows close parallels with Qumran

texts; cf. also 1 Cor.7.29-31 where Paul refers to biblical and eschatological time together; see D. Flusser, *Introduction*, xv.

25 The passage in Eph.5.14f is frequently understood as an early baptismal hymn. See K. Kuhn, *Ephesians*.

26 Cf. Rom.6.16, 19, 21, 23, 12.1, Eph.2.1, 5, 1QS 4.2-21, 5.1-5, 7-11, 1QH 11.10-14, 13.11-12. The "renewal" of resurrection is described in terms of the "light" which destroys the darkness of evil deeds; cf. vss.12-13, Jn.1.4-5, Acts 26.18, 2 Cor.4.4-6, 1 Pet.2.9-10, 1 Jn.1.5-10, 2.8-11, CDC[b] 2.3f, Test.Naph.2.10.

27 K. Kuhn, *Ephesians*, 124-25.

28 Cf. Isa.2.12, 13.6f, Jer.46.10f, Lam.2.22, Ezek.30.3f, Joel 1.15, 2.1ff, Amos 5.18, Zeph.1.7ff, 1 Pet.2.12, 2 Pet.3.7f, 1 Jn.4.17, Jude 6, Rev.6.17, 16.14, 1QS 4.20, 26, 9.23, 26, 10.19-20.

29 See the references and comments on 2.19.

30 Cf. Isa.2.12, 13.6, Joel 2.11, Mal.3.2, 1QS 3.18, 4.15-19, 25-26, 9.23, 10.19-20.

31 Cf. Job 29.14, Ps.93.1, 104.1, Isa.51.9-10, 52.1, 59.17, 61.10, 63.1-2, Dan.7.9.

32 Cf. Pes.Rab.36.1, 37.1f, *Yalkut ha-Makiri* on Isa.61.10. See B. Young and D. Flusser, "Messianic Blessings in Jewish and Christian Texts," in *Judaism*, 280-300. Cf. also the comments on 1.2-4 and 3.21-23 for the midrashim which speak of the Messiah's glory and righteousness. Two of the qualities or possessions which Adam lost when he sinned, and which will be restored when the Messiah comes, are said to be his luster and the luminaries (both forms of light) (cf. Gen.R.12.6). The parallel in Pesikta Rabbati (37) refers to God's clothing of the "Messiah of Ephraim" (or Joseph; cf. Pes.Rab.36.1), whom he calls "our Righteousness" (cf. Jer.23.6). Yeshua identifies himself with the "bridegroom" of Isa.61.10 (cf. Mt.9.15, 25.1-13 [where the "day" and the "hour" refer to his unexpected arrival]); cf. also Jn.3.29, Rev.18.23. The bridegroom was therefore also a figure (cf. the Song of Songs) for the Messiah to come (cf. PRK 22.5, PShev.4, 35c, Ex.R.15.31, Dt.R.2.37). His diadem was then interpreted as the light (cf. Jn.1.9, 8.12) which he would restore to mankind.

33 The Testament of the Twelve Patriarchs is closely connected to the Qumran literature, and therefore to the conflict between the "sons of light" and the "sons of darkness." The community expected a priestly Messiah and a kingly (Davidic) Messiah as reflected in the Testament of Levi here (cf. 1QS 9.11, CDC 14.19, CDC[b] 1.10-11, 2.1). The idea of light is based on the reference to the "diadem," whose "splendor" was interpreted as light. The same, or a similar, tradition is reflected in the Book of Revelation (cf. 4.3-4, 21.19-27), where the foundation stones of the

city walls (of the new Jerusalem) are adorned with precious stones and the glory of God and the Lamb give it its light. A passage in Pseudo-Philo associates this tradition with the end times foretold by the prophets: "And then I will take those [stones] and many others better than they are from where *eye has not seen nor has ear heard* and it has not entered into the heart of man, until the like should come to pass in the world. And the just will not lack the brilliance of the sun or the moon, for the light of those most precious stones will be their light" (*Biblical Antiquities*, 26.13b); cf. Isa.64.4, Mt.13.11, 13, Mk.4.10, 12, Lk.8.10, 1 Cor.2.9, 1 Pet.2.9, 1QpHab 7.1-5, San.99a, Ber.34b, Shab.63a. Flusser connects all these passages with the messianic blessing in PRK S6.5, and suggests that the New Testament texts specifically refer to the coming of the Messiah. See D. Flusser, *Messianic*. Those who are faithful to God in being baptized into Yeshua's death and resurrection (cf. 6.2ff) are then clothed with the same righteousness with which God clothes Yeshua (cf. also 1 Thess.5.8, Rev.16.15, 1QS 3.6-12, 4.20-21).

ROMANS

14

Introduction

Paul develops the principles which he has raised in chapters 12 and 13 with regard to the community's internal relationships (cf. Jews and Gentiles). He brings the two examples of dietary laws and festivals in order to demonstrate not only that Jews and Gentiles must respect one another's observances, but also that loving one's neighbor takes precedence over observing God's commandments (if and when the circumstance arises), because God's ordinances are not sacred in and of themselves, and because God may be "sanctified" in and through things which He has not commanded (verses 1-2). Paul appeals to numerous rabbinic halakhot regarding the value of peace which support this injunction (verses 13-20), and lays down the comprehensive principle that everything that the believer does must be done in order to sanctify God (out of "faith") as best he understands His character, and in order to respect his brothers (verses 21-23).

Verse 1:
"Accept the one who is weak in faith": cf. 15.1, 7, 1 Cor.8.9ff, 9.22, 1 Thess.5.14.

Paul continues in chapter 14 the theme of "loving one's neighbor as oneself" which he introduced in chapter 12. Here he picks up the idea of the "measure of faith" which God allots to each believer (12.3), and relates it to faithfulness in love and single-mindedness in regard to the eating habits and holy days observed within the early communities. He lays down the principle that everything that one does must be according to his "conscience," namely out of his commitment to love his neighbor and to seek his good[1] He uses the terms "weakness" and "strength" of faith in terms of the "measure of faithfulness" in love which each believer should exercise (cf. 12.3-6): those who have the "strength of faith" to respect other people's commitments when they differ from their own; and those who do not have the "strength of faith" to accept alternate principles as being legitimate in God's eyes (the "weak").

The two categories of the "weak" and the "strong" do not automatically run parallel to the distinction between Jews and Gentiles, although they reflect certain difficulties created by the respective cultural and religious sensibilities of Jewish and Gentile believers.[2] Observance of the Torah (and/or rabbinic *halakhah*) is a biblical principle for the Jewish believer. His choice is between holding strictly to his understanding of scriptural principles and a willingness to "compromise" them for the sake of respecting his brothers in faithfulness. For the Gentile believer, on the other hand, the choice is between a conviction that meat offered to idols, for example, does not engage him in any act of idolatry itself and between respecting the sensibility of a brother who understands this as, at the very least, tolerating idolatry (and at worst as engaging in it). Since both groups ground their principles upon biblical injunctions (observance of Torah and renunciation of idolatry), to compromise either set of principles presents a serious dilemma. Only the individual himself can decide to which principle he will give priority. Paul's argument is that the supreme guiding principle for the community should be that each person behaves according to his "conscience." This guides him to love his brother; each believer must respect his brother before himself, be single-minded in his love and seek the good of his fellowmen. This principle takes precedence over all the other principles to which an individual commits himself.

"Not for . . . passing judgment": cf. Mt.7.1, Lk.6.37, 12.14, Rom.2.1f, 12.3, 14.13; 1QS 10.18f; PA 1.6, 2.4, Shab.127a-b, Shevu.30a.

The practice of loving one's neighbor single-mindedly (cf. "for conscience' sake" [13.5]) excludes the possibility of condemnation (cf. 8.1, 12.9f, 14.18). This is the "sound judgment" which a person exercises in accordance with the "measure of faithfulness" which God gives him (cf. 12.3). This faithfulness in love does not "pass judgment" on (condemn or criticize) a brother (cf. 1 Cor.13.4-7), but respects him because he possesses the same human nature as one's own (cf. the principle of מידה כנגד מידה; *middah ke-neged middah*; a "measure for measure"):

> And these are the ways of these (Spirits) in the world. It is < of the Spirit of truth > to enlighten the heart of man, and to level before him the ways of true righteousness, and to set fear in his heart of the judgment of God. And (to it belong) the spirit of humility and forbearance, of abundant mercy and eternal goodness, of understanding and intelligence, and almighty wisdom with faith in all the works of God and trust in His abundant grace. . . . (1QS 4.2-4)

"Opinions": cf. Mt.15.19, Lk.2.35, 5.22, 6.8, 9.47, 24.38, Rom.1.21, Phil.2.14, 1 Tim.2.8, Jas.2.4; CDC 7.1-6, 8.5-6, 9.2-5, CDC[b] 1.18.

The Greek term διαλογισμος (*dialogismos*), "opinion," derives from the root λογος (*logos*), which relates to "reason" or "reasoning." In the New Testament, the term is frequently used to refer not merely to dubious speculations (cf. Rom.1.21f) but to the division and dissension to which "judgments" often lead.[3] Such "strife and jealousy" (cf. 13.13) were *halakhically* forbidden within the Qumran community:

> To no man will I render the reward of evil, with goodness will I pursue each one; for judgment of all the living is with God, and He it is who will pay to each man his reward. . . . I will be without malice and wrath towards those that are converted from rebellion. . . . And I will not keep Belial in my heart; no folly shall be heard within my mouth, and on my lips shall be found no criminal deceit or falsity or lies. But on my tongue shall be fruit of holiness and no abominations shall be found on it. I will open my mouth in thanksgiving, and my tongue shall ever recount the deeds of God . . . I will cause vain words to cease from my lips, and defilement and perfidy from the understanding of my heart. (1QS 10.17-24)

Verse 2:

"One man has faith . . . eats vegetables": cf. Dan.10.3, Mt.3.4, Mk.1.6, Rom.12.3; Asc.Isa.2.11, Test.Jud.15.4, 4 Ez.9.24f; Tos.Sot.15.11, Mid.Ps.137.6; Philo, De Vit.Cont.73f, De Prov.70.

In chapter 12, Paul encourages the members of the community to serve one another according to the "measure of faithfulness" which God has allotted to each person. Here he applies the believers' faithfulness to various social issues which cause divisions among them. The reference to "vegetables" (and thus to "meat" by contrast) most likely relates to the problems associated with food offered to idols; vegetarianism was not a religious or "theological" issue per se during the Second Temple period. The Jewish believer's sensitivities derive from extensions or "fences" against the possibility of idolatry and/or from traditional interpretations concerning *kashrut* (the laws concerning clean and unclean animals and ritual slaughtering), as well as the laws concerning ritual purity.[4] To exclude meat from one's diet was a solution to those who doubted the origin of meat, its method of slaughter, and the possibility that it might have been offered to idols before sale in the market.[5] When the "weak" person refrains from eating food that has been offered to idols, Paul considers him in effect to question whether God has more power than the idol. Although he may deny that idols have substance, by his refusal to eat he "weakens the Power on high" (cf. 1.20), and thus raises questions regarding God's sovereignty. He is also less "faithful" to his brethren in his love towards them, since if he is not convinced that God's power is stronger than idol worship, he would find it difficult to believe that God accepts those who "engage" in it even indirectly.[6]

Verse 3:

"Let not him who eats . . . accepted him": cf. Prov.21.2, Lk.18.9, 1 Thess.5.14; 1QS 4.3-4, 7.9, CDC 7.1-5, 8.5-6.

Paul gives the grounds upon which each person must respect his brethren. God accepts the convictions of each individual when they are subject to His will. When a person knows that God accepts his convictions, he also knows that God accepts the convictions of his brethren. "has faith" that God permits him to eat whatever he "sanctifies" before God, since God determines the meaning both of "clean" and "unclean." Both God and the individual believer can therefore accept divergent convictions and observances within the community. When an act which appears to compromise one's principles, e.g., not eating meat that is suspected or known to have been offered to idols (if one is convinced that "all things are clean"); or eating meat that has been offered to idols when one is convinced that it is unclean—when that act is performed as an act of conscience, in respect for a brother who holds a contrary view, it becomes a sign of strength (faith or love). The "strength" of a person's conscience—and not his "weakness"—may thus be exhibited in his willingness not to eat, so as not to cause a stumbling block to a brother:

> But those who are converted from the sin of J[a]c[ob], who have kept the Covenant of God, they will then speak one with another to justify each man his brother by supporting their steps in the way of God. And God will heed their words and will hear, and a reminder will be written [before Him] of them that fear God and of them that revere His Name, until Salvation and Justice are revealed to them that fear God. [And] you will distinguish anew between the just and the wicked, between him that has served God and him that served Him not. (CDCb 2.17-21)

By deferring to the "weaker" brother, the believer offers his body as a "living sacrifice" to "prove the will of God [as] good and acceptable and perfect" (12.2). He "proves" God's will (cf. 3.4f) by showing love and respect towards his brethren. God's will is therefore not only expressed in His Word (Scripture; cf. 15.4) to which He demands obedience, but is also found in loving one's brother by accepting his set of priorities and principles.[7]

Verse 4:

"Who are you . . . another?": cf. 1 Sam.2.25, Prov.30.10, Mt.7.1, Rom.2.1f, 6.6ff, 12.16f, 13.8, 13, 14.1, Eph.6.5-9, Col.2.16; 1QS 10.18f; PA 1.6, 2.4, Shab.127b, Kid.39b.

Paul integrates the principle of loving one's neighbor as oneself into the motif of the "two masters" (Two Spirits or Ways), which he introduces in chapter 6.[8] Since every man must choose to obey either His Creator or his own (evil) inclination, when he chooses to serve God, God becomes his master. This means that no man possesses the right to judge another brother, because each man is responsible to God alone. Once again, Paul makes use of the "new" interpretation of Leviticus 19.18 (cf. 12.9f) to establish the principle of "conscience" or loving and respecting one's neighbor, reflecting numerous similar rabbinic texts:

> Joshua b. Perahiah used to say: . . . judge all men in the scale of merit. . . . Hillel said: . . . judge not thy fellow-man until thou hast reached his place. . . . Our Rabbis taught: He who judges his neighbor in the scale of merit is himself judged favorably [by God and by men]. (PA 1.6, 2.4, Shab.127b)[9]

The fact that God has created all men in His image, and that part of loving Him includes loving one's fellow-man means that all men should treat each other as equal in God's eyes:

> And I am commanding this, my sons, that you might perform righteousness and uprightness upon the earth so that the Lord will bring upon you everything which the Lord said that he would do for Abraham and for his seed. And among yourselves, my sons, be loving of your brothers as a man loves himself, with each man seeking for his brother what is good for him, and acting together on the earth, and loving each other as themselves. . . . And now I will make you swear by the great oath—because there is not an oath which is greater than it, by the glorious and honored and great and splendid and amazing and mighty name which created heaven and earth and everything together—that you will fear him and worship him. And (that) each one will love his brother with compassion and

> righteousness and no one will desire evil for his brother from now and forever all the days of your lives so that you will prosper in all your deeds and not be destroyed. And if either of you seeks evil against his brother, know that hereafter each one who seeks evil against his brother will fall into his hands and be uprooted from the land of the living and his seed will be destroyed from under heaven. (Jub.36.3-9)[10]

All men stand as individuals before God, because He accepts each person according to own principles. No man is responsible to another for his understanding of God's desires, and therefore no one may therefore judge another person's commitments or his priorities. Paul emphasizes that each person has the liberty to choose and organize his personal priorities (according to God's will). Paul argues that this choice is personal and inviolable, subject only to God's judgment and not to that of another man.

"To his own master . . . stand": cf. 2.16, 5.2, 9.11, 11.15, 22, 14.10, 1 Cor.10.12, 16.13, 2 Cor.1.24, 2 Cor.5.10, Eph.6.14; PA 2.14, 3.1, 4.22, Lev.R.29.3, Hag.5a.

Paul appeals to the midrash of the "two masters" (cf. chapter 6), according to which a man must either "anger" his own evil inclination to be obedient to God, or "anger" God in obeying his own inclination. Now he applies to the midrash the principle of loving one's neighbor: not only can a person serve only one master, but his allegiance to one master also makes him accountable only to his own master. God's "acceptance" is His "calling" (cf. 11.11, 15) of men, who "stand" (cf. 5.2) on the basis of their "election" by God:

> He [R. Eleazar Ha-Kappar] used to say, The born [are destined] to die, the dead to be brought to life, and the living to be judged; [it is, therefore, for them] to know and to make known, so that it become known, that He is God, He the Fashioner, He the Creator, He the Discerner, He the Judge, He the Witness, He the Complainant, and that He is of a certainty to judge, blessed be He, before Whom there is no unrighteousness, nor forgetting, nor respect of persons, nor taking of bribes, for all is His. And know that all is according to the reckoning. And let not thy [evil] inclination assure thee that the grave is a place of refuge for thee; for without thy will wast thou fashioned, without thy will wast thou born, without thy will livest thou, without thy will wilt thou die, and without thy will art thou of a certainty to give an account and reckoning before the King of the King of Kings, blessed be He. (PA 4.22)

Verse 5:
"One man regards . . . every day (alike)": cf. Gal.4.10, Col.2.16; 1QS 1.8-9, 3.10, 9.13-14, 10.1-11; Philo, De Spec.Leg.2.41f.

Paul gives a further example of the ways in which God's commandments are subject to the highest principle of loving one's neighbor. "Days" include fast days enjoined in the Torah and/or by the Sages (cf. *Ta'anit*), or other minor remembrances (cf. Judg.11.40); days considered to be under lucky, or unlucky stars according to the astrological calendar; or to the pagan holidays dedicated to the numerous gods within the Roman pantheon.[11] In Galatians 4.10, Paul specifies "days," "months," "seasons" and "years;" and Colossians 2.16 speaks of "festivals," "new moons," and "Sabbaths." Certain (Jewish and Gentile) Hellenistic circles practiced a religiously-based vegetarianism combined with abstinence from wine, and a belief in astrology connected with a fear of demons which made some days lucky and others unlucky.[12] Paul's argument here is influenced on the one hand by Hellenistic Jewish ideas such as Philo's, and by a debate between the two Pharisaic schools of *Beit Shammai* and *Beit Hillel*. Philo associates religious dietary habits with the observance of holy days:

> There are in all ten feasts which are recorded in the law. The first, the mention of which may perhaps cause some surprise, is the feast of every day. . . . When the law records that every day is a festival, it accommodates itself to the blameless life of righteous men who follow nature and her ordinances. And if only the vices had not conquered and dominated the thoughts in us which seek the truly profitable dislodged them from each soul—if instead the forces of the virtues had remained unvanquished throughout, the time from birth to death would be one continuous feast . . . Such men filled with high worthiness, inured to disregard ills of the body or of external things, schooled to hold things indifferent as indeed indifferent, armed against the pleasures and lusts, ever eager to take their stand superior to the passions in general . . . such men, we say, in the delight of their virtues, naturally make their whole life a feast . . . and the true sense [of the word "feast"] is, to find delight and festivity in the contemplation of the world and its contents and in following nature and in bringing words into harmony with deeds and deeds with words. And therefore it was a necessary pronouncement that the feasts belonged to God alone, for God alone is happy and blessed, exempt from all evil, filled with perfect forms of good, or rather, if the real truth be told, Himself the good, Who showers the particular goods on heaven and earth. (Philo, De Spec.Leg.2.41-53)[13]

Similarly, the writings connected with the community at Qumran reflect many of the semi-pagan and/or Hellenistic influences on Second Temple Jewish ideas concerning the feasts and festivals:

> I will sing the Decree with the seasons: at the beginning of the dominion of light, during its circling, and when it vanishes towards its appointed dwelling-place; at the beginning of the watches of darkness when He opens their reservoir and sets them up on high, and in their circling when they vanish before the light; when the (heavenly) lights appear from out of the realm of holiness, (and) when they vanish towards the dwelling-place of glory; at the seasons' entry, on the days of the new moon, the circling of the seasons being in harmony with the bonds binding one new moon to another, for the moons are renewed and grow according to the infinite holiness of the sign N, according to the key of His everlasting favour, according to the beginning of the seasons for all time to come; at the beginning of the months according to the seasons on which they depend; and (on the) days of holiness [*Shabbatot*], on their appointed date with reference to the seasons on which they depend. (1QS 10.1-5)[14]

Paul's reference to the man who "regards [judges] every day alike" relates to the practice of judging each day as equally sacred. This issue was the basis of the controversies between *Beit Hillel* and *Beit Shammai*, who debated the propriety of distinguishing between "secular" (profane) weekdays and "holy" days (i.e., *Shabbat*):

> It was taught: They related concerning Shammai the Elder [that] all his life he ate in honour of the Sabbath. [Thus] if he found a well-favoured animal he said, Let this be for the Sabbath. [If afterwards] he found one better favoured he put aside the second [for the Sabbath] and ate the first. But Hillel the Elder had a different trait, for all his works were for the sake of heaven, for it is said: *Blessed be the Lord, day by day* (Ps.68.19). It was likewise taught: Beth Shammai say: *From the first day of the week [prepare] for the Sabbath*; but Beth Hillel say: *Blessed be the Lord, day by day*. . . . As early as the first day of the week, Shammai the Elder used to purchase wood for the Sabbath. Hillel the Elder had a another and better idea of conduct, for he used to say: "Let each of your deeds be for Heaven's sake." . . . (Betza 16a, Pes.Rab.23.)[15]

Hillel's "greater criterion" corresponds here to Paul's principle of "strong" faith. Acts performed לשם שמים (*le-shem shamayim*), "for the sake of heaven," are those done לשמה (*lishmah*), for their own sake and without ulterior motives. The controversy between the two Pharisaic schools suggests that Beit Hillel granted to "profane" weekdays the same sanctity given to Shabbat. Beit Shammai, on the other hand, regarded granting sanctity to "secular" days as a degradation of God's sovereignty and glory. Their controversy is based on Beit Hillel's view that God would not allow His Sabbath to be profaned, a view which Beit Shammai could not accept on trust. Instead, they took upon themselves the responsibility for observing God's will "literally" or "according to the letter" of the law (cf. 2.29 and 7.6). Paul's description of the "weak" in faith (love) corresponds to *Beit Shammai's* position, which held that men must strengthen God's hand, as it were, by defending His statutes; the "strong" in faith (love) correspond to *Beit Hillel*, who judged God to be strong enough to bear the priorities established by each individual's conscience and convictions. Paul sums up his principle in the statement: "Let each man be fully convinced in his own mind."[16] In similar fashion to the ruling following the בת קול (*bat kol*), the heavenly voice which declared both the words of Beit Hillel and of Beit Shammai to be the "words of the Living God" (cf. Eruv.13b), Paul maintains that the "weak" and the "strong" are both accepted by God, whom He makes to stand together equally by Him in His body. The relations between Beit Hillel and Beit Shammai (according to the extant sources) are themselves an example of Paul's injunction:

> . . . Even though the school of Shammai disagree with the school of Hillel [in various fundamental issues in marriage law without reaching a compromise], Beit Shammai did not refrain from marrying women from Beit Hillel, but rather followed ways of truth and peace [דרכי שלום] between one another . . . Despite the fact that [in a great number of cases] these [Beit Shammai] forbid and these [Beit Hillel] permit, they did not refrain from preparing their ritually pure foods together, in order to fulfill what is written: *Every way of a man is pure in his own eyes but the Lord pondereth the hearts* (Prov.21.2). (Tos.Yev.1.10-11)[17]

Verse 6:
"Observes . . . for the Lord": cf. Prov.3.6, 1 Cor.10.31, Eph.5.15-20, 6.5f, Col.3.17, 22f; PA 2.2, 12, 4.11, Ned.62a.

Paul repeats Hillel's "better idea of conduct" to do everything "for the sake of heaven" (cf. Ps.68.19); "heaven" is a circumlocution for God (cf. the "kingdom of God," or the "kingdom of heaven"). The idea of doing something

לשמה (*lishmah*), for its own sake or לשם שמים (*le-shem shamayim*), for the sake of heaven, is related to the "intention" (כונה ; *kavvanah*) behind the action:

> R. Eliezer son of R. Zadok said: Do [good] deeds for the sake of their Maker, and speak of them for their own sake. Make not of them a crown wherewith to magnify thyself, nor a spade to dig wit. (Ned.62a)[18]

Hillel's prooftext from Psalm 68.19 follows Psalm 68.18, to which Paul appeals in Ephesians 4.7-8. Paul was educated by Gamaliel the Elder (Acts 5.34, 22.3) who, being from Beit Hillel, was presumably familiar with this tradition, which is similar to Paul's statements on the "gifts" of service in 12.1f.[19]

"Gives thanks to God": cf. Ps.68.19, 100.4, Mt.14.19, Rom.1.25, 1 Cor.10.30, 2 Cor.11.31, 1 Tim.4.4-5; 1QS 6.4-6, 1QS a 2.17-22; PA 3.3, Tos.Ber.4.1, 7.1.

In Jewish eyes, eating food which a pagan considers to have been consecrated to his god affirms idolatrous practices. According to the majority *halakhic* ruling, such food can neither be eaten nor sanctified by a blessing, since the blessings recited over meals thank God for His provision and thus acknowledge His sovereignty:

> One should not savour anything until one has blessed, as it is said, *The earth is the Lord's and its fullness* (Ps.24.1). . . . If three have eaten together, they are obliged to summon (each other to say grace after meal [ברכת המזון] together). . . . One says Amen after an Israelite who says a benediction [over the food and wine], but not after a Samaritan until he has pronounced the full blessing. (Tos.Ber.4.1, Ber.7.1, Tos.Ber.3.26)[20]

According to *Beit Hillel*, the blessings over meals provide another example in which a person may honor God in all things, including what he eats:

> R. Simeon [b. Yochai] said, If three have eaten at one table and have not spoken thereat words of Torah, [it is] as if they had eaten sacrifices [offered] to the dead, for [of such persons] it is said, *For all tables are full of filthy vomit, [they are] without the All-Present* (Isa.28.8). But, if three have eaten at one table, and have spoken thereat words of Torah, [it is] as if they had eaten at the table of the All-Present, blessed be He, as it is said, *This is the table before the Lord* (Ezek.41.22). (PA 3.3)

Paul follows this principle, and combines it with loving one's neighbor. Each person must subject his principles regarding his eating practices to the higher demand of loving his fellow-man, since God makes everyone "stand" according to his personal convictions (cf. verse 4). If a person eats food with the intention of "blessing" God, the substance of the food and the nature ascribed to it (such as whether it was offered to idols) lose their significance. Just as weekdays as well as "holy" days are sanctified, so also can God "sanctify" by the "blessing" a person makes over what he eats.[21] If a person's intention is to "observe for the Lord," he will be able to love his neighbor by "sanctifying" all the ways in which he serves God:

> Bar Kappara expounded: What short text is there upon which all the essential principles of the Torah depend? *In all thy ways acknowledge Him and He will direct thy paths* (Prov.3.6). (Ber.63a)[22]

Verses 7-8:
"Not one of us lives . . . for the Lord": cf. Mt.16.25, 20.28, Lk.20.38, Jn.12.24, Rom.5.6-8, 6.2, 10-11, 12.1, 2 Cor.5.15, Gal.2.20, Phil.1.21, 3.8, 1 Thess.5.10, 1 Tim.2.6; 4 Macc.7.19; ARNb 32, Sifra 88b, Tamid 32a.

Paul again refers to the theme of the two masters (cf. chapter 6), since in order to "live for God" a man must "anger" (disobey) his own evil inclination by "putting it to death" (cf. 6.3, 6, 11, 17, 22, 8.5-14):

> He [Rabbi Judah the Prince] used to say: If you have done His will as though it were your will, you have not yet done His will as He wills it. But if you have done His will as though it were not your will, then you have done His will as He wills it. Is it your wish not to die? Die, so that you may not need to die. Is it your wish to live? Do not live, so that you may live. It is better for you to die in this world, where you will die against your will, than to die in the age to come, where, if you wish, you need not die. (ARNb 32)

When a person "lives to God" and offers himself as a "living sacrifice" (12.1) to "prove" what is "good and acceptable and perfect" (12.2), he also "proves his "intention" to sanctify all things. Everything which God has created is in fact "good" (cf. Gen.1.31, Ps.24.1, 50.12, 104.24), and therefore "acceptable" both for men and before God.

Verse 8:
"We are the Lord's": cf. Job 13.15, Ps.95.7, 100.3, Isa.40.11, Ezek.34.30-31.

Verses 6-8 appear to be based on Psalm 100, which Paul cites in a similar fashion as the Sages appeal to Psalm 24.1 (cf. Tos.Ber.4.1):

> Shout joyfully to the Lord, all the earth. Serve the Lord with gladness; come before Him with joyful singing. Know that the Lord Himself is God; it is He who has made us, and not we ourselves; (we are) His people and the sheep of his pasture. Enter His gates with thanksgiving, (and) His courts with praise. Give thanks to Him; bless His name. For the Lord is good; His lovingkindness is everlasting, and His faithfulness to all generations. (Ps.100)

The reference to blessing God's name recalls Psalm 24.1 (cf. verse 6), and indicates that Paul applied the principles of blessing (sanctifying) food to men as well, a theme which he introduces in the subsequent verses.[23]

Verse 9:

"For to this end . . . living": cf. Acts 10.42, Rom.4.24-25, 6.4f, 7.24-25, 8.11, 32, 10.9-13, 1 Cor.3.23, 15.20ff, 2 Cor.10.7, Gal.3.29, 1 Thess.4.14, 5.10, 2 Tim.4.1, 1 Pet.4.5, Rev.1.18, 2.8.

Paul refers again to the midrash of the two masters, which in chapter 6 he links with baptism and Yeshua's resurrection. The power which God demonstrated in raising Yeshua from the dead (cf. 4.24-25, 8.11) is the same power which gives new life to the person who serves his Creator by putting his evil inclination to death. "Lord" corresponds here to "Judge," as in the צדוק הדין (*tziduk ha-din*) burial prayer:

> Just art thou, O Lord, in ordering death and restoring to life, in whose hand is the charge of all spirits; far be it from thee to blot out our remembrance: O let thine eyes mercifully regard us; for thine, Lord, is compassion and forgiveness. . . . We know, O Lord, that thy judgment is righteous: thou art justified when thou speakest, and pure when thou judgest . . . just art thou, O Lord, and righteous are thy judgments. O true and righteous Judge! Blessed be the true Judge, all whose judgments are righteous and true. The soul of every living thing is in thy hand; thy might is full of righteousness. (PB, p.1077).

Since God is the God of all (cf. 3.29-30, 10.9-13), and has created all men equal in His sight, each man must therefore respect his fellow-man as himself, knowing that he has no right to judge him.[24]

Verses 10-12:
"Judge . . . to God": cf. Isa.45.23, Phil.2.10f; Ps.-Phoc.52; PA 4.22.

Paul appeals to Isaiah 45.23 (cf. Phil.2.10-11), in order to demonstrate that all men will give an account for their actions before God's judgment seat. Each individual is accountable to God alone for his conduct, and therefore no man can judge his brother:

> A person should not say in his mind, "since these prohibit and these permit, why is it that I study?" Scripture teaches us: "They were given by One Shepherd" (Eccl.12.11): One Shepherd received them; One God created them. So too you. make your heart into many chambers and enter the words of (both) those (who rule) pure and those (who rule) impure. (Tos.Sot.7.12)[25]

Verse 13:
"Obstacle . . . way": cf. Lev.19.14, Isa.8.14, Mt.18.6ff, Rom.9.33, 1 Cor.8.9, 13, 10.22-26, 32, 1 Pet.2.8, 1 Jn.2.10, Rev.2.14; 1QS 3.24, 5.24-6.1, 10.17-11.2, CDC 6.20-7.3, CDCb 2.17-18, 1QH 2.8; Test.Ben.4.2-5, 6.1f; Sifra Ked.88d, PDem.3, 23b, Pes.22b, AZ 6a-b, Ned.81a.

In this verse, Paul may be associating Isaiah 8.14 (and 28.16) with Leviticus 19.14, and perhaps intends to apply the "stumbling block" of unbelief here to those who do not accept their fellow-man in love.[26] He understands Leviticus 19.14 through the "new" interpretation of Leviticus 19.18 (cf. 12.9ff), and repeats the negative formulation of the "Golden Rule"—do not do to others what you do not wish them to do to you:

> . . . the Council of the Community shall be established in truth as an everlasting planting. It is the House of holiness for Israel and the Company of infinite holiness for Aaron; they are the witnesses of truth unto Judgment and the chosen of Loving-kindness appointed to offer expiation for the earth and to bring down punishment upon the wicked. It is the tried wall, the precious corner-stone; its foundations shall not tremble nor flee from their place. It is the Dwelling of infinite holiness for Aaron in < eternal > Knowledge unto the Covenant of justice and to make offerings of sweet savour. . . . I will be without malice and wrath towards those that are converted from rebellion . . . I will apportion the Precept with the measuring cord of the times and [. . .] righteousness full of loving charity towards the disheartened and strengthening the hands of those whose [heart] is troub[led]; [teaching] understanding to those whose spirit has

gone astray, instructing in the doctrine those that murmur. . . . (1QS 8.5-9, 10.20-21, 25-11.1)[27]

Several talmudic passages also raise the same issue of eating habits in warning against causing one's fellow-man to stumble through putting an obstacle before his customary practice:

R. Nathan said: How do we know that a man must not hold out a cup of wine to a Nazirite or the limb of a living animal to the children of Noah? Because it is stated, *thou shalt not put a stumbling-block before the blind* (Lev.19.14). (Pes.22b)[28]

Such conduct is summed up in a *halakhah* attributed to R. Gamaliel, Paul's teacher:

. . . no person may be fed with what is forbidden to him. Who is the author of what was taught: Things that are in themselves permissible, and yet are treated by others as forbidden, you may not treat them as permitted in order to nullify them? Who is the author?—R. Gamaliel. (Ned.81b)[29]

This *halakhah* is reinforced by another ruling to which Paul alludes, one which demands respect for the essential dignity of each person:

Come and hear. 'Great is human dignity, since it overrides a negative precept of the Torah'. Why should it? Let us apply the rule, 'There is no wisdom nor understanding nor counsel against the Lord?—Rab b. Shaba explained the dictum in the presence of R. Kahana to refer to the negative precept of 'thou shalt not turn aside' (Dt.17.11). The negative precept of 'thou shalt not turn aside' is also from the Torah! Said R. Kahana: If a great man makes a statement, you should not laugh at him. All the ordinances of the Rabbis were based by them on the prohibition of 'thou shalt not turn aside' but where the question of [human] dignity is concerned the Rabbis allowed the act. (Ber.19b)[30]

Verse 14:
"I know . . . in the Lord Yeshua": cf. 8.38, 14.5, 9, 1 Cor.7.10, 17, 11.2, 23, 15.3, Gal.5.10, 2 Thess.3.4.

As in 9.1-2 and 11.1, Paul uses his own practice and life as an example of the need to love and respect one's fellow man. He knows that he is committed to his personal convictions, which God accepts. He also knows that, just as he holds certain convictions, so too do his brethren. They also are convinced before God, and are accepted by Him. Since both Paul and his brethren are created by God and are to give an account to Him for their deeds (cf. verse 10), Paul's overriding commitment is to love his brethren and to respect their personal priorities and commitments.[31] Yeshua is the Lord of both the dead and the living (verse 9), because he judges man to life or to death (cf. Jn.3.16-18). Paul's conviction "in the Lord Yeshua" corresponds to performing deeds "for the Lord" in verse 6, and establishes the framework in which different people may hold divergent opinions. God, however, will make each one "stand" when they seek to serve Him in faithfulness through Yeshua.[32]

"Nothing is unclean in itself . . . ": cf. Prov.16.2, 21.2, Mt.15.11, 20, Mk.7.19, Acts 10.15, Rom.14.20, 1 Cor.8.8, 10.25-26, Tit.1.15; 4 Macc.5.8; PA 2.2, 12, 3.3, ARNb 30, Pes.Rab.23.1, Lev.R.34.3, PKid.1, PKil.9.1, PBer.8, 12a, PYev.1, 3b, Tos.Yev.1.10-11, Ber.63a, Yev.14b, Kid.58d, Betza 16a, Pes.50b-51a,

Paul's personal conviction follows the principle that God sanctifies what He will, even that which in other circumstances He may have pronounced "unclean":

> A heathen questioned Rabban Johanan ben Zakkai, saying: The things you Jews do appear to be a kind of sorcery. A heifer is brought, it is burned, is pounded into ash, and its ash is gathered up. Then when one of you gets defiled by contact with a corpse, two or three drops of the ash mixed with water are sprinkled upon him, and he is told, "You are cleansed!" Rabban Johanan asked the heathen: "Has the spirit of madness ever possessed you?" He replied: "No." "Have you ever seen a man whom the spirit of madness has possessed?" The heathen replied: "Yes." "And what do you do for such a man?' 'Roots are brought, the smoke of their burning is made to rise about him, and water is sprinkled upon him until the spirit of madness flees." Rabban Johanan then said: "Do not your ears hear what your mouth is saying? It is the same with a man who is defiled by contact with a corpse—he, too, is possessed by a spirit, the spirit of uncleanness, and, [as of madness], Scripture says, I will cause [false] prophets as well as the spirit of uncleanness to flee from the Land (Zech.13.2)." Now when the heathen left, Rabban Johanan's disciples said: "Our master, you put off that heathen with a mere reed of an

> answer, but what answer will you give us?" Rabban Johanan answered: "By your lives, I swear: the corpse does not have the power by itself to defile, nor does the mixture of ash and water have the power by itself to cleanse. The truth is that the purifying power of the Red Heifer is a decree of the Holy One. The Holy One said: 'I have set it down as a statute, I have issued it as a decree. You are not permitted to transgress My decree. This is the statute of the Torah' (Num.19.1). (PRK 4.7)[33]

This theme, that God may sanctify what is "profane," forms the basis for Paul's principle of love and respect for one's neighbors.

Verse 15:
"If because of food . . . hurt": cf. Lev.25.17, Dt.6.18, Prov.2.20, 3.17, Ps.34.15, Prov.3.17; 1QS 3.18-4.26; Test.Zev.5.1, Test.Iss.5.2, 7.6, Test.Dan 5.3, Jub.36.7f; PA 1.12, PGit.6.6, PBer.3.1, Shev.5.9, Ber.19b-20a, Ned.62a, 81b, Shab.81b, 94b, Men.37b, BK 99b, 30b, 58b, 83a, Ket.97a; Did.1.2.

The *halakhot* which rule that it is forbidden to "treat as permitted what for your brother is forbidden" (cf. Ned.81b; see verse 13) are also linked to the rabbinic injunction against אונאה (*'ona'ah*) or "wrongdoing":

> Our Rabbis taught: *Ye shall not therefore wrong one another* (Lev.25.17); Scripture refers to verbal wrongs. You say, 'verbal wrongs'; but perhaps that is not so, monetary wrongs being meant? When it is said, *And if thou sell aught unto thy neighbour, or acquirest aught of thy neighbour [ye shall not wrong one another]* (Lev.25.14), monetary wrongs are already dealt with. Then to what can I refer, *ye shall not therefore wrong each other?* To verbal wrongs. E.g., If a man is penitent, one must not say to him, 'Remember your former deeds.' If he is the son of proselytes, he must not be taunted with, 'Remember the deeds of thy ancestors.' If he is a proselyte and comes to study the Torah, one must not say to him, 'Shall the mouth that ate unclean and forbidden food, abominable and creeping things, come to study the Torah which was uttered by the mouth of the Omnipotence!' . . . If ass-drivers sought grain from a person, he must not say to them, 'Go to so and so who sells grain,' whilst knowing that he has never sold any. R. Judah said: One must also not feign interest in a purchase when he has no money, since this is known to the heart only, and of everything known only to the heart it is written, *and thou shalt fear thy God* (Lev.25.17). (BM 58b)[34]

The injunction to "walk according to love" according to the Spirit of Truth (the doctrine of the Two Spirits or Ways) is thus expressed in a series of halakhot, according to the rabbinic principles of "loving one's fellow-man;" "intention;" "wrongdoing;" "kavod ha-briot" [respect for creation]; the "image" of God; לפנים משורת הדין (*lifnim mi-shurat ha-din*; within the strict letter of the law); honoring one's fellow-men; and "pursuing peace" [דרכי שלום] (see verse 19).

"Do not destroy with your food": cf. 20, 1 Cor.8.11, Eph.4.29-30; PBer.3.1, PKil.9.1, Ned.81b, Ber.19a-20a, Men.37b, Shab.81b, 94b.

The Greek verb λυπεω (*lupeo*, "to destroy") means "to offend" or "to aggrieve" and corresponds to the Hebrew term אונאה (*'ona'ah*), "wrongdoing" (see above). Just as there is wrongdoing in words (cf. Eph.4.29), there can also be "wrongdoing" in eating. A person should not be "fed with what is forbidden to him," nor may he treat things which are forbidden "as permitted in order to nullify them" (cf. Ned.81b), because food in itself does not "offend" or destroy:

> R. Eleazar ben Azaria exclaims: Whence do we know that a man should not say, I do not wish to dress in mixed garments [*sha'atnez*], I do not want to eat pork, I do not wish to commit illicit sexuality—but I wish to and what can I do? For my Father in heaven decreed (these prohibitions) on me thus. (Sifra Ked.88b)

What God commands regarding certain foods, certain acts, certain practices gives them a particular significance. But God Himself does not require a person's obedience to such ordinances if in observing them he replaces his love for God (through loving his fellow-men) with the act of observance itself.[35]

"For whom the Messiah died": cf. 5.6, 14, 14.9.

Paul understands that refusing to respect another person's principles is tantamount to denying him God's "salvation." If a person refuses to accept a brother's commitments, he in fact declares that God also does not accept him. If Yeshua died on behalf of all mankind, every man is redeemed through the love He expressed towards them in sending His son to atone for them while they were still hostile to Him (cf. 5.6-10).

Verse 16:

"Therefore . . . evil": cf. Ex.32.12, Ps.34.12-14, Mal.2.17, Rom.12.9, 17, 21, 14.20, 1 Cor.10.30, Tit.2.5, 1 Pet.2.12, 3.10-16; Test.Ben.4.2f, 6.5f; Sifra Ked.76b, Mid.Ps.52.1, Tos.BK 10.15, BK 94a, Yoma 86a.

Paul restates the idea that a person may not treat things which are forbidden "as permitted in order to nullify them" (cf. Ned.81b).[36] What a person "vows" to observe is "sacred." He may not be forced to violate his own convictions in abiding by the divergent views of another person, nor must he be compelled to redefine his principles to suit the convictions of his brother. Paul claims that the only grounds for "compromise" in this regard are those of love and respect for one's brother, for whom Yeshua gave his own life. The phrase "to speak evil of" is literally βλασφημεω (*blasphemeo*), "to blaspheme." Any behavior which causes "stumbling" or an "offense" (cf. verse 13) "profanes" God's name (cf. חילול ה'; *chilul ha-Shem*), in the same way as God declares, according to the midrashic interpretation of Leviticus 19.18, that He will judge a man for not loving himself if he does not love his brother.[37]

Verse 17:

"For the kingdom . . . Holy Spirit": cf. 1 Cor.6.9f, 8.8, 15.50, Gal.5.21, Eph.5.5; 1QS 4.2-11; PRK 4.7, Git.59a-b.

Paul repeats the principle that all things can be acceptable to God if they are observed for His sake (cf. verse 6). "Eating and drinking" represent the "ritual" aspect of the commandments. God's will is best served not by "rote" observance but by "sanctifying" all of one's thoughts and acts before Him by "walking in the Spirit according to love":

> It is < of the Spirit of Truth > to enlighten the heart of man, and to level before him the ways of true righteousness, and to set fear in his heart of the judgment of God. And (to it belong) the spirit of humility and forbearance, of abundant mercy and eternal goodness, of understanding and intelligence, and almighty wisdom with faith in all the works of God and trust in His abundant grace, and the spirit of knowledge in every design and zeal for just ordinances, and holy resolution with firm inclination and abundant affection towards all the sons of truth, and glorious purification from hatred of all the idols of defilement, and modesty with universal prudence, and discretion . . . . And as for the Visitation of all who walk in this (Spirit), it consists of healing and abundance of bliss, with length of days and fruitfulness, and all blessings without end, and eternal joy in perpetual life, and the glorious crown and garment of honour in everlasting light. (1QS 4.2-8)

"Righteousness and peace" are the paths of לפנים משורת הדין (*lifnim mishurat ha-din*), "within the strict letter of the law" or being "in the Spirit": "You should diligently keep the commandments of the Lord your God, and

His testimonies and His statutes which He has commanded you. And you shall do what is right and good in the sight of the Lord . . ." (Dt.6.17-18). The teachers of the *halakhah* did not read these verses as having only one meaning: do the right and good by keeping My commandments. The words 'Ye shall do the right and the good" were understood as an additional commandment. In addition to observing the laws of the Torah, also do the right and the good. This could mean that it is sometimes necessary to go beyond the law, which in itself is right and good, in order to do what is right and good.[38]

Verse 18:
"For he who . . . approved by men": cf. Lev.19.18, Dt.6.5, Jn.12.26, Acts 20.19, 24.14, Rom.6.18, 22, 7.6, 12.1-2, 11, 14.3, 6-8, 2 Cor.3.6, 8.21, 11.23, Eph.4.12, 5.10, Phil.1.10, 4.8, 1 Pet.2,12; 1QS 5.9, 8.4-10; Sir.27.30-28.7, PA 3.10, 4.1, 6.1, ARNa 16, ARNb 26.

The phrase "in this way" refers to the principle of "sanctifying the profane" according to the various principles and ways which Paul enumerates in chapters 12-15. He expresses the idea that the believer should offer up his body as a "living and holy sacrifice, acceptable to God" (12.1) in terms of the "Golden Rule" (cf. 12.9f), so that in loving one's fellow-man one is rewarded by and loves God Himself:

> He [R. Hanina b. Dosa] [also] used to say: Anyone from whom the spirit of [his fellow-] creatures derives satisfaction, from him the Spirit of the All-Present [too] derives satisfaction. But anyone from whom the spirit of [his fellow-] creatures derives no satisfaction, from him the Spirit of the All-Present [too] derives no satisfaction. . . . R. Joshua said: An evil eye, the evil inclination, and hatred for [one's fellow-] creatures put a man out of the world. . . . A favourite saying of Abaye was: A man should always be subtle in the fear of heaven. *A soft answer turneth away wrath* (Prov.15.1), and one should always strive to be on the best terms with his brethren and his relatives and with all men and even with the heathen in the street, in order that he may be beloved above and well-liked below and be acceptable to his fellow creatures. (PA 3.10, 2.11, Ber.17a)[39]

Verse 19:
"Pursue the things which make for peace": cf. Ps.34.14, Rom.12.17-18, Heb.12.14, 1 Pet.3.11; PA 1.12, ARNa 16, ARNb 24, San.6a.

Paul appeals to another rabbinic principle, known as דרכי שלום (*darkei shalom*), "the paths of peace" (cf. Ps.34.14):

> The following rules were laid down in the interests of peace [lit. 'on account of ways of peace']. A priest is called up first to read the law and after him a Levite and then a lay Israelite, in the interests of peace. An 'erub is placed in the room where it has always been placed, in the interests of peace. The pit which is nearest the [head of the] watercourse is filled from it first, in the interests of peace. [The taking of] beasts, birds and fishes from snares [set by others] is reckoned as a kind of robbery, in the interests of peace. R. Jose says that it is actual robbery. [To take away] anything found by a deaf-mute, an idiot or a minor is reckoned as a kind of robbery, in the interests of peace. R. Jose says: It is actual robbery. If a poor man gleans on the top of an olive tree, [to take the fruit] that is beneath him is counted as a kind of robbery. R. Jose says it is actual robbery. The poor of the heathen may not be prevented from gathering gleanings, forgotten sheaves, and the corner of the field, in the interests of peace. (Git.59a-b)[40]

The "paths of peace" prohibit a man from judging his brother for his personal convictions, and preclude any conduct or behavior which might cause him to "stumble" in his walk before God. Paul summarizes all the principles with the statement that "sin"—which incurs judgment and punishment—occurs when a person is not convinced of his principles in God's sight, or is influenced by the opinions of others to act in a way contrary to his "conscience" (cf. verse 23).

"The building up of one another": cf. 12.3f, 15.2, 1 Cor.10.23, 14.3, 26, 2 Cor.12.19, Eph.4.12, 1 Thess.5.11.

Paul continues using the metaphor of the "living stones" which are "built up" into a "spiritual house (cf. Rom.12.1f, 1 Pet.2.5f).[41] The intent to "build up" one another, through faithfulness in love, is the antithesis of "destroying" one's brethren (cf. verse 15), so that "peace" and "edification" are both examples of loving one's fellow-man:

> R. Eleazar said in the name of R. Hanina: The disciples of the wise increase peace in the world, as it says, *And all thy children shall be taught of the Lord, and great shall be the peace of thy children.* Read not banayik [thy children] but bonayik [thy builders]. *Great peace have they that love Thy law, and there is no stumbling for them. Peace be within thy walls and prosperity within thy palaces* (Ps.119.165). *For my brethren and companions' sake I will now say, Peace be within thee* (Ps.122.7). *For the sake of the house of the Lord*

> *our God I will seek thy good* (ibid., 8). *The Lord will give strength unto His people, the Lord will bless His people with peace* (Ps.29.11). (Ber.64a)[42]

Verse 20:

"Tear down the work of God": cf. Gen.2.2, Ps.119.126, Eccl.3.11, 8.17, 11.5, Jn.6.28, 9.4; 1QH 16.8.

Paul appeals to another similar rabbinic principle, whose claim it is that it is "time to work for the Lord." This prooftext from Psalm 119.126 which is quoted in the Mishnah, is explained in the Gemara:

> . . . IT ALSO SAYS, 'IT IS TIME TO WORK FOR THE LORD; THEY HAVE MADE VOID THY LAW' (PS.119.126). R. NATHAN SAYS: [THIS MEANS] THEY HAVE MADE VOID THY LAW BECAUSE IT IS A TIME TO WORK FOR THE LORD. . . . Raba said: The first clause of this verse can be taken as explaining the second, and the second can be taken as explaining the first. 'The first clause may be taken as explaining the second', thus: It is time to work for the Lord. Why? Because they have made void Thy law. 'The second clause may be taken as explaining the first', thus: They have made void Thy law.' Why Because it is time to work for the Lord. (Ber.9.1 [Mishnah] and 63a)

The Sages claimed, in other words, that there are times when they possessed the authority to institute observances instead of God: "At times, it is permitted to suspend a biblical law even by an action whose purpose is altogether humanly social. We read in a Mishnah: 'It was established [by the sages] that one greet one's fellow man with the name of God. For thus we read in the Bible: "And behold, Boaz came from Bethlehem and said to the harvesters: God be with you."' This practice, reintroduced in Mishnaic times, was not at all self-evident. According to the Torah, one must not take the name of God in vain. In order to justify this form of greeting, the Mishnah quotes the verse, 'It is time to do for the Eternal One,' which one of its teachers, Rabbi Nathan, interprets: 'Dissolve the law, in order to act for God.' In this instance, the explanation of Rashi is most revealing. He writes: At times one abolishes the words of the Torah in order to do for God. So this one, too, whose concern is with the well-being of his fellow man, is doing the will of God. For it is written, 'Seek peace and pursue it.' It is permissible to dissolve the Torah and do what appears to be forbidden.' To some extent this is an exceptional case of 'it is time to do for God.' There is no real suspension of any law.

Because of the divine commandment, 'Seek peace and pursue it,' one is actually urged to greet one's neighbor with the divine name. Far from taking His name in vain, one actually does the will of God. What one does, then, appears on the surface as if one were violating a commandment."[43]

"All things indeed are clean . . . ": Paul clearly states that all food may be sanctified by the intention of the one who eats it, as he has argued throughout the chapter.[44]

"They are evil . . . "

Paul indicates that he is using the term "clean" in the sense of "permissible," rather than as a strictly ritual term, since the opposite of clean (תהור; *tahor*) is impure (תמא; *tamei'*) rather than "evil." When a person gives offense to his brother by what he eats, then the action (not, in fact, even the food) becomes wrong, and should not be engaged in.[45]

Verse 21:

"It is good . . . stumbles": cf. vss.13-16.

Paul restates his injunction to do good to one's fellow-man so that he may "stand" before God; no one has the right to make another person "fall" and be "destroyed."[46] A person must act wholeheartedly and single-mindedly in order not to hurt his brethren through his hypocritical attitudes:

> The law, 'Thou shalt not set a stumbling block before the blind' (Lev.19.14), is extended to mean, 'You must not hide part of your intention in giving advice to a man.' You must not say, 'Sell your field, and buy a donkey,' when you are really intending to circumvent him, and get his field [i.e., by buying his field from him]. Perhaps you will reply, 'I gave him good advice' [i.e. it was really to his interest to sell his field and get the donkey]. [No, even so, you must not act thus.] This is a matter delivered to the heart, as it is said, *thou shalt fear thy God* (Lev.25.17). . . . What constitutes profanation of the Name?—Rab said: If, e.g., I take meat for the butcher and do not pay him at once. . . . R. Eliezer b. Jacob says: If one misappropriated a se'ah of wheat and kneaded it and baked it and set aside a portion of it as hallah [the priestly portion], how would he be able to pronounce the benediction? He would surely not be pronouncing a blessing but pronouncing a blasphemy, as to such a one could be applied the words: *The robber pronounceth benediction [but in fact] contemneth the Lord* (Ps.10.3). . . . (Sifra Ked.76b, Yoma 86a, BK 94a)[47]

Verse 22:

"The faith which you have . . . approves": cf. 2.15-16, 12.3, 1 Jn.3.19-21.

Paul picks up the theme of "faithfulness" from 12.3ff.[48] "Faithfulness" refers both to a person's "conviction" that God is able to take care of Himself, as it were—to allow men to "sanctify" what others may consider to be "profane"—and to his willingness to love and respect his brothers' convictions even when they differ from his own.

"Happy . . . does not condemn himself": cf. Ps.1.1, 2.12, 32.1-2, 34.8, 40.4, 106.3, 112.1, 128.1, Isa.56.2, Jer.17.7, Prov.3.13, Mt.5.3-12, Lk.11.28, Rom.2.14-15, 4.7, 8.1, 34-39, Jas.1.12, 1 Jn.3.18-24, Rev.16.15, 19.9, 20.6, 22.7, 14; Mekh.Bachod.9, TBE p.18, Ruth R.2.7, Ber.17a.

Paul picks up the theme of blessing from verse 6, and uses it to say that he who blesses (sanctifies) God through what he eats or what he observes is himself "blessed":

> Happy is the person who reverences the name of the LORD, and who serves in front of his face always, and who organizes his gifts with fear, offerings of life, and who in this life lives and dies correctly! Happy is he who carries out righteous judgment, not for the sake of payment, but for justice, not expecting anything whatever as a result; and the result will be that judgment without favoritism will follow for him. Happy is he who clothes the naked with his garment, and to the hungry gives bread! Happy is he who judges righteous judgment for orphan and widow, and who helps anyone who has not been treated justly! Happy is he who turns aside from the secular path of this vain world, and walks in the right paths, and who lives that life which is without end! Happy is he who sows right seed, for he shall harvest sevenfold! Happy is he in whom is the truth, so that he may speak the truth to his neighbor! Happy is he who has compassion on his lips and gentleness in his heart! Happy is he who understands all the works of the LORD, performed by the LORD, and glorifies him! (2 En.42.6-14)[49]

God gives His blessing to the person who blesses God in whatever he eats and whatever he does.[50] The person who is blessed is the person who knows that what he sanctifies is acceptable in God's eyes, since he thus "proves" God's will as "good and acceptable and perfect" (cf. 12.2).[51]

Verse 23:

"Doubts . . . faith": cf. vss.1-3; PA 3.4, 7, 8.

The verb διακρινω (*diakrino*, "to be condemned") means "to make a distinction," "to distinguish," or "to discern." If a person discriminates between what he eats, with whom he eats it, or when he eats it, and acts contrary to his convictions in doing so, he condemns himself. Several sayings in *Aboth* speak of similar circumstances in which an individual can "endanger his life" through doing things which in themselves are not harmful but which transgress the priorities which he has chosen for himself:

> R. Hanina b. Hakinai said: He who keeps awake at night, and he who walks on the way alone and makes room in his heart for that which is futile, lo, this [man] incurs guilt [expiable] by his life [מתחייב בנפשו]. . . . R. Simeon said: When one, walking on the road, rehearses [what he has learnt], and breaks off from his rehearsing, and says, 'How fine is this tree!' [or] 'How fine is this newly ploughed field!' Scripture accounts it to him as if he had incurred guilt [expiable] by his life. (PA 3.4, 7)[52]

In a similar way, the person who is not convinced that God's will is proved to be "good and acceptable and perfect" by his "sanctification" of otherwise unclean things does not act out of the knowledge that God is strong enough to let men understand and interpret His commandments according to their own convictions ("faithfulness"). In that case, an individual's faithfulness or love is "weak," both towards God and towards his fellow men. Each person must be fully convinced in his own mind of what is right and must act in accordance with his conviction. His "faithfulness in love" will "prove" him able to alter his behavior when circumstances demand it. The person whose faithfulness and love is "strong"—who does not doubt God, himself, or his brother—not only accepts his brothers' opinions and conduct but also respects their behavior when it runs contrary to his own convictions.

"Whatever is not from faith is sin": cf. Dt.23.22, 24.15, Prov.16.2-3, 21.2, Jas.4.17; Mid.Ps.30.2, 31.8, Num.R.8.5, RH 28b.

Paul summarizes the various principles to which he has appealed throughout chapters 12-14 in relation to "faithfulness in love," and turns his statement in verse 14 ("to him who thinks anything to be unclean, to him it is unclean") into an even broader *halakhic* principle. He claims that any conduct which runs contrary to an individual's convictions before God is "sin" for him (cf. Jas.4.17). His summarizing statement covers the two interrelated aspects of a person's individual convictions before the Lord: those things which he feels may be sanctified and those which he regards as inviolably commanded by God; and his ability and willingness to love his fellow-man, since he acknowledges that they also hold their convictions before God, even when the things which they "sanctify" do not correspond to his own commitments. In both these areas, whatever a man sanctifies before God, and whomever he accepts and respects, must be based upon his personal conviction. "Doubting" or "condemnation," either of himself or of his fellow-man, cannot please God since it does not "prove" His will to be "good and acceptable and perfect" (12.2). The principle of "sanctification" thus directly influences the definition of "sin." A certain object or action is not "clean" or "unclean" in itself, but may be "sanctified" by a person's attitude. Lack of sanctification causes the same or a similar object or action to become a "sin"—a "profanity"—for the person who is not committed to it before God. Whatever action a person takes which he has not resolved in his mind, and to which he is not committed before God, does not please Him. God looks for each individual's personal commitment to love Him and demands that each person "stand" before Him on his commitment to his own principles:

> All the ways of a man are clean in his own sight, [and] the Lord weights the motives [lit. spirits]. Commit your works to the Lord, and your plans will be established. (Prov.16.2-3; cf. 21.2)

> TO COMMIT A TRESPASS (Num.5.6). Trespass in all cases denotes nought but breach of faith. Scripture confirms this when it says, And they broke faith with the God of their fathers (1 Chron.5.25) and when it says, But the children of Israel committed a breach of faith concerning the devoted thing (Josh.7.1) and when it says, So Saul died for the breach of faith which he committed . . . because of the word of the Lord, which he kept not (1 Chron.10.13). (Num.R.8.5)

Endnotes Chapter 14

1 Paul uses the actual term "conscience" only in 12.5 and 13.5, and not at all in chapter 14. Although many commentators assume that Paul is speaking of matters of conscience in this chapter, he describes his theme here more specifically in terms of "faithfulness in love" to one's brethren. In

1 Corinthians 8, on the other hand, he focuses upon the substantive issues of food offered to idols. The principle of "acceptance" clearly derives from the ideas expressed in chapters 12-13, namely of brotherly love, respect, and faithfulness within the community; cf. also 1 Cor.10.25f.

2 The traditional interpretation of chapter 14 identifies the "weak in faith" as those Jewish believers who ascribe power to food offered to idols and lack "faith" that God has permitted all foods to be eaten; the "strong in faith" are those who are willing to eat any foods, including those which God prohibits in the Torah. Cf. also the controversy between Beit Hillel and Beit Shammai over food preparations for Shabbat. The "Eighteen Decrees" designed to regulate social intercourse between Israel and the Gentiles, and were passed on a day on which Beit Shammai outnumbered Beit Hillel. The decrees thus strengthened the separation between Israel and the Gentile nations; cf. Tos.Shab.1.16, Shab.1.4, PShab.1, 3c, Shab.17a, 153b. See verse 5.

3 See also the comments on 13.13 and 16.17-20.

4 See P. Tomson, Paul. The issues of kashrut and purity regulations may be subsumed as "fences" against idolatry, but they are also issues in their own right. Laws of ritual purity are not directly relevant here, however, since strict purity could not be maintained outside Israel, given the decree of impurity ascribed to Gentile lands; cf. PShab.1, 3d, PPes.1, 27d, Shab.14b-15a, Hag.25a, Eruv.30b. See G. Alon, Jews, Judaism and the Classical World (Jerusalem: Magnes Press, 1977), 146-89, 190-234.

5 Cf. 1 Cor.8.4f, 10.19ff, AZ 2.3, 5, PShab.1, 3c, AZ 32b, 38a, 39a-b. Paul speaks of "faith" in this verse as the belief that God is greater than His commandments. A person's "faith" is not his willingness to eat certain foods (e.g., meat that has been offered to idols), but his conviction that God accepts his personal convictions when they are subjected to His will; (see below.) Neither does Paul permit a person to eat food prohibited by God in the Torah on the grounds that living "under grace" has made the Torah obsolete.

6 Paul does not only call for "tolerance" on the part of the Gentiles, but for mutual love and respect from both Jews and Gentiles. The comparison with 1 Corinthians 8-10 shows that the categories of "weak" and "strong" are relative and cross the Jewish-Gentile divide. In 1 Corinthians 8-10 the Gentile believers are the "delicate" brothers; in Romans 14-15, the "delicate" are the Jewish believers.

7 God's will is therefore both "absolute" (in His Word) and "relative" (according to the convictions of each believer).

8 See the comments on 6.2ff.

9 These sayings relate to Hillel's other "proselytizing" teachings, which were designed to bring a person close to God by relating to him in his present position. Here Paul applies this principle to the brethren within the community, rather than to "outsiders."

10 This passage is based upon the "oaths" in Lev.19.18 and Dt.6.5, through which God commands the people to love Him and their fellow-man; cf. Sir.27.30-28.7, ARNb 26, Ber.Rab.24.7, Shab.31a. (God also swears by an oath that all men will acknowledge His sovereignty in the prooftext of Isa.45.23, in verse 11.) Simeon ben 'Azzai disputes R. Akiba's view that the basis of the כלל גדול (*kelal gadol*) should be Lev.19.18, and argues that the "greatest principle of the Torah" should rather be based on Gen.5.1: "This is the book of the generation of Adam. In the day when God created man, He made him in the likeness of God" (cf. Sifra Ked.39b). Love of one's fellow-man, according to ben 'Azzai, is based upon man's creation in God's image, instead of on loving one's neighbor "as oneself."

11 See M. Hengel, Judaism and Hellenism (London: SCM, 1974), 1:234ff.

12 Cf. M. Hengel, Judaism.

13 The idea of the "feast of every day" is based on Num.28.2f, which describes the daily offerings. Philo's interpretation treats the biblical feasts as examples of and for virtuous conduct, thus stripping them of their ritual and literal dimensions. Paul's thought is close to Philo's only to the extent to which his concern lies with the attitude of the observer as much as with his practical observance. Cf. also Tos.BK 7.2-9, PRK 4.7, Sifra Ked.88b.

14 Cf. Jub.4.17ff, 6.17ff, 1 En.69.16-25, 72.1-74.17, 78.10-82.20. The Hebrew letter nun (N) carries the numerical value of 50, a number considered by the Pythagoreans as "the holiest and most substantial of numbers, since it formed the power (of the square) of the right-angled triangle, the principle of the generation of the universe" (Philo). The calculation of the Qumran calendar appears in some way to have been based on this number.

15 Cf. PA 2.2, 12, ARNb 30, Lev.R.34.3. For a discussion of the major theological distinctives between *Beit Hillel* and *Beit Shammai*, see S. Safrai, The Literature of the Sages (Philadelphia: Fortress Press, 1987), 185-99.

16 Cf. the parallel Hebrew terms דעת, כונה, and מחשבה (*da'at, kavvanah,* and *machshevah*) which correspond to the Greek συνειδησις (*suneidesis*; "conscience"); see verse 6. Paul states this principle most clearly in 1 Corinthians 13, where he says that without love, no deed pleases God. Romans 14, although less well-known and quoted, is as equally important as 1 Corinthians 13 for an understanding of the "principles" of love.

17 Cf. PKid.1, 58d, PYev.1, 3b, Yev.1.4, 14b, Eduy.4.8.

18 Cf. PA 1.13, 4.5. Tomson argues (Paul, 212f) that the concepts of כונה (*kavvanah*; intention) (together with מחשבה [*machshevah*; thinking] and דעת [*da'at*; knowing]) arose coincidentally with the Latin word *conscienta*, which translates the Greek term συνειδησις or "conscience." "Conscience" thus corresponds to loving one's fellow-man through acting selflessly and without ulterior motives, with a single-mindedness and purity of motive (intention); cf. also Sifra Vayikra 13a, Ber.5.1, 17a, Men.13.11, 110a, Yoma 42a, Shevu.15a.

19 Cf. also the Job midrash in Shab.89a in Rom.10.6-12, which also appeals to Psalm 68.

20 The term "Samaritan" (כותי; *kuti*) might stand here, as in other places, for גוי; *goi*—heathen) or מין (*min*; heretic), under the influence of medieval Christian censorship. More likely, however, it refers to the actual Samaritan practice of invoking Mount Gerizim in place of Jerusalem (cf. Jn.4.20f). The Sages also used Ps.24.1 as a proof text for God's righteous judgment (cf. Rom.14.9):

> *Defend the poor and fatherless: do justice to the afflicted and needy* (Ps.82.3). Here Scripture does not say "Have mercy on the afflicted and needy," but *Do justice to the afflicted and needy*, that is, "Make just your judgment of him. Say not, because the poor man is fatherless or afflicted, 'Let what belongs to the rich man be given to him.' For *The earth is the Lord's and the fullness thereof* (Ps.24.1), and therefore, in giving judgment, if you unjustly take anything away from a rich man and give it to a poor man, you rob Me, for you give to the poor man what belongs to Me. All the earth is Mine, and I meant the rich man to have his riches. Yet you would take away what is his." (Mid.Ps.82.2)

21 Cf. 1 Tim.4.4-5: "For everything created by God is good, and nothing is to be rejected, if it is received with gratitude; for it is sanctified by means of the word of God and prayer."

22 To know God and His character (cf. Jer.9.23-24) is the whole τελος (*telos*) or goal of Torah-observance (cf. 10.4). All God's commandments can therefore be "uprooted" when conduct appropriate to God's attributes is perceived as befitting the circumstances; or something can be instituted or observed which He has not directly commanded.

23 See also verse 16 (cf. 1 Cor.10.30), where Paul picks up the motif of "a good thing," also influenced, perhaps, by Psalm 100. The motif begins in

Romans 12, with Paul's injunction not to "be overcome with evil, but overcome evil with good" (12.21).

24 Paul builds here upon his argument in chapters 12-13, in which he demonstrates that God judges men for lack of love of their brethren.

25 See the comments on verses 3ff and on 2.1. The rabbinic principles of "uprooting" biblical commandments, and it being "time to act for God" (cf. Ps.119.126), which deal with overturning and/or ignoring biblical injunctions at certain times and in certain circumstances are perhaps also relevant; cf. Yev.90a-b, Yoma 69a, Ber.54a, 63a, Git.60a; also their discussions of Dt.17.9, "to the judge that will be in those days," according to which each generation possesses the authority to make its own decisions and rulings; cf. RH 25b.

26 Paul appeals to both passages from Isaiah in Rom.10.9f, where he establishes the gift of redemption for "all men."

27 See also the comments on 12.9ff.

28 A Nazirite is forbidden to drink wine (Num.6.3) and the Noachide is forbidden to eat the limb from a living animal (Gen.9.4).

29 Cf. Pes.50b-51a, PBer.8, 12a. The context of R. Gamaliel's ruling is the annulment of vows: "what is forbidden" is literally something from which a person has vowed to abstain. The principle also applies, however, to forcing people to violate their own principles. It recognizes that things may be regarded as permissible or forbidden by different people, and that these differences must be respected.

30 Cf. PKil.9.1, PBer.3.1, Shab.81b, 94b, Men.37b. The passage also deals with the issue of the basis on which the Rabbis made their rulings equally authoritative with those of the Torah itself, so that Rab b. Shaba interprets the words "negative precept of the Torah" to mean "rabbinical ordinances deriving their sanction from this negative precept of the Torah." Even where this was the case, however, the Gemara claims that human dignity overrides both rabbinic and biblical ordinances; see also the comments on 12.9f and 13.7.

31 Paul's own conviction in 8.35-39 is precisely that nothing is able to separate men from God's love in Yeshua.

32 Tomson suggests the possibility that the phrase refers to a tradition "of the Lord," i.e., certain *halakhic* traditions to which Paul refers at significant points. See P. Tomson, Paul, 240-41.

33 The story indicates how Jewish sensibilities of the time distinguished between divine law and personal conviction or priorities; cf. the related debate concerning טעמי המצוות (*ta'amei ha-mitzvot*) or the reasons for the commandments: E.E. Urbach, Sages, [321-47], 365-99. (Cf. also the

affinity of Rabban Johanan's explanation to his close disciples with Yeshua's explanation of his "parable" of what is "clean" to the twelve in Mk.7.14ff; cf. Mt.13.36, 15.15f.)

34 The prooftext from Lev.25.17 is brought in order to demonstrate that man cannot know whether another person's intentions are legitimate or not, since they are concealed, but God knows (cf. Rashi). The phrase "entrusted [known] to the heart" may also denote matters left to ethical research and conviction, which cannot be mastered, weighed, or determined by will, but by a delicate perception, fine tact, and a sensitiveness of nature; see the Soncino note to this passage.

35 Paul may also be referring to the possibility of "destroying" a person's reputation or his faithfulness to God in Yeshua. Eating what a brother regards as forbidden may "consume" his personal convictions and commitments before God, and cause him to doubt.

36 Paul may also here be rephrasing and developing the theme of repaying evil with good (cf. chapter 12).

37 Cf. ARNb 26; see the comments on 12.9ff. The frequent talmudic appeal to good conduct before the Gentiles on account of חילול ה' is reflected also in 1 Pet.2.12: "Keep your behavior excellent among the Gentiles, so that in the thing in which they slander you as evildoers, they may on account of your good deeds, as they observe (them), glorify God in the day of visitation;" see verse 20.

38 See E. Berkovits, Not, 26-27, and the comments on 2.25-29.

39 Cf. TBE p.127, p.156, [EZ] p.167, p.197, [S] p.4.

40 The examples given are all illustrations of *halakhic* rulings which protect the rights of certain "minority" or disadvantaged groups. Several of the rulings actually deviate from the general law, as in לפנים משודת הדין (*lifnim mi-shurat ha-din*; see above). Similar principles include כבוד הבריות (*kevod ha-briot*), "respect for the creation," which is invoked where fulfillment of rabbinic restrictions (and perhaps even biblical injunctions) might otherwise infringe on a person's dignity; and דרכי נועם (*darkhei no'am*), "ways of pleasantness," which is invoked for an interpretation of a biblical commandment so that it will not conflict with "the ways of pleasantness and peace" (Prov.3.17). The Torah itself is ultimately also regarded as being given "for the sake of the ways of peace" (cf. Git.59b).

41 The metaphor of "edification" recalls the motifs of "planting" and of the "body" as a "house" or "temple" in Qumran and the New Testament; cf. 1 Cor.3.16-17, 12.12f, 2 Cor.6.14ff, 1 Tim.3.15, Heb.3.6, 1 Pet.2.3-6; 1QS 5.5ff, 8.4ff, 9.3ff, 4QFlor.1.6f, 4QpIsa.d frag.1; see the comments on 12.4f.

The Sages referred also to the principle of שלום בית (*shelom beit*), "for the sake of peace in the house" in parallel to דרכי שלום (*darkei shalom*); see the comments on verse 19.

42 The word "builders" refers to "learned men."

43 E. Berkovits, Not, 66; cf. also 57-64.

44 See especially the comments on verse 14.

45 See the comments on verse 16.

46 Paul appeals to the same language of stumbling and falling in regard to Israel's election in chapters 9-11. There the Gentiles may not return evil for evil, but in loving their "neighbor" they will themselves be accepted (approved, elected) by God as part of His people and cause Israel also to be provoked to jealousy and made to stand "irrevocably" before their own God. Similarly, Yeshua is the "stumbling-block" or "testing-stone" through whom man receives or rejects his redemption.

47 The same "rule" of "There is no wisdom and no understanding and no counsel against the Lord" (Prov.21.30) is used as the prooftext for the two (interrelated) principles of חילול ה׳, "wherever a profanation of God's name is involved no respect is paid to a teacher," and "great is human dignity, since it overrides a negative precept of the Torah" (cf. Ber.19b).

48 See verses 1f.

49 This type of moral instruction by "beatitude" (אשרי; *'ashrei*), "blessed are . . . " formed a distinct genre in contemporary Jewish literature (cf. Deuteronomy 28, Mt.5.3-12, Lk.6.24-26, and especially 1 En.94-103). It relates the form of eternal reward to a person's temporal behavior, so that it contains both the positive and negative expressions of the Golden Rule. Flusser has demonstrated the influence of the Qumran texts (cf. 1QH 18.14-15) on the New Testament beatitudes (in Judaism, 102-47), and they clearly reflect the doctrine of the Two Ways in which the righteous are "blessed" and the wicked are "cursed" (cf. also Rom.12.14). The expression is used in Ps.32.1-2, which Paul quotes in 4.7: "How blessed is he whose transgression is forgiven, whose sin is covered! How blessed is the man to whom the Lord does not impute iniquity, and in whose spirit there is no deceit!" (The phrase "offerings of life" is obscure, and the variant texts do not clarify it. It is remarkably close, however, to Paul's phrase "a living and holy sacrifice" in 12.1, as the thought of Romans 12 resembles that of Romans 14 in general.)

50 "Faithfulness" (love or "conscience") (cf. verses 1ff) in this context is the opposite of "condemnation" (cf. 8.1, 13.2).

51 He is also "blessed" because he is accepted and "approved" by God; he does not stumble or fall and is not destroyed. He may also literally not

"condemn himself" in the sense that God will not punish him because he has not loved Him in loving his fellow-man (see 12.10).

52 Most commentators agree that the actions denounced here are not wrong or evil in themselves. The third clause ("and makes room in his heart . . . ") is therefore frequently adduced not as a third category of person but as a qualification of the first two clauses. The phrase התחייב בנפשו is variously translated as "incurs guilt [expiable] by his life," "is mortally guilty," "incurs guilty responsibility for his life," "is guilty against himself," "guilty against his own soul." The reference to "Scripture" accounting guilt to a man is sometimes deleted, since no prooftext is given, and replaced with the impersonal "they account. . . ." The parallel with Paul's thought in Romans can be seen from the fact that, according to R. Simeon's implication, it is only because learning is so much more important that breaking off from study deserves such severe condemnation. It is also possible to infer that the expression "guilty against himself" refers to the condemnation which a person brings against himself, punishable by the "heavenly court" (as if, perhaps it were a violation of לפנים משורת הדין (*lifnim mi-shurat ha-din*), a moral code beyond the Torah) but not by the (human) *Beit Din* (as an enforceable biblical or rabbinic regulation). Paul speaks of "futile speculations" in 1.21, and he may be referring to the same idea as R. Simeon here, when he describes deeds done out without faithfulness as performed out of "doubt."

ROMANS 15

Introduction

Paul applies the principles he has laid out in chapter 14 (verses 1-2) also to scriptural interpretation (verses 4-6), and demonstrates how Yeshua's honoring of God (verse 3), which brought also the Gentiles into God's kingdom in fulfillment of the hope of resurrection (cf. chapter 4), is the example for the members of the community (verses 7-13). He then returns to the theme of gaining fruit from the community in Rome (cf. chapter 1), justifying his appeal for a financial contribution (verses 25-27) on the grounds of his priestly ministry (apostleship) to the Gentiles (verses 15-21). He explains the reason for his longing to visit the Roman community, and for his deferment of the trip in order to bring the contribution he has gathered from the Gentiles to the Temple in Jerusalem (verses 22-29), as well as not wishing not encroach on other people's territory of evangelism. Finally, he asks for the community's prayers for the completion of his mission, which would enable him to visit Rome on his way to Spain (verses 30-33).

Verse 1:
"Now we who are strong . . . ourselves": cf. 12.10f, 13.7ff, 14.1-23, Gal.6.2, 1 Thess.5.14.

Paul returns to the injunctions of the previous chapter (cf. 14.1-2), and continues the theme of "weakness" and "strength" in faithfulness. Here he identifies himself as one who is "strong" (cf. 14.14), because he is convinced of his own commitments before God. This principle of "sanctification" (cf. also 15.16) forms the basis for each person's need to love and respect his neighbor. Paul's "strength" lies in his willingness to accept other people when their convictions run contrary to his own. He is able to do so because he knows that just as God accepts his convictions He also accepts the convictions of his brethren. Those whose faithfulness in love is "weak" are those who do not believe that God is strong enough to defend His commandments, and therefore insist that the commandments are inviolable and must be observed as they are given.[1] It is difficult for such people to accept the convictions of their brothers, since they see them as openly violating the direct commandments of God. Paul perceives this attitude, however, as one of "pleasing ourselves" rather than being pleasing ("acceptable") to God (cf. 12.2, 14.18). Each person is obligated, as his "living and holy sacrifice" (cf. 12.1-2), to serve his brethren (cf. 12.9f). "Pleasing ourselves" is not merely a selfish act (although it expresses the principle of the Golden Rule—not to do to others what you do not wish them to do to yourself)—but it also "destroys" another man, for whose redemption Yeshua gave himself as a ransom (cf. 14.15).

Verse 2:

"Let each of us . . . edification": cf. 12.10, 14.19, 1 Cor.9.22, 10.22-26, 33, 14.3f, 26, 2 Cor.12.19, 13.9, Eph.4.12, Phil.2.3-4; 1QS 4.5, 5.3-4, CDC 6.20-21, CDCb 2.17-18, PA 2.4, 10.

The "building up" of the Body as "living stones" (cf. 12.1f) is based upon loving one's neighbor, the "spiritual service of worship" which binds the community together in "one accord."[2]

Verse 3:

"For even the Messiah did not please himself . . . ": cf. Ps.69.9, Isa.50.6, 53.3-12, Rom.5.6-7, 12.2-3, 14.5, 9, 15, 2 Cor.8.9, Phil.2.5-8, 1 Tim.2.6, Tit.2.14; 1QH 3.6ff, 8.8ff, 9.24-28.

Paul demonstrates that Yeshua's own example was to give his life as a ransom for mankind (cf. Mt.20.28, 1 Tim.2.6), and his "faithfulness in love" is the model for all his followers. Since the Messiah died to save man who was his enemy and hostile to God, the members of his Body should accept the diverse convictions held by their brethren. Paul understands the "reproaches" of the prooftext in Psalm 69.9 in the sense of Psalm 22.6 and Isaiah 53.4-5: "But I am a worm, and not a man, a reproach of men and despised by the people. . . . Surely our griefs [sickness] he Himself bore, and our sorrows [pains] he carried . . . . He was pierced through for our transgressions, he was crushed for our iniquities; the chastening for our well-being [peace] (fell) on Him." No greater love exists than to put a brother's life before one's own (cf. 5.6-7).

Verse 4:

"Whatever was written . . . hope": cf. 2.18, 4.23, 1 Cor.9.10, 10.6, 11, 2 Tim.3.16, 1 Pet.1.12; 1QS 9.18-20, 1QSa 1.7, CDC 13.7-8; Sir.Prologue, 24.33.

Paul expands the prooftext in verse 3 (Ps.69.9), and applies the attributes of the Messiah to scriptural instruction. He first justifies his exegesis of Scripture, in which he applies the messianic implications of

Psalm 22.6 to Psalm 69.9 according to the principle of גזרה שווה (*gezerah shavah*), or "verbal analogy."[3] Yeshua's attitude (cf. Isaiah 53) is an example for each person to respect his brother and love his neighbor. Moreover, everything written in the Torah, of which Yeshua is the τελος (*telos*; goal) was given in order to give "hope" to those who live in later generations, and perseverance and encouragement are the direct source of love and respect for one's neighbor. Paul does not specify the particular circumstances under which the believing community appears to be labouring, but they may be similar to those described in the first book of Maccabees:

> At which time Onias treated the ambassador that was sent honorably, and received the letters, wherein declaration was made of the league and friendship. Therefore we also, albeit we need none of these things, for that we have the holy books of scripture in our hands to comfort us, have nevertheless attempted to send unto you for the renewing of brotherhood and friendship. . . (1 Macc.12.8-9)

"Instruction" through God's word "builds up" those who receive it: " . . . the whole of the Law is also for the purpose of promoting peace" (Git.59b). Those who wish to edify their brethren and build them up in love are themselves "built up" by God's word, which teaches them to love their fellow-man (cf. Lev.19.18), since the Torah guides a man into the paths of righteousness (cf. Prov.2.20, 3.17).

Verse 5:

"God who gives . . . Yeshua": cf. 5.3-5.

Paul describes God as the "author" of the "Word" of encouragement and perseverance—both in the Torah and in Yeshua. The purpose of encouragement is to create hope in love, so that there will be acceptance, respect, and the seeking of good for all men, in the same way as Yeshua offered his life on behalf of mankind. Here Paul perceives the Torah not as arousing (the knowledge of) sin (cf. 3.20, 4.15, 5.20) but as an encouragement to be of the "same mind," serving one another in love and respecting one's brethren:

> . . . those who are converted from the sin of J[a]c[ob], who have kept the Covenant of God, they will then speak one with another to justify each man his brother by supporting their steps in the way of God. And God will heed their words and will hear, and a reminder will be written [before Him] of them that fear God and of them that revere His Name, until Salvation and Justice are revealed to them that fear [God] . . . and

> who have let themselves be instructed in the first ordinances by which the men of the Unique (one) were judged and who have lent their ear to the voice of the Teacher of Righteousness, and have not disputed the precepts of righteousness when hearing them, they will rejoice and be glad and their heart will be strong and they will bear it away over all the sons of the world. And God will forgive them, and they will see His salvation because they sought refuge in His holy Name. . . . For all who walk in these (precepts) in holy perfection, obeying His instructions, the Covenant of God is assurance that they will live for a thousand generations. (CDCb 2.17-20, 31-35, CDC 7.4-6)

Verse 6:

"With one accord . . . ": cf. Jn.17.21f, Acts 2.44-47, 1 Cor.1.10, 2 Cor.13.11, Phil.2.2f, 1 Pet.3.8; 1QS 9.23-26, 10.6ff, CDC 6.20-7.1, CDCb 2.17-18, 1QM 13.8ff, 18.6f, 19.1f, 1QH 1.27-31, 3.22-23.

Paul repeats his injunction to be of the "same mind" (cf. 12.16), urging the community to glorify God in the "one accord" they have gained through loving and respecting the different members of the Body. This accord directly leads to praising God together for His wondrous works:

> It is Thou who hast created breath on the tongue and known the words of the tongue and determined the fruit of the lips before they ever were. And Thou hast set out words on a measuring-cord and measured the breathing of the breath from the lips and hast sent out sounds according to their mysterious (laws) and breathings of breath according to their harmony; that Thy glory might be made known and Thy wonders told in all Thy works of Truth and [judgments] of righteousness, and that Thy Name might be praised by the mouth of all men, and that they might know Thee according to the measure of their understanding, and might bless Thee for ever and ever. (1QH 1.27-31)

Loving one's neighbor and respecting his convictions is both a measure of the unity of the Body of the Messiah (cf. 12.3f), and an expression of God's glory—the offering of a "living and holy sacrifice," a "spiritual service of worship," which, through the "renewing of [the] mind" proves the will of God to be "good and acceptable and perfect" (12.1-2).[4]

Verse 7:

"Wherefore . . . glory of God": cf. 14.1-4, 8f, 1 Cor.10.31, Phil.2.11, Phlm.17.

Yeshua's acceptance of the person who repents and is united with him in baptism (cf. chapter 6) demonstrates how the believer is made part of God's glory.[5] Paul also returns to the thought of both 14.3, where he speaks of God's acceptance of each individual, and 14.15, where he demonstrates that Yeshua's death and resurrection "prove" God's love and acceptance of all men, which must be copied in the believer's conduct.[6]

Verses 8-12:
"For I say . . . hope": cf. Dt.32.43, 2 Sam.22.50, Ps.117.1, Isa.11.10, 61.1-3, Mt.9.8, Jn.7.22, Acts 2.26, 4.21, 7.8, Rom.3.29-30, 4.11-12, 11.28-32, 1 Cor.7.18, 2 Cor.9.13, Gal.1.24, 2.7-9, Eph.2.11, Phil.3.3, Col.3.11; Odes Sol.31.13, Hell.Syn.Pray.12.67; Mid.Ps.100.1.

Paul again states that the members of the community are obligated to accept one another because Yeshua has broken down the "barrier of the dividing wall," and made both Jews and Gentiles into one new creature (cf. Eph.2.12ff). He picks up the theme of chapters 8-11 in which he describes Israel's election as the "paradigm" (the pattern or model), for the early community. Israel's election by God demonstrates His plan of salvation for (His "acceptance" of) all mankind. Paul respectively refers to Israel and the Gentiles metonymically as the "circumcision" and the "uncircumcision" (one of their attributes designates their whole identity).[7] God has given His Word to Israel (cf. 3.2), to whom belong the "fathers" and the "promises" (cf. 9.4-5). The "three things upon which the world rests" (cf. PA 1.2, 18) are therefore Israel's possessions. Israel's transgression incurs "riches for the Gentiles;" their obedience brings, how much the more, resurrection and new life for the whole world.[8] Yeshua became a servant to Israel so that the Gentiles would also bow the knee and confess Yeshua's Lordship (cf. Isa.45.23, Phil.2.11). God's unity (cf. 3.29-30) is thus reflected in the "like-mindedness" of those who share Yeshua's attitude and love their fellow-man:

> He is our God; there is none else: in truth he is our King; there is none besides him; as it is written in his Torah, And thou shalt know this day, and lay it to thine heart, that the Lord he is God in heaven above and upon the earth beneath: there is none else. We therefore hope in thee, O Lord our God, that we may speedily behold the glory of thy might, when thou wilt remove the abominations from the earth, and heathendom will be utterly destroyed, when the world will be perfected under the kingdom of the Almighty, and all the children of flesh will call upon thy Name, when thou wilt turn unto thyself all the evil-doers upon the earth. Let all the inhabitants of the world perceive and know that unto thee every knee must bow,

> every tongue must swear allegiance. Before thee, O Lord our God, let them bow and worship; and unto thy glorious Name let them give honour; let them all accept the yoke of thy kingdom, and do thou reign over them speedily, and for ever and ever. For the kingdom is thine, and to all eternity thou wilt reign in glory; as it is written in thy Torah, THE LORD SHALL REIGN FOR EVER AND EVER (Ex.15.18). And it is said, AND THE LORD SHALL BE KING OVER ALL THE EARTH: IN THAT DAY SHALL THE LORD BE ONE, AND HIS NAME ONE (Zech.14.9). (PB, Alenu Prayer, p.553)

Verse 13:

"The God of hope fill you . . . ": cf. Lk.2.25, 38, Acts 2.26, Rom.4.18, 5.3-5, 12.12, 14.7, 15.4, 1 Cor.13.7, 13, Eph.4.4, 1 Tim.4.10, Heb.11.1, 1 Pet.1.3; Ex.R.21.8.

Paul sums up the theme of hope in verse 4, and appeals to Isaiah 11.10 (LXX): "In Him shall the Gentiles hope."[9] The "God of hope" is the God who gives hope because He is the source of redemption and resurrection (cf. 4.17) for both Israel and the Gentile nations:

> For to God belongs my justification, and the perfection of my way, and the uprightness of my heart are in His hand: by His righteousness are my rebellions blotted out. For He has poured forth from the fount of His Knowledge the light that enlightens me, and my eye has beheld His marvels and the light of my heart pierces the Mystery to come . . . . From His wondrous Mysteries is the light in my heart, in the everlasting Being has my eye beheld Wisdom: because Knowledge is hidden from men and the counsel of Prudence from the sons of men. The fountain of righteousness, the reservoir of power, and the dwelling-place of glory are denied to the assembly of flesh; but God has given them as an everlasting possession to those whom He has chosen. He has granted them a share in the lot of the Saints, and has united their assembly, the Council of the Community, with the Sons of Heaven. And the assembly of the holy Fabric shall belong to an eternal planting for all time to come. (1QS 11.2-9)

"By the power of the Holy Spirit": cf. 15.19, 1 Cor.2.4; 1QS 4.2-8, 20-21, 1QH 4.31-32, 16.11-12, 17.17, 26; Mekh.Beshall.7, Sot.9.15.

Paul's injunction to "walk according to love" (cf. 14.15) is based upon the doctrine of the Two Spirits or Two Ways, according to which the person who is faithful to God in Yeshua puts his evil inclination to death in his baptism, and is indwelt by God's Spirit to serve God in newness of life (cf. 6.3-6). The "hope" of the Spirit is the hope of "creation" and resurrection, which "gives life to the dead and calls into being that which does not exist" (cf. 4.17):

> And I, I know that righteousness is not of man, nor of the sons of men perfection of way; to the Most High God belong all the works of righteousness, whereas the way of man is not firm unless it be by the Spirit which God has created for him to make perfect a way for the sons of men, that all His works may know the might of His power and the greatness of His mercy to all the sons of His loving kindness. . . . For Thou hast established my spirit and knowest my meditation. And Thou hast comforted me in my confusion and in pardon I delight; and I was comforted for the original sin. And I knew there was hope in Thy [fav]ours and expectation in the greatness of Thy might . . . they shall recount Thy glory in all Thy dominion. For Thou hast caused them to see what they had not known [by bringing to an end the] former [things] and by creating things that are new, by setting aside the former covenants and by [set]ting up that which shall remain for ever. For Th[ou] art a God of eternity . . .] and shalt be for ages without end. (1QH 4.30-33, 9.12-14, 13.11-13)

Verse 14:
"Concerning you, my brethren . . . ": cf. 8.38, 14.14, 2 Cor.1.14-15, Phil.1.1ff, 2.16, 1 Thess.2.17-20, 3.9-13.

Paul is himself "convinced" that his readers accept the principles which he has laid out in chapter 14. He also appeals here, however, to his authority as an apostle in addressing a community which he has not personally founded, but towards which he feels spiritual responsibility. He wants to be assured that the community in Rome will imitate him in loving both him and their own brethren.

"Full . . . filled . . . ": cf. 11.25, 12.2, 21, 15.13, 1 Cor.1.5, 8.1, 7, Eph.4.13, 5.9; 1QS 4.3-5, 5.25-26, 9.17, 10.24, 11.3-9, 15-16, CDC 9.2-7, 1QH 4.27-28, 11.12, 12.12-13, 13.13-14.

Paul knows that loving one's fellow-man is founded upon the attributes of goodness and knowledge.[10] The term "admonishing" in this context refers not only to the exercising of authority, but also to loving one's neighbor. Paul is convinced that the members of the Roman community are "also able to admonish one another," since they are "filled" ("full") with "doing good" to one another rather than eager to repay "evil" with evil (cf. 12.9f). Paul may also mean that despite his injunction for each person to respect his brothers' opinions they must also reprove one another for those things which are not "proper" (cf. 1.28):

> They shall reprove each other in truth and humility and loving charity one towards the other. Let no man speak to his < brother > with anger, or ill-temper, or disrespect, or impatience, or a spirit of wickedness. And let no man hate him [in the perver]si[ty] of his heart; he shall be reproved on the very same day. And thus a man shall not bear a fault because of him. (1QS 5.25-6.1; cf. CDC 7.2-3, 9.2-8)[11]

Verse 15:

"Written very boldly . . . ": cf. 12.3, 1 Cor.4.14-17, 7.10-11, 14.37-38, 2 Cor.2.9, 4.9, 2 Pet.1.12.

Paul acts on his "conviction" that the community in Rome shares his views. His "boldness" not only reflects the "strength" (cf. 14.2) of his convictions, but also his "acceptance" of those who hold different opinions. He is willing and sees fit to love these brethren and also to admonish them (cf. verse 14), just as the Qumran community were "instructed" (cf. verse 4) to seek the good of their opponents and to reprove their own brethren (cf. 1QS 5.25, 9.16-23, 10.17-25). Paul re-asserts his authority (cf. 12.3) in appealing to his scriptural and apostolic mandate to bring the gospel also to the Gentiles (cf. verses 9-12):

> And [Thou hast] created [me] for Thy sake to fulfil the Law, and [to te]a[ch by] my mouth the men of Thy council in the midst of the sons of men, that Thy marvels may be told to everlasting generations and [Thy] mighty deeds be [contemp]lated without end. And all the nations shall know Thy truth and all the peoples, Thy glory. For Thou hast caused [them] to enter Thy [glo]rious [Covenant] with all the men of Thy council and into a common lot with the Angels of the Face; and none shall treat with insolence the sons [. . .] [. . .]and they shall be converted by Thy glorious mouth and shall be Thy princes in the lo[t of light]. . . . [And] Thou [in] Thy righteousness hast appointed me unto Thy Covenant. And I have held fast to Thy truth and have [clung to Thy Covenant]. And Thou hast made of me a father to the sons of Grace and as a foster-father to the men of good omen; and they have opened their mouth as a ba[be to its mother's breasts] and as a child delighting in the breasts of its nurses. (1QH 6.10-14, 7.19-22)[12]

The verse is elliptical, since Paul neglects to specify what exactly he wishes to remind the community of, unless the "reminder" itself conveys that wish ("so as to remind you again . . ."). He seems to take the thought up again in verse 17, however, where he in fact manifests doubt concerning his own convictions. Although he is convinced of his calling to bring the Gentiles into the kingdom of God, he feels that certain people are threatening this conviction. Since he also feels that this calling is the basis of his authority, such questioning of his ministry can shake the foundation of his teaching. He must know that God has indeed brought the Gentiles to the "obedience of faithfulness" (cf. verse 18) in order to be assured that his authority and teaching are "acceptable" (cf. 12.2, 14.14) in God's eyes.

Verse 16:
"To be a minister . . . ": cf. Ex.19.6, Isa.55.1ff, 61.6, 66.18-24, Acts 9.15, Rom.1.5, 12.8, Gal.2.9, Eph.3.1ff, Phil.2.17, Col.1.25f, 1 Pet.2.5, 9, Rev.1.6; 1QS 4.20-21, 8.4-10, 9.3-6, 4QFlor.1.1-6, 4QpIsa.d 11-12.

Paul returns to the theme of 12.1-2, in the context of his calling to the Gentiles. His authority comes from his "commission" to bring the Gentiles to the "obedience of faithfulness." He imitates Yeshua's role as a "servant . . . for the Gentiles" (cf. verse 8). His "ministry" is a priestly one, to offer sacrifices and to intercede on behalf of the people (cf. 12.1-2):

> It is the House of holiness for Israel as an everlasting planting and the Company of infinite holiness for Aaron; they are the witnesses of truth unto Judgment and the chosen of Loving-kindness appointed to offer expiation for the earth . . . and to make offerings of sweet savour . . . and they shall be accepted as expiation for the earth and to decree the judgment of wickedness with no perversity remaining. (1QS 8.5-10)

Paul is a part of the people of Israel, whom God has chosen to be a "kingdom of priests and a holy nation" before Him (cf. Ex.19.6). Since, however, he is not from a priestly tribe, but a Benjamite (cf. 11.1, Phil.3.5), he feels it necessary to stress that his priestly calling is based on God's "grace" (cf. 12.3, 15.15), and that his "offering" of the Gentiles fulfils the prophetic passages in Isaiah 61.6 and 66.18-24.[13] The nations are Israel's offering to God when His people return to their God and the Land, in fulfilment of her priestly task to serve the nations. The fact that Paul addresses this issue so soon after he appeals to the halakhot concerning love and peace in chapter 14 also suggests that he sees his ministry to the Gentiles as their "sanctification."[14] God "accepts" his offering and "sanctifies" the Gentiles through giving them His Spirit, "calling them into being" from "not-My people" (cf. Hos.1.10, Rom.4.17) by bringing them into the commonwealth of Israel.

"Offering of the Gentiles": cf. Isa.66.18-24, Rom.12.1-2, 14.18, Eph.1.4, Col.1.22, 1 Pet.2.5.

Paul appeals to Isaiah 66.18-24, in which the priestly tasks of Israel and the Gentiles are interlinked, and which reflects God's plan to provoke Israel to jealousy through the Gentile nations. Both Jewish and Gentile believers serve before God, bringing him "living and holy sacrifices" as they walk in the Spirit, and serve the Creator instead of their own evil inclination:

> They {the Gentiles} will come with their gifts, silver, gold and precious stones, with all the treasures from their countries to glorify thy people and Zion, thy holy city and thy marvellous house. . . . O Zion, rejoice greatly! Appear amid shouts of joy, O Jerusalem! Show yourselves, O all you cities of Judah! Open [thy] gat[es] for ever, for the riches of the nations to enter in! (4Q207 4.10f, 1QM 12.13-14)

"Sanctified by the Holy Spirit": cf. Ex.28.41, 29.7, 30.25-31, 8.1ff, 12.1-2, 14.14, 23, 1 Tim.4.4-5; Jub.1.22-23, Odes Sol.11.1-3; DEZ 3.6, 6.5, Sot.9.15, Ned.20a.

Paul's ministry as a priest is to consecrate his offering before God. The Gentiles who become faithful to God in Yeshua are "sanctified" (consecrated) because God makes those who were once "not-My-people" (cf. Hos.1.10, Rom.4.17) part of His elect, and includes them in the "commonwealth of Israel (cf. Eph.2.12ff, 3.1f).[15] The Gentile believers "prove what the will of God is, that which is good and acceptable and perfect" (cf. 12.2):

> When these things come to pass in Israel according to all the appointed times for the Institution of the Spirit of holiness (founded) in accordance with eternal Truth, they shall expiate guilty rebellion and sinful infidelity and (procure) Loving-kindness upon earth without the flesh of burnt offering and the fat of sacrifice, but the offering of the lips in accordance with the law shall be as an agreeable odour of righteousness, and perfection of way shall be as the voluntary gift of a delectable oblation. (1QS 9.3-4)

Verse 17:

"Therefore . . . boasting": cf. 2 Cor.10.13-18, Phil.3.3, Heb.2.17, 5.1.

Paul's reference to "boasting" reflects his concern over his authority, so that this verse may pick up the thread of the uncompleted sentence in verse 15 ("so as to remind you again . . . "), and relate to Paul's ministry to the Gentiles. Here Paul describes his "offering" of the Gentiles in the technical phrase τα προς θεον (ta pros theon), "the things that pertain to God," which in Jewish literature frequently describes the priestly office (cf. Heb.2.17, 5.1). His "offering" consists of the Gentile believers themselves, who have become faithful to God in Yeshua (cf. verse 16), but this offering is also possibly the "contribution" which he was intending to collect from the communities in Macedonia and Achaia for the "saints in Jerusalem."[16]

Verse 18:
"For I will not presume . . . me": cf. Acts 15.12, 21.19, 2 Cor.10.12ff.

As Yeshua has become the servant both of the "circumcision" and the "uncircumcision" (cf. verse 9) in order to make them into one body, so Paul claims Yeshua alone as his authority for his commission to the Gentiles (cf. Acts 9.15). He associates his "boasting" with his bringing the Gentiles to the "obedience of faith," and may "boast" (cf. 3.27) in the fact that God uses him to accomplish His work. Everything which he teaches is approved by God (cf. 14.3-4, 18), since it results in the obedience of the Gentiles to faithfulness to God in Yeshua.

"Obedience of the Gentiles . . . ": cf. Gen.49.10, Ps.2.6-9, 72.8-11, Isa.42.6-13, 49.6-7, 51.4-5, Rom.1.5, 2.13, 5.19, 6.16, 16.19, 26, 2 Cor.10.6, 1 Pet.1.2; CDC 7.18-21, 1QH 6.10-13; Gen.R.97 [NV], 98.8, 99.8.

Although the phrase "obedience (to faithfulness)" does not refer exclusively in the New Testament to the Gentiles (cf. Acts 6.7), it is directly associated with God's plan of redemption in which the Gentiles provoke Israel back to the God of their fathers.[17] The phrase "obedience to faithfulnes" is based upon the messianic blessing in Genesis 49.10, which speaks of the obedience (יקהת; *yikhat*) of the nations to Shiloh. This theme is developed in the prophets, and particularly in the Servant Songs in Isaiah (cf. verse 8):

> UNTIL SHILOH COMETH [Gen.49.10]. This indicates that all the nations of the world will bring a gift to Messiah the son of David, as it says, *In that time shall a present be brought (yubal shay) unto the Lord of Hosts* (Isa.18.7). 'Transpose *yubal shay* and expound it, and you find that it reads Shiloh.' . . . UNTIL SHILOH COMETH: he to whom kingship belongs (*shelo*). AND UNTO HIM SHALL THE OBEDIENCE OF THE PEOPLES BE—him to whom the nations of the world will flock (*mithkahalin*), as it says, *The root of Jesse, that standeth*

> *for an ensign of the peoples, unto him shall the nations seek* (Isa.11.10). (Gen.R.97 [NV], 99.8)[18]

The "faithfulness" of the Gentile believers "proves" Paul's ministry and his teaching. His offering is "acceptable" before God for his sake (his teaching is accepted) and for the sake of those whom he offers (the Gentiles are "sanctified").

"By word and deed . . . ": cf. Acts 1.8, 1 Cor.2.4-5, 2 Cor.10.11, 12.12, 13.3, 1 Thess.1.5.

Paul's teaching has brought forth fruit (cf. 1.13, 8.23) in the Gentiles' imitation of his principles and loving their fellow-man (cf. chapter 14).

Verse 19:

"In the power of . . . the Spirit": cf. Dt.13.1-2, 28.46, Mic.3.8, Lk.1.17, 4.14, Jn.4.48, Rom.1.4, 17, 1 Cor.1.18, 24, 2.4, 5.4, Eph.1.19, 2.2, 3.7, 16, 4.10, 2 Tim.1.7; 1QS 11.19f, 1QM 10.5, 11.5, 1QH 4.32, 7.9f, 14.23, 18.8f.

In chapter 1, Paul describes his commission as an apostle as the preaching of the gospel, which is the "power of God for salvation to everyone who believes" (1.16). Here he returns to this theme, and speaks of the manifestation of the "power of the Spirit" in "signs and wonders."19 In his preaching of Yeshua, the power of God, God has demonstrated His power both in Paul's own teaching, and in the obedience of the Gentiles to Yeshua:

> And through me Thou hast illumined the face of many and caused them to grow until they are numberless; for Thou hast given me to know Thy marvellous Mysteries and hast manifested Thy power unto me in Thy marvellous counsel and hast done wonders to many because of Thy glory and to make known Thy mighty works to all the living . . . to the Most High belong all the works of righteousness, whereas the way of man is not firm unless it be by the Spirit which God has created for him to make perfect a way for the sons of men, that all His works may know the might of His power and the greatness of His mercy to all the sons of His loving-kindness. (1QH 4.27-33)

"From Jerusalem . . . as far as . . . ": cf. Acts 22.17-22, Gal.1.18, 2.1.

Jerusalem served as the central place of Jewish worship throughout Jewish history. The Sanhedrin met in the Temple, to which thousands of pilgrims came up to celebrate the great Feasts of Passover, Shavuot, and Sukkot (שלוש הרגלים; *shalosh ha-regelim*).[20] Paul looked to Jerusalem for his own authority, since it was also the home of the "mother church" of the early community. On his escape from Damascus, where he was baptised, Paul went up to Jerusalem (cf. Acts 9.26), until persecution forced him to leave again for Tarsus from Caesaria. He visited Thessalonika on his subsequent journeys, and Illyria or Dalmatia formed the upper reaches of this region of Macedonia, bordering the Adriatic sea. The mountain region to the north of Thessalonika towards Illyria might therefore represent the furthermost reaches of his evangelism, where he has preached Yeshua, the power of God for salvation, to the Gentiles. Their offering (of themselves and their financial contribution) has proved their obedience to Yeshua.

Verses 20-21:
"I aspired . . . understand": cf. Ps.102.15, Isa.45.23, Zech.14.9, Jn.17.6, 11, Acts 4.12, 1 Cor.3.8-15, 2 Cor.10.13-18, Eph.1.21, Phil.2.9-11.

Paul "names" Yeshua in his preaching of the gospel, which is the power of God for salvation (cf. 1.16). Yeshua's "name" expresses and manifests this "power," according to which Israel and all the nations acknowledge him to be Lord, and bow their knee to him (cf. 10.9, 14.11, Phil.2.10). Paul is anxious not to encroach upon "territory" where the gospel has already been preached by other people, in adherence to the principle of not "building upon another man's foundation." As each believer has his own measure of service (cf. 12.3), so Paul is also bound in his ministry: he is careful not to infringe on other men's labours. According to 1 Corinthians 3.10, he does not hold the principle that laying a foundation and building upon that foundation are mutually exclusive ministries, but allows that someone may build upon his own "foundation" (the establishment of a community). If someone does "build," however, he must recognize the work and authority of the person who laid the foundation.[21] Since he himself wishes to preach wherever he goes, he now feels constrained from going to Rome, where the community had been founded by someone else.[22] Paul's prooftext from Isaiah 52.15 refers to the Gentiles ("kings"), so that he has a direct precedent for his preaching to those who "had not been told . . . had not heard" of the Messiah.

Verse 22:
"For this reason . . . ": cf. 1.13, 1 Thess.2.18.

Paul explains his absence from Rome as the result of his determination not to impinge upon someone else's territory. He describes this principle here, however, as though it were a "hindrance" rather than a policy to which he is committed.[23] Nevertheless, he seems to retain his adherence to the principle of non-encroachment, since he returns to the same theme in verse 23.

He has, in fact, exhausted the territory which has not been evangelized, and has also harbored a desire to visit the community in Rome. These additional factors enable him to plan to visit Rome on his way to Spain.

Verse 23:
"No further place . . . "

Paul considers that he has preached as far as he is able without violating his principle of not preaching to those who have already heard the gospel. He obviously feels free to proceed to Rome, where for many years he has desired to visit.

Verse 24:
"Whenever I go to Spain . . . ": cf. vs.28.

Paul hints here that his longing to visit Rome might have been dependent upon his plans to travel to Spain; he will visit Rome, he suggests in other words, only if and when he goes to Spain.[24] This suggestion runs counter to his statements in 1.10-13 and 15.23, however, since his desire to visit the community in Rome appears to be one factor in his willingness to compromise his principle of non-interference in the ministry of other preachers (evangelists). Paul then introduces his intention of going up to Jerusalem before reaching either Rome or Spain. Spain is known in talmudic literature as "Hispania" (איספניא [*'Ispania'*] or איספמיא [*'Ispamia'*]), Hebrew terms possibly derived from the Phoenician סיף-ימא (*Sif-Yama'*), "the end of the sea." It is described as the furthest place to which an owner of land was likely to go.[25] A three year limit was placed on a certain category of title-claimance, for example, since that was considered sufficient time for an owner to travel to Spain. While a leasor occupied his property for one year, an agent could reach Spain (a year's travel) to notify the owner of the occupancy, who would then have time to return by the end of the next (third) year in order to raise his claim (cf. BB 3.2). R. Eleazar interprets the verse in Genesis 12.3, "in you all the families of the world shall be blessed" (interpreting "families" as "nations" according to Gen.18.18), to include "even the ships that go from Gaul to Spain are blessed only for Israel's sake" (Yev.63a).[26] Spain represents for Paul also the furthest point of the world where the gospel must be preached (cf. Acts 1.8).

"Helped on my way there": cf. 1.10-13.

Paul anticipates receiving some spiritual encouragement from the community in Rome (whom he also wants to encourage on his part in imparting to them a "spiritual gift"). It is also likely, however, that he hopes for a financial contribution, possibly for his personal needs, but more importantly for the gift which he intends to convey to Jerusalem from the congregations in Macedonia and Achaia (cf. verses 25-28).

Verses 25-26:
"But now . . . Jerusalem": cf. Acts 19.21, 20.16, 22, 24.17, 1 Cor.16.1f.

Paul repeats his need first to go to Jerusalem in the same phrase ("but now") from verse 23, where in fact he intends to go directly to Rome. "But now" he counters that intention with the prior and more immediate need to go first to Jerusalem. Visiting Jerusalem is in fact Paul's most central concern. In Acts 20.16, he says that he is hastening back to Jerusalem to celebrate Shavuot (Pentecost) (cf. 1 Cor.16.8), having passed through Macedonia and Achaia both on his way to Greece and on his return. He is particularly anxious to be in Jerusalem for Shavuot since he is bringing the contribution from the congregations in Macedonia and Achaia as a "first fruit" to the Temple on the Feast (Rom.15.26, 2 Cor.8.1f). His longing to visit Rome on his way to Spain can only in fact be accomplished after he has made the necessary pilgrimage to Jerusalem.[27]

Verse 26:
"Serving . . . the poor among the saints in Jerusalem": cf. Ex.19.6, Dt.7.6, Dan.7.25, Mt.27.52, Acts 24.17, 26.10, Rom.1.7, 15.26, 16.15, 1 Cor.1.2, 6.2, 16.1ff, 2 Cor.8.4, 9.1, 12, Gal.2.10, Eph.1.1, 4, 15, 2.19; 1QS 5.13, 18, CDC 4.6, 6.16, 1QM 11.9-10, 12.1, 4, 7, 14.12, 1QH 4.25, 5.22, 11.11-12, 18.14-15, 1QpHab 12.2-10; PSan.6.9, Shab.86a, 105a, Pes.83b, Ket.65b, San.109b, Hul.7b.

The designation of God's people as "saints" (קדושים; *kedoshim*) is common to the Tanakh, Qumran and the New Testament writings.[28] Paul's service to the saints is his offering of the Gentiles (cf. verse 16) to Israel in fulfilment of the prophetic texts (cf. Isa.56.6-8, 66.18ff). The "saints" are therefore not the congregation in Jerusalem, but the poor among the people in general, who are given charity from contributions through the Temple. Paul is bringing this offering to the Temple for the poor among God's people both on behalf of the Gentiles (they have collected and contributed the money), and to represent the Gentiles' offering of themselves (cf. 12.1). It is his "first fruit" at the Feast of Shavuot (the Feast of the first fruit; cf. Num.28.26, Dt.16.9-12) and this determines his need first to go to Jerusalem.[29]

Verse 27:

"Indebted to them . . . ": cf. Rom.1.14, 11.11-13, 13.8, 1 Cor.9.11, Gal.6.6; Pes.Rab.15.5.

Paul's own "obligation" is to preach the gospel to both Jews and Gentiles (1.14). He further declares in 13.8 that no man should "owe" anything but love, and in 11.12-15 he describes the "debt of love" which the Gentiles owe to Israel for the redemption of the whole world (cf. 11.12-15). This principle reflects the doctrine of the Two Ways (Spirits), which runs through the whole letter. According to this view, when a person shares spiritual things with his brother, he should also share with him material things; if he has shared material things with him, he must also share spiritual things:

> Thou shalt not turn away the needy, but thou shalt share everything with thy brother, and shalt not say that it is thine own, for if you are sharers in the imperishable, how much more in the things which perish. [For the Lord's will is that we give to all from the gifts we have received.] (Did.4.8)[30]

If a person shares with someone his material treasures (things which are "mortal" or perishable), how much more ought he also to share with them his spiritual or immortal (imperishable) treasures. Paul suggests that common sharing in spiritual wealth "obliges" one to share one's material wealth also (and vice versa; cf. 1QS 1.12-13).

Verse 28:

"Put my seal . . . ": cf. Jn.3.33, Rom.4.11.

Paul refers here to the "seal" of the "first fruits" which he is bringing to the Temple on behalf of the Gentiles (cf. 15.16). The seal (חותם; *chotam*) was used for various purposes: it was engraved on the signet-ring of the king or other person in authority (cf. RH 24b, Yev.120a); it referred to the completion of a benediction, the signature on a letter or a verdict (cf. Ber.1.4, Ta'anit 2.3); and it functioned as the mark of the slave which he wore around his neck (cf. Shab.58a). The "seals" of the Temple, however, were four or five in number, and were used as "tokens" for the Temple currency which people received in exchange for the animal sacrifices which they brought to offer at the Temple:

> There were four seals in the Temple and on them was inscribed 'Calf', 'Ram', 'Kid', 'Sinner'. Ben Azzai says: There were five and on them was inscribed in Aramaic, 'Calf', 'Ram', 'Kid', 'Poor sinner',

> and 'Rich sinner' . . . If any wished for drink-offerings he would go to Johanan [b. Phineas] who was [officer] over the seals and give him money and receive from him a seal; he would then go to Ahijah who was over the drink-offerings and give him the seal and from him receive drink offerings. And in the evening the two came together and Ahijah brought out the seals and took their corresponding value in money [מעות]; and if there was any surplus the surplus fell to the Temple, and if there was any lack Johanan paid it from his own means, since the Temple has the upper hand. If a man lost his seal they made him wait until evening; if they found [money left over] enough for his seal they gave him a seal, but if they did not find enough he received none. And the name of the day was inscribed thereon because of defrauders. (Shek.5.3-5)

Paul's expression to "put my seal on their fruit" may thus reflect his intention to change the contribution collected from the Gentile believers in Macedonia and Achaia into Temple currency as a form of offering.[31]

Verse 29:
"Fulness of the blessing of the Messiah": cf. Gen.12.2, 22.17, 28.4, Dt.11.26f, 30.1f, 33.23, Ps.129.8, 133.3, Prov.10.22, Isa.44.3, Jn.1.16, Rom.11.12, 15.14, Gal.3.14, Eph.1.3, 23, 3.19, 4.13, Col.1.19, 2.9, Heb.6.14f, 1 Pet.3.9, Rev.5.12, 7.12.

The "blessing of the Messiah" is God's promise to Abraham that in his "seed" (cf. Gal.3.16) all the nations of the world would be "blessed." Paul appeals to this blessing in his promise to come to Rome on his way to Spain—to the "remotest part of the earth" (cf. Acts.1.8).32 The "fulness" of the blessing is its completion (fulfilment) and its richness (cf. 11.12). Its τελος (*telos*) or goal is "in order that in the Messiah Yeshua the blessing of Abraham might come to the Gentiles, so that we [Jews and then also Gentiles] might receive the promise of the Spirit through faith" (Gal.3.14). Paul might also have in mind his offering of the Gentile believers and their contribution, since God's blessing is given over the first fruits offered to the priests: "And the first of all the first fruits of every kind, from all your contributions [heave-offerings], shall be for the priests; you shall also give to the priest the first of your dough [coarse meal] to cause a blessing to rest on your house" (Ezek.44.30). The "fulness of the blessing of the Messiah" then parallels Paul's statements in 12.3 and 15.15, and indicates Paul's authority as a שליח (*shaliach*) in that Paul's ministry has been "stamped" or "sealed" with the "blessing" of Yeshua.[33] Paul wishes to pass on this blessing or grace to the community in Rome by imparting a spiritual gift to them which will bring fruit through their faithfulness to God.[34] Paul tells the community in Rome that he will come with full authority to impart gifts which will produce fruit (cf. the "fruit of the Spirit" [Gal.5.22]). This verse thus sums up the themes of God's "creation" (election) of the Gentiles, which will provoke Israel back to serving their Creator through jealousy for their own God.

Verse 30:

"Now I urge you . . . by the love of the Spirit . . . ": cf. 12.1, 16.17, 1 Cor.1.10, 2 Cor.1.11, 10.1, Gal.5.22, Col.1.8, 4.12, Phlm.22.

Paul exhorts the community in Rome to "help" him (cf. verse 24) by praying that he might accomplish the work which the Lord has given to him. The phrase "love of the Spirit" is a Semitism similar to "the poor in spirit" (cf. Mt.5.3), and refers both to the love which comes from the Spirit of God, and to those who love (walk according to) the Spirit of holiness (cf. 8.1ff). Paul picks up the theme of loving one's neighbor from chapters 12-15, and now requests that the community in Rome manifest their love of the brethren by praying together with Paul. Paul's specific request is to be "delivered from those who are disobedient in Judea," and for his "service to Jerusalem."

Verse 31:

"Delivered from those who are disobedient in Judea": cf. Jn.3.36, Acts 20.22-25, 21.13, Rom.2.8, 2 Cor.1.10, 1 Thess.2.14-16, 2 Thess.2.12, 3.1-2, 2 Tim.3.11, 4.17; CDC 1.12-21, 5.11-14, 8.1-10, CDCb 1.15-26, 1QpHab 2.1-10, 5.9-12, 8.1-12.10.

The phrase "those who are disobedient in Judea" refers to those opposed to Paul's commission to bring his offering of the Gentiles and their financial contribution to the Temple in Jerusalem. In the New Testament, the Greek verb ἀπειθεω (*apeitheo*), "to be disobedient," often refers to "unfaithfulness," or the refusal to be faithful, and thus carries the connotation of people who are opposed to those who are faithful to Yeshua.[35] Paul must travel through Judea in order to reach Jerusalem, and he apparently anticipates opposition on the way from Jewish sources antagonistic to his mission.[36] Such interference might be expected from Jews who held exclusivist attitudes and who thus imposed strict conditions on Gentile conversion to Judaism; this attitude might have also been reinforced by the fact that these Gentiles were part of the early church, and believed that Yeshua was the Messiah. Paul's opposition here is therefore not from the "Judaizers" within the messianic movement (cf. Acts 11.2) but from non-believing Jews opposed to his mission to the Gentiles.[37] The Book of Acts reflects the dangers in travelling to

Jerusalem in the period leading to the outbreak of the war in 66-70 C.E. Josephus records that under the Procuratorship of Felix, before whom Paul was tried in Caesarea (cf. Acts 23-24), the religious and political fanatics (ὁι γοητες και ληστρικοι; *hoi goetes kai lestrikoi*) "incited numbers to revolt, exhorting them to assert their independence, and threatening to kill any who submitted to Roman domination and forcibly to suppress those who voluntarily accepted servitude. Distributing themselves in companies throughout the country, they looted the houses of the wealthy men, murdered their owners, and set the villages on fire. The effects of their frenzy were thus felt throughout all Judaea, and everyday saw this war being fanned into fiercer flame."[38] The activity of both Zealot groups and the Sicarii was widespread in Jerusalem and Judea. Paul was at risk precisely because he was travelling to and visiting not merely Gentile communities, but also synagogues in the Diaspora, whose members he encouraged to accept Gentile participation in the "commonwealth of Israel."

Verse 32:
"Come to you in joy . . . ": cf. Acts 18.21, Rom.1.10-12, 15.24.

Paul feels that he will be able to visit Rome only after he has successfully completed his trip to Jerusalem.[39] Once he has received confirmation of his mission to the Gentiles, having brought their offering as a first fruit to Israel, he may continue in the knowledge of God's will for his commission. Spain is the furthermost point of that mission, and Rome is his long-desired stop on the way, where he may be refreshed in the company of the community of the believers.

Verse 33:
"Now . . . Amen": cf. Isa.9.6, 26.12, 48.18, 54.10, 66.12, Rom.16.20, 2 Cor.13.11, Phil.4.9, 1 Thess.5.23, Heb.13.20; Test.Dan 5.2.

Paul closes the body of his letter with his request for prayer that God would allow him to bring his offering of the Gentiles to the Temple in Jerusalem on behalf of his nation. This is the culmination of his commission to preach the "gospel concerning God's son" which is the "power of God for salvation to every one who believes, to the Jew first and also the to Greek" (1.16). The "God of peace" will assure him a way of peace in order to bring the offering of the Gentiles to the Temple through Judaea; His peace has reconciled men to him through the death and resurrection of Yeshua; and made Jews and Gentiles into one "new man" in Yeshua's breaking down of the "barrier of the dividing wall" (the "middle wall of partition"); and in walking in the "ways of peace" all those who are faithful to God in Yeshua, both Jews and Gentiles, are committed to loving their neighbor and respecting the opinions of their brothers. Thus in this phrase Paul sums up all the basic themes of his letter.

Endnotes Chapter 15

1 This means that there can be only one "true" interpretation of Scripture, which such people alone possess. The principle of "sanctification" is therefore also directly concerned with the issue of hermeneutics, and the need, nature, and extent of the human understanding of God's word.

2 See the comments on 12.9ff, 14.1ff, and 14.19.

3 The same Hebrew root (חרפה; *cherpah*) is used in both verses, and Paul transposes the messianic context of Ps.22.6 on to Ps.69.9.

4 Cf. PA 1.2: " . . . The world is based upon three things: the Torah, Divine Service, and the practice of kindliness." The Torah (verse 4) is the source of perseverance and encouragement; worship (verse 6) is the basis of unity and brotherly love (cf. Acts 2.46-47); and these two lead in turn to דרך ארץ (*derekh 'eretz*) and to גמילות חסדים (*gemilut chasadim*), works of charity and lovingkindness (verse 7); cf. also Sot.9.15.

5 See the comments on 3.23 and 8.17.

6 Man's "sanctification of God's name" (קדוש ה'; *kiddush ha-Shem*) can in some sense therefore also parallel the believer's "sanctification" ("glorification") of everyday things (cf. chapter 14).

7 Circumcision and covenant were considered synonymous in Second Temple Judaism; cf. Gal.2.7-9, Jub.15.25-34, PA 3.11, Ex.R.38.8. In distinction, the "party of (ἐκ; *ek*) circumcision" ordinarily (although not exclusively) refers in the New Testament to "Judaizing" believers who insist that Gentile believers must be circumcised and observe Torah and mitzvot; cf. Acts 15.5, Gal.2.12.

8 See also the comments on 3.29-31, 9.4-5, and 11.25-32.

9 The Hebrew masoretic text reads: ". . . the nations will resort to the root of Jesse, who will stand as a banner for the peoples; and His resting place will be glory." The LXX understands the "banner" to refer to "salvation" (cf. Num.21.8-9).

10 See the comments on 12.21, and on chapter 14.

11 See also the comments on 13.11-14.

12 Cf. Rom.1.5, 1 Cor.3.10, 4.14, 1 Thess.2.7-8, 1QH 2.17-18, 6.10-13, 8.16, 36, 18.10-12.

13 The offering is also associated with the "sweet savour" which symbol-

izes God's acceptance of the offering; cf. Gen.8.20-21, Ex.29.18, 25, Eph.5.2, Phil.4.18.

14 See the comments on 14.14.

15 For the idea of sanctifying the "profane," see the comments on chapter 14.

16 See the comments on verse 26.

17 See the comments on 1.5.

18 The Hebrew יבוא שילה (*yavo' Shiloh*), "until Shiloh comes," can be transposed into יובל שי (*yuval shai*), "a present will be brought." The midrash renders Num.24.17 as "Until he cometh to whom the present belongs;" שילה (*Shiloh*) can be read phonetically as שלו (*shelo*), "belonging to him." The author of the midrash apparently equates "obedience" (יקהת) with the "ensign" (נס) in Isal.11.10, since it parallels the " . . . of the peoples" in Gen.49.10, and apparently associates it with the root verb קהל (*kahal*), "to congregate," which carries the same sense for him as the "seeking" of the nations (ידרשו; *yidreshu*) in Isa.11.10.

19 The expression "signs and wonders" (אתות ומופתים; *'otot u-moftim*) is the traditional biblical phrase for miracles which attest to God's presence and interventions; cf. Dt.4.34, 7.19, 13.2, 26.8, 28.46, 29.2, Isa.20.3, Jer.32.21.

20 Cf. S. Safrai, "Pilgrimage to Jerusalem at the Time of the Second Temple," Immanuel 5 (1975), 51-62.

21 Paul thus considers "preaching" to be a principle of foundation-laying.

22 Paul thus also refrained from "boasting" (cf. verse 17) in regard to evangelism, which could easily become a means of making note of success where another person was less effective. Evangelizing was also a geographical matter in the early history of the messianic community. "Boasting" could also be manifested in the claim to have been to the most places, or to the furthest distance.

23 In 1.13, Paul indicates that his desire to visit the community in Rome has been frustrated, but gives no details of the cause. However, in 1 Thess.2.18 he ascribes the source of his hindrance to the work of Satan.

24 The modifiers in this verse ("whenever" and "in passing") both seem to weaken Paul's intention to visit Rome for its own sake (cf. also verse 28). A further sign of "indecision" regarding his desire to visit Rome is reflected in verse 22, where he leaves his thought hanging in mid-air. These factors may arise from his wish not to offend the community in Rome; alternatively, he makes the textual digression because reaching Spain, which is still unevangelized territory, is ultimately more important to him than his desire to visit the community in Rome.

25 This is reflected in the story of Jonah. In order to flee as far as possible in the opposite direction of Nineveh, where God had commanded him to preach, Jonah caught a ship to Tarshish (probably Tartessus), in South West Spain. Tarshish maintained a mineral trade with Tyre, and was apparently an ancient Semitic colony (cf. Isa.23.1).

26 For R. Eleazar's interpretation of the "blessing" in Gen.12.3 in relation to the "grafting" of the Gentiles into the people of Israel, see the comments on 11.17.

27 Shavuot is one of the three feasts which require pilgrimage (עליה לרגל; *'aliyah le-regel*) to Jerusalem (Ex.23.15, Num.15.15); cf. S. Safrai, Pilgrimage.

28 See the references above, and the comments on 1.7.

29 See also the comments on verse 28, on Paul's "sealing" of the fruit.

30 Cf. Lk.16.101-12, 1 Cor.15.42ff, PA 5.10, Ep.Barn.19.8. For the inclusion of the bracketed sentence and for the thought represented in the Didache, see D. Flusser, Jesus'; see also the comments on 1.14.

31 Although Paul is bringing a financial contribution rather than an animal sacrifice, Acts 24.17 indicates that he brought both alms and offerings "to my nation."

32 Cf. especially R. Eleazar's midrash in Yev.63a, where he connects God's promise to Abraham, that in him all the nations of all the earth would be blessed (Gen.12.3, 18.18) to both the "grafting in" of Ruth and Naama to the royal ancestors of Israel, and to the ships which sail from Gaul to Spain; see the comments on 11.17.

33 Cf. the function of the seal as the "amen" to a blessing; see the comments on verse 28.

34 In this context, the idea of "blessing" also picks up the theme of loving one's fellow-man and seeking their good in chapters 13-14: "Not returning evil for evil, or insult for insult, but giving a blessing instead; for you were called for the very purpose that you might inherit a blessing" (1 Pet.3.9).

35 The same sort of "disobedient" people are identified in the Qumran texts as the Jerusalem Priestly Establishment and the Romans ("Kittim"); see the references above.

36 1 Thess.2.16 indicates that some of the Jewish opposition was directed against the witness to the Gentiles (cf. Acts 13.45f). The "Jews" (ὁι 'Ιουδαιοι) in 1 Thess.2.14-16 are "Judeans," those who are inhabitants of "Judea," just as they are in John, so that when Paul describes those who are disobedient "in Judea" he also identifies them as being Jewish. Cf. M. Lowe, "Who Were the IOYDAIOI," Novum Testamentum 18.2 (n.d.), 101-29.

37 This is confirmed by the fact that Paul perceives the success of his mission, or the "deliverance" from those who oppose it, in terms of bringing his gifts and offerings to the Temple.

38 Jos.Bell.2.264-65; cf. Ant.20.172-76; see E. Schürer, History, 3:231-32.

39 See the comments on verses 22-25.

ROMANS

16

Introduction

Paul concludes his letter by recommending Phoebe, who will deliver it, to the congregation, and sends greetings to the members of the various groups of believers (Jews and Gentiles) in Rome, both those in the congregation to whom he is writing and those who meet in different groups (verses 3-16). Those working with him also send their greetings (verses 21-23), and his scribe, Tertius, adds his own greetings (verse 22). Paul inserts one final warning against false teachings which spread strife, based on another Qumran homily (verses 17-20), and ends with a benediction (doxology) to the God who promised to bless the nations of the world through Abraham, thus bringing the whole world to obedience through His Messiah, Yeshua (verses 25-27).

Verse 1:

"I commend to you . . . ": cf. Acts 18.18, 2 Cor.3.1.

Paul adds an addendum to his letter, greeting all those whom he knows in Rome, both in the community to which he writes and those who are part of the wider community of believers in Rome. He mentions first of all Phoebe, the person who is presumably bringing his letter to the community. To "commend" or "recommend" is the ordinary word for "to introduce" in written correspondence of that period; letters of recommendation were standard for travelers, and particularly for women during this period.[1] Paul asks the Roman congregation to accept Phoebe as Paul's approved שליח (*shaliach*; cf. "the agent is as the one who sends him" [Ber.5.5]). Although nothing more is known of Phoebe herself, Paul visited the congregation in Cenchrea, Corinth's eastern port city, on his second journey (c. 52 C.E.). Paul was writing from the house of Gaius in Corinth (verse 23), presumably the same person whom he baptized at Corinth (1 Cor.1.14). At the time, Corinth was the center of evangelizing activity for the entire region of Achaia (cf. 15.26, 2 Cor.1.1); Cenchraea was also the port nearest to Ephesus, with its large Jewish population.

"Servant"

This is the only direct reference to "deaconess" (in contrast to "deacon") in the New Testament.[2] Although 1 Timothy 3.8f evidently refers to deaconesses, the term itself is not otherwise used in the feminine. According to 1 Timothy 3.8f, deaconesses are required to be "dignified, not malicious gossips, but temperate, faithful in all things." Paul acknowledges that Phoebe possesses these qualities, and is recognized by the congregation in Cenchrea as a deaconess. He wishes the congregation in Rome to receive her with the same recognition and authority.

Verse 2:

"Receive her in the Lord . . . ": cf. Phil.2.29.

Paul's commendation is not merely for Phoebe's sake, but also on his own behalf. His request is that she be greeted specifically as his "agent," and treated accordingly. The expression "in the Lord" signifies "a sister in the Lord," one who belongs to the body of the Messiah. "In a manner worthy of the saints" acknowledges her status as a deaconess.

"Help . . . helper": cf. 15.24.

Paul wishes for the same help for his "agent" as for himself (cf. 15.24), but he prefaces the request with the promise that Phoebe has already proven herself as the helper of others, including himself. The Greek word προστατις (*prostatis*), "helper" (suggested by the term παραστετη [*parastete*; "assistant" or "supporter"]) corresponds to the Latin word *patronus* ("patron"). The role of the patron included giving a small dole of gifts or money. He also rendered assistance in need, welcomed his client from time to time to his house and table, and offered legal protection if it was needed. The patron and client relationship operated between former masters and freedmen, rich and poor, generals and conquered peoples, aristocrats and *collegia* or clubs. Beginning from the slave and up to the aristocrat, every individual could find someone more powerful than himself, up to the emperor.[3] Paul describes Phoebe in the terms of a patroness, someone who gave aid and who had the resources to do so. The New Testament office of deacons and deaconesses may well have been modeled on this Roman "clientele system," so that the roles of deacon(ess) and patron(ess) merged into one another.

Verse 3:

"Greet Prisca and Aquila . . . ": cf. Acts 18.2-3, 18, 26, 1 Cor.16.19, 2 Tim.4.19.

Aquila was born in Pontus, and was part of the Jewish community of Rome forced to leave the city, with his wife, Prisca or Priscilla, following the

Emperor Claudius' edict in 52 C.E.[4] The couple apparently settled in Corinth, where they met Paul, who worked in the same trade of tent-making (cf. Acts 18.3). They traveled with Paul to Ephesus on his return to Antioch on his second journey, and remained there (cf. Acts 18.18-19). They later returned to Corinth, where they had a house-church, and were back in Ephesus when Paul wrote his second letter to Timothy (cf. 2 Tim.4.19). The numerous Latin inscriptions which mention both or one of the names Aquila and Prisca/Priscilla make it likely that they were the freedmen of a noble Roman family.[5] The frequent mention of the couple in the New Testament epistles reflects their prominence within the believing community. The long list of greetings with which this verse begins is a further source of Paul's "introduction" or recommendation (authority) to the community in Rome. It also importantly reflects the mixed Jewish and Gentile character of the congregation.

Verse 4:
"For my life risked their own necks . . . ": cf. Acts 15.26.

Paul gives no specific details of the event in which his life was threatened, although he lists a history of his hardships in 2 Corinthians 6.5 and 11.23; it is possible to surmise that the particular incident to which he alludes here occurred at Ephesus (cf. 1 Cor.15.32). The tenor of the statement suggests that it was not so much a public event, with consequent effects upon the community at large, as much as a personal affair. The thanks which Paul feels are due to Aquila and Priscilla from "all the churches of the Gentiles" are based on Paul's role as an apostle to the Gentiles, who should be grateful that Aquila and Priscilla saved his life and enabled him to preach the gospel to them.

Verse 5:
"The church that is in their house": cf. Acts 12.12, 1 Cor.16.19, Col.4.15, Phlm.2; Act.Paul 2.7.

The term ἐκκλησια (*ekklesia*), "church," refers primarily to the people and not to a building.[6] House-groups were the normal form of meeting in the first centuries (cf. Acts 12.12, 1 Cor.16.19, Col.4.15), although there is some witness of outdoor gatherings (cf. Just.*Apol.*1.67 [C2]). Frequently, private room(s) were offered on a regular basis by wealthy patrons, one of whom might have been Nympha (Col.4.15; cf. Acts of Justin 2); Phoebe, on the other hand, is not said to have hosted the congregation in her own house. There were therefore probably several congregations in the larger cities (cf. Paul's greeting to various groups in Rome in verses 14-15). At a later historical stage, a house which had been used as a meeting place might be acquired and remodeled as a church building. The earliest example of such premises is the meeting-place at Dura Europos (C3).[7]

"Epaenetus . . . the first convert . . . from Asia": cf. 1 Cor.16.15, Heb.12.23, Jas.1.18, Rev.14.4.

Epaenetus was a fairly common name and occurs in archaeological inscriptions from Asia Minor. Although particular status was imputed to several of the first believers by the early communities, and described as the "first fruits" of obedience amongst the Gentiles (cf. 1 Cor.16.15), nothing more is known about this Epaenetus. Paul describes him as the ἀπαρχη (*aparkhe*) or "first fruits" of the gospel (cf. 1.13, 8.23, 15.16). In the pagan world, individuals who were offered to deities could easily be substituted by first fruits: men who dedicated themselves to the service of the sanctuary or who were given to the temple as temple servants were in fact called "first fruits" (ἀπαρχαι).[8] No reason is suggested for Epaenetus' move to Rome, but such travelling was not unusual, as is witnessed by the wanderings of Aquila and Priscilla (see above).[9] Travelling was apparently a sufficiently commonplace activity that acquaintances could be made and kept in touch with in many places.

Verse 6:

"Mary": The manuscript evidence attests to Mary as both a Jewish (cf. "Miriam") and a Roman name.[10] Since Paul designates Andronicus and Junias as "fellow Jews" in the following verse, the lack of a similar designation for Mary may indicate that she was not Jewish. Paul asks the Roman congregation to treat her well since she has served them conscientiously, although he does not indicate the source of his own acquaintance with her.

Verse 7:

"Andronicus and Junias . . . ": cf. 9.3.

Junias might either be a masculine contraction of Junianus, or the feminine form, Junia. If it is a feminine name (quite common in Roman circles) the two might be a couple like Prisca and Aquila. Andronicus is a Greek name, suggesting that he was possibly a freedman.[11] The term "my kinsmen" obviously refers to fellow-Jews, as in 9.3 (cf. also 16.11, 21).

"Fellow prisoners": cf. Col.4.10, Phlm.23.

Andronicus and Junias are not mentioned otherwise as fellow-prisoners, and nothing is known of the circumstances of their imprisonment. They were not necessarily imprisoned at the same time as Paul, and he might be referring loosely to the fact of their having been jailed, presumably for their faithfulness to Yeshua. Paul was not imprisoned in Corinth, and makes no mention of fellow-believers in the Philippian jail. The proposition that they became believers when in prison is refuted by the subsequent statement that they came to faith in Yeshua before Paul himself.[12]

"Outstanding among the apostles": cf. Mk.3.14f, Lk.6.13, Acts 1.21-22, 14.4, 14, 1 Cor.12.28, 2 Cor.8.23, 11.5, 13, Gal.1.19, Eph.4.11; Did.11.3ff.

The Greek word ἐπισημος (*episemos*) means "outstanding" or "prominent." Some commentators modify the implications of this verse to make Andronicus and Junia(s) "well-known among" or "esteemed by" the apostles, in order to resolve the difficulty of the possibility that Junias is a woman, and that women apostles were thus known in the early community. The qualifications which the New Testament texts lay down for apostleship (twelve, in correspondence with the twelve tribes, and qualified by having seen Yeshua in the flesh; cf. Acts 1.21-22) are not absolute. Paul himself does not fit the generally recognized criteria, and often had to defend his apostolic authority.[13] It is therefore reasonable to understand that Andronicus and Junia(s) were considered (or, at the very least, considered themselves to be) apostles, possibly in the sense of "community apostles" or representatives ("missionaries"), as in the "sending out" of congregational members to establish new communities (cf. Acts 15.30, 33, 17.10, 14). The function of "women ministering to women" was probably already practiced in synagogues where, although women were confined to their own "court" (cf. Mid.2.5, Suk.51b, Hag.16b), they were allowed to be agents (שליחים; *shelichim*) for betrothal (cf. Ked.52a), and to "lay hands" on the sacrifices "optionally," in other words, neither as an obligatory precept (חובה; *chovah*), nor as a meritorious religious act (מצוה; *mitzvah*), but as a religiously indifferent act performed for their own gratification (cf. Hag.16b). The idea of "apostleship" possibly reflects here the Jewish custom of sending rabbinic representation to the Diaspora.[14] Letters of recommendation were commonly carried by such representatives (cf. Acts 9.1f, 18.27, PHag.76d), even if the talmudic witness is of a later period. Hanna b. Adda (c.340) is described as שליח ציון (*shaliach Tziyon*), or "Zion's messenger" in Beza 25b, which Rashi explains in reference to the Rabbi Hanna's frequent travelling between Babylon and Eretz Israel in order to provide the latter, in its decaying state, with funds from abroad.[15] It was common practice to send such representatives in pairs, as in this verse.[16]

Verse 8:

"Ampliatus, my beloved . . .": cf. Mt.3.17, 17.5, Jn.13.23, 19.26, 20.2, Rom.16.9, 12, Eph.1.6, Col.1.13, 2 Tim.1.2, Phlm.16, Jude 1.

The appellation "beloved" is originally used in the account of the "binding of Isaac," where God commands Abraham to sacrifice "your son, your only son, whom you love" (Gen.22.2). Ampliatos (or Amplias) was a common Roman slave name. It appears on a second century inscription in a Christian catacomb in the cemetery of Domitilla, together with references to other members of the Domitillan family, which was a prominent Roman household. The additional inscriptions there clearly suggest that members of this family were believers in Yeshua the Messiah.[17] This, together with the fact that the name Ampliatus occurs without any other description, which suggests that he was probably a slave, might indicate that Ampliatus was well-known in the Roman communities and was connected with a noble Roman family associated with the faith.[18]

Verse 9:

"Urbanus . . . and Stachys"

Urbanus is another common Roman slave name. Strachys is a rare Greek name, although known among members of the Imperial household.[19]

Verse 10:

"Appeles, the approved in the Messiah": cf. Rom.14.18, 1 Cor.11.19, 2 Cor.10.18, 13.7, 2 Tim.2.15.

Appeles was both a slave and a Jewish name. The Greek noun δοκιμος (*dokimos*), "approved" (cf. 14.18, 22) reflects the Hebrew term בחון (*bachun*), "well-tested" or "favoured": Israel "are the children of Thy favoured ones . . . the children of My tried ones, they are the children of Abraham, Isaac, and Jacob" (Pes.87a, b). The appellation "approved" is synonymous with "beloved," in verses 8 and 9.

"(Household) of . . . Aristobulus": cf. vs.11.

Some scholars have speculated whether this might refer to Aristobulus the grandson of Herod the Great. Josephus recounts that Aristobulus was a friend and adherent of Claudius (41 C.E.), who died in Rome (cf. Jos.*Bell.*2.221-22, *Ant.*20.10-12). Aristobulus himself could have still been alive when Paul wrote. If, however, he had already died, his "household" (ὁι Ἀριστοβουλου; *hoi Aristoboulou*; "those of [the house] of Aristobulus") could have retained his name even after it had been merged with the imperial household.[20]

Verse 11

"Herodian, my kinsman"

A Jewish believer, but without any traceable connection to the Herodian family, even if the Aristobulus mentioned above was from the Herodian family.

"(Household) of Narcissus"

Narcissus was another common slave and freedman's name.[21] Paul distinguishes between believing and non-believing members of Narcissus' household, but this does not necessarily mean that his previous references are to whole households who had believed.

Verse 12:

"Tryphaena and Tryphosa"

These names are traditionally identified as referring to two sisters, perhaps because of the similarity of name, although there is no evidence to support the assumption. The name "Tryphaena" is known from Queen Tryphaena, widow of Cotys, King of Thrace, who was the mother of Polemo II, and was herself a great-niece of Claudius, who is referred to in the apocryphal Acts of Paul (2.27ff).[22]

"Persis"

This name occurs in contemporary inscriptions as that of a freedwoman.[23] Paul is very sensitive to the contribution of the women in the early congregations, and makes a point of noting their hard work.

Verse 13:

"Rufus": cf. Mk.15.21.

This Rufus is traditionally identified with the son of Simon of Cyrene (cf. Mk.15.21), although Rufus was a common slave name.[24] Paul's referral to him as ἐκκλεκτος (*ekklektos*; "choice" or "chosen") probably indicates that Paul held him in particular affection; or his general regard for Rufus' commitment and walk in the Lord. In the same way as Yeshua had commended John, "the beloved disciple," to take his place in Mary's affections (cf. Jn.19.26), Paul appears to regard Rufus' mother as a mother-figure.

Verse 14:

"Greet . . . "

The names in this verse belong to slaves and/or freedmen. They are all male, and the reference to the "brethren with them" appears to indicate a separate, independent congregation or house-group, as does the similar expression in the following verse.[25]

Verse 15:

"Greet . . ."

Another small congregation, distinguished at least in this greeting by the reference to women.[26]

Verse 16:

"Holy kiss": cf. Gen.29.11, 33.4, 45.14-15, Lk.7.45, 15.20, 20.37, 22.47, 1 Cor.16.20, 2 Cor.13.12, 1 Thess.5.26, 1 Pet.5.14.

The custom of greeting people with a kiss is reflected in the gospels (cf. Lk.7.45). Foot kissing is mentioned as expressing an effusion of gratitude or supplication (cf. Lk.22.47), so that kissing on the cheek can be gathered to have been the normal manner of greeting and parting.[27] In the early community, the "holy kiss" was primarily an expression of fellowship (cf. the epithet "holy"), acknowledging the bond created between those "in the Messiah." The kiss was both physical and symbolic. The greeting became a regular feature of the liturgical practice of the early church, including the baptismal ceremony, and was also associated with the "kiss of peace."[28] The "holy kiss" was a sign of brotherhood, and, in connection with the Lord's supper, designated those who were allowed to participate from those who were not (i.e., the "holy" or "saints"). This practice may have been influenced by the community at Qumran, who placed a "curse" (ἀναθεμα; *anathema*; cf. 1 Cor.16.22) on those members whose "impurity of malice" excluded them from the communal meal:

> . . . during the first year he shall not touch the Purification of the Many, and during the second year he shall not touch the Banquet of the Many. . . . And these are the precepts for the man of understanding, that he may walk in them in the company of all the living according to the law proper to each time; and it is according to this law that the race of Israel shall walk that it may not be cursed. . . . Let not (the wicked) enter the water to touch the Purification of the holy, for a man is not pure unless he be converted from his malice. . . . Truly, they shall be careful to act according to the exact tenor of the Law in the time of wickedness, to separate themselves from the sons of the Pit . . . to distinguish between the unclean and the clean, and to make known (the distinction) between sacred and profane . . . to set holy things apart according to their

> exact tenor; to love each man his brother as himself, and to support the hand of the needy, the poor, and the stranger, and to seek each man the well-being of his brother, and not to betray, each man him who is flesh of his flesh . . . to bear no malice from one day to the next; and to be separated from all uncleanness according to their ordinance, and not to defile each man his Holy Spirit. . . . (1QS 7.19-20, CDC 12.21-22, 1QS 5.13-14, CDC 6.14-7.4) [29]

"All the churches of the Messiah greet you": cf. Acts 11.22, 20.28, 1 Cor.1.2, 11.16, 14.33, 15.9, 16.1, 19, 2 Cor.8.1, Gal.1.22, Eph.5.23, Col.1.18, 24, 1 Thess.2.14, 2 Thess.1.4, 1 Tim.3.15, Rev.1.4.

Paul might be conveying the kiss of greeting to the communities in Rome on behalf of all those communities with whom he is in fellowship. The phrase "the churches of the Messiah" combines an adjective of belonging ("of the Messiah," "of God . . .") with an identity of location (at Corinth, of Asia . . .), and indicates that each congregation was recognized first of all as part of the body of the Messiah and then by its geographical location.

Verse 17:

"Now I urge you . . . ": cf. 12.1, 1 Cor.1.10.

Immediately after delivering the kiss of greeting and peace and encouraging the communities to live in peace, Paul warns against the causes of strife between the brethren.

"Keep your eye on . . . ": cf. Mt.16.23, 18.7f, Lk.17.1, Rom.14.13, 1 Cor.3.3, Gal.5.11, 20, 1 Jn.2.10, Rev.2.14.

The "dissensions and hindrances" about which Paul warns the congregation are possibly the result of strife caused by those who spread false teachings amongst the community, just as he proclaims a curse against "any man preaching to you a gospel contrary to that which you received" in Galatians 1.6-9, and names "certain men" as from the "party of the circumcision" (Gal.2.12; cf. Acts 11.2). There were people within the various communities who spread dissension and strife by preaching "another gospel" (cf. Acts 15.1, 24, Gal.1.6, 5.10, 1 Tim.1.3ff, 6.3-6).[30] The Greek idiom "to keep your eye upon" (σκοπειν τους τας διχοστασιας; *skopein tous tas dichostasias*) means to be on guard against and keep watch for, as it does in modern English.

"Contrary to the teaching which you learnt": cf. Rom.6.17, 1 Cor.11.2, Gal.1.6f, 3.1f, 2 Thess.3.6, 1 Tim.1.3f, 6.3-6, 2 Tim.1.13, 3.14f; 1QS 2.11f, 3.1-6, 5.11-13, 7.16ff, 8.16-19, 21-24, CDC 7.9ff, 8.1ff, 15.12f, CDC[b] 1.5ff.

"Dissensions and hindrances" are themselves what is contrary to the "mind of the Messiah."[31] The "teaching" (Torah" or "instruction") of the gospel encourages harmony instead of strife:

> It is < of the Spirit of truth > to enlighten the heart of man. . . . And (to it belong) the spirit of humility and forbearance, of abundant mercy and eternal goodness, of understanding and intelligence, and almighty wisdom with faith in all the works of God . . . and abundant affection towards all the sons of truth . . . . But to the Spirit of perversity belong cupidity, and slackness in the service of righteousness, impiety and falsehood, pride and haughtiness, falsity and deceit, cruelty and abundant wickedness, impatience and much folly, and burning insolence . . . and a blaspheming tongue, blindness of eye and hardness of ear, stiffness of neck and heaviness of heart causing a man to walk in all the ways of darkness, and malignant cunning. (1QS 4.2-11)

"Turn away from them": cf. 1 Cor.5.9, 11, 2 Cor.6.14f, 1 Thess.5.21-22, 2 Thess.3.6, 14, 2 Tim.3.5; 1QS 1.3-18, 5.10-20, 9.9, 20-21, CDC 6.14-7.6, CDC[b] 1.17-26.

Paul's warning against factionalism, strife, dissension, and false teaching naturally follows upon his greetings, which emphasize the unity and fellowship within the community:

> And let him keep true Knowledge and right Justice for them that have chosen the Way. He shall guide each man in Knowledge according to his spirit . . . that they may walk with one another in perfection in all that has been revealed to them. This is the time to *prepare the way* {Isa.40.3} to go into the desert. And he shall instruct them in all that has been found that they may do it at this time, and that they may be separated from all who have not departed from all perversity. And these are the norms of conduct for the man of understanding in these times, concerning what he must love and how he must hate. Everlasting hatred for the men of the Pit because of their spirit of hoarding. He shall surrender his property to him and the wages of the work of his hand, as a slave to his master and as a poor man in the presence of his overlord. But he shall be a man full of zeal for the Precept, whose time is for the Day of Vengeance. (1QS 9.18-23)[32]

Verse 18:

"Slaves . . . flattering": cf. 6.6, 12, 16, 19, 7.14f, Eph.5.6, Phil.3.19, Tit.1.10, 2 Pet.2.3, 18; 1QH 2.14f, 32, 4.9f, 16f, 5.24, 27, 4QpNah 7.

Paul knows that he is a "bond-servant" of Yeshua (1.1), and here refers back to the midrash on the "two masters," which he introduces in chapter 6.[33] Those who create strife and dissension are those who refuse to present their members to righteousness, and unless they "become obedient from the heart to that form of teaching to which [they were] committed," are "slaves of sin" (cf. 6.17). Paul adopts similar terms of vilification as found in the Qumran texts for such people who disobey God and turn others away from His truth:

> And they, interpreters of falsehood and seers of deceit, devised plans of Belial against me, bartering Thy Law which Thou hast graven in my heart for the flattering words (which they speak) to Thy people . . . and I became a spirit of jealousy to all those who seek sm[ooth] things . . . Thou hast delivered me from the envy of the interpreters of falsehood and from the congregation of them that seek smooth things. (1QH 4.10, 2.15, 32)[34]

"Deceive . . . unsuspecting"

Paul perceives a threat to the early communities from within, from people liable to beguile and flatter with soft words in order to draw the "saints" astray from the "teaching which you have learnt." The "unsuspecting" are the innocent and simple, the "poor" who cleave to the ways of God and to His word, and who are preyed upon by wolves in sheep's clothing.[35]

Verse 19:

"Report of your obedience . . . ": cf. 1.5, 8, 15.19, 16.26.

Paul is convinced (cf. 15.14) of the "unsuspecting" hearts of the congregations of those who are faithful to God in Yeshua. He knows and has received reports that, despite the threat of those who would try to lead God's people astray, the believers in Rome have remained faithful to Yeshua and to one another.[36]

"Wise . . . evil": cf. Gen.3.1, Jer.4.22, Mt.10.16, Lk.16.1-13, Rom.12.16-21, 14.16, 20, 1 Cor.14.20, Phil.2.15, Heb.5.14; 1QS 1.8, 3.9, 4.2-6, 8.9, 20; Mid.Ps.119.1.

Paul continues the theme of the Two Ways, here expressed in terms of being innocent in the face of evil:

And these are the norms of conduct for the man of understanding in these times, concerning what he must love and how he must hate. Everlasting hatred for all the men of the Pit because of their spirit of hoarding! He shall surrender his property to them and the wages of the work of his hands, as a slave to his master and as a poor man in the presence of his overlord. But he shall be a man full of zeal for the Precept, whose time is for the Day of Vengeance. . . . I will not envy from a spirit of wickedness and my soul shall not covet the riches of violence. As for the multitude of the men of the Pit, I will not lay hands on them till the Day of Vengeance; but I will not withdraw my anger from perverse men, I will not be content till He begins the Judgment. I will be without malice and wrath towards those that are converted from rebellion, but merciless to those that have turned aside from the way; I will not comfort them that are smitten until their way is perfect. I will not keep Belial in my heart; no folly shall be heard within my mouth, and on my lips shall be found no criminal deceit or falsity or lies. But on my tongue shall be fruit of holiness and no abominations shall be found on it. I will open my mouth in thanksgiving, and my tongue shall ever recount the deeds of God, together with the unfaithfulness of men until the destruction of their rebellion. I will cause vain words to cease from my lips, and defilement and perfidy from the understanding of my heart. With wise reflection I will conceal Knowledge; with understanding prudence I will guard [it] within firm bounds, to keep the faith and the law strictly according to the righteousness of God. (1QS 9.21-23, 10.19-25)[37]

R. Judah said in the name of R. Simon: With Me they are innocent like doves, but with the nations they are cunning like serpents. (Cant.R.2.14.1)

Verse 20:

"God of peace": cf. 12.18ff, 14.17, 19, 15.33.

Paul returns to his greeting and blessing of peace in 15.33, emphasizing the fact that it is God who is the source of peace in the face of strife and dissension.[38]

"Will soon crush Satan under your feet": cf. Gen.3.1, 15, Rom.12.19, 2 Cor.11.13f; 1QS 3.23, 4.18-19, 1QM 11.8ff, 13.9ff, 14.4ff, 15.1ff, 17.1ff, 18.1ff; Test.Sim.6.6, Test.Levi 18.12.

Paul specifically associates God's peace here with the "crushing" of Satan and the forces of evil. He indirectly introduces the theme of the serpent in verse 19 (cf. "wise in what is good"), since in the LXX the serpent is characterized as φρονιμωτατος (*phronimotatos*), "clever," the word with which Yeshua describes the "sons of the world" who are "cleverer" (φρονιμωτεροι; *phronimoteroi*) than the "sons of light" (Lk.16.8).[39] Paul recalls the principle of "non-retaliation" he introduced in 12.9ff, and once again refers to the Day of Vengeance which brings to an end the period of submission (cf. 13.11-14). Here he again uses terms from Genesis 3.15 to assure the community in Rome that God's final victory over the forces of darkness and evil and the spirits of Belial will soon be accomplished:

> And She who is big with the Asp is prey to terrible anguish and the billows of the Pit (are unleashed) unto all the works of terror. And they shake the foundation of the rampart like a ship on the face of the waters, and the clouds roar in a noise of roaring. And they that live in the dust are, like them that sail the seas, terrified because of the roaring of the waters. And their wise men are for them like sailors in the deeps, for all their wisdom is destroyed because of the roaring of the waters, because of the boiling of the deeps upon the fountains of the waters. [And] the waves [are turb]ulent (rearing) into the air and the billows resound with the roaring of their voice. And Sh[eo]l [and Abaddon] open in the midst of their turbulence [and al]l the arrows of the Pit (fly out) in their pursuit; they let their voice be heard in the Abyss. And the gates [of Sheol] open [to all] the works of the Asp, and the doors of the Pit close upon her who is big with Perversity, and the everlasting bars upon all the spirits of the Asp. (1QH 3.12-18)[40]

"The grace of . . . ": cf. 1.5, 5.15f, 6.23, 12.3, 15.15.

The doxological ending sets the "seal" or "amen" (cf. 15.28) on God's ultimate victory over Satan and evil. By his death and resurrection, Yeshua has conquered death and brought forth the "first fruits" of the Kingdom of God in the lives of those who are faithful to God in his Messiah (cf. 1 Corinthians 15).

Verse 21:

"Timothy, my fellow-worker": cf. Acts 16.1, 17.14f, 1 Cor.4.17, 16.10, 2 Cor.1.1, 19, Col.1.1, 1 Thess.1.1, 3.2, 6, 1 Tim.1.2, Phlm.1, Heb.13.23.

Paul follows his warnings against strife and his assurance of final victory with further greetings to his acquaintances in the Roman communities.[41]

Timothy was Paul's closest and most trusted brother in the Lord, who was faithful in accompanying Paul on his journeys, in his imprisonment, and in being sent on his behalf to encourage other communities (see the references above).

"Lucius": cf. Acts 13.1.

It is not clear whether this Lucius is the one mentioned in Acts 13.1, who is identified as being from Cyrene, as is Rufus the son of Simon of Cyrene (cf. Mk.15.21).[42]

"Jason": cf. Acts 17.5-7, 9.

The Jason referred to in Acts was a prominent believer in Thessalonica, well-known in the early communities, and a close friend of Paul (cf. Acts 17.5-7, 9).

"Sosipater": cf. Acts 20.4.

The Sosipator (or Sopater) mentioned in Acts 20.4 was a native of Berea, close to Thessalonica. It is possible that he visited Paul in Corinth and traveled with him, temporarily or permanently. Lucius, Jason, and Sosipater are all identified as Jewish believers.

Verse 22:

"I, Tertius . . . ": cf. 1 Cor.16.21, Gal.6.11, Col.4.18, 2 Thess.3.17.

Paul was accustomed to an amanuensis or scribe, and now adds personal greetings in his own hand. The use of a secretary even for private letters was common. Here Tertius also adds his own greetings, indicating that he was acquainted with some of the members of the communities in Rome.

Verse 23:

"Gaius, host to me . . . ": cf. (Acts 19.29, 20.4), 1 Cor.1.14.

Most commentators identify Paul's host with the Gaius whom he baptized at Corinth (cf. 1 Cor.1.14). It would perhaps be natural for Paul to stay at the house where the congregation also met. Luke identifies a Gaius "from Derbe" in Acts 19.29, perhaps distinguishing him thus from this Gauis, who lived in Corinth.

"Erastus": cf. Acts 19.22, 2 Tim.4.20.

Paul identifies Erastus as the "city treasurer" of Corinth. An inscription discovered on the plaza of the theatre in Corinth, dated around 50 C.E., has provided external witness of this Erastus, which reads: "Erastus in return for his aedileship laid (the pavement) at his own expense." The term "aedileship" refers to the function of "business manager," a public figure responsible for the upkeep and welfare of city property, as well as for commercial and financial litigation. The date is appropriate for the period at which Paul was writing, and the name sufficiently infrequent as to make the identification with this Erastus very likely. The use of the word οἰκονομος (*oikonomos*), "city treasurer," in place of the customary Greek term ἀγορανομους (*agoranomous*), is further explained by the particular circumstances in Corinth. Since the public games which were a normal part of the aedile's responsibility were administered separately in Corinth, the tasks of the Corinthian aediles were limited to local economic affairs.[43]

"Quartus"

Nothing more is known of him at all.

Verse 24:

"The grace . . . ": cf. 11.36, 16.20, Gal.1.5.

This verse (doxology) does not appear in many of the manuscripts, and adds no weight to the epistle.

Verses 25-26:

"Now to Him . . . obedience of faith": cf. 1.2, 15.16, 11.36, 1 Cor.2.1, 7, 4.1, Gal.1.5, Eph.1.4, 9, 3.1-12, 20, Col.1.26f, 2 Tim.1.9, 1 Pet.1.10-13, Jude 24; PRK 3.12, DEZ 1.18, Pes.Rab.33.6, Mid.Ps.72.6, 90.12, 93.3, Lam.R.1.16.51, Ber.34b, Pes.54a, Ned.39a, San.98b.

The final verses of the chapter recapitulate the main themes of the letter as a whole. Most importantly, Paul recapitulates 1.1-6 and 16-17, thereby enclosing the contents of the letter in the theme of God's election (creation) of the Gentiles to provoke Israel back to their God through jealousy. The gospel "reveals" the righteousness of God (1.17, 3.21), whose "mystery" relates specifically to the election (creation) of the Gentiles (cf. Ephesians 3).[44]

Verse 27:

"To the only wise God . . . ": cf. Rom.11.33, 1 Cor.1.24, 30, Eph.3.10, Col.2.3.

Paul sums up the letter with a doxology which relates the theme of wisdom in verses 17-20 to God Himself, through Yeshua, who is the wisdom of God, and who has revealed the mystery of salvation, leading to the obedience of faith: "We preach Messiah crucified, to Jews a stumbling block, and to Gentiles foolishness, but to those who are the called, both Jews and

Greeks, Messiah the power of God and the wisdom of God. Because the foolishness of God is wiser than men, and the weakness of God is stronger than men" (1 Cor.1.23-25).

Endnotes for Chapter 16

1 Cf. E. Käsemann, *Commentary*, 410.

2 Paul also refers to the ἐκκλησια (*ekklesia*) or the "church" (cf. verse 5) only in this chapter of the letter.

3 See E. Ferguson, *Backgrounds*, 45.

4 Cf. Acts 18.2. Priscilla is a diminutive form of Prisca.

5 See Sanday and Headlam, *Romans*, 418-20.

6 Cf. the transposition of the metaphor of the "building" or "temple" to the people in Qumran and in the New Testament epistles; cf. 1 Cor.3.16-17, 2 Cor.6.14-7.1, Eph.2.18-22, 1 Tim.3.15, Heb.12.18-24, 1 Pet.2.3-6, 1QS 5.5f, 8.4f, 9.3f, 4QFlor.1.6f, 1QpHab 12.1f.

7 Church buildings are also mentioned in the apocryphal Act.Philip 7.88, 9.147. See E. Ferguson, *Early Christians Speak* (Abilene: Abilene Christian University Press, 1981), 76, 81f.

8 See TDNT 1:485.

9 Paul does not elaborate on the circumstances in which he knows most of the people whom he greets.

10 See Sanday and Headlam, *Romans*, 422.

11 The name is found listed amongst members of the Imperial household and as the name of a slave; cf. Sanday and Headlam, *Romans*, 422. For the custom of Hellenizing Jewish names, see the midrash in Lev.R.32.5: "They did not change their name, having gone down [to Egypt] as Reuben and Simeon, and having come up as Reuben and Simeon. They did not call Judah 'Leon', nor Reuben 'Rufus', nor Joseph 'Lestes', nor Benjamin 'Alexander'."

12 Paul's history of hardships in 2 Cor.11.23 also leaves room for unidentified imprisonings when he might have made the acquaintance of the two believers.

13 Cf. Acts 14.4, 14, 1 Cor.12.28, 2 Cor.11.5, 12.10 13, Gal.1.11-2.9, Eph.4.11.

14 Cf. Yev.16.7, Tos.Meg.2.5, PHag.76c-d, 3f, PNed.42b, 22f, PHor.48a, 39ff.

15 Klausner suggests applying this function to Paul himself. See J. Klausner, *From Jesus to Paul*, quoted in H.J. Schoeps, *Paul* (Philadelphia: Westminster Press, 1961), 69.

16 Cf. the Venosa inscription ("*duo apostuli*" together with "*duo rebbites*"); Mt.11.2, Mk.6.7, Lk.10.1; and the זוגות (*zugot*) or pairs in PA 1.1f, Hag.16b.

17 See Sanday and Headlam, *Romans*, 424.

18 Ibid.

19 See Sanday and Headlam, *Romans*, 425.

20 Cf. the households of the "Maecenatiani," "Amyntiani," "Agrippiani," and "Germaniciani;" see Sanday and Headlam, *Romans*, 425.

21 Ibid.

22 See Sanday and Headlam, *Romans*, 426.

23 Ibid.

24 Rufus was the common Latin/Greek equivalent of Reuven; cf. Lev.R.32.5.

25 For the particular names, see Sanday and Headlam, *Romans*, 427.

26 For the particular names, see Sanday and Headlam, *Romans*, 427-28.

27 The father's kiss in Lk.15.20 is an act of forgiveness and acceptance.

28 See TDNT 9:138-45.

29 The affinities of the "Banquet of the Many" with the "Lord's supper" have been noted by many scholars; cf. Acts 2.42, 46, 20.7, 1 Cor.11.20f, Jude 12, 1QS 6.4-5, 1QS[a] 2.11-23; see G. Kuhn, "The Lord's Supper and the Communal Meal at Qumran," in *The Scrolls and the New Testament*, ed. K. Stendahl (NY: Harper, 1957), 65-93.

30 Most of these dissensions came either from Jewish believers who emphasized the need for Gentile believers to be circumcised ("Judaizers"), or from certain gnostic teachings; cf. the references below.

31 Cf. Rom.12.16, 1 Cor.1.10, Phil.2.2, 5, 4.2, 1 Tim.3-5. Paul might also be acknowledging here that the gospel which the communities in Rome had received was in accordance with his own preaching, even though he had not preached it to them personally.

32 Paul again picks up the theme of non-retaliation in 12.9ff; see the comments on 12.9ff and chapter 13.

33 See the references at 6.6 et al.

34 Cf. also the similarity between Phil.3.19, "whose god is their appetite," and the fragmentary text in 1QpHab 4.9f on Hab.1.2, "and it made of its might its god."

35 Cf. Mt.7.15, Acts 20.29-30, 1QS 11.7, CDC 1.18, 1QM 11.9, 13, 12.1f, 13.14, 14.7, 1QH 5.22, 7.22-23, 18.14-15, 1QpHab 12.2-10, 4QpNah.1-11. The Greek term εὐλογια (*eulogia*), "flattering," usually means "blessing," "benediction," or "benefit." Paul obviously uses it negatively here, perhaps in a reflection of other common euphemisms in rabbinic literature, in which either the opposite sense is used or the appellation is

displaced; cf. Ber.11b, San.46b, 96a, Shab.30b. His meaning is nevertheless substantiated by the parallels from Qumran.

36 For the phrase "obedience of the Gentiles," see the comments on 1.5 and 15.18.

37 This further confirms the Qumran influence on this passage, since Yeshua praised the "unrighteous servant" for acting shrewdly: "for the sons of this age are more shrewd in relation to their own kind than the sons of light" (Lk.16.1-13). As Flusser has demonstrated (*Jesus*), Yeshua is referring to the Essenes (the "sons of light"), and Luke directly connects the parable with Yeshua's saying concerning the two masters. The conjunction of wisdom and innocence here thus becomes an injunction to be careful about whom the congregations associate with, on the assumption that they should not separate themselves from the rest of the community, as did the Essenes. The encouragement to fellowship with one another demands the warning to be "wise in what is good and innocent in what is evil." Paul therefore builds here on the material from 12.9ff.

38 See also the comments on 12.18 and 14.17-19.

39 Paul probably appeals to a Qumran tradition here also, therefore (cf. verses 17-20). The "sons of light" is the name used most frequently in Qumran to designate the community, who are engaged in a battle against the "sons of darkness." For the background to the parable of the Unjust Steward, see D. Flusser, *Jesus*.

40 The "Asp" refers to Belial or Satan, by allusion to the serpent of Gen.3 (cf. Rev.12.9). All the "works of the Asp" are the creatures of Belial, the damned who are to be shut up in Sheol forever. "She" is the "Mother of the Messiah" (cf. Isa.7.14, Jer.13.21, Mic.5.2, Rev.12) whose birth-pangs bring forth the new world (cf. Jn.16.21, Rom.8.23). This is the end of the dominion of Belial (cf. 1QS 2.19) and his demons, and the advent of the exclusive reign of God and Goodness.

41 This break in the list of greetings raises a problem with verses 17-20. It seems likely that the thought of the "greetings" from all the communities reminds Paul of difficulties of strife and dissension, so that he is compelled to digress and repeat some of his injunctions from chapters 12f.

42 See also verse 13.

43 See E. Ferguson, *Backgrounds*, 33.

44 See the comments on 1.2, 5, and 11.25.

ABOUT THE AUTHORS

JOSEPH BARUCH SHULAM (Chief Editor)

Joseph Shulam was born in Sofia, Bulgaria on March 24, 1946. His family immigrated to Israel in 1948, where they settled in Jerusalem. In 1962, he came to faith in Jesus the Messiah. He was educated at Hebrew University in Jerusalem, where he received a B.A. in Bible and Bible Archeology. He later came to the United States and studied at David Lipscomb College in Nashville, Tennessee, where he received a B.A. in Chemistry and Biblical Studies. Upon completion of his B.A., he returned to Israel where he has since been involved in the local Messianic Jewish community. He continued his studies at the Hebrew University, and received an M.A. in the History of Jewish Thought in the Second Temple Period. From 1972–1975, he studied Rabbinics and Jewish Thought at the Diaspora Yeshiva in Jerusalem. Mr. Shulam is the Director of *Netivyah Bible Instruction Ministry* in Jerusalem. Netivyah is an Israeli-government recognized organization, established by Mr. Shulam for the purposes of studying and teaching the Jewish background of the New Testament, providing a bridge between Jews and Christians and Judaism and Christianity, and nurturing the Messianic Jewish community in Israel. Mr. Shulam is also the Elder of *Congregation Roeh Israel*, also located in Jerusalem. In addition to Biblical Studies, he lectures worldwide on such subjects as the First Century Church in Jerusalem, the Jewish Roots of the New Testament, and Contemporary Middle East Politics. He was an adjunct professor at Abilene Christian University (ACU), and directed the ACU. graduate extension program in Jerusalem in 1988. Joseph Shulam is married to Marcia Saunders Shulam, and they have two children.

HILARY LE CORNU (Research)

Hilary Le Cornu was born in Jersey, Channel Islands, in 1959. She graduated with honors from Edinburgh University in 1983 with an M.A. in Religious Studies. While pursuing her M.A., she received a certificate in Judaic Studies from the One Year Program at the Hebrew University in Jerusalem, where she is currently completing her Ph.D. in the Department of Comparative Religion. Miss Le Cornu has been residing in Jerusalem since 1983. In 1986, she began working as Joseph Shulam's Research Assistant as part of the staff of *Netivyah Bible Instruction Ministry*. She also participated in a four-member Interfaith Reconciliation Program to Rome and the U.S.A. in 1984. She served for a number of years as a volunteer coordinator for the Holocaust Education Seminar at *Yad VaShem*, and taught a course on Religious Pluralism for the Jerusalem Extension Program of Abilene University in 1988. She spent several years as Adminstrative Officer of the *Messianic Midrasha* in Israel, and is currently working as a freelance editor and proofreader.